A COMMENTARY ON
THE COLLECTED POEMS
OF W. B. YEATS

A COMMENTARY ON THE COLLECTED POEMS OF W. B. YEATS

A. Norman Jeffares

First edition 1968
Reprinted 1971, 1974, 1977, 1979

Published by
THE MACMILLAN PRESS LTD
London and Basingstoke
Associated companies in Delhi Dublin Hong Kong Johannesburg Lagos
Melbourne New York Singapore Tokyo

ISBN 0 333 02266 1

Printed in Hong Kong

TO ADÈLE CROWDER

Contents

Preface

THIS commentary is intended to assist the reader of Yeats's *Collected Poems* (page references to the second edition (1950) are given in the margin in bold face type). It attempts to date the composition of poems where this is possible and to give the place of first publication. Yeats's prose has been quoted where it throws light on the meaning of particular poems : thus his notes to early editions are included as well as passages from his critical and autobiographical prose. Abbreviations of the titles of works cited are given in a list on pp. ix–xii. His inconsistencies in spelling have been retained ; an appendix gives his views on the pronunciation and spelling of Gaelic names. For help in annotating them I am deeply indebted to Dr Brendan Kennelly.

The commentary owes much to the helpful kindness of Mrs Yeats, who allowed the editor access to Yeats's library and manuscripts. Readers will be able to supplement the bibliographical information by referring to *The Variorum Edition of the Poems of W. B. Yeats* (ed. Allt and Alspach). *A Concordance to the Poems of W. B. Yeats* (ed. Parrish and Painter) affords a quick means of comparing the images and symbols used by the poet. The commentary has, for reasons of space, avoided critical comment or judgement, and has been confined to providing information which will help readers to assess the effects of Yeats's sources, his wide and unusual reading, and his life — and to understand some factual meanings of poems and the circumstances in which some poems were written. Much — despite the continuing, specialised work on Yeats by critics and scholars — remains uncertain and obscure. And the poet himself would probably not have objected to this situation : 'I don't want them', he once remarked to his wife, 'to know all about everything.' It is largely thanks to her work, her care in preserving his manuscripts and library, her unselfish readiness to help scholars in their enquiries, that we can piece our thoughts about his work into our own individual views of his great poetic achievement.

Lédenon, France.   A. NORMAN JEFFARES
   1967

Acknowledgement

THE quotations from the work of W. B. Yeats are reprinted by kind permission of Mr Michael Butler Yeats.

Abbreviations

MRD	*Michael Robartes and the Dancer* (1921)
NP	*New Poems* (1938)
OB	*October Blast* (1927)
OTB	*On the Boiler* (1939)
P (1895)	*Poems* (1895)
PASL	*Per Amica Silentia Lunae* (1918)
PW	*Poetical Works*, 2 vols (1906 ; 1907)
PWD	*Poems Written in Discouragement* (1913)
RIT	*Representative Irish Tales*
RPP	*Responsibilities : Poems and a Play* (1914)
SPF	*Seven Poems and a Fragment* (1922)
SSY	*The Senate Speeches of W. B. Yeats*, ed. Donald R. Pearce (1960)
TSR	*The Secret Rose* (1897).
VE	*The Variorum Edition of the Poems of W. B. Yeats*, ed. Peter Allt and Russell K. Alspach (1957)
VPl	*The Variorum Edition of the Plays of W. B. Yeats*, ed. Russell K. Alspach (1966)
W & B	*Wheels and Butterflies* (1934)
WPM	*Words for Music Perhaps and Other Poems* (1932)
WO	*The Wanderings of Oisin and Other Poems* (1889)
WR	*The Wind Among the Reeds* (1899)
WS	*The Winding Stair and Other Poems* (1933)
WSC	*The Wild Swans at Coole* (1917)
WWP	*The Words upon the Window-pane* (1934)
Y & TSM	*W. B. Yeats and T. Sturge Moore. Their Correspondence* 1901–1937, ed. Ursula Bridge (1953)

OTHER BOOKS

B	*A Bibliography of the Writings of W. B. Yeats*, ed. Allan Wade, 2nd ed. (1958)
BL	J. Stallworthy, *Between the Lines* (1963)
ED	Richard Ellmann, *Eminent Domain* (1967)
HG	*An Honoured Guest*, ed. Denis Donoghue and J. R. Mulryne (1965)
HI	Edmund Curtis, *A History of Ireland* (1936)
HS	C. M. Bowra, *The Heritage of Symbolism* (1943)

List of Abbreviations

ICL	Birgit Bjersby, *The Interpretation of the Cuchulain Legend in the Works of W. B. Yeats* (1950)
IER	*In Excited Reverie*, ed. A. Norman Jeffares and K. G. W. Cross (1965)
IP	D. J. Gordon, *W. B. Yeats, Images of a Poet* (1961)
IY	Richard Ellmann, *The Identity of Yeats* (1954)
LT	T. R. Henn, *The Lonely Tower* (1950 ; rev. ed. 1965). References are to the 1965 edition.
LTHS	John Butler Yeats, *Letters to his Son W. B. Yeats and others* (1944)
PYP	George Brandon Saul, *Prolegomena to the Study of Yeats's Poems* (1957)
RG	John Unterecker, *A Reader's Guide to W. B. Yeats* (1959)
RI	Frank Kermode, *Romantic Image* (1957)
SQ	Maud Gonne MacBride, *A Servant of the Queen* (1938)
TM	Peter Ure, *Towards a Mythology* (1946)
WBY	J. M. Hone, *W. B. Yeats 1865–1939* (1942 ; rev. ed. 1962). References are to the 1962 edition.
WMA	Giorgio Melchiori, *The Whole Mystery of Art* (1960)
Y & GI	Donald T. Torchiana, *Yeats and Georgian Ireland* (1966)
Y & T	F. A. C. Wilson, *W. B. Yeats and Tradition* (1958)
YCE	*W. B. Yeats 1865–1939 Centenary Essays*, ed. D. E. S. Maxwell and S. B. Bushrui (1965)
YI	F. A. C. Wilson, *Yeats's Iconography* (1960)
Y:M & M	Richard Ellmann, *Yeats : the Man and the Masks* (1948 ; rev. ed. 1961). References are to the 1948 edition.
Y:M & P	A. Norman Jeffares, *Yeats : Man and Poet* (1949, rev. ed. 1962). References are to the 1962 edition.
YP & T	A. G. Stock, *W. B. Yeats His Poetry and Thought* (1961, rev. ed. 1964). References are to the 1964 edition.
YTLP	Thomas Parkinson, *W. B. Yeats : the Later Poetry* (1964)

JOURNALS

BR	*British Review*
D	*The Dome*
DM	*Dublin Magazine*
DUR	*Dublin University Review*

ER	*English Review*
IM	*Irish Monthly*
IR	*Irish Review*
LM	*London Mercury*
LR	*London Review*
N	*The Nation*
NO	*National Observer*
NR	*New Review*
P(*Ch*)	*Poetry* (Chicago)
RES	*Review of English Studies*
S	*The Savoy*
SO	*Scots Observer*
SR	*Saturday Review*
TB	*The Bookman*
UI	*United Ireland*

Chronology of Yeats's Life

1865   William Butler Yeats, the son of John Butler Yeats and his wife, Susan (*née* Pollexfen), born at Georgeville, Sandymount Avenue, Dublin, 13 June.

1867   John Butler Yeats moves with his family to 23 Fitzroy Road, Regent's Park, London. Robert (d. 1873), John Butler (Jack), Elizabeth Corbet (Lolly) were born here. Susan Mary (Lily), the elder daughter, was born at Enniscrone. Frequent visits were made to Sligo to Mrs Yeat's parents, the Pollexfens.

1874   The family moves to 14 Edith Villas, West Kensington.

1876   The family moves to 8 Woodstock Road, Bedford Park.

1877   Yeats goes to the Godolphin School, Hammersmith. Holidays spent in Sligo.

1880   John Butler Yeats's income declines because of Land War and decline in economy.

1881   Family returns to Ireland, is lent Balscadden Cottage, Howth, Dublin. W. B. Yeats goes to the High School, Harcourt Street, Dublin (until 1883).

1882   Family moves to Island View, small house overlooking Howth Harbour. Yeats thinks himself in love with his cousin Laura Armstrong.

1884   W. B. Yeats enters School of Art, Dublin.

1885   Family moves to 10 Ashfield Terrace, off Harold's Cross Road, Dublin. First published poems (and Charles Johnston's article on esoteric Buddhism) appear in *Dublin University Review*. Founder member of Dublin Hermetic Society. Becomes friend of Katharine Tynan and John O'Leary.

1886   First experience of séance. Attacks Anglo-Irish, begins to read Irish poets who wrote in English and translations of Gaelic sagas.

1887   Family moves to 58 Eardley Crescent, Earls Court, London. Mrs Yeats has two strokes. W. B. Yeats visits William Morris at Kelmscott House. Joins London Lodge of Theosophists.

1888   Family installed in 3 Blenheim Road, Bedford Park (J. B. Yeats's home till 1902). Last of Yeats family land sold in accordance with Ashbourne Act (1888). Contributions to American journals. Visits Oxford to work in Bodleian. Joins esoteric section of Theosophists.

1889   Mild collapse. Prepares selections for Walter Scott. *The Wanderings of Oisin and Other Poems*. Visits W. E. Henley, meets Oscar Wilde, John Todhunter, York Powell, John Nettleship, and Edwin Ellis (with whom he decides to edit Blake's poems). Edits *Fairy and Folk Tales of the Irish Peasantry*. Maude Gonne visits Bedford Park; he falls in love with her; offers to write *The Countess Cathleen* for her.

1890   'The Lake Isle of Innisfree.' Asked to resign from Theosophists. Meets Florence Farr, who was acting in John Todhunter's *A Sicilian Idyll*.

1891   *Representative Irish Tales*. *John Sherman and Dhoya*. The Rhymers' Club founded in London. Friendship with Johnson and Dowson. Asks Maud Gonne to marry him. She goes to France. He meets her on her return on ship with Parnell's body. Writes poem on Parnell. Founds London-Irish Literary Society with T. W. Rolleston. Founds National Literary Society in Dublin with John O'Leary as President.

1892   *The Countess Kathleen and Various Legends and Lyrics*. *Irish Fairy Tales*.

1893   *The Celtic Twilight*. *The Works of William Blake* (ed. Ellis and Yeats, 3 vols).

1894   First visit to Paris; stays with MacGregor Mathers and proposes to Maud Gonne again. Sees *Axel*. Meets 'Diana Vernon'. Revises *The Countess Cathleen* in Sligo while staying with George Pollexfen and conducting experiments with symbols. *The Land of Heart's Desire* produced. Visits Gore-Booths at Lissadell.

1895   *Poems*. Not on good terms with Dowden and Mahaffy. Lionel Johnson drinking heavily. Shares rooms in the Temple with Arthur Symons for a few months (between 1895 and 1896, date uncertain).

1896   Takes rooms in Woburn Buildings ; affair with 'Diana Vernon' lasts a year. Visits Edward Martyn with Arthur Symons, meets Lady Gregory, visits Aran Islands. Meets Synge in Paris, when there to found order of Celtic Mysteries. Member of I.R.B.; forms idea of uniting Irish political parties.

1897   *The Adoration of the Magi. The Secret Rose.* Disturbed by effects of Jubilee Riots in Dublin. Visits Coole ; collects folklore there with Lady Gregory ; writing *The Speckled Bird* (unpublished novel).

1898   Accompanies Maud Gonne on tour of Irish in England and Scotland. Forms idea of creating Irish Theatre with Lady Gregory and Edward Martyn. 'Spiritual marriage' with Maud Gonne.

1899   *The Wind Among the Reeds.* In Paris, again proposes marriage to Maud Gonne. *The Countess Cathleen* and Martyn's *Heather Field* produced in Ancient Concert Rooms, Dublin, as programme of Irish Literary Theatre.

1900   Proposes marriage to Maud Gonne in London. Leaves I.R.B. (probably in 1900), Forms new order of Golden Dawn after trouble with Mathers and Aleister Crowley. Helps George Moore to rewrite Martyn's *The Tale of a Town*, which became *The Bending of the Bough*.

1901   Proposes marriage to Maud Gonne again.

1902   Lectures on the psalteries. *Diarmuid and Grania* written in collaboration with George Moore. Becomes President of Irish National Dramatic Society. *Cathleen ni Houlihan* performed in Dublin with Maud Gonne in title role.

1903 **Maud Gonne marries John MacBride.** *The Countess Cathleen, The Pot of Broth* and *The Hour Glass* produced in visit of Irish National Dramatic Company to London. First lecture tour in U.S., arranged by John Quinn.

1904 Abbey Theatre opens with Yeats as producer-manager. *The King's Threshold* and *On Baile's Strand*.

1905 Limited company replaces National Theatre. Co-director with Lady Gregory and Synge. *Stories of Red Hanrahan*.

1906 *Poems 1895–1905*.

1907 Crisis over Synge's *The Playboy of the Western World*. Visits Italy with Lady Gregory and her son. Works on *The Player Queen*. Father goes to New York.

1908 *Collected Works* (in 8 vols). Stays with Maud Gonne in Paris. Meets Ezra Pound.

1910 Resigns managership. Crisis in affair with Mabel Dickinson. *The Green Helmet and other poems*.

1911 Accompanies Abbey players to U.S. Meets Georgie Hyde-Lees.

1912 Stays with Maud Gonne in Normandy.

1913 Receives Civil List pension of £150 p.a. *Poems Written in Discouragement* (dealing with Lane Gallery controversy). Stays at Stone Cottage, Holmans Hatch, Sussex, in autumn with Ezra Pound.

1914 Visits U.S. (January). Returns for Ezra Pound's marriage to Mrs Shakespear's daughter. Investigates miracle at Mirebeau with Maud Gonne MacBride and the Hon. Everard Feilding (May). *Responsibilities: poems and a play*. Becomes interested in family history; finishes *Reveries* (first part of *Autobiographies*).

1915 Hugh Lane goes down with *Lusitania*. Refuses knighthood.

1916   With Ezra Pound (winter). First of the *Plays for Dancers* produced in Lady Cunard's house, London (March). Easter Rising, writes 'Easter 1916'. In Normandy proposes marriage to Maud Gonne. Reads French poets with Iseult Gonne.

1917   Buys Castle at Ballylee. Proposes to Iseult Gonne. Marries Georgie Hyde-Lees on 20 October. *The Wild Swans at Coole.*

1918   They stay at Oxford, then Glendalough, then visit Sligo ; stay at Coole (and supervise restoration of tower), later at 73 St Stephen's Green (Maud Gonne's house) until December. *Per Amica Silentia Lunae.*

1919   Anne Butler Yeats born (26 February) in Dublin. Summer at Ballylee. Winter spent in Oxford in Broad Street.

1920   American lecture tour until May. Yeats in Ireland in autumn.

1921   Michael Butler Yeats born (22 August). *Michael Robartes and the Dancer. Four Plays for Dancers.*

1922   Buys Georgian house, 82 Merrion Square, Dublin. J. B. Yeats dies in New York. D.Litt. of Dublin University. Spends summer at Ballylee. *The Trembling of the Veil. Later Poems. The Player Queen.* Becomes Senator of Irish Free State.

1923   Nobel Prize for Poetry. Visits Stockholm in December for award of Nobel Prize.

1924   *Essays. The Cat and the Moon and certain poems.* Year mainly spent in final work on *A Vision.* Reading history and philosophy. High blood pressure. Visits Sicily (November).

1925   Visits Capri, Rome, Milan (February). May at Ballylee. Reading Burke and Berkeley. Speech on divorce in Senate. *A Vision* (dated 1925, published January 1926).

1926   *Estrangement.* Chairman of Coinage Committee in Senate. Visits St Otteran's School in Waterford ('Among School Children').

1927   Ballylee in summer. *October Blast*. Congestion of lungs. (October). Algeciras, Seville (lung bleeding). Cannes.

1928   Cannes (till February). *The Tower*. Rapallo (April). Dublin house sold. Ballylee (June). Furnished house at Howth (July). Last Senate Speech (July).

1929   Rapallo (winter). Summer in Ireland, in flat (Fitzwilliam Square, Dublin), at Coole and Ballylee, then at Howth. *A Packet for Ezra Pound* (August). *The Winding Stair* (October). Rapallo. Malta fever (December). Ezra Pound and George Antheil at Rapallo.

1930   Portofino (April). Writes 'Byzantium'. Renvyle, Connemara (June). Coole. *Words upon the Window-pane* produced at Abbey Theatre (November). Visits Masefield at Boar's Hill, Oxford, thirtieth anniversary of their first meeting. Spends winter in Dublin, in furnished house on Killiney Hill.

1931   Writes 'The Seven Sages'. D.Litt. at Oxford (May). Writes much verse at Coole in summer. Broadcast B.B.C. Belfast (September). Spends winter at Coole, reading Balzac ; Lady Gregory dying.

1932   Works on 'Coole Park and Ballylee 1931'. Winter and spring at Coole. Lady Gregory dies. Foundation of Irish Academy of Letters (September). Last American tour (October). *Words for Music Perhaps and other poems* (November). Leases Riversdale, Rathfarnham, Co. Dublin.

1933   Interested in O'Duffy's blueshirt movement. *The Winding Stair and other poems* (September), *Collected Poems* (November).

1934   Steinach operation. Rapallo (June). Rome (autumn). *Wheels and Butterflies*. *Collected Plays*. *The King of the Great Clock Tower*.

1935   Majorca (winter). Shri Purohit Swami collaborates in translation of *Upanishads* there. *Dramatis Personae*. *A Full Moon in March* (November).

1936   Seriously ill ; heart missing beat (January) ; nephritis.

Returns to Riversdale. Broadcasts on modern poetry, B.B.C., London (summer). *Oxford Book of Modern Verse (1892–1935)*.

1937   Elected member Athenaeum. Broadcasts B.B.C. London. (April, July, September) *A Speech and Two Poems* (August). Visits Lady Gerald Wellesley. *A Vision* (October). Mentone (winter). *Essays 1931–1936* (December).

1938   *The Herne's Egg* (January). Visits Sussex, stays with Lady Gerald Wellesley, and with Edith Shackleton Heald. *New Poems* (May). Sussex (June). Last public appearance at Abbey Theatre for performance of *Purgatory* (August). Maud Gonne visits him at Riversdale (late summer). Sussex (September).

1939   Dies 28 January, buried at Roquebrune. *Last Poems and Two Plays* (June). *On the Boiler*.

1948   Body reinterred at Drumcliffe Churchyard, Sligo.

The Contents of the Collected Poems

Page numbers in bold are those of the *Collected Poems*; those of the Commentary are in ordinary figures

LYRICAL

The Contents of the Collected Poems

The Contents of the Collected Poems

The Wild Swans at Coole (1919)

The Contents of the Collected Poems

The Contents of the Collected Poems

NARRATIVE AND DRAMATIC

Miles

ULSTER

BELFAST

CO. DOWN

ARMAGH

Ballyshannon

Innismurray

Killala Bay

SLIGO
Ben Bulben
Glencar L.
L. Gill
Dromahair

Enniscrone

Ox Mountains

Ballisodare

Boyle   L. Key

CO. MAYO

French Park   Cruachan

Westport   CONNAUGHT   Elphin

Cro-Patrick   Moore Hall

Drogheda

R. Boyne

Hill of Tara

Lissoy

L. Corrib

ATHLONE

DUBLIN

Howth
Sandymount
Rathfarnham

GALWAY

Tulira   Loughrea

Aran Islands

Durras House   Ballylee

Gort   Coole Park   L. Derg

CO. CLARE

R. Liffey

LEINSTER

Two Rock Mountain

Glendalough

WICKLOW

Kilkenny

LIMERICK

MUNSTER   Cashel

Tipperary

WEXFORD

CORK

Ballylee *(W. B. Yeats)*

Sandymount *(Yeats's birthplace)*

Rathfarnham *(Yeats's last Irish residence)*

Aran Islands *(J. M. Synge)*

Coole Park *(Lady Gregory)*

French Park *(Douglas Hyde)*

Tulira *(Edward Martyn)*

Lissoy *(? The Deserted Village)*

Moore Hall *(George Moore)*

Elphin *(Oliver Goldsmith)*

Cloyne *(Bishop Berkeley)*

Ballyshannon *(Wm. Allingham)*

YEATS'S IRELAND

YEATS'S SLIGO

LYRICAL

Crossways was a heading first given by Yeats to a group of poems in *P* (1895), most of which were taken from an earlier volume (*WO*), with the exception of two ballads, 'The Ballad of Father O'Hart' and 'The Ballad of the Foxhunter', which, as Yeats wrote in the Preface to *P* (1895), were 'written at the same time, though published later', in *CK*. The title *Crossways* was adopted because in these poems he 'tried many pathways' (*P* (1895)). Yeats commented, in a note dated 1925, that

> Many of the poems in *Crossways*, certainly those upon Indian subjects or upon shepherds and fauns, must have been written before I was twenty, for from the moment I began *The Wanderings of Oisin*, which I did at that age, I believe, my subject matter became Irish. (*CP*)

THE SONG OF THE HAPPY SHEPHERD   7

This poem was written in 1885 and first appeared in *DUR* (Oct. 1885). It was entitled 'An Epilogue. To "The Island of Statues" and "The Seeker". *Spoken by a Satyr, carrying a sea-shell*'. Later, it was entitled 'Song of the Last Arcadian (*He carries a sea-shell*)' in *WO*.

1 *Arcady* : from Arcadia in the Peloponnesus, a pastoral paradise in Greek literature. Yeats commented : 'When I first wrote I went here and there for my subjects as my reading led me, and preferred to all other countries Arcadia and the India of romance.' (*CW* 1). His Arcadian ideas probably came from Spenser.

4 *Grey Truth* : in his teens Yeats began

> occasionally telling people that one should believe whatever had been believed in all countries and periods, and only reject any part of it after much evidence, instead of starting all over afresh and only believing what one could prove. (*A* 78)

He had grown to hate science 'with a monkish hate' (*A* 82). He had made himself a new religion :

> almost an infallible Church of poetic tradition, of a fardel of stories, and of personages, and of emotions, inseparable from their first expression, passed on from generation to generation by poets and painters with some help from philosophers and theologians . . . I had even created a dogma : 'Because those imaginary people are created out of the deepest instinct of man, to be his measure and his norm, whatever I can imagine those mouths speaking may be the nearest I can go to truth'. (*A* 116)

9 *Chronos* : Kronos or Cronos, one of the Titans, a son of Uranus and Ge, who conspired against his father with his brothers and sisters. He succeeded Uranus as ruler of the Universe and was himself overthrown by his own son, Zeus. The Roman god Saturn was identified with Kronos : he was thought to have been an early king at Rome, his rule so benign that his reign was known as the Golden Age. It is possible Yeats had Milton's *Paradise Lost*, 1 510–21, in mind (see note on line 29 of this poem), which connects Saturn with Mount Ida, Olympus, Delphi, Dodona and the Celtic isles.

10 *Words alone* : A. G. Stock (*YP & T* 10–11) compares these lines to Spenser's *The Ruines of Time*, 400–6, where deeds are described as dying :

> But wise wordes taught in numbers for to runne,
> Recorded by the Muses, live for ay.

12 *Word be-mockers* : the warring kings who are men of action : their memory lives on in the words of the dreaming poets. In the first version of the poem this line was included after line 13 'They were of no wordy mood'.

Rood : Cross

16 *entangled story* : the first version reads 'In the verse of Attic story'.

29   *optic glass* : an echo of Milton's description in *Paradise Lost*,   **8**
1 286–91, of Galileo's use of the telescope :

> the moon, whose orb
> Through optic glass the Tuscan artist views
> At evening from the top of Fesole
> Or in Valdarno, to descry new lands,
> Rivers or mountains, in her spotty globe.

31   *sooth* : truth

36   *shell* : cf. lines 18–25 'The Sad Shepherd' (*CP* 9).   The happy
shepherd's fretful words are reworded by the shell.   The sad
shepherd's words were changed to an inarticulate moan.

56   *poppies* : the juice of poppies possesses narcotic properties.

THE SAD SHEPHERD   **9**

This poem was written in 1885 and first appeared in *DUR* (Oct.
1886).   It was then entitled 'Miserrimus'.   This was also the title
of a Godwinian tale of a fiend, dedicated to Godwin by E. M.
Reynolds and published in 1832.

18   *a shell* : cf. 'The Song of the Happy Shepherd' (*CP* 7).   See
note (p. 5) on line 36 of that poem.

26   *sad dweller* : the shell

THE CLOAK, THE BOAT, AND THE SHOES   **10**

The original title was 'Voices' in *DUR* (March 1885).   The poem
was untitled in the play *The Island of Statues*, where it opens Act II,
scene iii, and untitled also in *WO*.   Yeats described *The Island of
Statues* as 'an Arcadian play in imitation of Edmund Spenser' ; he
read it aloud 'to a gathering of critics who were to decide whether
it was worthy of publication in the College magazine' (*A* 92).
The text is included in *VE*, which gives details of its printings on
p. 644.   In the early printings the song is sung by six voices in
turn, the lines divided thus : 1 ; 2–5 ; 6 ; 7–10 ; 11 ; 12–15.
The voices are described by the enchantress as being 'the flowers'
guardian sprights'.

10 ANASHUYA AND VIJAYA

This poem first appeared in *WO* ; its original title was 'Jealousy'. In *P* (1895) it is dated 1887. Yeats commented, in a note dated 1925, that the

> little Indian dramatic scene was meant to be the first scene of a play about a man loved by two women, who had the one soul between them, the one woman waking when the other slept, and knowing but daylight as the other only night. It came into my head when I saw a man at Rosses Point (in Sligo) carrying two salmon. 'One man with two souls,' I said, and added, 'O no, two people with one soul.' I am now once more in *A Vision* busy with that thought, the antithesis of day and night and of moon and sun. (*CP*)

F. F. Farag, 'Oriental and Celtic Elements in the Poetry of W. B. Yeats', in *YCE*, remarks that Yeats has evidently taken the name 'Anashuya' from Kalidasa's play *Sakuntala* which he read in the translation of Monier Williams.

11 14 *Brahma* : the supreme God of Hindu mythology

12 26 *Kama* : Yeats's footnote reads 'The Indian Cupid' in *WO* and his note in *P* (1895) reads '*The Indian Eros*'.

13 66–75 *the parents of the gods* : Richard Ellmann (*Y:M & M* 71) comments that these lines celebrate the Tibetan adepts Koot-Hoomi and Morya, the masters of Madame Blavatsky whom Yeats saw on her door in poorly drawn pictures supposed to have been telepathically projected. (See *A* 176.) Madame Blavatsky (Helena Petrovna Blavatsky, 1831–91) was born in Russia, married General Blavatsky, founded the Theosophical Society with Colonel Olcott in 1875 and wrote several books about theology, *Isis Unveiled* (1877) and *The Secret Doctrine* (1888–97) being perhaps the best known. Yeats's schoolfriend Charles Johnston read books by A. P. Sinnett (1840–1921), *The Occult World* (1881) and *Esoteric Buddhism* (1883), and then read a paper on Theosophy at the Dublin Hermetic Society in 1885, which Yeats heard. Johnston was indignant when Madame Blavatsky was denounced as a charlatan before the Society for Psychical Research in London in 1885, and he founded a Dublin Lodge in 1886. Yeats and George Russell refused to join, but when Yeats's family moved to London in May 1887 Yeats was impressed by Madame Blavatsky and joined the London Lodge. He joined the Esoteric Section of the Lodge in 1888 (about December), but was asked to resign (probably in the autumn) in 1890, as he 'was causing discussion and disturbance'. He hated all abstraction and had begun a series of experiments in his search for some kind of certainty. Yeats found support in the Society for his opposition to materialism, the 'grey truth' of 'The Sad Shepherd' (*CP* 9) and he wrote a lively account of Madame Blavatsky in *A* 173–82.

THE INDIAN UPON GOD

This poem was written in 1886 and first appeared in *DUR* (Oct. 1886). Its original title was 'From the Book of Kauri the Indian — Section v. On the Nature of God.' In *WO* the title is 'Kanva, the Indian, on God'. *P* (1895) gives the date of the poem as 1886. It is possible that this poem and 'The Indian to his Love' (*CP* 15) were inspired by the Brahmin Theosophist Mohini M. Chatterjee, who visited Dublin in 1885 and gave a lecture to the Hermetic Society, a group of young men who had taken a room in York Street, Dublin, as their headquarters. They included A E (George Russell, 1867–1935), a poet, essayist, painter and mystic, an active member of the Irish literary renaissance and the Home Rule movement, and a founder of the Abbey Theatre. He worked with Sir Horace Plunkett in the foundation of the Irish Cooperative Movement, and edited the *Irish Statesman*. Yeats first met him when he was a pupil at the School of Art in Dublin. Another member was Charles Johnston, son of the M.P. for Ballykilbeg, Northern Ireland, a brilliant fellow pupil of Yeats's at the High School, Dublin, who married Madame Blavatsky's niece. Claude Wright and Charles Weekes were also members of the group. Their purpose was to study Eastern philosophy. A poem 'Kanva on Himself', included in *WO*, puts into verse a saying of the Brahmin in reply to a query as to whether one should pray :

No, one should say before sleeping : 'I have lived many lives,
I have been a slave and a prince. Many a beloved has sat upon

my knees and I have sat upon the knees of many a beloved.
Everything that has been shall be again.'

> Now wherefore hast thou tears innumerous?
> Hast thou not known all sorrow and delight
> Wanderings of yore in forests rumorous,
> Beneath the flaming eyeballs of the night,
>
> And as a slave been wakeful in the halls
> Of Rajas and Mahrajas beyond number?
> Hast thou not ruled among the gilded walls?
> Hast thou not known a Raja's dreamless slumber?
>
> Hast thou not sat of yore upon the knees
> Of myriads of beloveds, and on thine
> Have not a myriad swayed below strange trees
> In other lives? Hast thou not quaffed old wine
>
> By tables that were fallen into dust
> Ere yonder palm commenced his thousand years?
> Is not thy body but the garnered rust
> Of ancient passions and of ancient fears?
>
> Then wherefore fear the usury of Time,
> Or Death that cometh with the next life-key?
> Nay, rise and flatter her with golden rhyme
> For as things were so shall things ever be.

This poem's theme is recaptured in 'Mohini Chatterjee' (*CP* 279),
written in February 1929, where it is far better handled. F. F.
Farag (*YCE* 40) points out that Mohini meant that one 'should
realise the permanence of the soul in the eternal essence amidst all
the transient forms through which it has passed'. Other poems
dealing with reincarnation are 'Fergus and the Druid' (*CP* 36),
'He mourns for the Change that has come upon him and his
Beloved' (*CP* 68), and 'Broken Dreams' (*CP* 172). See also the
note (p. 10) on 'Ephemera' (*CP* 16).

15   THE INDIAN TO HIS LOVE

This poem was written in 1886 and first appeared in *DUR* (Dec.
1886).

3   *The peahens dance*: Yeats replied (to a critic's objections that
peahens do not dance) that they 'dance throughout the whole of

Indian poetry. If I had *Kalidasa* by me I could find many such dancings. As to the poultry yards, with them I have no concern. The wild peahen dances or all Indian poets lie' (*L* 109, quoted by F. F. Farag, *YCE* 38-9).

THE FALLING OF THE LEAVES   16

This poem first appeared in *WO*. Its original title was 'Falling of the Leaves'. In 1907 Yeats wrote in 'Speaking to the Psaltery':

> Sometimes one composes to a remembered air I wrote and I still speak the verses that begin 'Autumn is over the long leaves that love us' to some traditional air, though I could not tell that air or any other on another's lips . . . (*E & I* 21)

Yeats was tone-deaf; he often composed by repeating the words aloud in a form of chant. He described the process clearly in *BS*:

> Every now and then, when something has stirred my imagination, I begin talking to myself. I speak in my own person and dramatise myself, very much as I have seen a mad old woman do upon the Dublin quays, and sometimes detect myself speaking and moving as if I were still young, or walking perhaps like an old man with fumbling steps. Occasionally, I write out what I have said in verse, and generally for no better reason than because I remember that I have written no verse for a long time. I do not think of my soliloquies as having different literary qualities. They stir my interest, by their appropriateness to the men I imagine myself to be, or by their accurate description of some emotional circumstance, more than by any aesthetic value. When I begin to write I have no object but to find for them some natural speech, rhythm and syntax, and to set it out in some pattern, so seeming old that it may seem all men's speech, and though the labour is very great, I seem to have used no faculty peculiar to myself, certainly no special gift. I print the poem and never hear about it again, until I find the book years after with a page dog-eared by some young man, or marked by some girl with a violet, and when I have seen that, I am a little ashamed, as though somebody were to attribute to me a delicacy of feeling I should but do not possess. What came so easily at first, and amidst so much drama, and was written so laboriously at the last, cannot be counted among my possessions. (*A* 532-3)

J. M. Hone quotes Cecil Salkeld's description of Yeats composing :

Coming down to breakfast, Madame Gonne MacBride smiled at me and said : 'Willie is booming and buzzing like a bumble bee . . . that means he is writing something. . . . .' To my great surprise, Yeats, who appeared shortly, obviously preoccupied and absent-minded, asked me if I would walk up the glen with him. We walked, treading our way among boulders and small stones along the river bank for nearly half an hour in silence. By that I mean no word was spoken ; but, all the while Yeats kept up a persistent murmur — under his breath, as it were. Suddenly, he pulled up short at a big stone and said : 'Do you realise that eternity is not a long time but a *short* time . . . ?' I just said, I didn't quite understand. 'Eternity,' Yeats said, 'Eternity is in the glitter on the beetle's wing . . . it is something infinitely short. . . .' (*WBY* 326–7)

16 EPHEMERA

This poem was written in 1884. It was originally entitled 'Ephemera. An Autumn Idyl', and first appeared in *WO*.

17 21 *other loves* : Yeats frequently used the idea of reincarnation in his poetry. Some of his interest in it was derived from George Russell and some from Mohini M. Chatterjee. But his belief in reincarnation was at the mercy of his sceptical intelligence. He wrote : 'Ought I not to say "The whole doctrine of the reincarnation of the soul is hypothetic ; it is the most plausible of the explanations of the world but can we say more than that ?"' (unpublished Autobiography)

17 THE MADNESS OF KING GOLL

This poem was written in 1884 and it first appeared in *The Leisure Hour* (Sept. 1887) entitled 'King Goll, An Irish Legend'. Subsequent titles were in *Poems and Ballads of Young Ireland* (1888). 'King Goll (*Third Century*)', and in *WO* 'King Goll (Third Century)'. Yeats's note reads 'In the legend King Goll hid himself in a valley near Cork where it is said all the madmen in Ireland would gather were they free, so mighty a spell did he cast over that valley' (*P* (1895)). Goll means one-eyed in Irish, and the name appears in the Fenian and mythological cycles. The poem was altered extensively and *VE* 81–6 should be consulted for the changes.

2   *Ith* : possibly Ith, a plain near Raphoe, Co. Donegal.
Emain : Yeats glossed this as 'the capital of the Red branch kings' (*P* (1895)), and their 'chief town' (*P* (1895 ; rev. 1899)).   The 'Red Branch' cycle of Irish tales was probably transmitted orally early in the Christian period, written down by monks in the seventh or eighth centuries and incorporated in late manuscripts between the eleventh and fifteenth centuries.   The ruins of Emain Macha are still to be seen some miles south-west of Armagh. Warriors came there each summer for training at Conchubar (or Conor) MacNessa's court, he being King of Ulster.

3   *Inver Amergin* : Amergin was the poet of the Milesian invaders of Ireland, who were traditionally thought to have come from Spain about the time of Alexander the Great.   Mileadh's three sons, Heber, Heremon ['the ancestors of the merely human inhabitants of Ireland' (*P* (1895)) 'according to mythology' (*P* (1895 ; rev. 1899))] and Ir conquered the Tuatha de Danaan, or tribes of the goddess Dana, who were traditionally divine masters of magic. Yeats described them as follows :

> Tuath De Danaan means the Race of the Gods of Dana.   Dana was the mother of all the ancient Gods of Ireland.   They were the powers of light and life and warmth, and did battle with the Formoroh, or powers of night and death and cold. Robbed of offerings and honour, they have gradually dwindled in the popular imagination until they have become the Faeries. (*P* (1895)).

Elsewhere he calls them 'Gods of Danu.   They were . . . become Faeries' (*P* (1895 ; rev. 1899)).

The other inhabitants were the Firbolgs, a short dark plebeian people, described by Yeats as 'an early race who warred vainly upon the Formornians, or Fomorah before the coming of the Tuath de Danaan'.   Certain Firbolg kings, killed at Southern Moytura, are supposed to be buried at Ballisodare, Co. Sligo.   It is by their graves that Usheen and his companions rode ; 'Usheen was the poet of the Fenian cycle of legend as Fergus was the poet of the Red Branch Cycle' (*P* (1895)).   The Fianna are thought to have been a body of infantry, although horsemen are mentioned in the cycle. They were particularly prominent in the reign of Cormac MacArt, whose supposed son-in-law Finn MacCumhall was their leader ; and are thought to have been put down in the Battle of Gabhra (A.D. 297). MS. evidence suggests twelfth-century composition for the tales and ballads, though some may have been composed in the eighth century.

Yeats explained Fomoroh as meaning

> from under the sea, and is the name of the gods of night and death and cold. The Fomoroh were misshapen and had now the heads of goats and bulls, and now but one leg, and one arm that came out of the middle of their breasts. They were the ancestors of the evil faeries and, according to one Gaelic writer, of all misshapen persons. The giants and the leprechauns are expressly mentioned as of the Fomoroh. (*P* (1895))

4 *the world-troubling seamen* : G. B. Saul (*PYP* 46) speculates that these are the Milesians, but they are more likely Formorians.

9 *Ollave* : an Irish poet, of the highest grade of the order of Filidh who were the hereditary keepers of the lore and learning ot Ireland (*HI* 2–3)

11 *Northern cold* : Yeats comments, 'The Fomoroh, the powers of death and darkness and cold and evil, came from the north.'

19 45 *The grey wolf* : the last wolf in Ireland was reputed to have been killed in the eighteenth century.

49 *a little town* : reminiscent of Allingham's 'The Winding Banks of Erne'

55 *tympan* : kettle-drum, in original version of poem a harp

62 *Orchil* : a Formorian sorceress (*P* (1895)). Yeats wrote, 'I forget whatever I may have once known about her' (*P* 1895 ; rev. 1899)).

20 THE STOLEN CHILD

This poem first appeared in *IM* (Dec. 1886). Yeats's note read :

> The places mentioned are round about Sligo. Further Rosses is a very noted fairy locality. There is here a little point of

rocks where, if anyone falls asleep, there is danger of their waking silly, the fairies having carried off their souls. (*FFT*)

2   *Sleuth Wood*: this wood lies between Lough Gill and Dromahair. Yeats described it in 'The Heart of the Spring'; 'Sleuth Wood away to the south looked as though cut out of green beryl, and the waters that mirrored it shone like pale opal' (*M* 175).

9–12   *Come away, O human child*: Yeats wrote to Katharine Tynan, on 14 March 1888, that in the process of correcting his poems he had noticed things about his poetry he had not known before, that it was

> almost all a flight into fairyland from the real world. . . . The Chorus to the 'Stolen Child' sums it up — that it is not the poetry of insight and knowledge but of longing and complaint — the cry of the heart against necessity. I hope some day to alter that and write poetry of insight and knowledge. (*L* 63)

This poem probably marks the shift from Arcadian and Indian scenes to Irish — Yeats wrote later that for such reasons as those in 'Ireland and the arts' (*E & I* 203) he convinced himself that he should never 'go for the scenery of a poem to any country but my own, and I think that I shall hold to that conviction to the end' (*CW* 1).

15   *Rosses*: Yeats described this area in Sligo as 'a little seadividing, sandy plain, covered with short grass, like a green tablecloth and lying in the foam midway between the round cairnheaded Knocknarea and "Ben Bulben"' (*M* 88). It had its supernatural aspects:

> At the northern corner of Rosses is a little promontory of sand and rocks and grass: a mournful, haunted place. Few countrymen would fall asleep under its low cliff, for he who sleeps here may wake 'silly', the Sidhe having carried off his soul. There is no more ready short-cut to the dim kingdom than this plovery headland, for, covered and smothered now from sight by mounds of sand, a long cave goes thither 'full of gold and silver, and the most beautiful parlours and drawingrooms'. Once, before the sand covered it, a dog strayed in, and was heard yelping helplessly deep undergound in a fort far inland. These forts or raths, made before modern history

had begun, cover all Rosses and all Columcille. The one where the dog yelped has, like most others, an underground beehive chamber in the midst. Once when I was poking about there, an unusually intelligent and 'reading' country-man who had come with me, and waited outside, knelt down by the opening, and whispered in a timid voice, 'Are you all right, sir?' I had been some little while underground, and he feared I had been carried off like the dog. (*M* 88–9)

21   29   *Glen-Car* : Glencar Lake lies to the north-east of Sligo.

22   TO AN ISLE IN THE WATER

This poem first appeared in *WO*.

22   DOWN BY THE SALLEY GARDENS

This poem first appeared in *WO*. Its original title was 'An Old Song Re-sung' and Yeats's footnote explained that 'This is an attempt to reconstruct an old song from three lines imperfectly remembered by an old peasant woman in the village of Ballysodare, Sligo, who often sings them to herself' (*P* (1895)). He later called it 'an extension of three lines sung by an old woman at Ballisodare' and a letter to Katharine Tynan, written after 6 September 1888, suggests that the lines were 'Old Irish verse' (*L* 86). A letter to Dorothy Wellesley of 25 September 1935 commented that the Irish Free State army marched to a tune called 'Down by the Salley Garden' without knowing that the march was 'first published with words of mine, words that are now folklore' (*DWL* 29). The source of the poem has been given by H. E. Shields, 'Yeats and the "salley gardens"', *Hermathena*, C1 (Autumn 1965), 22–6. It is not 'Going to Mass last Sunday' (as stated by Colin O'Lochlainn, *Anglo-Irish Song-Writers* (1950), 17) but 'The Rambling Boys of Pleasure', an Anglo-Irish broadside ballad, the text of which is in the National Library, Dublin. Mr Shields gives several versions and says it was written to the Irish metre of, for example, *An beinnsín luachra* ; he obtained his source from Mr. Paddy Tunney.

I

You rambling boys of pleasure, give ear unto these words I write
For I own I am a rover and in rambling I take great delight.

I've set my heart on a fair young girl though oftentimes she
    does me slight
But my mind is never easy but when my own girl is in my sight.

II

Down by yon flowery garden my love and I we first did meet.
I took her in my arms and to her I gave kisses sweet.
She bade me take life easy just as the leaves fall from the tree
But I being young and foolish with my own darling did not
    agree.

III

The second time I met my love I vowed her heart was surely
    mine
But as the weather changes my darling girl she changed her
    mind.
Gold is the root of evil although it wears a glittering hue :
Causes many a lad and lass to part though their hearts like mine
    be e'er so true.

IV

I wish I was in Americay and my true love along with me,
Money in my pocket to keep us in good company,
Liquor to be plenty, a flowing bowl on every side
Hard fortune ne'er would daunt me for I am young and the
    world is wide.

Mr Shields quotes two other stanzas and remarks that Yeats
would probably not have liked the rest of the ballad and 'retained
only the most strikingly poetic lines'.

1   *salley* : willow

THE MEDITATION OF THE OLD FISHERMAN   23

This poem was written in June 1886 and first appeared in *IM*
(Oct. 1886). Yeats commented that 'This poem is founded upon
some things a fisherman said to me when out fishing in Sligo
Bay' (*P* (1895)). He is elsewhere described as 'a not very old
fisherman at Rosses Point' (*CW* 1).

6   *creel* : wicker basket for fish, or in Ireland, for turf (peat)

23 THE BALLAD OF FATHER O'HART

This poem first appeared in *Irish Minstrelsy* (ed. H. Halliday Sparling, 1888); it was then entitled 'The Priest of Coloony'. 'Father O'Hart' was the title used in *CK*. Yeats appended to the text of the poem a brief note which reads:

> Coloony is a few miles south of the town of Sligo. Father O'Hart lived there in the last century, and was greatly beloved. These lines accurately record the tradition. No one who has held the stolen land has prospered. It has changed owners many times. (*FFT* 220)

This comment was expanded in the notes:

> Father O'Rorke is the priest of the parishes of Ballysadare and Kilvarnet and it is from his learnedly and faithfully and sympathetically written history of these parishes that I have taken the story of Father John, who had been priest of these parishes, dying in the year 1739. Coloony is a village in Kilvarnet.
>
> Some sayings of Father John's have come down. Once when he was sorrowing greatly for the death of his brother, the people said to him, 'Why do you sorrow so for your brother when you forbid us to keen?' 'Nature', he answered, 'forces me, but ye force nature.' His memory and influence survives, in the fact that to the present day there has been no keening in Coloony.
>
> He was a friend of the celebrated poet and physician, Carolan. (*FFT* 324)

In a later volume Yeats further glossed the poem:

> The robbery of the lands of Father O'Hart was one of those incidents which occurred sometimes, though but rarely, during the time of the penal laws. Catholics, who were forbidden to own landed property, evaded the law by giving some honest Protestant nominal possession of their estates. There are instances on record in which poor men were nominal owners of unnumbered acres. (*CK*)

2 *penal days*: Penal laws against Roman Catholics existed in Ireland after the 1560 Parliament but 'the amount of persecuting statutes in Ireland was actually small compared to England' (*HI* 224). Yeats, however, is referring to a series of measures enacted

against Catholics, after William and Mary came to the throne up to 1727. They were not repealed until 1829.

3 *shoneen* : Yeats's footnote read 'upstart' ; his note was longer :
Shoneen is the diminutive of shone (Ir. *Séon*). There are two Irish names for John — one is *Shone*, the other is *Shawn* (Ir. *Séaghan*). Shone is the 'grandest' of the two, and is applied to the gentry. Hence *Shoneen* means 'a little gentry John', and is applied to upstarts and 'big' farmers, who ape the rank of gentleman. (*FFT*)

6 *Sleiveens* : Yeats's footnote read 'mean fellow'; his note was **24** longer :
Sleiveen, not to be found in the dictionaries, is a comical Irish word (at least in Connaught) for a rogue. It probably comes from *sliabh*, a mountain, meaning primarily a mountaineer, and in a secondary sense, on the principle that mountaineers are worse than anybody else, a rogue. I am indebted to Mr Douglas Hyde for these details, as for many others. (*FFT*)

13 *only* : except

22 *keeners* : professional mourners who utter the keen for the dead at wakes and funerals in Ireland. From Ir. *Caoinim*, I wail.

27 *Colooney* : Yeats commented : 'a few miles south of the town of Sligo'

30 *Knocknarea* : 'round cairn-headed Knocknarea', the 'hill of the executions', a mountain overlooking Sligo, where Queen Maeve is supposed to be buried. She was a Queen of Connaught who invaded Ulster in the Cattle Raid of Cooley, the central story of the Red Branch cycle told in the *Táin Bó Cuálgne*.

31 *Knocknashee* : this may be Knocknashee Common in the parish of Achonry in the Barony of Leyny, Co. Sligo. There is a Knocknashee in Boyle, Co. Roscommon.

35 *Tiraragh* : this may be Teeraree (*Tír a ríg*), a townland in the **25** parish of Kilmorgan, Co. Sligo

36 *Ballinafad* : a village in the parish of Aughanagh, on the Sligo road near Boyle

37 *Inishmurray* : an island in the Atlantic, now uninhabited

THE BALLAD OF MOLL MAGEE

This poem first appeared in *WO*, but Katharine Tynan told Allan Wade she thought it appeared in *The Gael* (1887). See *B* 20. It was derived from a sermon preached in the chapel at Howth [then a fishing village, now a suburb on the northern side of the headland and peninsula which forms the northern arm of Dublin Bay]. (*PW* 11).

6 *say* : sea

7–9 *saltin' herrings . . . saltin' shed* : Howth herrings were supplied by a local fishing fleet and the salting sheds lined one of the piers of the harbour.

26 24 *Kinsale* : fishing port in Co. Cork

32 *boreen* : Ir. for lane

27 48 *keenin'* ; see note (p. 17) on line 22 'The Ballad of Father O'Hart' (*CP* 23)

49 *she* : Saul (*PYP* 50) comments that this refers to the dead child.

27 THE BALLAD OF THE FOXHUNTER

The original title was 'The Ballad of the Old Fox-hunter' in the first published version, in *East and West* (Nov. 1889). The second printing, in *UI* (28 May 1892), added 'An incident from Kickham's "Knocknagow"' and Yeats's note remarked that the ballad founded on this incident from *Knocknagow* was probably in its turn a transcript from Tipperary tradition. C. J. Kickham (1826–82) author and journalist, member of Young Ireland movement 1848, joined the Fenian movement 1860, was condemned to fourteen years

penal servitude in 1865, and released after four years. He wrote
ballads as well as the novel *Knocknagow* (1879). Yeats read *Knock-nagow* when he was collecting material for *RIT* and included items
from it in that volume. He also used material from it in *WO*.
The following pages are the source for the poem.

Dr. Kiely was astonished to find his patient in a chair on the
lawn, propped up with pillows. His son, a tall, cadaverous-looking man with grizzled hair and beard, stood on one side
of the chair, and a saintly looking though somewhat spruce
young clergyman at the other. Two graceful young ladies
stood a little apart, looking very sad and interesting, but not
altogether oblivious of the handsome young clergyman's
presence.

'Blow, Rody, blow,' muttered the poor old invalid. And the
horn sounded, and the woods gave back the echo.

'O sweet Woodlands, must I leave you?' exclaimed the old
foxhunter in tones of the deepest grief.

'You're going to a better place,' said the clergyman, im-
pressively.

'Yoix! Tallyho!' cried the invalid, faintly. 'Blow, Rody,
blow.'

'Don't ax me, sir,' returned the huntsman, after putting the
horn to his lips and taking it away again ; 'my heart is ready to
burst.'

'O sweet Woodlands, must I leave you?' his master exclaimed again.

'My dear sir,' the clergyman repeated, stooping over him
and placing his gloved hand gently upon his shoulder, 'my
dear sir, you are going to a better place.'

The invalid turned round and looked earnestly into the
young clergyman's face, as if he had until then been unconscious of his presence.

'You're going to a better place ; trust me, you're going to a
better place,' the clergyman repeated fervently.

'Ah!' replied the old foxhunter, with a sorrowful shake of
his head, and looking earnestly into the parson's face — 'ah!
by G——, I doubt you!'

The parson's look of consternation brought a grim smile
into the hard features of Mr. Sam Somerfield, as he adjusted his
father's nightcap, which was displaced by the effort to turn
round to look at his spiritual director.

The dying foxhunter seemed to drop suddenly into a doze,

from which a low fretful whine from one of the hounds caused
him to awake with a start. 'Poor Bluebell ; poor Bluebell,'
he murmured. The hound named wagged her tail, and coming
close to him, looked wistfully into his face. The whole pack
followed Bluebell, waving their tails, and with their trustful
eyes appeared to claim recognition, too, from their old master.
But his head drooped, and he seemed falling asleep again. He
roused himself, however, and gazed once more upon the fine
landscape before him, and again called upon the huntsman to
sound the horn. The huntsman put it to his lips, and his chest
heaved as he laboured for breath ; but no sound awoke the
echoes again.

'God knows I can't, sir,' he cried at last, bursting into
tears. The huntsman's emotion moved the two young ladies
to tears, and they came nearer to their grandfather's chair,
and looked anxiously into his face. Dr. Kiely laid his finger on
the old man's wrist, and turned to whisper something to his
son, who was still standing by the chair. But the doctor drew
back, as if the eye of a murderer were upon him. Mr. Sam
Somerfield's face was ashy pale and his lips vivid, while a
baleful light glared from under his shaggy brows, which were
dragged together in puckered folds. His daughters, too, were
terrified, and wondered what could have brought that shock-
ing expression into their father's face. But guided by his eyes
they turned round and saw that Mr. Lowe was standing near
them : then they understood that terrible look.

The young girls gazed upon the woods and groves and
undulating meadows, just as their grandfather had done. And
the expression in the bright eye of youth and in the dimmed
eye of age was the same.

'Ah,' said the younger girl, as her sister's eyes met hers, 'it
is a sweet place.'

Turn round, young ladies, and look through that arched
gateway to yon sloping hillside, speckled with white sheep,
upon which the sun shines so brightly. There were many
happy homes along that green slope not many years ago.
There is not one now. You remember the last of them — the
old farm-house in the trees, with its cluster of cornstacks ;
and the square orchard, that looked so pretty in the spring-
time ; and the narrow boreen leading to the road between
tangled wild roses and woodbines ? You remember the children who peered shyly at you from under their brown arms
when you rode by upon your pretty ponies ? You remember

what a rage your papa was in when the man who lived there refused to give up the old lease ; and how he swore when the old lease had expired, and the 'scoundrel' — that was the word — refused to go until the sheriff and police and military drove him away ?

To be sure, his father, and grandfather, and great-grandfather had lived there before him. He paid your papa fifty gold guineas every year, and was willing to pay half as many more if he were allowed to toil on there to the end of his days ; though old people remembered when that productive little farm was covered with furze and briers, with patches of green rushes here and there in the marshy places. Well, he should go ; and the children — but what do you care for such things ? We merely meant to remind you that, to that poor man and his wife and children, their place, too, was 'a sweet place.'

'I suppose,' thought Mr. Sam Somerfield, 'he came here purposely to watch till the breath is out of him, in order that I may be hunted without an hour's delay.' Then fixing his eyes upon the old man with a look in which pity and hatred seemed blended, he continued, 'What right had he to take such a lease ? He cared only for himself. Why wasn't it *my* life he got it for ? He might have died, and died an old man, twenty years ago. And I wish to heaven he did die twenty years ago, before my heart was rooted in it.'

An old blind hound, lying on a mat near the door, raised his head, and uttered a long dismal howl. The whole pack took up the cry ; and, as it passed like a wail of sorrow over the hills, the old foxhunter fell back in his chair — dead !

The huntsman threw himself from his horse ; and, with the help of two or three other servants, carried his old master into the house.

'O papa, poor grandpapa is gone !' the young girls exclaimed, flinging their arms round their father's neck.

He bent down as they clung to him, looking quite helpless and stupefied. But, when he saw the horse from which the huntsman had dismounted, walk to a square stone near the end of the house, and stand quietly beside it, and thought that 'old Somerfield' would never mount his hunter from that stone again, the tears ran down his hard, yellow cheeks, and fell upon his children's hair.

(*Knocknagow*, 491–4)

The Rose

The Rose was a heading used first by Yeats in *P* (1895) for a group of some shorter poems taken from *CK*. Yeats wrote in 1925 that on reading the poems in *The Rose* for the first time for several years he noticed that the quality symbolised as The Rose differed from the Intellectual Beauty of Shelley and of Spenser in that he had imagined it as suffering with man and not as something pursued and seen from afar.

It must have been a thought of my generation, for I remember the mystical painter Horton [W. T. Horton (1864–1919) a black-and-white artist of a mystic nature, whose *A Book of Images* (1898) contained an Introduction by Yeats] whose work had little of his personal charm and real strangeness, writing me these words, 'I met your beloved in Russell Square and she was weeping', by which he meant that he had seen a vision of my neglected soul. *(CP)*

The poems in the section named *The Rose* were printed because in them 'he has found, he believes, the only pathway whereon he can hope to see with his own eyes the Eternal Rose of Beauty and of Peace' *(P* (1895)).

35 TO THE ROSE UPON THE ROOD OF TIME

This poem first appeared in *CK*.

1 *Red Rose*: Yeats used roses decoratively in very early poems, but by 1891 he had begun to use the rose as an increasingly complex symbol. In doing so he was influenced by current English poetic practice and by the work of Irish poets in whose work it had stood for Ireland : 'It has given a name to more than one poem, both Gaelic and English, and is used, not merely in love poems but in addresses to Ireland, as in De Vere's line, "The little black rose shall be red at last", and in Mangan's "Dark Rosaleen". I do not

of course, use it in this latter sense' (*CK*). Rose was the name of a girl with black hair in Irish patriotic poetry; she was Róisín Dubh, Dark Rosaleen, and personified Ireland. Yeats also alluded to the use of the Rose symbol in religious poems 'like the old Gaelic which speaks of "the Rose of Friday" meaning the Rose of Austerity' (*P* (1895)). He added that he had written a good deal on it in the notes to *WR* and these notes are included in this volume's comments on 'The Poet pleads with the Elemental Powers' (*CP* 80), 'He thinks of his Past Greatness . . . ' (*CP* 81), 'He hears the Cry of the Sedge' (*CP* 75). The Rose symbolises spiritual and eternal beauty. Its meaning as a symbol was intensified by Yeats's membership of the Golden Dawn, an occult society or Rosicrucian order (See note (p. 141) on 'The Mountain Tomb' (*CP* 136)) into which he was initiated by MacGregor Mathers, the author of *The Kabbalah Unveiled*, on 7 March 1890. See note (p. 316) on 'All Souls' Night' (*CP* 256). From him and from the rituals of the Golden Dawn (which included Egyptian, Kabbalist and Christian imagery) Yeats learned of a series of geometric symbols that he could classify according to the four elements, and what the ancients called the fifth element and sub-divisions of these. In his unpublished Autobiography he wrote : 'I allowed my mind to drift from image to image and these images began to affect my writing, making it more sensuous and vivid.' In the Rosicrucian symbolism a conjunction of rose (with four leaves) and cross forms a fifth element — a mystic marriage — the rose possessing feminine sexual elements, the cross masculine ; the rose being the flower that blooms upon the sacrifice of the cross. The Rose was a central symbol in the Order of the Golden Dawn, and Ellman (*Y:M & M* 97), quotes Stanislas de Guaïta (who founded in Paris in 1888 a Kabbalistic Order of the Rosy Cross) who wrote in *Rosa Mystica* :

The Rose that I invite you to pluck — sympathetic friend who turn these pages — does not flower on the shores of faraway countries ; and we shall take, if you please, neither the express train nor the transatlantic steamer.

Are you susceptible to a deep emotion of the intellect? and do your favourite thoughts so haunt you as to give you at times the illusion of being real? . . . You are then a magician, and the mystic Rose will go of her own accord, however little you desire it, to bloom in your garden.

Yeats wrote to Ernest Boyd in February 1915 that his interest in mystic symbolism did not come from Arthur Symons or any other contemporary writers but from his own study of the mystic tradition which dated from 1887; he had found in writers such as Valentin Andrea authority for his use of the Rose (*L* 592). Wade commented that Yeats probably read Johannes Valentine Andreae or Andreas (1586–1654) the German theologican and mystic, in Foxcroft's translation of *The Hermetic Romance or the Chymical Wedding* (1690) originally written in High Dutch by C[hristian] R[osenkreuz]; this was reprinted in A. E. Waite, *The Real History of the Rosicrucians* (1887). In July 1892 Yeats wrote to John O'Leary that he could not have written his Blake book nor *The Countess Cathleen* had he not made magic his constant study — 'The mystical life is the centre of all that I do and all that I think and all that I write.' The study of magic was 'next to my poetry, the most important pursuit of my life' (*L* 210).

The Rose symbolism had other elements: physical and spiritual, pagan and Christian, and Yeats described them in an autobiographical passage:

> I planned a mystical Order . . . and for ten years to come my most impassioned thought was a vain attempt to find philosophy and to create ritual for that Order. I had an unshakable conviction, arising how or whence I cannot tell, that invisible gates would open as they opened for Blake [see note (p. 31) on 'The Rose of Peace' (*CP* 41). 'The Blessed' (*CP* 75) has his association of holiness with passion, an idea also contained in 'The Secret Rose' (*CP* 77), where the Rose symbolises spiritual beauty], as they opened for Swedenborg, as they opened for Boehme, and that this philosophy would find its manuals of devotion in all imaginative literature and set before Irishmen for special manual an Irish literature which, though made by many minds, would seem the work of a single mind, and turn our places of beauty or legendary association into holy symbols. I did not think this philosophy would be altogether pagan, for it was plain that its symbols must be selected from all those things that had moved men most during many, mainly Christian, centuries.
>
> I thought for a time I could rhyme of love, calling it *The Rose* because of the Rose's double meaning; of a fisherman who had 'never a crack' in his heart; of an old woman complaining of the idleness of the young, or of some cheerful

fiddler, all those things that 'popular poets' write of, but that I must some day — on that day when the gates began to open — become difficult or obscure. With a rhythm that still echoed Morris I prayed to the Red Rose, to Intellectual Beauty. [He then quoted from the second stanza of 'To the Rose upon the Rood of Time'.] (*A* 253)

The 'mystical Order' was to include Maud Gonne ; Yeats's uncle George Pollexfen and MacGregor Mathers were helpful but the idea was his own, and in the 1890s he envisaged the order centring on an empty castle on the Castle Rock in Lough Key which he had seen when visiting Douglas Hyde :

There is a small island entirely covered and still [indecipherable] empty castle. The last man who lived there had been Dr Hyde's father who when a young man had lived there for a few weeks. All round it were the wooded and hilly shores — a place of great beauty. I believed that this castle could be hired for little money and I had long dreamed of a king, an Irish Eleusis or Samothrace. An obsession more constant than anything but my love itself was the need of mystical writing a retired system of evocation and meditation — to reunite the perception of the spirit, of the divine with natural beauty. I believed that instead of thinking of Judaea as holy we should [believe] our own land holy and most holy when most beautiful. Commerce and manufacture have made the world ugly. The death of pagan nature worship had robbed visible beauty of its inviolable sanctity and I was convinced that all lonely and lovely places were crowded with invisible beings and that it would be possible to communicate with them. I meant to interest young men and women in the worship which would unite the radical truths of Christianity with those of a more ancient world, and to use the Castle Rock for these occasional retirements from the world. For years to come I was in my thoughts as in much of my writing to seek alone to bring again imaginative life in the old sacred places. Slieve Knocknarea all that old reverence that hung above all conspicuous hills. But I wished by writing and thought of the school I founded . . . I believed we were about to have a revelation. Maud Gonne entirely shared this idea and I did not doubt that in carrying this out I should win her for myself. Politics were merely a means of meeting her but this was a link so perfect that would restore at once even in a quarrel the sense of intimacy. At every moment of leisure we obtained

in visions long lists of various symbols that corresponded to
the cardinal points and all the old gods and heroes took place
gradually in the symbolic fabric that had for its centre the four
tales bringing the Tuatha de Danaan the sword the stone the
pen and the cauldron which related themselves in my mind to
the Irish of the Tarot cards.   (Unpublished MS., cf. *A* 253)

This Order of Celtic mysteries was regarded by Yeats as a means
of escaping from active life and politics as well as a means of gaining
Maud Gonne's love.   He wrote to George Russell (AE) on 23
January 1898 :

I am deep in 'Celtic Mysticism', the whole thing is forming
an elaborate vision.   Maude Gonne and myself are going for
a week or two perhaps to some country place in Ireland to
get as you do the forms of gods and spirits and to get some
sacred earth for evocation.   Perhaps we can arrange to go
somewhere where you are so that we can all work together.
Maud Gonne has seen a vision of a little temple of the heroes
which she proposes to build somewhere in Ireland when '98
is over [celebrations to commemorate Wolfe Tone and the
Rebellion of 1798] and to make the centre of our mystical and
literary movements.   (*L* 295)

The Rose also symbolises Maud Gonne, who told the present
editor that Yeats intended to allude to her by the symbol, and
through her to Ireland.   In 'The Rose upon the Rood of Time'
the Rose is eternal beauty and something of its meaning is indicated in his remark that Timon of Athens and Cleopatra sorrow
for all men's fate.   'Tragic joy' was a quality Yeats appreciated
and he wrote of it :

That shaping joy has kept the sorrow pure, as it had kept it
were the emotion love or hate, for the nobleness of the arts is
in the mingling of contraries, the extremity of sorrow, the
extremity of joy, perfection of personality, the perfection of
its surrender, overflowing turbulent energy, and marmorean
stillness ; and its red rose opens at the meeting of the two
beams of the cross, and at the trysting-place of mortal and
immortal, time and eternity.   (*E & I* 255)

3   *Cuchulain* : the 'Hound of Culain', the hero of the Red Branch
(or Ulster, or Conorian) cycle of tales.   In *The Tragical Death of
Conlaech* the hero kills his own son.   Yeats also spelt the name

Cuhoollin and Cuchullin, and commented that it is pronounced Cuhoolin (see Appendix : Gaelic Names, p. 539) and remarks that his poem is founded on a West of Ireland legend given by Curtin in *Myths and Folklore in Ireland* adding that the bardic tale of the death of Cuchulain is very different (*CK*). See also 'Cuchulain's Fight with the Sea' (*CP* 37) and the plays *On Baile's Strand* and *The Only Jealousy of Emer*. Birgit Bjersby (*ICL*) gives a useful account, and Brendan Kennelly, 'The heroic ideal in Yeats's Cuchulain plays', *Hermathena*, C 1 (Autumn 1965), 13-21, is also stimulating.

5   *Fergus* : Fergus MacRoy, also from the Red Branch cycle, was King of Ulster ; he was tricked out of his crown by Ness the mother of Concobar. The story is told in the Book of Leinster, translated by Whitley Stokes, *Eriu*, IV, 22. Yeats remarked that he was the poet of the cycle and that he gave up his throne that he might live at peace hunting in the woods (*P* (1895)).

20   *the bright hearts* : Yeats wrote 'I do not remember what I meant by "the bright hearts" but a little later I wrote of spirits "with mirrors in their hearts"' (*A* 255).

23   *Eire*: Eire, or Ireland, originally a name of a queen of the Tuatha de Danaan or tribes of the goddess Dana

FERGUS AND THE DRUID   **36**

This poem first appeared in *NO* (21 May 1892).
1   *Fergus* : see note (p. 27) on 'To the Rose upon the Rood of Time' (*CP* 35). Yeats suggested that his source for the legend was Sir Samuel Ferguson, *P* (1895 ; rev. 1899). He commented that 'the proud dreaming king' of 'The Secret Rose' (*CP* 77) was founded upon Fergus, the son of Roigh, the legendary poet of 'the quest of the bull of Cualg[n]e' as he was in the ancient story of Deirdre and in modern poems by Sir Samuel Ferguson. Fergus married Ness (or Nessa) and Ferguson 'makes him tell how she took him "captive in a single look"' :

> I am but an empty shade,
> Far from life and passion laid ;
> Yet does sweet remembrance thrill
> And my shadowy being still.

Presently, because of his great love, he gave up his throne to Conchobar, her son by another, and lived out his days feasting, and fighting, and hunting. His promise never to refuse a feast from a certain comrade, and the mischief that came by his promise, and the vengeance he took afterwards, are a principal theme of the poets (*W*R).

8   *Druid* : cf. line 4 'To the Rose upon the Rood of Time' (*CP* 35)

Red Branch kings : the Red Branch heroes served Conchubar King of Ulster at his court Emain Macha.

10   *Conchubar* : Yeats also spelt the name Conhor and Concobar and described him as king of all Ireland in the time of the Red Branch kings (*P* (1895)). He is the central figure in the saga *The Fate of the Children of Usna* from which Yeats and Synge among other Irish writers quarried their Deirdre plays.

37   35   *quern* : apparatus for grinding corn, usually consisting of two circular stones, the upper turned by hand

40   *slate-coloured thing* : the little bag of dreams of line 29, described in early versions as a 'small slate-coloured bag of dreams'

37   CUCHULAIN'S FIGHT WITH THE SEA

This poem first appeared in *UI* (11 June 1892) with the title 'The Death of Cuchulain'; it was extensively revised and *VE* 105 should be consulted. The last version is strengthened.

2   *Emer* : Emer of Borda, spelt Emir in the original version, the daughter of Forgael, was Cuchulain's wife. His wooing is told in *The Wooing of Emer* in the *Book of the Dun Cow*. This poem derives from J. Curtin, *Myths and Folklore in Ireland* (*CK*), from oral tradition, and from a ninth-century tale in *The Yellow Book of Lecan* where Cuchulain's son is by Aoife (with whom the hero had an affair when he was having advanced training in arms with Scathach, an Amazon) not by Emer. Other tales concerning their married life are *The Sickbed of Cuchulain* (in which Emer has her

only jealousy of another woman, Fand, the wife of Manannan MacLir), and *Bricriu's Feast* (which deals with questions of precedence between Cuchulain and two other warriors and their wives). Bjersby, (*ICL* 23-7), discusses other possible sources, among them Sir Samuel Ferguson.

raddling: this can mean either to dye with red ochre, or to weave or intertwine: 'dyeing cloth' was originally intended as the first three lines read:

> A man came slowly from the setting sun,
> To Emer of Borda, in her clay-piled dun
> And found her dyeing cloth with subtle care . . .

dun: fortress

3   *that swineherd*: the original version included the line 'I am Aileel, the swineherd, whom you bid' and Aileel was spelt Aleel in later versions.

6   *web*: woven stuff

7   *raddled*: red with dye

16   *one sweet-throated*: Eithne Inguba, Cuchulain's young mistress   **38**

18   *her son*: Finmole in early versions (see note on line 68)

21   *herd*: herdsman

33   *The Red Branch*: Conchubar and his army

40   *young sweetheart*: Eithne Inguba   **39**

68   *Cuchulain I*: the original version read 'I am Finmole mighty   **40** Cuchulain's son'.

72   *sweet-throated maid*: Eithne Inguba

THE ROSE OF THE WORLD   **41**

This poem first appeared in *NO* (2 Jan. 1892) entitled 'Rosa Mundi'.

4 *Troy* : this poem was written to Maud Gonne, later (*c.* 1903–14) frequently identified with Helen of Troy, and with Deirdre. At the time Yeats was full of John Todhunter's play *Helen of Troy*.

5 *Usna's children* : Deirdre, the daughter of King Concobar's storyteller, prophesied she would bring great suffering upon Ulster. Concobar prevented her death at the hands of the Ulstermen by saying she was to be brought up to be his future queen. Despite isolation with a nurse, Lavarcam, she fell in love with Naoise, one of the Red Branch heroes. He escaped with her to Scotland (along with his brothers, the other sons of Usna, who were Ainle and Ardan) where they lived happily for some years. Conchobar then sent Fergus to offer a peaceful return. Deirdre opposed the return, but Naoise insisted and they were separated from Fergus (for whom it was *geasa* — an equivalent to *tabu* — not to be able to refuse an invitation to a feast). See notes (p. 28) on 'Fergus and the Druid' (*CP* 36). Conchobar then had the sons of Usna beheaded, contrary to the promise he had made to Cathbad the Druid, who had used spells to bring about their capture. Yeats referred to Deirdre's beautiful lament over the bodies of the children of Usna which had been finely translated by Sir Samuel Ferguson in his *Deirdre* (P (1895)). Cathbad cursed Conchobar and Emania, and this curse was worked out in the legend of the *Táin Bó Cualgne*. Deirdre, in one version of the legend, stabbed herself ; in another was forced to live a year with Conchobar, who intended to hand her on to Owen (who killed Naoise, her husband), but killed herself by leaping from a chariot in which both men were travelling with her. Yeats's note reads: 'the quality symbolised in such poems . . . differs from the intellectual beauty of Shelley and of Spenser in that it is imagined as suffering, with man and not as something pursued from afar'.

13 *Weary and kind* : the poem was first composed of two stanzas. Yeats recited it to George Russell (AE) and some friends in this original form after he and Maud Gonne had returned from walking a long distance in the Dublin mountains. Yeats was worried because she had been exhausted by walking on the rough mountain roads, and added the third stanza, much to George Russell's disapproval. The latter told Professor E. R. Dodds (to whom the

present editor is indebted for this information) that he disliked these lines for their sentimentality and especially for the incongruity of the words 'weary and kind'. He thought the word 'kind' meaningless in its context and explained that it was there because Maud Gonne, though tired and footsore, was in a gentler mood than usual after the long walk. He also thought it ridiculous to call the world of human experience 'a grassy road' and told the story to illustrate how fine poetry can be ruined by the intrusion of the transient and incidental.

THE ROSE OF PEACE   41

This poem first appeared in *NO* (13 Feb. 1892). Its original title was 'The Peace of the Rose'.

1   *Michael*: the archangel

4   *deeds*: in the war between God and Satan, of which Yeats read in *Paradise Lost*

16   *Heaven with Hell*: Swedenborgian but also reminiscent of   42
Blake's juxtapositions though not the 'paradoxical violence' of *The Marriage of Heaven and Hell*. Cf. *E* 44.

THE ROSE OF BATTLE   42

This poem first appeared in *CK*; its title then was 'They went forth to the Battle but they always Fell'.

A FAERY SONG   43

Sung by the people of Faery over Diarmuid and Grania,
in their bridal sleep under a Cromlech

This poem first appeared in *NO* (12 Sept. 1891).

Subtitle: The earlier versions state the song was sung by 'the good people' over the author Michael Dwyer and his bride, who had escaped into the mountains. (Michael Dwyer was a rebel leader in the 1798 rebellion who operated in the Wicklow mountains.) *The Pursuit of Diarmuid and Grania* is one of the Fenian cycle of tales. The Fianna (Yeats described the Fenians as 'a great military order of which Finn was chief' in *P* (1895; rev. 1899) are generally supposed to have been a body of infantry (though there is some

mention of horsemen in the cycle) who were particularly prominent in the reign of Cormac Mac Art, whose supposed son-in-law
Finn MacCumhall (Yeats spelt his name Fion) was their leader.
Their power was supposed to have been broken in the Battle of
Gabhra, A.D. 297 (Yeats spelt it Gavra). MS. evidence points to
twelfth-century composition for the tales and ballads, though some
of them may have been composed in the eighth century. In the
tale Finn, an ageing widower, decided to marry Grania (Grainne)
the daughter of Cormac Mac Art, but she preferred a younger man
and offered herself, after she had drugged the other banqueters at
her betrothal feast, to Diarmuid and Oisin. Both refused, but she
put Diarmuid under *geasa* to elope with her that night, which he
did unwillingly. Finn pursued them with the Fianna, who tried
to protect Diarmuid and Grania from him, but he eventually killed
Diarmuid by treachery and Grania transferred her attentions back
to him. Yeats described her as a beautiful woman

> who fled with Dermot to escape from the love of aged Finn.
> She fled from place to place over Ireland, but at last Dermot
> was killed at Sligo upon the seaward point of Benbulben, and
> Finn won her love and brought her, leaning upon his neck,
> into the assembly of the Fenians, who burst into inextin-
> guishable laughter. (*P* (1895))

Cromlech: a prehistoric stone construction consisting of one large
stone laid upon several upright stones

5   *these children*: the lovers Diarmuid and Grania. See also Yeats's
story 'Hanrahan's Vision' (*M* 246–52).

44   THE LAKE OF INNISFREE

This poem was written in 1890 and first appeared in *NO* (13 Dec.
1890). It was written in Bedford Park, a London suburb, and a
passage in 'Ganconagh's'[1] [Yeats's] novel *John Sherman* (1891) gives

---

1 Yeats annotated the word in *FFT* 323–4, pointing out that it was not to
be found in dictionaries and meant a 'love-talker'. He quoted O'Kearney for
the description 'another diminutive being of the same tribe as the Lepracaun
but, unlike him, he personated love and idleness, and always appeared with a
dudeen [clay pipe] in his jaw in lonesome valleys, and it was his custom to
make love to shepherdesses and milkmaids. It was considered very unlucky
to meet him . . .'

an insight into the personal feelings underlying the poem :

> Delayed by a crush in the Strand, he heard a faint trickling of water near by ; it came from a shop window where a little water-jet balanced a wooden ball upon its point. The sound suggested a cataract with a long Gaelic name, that leaped crying into the gate of the winds at Ballagh. . . . He was set dreaming a whole day by walking down one Sunday morning to the borders of the Thames a few hundred yards from his house — and looking at the osier-covered Chiswick eyot. It made him remember an old day-dream of his. The source of the river that passed his garden at home was a certain wood-bordered and islanded lake, whither in childhood he had often gone blackberrying. At the further end was a little islet called Innisfree. Its rocky centre, covered with many bushes, rose some forty feet above the lake. Often when life and its difficulties had seemed to him like the lessons of some elder boy given to a younger by mistake, it had seemed good to dream of going away to that islet and building a wooden hut there and burning a few years out rowing to and fro fishing, or lying on the island slopes by day, and listening at night to the ripple of the water and the quivering of the bushes — full always of unknown creatures — and going out at morning to see the island's edge marked by the feet of birds.

Yeats described himself as 'very homesick in London' when he made the poem, in a letter of 30 November 1922, replying to schoolgirls who had asked if Innisfree was a real island (*WBY* 39), and is explicit elsewhere :

> I had still the ambition, formed in Sligo in my teens, of living in imitation of Thoreau on Innisfree, a little island in Lough Gill, and when walking through Fleet Street very homesick I heard a little tinkle of water and saw a fountain in a shop-window which balanced a little ball upon its jet, and began to remember lake water. From the sudden remembrance came my poem *Innisfree* my first lyric with anything in its rhythm of my own music. I had begun to loosen rhythm as an escape from rhetoric and from that emotion of the crowd rhetoric brings, but I only understood vaguely and occasionally that I must for my special purpose use nothing but the common syntax. A couple of years later I would not have written that first line with its conventional archaism — 'Arise and go' — nor the inversion in the last stanza. (*A* 153)

Elsewhere Yeats suggested that Thoreau may have had some influence on the desire for solitary life expressed by the poems and linked the island again with the local legends :

> My father had read to me some passage out of *Walden*, and I planned to live some day in a cottage on a little island called Innisfree, and Innisfree was opposite Slish Wood. . . . I thought that having conquered bodily desire and the inclination of my mind toward women and love, I should live, as Thoreau lived, seeking wisdom.   There was a story in the county history [William Gregory Wood-Martin, *History of Sligo* (1882)] of a tree that had once grown upon that island guarded by some terrible monster and borne the food of the gods.   A young girl pined for the fruit and told her lover to kill the monster and carry the fruit away.   He did as he had been told, but tasted the fruit ; and when he reached the mainland where she waited for him, he was dying of its powerful virtue. And from sorrow and remorse she too ate of it and died.   I do not remember whether I chose the island because of its beauty or for the story's sake, but I was twenty-two or three before I gave up the dream.   (*A* 71-2)

Katharine Tynan probably discussed Thoreau with him ; she included a poem 'Thoreau at Walden' in her *Louise de la Vallière and other Poems* (1885), and on 21 December 1888 Yeats wrote to her enclosing 'two verses I made the other day' — an early version of the first two stanzas of the poem about the little rocky island with a legended past : 'In my story [*John Sherman*] I make one of the characters whenever he is in trouble long to go away and live alone on that Island — an old day dream of my own' (*L* 99). The island attracted Yeats because of its association with Irish legend and folk-lore.   These are discussed by Russell K. Alspach, *Yeats and Innisfree* (1965).   A poem 'The Danaan Quicken Tree' printed in *TB* (May 1893) had a note after the title explaining these associations which runs :

> It is said that an enchanted tree grew once on the little lake-island of Innisfree, and that its berries were, according to one legend, poisonous to mortals, and according to another, able to endow them with more than mortal powers.   Both legends say that the berries were the food of the *Tuatha de Danaan*, or faeries.   Quicken is the old Irish name for the mountain ash.   The Dark Joan mentioned in the last verse is a famous

faery who often goes about the roads disguised as a clutch of chickens. Niamh is the famous and beautiful faery who carried Oisin into Faeryland. *Aslauga Shee* means faery host.

1 *I will arise* : cf. the parable of the prodigal son, Luke xv. 18 : 'I will arise and go to my father.'

9 *night and day* : cf. the cleansing of the unclean spirits, Mark v. 5 : 'And always, night and day, he was in the mountains.'

A CRADLE SONG   **45**

This poem first appeared in *SO* (19 April 1890). Early versions had an epigraph:

> '*Cloth yani nu von gilli beg,*
> *?N heur ve thu more a creena*'

'*Cloth*' was altered to '*Coth*' in *CK*. Early versions (*VE* 118) show how Yeats's rewriting strengthened the poem. It was altered by W. E. Henley (1849–1903), the editor of *SO*, in its early state.

7 *The Sailing Seven* : the planets

11–12 *That I shall miss you when you have grown* : Yeats wrote to Katharine Tynan that the last two lines were suggested by a Gaelic song quoted in Gerald Griffin's novel *The Collegians* (*L* 148). Gerald Griffin (1803–40) was an Irish novelist, poet and dramatist.

THE PITY OF LOVE   **45**

This poem first appeared in *CK*.

THE SORROW OF LOVE   **45**

This poem was written in October 1891 and first appeared in *CK*. Yeats described it as one of several altogether new poems produced by rewriting (*Early Poems and Stories* (1925)). *VE* 119 gives different versions of the poem ; it is one of the best known examples of Yeats's rewriting of his earlier work.

5 *A girl arose* : presumably Helen of Troy, but the poem also **46** relates to Maud Gonne's beauty.

6   *Odysseus* : son of Laertes, king of the Island of Ithaca, a suitor of Helen and married to Penelope.   He took part in the Greek expedition to recover Helen from Troy where Paris took her from Menelaus.   He took nearly twenty years to return to Ithaca after the sack of Troy, his adventures being recounted in Homer's *Odyssey*.

7   *Priam* : Son of Laomedon, was the last king of Troy and father of many children, among whom were Hector, Paris, and Cassandra ; he was killed by Neoptolemus, the son of Achilles, after the fall of Troy.

46   WHEN YOU ARE OLD

This poem was written on 21 October 1891 and first appeared in *CK*.   It was written to Maud Gonne, and is founded upon, but is not a translation of, Ronsard's 'Quand Vous Serez Bien Vieille', *Sonnets pour Hélène*, II (1578).

46   THE WHITE BIRDS

This poem first appeared in *NO* (7 May 1892).   The title in this printing had a note after it which read '(*The birds of fairyland are said to be white as snow.   The Danaan Islands are the islands of the fairies*.)'   'The Danaan Shore is, of course, *Tier-nan-Oge*, or fairyland.' (*CK*)

Madame MacBride (to whom, as Maud Gonne, the poem was written) told the present editor that she and Yeats had been walking on the cliffs at Howth one afternoon (the day after Yeats had first proposed to her and been rejected) and were resting when two seagulls flew over their heads and on out to sea.   She had said that if she was to have the choice of being any bird she would choose to be a seagull above all, a commonplace remark, but 'in three days he sent me the poem with its gentle theme, "I would that we were my beloved, white birds on the foam of the sea".'

2   *meteor* : because meteors do not last long in the sight of the onlooker

47   3   *blue star of twilight* : Venus

5   *the lily and rose* : the lily is a masculine symbol, the rose feminine.

9 *Danaan* : fairy. See Yeats's note (p. 48), 'The Hosting of the Sidhe' (*CP* 61).

A DREAM OF DEATH   **47**

This poem first appeared in *NO* (12 Dec. 1891), the title being 'An Epitaph'.

1 *one* : Maud Gonne, who had gone to France to recover from fatigue caused by her aiding victims of evictions in Donegal, where there was a famine. She had a tendency to tuberculosis. Her comment on the poem was, 'I was getting steadily better and was greatly amused when Willie Yeats sent me a poem, my epitaph he had written with much feeling' (*SQ* 147). Cf. 'He wishes his Beloved were Dead' (*CP* 80).

strange place : the south of France where Maud Gonne was convalescing

11 *thy first love* : perhaps Laura Johnston, a red-headed cousin   **48** with whom Yeats fell in love when the Yeatses lived at Howth :

> . . . I saw a great deal of her and was soon in love. I did not tell her I was in love, however, because she was engaged. She had chosen me for her confidant and I learned all about her quarrels with her lover. Several times he broke the engagement off, and she fell ill, and friends had to make peace. . . . I wrote her some bad poems and had more than one sleepless night through anger with her betrothed.
> (*A* 76)

THE COUNTESS CATHLEEN IN PARADISE   **48**

This poem first appeared in *NO* (31 Oct. 1891) with the title 'Kathleen'. This was altered to 'Song' in *CK*. This song was from scene v of *The Countess Cathleen* ; the title used in *P* (1895) was 'A Dream of a Blessed Spirit'. The poem was renamed 'The Countess Cathleen in Paradise' because, as Yeats commented in 1926, he had rewritten it so much (see *VE* 124), that it was 'almost a new poem' (*P* (1895 ; rev. 1927)). See also a letter to Olivia Shakespear, written in October 1927, stating he had rewritten 'a poor threadbare poem of his youth ... it is almost a poem for children . . . I like the last verse, the dancer Cathleen has become heaven itself.' (*L* 731). Yeats initially wrote *The Countess Cathleen* to convince Maud Gonne that he could write for a public audience ; the play illustrates Cathleen's 'sad resolve' to aid the famine-crazed folk (which was like Maud Gonne's desire to help the Donegal peasants). His play was founded on 'The Countess Kathleen O'Shea', *FFT*, 232–35, which was 'quoted in a London-Irish newspaper'.

The poet in the play, Kevin (Aleel), in his relationship to Cathleen, is not unlike Yeats *vis-à-vis* Maude Gonne, despairing of persuading her to marry him and to give up the politics that were, he thought, swamping her noble qualities : he is tired of his soul, but he tries to stop Cathleen selling hers. In old age Yeats records this in 'The Circus Animals' Desertion' (*CP* 391) :

> And then a counter-truth filled out its play,
> *The Countess Cathleen* was the name I gave it;
> She, pity-crazed, had given her soul away,
> But masterful Heaven had intervened to save it.
> I thought my dear must her own soul destroy,
> So did fanaticism and hate enslave it,
> And this brought forth a dream and soon enough
> This dream itself had all my thought and love.

He wrote in his Preface that the chief poem was an attempt to mingle personal thought and feeling with the beliefs and customs of Christian Ireland, whereas his earlier book *The Wanderings of Oisin* had tried to record the effect on his imagination of the pre-Christian cycle of legends. He hoped Ireland, having a huge body of tradition behind her in the depths of time, would draw inspiration from the double fountainhead of the Christian and Pagan cycles, and make for herself 'a great distinctive poetic literature'. She already had many moving songs and ballads which are quite her own, and *The Countess Cathleen*, like *The Wanderings of Oisin*, was an attempt to write a more ample method to feeling 'not less national, Celtic and distinctive' (*CK*).

7   *mournful* : an alteration from the first version of the line ('For she needs not her sad beauty'), the adjective used in line 5 of 'The Sorrow of Love' (*CP* 45)

13 *angels seven*: the detail is reminiscent of Rossetti, the original version of the line reading, 'And her guides are angels seven'.

WHO GOES WITH FERGUS? 48

This poem first appeared in *CK* and is a lyric in the second scene of the play *The Countess Cathleen*.

1 *Fergus*: see note (p. 27) on 'Fergus and the Druid' (*CP* 36)

9 *rules the brazen cars*: Fergus uses chariots for his peaceful, 49 poetic pursuits, and the wood is presumably a place in which the cares of life could be escaped.

THE MAN WHO DREAMED OF FAERYLAND 49

This poem first appeared in *NO* (7 Feb. 1891).

1 *Dromahair*: Dromohair, in Co. Leitrim

8 *world-forgotten isle*: akin to the first of the four paradises to which Niamh brings Oisin in 'The Wanderings of Oisin', II, 193–357. Cf. George Mills Harper, *Yeats's Quest for Eden* (1965), 302–5.

13 *Lissadell*: Lissadell (spelt Lisadill and Lisadell in early versions), home of the Gore-Booth family in Sligo. See 'In Memory of Eva Gore-Booth and Con Markiewicz' (*CP* 263).

14 *money cares and fears*: as a young man Yeats spent many summers in Sligo through lack of funds, sometimes staying with his mother's family, later with his uncle George Pollexfen.

16 *hill*: the hill of Lugnagall, see line 37

21 *the golden or the silver skies*: solar and lunar principles when 50 fused are an alchemical emblem of perfection (see *Y & T* 219). Yeats distinguished between solar meaning, according to what he learned from MacGregor Mathers (see note, p. 316, on 'All Souls' Night' (*CP* 256)) 'elaborate, full of artifice, rich, all that resembles the work of a goldsmith, whereas . . . lunar . . . is simple, popular, traditional, emotional' (*A* 371).

The poem displays Yeats's symbolist technique developing in richness ; the gold and silver of the first stanza are blended in the second with its dancer and its golden and silver skies and the sun and moon. The symbols gradually attain their power by repetition and the idea of blessedness, of perfection, is created. Poems like this and 'The Song of Wandering Aengus' (*CP* 66) with 'The silver apples of the Moon, the golden apples of the Sun'; 'He wishes for the Cloths of Heaven' (*CP* 81) with its cloths 'Enwrought with golden and silver light'; and 'The Happy Townland' (*CP* 94) with its 'golden and silver wood', are later caught up in the fuller symbolism of poems like 'Under the Round Tower' (*CP* 154) with its 'sun and moon', its 'golden king and silver lady'; 'The Tower' (*CP* 218) where the sunlight and moonlight seem 'one inextricable beam' of perfection, and 'Those Dancing Days are Gone' (*CP* 302) with '. . . *the sun in a golden cup, The moon in a silver bag.*'

22 *a dancer* : represents fairyland and blessedness. Cf. line 45, where the symbols represent Innocence by the dreamless wave, an idea recaptured later in 'To a Child dancing in the Wind' (*CP* 136). It becomes more important in poems like 'The Double Vision of Michael Robartes' (*CP* 192), 'Among School Children' (*CP* 242), and even in the ironic fusion of 'News for the Delphic Oracle' (*CP* 376) with its 'golden codgers' and 'all the silver dew'.

23 *sun and moon* : see note on line 21

25 *Scanavin* : Padraic Colum has informed the editor that Scanavin, Knockfefin and Crevroe are three small townlands in Co. Sligo. See notes (p. 526) on line 179 'The Wanderings of Oisin' III (*CP* 409).

33 *silver fret the gold* : cf. note on line 21

35 *lover there by lover* : cf. the 'lover by lover' of 'The Wild Swans at Coole' (*CP* 147)

37 *the hill of Lugnagall* : 'The Curse of the Fires and of the Shadows' is a story of the death of five Puritan troopers who attacked an Abbey and were subsequently led by a (fairy ?) piper

to their deaths. Their route led them in pursuit of two rebels along 'the road between Ben Bulben and the great mountain spur that is called Cashel-na-Gael' (*M* 182). Their guide led them to

the brink of the abyss that is now called Lugnagall, or in English the Steep Place of the Strangers. The six horses sprang forward, and five screams went up into the air, and a moment later five men and five horses fell with a dull crash upon the green slopes at the foot of the rocks. (*M* 183)

41 *spired*: a use which anticipates the later 'spiring' in 'Demon and Beast' (*CP* 209)

47 *God burn Nature*: this idea of God burning time was used in 'He tells of the Perfect Beauty' (*CP* 74); the idea of the world burning out 'like a candle that is spent' was also used in 'The Death of Hanrahan' (*M* 260), and in 'In Memory of Eva Gore-Booth and Con Markiewicz' (*CP* 263), '. . . strike a match, And strike another till time catch'.

THE DEDICATION TO A BOOK OF STORIES SELECTED FROM **51**
THE IRISH NOVELISTS

This poem first appeared in *RIT*. Yeats called it, even in its re-written form, 'a sheaf of wild oats' (*Irish Statesman* (8 Nov. 1924)). It was originally entitled 'Dedication'.

1 *green branch*: *bell-branch*, Yeats explained as a legendary branch whose shaking cast all men into a gentle sleep (*P* (1895)). See line 12.

2 *Eire*: Eire, spelt Eri in early version, see note (p. 27) on line 23 'The Rose upon the Rood of Time' (*CP* 35)

THE LAMENTATION OF THE OLD PENSIONER **52**

This poem first appeared in *SO* (15 Nov. 1890) entitled 'The Old Pensioner'. It is another drastically rewritten poem. The original version runs as follows:

> I had a chair at every hearth
> When no one turned to see,
> With 'Look at the old fellow there;
> And who may he be?'
> And therefore do I wander on,
> And the fret lies on me.

> The road-side trees keep murmuring.
> Ah, wherefore murmur ye,
> As in the old days long gone by,
> Green oak and poplar tree ?
> The well-known faces are all gone,
> And the fret lies on me.

Of this Yeats said it was 'little more than a translation into verse of the very words of an old Wicklow peasant' (*CK*). Yeats used the experience in *CT* also :

A winter or two ago he spent much of the night walking up and down upon the mountain talking to an old peasant who, dumb to most men, poured out his cares for him. Both were unhappy : X because he had then first decided that art and poetry were not for him, and the old peasant because his life was ebbing out with no achievement remaining and no hope left him. Both how Celtic ! How full of striving after a something never to be completely expressed in word or deed. The peasant was wandering in his mind with prolonged sorrow. Once he burst out with, 'God possesses the heavens but He covets the earth' and once he lamented that his old neighbours were gone and that all had forgotten him : they used to draw a chair to the fire for him in every cabin, and now they said 'Who is that old fellow there ? ' 'The fret (Irish for doom) is over me,' he repeated, and then went on to talk once more of God and Heaven. More than once he said, waving his arm towards the mountain, 'Only myself knows what happened under the thorn-tree forty years ago' ; and as he said it the tears upon his face glistened in the moonlight. This old man always rises before me when I think of X. Both seek — one in wandering sentences, the other in symbolic pictures and subtle allegoric poetry — to express something that lies beyond the range of expression ; and both, if X will forgive me, have within them the vast and vague extravagance that lies at the bottom of the Celtic heart. The peasant visionaries that are, the landlord duellists that were, and the whole hurly burly of legends — Cuchullin fighting the sea for two days until the waves pass over him and he dies, Caolte storming the palace of the Gods, Oisin seeking in vain for three hundred years, to appease his insatiable heart with all the pleasures of faeryland, these two mystics walking up and down upon the mountain uttering the central dream of their souls

in no less dream-laden sentences, and this mind that finds X
so interesting — all are a portion of that great Celtic phan-
tasmagoria whose meaning no man has discovered nor any
angel revealed. (*CT* 23). A different version is given in
M 13 ff.

X is George Russell (A E), and another note places the conversation
as occurring on the Two Rock Mountain, south-west of Dublin.
See also 'My friend's Book' (*E & I* 412–13) for A E's meditating
there.

THE BALLAD OF FATHER GILLIGAN   52

This poem first appeared in *SO* (5 July 1890) with the title 'Father
Gilligan / A Legend told by the people of Castleisland, Kerry'.
    Yeats commented that the ballad was written to a modification
of the air *A Fine Old English Gentleman* (*E & I* 21).

25 *Mavrone* : cry of grief. In *The Book of the Rhymers' Club* (1892)   53
this appears as 'Ochone, ochone !', a similar cry.

THE TWO TREES   54

This poem first appeared in *CK*.

2 *The holy tree* : the Sephirotic tree of the Cabbala and the tree
of knowledge. Two other early poems deal with the tree of life,
'He thinks of his Past Greatness when a Part of the Constellations of Heaven' (*CP* 81) and 'He hears the Cry of the Sedge'
(*CP* 75). Ellmann (*IY* 76) comments:

    The Kabbalah is helpful in interpreting his poem 'The Two
    Trees', because the Sephirotic tree has two aspects, one
    benign, the reverse side malign. On one side are the *Sephiroth*,
    on the other the dead *Qlippoth*. Since the Kabbalists consider
    man to be a microcosm, the double-natured tree is a picture
    both of the universe and of the human mind, whose faculties,
    even the lowest, can work for good or ill. Yeats can therefore
    write,
                Beloved, gaze in thine own heart,
                The holy tree is growing there . . .

and at the same time warn her not to look in 'the bitter glass', where the tree appears in its reverse aspect :

> For there a fatal image grows,
>> With broken boughs and blackened leaves,
> And roots half-hidden under snows
>> Driven by a storm that ever grieves.

Although the poem is comprehensible without the esoteric source, the source helps to explain how it came to be written. F. Kermode (*RI* 96) suggests Blake as a source :

> Love and harmony combine,
> And around our souls entwine,
> While thy branches mix with mine,
> And our roots together join.
>
> Joys upon our branches sit,
> Chirping loud, and singing sweet ;
> Like gentle streams beneath our feet
> Innocence and virtue meet.
>
> Thou the golden fruit dost bear,
> I am clad in flowers fair ;
> Thy sweet boughs perfume the air,
> And the turtle buildeth there.
>
> There she sits and feeds her young,
> Sweet I hear her mournful song ;
> And thy lovely leaves among,
> There is love ; I hear his tongue.
>
> There his charming nest doth lay,
> There he sleeps the night away;
> There he sports along the day,
> And doth among our branches play.

He regards this tree (in a poem of innocence) as the Tree of Life, and thinks Yeats drew upon Blake's later 'Art is the Tree of Life . . . Science is the Tree of Death', trying to incorporate in 'The Two Trees' the ideas in 'Blake's illustrations to Dante', that the good tree is desire and divine energy, the bad is morality and nature, the fallen world, selfhood and abstraction. Yeats wrote:

> The kingdom that was passing was, he held, the kingdom of the Tree of Knowledge ; the kingdom that was coming was the kingdom of the Tree of Life : men who ate from the Tree of Knowledge wasted their days in anger against one another,

and in taking one another captive in great nets; men who
sought their food among the green leaves of the Tree of Life
condemned none but the unimaginative and the idle, and
those who forget that even love and death and old age are an
imaginative art. (*E & I* 130)

Kermode explains as the Tree of Life or Imagination 'the holy
tree' of the poem, inhabited by love, growing in the heart of a
beautiful woman who does not think. If she does so she is breaking
her beauty by an act of homage to the abstract, bartering beauty
for argument, for the Tree of the Fall. This is depicted in the
lines which follow 'Gaze no more in the bitter glass . . .'. Kermode
thinks the poem one of the few improved by revision because
Yeats only emphasised the difference between the anti-intellectual
tree and the 'dead rottenness' of the second tree.

In an essay on Magic (*E & I* 28-52) Yeats described how he saw
a young Irishwoman cast into trance who thought in her waking
state the apple of Eve the kind bought in a grocer's shop, but in
trance saw the Tree of Life with ever-sighing souls moving in its
branches instead of sap, and all the fowls of the air among its
leaves with a white fowl on its highest bough wearing a crown.
When Yeats returned home he took from the shelf a translation
[by MacGregor Mathers in *The Kabbalah Unveiled*] of *The Book of
Concealed Mystery*, an old Jewish book, 'and cutting the pages
came upon this passage, which I cannot think I had ever read:
"The Tree . . . is the Tree of the Knowledge of Good and Evil . . .
in its branches the birds lodge and build their nests, the souls and
the angels have their place"' (*E & I* 44).

13   *circle*: Yeats elsewhere described the Tree of Life as a geo-   55
metrical figure made up of ten circles or spheres called Sephiroth
joined by straight lines, and added that once men must have
thought of it as 'like some great tree covered with its fruit and its
foliage', but he thought at some period it had lost its natural form
(*A* 375).

13-18   The original version reads:

> There, through bewildered branches, go
> Winged Loves borne on in gentle strife
> Tossing and tossing to and fro
> The flaming circle of our life.

> When looking on their shaken hair
> And dreaming how they dance and dart . . .

16 *ignorant* : is here a virtue compared to the 'unresting thought' of line 34.

22 *the demons* : perhaps of abstract thought. The soul was likely to be ambushed on its road to truth. 'Abstract thought' which devoured the freedom and pride of life and hunger for miracles were listed in Yeats's opening address to the Hermetic Society of June 1885. See *Y : M & M* 43.

25 *a fatal image* : this is the Tree of Knowledge as opposed to the Tree of Life. See Yeats's comment on Blake, quoted earlier.

56 TO SOME I HAVE TALKED WITH BY THE FIRE

This poem first appeared in *TB* (May 1895) with a sub-title *The Dedication of a new book of verse.*
1 *Danaan* : see note (p. 37) on line 9 'The White Birds' (*CP* 46) and Yeats's note (p. 48) on 'The Hosting of the Sidhe' (*CP* 61)

56 TO IRELAND IN THE COMING TIMES

This poem first appeared in *CK*. The title then read 'Apologia addressed to Ireland in the coming days'. This poem is in part a defence of the obscurity caused by 'a passion for the symbolism of the mystical rose which has saddened my friends', in part an explanation of Yeats's attitude to the role of literature in the struggle for Irish independence, in part a love poem to Maud Gonne. He argued that his patriotism was to be considered as being no less than that of the Young Irelanders and patriotic writers of the past.

4 *rann* : a verse of a poem in Irish, not the whole poem

57 18 *Davis, Mangan, Ferguson* : Yeats discussed the part played by these writers in a letter in *UI* (10 Sept. 1892). Thomas Osborne Davis (1814–45) founded *N* in 1842, and was leader of the Young Ireland party. He wrote poems and prose of a popular, patriotic kind. James Clarence Mangan (1803–49), was a romantic Irish

poet and essayist, who wrote prolifically for the magazines and journals of his period, sometimes translating, sometimes adapting Irish material and German. Sir Samuel Ferguson (1810–86) was an Irish lawyer, poet and antiquary who translated the Gaelic legends in a masculine manner truer to the originals than Yeats's twilight style.

20 *more than their rhyming tell* : Yeats wanted to recreate the old mythology by infusing new life into it, to reach beyond nationality into universality. His interest in the occult and in symbolism added a new dimension to the material he was handling and gave the touch of mystery he required. See note (p. 48) on *WR* (*CP* 59).

The Wind Among the Reeds

YEATS introduced this volume in *CW* I in 1906 with the comment that he had so meditated on the images that had come to him in writing 'Ballads and Lyrics', 'The Rose' and 'The Wanderings of Oisin' and other images from Irish folklore that they had become true symbols. He had when awake, but more often in sleep, moments of vision; 'a state very unlike dreaming, when these images took upon themselves what seemed an independent life and became a part of a mystic language, which seemed always as if it would bring me some strange revelation.' Being troubled by what was thought to be reckless obscurity he tried to explain himself in lengthy notes into which he put 'all the little learning I had, and more wilful phantasy than I now think admirable, though what is most mystical still seems to me the most true'.

61 THE HOSTING OF THE SIDHE

This poem was written on 29 August 1893, and first appeared in *NO* (7 Oct. 1893) with the title 'The Faery Host'. Yeats's note covers the following words : Sidhe, Knocknarea, Clooth-na-Bare, Caolite and Niamh, and is quoted in full :

> The powerful and wealthy called the gods of ancient Ireland the Tuatha De Danaan, or the Tribes of the goddess Danu, but the poor called them, and still sometimes call them, the Sidhe, from Aes Sidhe or Sluagh Sidhe, the people of the Faery Hills, as these words are usually explained. Sidhe is also Gaelic for wind, and certainly the Sidhe have much to do with the wind. They journey in whirling winds, the winds that were called the dance of the daughters of Herodias in the Middle Ages, Herodias doubtless taking the place of some old goddess. When the country people see the leaves whirling on the road they bless themselves, because they believe the Sidhe

to be passing by. They are almost always said to wear no covering upon their heads, and to let their hair stream out; and the great among them, for they have great and simple, go much on horseback. If any one becomes too much interested in them, and sees them over much, he loses all interest in ordinary things. I shall write a great deal elsewhere about such enchanted persons, and can give but an example or two now.

A woman near Gort, in Galway, says: 'There is a boy, now, of the Cloran's; but I wouldn't for the world let them think I spoke of him; it's two years since he came from America, and since that time he never went to Mass, or to Church, or to fairs, or to market, or to stand on the cross roads, or to hurling, or to nothing. And if anyone comes into the house, it's into the room he'll slip, not to see them; and as to work, he has the garden dug to bits, and the whole place smeared with cow dung; and such a crop as was never seen; and the alders all plaited till they look grand. One day he went as far as the chapel; but as soon as he got to the door he turned straight round again, as if he hadn't power to pass it. I wonder he wouldn't get the priest to read a Mass for him, or something; but the crop he has is grand, and you may know well he has some to help him.' One hears many stories of the kind; and a man whose son is believed to go out riding among them at night tells me that he is careless about everything, and lies in bed until it is late in the day. A doctor believes this boy to be mad. Those that are at times 'away', as it is called, know all things, but are afraid to speak. A countryman at Kiltartan says, 'There was one of the Lydons — John — was away for seven years, lying in his bed, but brought away at nights, and he knew everything; and one, Kearney, up in the mountains, a cousin of his own, lost two hoggets, and came and told him, and he knew the very spot where they were, and told him, and he got them back again. But *they* were vexed at that, and took away the power, so that he never knew anything again, no more than another.' This wisdom is the wisdom of the fools of the Celtic stories, that was above all the wisdom of the wise. Lomna, the fool of Fiann, had so great wisdom that his head, cut from his body, was still able to sing and prophesy; and a writer in the 'Encyclopaedia Britannica' writes that Tristram, in the oldest form of the tale of Tristram and Iseult, drank wisdom, and madness the shadow of wisdom, and not love, out of the magic cup.

The great of the old times are among the Tribes of Danu, and are kings and queens among them. Caolte was a companion of Fiann; and years after his death he appeared to a king in a forest, and was a flaming man, that he might lead him in the darkness. When the king asked him who he was, he said, 'I am your candlestick.' I do not remember where I have read this story, and I have, maybe, half forgotten it. Niam was a beautiful woman of the Tribes of Danu, that led Oisin to the Country of the Young, as their country is called; I have written about her in *The Wandering[s] of Usheen*; and he came back, at last, to bitterness and weariness.

Knocknarea is in Sligo, and the country people say that Maeve, still a great queen of the western Sidhe, is buried in the cairn of stones upon it. I have written of Clooth-na-Bare in *The Celtic Twilight*. She 'went all over the world, seeking a lake deep enough to drown her faery life, of which she had grown weary, leaping from hill to hill, and setting up a cairn of stones wherever her feet lighted, until, at last, she found the deepest water in the world in little Lough Ia, on the top of the bird mountain, in Sligo.' I forget, now, where I heard this story, but it may have been from a priest at Collooney. Clooth-na-Bare would mean the old woman of Bare, but is evidently a corruption of Cailleac Bare, the old woman Bare, who, under the names Bare, and Berah, and Beri, and Verah, and Dera, and Dhira, appears in the legends of many places. Mr O'Grady found her haunting Lough Liath high up on the top of a mountain of the Fews, the Slieve Fuadh, or Slieve G-Cullain of old times, under the name of the Cailleac Buillia. He describes Lough Liath as a desolate moon-shaped lake, with made wells and sunken passages upon its borders, and beset by marsh and heather and gray boulders, and closes his 'Flight of the Eagle' with a long rhapsody upon mountain and lake, because of the heroic tales and beautiful old myths that have hung about them always. He identifies the Cailleac Buillia with that Meluchra who persuaded Fionn to go to her amid the waters of Lough Liath, and so changed him with her enchantments, that, though she had to free him because of the threats of the Fiana, his hair was ever afterwards as white as snow. To this day, the Tribes of the Goddess Danu that are in the waters beckon to men, and drown them in the waters; and Bare, or Dhira, or Meluchra, or whatever name one likes the best, is, doubtless, the name of a mistress among them. Meluchra was daughter of Cullain; and Cullain Mr O'Grady calls, upon I know not what authority, a form of

Lir, the master of waters. The people of the waters have been in all ages beautiful and changeable and lascivious, or beautiful and wise and lonely, for water is everywhere the signature of the fruitfulness of the body and of the fruitfulness of dreams. The white hair of Fionn may be but another of the troubles of those that come to unearthly wisdom and earthly trouble, and the threats and violence of the Fiana against her, a different form of the threats and violence the country people use, to make the Tribes of Danu give up those that are 'away'. Bare is now often called an ugly old woman; but Dr Joyce says that one of her old names was Aebhin, which means beautiful. Aebhen was the goddess of the tribes of northern Leinster; and the lover she had made immortal, and who loved her perfectly, left her, and put on mortality, to fight among them against the stranger, and died on the strand of Clontarf. (*WR*)

3 *Caoilte*: cf. Yeats's note (p. 78) on 'The Secret Rose' (*CP* 77), and his note on this poem quoted above. Though Yeats described him there as a companion of Fiann, he was also a comrade of Oisin, the son of Finn. He was the swiftest runner of the Fianna.

4 *Niamh*: cf. 'The Wanderings of Oisin' (*CP* 409 ff.) and 'News for the Delphic Oracle' (*CP* 376), where she is described as 'Man-picker'; and 'The Circus Animals' Desertion' (*CP* 391) where she is the 'faery bride'. In the Fenian tale, *Oisin in the Land of the Young*, Niamh, who is extremely beautiful, spirits Oisin off to the land of the Young for three hundred years.

11–12 *between him and the deed ... and the hope*: a passage in Yeats's *Pages from a Diary written in 1930* seems to link this poem and these lines with 'The Everlasting Voices' (*CP* 61), and 'To his Heart, bidding it have no Fear' (*CP* 71). In it Yeats suggested that his conceptions, one of reality as a congeries of beings, another of reality as a single being, alternate in emotion and history and cannot be reconciled by human reason because it is always subject to one or the other. He saw himself as driven to a moment 'which is the realisation of myself as unique and free, or to a moment which is the surrender to God of all that I am'. He thought there were historical cycles in which one or the other predominated, and that a cycle was approaching where all would be as particular and

concrete as human intensity would permit. He had tried again
and again

> to sing that approach — *The Hosting of the Sidhe*, 'O Sweet
> Everlasting Voices' and those lines about 'The lonely,
> majestical multitude' — and have almost understood my
> intention. Again and again with remorse, a sense of defeat,
> I have failed when I would write of God, written coldly and
> conventionally. Could those two impulses, one as much a
> part of the truth as the other, be reconciled, or if one or the
> other could prevail, all life would cease. (*E* 305)

61 THE EVERLASTING VOICES

This poem was written on 29 August 1895 and first appeared in
NR (Jan. 1896) with the title 'Everlasting Voices'.

1 *everlasting Voices, be still*: In one of Yeats's stories, Hanrahan,
when he is dying, hears 'faint joyful voices' and he asks who they
are, to receive the reply, 'I am one of the lasting people, of the
lasting unwearied Voices, that make my dwelling in the broken
and the dying and those that have lost their wits; and I came
looking for you, and you are mine until the whole world is burned
out like a candle that is spent . . .' (*M* 260). Another essay, 'The
Golden Age', refers to Yeats seeming to hear a voice of lamentation
of the Golden Age. It told him that humans were imperfect and
incomplete, that the world was once perfect and kindly and that
the kindly and perfect world still existed but 'buried like a mass of
roses under many spadefuls of earth'. The fairies and more
innocent spirits dwelt within it and lamented over the fallen world
of humanity 'in the lamentation of the wind-tossed reeds' in the
song of birds, the moan of waves, and the cry of the fiddle. It is
said that 'if only they who live in the Golden Age could die we
might be happy, for the sad voices would be still; but they must sing
and we must weep until the eternal gates swing open'. (*M* 104–5)

62 THE MOODS

This poem first appeared in *TB* (Aug. 1893). Yeats's essay on 'The
Moods', dated 1855, provides a prose gloss upon the poem. It
reads:

Literature differs from explanatory and scientific writing in being wrought about a mood, or a community of moods, as the body is wrought about an invisible soul; and if it uses argument, theory, erudition, observation, and seems to grow hot in assertion or denial, it does so merely to make us partakers at the banquet of the moods. It seems to me that these moods are the labourers and messengers of the Ruler of All, the gods of ancient days still dwelling on their secret Olympus, the angels of more modern days ascending and descending upon their shining ladder; and that argument, theory, erudition, observation, are merely what Blake called 'little devils who fight for themselves,' illusions of our visible passing life, who must be made serve the moods, or we have no part in eternity. Everything that can be seen, touched, measured, explained, understood, argued over, is to the imaginative artist nothing more than a means, for he belongs to the invisible life, and delivers its ever new and ever ancient revelation. We hear much of his need for the restraints of reason, but the only restraint he can obey is the mysterious instinct that has made him an artist, and that teaches him to discover immortal moods in mortal desires, an undecaying hope in our trivial ambitions, a divine love in sexual passion. (*E & I* 195)

3 *mountains and woods*: these lines are close to a passage in 'The Death of Hanrahan':

I am young, I am young; look upon me, mountains; look upon me, perishing woods, for my body will be shining like the white waters when you have been hurried away. You and the whole race of men, and the race of the beasts, and the race of the fish, and the winged race, are dropping like a candle that is nearly burned out . . . (*M* 254)

4 *have their day*: a passage in the essay 'Rosa Alchemica' illustrates these lines with the picture given to six students in a book of alchemical doctrines. If they were to imagine the semblance of a living being it was at once possessed by a wandering soul which went hither and thither working good or evil, until the moment of its death had come:

If you would give forms to the evil powers, it went on, you were to make them ugly, thrusting out a lip with the thirsts of life, or breaking the proportions of a body with the burdens of life; but the divine powers would only appear in beautiful shapes, which are but, as it were, shapes trembling out of existence, folding up into a timeless ecstasy, drifting with half-shut eyes into a sleepy stillness. The bodiless souls who descended into these forms were what men called the moods; and worked all great changes in the world; for just as the magician or the artist could call them when he would, so, they could call out of the mind of the magician or the artist, or if they were demons, out of the mind of the mad or the ignoble, what shape they would, and through its voice and its gestures pour themselves out upon the world. In this way all great events were accomplished; a mood, a divinity or a demon, first descending like a faint sigh into men's minds and then changing their thoughts and their actions until hair that was yellow had grown black, or hair that was black had grown yellow, and empires moved their border, as though they were but drifts of leaves. (*M* 285)

6 *fire-born moods*: Yeats wrote in 'Anima Mundi' 'in the condition of fire is all music and all rest' (*M* 357) when he distinguished between terrestrial reality and the condition of fire.

7 *fallen away*: The essay 'Anima Mundi' continued:

All power is from the terrestrial condition, for there all opposites meet and there only is the extreme of choice possible, full freedom. And there the heterogeneous is, and evil, for evil is the strain one upon another of opposites; but in the condition of fire is all music and all rest. Between is the condition of air where images have but a borrowed life, that of memory or that reflected upon them when they symbolise colours and intensities of fire: the place of shades who are 'in the whirl of those who are fading . . . .'
After so many rhythmic beats the soul must cease to desire its images, and can, as it were, close its eyes.
When all sequence comes to an end, time comes to an end and the soul puts on the rhythmic or spiritual body or luminous body and contemplates all the events of its memory [cf. 'The Man and the Echo' (*CP* 393), where Yeats contemplates events in his life, arranges all in one clear view, 'Then stands in judgment on his soul'] and every possible impulse in an eternal possession of itself in one single moment. That condition is alone animate, all the rest is fantasy, and from thence come all the passions and, some have held, the very heat of the body. (*M* 356–7)

He then quoted the present poem, but 'A Meditation in Time of War' (*CP* 214) gives a similar idea. Cf. also *AV* (B) 225 ff.

THE LOVER TELLS OF THE ROSE IN HIS HEART 62

This poem first appeared in *NO* (12 Nov. 1892) with the title 'The Rose in my Heart'. In *WR* the title was 'Aedh tells of the Rose in his Heart'. Yeats's note in that volume explained that 'Aedh' (Aodh), 'Hanrahan,' and 'Michael Robartes' were personages in the stories of *TSR* but that with the exception of some of Hanrahan's and one of Aedh's poems, the poems were not from that book. He was using these personages more as principles of the mind than as actual personages. He thought it likely that only students of the magical tradition would understand him when he said that Michael Robartes was fire reflected in water, that Aedh, whose name is not only the Irish for Hugh but also for fire, was fire burning by itself:

> To put it in a different way, Hanrahan is the simplicity of an imagination too changeable to gather permanent possessions, or the adoration of the shepherds; and Michael Robartes is the pride of the imagination brooding upon the greatness of its possessions, or the adoration of the Magi; while Aedh is the myrrh and frankincense that the imagination offers continually before all that it loves. (*WR*)

4 *your image*: Maud Gonne's

6 *green knoll*: this may refer to his dream of creating a Celtic order of mysteries, centring on the island on Lough Key. See note (p. 24) on 'To the Rose upon the Rood of Time' (*CP* 35).

THE HOST OF THE AIR 63

This poem first appeared in *TB* (Nov. 1893), dated 1 October 1893, with the title 'The Stolen Bride'. Yeats's note after the title read:

> I heard the story on which this ballad is founded from an old woman at Balesodare, Sligo. She repeated me a Gaelic poem on the subject, and then translated it to me. I have always regretted not having taken down her words, and as some amends for not having done so, have made this ballad.

Any one who tastes fairy food or drink is glamoured and stolen by the fairies. This is why Bridget sets O'Driscoll to play cards. 'The folk of the air' is a Gaelic name for the fairies.

4 *Hart Lake* : a lake high up in the Ox Mountains, six or seven miles west of Ballisodare

8 *Bridget his bride* : In the story 'Kidnappers' Yeats used the same story (a footnote to the story pointed out that he had used the theme in a ballad in *WR*), and told how a young man going at nightfall to his house and his just married bride, met on his way a jolly company and with them his bride :

> They were faeries and had stolen her as a wife for the chief of their band. To him they seemed only a company of merry mortals. His bride, when she saw her old love, bade him welcome, but was most fearful lest he should eat the faery food, and so be glamoured out of the earth into that blood-less dim nation, wherefore she set him down to play cards with three of the cavalcade ; and he played on, realising nothing until he saw the chief of the band carrying his bride away in his arms. Immediately he started up, and knew that they were faeries, for all that jolly company melted into shadow and night. He hurried to his house, and as he drew near he heard the cry of the keeners [the original version of the poem included the following lines, placed after the present line 40 (which was altered from the original version) :
>> He knew now the folk of the air,
>> And his heart was blackened by dread,
>> And he ran to the door of his house ;
>> Old women were keening the dead.

In *Later Poems* (1924) Yeats commented, in a note dated 1899, that the poem was founded on an old Gaelic ballad, but in the ballad the husband found the keeners (see note (p. 17) on line 22 'The Ballad of Father O'Hart' (*CP* 24)) keening his wife when he got to his house and knew that his wife was dead. Some noteless Gaelic poet had made this into a forgotten ballad, some old verses of which my white-capped friend remembered and sang for me. (*M* 73 ff.)

Yeats's note reads :

> Some writers distinguish between the Sluagh Gaoith, the host of the air, and Sluagh Sidhe, the host of the Sidhe, and

describe the host of the air of a peculiar malignancy. Dr Joyce says, 'of all the different kinds of goblins . . . air demons were most dreaded by the people. They lived among clouds, and mists, and rocks, and hated the human race with the utmost malignity.' A very old Arann charm, which contains the words 'Send God, by his strength, between us and the host of the Sidhe, between us and the host of the air,' seems also to distinguish among them. I am inclined, however, to think that the distinction came in with Christianity and its belief about the prince of the air, for the host of the Sidhe, as I have already explained, are closely associated with the wind.

They are said to steal brides just after their marriage, and sometimes in a blast of wind. A man in Galway says, 'At Aughanish there were two couples came to the shore to be married, and one of the newly married women was in the boat with the priest, and they going back to the island ; and a sudden blast of wind came, and the priest said some blessed words that were able to save himself, but the girl was swept.'

This woman was drowned ; but more often the persons who are taken 'get the touch', as it is called, and fall into a half dream, and grow indifferent to all things, for their true life has gone out of the world, and is among the hills and the forts of the Sidhe. A faery doctor has told me that his wife 'got the touch' at her marriage because there was one of them wanted her ; and the way he knew for certain was, that when he took a pitchfork out of the rafters, and told her it was a broom, she said, 'It is a broom.' She was, the truth is, in the magical sleep to which people have given a new name lately, that makes the imagination so passive that it can be moulded by any voice in any world into any shape. A mere likeness of some old woman, or even old animal, some one or some thing the Sidhe have no longer a use for, is believed to be left instead of the person who is 'away' ; this some one or some thing can, it is thought, be driven away by threats, or by violence (though I have heard country women say that violence is wrong), which perhaps awakes the soul out of the magical sleep. The story in the poem is founded on an old Gaelic ballad that was sung and translated for me by a woman at Ballisodare in County Sligo ; but in the ballad the husband found the keeners keening his wife when he got to his house. She was 'swept' at once ; but the Sidhe are said to value those the most whom they but cast into a half dream, which may last for years, for they need the help of a living person in most of the things they do.   There are many stories of people who seem to die and be buried — though the country people will tell you it is but some one or some thing put in their place that dies and is buried — and yet are brought back afterwards.   These tales are perhaps memories of true awakenings out of the magical sleep, moulded by the imagination, under the influence of a mystical doctrine which it understands too literally, into the shape of some well-known traditional tale.   One does not hear them as one hears the others, from the persons who are 'away', or from their wives or husbands ; and one old man, who had often seen the Sidhe, began one of them with 'Maybe it is all vanity.'

Here is a tale that a friend of mine heard in the Burren hills, and it is a type of all :

'There was a girl to be married, and she didn't like the man, and she cried when the day was coming, and said she wouldn't go along with him.   And the mother said, "Get into the bed, then, and I'll say that you're sick."   And so she did. And when the man came the mother said to him, "You can't get her, she's sick in the bed:"   And he looked in and said, "That's not my wife that's in the bed, it's some old hag."   And the mother began to cry and to roar.   And he went out and got two hampers of turf and made a fire, that they thought he was going to burn the house down.   And when the fire was kindled, "Come out now," says he, "and we'll see who you are, when I'll put you on the fire."   And when she heard that, she gave one leap, and was out of the house, and they saw, then, it was an old hag she was.   Well, the man asked the advice of an old woman, and she bid him go to a faery-bush that was near, and he might get some word of her.   So he went there at night, and saw all sorts of grand people, and they in carriages or riding on horses, and among them he could see the girl he came to look for.   So he went again to the old woman, and she said, "If you can get the three bits of blackthorn out of her hair, you'll get her again."   So that night he went again, and that time he only got hold of a bit of her hair.   But the old woman told him that was no use, and that he was put back now, and it might be twelve nights before he'd get her.   But on the fourth night he got the third bit of blackthorn, and he took her, and she came away with him.   He never told the mother he had got her; but one day she saw her at a fair, and, says she, "That's my daughter; I know her by the smile and by the laugh of her," and she with a shawl about her head. So the husband said, "You're right there, and hard I worked to get her." She spoke often of the grand things she saw underground, and how she used to have wine to drink, and to drive out in a carriage with four horses every night. And she used to be able to see her husband when he came to look for her, and she was greatly afraid he'd get a drop of the wine, for then he would have come underground and never left it again. And she was glad herself to come to earth again, and not to be left there.'

The old Gaelic literature is full of the appeals of the Tribes of the goddess Danu to mortals whom they would bring into their country; but the song of Midher to the beautiful Etain, the wife of the king who was called Echaid the ploughman, is the type of all.

'O beautiful woman, come with me to the marvellous land where one listens to a sweet music, where one has spring flowers in one's hair, where the body is like snow from head to foot, where no one is sad or silent, where teeth are white and eyebrows are black ... cheeks red like foxglove in flower ... Ireland is beautiful, but not so beautiful as the Great Plain I call you to. The beer of Ireland is heady, but the beer of the Great Plain is much more heady. How marvellous is the country I am speaking of! Youth does not grow old there. Streams with warm flood flow there; sometimes mead, sometimes wine. Men are charming and without a blot there, and love is not forbidden there. O woman, when you come into my powerful country you will wear a crown of gold upon your head. I will give you the flesh of swine, and you will have beer and milk to drink, O beautiful woman. O beautiful woman, come with me!' (*W*R)

THE FISH

This poem first appeared in the *Cornish Magazine* (Dec. 1898) with the title 'Bressel the Fisherman'. 'Bressel' became 'Breasel' in *W*R. The poem was written to Maud Gonne.

6 *the little silver cords*: cf. 'their little silver heads', line 6 'The Man who dreamed of Faeryland' (*CP* 49), and 'a little silver trout' line 8 'The Song of Wandering Aengus' (*CP* 66).

65 THE UNAPPEASABLE HOST

This poem first appeared in *S* (Nov. 1896) under the title 'Two Poems concerning Peasant Visionaries'. (The other poem was 'The Valley of the Black Pig' (*CP* 73).) In *W*R it was entitled 'A Cradle Song'.

1 *Danaan children*: the Danaan children stand for the Tuatha de Danaan, the race of the gods of Dana, the mother of the ancient gods of Ireland, hence, in the popular imagination, fairies. See note (p. 11) on line 3 'The Madness of King Goll' (*CP* 17).

3 *the North*: presumably wind. The original version's third line ran: 'For winds will bear them gently when the eagle flies', and the second version published in the *Senate* (Nov. 1896) had 'For they will ride the winds when the gier-eagle flies'. Yeats's note reads:

> I use the wind as a symbol of vague desires and hopes, not merely because the Sidhe are in the wind, or because the wind bloweth as it listeth, but because wind and spirit and vague desire have been associated everywhere. A highland scholar tells me that his country people use the wind in their talk and their proverbs as I use it in my poem. (*W*R)

In the same volume he associated the North with night and sleep.

3 *ger-eagle*: geier-eagle, used (as gier eagle) in Authorised Version of the Bible to translate Hebrew *raham*, a kind of vulture. Cf. Lev. xi. 18.

8 *flaming West*: Yeats associated the West, the place of sunset, with fading and dreaming things (*W*R).

65 INTO THE TWILIGHT

This poem was written on 31 June (1893 ?) and first appeared in *NO* (29 July 1893) with the title 'The Celtic Twilight'. It was published as the last item with the title 'Into the Twilight' in *CT*.

5 *Eire*: see note (p. 27) line 23 'To the Rose upon the Rood of Time' (*CP* 35)

This poem was written on 31 January (1893 ?) and first appeared in the *Sketch* (4 Aug. 1897) with the title 'A Mad Song'; it appeared without a title in the story 'Red Hanrahan's Vision' in *McClure's Magazine* (March 1905). Yeats's note reads :

> The Tribes of the goddess Danu can take all shapes, and those that are in the waters take often the shape of fish. A woman of Burren, in Galway, says, 'There are more of them in the sea than on the land, and they sometimes try to come over the side of the boat in the form of fishes, for they can take their choice shape.' At other times they are beautiful women ; and another Galway woman says, 'Surely those things are in the sea as well as on land. My father was out fishing one night off Tyrone. And something came beside the boat that had eyes shining like candles. And then a wave came in, and a storm rose all in a minute, and whatever was in the wave, the weight of it had like to sink the boat. And then they saw that it was a woman in the sea that had the shining eyes. So my father went to the priest, and he bid him always to take a drop of holy water and a pinch of salt out in the boat with him, and nothing could harm him.'
>
> The poem was suggested to me by a Greek folk song ; but the folk belief of Greece is very like that of Ireland, and I certainly thought, when I wrote it, of Ireland, and of the spirits that are in Ireland. An old man who was cutting a quickset hedge near Gort, in Galway, said, only the other day, 'One time I was cutting timber over in Inchy, and about eight o'clock one morning, when I got there, I saw a girl picking nuts, with her hair hanging down over her shoulders ; brown hair ; and she had a good clean face, and she was tall, and nothing on her head, and her dress no way gaudy, but simple. And when she felt me coming she gathered herself up, and was gone, as if the earth had swallowed her up. And I followed her, and looked for her, but I never could see her again from that day to this, never again.'
>
> The county Galway people use the word 'clean' in its old sense of fresh and comely. (*W* R)

R. K. Alspach, 'Two Songs of Yeats', *Modern Language Notes*, lxi, 395–400, considers that Yeats's note that the poem was suggested by a Greek folk song leads us to Lucy Garnett, 'The Three Fishes', *Greek Folk Poesy* (1896) which Yeats reviewed in *TB*

(Oct. 1896). Alspach also suggests as a source Samuel Lover's 'The White Trout' which was included in Yeats' *FFT*.

1 *I* : Yeats's note (p. 64) on 'He mourns for the Change that has come upon Him and his Beloved, and longs for the End of the World' (*CP* 68) explains that the 'man with a hazel wand' of that poem 'may well have been Angus, Master of Love', described by Yeats as the God of Youth, beauty and poetry, who reigned in Tir-nan-Oge, the country of the Young (*P* (1895)). He spelt the name Angus and Aengus.

2 *a fire was in my head* : Ellmann (*IY* 298) compares Symons's 'The Broken Tryst', 'That day a fire was in my blood'.

3 *hazel wand* : elsewhere Yeats commented that the hazel tree was the Irish tree of Life or of Knowledge, and in Ireland it was doubtless, as elsewhere, the tree of the heavens (*D* (Oct. 1898)).

13 *glimmering girl* : an image of Maud Gonne with whom Yeats associated apple blossom. His account of his first meeting with her in 1889 includes the image :

> How important it all seemed to me. How much would I have given so that she might think exactly right on all these great questions. And today all is faint to me beside a moment when she passed before a window dressed white and re-arranged a spray of flowers in a vase. Twelve years after I put this impression into verse ('She pulled down the pale blossoms') I felt in the presence of a great generosity and courage and a mind without rest, and when she and all the singing birds had gone, my melancholy was not the mere melancholy of love. I had what I thought was a clairvoyant perception (of some immediate disaster) but was I can see now but an obvious deduction of an immediate waiting disaster. . . . I was in love but had not spoken of love and never meant to speak of love as the months passed I gained a mastery of myself again. What wife would she make, I thought, what share could she have in the life of a student ? (Unpublished Autobiography)

Another description of this meeting was published :

> Her complexion was luminous, like that of apple-blossom through which the light falls, and I remember her standing

that first day by a great heap of such blossoms in the window. (*A* 123)

23–4   *The silver apples . . . The golden apples* : see note (p. 39) on   **67**
'The Man who dreamed of Faeryland' (*CP* 49)

THE SONG OF THE OLD MOTHER   **67**

This poem first appeared in *TB* (April 1894) and was described as 'an old woman complaining of the idleness of the young', one of the poems that 'popular poets' write (*A* 254).

2   *seed of the fire* : Yeats's note after the title in the original explained this as 'the Irish phrase for the little fragment of burning turf [peat] and hot ashes which remains in the hearth from the day before.'

THE HEART OF THE WOMAN   **67**

This poem was written in 1894 and first appeared in the *Speaker* (21 July 1894). It was untitled, and was included in the story, 'Those Who Live in the Storm' which was reprinted with the title 'The Rose of Shadow' in *TSR*.

4   *breast lies upon his breast* : cf. line 9 'He hears the Cry of the Sedge' (*CP* 75), line 4 'He wishes his Beloved were Dead' (*CP* 80), line 9 'He thinks of his Past Greatness when a Part of the Constellations of Heaven' (*CP* 81).

THE LOVER MOURNS FOR THE LOSS OF LOVE   **68**

This poem first appeared in *D* (May 1898) with the title 'Aodh to Dectora. Three Songs'. The others were 'He hears the Cry of the Sedge' (*CP* 75) and 'He thinks of Those who have spoken Evil of his Beloved' (*CP* 75).

2   *beautiful friend* : 'Diana Vernon' [the name presumably came from the heroine of Scott's *Rob Roy*], Mrs Olivia Shakespear, with whom Yeats had his first affair in 1896. The story is told in Yeats's unpublished Autobiography. See *Y:M & P* 100–3. The

identification of Diana Vernon and Mrs Shakespear is made explicit in *PYP* 66–7. Cf. note (pp. 310–11 on 'The Empty Cup' (*CP* 251).

6 *Your image* : Maud Gonne's. Cf. *Y:M & P* 102.

68 HE MOURNS FOR THE CHANGE THAT HAS COME UPON HIM AND HIS BELOVED, AND LONGS FOR THE END OF THE WORLD

This poem first appeared in *D* (June 1897) dated 'Sligo, June 1897' with the title 'The Desire of Man and Woman'. 'Mongan laments the Change that has come upon Him and His Beloved . . .' was the title given in *WR*. In his original note to 'He [in the first version, Mongan] thinks of his Past Greatness when a Part of the Constellations of Heaven' (*CP* 81), Yeats wrote: 'Mongan, in the old Celtic poetry, is a famous wizard and king who remembers his passed lives.' (*D* Oct. 1898).

In the original version the following note was printed after the title :

> In the old Irish story of Usheen's journey to the Islands of the Young, Usheen sees amid the waters a hound with one red ear, following a deer with no horns ; and other persons in other old Celtic stories see the like images of the desire of the man, and of the desire of the woman 'which is for the desire of the man', and of all desires that are as these. The man with the wand of hazel may well have been Angus, Master of Love ; and the boar without bristles is the ancient Celtic image of the darkness which will at last destroy the world, as it destroys the sun at nightfall in the west.

A fuller note in *WR* read :

> My deer and hound are properly related to the deer and hound that flicker in and out of the various tellings of the Arthurian legends, leading different knights upon adventures, and to the hounds and to the hornless deer at the beginning of, I think, all tellings of Oisin's journey to the country of the young. The hound is certainly related to the Hounds of Annwvyn or of Hades, who are white, and have red ears, and were heard, and are, perhaps, still heard by Welsh peasants, following some flying thing in the night winds ; and is probably related to the hounds that Irish country people believe will awake and seize the souls of the dead if

you lament them too loudly or too soon. An old woman told a friend and myself that she saw what she thought were white birds, flying over an enchanted place, but found, when she got near, that they had dogs' heads ; and I do not doubt that my hound and these dog-headed birds are of the same family. I got my hound and deer out of a last-century Gaelic poem about Oisin's journey to the country of the young. After the hunting of the hornless deer, that leads him to the seashore, and while he is riding over the sea with Niamh, he sees amid the waters — I have not the Gaelic poem by me, and describe it from memory — a young man following a girl who has a golden apple, and afterwards a hound with one red ear following a deer with no horns. This hound and this deer seem plain images of the desire of the man 'which is for the woman,' and 'the desire of the woman which is for the desire of the man,' and of all desires that are as these. I have read them in this way in *The Wanderings of Oisin*, and have made my lover sigh because he has seen in their faces 'the immortal desire of immortals.'

The man in my poem who has a hazel wand may have been Aengus, Master of Love ; and I have made the boar without bristles come out of the West, because the place of sunset was in Ireland, as in other countries, a place of symbolic darkness and death.— 1899. (*C W* 1)

1   *white deer with no horns* : cf. 'The Wanderings of Oisin' (*CP* 413) where the Land of Youth is described :

> We galloped ; now a hornless deer
> Passed by us, chased by a phantom hound
> All pearly white, save one red ear . . .

The source for the image is probably Brian O'Looney's translation of Michael Comyn's *The Lay of Oisin in the Land of Youth* (the Gaelic poem of the last century mentioned in Yeats's Notes) :

> We saw also, by our sides
> A hornless fawn leaping nimbly,
> And a red-eared white dog
> Urging it boldly in the Chase.

(See Russell K. Alspach, 'Some Sources of Yeats's "The Wanderings of Oisin"', *P.M.L.A.* (Sept. 1943).)

10   *the Boar* : cf. 'The Valley of the Black Pig' (*CP* 73)

the West: see note (p. 60) on 'The Unappeasable Host' (*CP* 65), and cf. line 5 'He bids his Beloved be at Peace' (*CP* 69), 'He reproves the Curlew' (*CP* 69). 'He wishes his Beloved were Dead' (*CP* 80).

69 HE BIDS HIS BELOVED BE AT PEACE

This poem was written on 24 September 1895 and first appeared in *S* (Jan. 1876), its title being '[Two Love Poems. The Shadowy Horses] Michael Robartes bids his Beloved be at Peace'. For Michael Robartes see note (p. 55) on 'The Lover tells of the Rose in his Heart' (*CP* 62). Yeats's note to this poem read:

> November, the old beginning of winter, or of the victory of the Fomor, or powers of death, and dismay, and cold, and darkness, is associated by the Irish people with the horse-shaped Púcas, who are now mischievous spirits, but were once Fomorian divinities. I think that they may have some connection with the horses of Mannannan, who reigned over the country of the dead, where the Fomorian Tethra reigned also; and the horses of Mannannan, though they could cross the land as easily as the sea, are constantly associated with the waves. Some neo-platonist, I forget who, describes the sea as a symbol of the drifting indefinite bitterness of life, and I believe there is like symbolism intended in the many Irish voyages to the islands of enchantment, or that there was, at any rate, in the mythology out of which these stories have been shaped. I follow much Irish and other mythology, and the magical tradition, in associating the North with night and sleep, and the East, the place of sunrise, with hope, and the South, the place of the sun when at its height, with passion and desire, and the West, the place of sunset, with fading and dreaming things. (*W*R)

3 *The North*: the Fomoroh, the gods of night and death and cold, the word meaning from under the sea, were of the north and winter, according to Yeats's note in *P* (1895).

9 *Beloved*: the poem was written to 'Diana Vernon'. See note (p. 63) on 'The Lover mourns for the Loss of Love' (*CP* 68).

10 *your hair fall over my breast*: cf. line 6 'The Travail of Passion' (*CP* 78) also written to 'Diana Vernon'

HE REPROVES THE CURLEW   **69**

This poem first appeared in *S* (Nov. 1896) with the title 'Windle-
straws I. O'Sullivan Rua to the Curlew [and II. Out of the Old
Days']. The poem was entitled 'Hanrahan reproves the Curlew'
in *W*R.

2 *water in the West*: see note (p. 60) on 'The Unappeasable
Host' (*CP* 65). Perhaps there is an echo here of the Neoplatonist
who 'describes the sea as a symbol of the drifting indefinite bitterness of life' in Yeats's note (p. 66) to 'He bids his Beloved be at
Peace' (*CP* 69). The West is the region 'of fading and dreaming
things'.

5 *breast*: see note (p. 66) on line 10 'He bids his Beloved be at
Peace' (*CP* 69)

6 *wind*: a symbol of vague desires, hopes

HE REMEMBERS FORGOTTEN BEAUTY   **69**

This poem first appeared in *S* (July 1896) with the title 'O'Sullivan
Rua to Mary Lavell'; in *W*R this became 'Michael Robartes
remembers Forgotten Beauty'. For Michael Robartes see note
(p. 55) on 'The Lover tells of the Rose in his Heart' (*CP* 62).

A POET TO HIS BELOVED   **70**

This poem was written in 1895 and first appeared in the *Senate*
(March 1896) with the title 'O'Sullivan the Red to Mary Lavell II
[and was accompanied by another poem, later entitled 'Aedh tells
of the Perfect Beauty', but printed under the title 'O'Sullivan the
Red to Mary Lavell I' in *The Senate*]. 'A Poet to his Beloved' was
used as title in *W*R.

HE GIVES HIS BELOVÈD CERTAIN RHYMES   **71**

This poem was written in 1895 and first appeared in a story, 'The
Binding of the Hair', in *S* (Jan. 1896) and was untitled. In *W*R
it was entitled 'Aedh [see note on 'The Lover tells of the Rose

in his Heart' (*CP* 62)] gives his Beloved certain Rhymes'. Yeats's note on *KGCT* comments that :

> In the first edition of *The Secret Rose* there is a story based on some old Gaelic legend. A certain man swears to sing the praise of a certain woman, his head is cut off and the head sings [somewhat parallel to the story of the horse Fallada in Grimm's Tales]. A poem of mine called 'He Gives His Beloved Certain Rhymes' was the song of the head.

Hone (*WBY* 123) comments that this poem was written to 'Diana Vernon', but it seems more likely — in view of lines 3–6 — to have been written to Maud Gonne.

71   TO HIS HEART, BIDDING IT HAVE NO FEAR

This poem first appeared in *S* (Nov. 1896) with the title 'Windle-straws II. Out of the Old Days' [the companion poem was 'He reproves the Curlew']. The present title was used in *WR*.

5   *the flame and the flood* : a phrase from the initiation ritual of the Golden Dawn. See note (p. 75) on line 7 'He hears the Cry of the Sedge' (*CP* 75).

71   THE CAP AND BELLS

This poem was written in 1893 and first appeared in *NO* (17 March 1894) with the title 'Cap and Bell'. The present title was used in *WR*. Yeats's note reads :

> I dreamed this story exactly as I have written it, and dreamed another long dream after it, trying to make out its meaning, and whether I was to write it in prose or verse. The first dream was more a vision than a dream, for it was beautiful and coherent, and gave me the sense of illumination and exaltation that one gets from visions, while the second dream was confused and meaningless. The poem has always meant a great deal to me, though, as is the way with symbolic poems, it has not always meant quite the same thing. Blake would have said 'The authors are in eternity,' and I am quite sure they can only be questioned in dreams. (*WR*)

3   *his soul* : the Jester offers the lady his soul and his heart (line 13) but she is not affected by either offering but by his cap and bells

(line 21). Yeats regarded this poem as the way to win a lady, but 'He wishes for the Cloths of Heaven' as the way to lose one. See *WBY* 152.

21   cap and bells: Yeats wrote in 1901 that he knew a man who   **72** was trying to bring an image of Angus, the Irish god of love, ecstasy and poetry, before his mind's eye : 'who changed four of his kisses into birds, and suddenly the image of a man with cap and bells rushed before his mind's eye, and grew vivid and spoke and called itself 'Aengus' Messenger' (*M* 115).

THE VALLEY OF THE BLACK PIG   **73**

This poem first appeared in *S* (April 1896) with the title 'Two Poems concerning Peasant Visionaries The Valley of the Black Pig' (the companion poem was 'A Cradle Song', later 'The Unappeasable Host'). A note after the title read :

> The Irish peasantry have for generations comforted themselves, in their misfortunes, with visions of a great battle, to be fought in a mysterious valley called, 'The Valley of the Black Pig,' and to break at last the power of their enemies. A few years ago, in the barony of Lisadell, in County Sligo, an old man would fall entranced upon the ground from time to time, and rave out a description of the battle ; and I have myself heard [it] said that the girths shall rot from the bellies of the horses, because of the few men that shall come alive out of the valley.

A longer note in *W*R read :

> All over Ireland there are prophecies of the coming rout of the enemies of Ireland, in a certain Valley of the Black Pig, and these prophecies are, no doubt, now, as they were in the Fenian days, a political force. I have heard of one man who would not give any money to the Land League, because the Battle could not be until the close of the century ; but, as a rule, periods of trouble bring prophecies of its near coming. A few years before my time, an old man who lived at Lisadell, in Sligo, used to fall down in a fit and rave out descriptions of the Battle ; and a man in Sligo has told me that it will be so great a battle that the horses shall go up to their fetlocks in blood, and that their girths, when it is over, will rot from their bellies for lack of a hand to unbuckle them. The battle

is a mythological battle, and the black pig is one with the bristleless boar, that killed Dearmod, in November, upon the western end of Ben Bulben ; Misroide MacDatha's son, whose [an errata slip in the first printing of *WR* read 'Misroide MacDatha's sow, whose'] carving brought on so great a battle ; 'the croppy black sow,' and 'the cutty black sow' of Welsh November rhymes (*Celtic Heathendom*, 509–516) ; the boar that killed Adonis ; the boar that killed Attis ; and the pig embodiment of Typhon (*Golden Bough*, II. 26, 31). The pig seems to have been originally a genius of the corn, and seemingly because the too great power of their divinity makes divine things dangerous to mortals, its flesh was forbidden to many eastern nations ; but as the meaning of the prohibition was forgotten, abhorrence took the place of reverence, pigs and boars grew into types of evil, and were described as the enemies of the very gods they once typified (*Golden Bough*, II. 26–31, 56–7). The Pig would, therefore, become the Black Pig, a type of cold and of winter that awake in November, the old beginning of winter, to do battle with the summer, and with the fruit and leaves, and finally, as I suggest ; and as I believe, for the purposes of poetry ; of the darkness that will at last destroy the gods and the world. The country people say there is no shape for a spirit to take so dangerous as the shape of a pig ; and a Galway black-smith — and blacksmiths are thought to be especially pro-tected — says he would be afraid to meet a pig on the road at night ; and another Galway man tells this story : 'There was a man coming the road from Gort to Garryland one night, and he had a drop taken ; and before him, on the road, he saw a pig walking ; and having a drop in, he gave a shout, and made a kick at it, and bid it get out of that. And by the time he got home, his arm was swelled from the shoulder to be as big as a bag, and he couldn't use his hand with the pain of it. And his wife brought him, after a few days, to a woman that used to do cures at Rahasane. And on the road all she could do would hardly keep him from lying down to sleep on the grass. And when they got to the woman she knew all that happened ; and, says she, it's well for you that your wife didn't let you fall asleep on the grass, for if you had done that but even for one instant, you'd be a lost man.'

It is possible that bristles were associated with fertility, as the tail certainly was, for a pig's tail is stuck into the ground in Courland, that the corn may grow abundantly, and the tails of pigs, and other animal embodiments of the corn genius, are dragged over the ground to make it fertile in different countries. Professor Rhys, who considers the bristleless boar a symbol of darkness and cold, rather than of winter and cold, thinks it was without bristles because the darkness is shorn away by the sun. It may have had different meanings, just as the scourging of the man god has had different though not contradictory meanings in different epochs of the world. [The note in *CW* reads: If one reads Professor Rhys' *Celtic Heathendom* by the light of Professor Frazer's *Golden Bough*, and puts together what one finds there about the boar that killed Diarmuid, and other old Celtic boars and sows, one sees that the Battle is mythological, and that the Pig it is named from must be a type of cold and winter doing battle with the summer, or of death battling with life. For the purposes of poetry, at any rate, I think it a symbol of the darkness that will destroy the world. . . .]

The Battle should, I believe, be compared with three other battles; a battle the Sidhe are said to fight when a person is being taken away by them; a battle they are said to fight in November for the harvest; the great battle the Tribes of the goddess Danu fought, according to the Gaelic chroniclers, with the Fomor at Moy Tura, or the Towery Plain.

I have heard of the battle over the dying both in County Galway and in the Isles of Arann, an old Arann fisherman having told me that it was fought over two of his children, and that he found blood in a box he had for keeping fish, when it was over; and I have written about it, and given examples elsewhere. A faery doctor, on the borders of Galway and Clare, explained it as a battle between the friends and enemies of the dying, the one party trying to take them, the other trying to save them from being taken. It may once, when the land of the Sidhe was the only other world, and when every man who died was carried thither, have always accompanied death. I suggest that the battle between the Tribes of the goddess Danu, the powers of light, and warmth, and fruitfulness, and goodness, and the Fomor, the powers of darkness, and cold, and barrenness, and badness upon the Towery Plain, was the establishment of the habitable world, the rout of the ancestral darkness; that the battle among the Sidhe for the harvest is the annual battle of summer and winter; that the battle among the Sidhe at a man's death is the battle between the manifest world and the ancestral darkness at the end of all things ; and that all these battles are one, the battle of all things with shadowy decay. Once a symbolism has possessed the imagination of large numbers of men, it becomes, as I believe, an embodiment of disembodied powers, and repeats itself in dreams and visions, age after age. (*W*R)

Yeats commented in 'The Tragic Generation' that it must have been some talk of MacGregor Mathers' (see note (p. 316) on 'All Souls' Night' *CP* 256) that made him write the poem. Mathers had announced in 1893 or 1894 the imminence of immense wars (*A* 336). Yeats also, in 1902, wrote that when he was discussing the Battle of the Black Pig with a Sligo countrywoman this seemed to her a battle between Ireland and England but to him an Armageddon which would quench all things in Ancestral Darkness again (*M* 111).

5 *cromlech* : a prehistoric structure of stones, usually consisting of one large uneven stone resting on several upright stones.

6 *grey cairn* : this may refer to Maeve's grave, the Cairn on Knocknarea, Sligo.

73 THE LOVER ASKS FORGIVENESS BECAUSE OF HIS MANY MOODS

This poem was written on 23 August 1895 and first appeared in *SR* (2 Nov. 1895) with the title 'The Twilight of Forgiveness', which was altered to 'Michael Robartes [see note (p. 55) on 'The Lover tells of the Rose in his Heart (*CP* 62)] asks Forgiveness because of his Many Moods'.

7 *O Winds* : Yeats's note read :

I use the wind as a symbol of vague desires and hopes, not merely because the Sidhe are in the wind, or because the wind bloweth as it listeth, but because wind and spirit and vague desire have been associated everywhere. A highland scholar tells me that his country people use the wind in their talk as I use it in my poem.

9   *tabors* :   small drums

13   *Niamh* :   the beautiful immortal who spirited Oisin away   **74**
to the Land of the Young, Tir-nan-Oge, for three hundred years.
Yeats used the Fenian tale *Oisin in the Land of the Young* as a source
for his own 'The Wanderings of Oisin' (*CP* 409 ff.).

16   *Phoenix* :   a mythical bird, fabled to be the only one of its
kind, which lived five or six hundred years in the Arabian desert.
It burnt itself to death on a funeral pyre but emerged with renewed
youth to live another cycle.

HE TELLS OF A VALLEY FULL OF LOVERS   **74**

This poem first appeared in *SR* (9 Jan. 1897) with the title 'The
Valley of Lovers' altered in *WR* to 'Aedh [see note (p. 55) on
'The Lover tells of the Rose in his Heart (*CP* 62)] tells of a Valley
full of Lovers'.

HE TELLS OF THE PERFECT BEAUTY   **74**

This poem was written in December 1895 and first appeared in
the *Senate* (March 1896) and twice (because proof sheets miscarried
and Yeats found the first reprint 'got a good deal on his nerves')
in *UI* (4 and 11 April 1896).   The poem was originally Stanza 1
of 'O'Sullivan the Red to Mary Lavell' but in *WR* this became
'Aedh [see note (p. 55) on 'The Lover tells of the Rose in his
Heart' (*CP* 62)] tells of the Perfect Beauty'.

5   *brood of the skies* :   the stars

7   *God burn time* :   see note (p. 41) on line 47 'The Man who
dreamed of Faeryland' (*CP* 49)

HE HEARS THE CRY OF THE SEDGE   **75**

This poem first appeared in *D* (May 1898) with the title 'Aodh
to Dectora.   Three Songs 1' [the companion poems were '2',

later 'The Lover mourns for the Loss of Love' (*CP* 68) and '3', later 'He thinks of those who have spoken Evil of his Beloved' (*CP* 75)]. The title was altered to 'Aedh [See note (p. 55) on 'The Lover tells of the Rose in his Heart' (*CP* 62)] hears the Cry of The Sedge'. Yeats's note, which also covers 'The Poet pleads with the Elemental Powers' (*CP* 80) and 'He thinks of his Past Greatness when a Part of the Constellations of Heaven' (*CP* 81), reads :

The Rose has been for many centuries a symbol of spiritual love and supreme beauty. The Count Goblet D'Alviella thinks that it was once a symbol of the sun, — itself a principal symbol of the divine nature, and the symbolic heart of things. The lotus was in some Eastern countries imagined blossoming upon the Tree of Life, as the Flower of Life, and is thus represented in Assyrian bas-reliefs. Because the Rose, the flower sacred to the Virgin Mary, and the flower that Apuleius' adventurer ate when he was changed out of the ass's shape and received into the fellowship of Isis, is the western Flower of Life, I have imagined it growing upon the Tree of Life. I once stood beside a man in Ireland when he saw it growing there in a vision, that seemed to have rapt him out of his body. He saw the garden of Eden walled about, and in the top of a high mountain, as in certain mediaeval diagrams, and after passing the Tree of Knowledge, on which grew fruit full of troubled faces, and through whose branches flowed, he was told, sap that was human souls, he came to a tall, dark tree, with little bitter fruits, and was shown a kind of stair or ladder going up through the tree, and told to go up ; and near the top of the tree, a beautiful woman, like the Goddess of Life associated with the tree in Assyria, gave him a rose that seemed to have been growing upon the tree. One finds the Rose in the Irish poets, sometimes as a religious symbol, as in the phrase, 'the Rose of Friday,' meaning the Rose of austerity, in a Gaelic poem in Dr Hyde's *Religious Songs of Connacht*, and, I think, was a symbol of woman's beauty in the Gaelic song, 'Roseen Dubh ;' and a symbol of Ireland in Mangan's adaptation of 'Roseen Dubh,' 'My Dark Rosaleen,' and in Mr Aubrey de Vere's 'The Little Black Rose.' I do not know any evidence to prove whether this symbol came to Ireland with mediaeval Christianity, or whether it has come down from Celtic times. I have read somewhere that a stone engraved with a

Celtic god, who holds what looks like a rose in one hand, has been found somewhere in England; but I cannot find the reference, though I certainly made a note of it. If the Rose was really a symbol of Ireland among the Gaelic poets, and if 'Roseen Dubh' is really a political poem, as some think, one may feel pretty certain that the ancient Celts associated the Rose with Eire, or Fotla, or Banba — goddesses who gave their names to Ireland — or with some principal god or goddess, for such symbols are not suddenly adopted or invented, but come out of mythology.

I have made the Seven Lights, the constellation of the Bear, lament for the theft of the Rose, and I have made the Dragon, the constellation Draco, the guardian of the Rose, because these constellations move about the pole of the heavens, the ancient Tree of Life in many countries, and are often associated with the Tree of Life in mythology. It is this Tree of Life that I have put into the 'Song of Mongan' under its common Irish form of a hazel; and, because it had sometimes the stars for fruit, I have hung upon it 'The Crooked Plough' and the 'Pilot star,' as Gaelic-speaking Irishmen sometimes call the Bear and the North star. I have made it an axle-tree in 'Aedh hears the Cry of the Sedge', for this was another ancient way of representing it. (*WR*)

This poem was written to Maud Gonne in a time of great strain and sorrow. Yeats wrote:

> Since my mistress had left me no other woman had come into my life and for nearly seven years none did. I was tortured with sexual desire and disappointed love. Often as I walked in the woods at Coole it would have been a relief to have screamed aloud. (unpublished Autobiography)

2 *lake* : perhaps the lake at Coole Park, Lady Gregory's house in Co. Galway

3 *sedge* : the echo of Keats's 'La Belle Dame sans Merci' ('The sedge is withered from the lake') is perhaps not unintentional.

7 *banners of East and West* : this line may relate to the initiation ceremony of The Order of the Golden Dawn. See V. Moore, *The Unicorn* (1954) 139.

75 HE THINKS OF THOSE WHO HAVE SPOKEN EVIL OF HIS BELOVED

This poem first appeared in *D* (May 1898) under the title 'Aodh to Dectora. Three Songs 3' [the companion poems being 1 & 2, later entitled 'The Lover mourns for the Loss of Love' (*CP*, 68) and 'He hears the Cry of the Sedge' (*CP* 75)]. The title became 'Aedh [see note (p. 55) on 'The Lover tells of the Rose in his Heart' (*CP* 62)] thinks of those who have spoken Evil of his Beloved' in *WR*.

5 *a mouthful of air*: the phrase was used by Yeats to describe faeries, 'nations of gay creatures, having no souls; nothing in their bright bodies but a mouthful of sweet air' ('Tales from the Twilight', *SO* (1 March 1890)). See *IY* 325. The phrase was used in Ganconagh's [Yeats's] novel *John Sherman* (1891): for 'what have we in this life but a mouthful of air' (see *PYP* 72) and in the lyric at the end of *At the Hawk's Well* as well as in the play *KGCT*, 'O, what is life but a mouthful of air?'

75 THE BLESSED

This poem first appeared in *The Yellow Book* (April 1897).

1 *Cumhal*: he appears as 'Cumhal the King' in the early versions of the poem, and as a pagan gleeman, Cumhal, the son of Cormac, who is crucified by monks in 'The Crucifixion of the Outcast' (*M* 147ff.).

2 *Dathi*: 'Dathi the Blessed' in the early versions of the poem is mentioned in 'The Crucifixion of the Outcast':

'I would,' mutters Cumhal, 'that the red wind of the Druids had withered in his cradle the soldier of Dathi who brought the tree of death out of barbarous lands, or that the lightning, when it smote Dathi at the foot of the mountain, had smitten him also...' (*M* 147).

77 36 *The Incorruptible Rose*: see notes (pp. 22 ff.) on 'To the Rose upon the Rood of Time' (*CP* 35), and 'He hears the Cry of the Sedge' (*CP* 75). Yeats regarded it as symbol of the highest spiritual ideal.

THE SECRET ROSE 77

This poem first appeared in *S* (Sept. 1896) with the title 'O'Sullivan Rua to the Secret Rose'; it was entitled 'To the Secret Rose' in *TSR*, 'The Secret Rose' in *WR*. Yeats's note reads:

I find that I have unintentionally changed the old story of Conchobar's death. He did not see the crucifix in a vision, but was told about it. He had been struck by a ball, made of the dried brain of a dead enemy, and hurled out of a sling; and this ball had been left in his head, and his head had been mended, the Book of Leinster says, with thread of gold because his hair was like gold. Keating, a writer of the time of Elizabeth, says: 'In that state did he remain seven years, until the Friday on which Christ was crucified, according to some historians; and when he saw the unusual changes of the creation and the eclipse of the sun and the moon at its full, he asked of Bucrach, a Leinster Druid, who was long with him, what was it that brought that unusual change upon the planets of Heaven and Earth. "Jesus Christ, the son of God," said the Druid, "who is now being crucified by the Jews." "That is a pity," said Conchobar; "were I in his presence I would kill those who were putting him to death." And with that he brought out his sword, and rushed at a woody grove which was convenient to him, and began to cut and fell it; and what he said was, that if he were among the Jews that was the usage he would give them, and from the excessiveness of his fury which seized upon him, the ball started out of his head, and some of the brain came after it, and in that way he died. The wood of Lanshraigh, in Feara Rois, is the name by which that shrubby wood is called.'

I have imagined Cuchullain meeting Fand 'walking among flaming dew.' The story of their love is one of the most beautiful of our old tales. Two birds, bound one to another with a chain of gold, came to a lake side where Cuchullain and the host of Uladh was encamped, and sang so sweetly that all the host fell into a magic sleep. Presently they took the shape of two beautiful women, and cast a magical weakness upon Cuchullain, in which he lay for a year. At the year's end an Aengus, who was probably Aengus the master of love, one of the greatest of the children of the goddess Danu, came and sat upon his bedside, and sang how Fand, the wife of Mannannan, the master of the sea, and of the islands of the dead, loved him; and that if he would come into the country of the gods, where there was wine and gold and silver, Fand, and Laban her sister, would heal him of his magical weakness. [In 'Mortal Help' Cuchullain 'won the goddess Fand for a while by helping her married sister and her sister's husband to overthrow another nation of the Land of Promise' (*M* 9).] Cuchullain went to the country of the gods, and, after being for a month the lover of Fand, made her a promise to meet her at a place called 'the Yew at the Strand's End,' and came back to the earth. Emer, his mortal wife, won his love again, and Mannannan came to 'the Yew at the Strand's End,' and carried Fand away. When Cuchullain saw her going, his love for her fell upon him again, and he went mad, and wandered among the mountains without food or drink, until he was at last cured by a Druid drink of forgetfulness.

I have founded the man 'who drove the gods out of their Liss,' or fort, upon something I have read about Caolte after the battle of Gabra, when almost all his companions were killed, driving the gods out of their Liss, either at Osraighe, now Ossory, or at Eas Ruaidh, now Asseroe, a waterfall at Ballyshannon, where Ilbreac, one of the children of the goddess Danu, had a Liss. I am writing away from most of my books, and have not been able to find the passage ; but I certainly read it somewhere. [But maybe I only read it in Mr Standish O'Grady, who has a fine imagination, for I find no such story in Lady Gregory's book. (*C W*, 1).]

I have founded 'the proud dreaming king' upon Fergus, the son of Roigh, the legendary poet of 'the quest of the bull of Cualg[n]e,' as he is in the ancient story of Deirdre, and in modern poems by Ferguson. He married Nessa, and Ferguson makes him tell how she took him 'captive in a single look.'

> 'I am but an empty shade,
> Far from life and passion laid ;
> Yet does sweet remembrance thrill
> All my shadowy being still.'

Presently, because of his great love, he gave up his throne to Conchobar, her son by another, and lived out his days feasting, and fighting, and hunting. His promise never to refuse a feast from a certain comrade, and the mischief that came by his promise, and the vengeance he took afterwards, are a principal theme of the poets. I have explained my imagination of him in 'Fergus and the Druid,' and in a little song in the second act of 'The Countess Kathleen.'

I have founded him 'who sold tillage, and house, and goods,' upon something in 'The Red Pony,' a folk tale in Mr Larmine's *West Irish Folk Tales*. A young man 'saw a light before him on the high road. When he came as far, there was an open box on the road, and a light coming up out of it. He took up the box. There was a lock of hair in it. Presently he had to go to become the servant of a king for his living. There were eleven boys. When they were going out into the stable at ten o'clock, each of them took a light but he. He took no candle at all with him. Each of them went into his own stable. When he went into his stable he opened the box. He left it in a hole in the wall. The light was great. It was twice as much as in the other stables.' The king hears of it, and makes him show him the box. The king says, 'You must go and bring me the woman to whom the hair belongs.' In the end, the young man, and not the king, marries the woman. (*W*R)

7 *great leaves* : the Rosicrucian emblem of the four-leaved rose. Yeats's half-belief in the possibility of some revelation was bound up with his proposed Order of Celtic Mysteries, and with it the hope of complete understanding between himself and Maud Gonne. Cf. the passage from *A*, which begins 'I had an unshakable conviction . . .' quoted below, note on line 28.

25 *so shining loveliness* : the poem was written to Maud Gonne.   **78**

28 *thy great wind* : this is probably a reference to the end of the world. Cf. 'He mourns for the Change that has come upon Him . . . and longs for the End of the World' (*CP* 68).

I had an unshakable conviction, arising how or whence I cannot tell, that invisible gates would open as they opened for Blake, as they opened for Swedenborg, as they opened for Boehme, and that this philosophy would find its manuals of devotion in all imaginative literature and set before Irishmen for special manual an Irish literature which, though made by many minds, would seem the work of a single mind, and turn our places of beauty or legendary association into holy symbols. I did not think this philosophy would be altogether pagan, for it was plain that its symbols must be selected from all those things that have moved men most during many, mainly Christian, centuries.

I thought for a time I could rhyme of love, calling it *The Rose*, because of the Rose's double meaning ; of a fisherman who had 'never a crack' in his heart ; of an old woman complaining of the idleness of the young, or of some cheerful fiddler, all those things that 'popular poets' write of, but that I must some day — on that day when the gates began to open — become difficult or obscure. With a rhythm that still echoed Morris I prayed to the Red Rose, to Intellectual Beauty. . . .   (*A* 254)

78   MAID QUIET

This poem first appeared, untitled, in the story 'The Twisting of the Rope', in *NO* (24 Dec. 1892). It was entitled 'O'Sullivan the Red upon his Wanderings' in *NR* (Aug. 1897) and 'Hanrahan laments because of his Wanderings' in *WR*, altered to 'The Lover mourns because of his Wanderings' in *PW* 1. The poem was reduced from twelve lines to eight and entitled 'Maid Quiet' in *CW*. 1. Yeats wrote of Hanrahan in John Quinn's copy of *Stories of Red Hanrahan* : 'Red Hanrahan is an imaginary name — I saw it over a shop, or rather part of it over a shop in a Galway village — but there were many poets like him in the eighteenth century in Ireland.' See (*B* 72). His note after the title in the first published version read :

'Gulleon's place of pride' [part of a line included in the original version] is the mountain now called 'The Fews', and once called 'Sleive Fua'. It is fabled to be his (Hanrahan's) tomb, and was doubtless the place of his worship, for Gulleon was Cullain, a god of the underworld. The 'pale deer' ['I would the pale deer had come' was a line from the original version] were certain deer hunted once by Cuchullain in his battle fury, and, as I understand them, symbols of night and shadow.

In his note on 'He mourns for the Change that has come upon Him and his Beloved, and longs for the End of the World' (*CP* 68) Yeats comments on this poem :

He [a solar mythologist] could certainly, I think, say that when Cuchullain, whom Professor Rhys calls a solar hero, hunted the enchanted deer of Slieve Fuadh because the battle fury was still on him, he was the sun pursuing clouds, or cold, or darkness. I have understood them in this sense in 'Hanrahan laments because of his wandering' and made Hanrahan long for the day when they, fragments of ancestral darkness, will overthrow the world. The desire of the woman, the flying darkness, it is all one ! The image — a cross, a man preaching in the wilderness, a dancing Salome, a lily in a girl's hand, a flame leaping, a globe with wings, a pale sunset over still waters — is an eternal act ; but our understandings are temporal and understand but a little at a time. (*WR*)

THE TRAVAIL OF PASSION   78

This poem first appeared in *S* (Jan. 1896) under the title 'Two Love Poems. The Travail of Passion' (the companion poem was 'The Shadowy Horses', later 'Michael Robartes (still later 'He') bids his Beloved be at Peace' (*CP* 69).) This poem was written to 'Diana Vernon', see note (p. 63) on 'The Lover mourns for the Loss of Love' (*CP* 68).

5 *Kedron* : spelt Kidron in early versions   79

THE LOVER PLEADS WITH HIS FRIEND FOR OLD FRIENDS   79

This poem first appeared in *SR* (24 July 1897) entitled 'The Poet pleads with his friend for old friends'.

1 *your shining days* : probably a reference to Maud Gonne's political work. Her power over crowds was at its height, and Yeats travelled to many public meetings with her in 1897 and 1898 in the cause of the '98 Association (of which he was President) which was formed to commemorate the 1798 Rebellion and its leader Wolfe Tone. Cf. 'Fallen Majesty' (*CP* 138), '. . . crowds gathered once if she but showed her face/And even old men's eyes grew dim'.

8 *all eyes but these eyes* : these lines were prophetic, in that after Maud Gonne married and she and her husband separated, she was

deserted by the mob. Cf. 'Fallen Majesty' again :

> '. . . this hand alone
> Like some last courtier at a gypsy camping-place
> Babbling of fallen majesty, records what's gone.'

Other poems recorded her power over others. Cf. 'Her Praise' (*CP* 168), 'The People' (*CP* 169) and 'Broken Dreams' (*CP* 172).

79 THE LOVER SPEAKS TO THE HEARERS OF HIS SONGS IN COMING DAYS

This poem was written in November 1895 and first appeared entitled, in the story 'The Vision of O'Sullivan' in *NR* (April 1896). It was entitled 'Hanrahan [see note (p. 55) on 'The Lover tells of the Rose in his Heart' (*CP* 62) and 'Maid Quiet' (*CP* 78)] speaks to the Lovers of his Songs' in *WR*.

6 *Attorney for Lost Souls* : Mary. The original version had 'Till Maurya ['Mary' in later versions] of the wounded heart cry out'.

80 THE POET PLEADS WITH THE ELEMENTAL POWERS

This poem first appeared in *TB* (Oct. 1892) entitled 'A Mystical Prayer to the Masters of the Elements, Michael, Gabriel, and Raphael'. In *The Second Book of the Rhymers' Club* (1894) 'Finvarra' replaced Michael, 'Feacra' Gabriel, and 'Caolte' Gabriel. The title became 'Aodh (Aedh) [see 'The Lover tells of the Rose in his Heart' (*CP* 62)] pleads with the Elemental Powers' in *WR*. Yeats's note after the title read :

> The Seven Lights are the seven stars of the Great Bear, and the Dragon is the constellation of the Dragon, and these, in certain old mythologies, encircle the Tree of Life, on which is here imagined the Rose of the Ideal Beauty growing before it was cast into the world. Three or four lines are taken from a poem of the author's on the same subject in 'The Second Book of the Rhymers' Club'.

1 *The Powers* : various conjectures have been made as to their identity. W. Y. Tindall, *Forces in Modern British Literature* (1947),

243 suggested Madame Blavatsky's elemental spirits; Saul (*PYP* 75) referred to the 'Heart of the Spring' (*M* 171) which described the beings who dwell 'in the waters and among the hazels and oak trees'. Henn (*LT* 252) saw stanza 1 as a Rosicrucian or Hermetic image. But the title suggests some correspondence between the three 'Masters of the Elements' and the Powers of wave and wind and fire, cf. line 7.

2 *the Immortal Rose*: partially the Rosicrucian symbol, but in Yeats's words the 'Rose of Ideal Beauty'.

3 *Seven lights*: the seven stars of the Great Bear

4 *The Polar Dragon*: the constellation of the Dragon. The 'Dragon of the Hesperides' is suggested by Wilson (*YI* 249). Ellmann (*IY* 78) remarks that if we look at the cover of *TSR* we find the serpent's folds encircling the trunk of the tree of life as if it were indeed the 'Guardian of the Rose'. He continues:

> In Kabbalism this serpent is the serpent of nature in its benign aspect, and the occultist is said to follow the serpent's winding path upwards through many initiations, corresponding to each of the *Sephiroth*, until he reaches the top of the tree. Since in the poem the polar dragon sleeps, like earth in the 'Introduction' to Blake's *Songs of Experience*, the meaning seems to be that the natural world has become uncoiled or detached from beauty.

For the tree of life see notes (p. 43) on 'The Two Trees' (*CP* 54).

9 *her I love*: Maud Gonne

HE WISHES HIS BELOVED WERE DEAD 80

This poem first appeared in the *Sketch* (9 Feb. 1898) with the title 'Aodh [see 'The Lover tells of the Rose in his Heart' (*CP* 62)] to Dectora', altered to 'Aedh to Dectora' in *WR*. This poem develops an idea in 'A Dream of Death' (*CP* 47) written when Maud Gonne was in France in 1891 convalescing from an illness. There is a passage in *CK* (where Kevin the poet is a projection of Yeats) which indicates the death imagery which came to him in moments of intense stress.

Sometimes he [Kevin] laid his head upon the ground.
They say he hears the Sheogues down below
Nailing four boards . . .
For love has made him crazy
And loneliness and famine dwell with him.

81 HE WISHES FOR THE CLOTHS OF HEAVEN

This poem first appeared in *WR* entitled 'Aedh [see note (p. 55) on 'The Lover tells of the Rose in his Heart' (*CP* 62)] wishes for the Cloths of Heaven'. Yeats remarked of this defeatist pre-Raphaelite poem that it was the way to lose a lady. See note (p. 69) on 'The Cap and Bells' (*CP* 71).

81 HE THINKS OF HIS PAST GREATNESS WHEN A PART OF THE CONSTELLATIONS OF HEAVEN

This poem first appeared in *D* (Oct. 1898) entitled 'Song of Mongan'. In *WR* it was entitled 'Mongan thinks of his Past Greatness'. Yeats's note after the title reads :

> Mongan, in the old Celtic poetry, is a famous wizard and king who remembers his passed lives. 'The Country of the Young' is a name in the Celtic poetry for the country of the gods and of the happy dead. The hazel tree was the Irish tree of Life or of Knowledge, and in Ireland it was doubtless, as elsewhere, the tree of the heavens. The Crooked Plough and the Pilot Star are translations of the Gaelic names of the Plough and the Pole star.

> See Yeats's note (pp. 73ff.) on 'He hears the Cry of the Sedge' (*CP* 75).

82 THE FIDDLER OF DOONEY

This poem first appeared in *TB* (Dec. 1892) dated November 1892.

3 *Kilvarnet*: originally 'My brother is priest of Kilbarnet'

4 *Mocharabuiee*: originally 'My cousin of Rosnaree' but altered in *WR* to 'Mocharabuiee'. Yeats's footnote reads 'pronounced as if spelt "Mockrabwee"'. The Gaelic *Machra Buidhe* means Yellow Plain.

20   *wave of the sea* : Henn (*LT* 305) compares Florizel's remark
to Perdita, *A Winter's Tale*, IV, iv :

> When you do dance, I wish you
> A wave o' the sea.

Cf. *The Countess Cathleen*, sc. 1, . . . 'singing like a wave of the sea'.

In the Seven Woods

YEATS wrote that he had made some of these poems

> walking about among the Seven Woods, before the big
> wind of nineteen hundred and three blew down so many trees,
> & troubled the wild creatures, & changed the look of things ;
> and I thought out there a good part of the play which follows
> [*On Baile's Strand*]. The first shape of it came to me in a
> dream, but it changed much in the making, foreshadowing, it
> may be, a change that may bring a less dream-burdened will
> into my verses. I never re-wrote anything so many times ;
> for at first I could not make these wills that stream into mere
> life poetical. But now I hope to do easily much more of the
> kind, and that our new Irish players will find the buskin and
> the sock. (*ISW*)

In the Seven Woods was the first book published by Elizabeth Corbet
Yeats's Dun Emer Press, later called the Cuala Press. The book
was printed in Caslon Old Face type, a type used for all the
seventy-eight books produced up to 1946. A brief note on the
history of the press is given in the catalogue compiled by R.O.
Dougan, *WB Yeats. Manuscripts and Printed Books exhibited in the
Library of Trinity College, Dublin 1956*, 17–18. See also *The Irish
Book* II, (1963) 43–52 and 81–90, and Liam Miller, 'The Dun Emer
and the Cuala Press', *The World of W.B. Yeats* (ed. Skelton and
Saddlemyer, 1965), 141–51. A brief comment is given by Robin
Skelton, 'Twentieth Century Irish Literature and the Private
Press Tradition' *Massachusetts Review* (Winter, 1964), 368–77.

85 IN THE SEVEN WOODS

This poem first appeared in *ISW*, dated August 1902.

1 *the Seven Woods*: in Lady Gregory's estate, Coole Park, Co.
Galway. Yeats described the woods in his 'Introduction to a
Dramatic Poem', a poem which first appeared in the *Speaker*

(1 Dec. 1900) and was entitled 'I walked among the Seven Woods of Coole' in *The Shadowy Waters* (1900). The poem opens :

> I walked among the seven woods of Coole ;
> Shan-walla, where a willow-bordered pond
> Gathers the wild duck from the winter dawn ;
> Shady Kyle-dortha ; sunnier Kyle-na-no
> Where many hundred squirrels are as happy
> As though they had been hidden by green boughs
> Where old age cannot find them ; Pairc-na-lee,
> Where hazel and ash and privet blind the paths ;
> Dim Pairc-na-carraig, where the wild bees fling
> Their sudden fragrances on the green air ;
> Dim Pairc-na-tarav, where enchanted eyes
> Have seen immortal, mild, proud shadows walk ;
> Dim Inchy wood, that hides badger and fox
> And marten-cat, and borders that old wood
> Wise Biddy Early called the wicked wood :
> Seven odours, seven murmurs, seven woods.

3 *lime-tree* : cf. line 2 'The New Faces' (*CP* 238) which describes Coole Park

6 *Tara uprooted* : the Hill of Tara in Co. Meath, the seat of the ancient Irish kings. Mr John Frayne has pointed out to me that Douglas Hyde, George Moore and Yeats wrote a letter to the *Times* (27 June 1902) which drew the attention of the public to the fact that labourers were destroying the site of the ancient Royal duns and houses 'apparently that the sect which believes the English to be descended from the ten tribes may find the Ark of the Covenant'.

7 *new commonness* : an allusion to the coronation of Edward VII and Alexandra

8 *paper flowers* : decorations in Dublin to celebrate the Coronation

12 *Great Archer* : Saul (*PYP* 77) glosses as Sagittarius. This hints at some revelation about to come. There is a possibility that the 'Quiet' of line 10 may refer to Maud Gonne, the archer being then some figure of love.

14 *Pairc-na-lee* : see note on line 1 above

85 THE ARROW

This poem was written in 1901 and first appeared in *ISW*.

1 *your beauty* : Maud Gonne's beauty. Yeats had first met her in 1889.

this arrow : it is possible that Yeats had in mind a Blakean meaning for the arrow. When he and Edwin Ellis edited *The Works of William Blake* (3 vols., 1893) they supplied a commentary on these lines of Blake's 'Preface' to *Milton* :

> Bring me my bow of burning gold :
> Bring me my arrows of desire :
> Bring me my spear : O clouds unfold !
> Bring me my chariot of fire.

The commentary ran : 'He shall return again, aided by the Bow, sexual symbolism, the arrow, desire, the spear, male potency, the chariot, joy.'

6 *apple blossom* : Yeats associated apple blossom with his memories of his first meeting with Maud Gonne. See note (p. 62) on 'The Song of Wandering Aengus' (*CP* 66), which quotes the accounts in his unpublished Autobiography and *Autobiographies* of this meeting.

86 THE FOLLY OF BEING COMFORTED

This poem first appeared in the *Speaker* (11 Jan. 1902). The poem refers to Maud Gonne and marks a newly emerging note of realism in Yeats's poetry.

1 *One that is ever kind* : possibly Lady Gregory

6 *patience* : Ellmann, (*Y:M & M* 161) quotes two drafts for a lyric written about 1897 which indicates Yeats's hopes and despair :

> O my beloved you only are
>   not moved by my songs
> Which you only understand
> You only know that it is
>   of you I sing when I tell
>   of the swan on the water
>   or the eagle in the heavens
>   or the faun in the wood.
> Others weep but your eyes
>   are dry.

II

O my beloved. How happy
I was that day when you
came here from the
railway, and set your hair
aright in my looking glass
and then sat with me at
my table, and lay resting
in my big chair. I am
like the children o my
beloved and I play at
marriage — I play
with images of the life
you will not give to me o
my cruel one.

9 *nobleness* : 'Her beauty . . . was incredibly distinguished', see
note (pp. 89–90) on 'Old Memory' (*CP* 86)

OLD MEMORY   **86**

This poem was written in November or December (probably the
third week of December) 1903 and first appeared in *Wayfarer's
Love* (ed. the Duchess of Sutherland, 1904). It was written when
Yeats was 'shut up in a railway train coming from Canada'. He
wrote to Lady Gregory, apropos of this poem, on 21 January
1904, that he thought a railroad train a good place to write in, if
the journey was long enough, the scenery being exhausted in two
or three hours, the newspaper — even an American one — in
the second two or three hours and then towards the end of the day

one can hardly help oneself but one has begun to write.
Indeed I think that if some benevolent government would
only . . . send one across the world one would really write
two or three dozen lyrics in the year. (*L* 427)

1 *her* : Maud Gonne, who married Major John MacBride in
Paris in February 1903

5 *The queens* : Yeats wrote that there was an element in Maud
Gonne's beauty that moved minds full of old Gaelic poems and
stories, because she looked as if she lived in some ancient civilisation where superiority of mind or body were part of public ceremonial,

were in some way the crowd's creation, as the entrance of the Pope into Saint Peter's is the crowd's creation. Her beauty, backed by her great stature, could instantly affect an assembly, and not, as often with our stage beauties, because obvious and florid, for it was incredibly distinguished, and if — as must be that it might seem that assembly's very self, fused, unified and solitary — her face, like the face of some Greek statue, showed little thought, her whole body seemed a master-work of long labouring thought, as though a Scopas [*fl.* 430 B.C., an architect and sculptor of Ephesus who made the mausoleum which Artemisia raised to her husband, one of the seven wonders of the world] had measured and calculated, consorted with Egyptian sages, and mathematicians out of Babylon, that he might outface even Artemisia's sepulchral image with a living norm. (*A* 364)

6 *he kneaded* : Yeats refers to his hopes of persuading Maud Gonne to give up politics and marry him, and his long work for the literary movement and his writing of poems for her — 'all was in her service'.

7 *the long years of youth* : he was twenty-three when he fell in love with Maud Gonne in 1889 at their first meeting.

8 *come to naught* : Maud Gonne's marriage to MacBride meant the end of his hopes.

87   NEVER GIVE ALL THE HEART

This poem first appeared in *McClure's Magazine* (December 1905).

1 *Never give* : this poem has affinities with Blake's 'Love's Secret' :

> Never seek to tell thy love
> Love that never told can be ;
> For the gentle wind doth move
> Silently, invisibly.
>
> I told my love, I told my love,
> I told her all my heart,
> Trembling, cold, in ghastly fears
> Ah ! she did depart !

12 *deaf and dumb and blind* : Yeats refers to his own hopeless passion.

14 *and lost*: another reference to Maud Gonne's marriage

THE WITHERING OF THE BOUGHS   87

This poem first appeared in the *Speaker* (Aug. 1900) with the title 'Echtge of Streams'.

6 *Echtge*: Sliab Aughty, mountain in Co. Galway

7–8 *No boughs . . . because of the wintry wind . . . my dreams*: Yeats commented elsewhere that Irish stories express the belief that as fruits and vegetables, trees, or plants decay on earth, they ripen among the faeries, and that dreams lose their wisdom 'when the sap rises in the trees, and that our dreams can make the trees wither' (*M* 116).

12 *Danaan*: see note (p. 11) on line 3 'The Madness of King   88
Goll' (*CP* 17)

17, 18 *swans . . . golden chains*: Baile and Aillinn were lovers but Aengus, the Master of Love, wished them to be happy in his own land among the dead so he told each the other was dead, their hearts were broken and they died. When they died they took the shape of swans linked with a golden chain 'the shape that other enchanted lovers took before them in the old stories'. See the 'Argument' and footnote on Aillinn in *Baile and Aillinn* (1903) (*CP* 457ff.) and lines 135–8 of the poem where the swans are 'Linked by a gold chain each to each.'

19 *A king and queen*: Baile and Aillinn

ADAM'S CURSE   88

This poem was written before 20 November 1902 and first appeared in the *Monthly Review* (Dec. 1902). It is written to Maud Gonne and is an autobiographical memory.

2 *That beautiful mild woman*: Maud Gonne's sister, Mrs Kathleen Pilcher

3 *And you and I*: Maud Gonne and Yeats

talked of poetry : The story of the poem's inspiration is contained in Madame MacBride's autobiography :

> While we were still at dinner Willie Yeats arrived to see me and we all went into the drawing-room for coffee. Kathleen [her sister, Mrs Pilcher] and I sat together on a big sofa amid piles of soft cushions. I was still in my dark clothes with the black veil I always wore when travelling instead of a hat, and we must have made a strange contrast. I saw Willie Yeats looking critically at me and he told Kathleen he liked her dress and that she was looking younger than ever. It was on that occasion Kathleen remarked that it was hard work being beautiful which Willie turned into his poem 'Adam's Curse'.
>
> Next day when he called to take me out to pay my customary visit to the Lia Fail, he said : 'You don't take care of yourself as Kathleen does, so she looks younger than you ; your face is worn and thin ; but you will always be beautiful, more beautiful than anyone I have known. You can't help that. Oh Maud, why don't you marry me and give up this tragic struggle and live a peaceful life ? I could make such a beautiful life for you among artists and writers who would understand you.'
>
> 'Willie, are you not tired of asking that question ? How often have I told you to thank the gods that I will not marry you. You would not be happy with me.'
>
> 'I am not happy without you.'
>
> 'Oh yes, you are, because you make beautiful poetry out of what you call your unhappiness and you are happy in that. Marriage would be such a dull affair. Poets should never marry. The world should thank me for not marrying you. I will tell you one thing, our friendship has meant a great deal to me ; it has helped me often when I needed help, needed it perhaps more than you or anybody know, for I never talk or even think of these things.'
>
> 'Are you happy or unhappy ?' he asked.
>
> 'I have been happier and unhappier than most, but I don't think about it. You and I are so different in this. It is a great thing to know one can never suffer again as much as one has suffered ; it gives one great calm and great strength and makes one afraid of nothing. I am interested in the work I have undertaken ; that is my life and I live, — while so many people only exist. Those are the people to be

pitied; those who lead dull, uneventful lives; they might as well be dead in the ground. And now, Willie, let us talk of the Lia Fail. You know I hate talking of myself; I am not going to let you make me. (*SQ* 328–30)

4 ... '*A line will take us hours maybe ; yet if it does not seem a moment's thought our stitching and unstitching has been naught* : Corinna Salvadori comments that these lines are an exact definition of *sprezzatura*, and draws attention to Yeats's comment on a group of dancers whose toil must have been long and difficult but whose movements were full of joy ('Certain Noble Plays of Japan' (*E & I* 223)), to his remark in *PASL* that it would be a hard toil to put what he had found into rhyme, and to his B.B.C. broadcast comment on 4 October 1932 'It gave me a devil of a lot of trouble to get into verse the poems that I am going to read'. (This is an echo of a remark by William Morris which he quoted elsewhere). She defines the word as a spontaneous improvisation, a careless rapture, but notes that Opdycke translated it as 'nonchalance' (*Yeats and Castiglione* 83–4).

19 *they do not talk of it at school* : cf. the final line of 'Michael **89** Robartes and the Dancer' (*CP* 197), 'They say such different things at school.'

20 *labour to be beautiful* : Yeats wrote in *Discoveries* of 'the heroic discipline of the looking-glass', regarding beauty as one of the most difficult of the arts (*E & I* 270). Cf. lines 7–8 'To a Young Beauty' (*CP* 157) 'You may, that mirror for a school'; and lines 14–15 'Michael Robartes and the Dancer' (*CP* 197) :

... your lover's wage
Is what your looking glass can show.

24 *compounded of high courtesy* : Yeats thought true love was a discipline that needed wisdom : 'Each divines the secret self of the other, and refusing to believe in the mere daily self, creates a mirror where the lover or the beloved sees an image to copy in daily life ; for love also creates the Mask.' (*A* 464)

90 RED HANRAHAN'S SONG ABOUT IRELAND

This poem first appeared, untitled, in the story 'Kathleen-ny-Houlihan', in *NO* (4 Aug. 1894). In *ISW* it was entitled 'The Song of Red Hanrahan' (having had the title 'Kathleen the Daughter of Hoolihan and Hanrahan the Red' in *TSR*). *VE* contains variant readings which show differences in the names of places in the poem. The poem may owe something to James Clarence Mangan's 'Kathleen-ny-Houlahan', *Irish Minstrelsy* (ed. H. Halliday Sparling), 141.

1 *Cummen Strand*: the southern shore of the estuary, to the northwest of Sligo

2 *left hand*: the left-hand side is unlucky in Irish, as in many other traditions.

5 *Cathleen, the daughter of Houlihan*: the poem is written to Maud Gonne (it was her favourite Yeats poem) who played the role of Cathleen, the old woman who symbolises a freed Ireland, in Yeats's play *Cathleen ni Houlihan* (1902). ('My subject is Ireland and its struggle for independence', the *United Irishman*, 5 May 1902). The last lines of the play describe her thus:

> *Peter*: Did you see an old woman going down the path?
> *Patrick*: I did not, but I saw a young girl, and she had the walk of a queen.

Yeats described her playing the part 'very finely, and her great height made Cathleen seem a divine being fallen into our mortal infirmity' (appendix ii, *Cathleen ni Hoolihan*).

6 *Knocknarea*: Irish, mountain of the Kings; mountain overlooking Sligo

7 *stones . . . Maeve*: Queen Maeve's supposed burial cairn is on the top of Knocknarea. See note (p. 50) on 'The Hosting of the Sidhe' (*CP* 61).

11 *Clooth-na-Bare* :   Lough Ia, Sligo.   Yeats   wrote   in   'The
Untiring Ones' :

Such a mortal too was Clooth-na-Bare [his footnote read
'Doubtless Clooth-na-Bare should be Cailleac Beare, which
would mean the old Woman Beare. Beare or Bere or Verah
or Dera or Dhera was a very famous person, perhaps the
Mother of the Gods herself. Standish O'Grady found her,
as he thinks, frequenting Lough Leath, or the Grey Lake on
a mountain of the Fews. Perhaps Lough Ia is my mishearing
or the story-teller's mispronunciation of Lough Leath, for
there are many Lough Leaths] who went all over the world
seeking a lake deep enough to drown her faery life, of which
she had grown weary, leaping from hill to lake and lake
to hill, and setting up a cairn of stones wherever her feet
lighted, until at last she found the deepest water in the world
in little Lough Ia, on the top of the Birds' Mountain at
Sligo.
The two little creatures may well dance on [they were
faeries, one like a young man, the other like a young woman],
and the woman of the log and Clooth-na-Bare sleep in peace,
for they have known untrammelled hate and unmixed love,
and have never wearied themselves with 'yes' and 'no', or
entangled their feet with the sorry net of 'maybe' and
'perhaps'. The great winds came and took them up into
themselves. (*M* 78)

14 *Rood* : cross

THE OLD MEN ADMIRING THEMSELVES IN THE WATER   **91**

This poem was written before 20 November 1902 and first appeared
in the *Pall Mall Magazine* (Jan. 1903).

UNDER THE MOON   **91**

This poem first appeared in the *Speaker* (15 June 1901).

1 *Brycelinde* : the forest in Brittany where Merlin was bewitched
by Viviane

2 *Avalon* : King Arthur was brought here after his death. It

was a mythical land like the Isles of the Blessed where the virtuous went after death. Cf. Sir Thomas Malory, *La Morte d'Arthur*, VIII, ch. 27 ; XII, chs. 7 and 9; and XXI, ch. 5. Yeats mocked at this poem in old age. See 'The Statesman's Holiday' (*CP* 389).

Joyous Isle : Saul (*PYP* 80) comments that this place occurs in the Agravain portion of the prose vulgate *Lancelot*. Lancelot is an Arthurian knight, the lover of Queen Guinevere, who, finding Arthur dead, seeks the Queen and discovers she has taken the veil. He then becomes a priest and guards Arthur's grave. On his death he is carried to Joyous Gard.

4 *Uladh* : Ulster, northern province of Ireland

Naoise : a son of Usna, a young warrior who carried off Deirdre to Scotland and was eventually killed by Conchobar on his return to Ireland with her and his brothers

6 *Land-under-Wave* : an Irish name for the underworld

7 *Seven old sisters*: perhaps the planets

8 *Land-of-the-Tower* : possibly the house of glass belonging to Aengus referred to in Yeats's footnote to *Baile and Aillinn* (1903) (*CP* 457), and 'the tower of glass' mentioned in 'The Harp of Aengus', first published in the *North American Review*, May 1900 and afterwards in *The Shadowy Waters* (1900). In the latter poem Edain came, in a fit of jealousy, from the hill of Midhir [her husband, a king of the Sidhe] and lived 'Beside young Aengus in his tower of glass' weaving harp strings out of his hair.

9 *Wood-of-Wonders* : as yet unidentified

11 *Branwen* : daughter of Llyr in the *Mabinogion*. Yeats read Lady Charlotte Guest's translation.

Guinevere : King Arthur's queen

92 12 *Niamh and Laban and Fand* : for Niamh see note (pp. 50–1) on 'The Hosting of the Sidhe' (*CP* 61); Laban was a sister of Fand, the wife of Manannan MacLir (Saul (*PYP* 81) remarks that she was changed to an otter by her magic well); Fand was loved by Cuchulain (see note (p. 77) on 'The Secret Rose' (*CP* 77)) though he returned to his mortal life in the end.

13 *wood-woman*: unidentified; as her lover was turned into a hawk, her love seems to have suffered as badly as that of the other women and goddesses.

14 *dun*: fort

THE RAGGED WOOD   **92**

This poem first appeared, untitled, in the story 'The Twisting of the Rope', *Stories of Red Hanrahan* (1904). It was entitled 'The Hollow Wood' in *CW*.

6, 7 *silver-proud queen-woman ... golden hood*: for the silver and gold symbols cf. 'The Song of Wandering Aengus' (*CP* 66)

O DO NOT LOVE TOO LONG   **93**

This poem was written before 23 February 1905 and first appeared entitled 'Do Not Love Too Long', in *The Acorn* (Oct. 1905).

8 *so much at one*: cf. lines 13–16 'Among School Children' (*CP* 242), 'it seemed that our two natures blent/Into a sphere from youthful sympathy'. Yeats is referring to his friendship with Maud Gonne.

9 *she changed*: probably a reference to Maud Gonne's marriage. Cf. the last line of 'Never give all the Heart' (*CP* 87).

THE PLAYERS ASK FOR A BLESSING ON THE PSALTERIES   **93**
AND ON THEMSELVES

This poem was probably written in June 1902 and first appeared in *ISW*.

Title The Psalteries: an instrument made by Arnold Dolmetsch for Yeats and Florence Farr (Florence Farr Emery, d. 1917 in

Ceylon, a member of the group of students of the occult who gathered round MacGregor Mathers (1854–1918)); it was 'half psaltery, half lyre' and contained all the chromatic intervals within the range of the speaking voice. Yeats wrote an essay on 'Speaking to the Psaltery' (*E & I* 13–27).

3. *O masters*: Yeats wrote to Arnold Dolmetsch on 3 June 1902 to say he was writing a 'Prayer to the Seven Archangels to bless the Seven Notes' (L 373). These 'masters' may therefore be the seven archangels. They are 'kinsmen of the Three in One' in line 14.

94 THE HAPPY TOWNLAND

This poem first appeared in *The Weekly Critical Review* (4 June 1903). It was entitled 'The Rider from the North' in *ISW*, but the original title was resumed in *Poems, 1899–1905*. In a radio talk of 1932 Yeats said the poem symbolised striving after an impossible ideal.

3 *the townland*: Paradise. Saul (*PYP* 83) links it with 'that happy townland' [Paradise] in *The Unicorn from the Stars*, Act II. C. M. Bowra (*HS* 190) thinks there is a folklore source for the Irish notion that certain men are 'away', entirely absorbed in the search for an earthly Paradise which is hidden behind the appearance of the visible world.

10 *golden and silver wood*: see note (p. 39) on 'The Man who dreamed of Faeryland' (*CP* 49).

14 *the world's bane*: Grace Jackson, *Mysticism in A E and Yeats in relation to Oriental and American Thought*, 162, considers the 'world's bane' may echo Blake's 'Jerusalem':

> When God commanded this hand to write
> In the shadowy hours of deep midnight,
> He told me that all I wrote should prove
> The bane of all that on earth I love.
>> (*The Works of William Blake* (1893) II, 224)

Yeats and Ellis in their note stress the meaning of 'bane', pointing out that Blake had his own career in mind in 'The Monk' as in 'Milton', that the line 'He told me that all I wrote should prove the bane of all that on earth I love' recalls lines written at Felpham at about the same time and sent in a letter to Mr Butts :

> Must my wife live in my sister's bane,
> And my sister survive on my love's pain ?

24 *golden and silver boughs* : see note, line 10

95

41 *Michael* : the Archangel

45 *Gabriel* : Saul points out that P. Gurd, *The Early Poetry of William Butler Yeats*, 83, links Gabriel with Bertrand, *La Religion des Gaulois*, with its figures 'with human heads and fish tails', and the 'old horn' (line 49) with one of hammered silver in the Dublin Museum. Yeats described Gabriel as the angel of the Moon in the Cabbala 'and might, I considered, command the waters at a pinch' (*A* 269).

97 *The Green Helmet and Other Poems*

THE poems of *The Green Helmet* (1910) are transitional; they are far from the languor and resignation, nostalgia and deliberate restriction of Yeats's earlier poetry. They echo a troubled period in the poet's life. The love poetry regrets the waste of spirit involved in loving Maud Gonne in vain (for she married John MacBride in Paris in 1903), yet excuses it because of her beauty in poems which are cold and simple in style, yet possess a dignity and symbolic rhetoric. The old ideal of romantic poetry had come to a stop, and there is an air of finality about the love poetry Yeats wrote after Maud's marriage: it is static, detached yet none the less poignant.

His other poems in this volume reveal an increasing poetic interest in public life: he had decided his Dionysiac phase was over and he must leave the modes of Mallarmé or Symons for an Apollonian activity: 'All things can tempt me from this craft of verse'. There are poems dealing with age, poems foreshadowing the political rhetoric which the Lane controversy would beget in his next volume; and there are poems which praise Coole and Lady Gregory.

This is varied work which reflects Yeats's own life increasingly; his work in the Abbey Theatre was demanding, and the poetry shows his occasional feeling of disappointment in the Irish audience, his frustration in love as well as the satiric and sensual side of his character. He was still forming a new style, stripping off the decoration of the old, but not yet managing to put all his interests together in his poetry, still feeling his way towards a fuller expression of himself.

HIS DREAM   **99**

This poem first appeared, entitled 'A Dream', in *N* (11 July 1908) dated July [1908] in *GH*. Several poems in this volume, including this one, were grouped under the general title 'Raymond Lully and his wife Pernella' corrected in an erratum slip to 'Nicolas Flamel and his wife Pernella'. A note after the title reads :

> A few days ago I dreamed that I was steering a very gay and elaborate ship upon some narrow water with many people upon its banks, and that there was a figure upon a bed in the middle of the ship. The people were pointing to the figure and questioning, and in my dream I sang verses which faded as I awoke, all but this fragmentary thought, 'We call it, it has such dignity of limb, by the sweet name of Death.' I have made my poem out of my dream and the sentiment of my dream, and can almost say, as Blake did, 'The Authors are in Eternity.'

A WOMAN HOMER SUNG   **100**

This poem was written between 5 and 15 April 1910 (in Yeats's Diary). It first appeared with some alterations in *GH*.

3 *her* : Maud Gonne

9 *being grey* : Yeats was nearly forty-five when he wrote the poem.

13 *shadowed in a glass* : he was celebrating her beauty — a duty he thought beautiful women should not shirk, but Maud Gonne seemed to him to hate 'her own beauty, not its effect on others, but its image in the mirror'. This passage commented (in terms of *AV*) that beauty is from the antithetical self and a woman 'can scarce but hate it, for not only does it demand a painful daily service, but it calls for the denial or the dissolution of the self' (*A* 365). [There follow some lines from an untitled poem not in *CP*]

> How many centuries spent
> The sedentary soul
> In toils of measurement
> Beyond eagle or mole,

> Beyond hearing or seeing
> Or Archimedes' guess,
> To raise into being
> That loveliness ?

100   WORDS

This poem was first written in prose in Yeats's 1908 Diary, section 10, probably on 22 January, as revised verses written on 23 January are to be added to the poem 'written yesterday'. The entry reads :

> To-day the thought came to me that P.I.A.L. [Maud Gonne] never really understands my plans, or nature or ideas. Then came the thought — what matter ? How much of the best I have done and still do is but the attempt to explain myself to her ? If she understood I should lack a reason for writing, and one can never have too many reasons for doing what is so laborious. (*WBY* 228)

The poem first appeared in *GH*.

2   *cannot understand* : Maud Gonne was always reproaching Yeats for not making his art into nationalist propaganda. She introduced him to Arthur Griffith of the Sinn Fein movement after she withdrew from the more extreme I.R.B. about the turn of the century, hoping to keep the literary movement in line with the policies of Sinn Fein. See *WBY* 173.

101   15   *poor words* : cf. 'The Choice' (*CP* 278) with its choice of 'Perfection of the life, or of the work'

101   NO SECOND TROY

This poem heads Yeats's Diary with the date December 1908 beneath it : it first appeared in *GH*.

1   *her* : Maud Gonne

2   *of late* : Maud Gonne withdrew from public life after the break-up of her marriage. See note on 'Against Unworthy Praise' (*CP* 103) p. 106.

3   *most violent ways* : before her marriage Maud Gonne was increasingly involved in anti-British activities ; she linked the I.R.B. (an Irish secret revolutionary association) with French military

intelligence; she offered a Boer agent in Brussels a plan to put bombs in British troopships bound for Africa. See *WBY* 169 and *Y:M & P* 133.

4 *little streets upon the great*: J. Hone, 'Yeats as political philosopher', *London Mercury* (April 1939) remarked that Yeats had come to distrust and quarrel with 'all the little semi-literary and semi-political clubs and societies out of which the Sinn Fein movement grew' (see notes (p. 102) on previous poem).

5 *courage equal to desire*: Conor Cruise O'Brien has also commented on this aspect of Yeats's attitude to politics in 'Passion and Cunning: an Essay on the Politics of W. B. Yeats', drawing attention to Yeats's picture of his political associates of the 'nineties: 'Men who had risen above the traditions of the countryman, without learning those of cultivated life, or even educating themselves and who because of their poverty, their ignorance, their superstitious piety, are much subject to all kinds of fear.' He comments that these views of Yeats are 'a classical statement of the Irish Protestant view of the rising Catholic middle-class' (*IER* 223).

8 *tightened bow*: sexual symbolism in Blake: see notes (p. 88) to 'The Arrow' (*CP* 85)

9 *not natural in an age like this*: Yeats described her in 'The Trembling of the Veil' as looking as if 'she lived in an ancient civilisation', her face was 'like the face of some Greek statue' (*A* 364), and elsewhere he described her as a classical impersonation of the spring, 'the Virgilian commendation "She walks like a goddess" made for her alone' (*A* 123).

10 *high and solitary and most stern*: cf. the description in 'The Trembling of the Veil' which described her beauty as backed by her great stature, . . . solitary . . . her face, like the face of some Greek statue, showed little thought (*A* 364).

12 *Troy for her to burn*: Bowra (*HS* 199) remarks 'His only symbol for her is Helen of Troy; for like Helen she is beyond praise or comment.'

102 RECONCILIATION

This poem was included in section 7 of Yeats's Diary, which was dated 26 February 1909, but Ellmann (*IY* 288) dates it September 1908. The entry reads, 'I made the following poem about six months ago and write it here that it may not be lost.' It first appeared in *GH*.

1 *you* : Maud Gonne

3 *ears being deafened* : Yeats was lecturing in Dublin and received the news of Maud Gonne's marriage to John MacBride just before the lecture. He gave the lecture but never knew what he said in it.

5–6 *a song about . . . kings, Helmets and swords* : possibly a reference to the plays *The King's Threshold* and *On Baile's Strand*

10 *pit* : originally 'a' pit not 'the' pit. Here (despite the possible ambiguity of 'pit' referring to the Abbey Theatre's pit) it probably means grave, as one of the MS. versions had an erased line, 'Trample in the dull lime after them.'

12 *barren thoughts* : another version of the poem written in the Diary between August 1910 and November 1911 contained these lines :

> But every powerful life goes on its way
> Too blinded by the sight of the mind's eye
> Too deafened by the cries of the heart
> Not to have staggering feet and groping hands.

102 KING AND NO KING

This poem was written on 7 December 1909, and first appeared in *GH*.

1 *but merely voice* : Ellmann (*IY* 252) using information given him by Allan Wade, has pointed out that this poem is based on the Beaumont and Fletcher play *King and No King* in which King Arbaces falls in love with his sister Panthea : he tells her

> I have lived
> To conquer men, and now am overthrown

Only by words, brother and sister. Where
Have those words dwelling ? I will find 'em out
And utterly destroy 'em ; but they are
Not to be grasped : let 'em be men or beasts,
And I will cut 'em from the earth ; or towns,
And I will raze 'em, and then blow 'em up :
Let 'em be seas, and I will drink 'em off,
And yet have unquenched fire left in my breast ;
Let 'em be anything but merely voice.

5   *Old Romance* : Arbaces is found to be an adopted child and 'No King', so he is finally able to marry Panthea and become King.

9   *that pledge you gave* : perhaps some vow Maud Gonne took not to marry, possibly in view of her relationship with Millevoye, a French Boulangist. There were reasons she could not marry, she told Yeats when he first proposed to her.

11   *your faith* : Maud Gonne became a Roman Catholic in 1897.

PEACE   **103**

This poem was written in May 1910 at Les Mouettes, Colville, Maud Gonne's house on the Normandy coast near Calvados. (It was destroyed in the Second World War.) It first appeared in *GH*.

3   *a hero's wage* : Maud Gonne had married Major John MacBride, who had fought for the Boers in the South African War.

8, 9   *All that sternness amid charm,* | *All that sweetness amid strength* : these opposing qualities in Maud Gonne troubled Yeats. Cf. 'Against Unworthy Praise' (*CP* 103) and 'The Tower' (*CP* 222) where he alludes to her as 'a great labyrinth'.

AGAINST UNWORTHY PRAISE   **103**

This poem was written at Colville, Calvados, and is dated 11 May 1910 in Yeats's Diary. It first appeared in *GH*.

2   *knave or dolt* : this may refer to the behaviour of the Abbey audience when disturbances over Synge's *The Playboy of the Western World* occurred in 1907.

4 *for a woman's sake* : an undated entry in section 10 of Yeats's Diary epitomises the main thought of the poem : 'How much of the best that I have done and still do is but the attempt to explain myself to her.'

104 13 *labyrinth* : cf. 'The Tower' (*CP* 222)

16, 17 . . . *slander, ingratitude, From self-same dolt and knave* : the Abbey audience hissed Maud Gonne when she appeared in the theatre in 1905 at a time when she was trying to obtain a separation from John MacBride. After she obtained this she virtually withdrew from public life.

104 THE FASCINATION OF WHAT'S DIFFICULT

The subject matter of this poem was contained in prose in Yeats's Diary in September 1909. The poem was probably written between that date and March 1910 ; it first appeared in *GH*.

1 *The fascination* : the prose draft reads :

Subject : To complain at the fascination of what's difficult. It spoils spontaneity and pleasure, and wastes time. Repeat the line ending difficult three times and rhyme on bolt, exalt, coalt, jolt. One could use the thought that the winged and unbroken coalt must drag a cart of stones out of pride because it is difficult, and end by denouncing drama, accounts, public contests and all that's merely difficult.

4 *our colt* : Pegasus, the winged horse who sprang from the blood of Medusa and flew to Heaven. Ovid relates a legend in which Pegasus lived on Helicon where he raised the Fountain of Hippocrene, after which the Muses made him their favourite.

6 *Olympus* : mountain in Greece, regarded as the home of the Gods in Greek mythology

8 *road-metal* : it is possible that Yeats got the image of Pegasus from T. Sturge Moore (1870–1944), who was a close friend of his at this period. Moore wrote

Swift, as a rule, used his Pegasus for a cart-horse, since it was strong, and he sorely importuned by the press of men and notions in need of condign punishment : but even when plodding in the ruts, its motion betrays the mettle in which it here revels. (*Art and Life* (1910) 76)

Another possible source is Heine :

> In the land of fable prances
> My beloved Pegasus.
> He's no useful, safely virtuous
> Cart-horse of your citizen.
> > (*Atta Troll*, III (1876) 9)

A DRINKING SONG   104

This poem is dated 17 February 1910 in Yeats's Diary : it first appeared in *GH*.

6 *I sigh* : the poem was written for *Mirandolina*, Lady Gregory's   105 adaptation of Goldoni's *La Locandiera*, and is a speech by Miran-dolina, an innkeeper who is flirting with the misogynist Captain. Clifford Bax's translation is perhaps nearer to the original spirit of Goldoni, whose original version read :

> Viva Bacco e viva Amore
> L'uno e l'altro ci consola :
> Uno passa per la gola
> L'altro va dagli occhi al cuore
> Bevo il vin ; cogli occhi poi . . .
> Faccio . . . quel che fate voi.
> > (*Commedie scelte*, 1891)

Bax's version reads :

> Wine and love ! With what sweet art
> Each can lay our sorrows flat !
> This goes down the throat, and that
> Down the eyes to take the heart.
> Look, I drink : and these eyes too
> Then do straightway what yours do.
> > Goldoni, *Four Comedies* (ed. Bax, 1922)

This leads better into the Captain's reception of the toast, which has a sentimental flavour in Yeats's version.

THE COMING OF WISDOM WITH TIME   105

This poem was written on 21 or 22 March 1909 in Yeats's Diary ; it was originally entitled 'Youth and Age' when it first appeared in *McClure's Magazine* (Dec. 1910). The present title was used in *GH*.

105   ON HEARING THAT THE STUDENTS OF OUR NEW
UNIVERSITY HAVE JOINED THE AGITATION AGAINST
IMMORAL LITERATURE

This poem was dated 3 April 1912 in Yeats's Diary, and entitled 'On hearing that the students of our New University having joined the Ancient Order of Hibernians are taking part in the Agitation against Immoral Literature'. The poem first appeared in *The Green Helmet and Other Poems* (1912) with the title 'On hearing . . . University have joined the Ancient Order of Hibernians and the Agitation against Immoral Literature'.

Title   New University : originally named the Royal University of Ireland. It was founded in 1908 on a federal basis, and became the National University of Ireland, composed of colleges in Dublin, Cork, Galway and Maynooth, that in Dublin being originally begun by Newman as Rector in 1854. It is 'new' as opposed to Trinity College, Dublin, founded by Queen Elizabeth I in 1591.

105   TO A POET, WHO WOULD HAVE ME PRAISE CERTAIN BAD
POETS, IMITATORS OF HIS AND MINE

This poem was written in Yeats's Diary between 23 and 26 April [1909], Section 166. It was headed 'To AE, who wants me [to] praise some of his poets imitators of my own.' It first appeared in *GH*.

1   *You* : Yeats's friend George Russell (A E), who had a literary circle in Dublin. 'Seumas O'Sullivan', a member of it, replied, 'Where's the wild dog which ever knew his father?'

106   THE MASK

The text of this poem was written in Yeats's Diary between August 1910 and May 1911. It first appeared in *GH* entitled 'A Lyric from an Unpublished Play'. It is a lyric from *The Player Queen* (1922). The parts are allocated to man and woman more clearly in the play, e.g. the man speaks lines 1–2, 6–7, 11–12, and the woman replies.

1 *that mask* : Yeats wrote 'What I have called "the Mask" is an emotional antithesis to all that comes out of their [subjective men] internal nature' (*A* 189).

UPON A HOUSE SHAKEN BY THE LAND AGITATION   **106**

Yeats's Diary included a prose draft for this poem dated 7 August [1910], the text of the poem and an explanation of it. The poem first appeared, entitled 'To a Certain Country House in Time of Change' in *McClure's Magazine* (Dec. 1910). It was entitled 'Upon a Threatened House' in *GH*. The draft read :

> Subject for a Poem. A Shaken House. How should the world gain if this house failed, even though a hundred little houses were the better for it, for here power has gone forth, or lingered giving energy, precision ; it gives to a far people beneficent rule ; and still under its roof loving intellect is sweetened by old memories of its descents from far off ; how should the world be better if the wren's nest flourish and the eagle's house is scattered.

The explanation read :

> I wrote this poem on hearing the result of reduction of rent made by the courts. One feels that when all must make their living they will live not for life's sake but the work's and all be the poorer. My work is very near to life itself and my father's very near to life itself but I am always feeling a lack of life's own values behind my thought. They should have been there before the stream began, before it became necessary to let the work create its values. This house has enriched my soul out of measure because here life moves within restraint through gracious forms. Here there has been no compelled labour, no poverty-thwarted impulse.

1 *this house* : Coole Park, Lady Gregory's house in Co. Galway, now demolished

4 *the lidless eye* : this line refers to a belief that only an eagle can stare into the sun without blinking. Yeats uses the eagle as a symbol for an active objective person.

5 *eagle thoughts*: cf. Blake's lines, 'The Eagle, that doth gaze upon the sun' ('King Edward the Third', *The Poems of William Blake* (ed. Yeats) 29) and

> As the wing'd eagle scorns the towery fence . . .
> Then, bosomed in an amber cloud, around
> Plumes his wide wings, and seeks Sol's palace high

('An Imitation of Spenser', poetical sketches, *The Poems of William Blake* (ed. Yeats) 14)

and

> And the eagle returns . . .
> Shaking the dust from his immortal pinions to awake
> The sun that sleeps too long.

(Visions of the Daughters of Albion, The Prophetical Books, *The Poems of William Blake* (ed. Yeats), 181)

There is also Blake's query '[Ask] the winged eagle why he loves the sun ?' (*The Poems of William Blake* (ed. Yeats) 182).

8 *Mean roof-trees*: the cottages whose inhabitants would farm more of the estate. In September 1910 Yeats's Diary contains thoughts upon the contrasts of Irish life. Synge, exalted to the aristocracy of writers and persecuted by the mob, is like Coole Park threatened by the growing powers of the cottages (cf. 'Estrangement', *A* 482). Yeats wrote :

> I thought of the house [Coole Park] slowly perfecting itself and the life within it in ever increasing intensity of labour and then of it probably sinking away, things courteous incomplete or rather sheer weakness of will, for ability has not failed in young Gregory, and I said to myself : Why is life a perpetual preparation for something that never happens ? Even an Odyssey only seems a preparation, a thing of ruined reminiscence. It is not always the tragedy of the great that they see before the end the small and weak in friendship or in enmity pushing them from their place and ruining what they have built and doing one or the other in mere lightness of mind.

107   10 *The gifts that govern men*: Sir William Gregory (1817–92), Lady Gregory's husband, a politician, had served as Governor of Ceylon.

11   *a written speech* : Lady Gregory's plays and her two books of
Irish legends, *Gods and Fighting Men* and *Cuchulain of Muirthemne*

AT THE ABBEY THEATRE   **107**

This poem was written in Paris in May 1911. A note to this effect,
dated 17 August 1911, is in Yeats's Diary ; the poem first appeared
in *IR* (Dec. 1912) and *The Green Helmet and Other Poems* (1912).

Title : *Ronsard* : the poem is very close to the original sonnet:

> Tyard, on me blasmoit, à mon commencement,
> Dequoy j'estois obscur au simple populaire,
> Mais on dit aujourd'huy que je suis au contraire,
> Et que je me démens, parlant trop bassement.
>   Toy de qui le labeur enfante doctement
> Des livres immortels, dy-moy, que doy-je faire ?
> Dy-moi, car tu sçais tout, comme doy-je complaire
> A ce monstre testu, divers en jugement ?
>   Quand je tonne en mes vers, il a peur de me lire ;
> Quand ma voix se desenfle, il ne fait qu'en mesdire.
> Dy-moy de quel lien, force, tenaille, ou clous
>   Tiendray-je ce Proté qui se change à tous coups ?
> Tyard, je t'enten bien, il le faut laisser dire,
> Et nous rire du luy, comme il se rit de nous.
>   (*Œuvres complètes*, 1, 116 (1950))

1   *Craoibhin Aoibhin* : Irish for 'Little Pleasant Branch', the pen
name of Dr Douglas Hyde (1860–1949), a poet, translator, politician, and first President of Eire. Yeats thought he had not fulfilled
his early promise, and while praising his first book of verse thought
he had not critical capacity but an uncritical folk genius : 'He
had much frequented the company of old countrymen, and had so
acquired the Irish language, and his taste for snuff, and for moderate
quantities of a detestable species of illegal whiskey [potheen] distilled from the potato by certain of his neighbours' (*A* 217). He
wrote out of an imitative sympathy ; he was to create a popular
movement (the Gaelic League) but Yeats none the less mourned
for '"the greatest folklorist who ever lived" and for the great poet
who died in his youth.' Yeats thought his incapacity for criticism
made him 'the cajoler of crowds, and of individual men and women
. . . and for certain years young Irish women were to display his

pseudonym, "Craoibhin Aoibhin", in gilt letters upon their hat-bands' (*A* 219). Cf. 'Coole Park, 1929' (*CP* 273):

> There Hyde before he had beaten into prose
> That noble blade the Muses buckled on . . .

11   *Proteus* : in Greek legend an old man of the sea who tended Poseidon's flocks. He had the gift of prophesy but he was difficult to consult because he could change his shape at will.

107   THESE ARE THE CLOUDS

This poem, which was written in May 1910, first appeared in *GH*.

3   *the weak lay hand on what the strong has done* : cf. notes on 'Upon a House shaken by the Land Agitation' (*CP* 106). Yeats wrote in his Diary when he was at Stone Cottage in 1914 : 'A long continuity of culture like that at Coole could not have arisen and has not arisen in a single Catholic family in Ireland since the Middle Ages.'

4   *lifted* : originally 'builded', probably a reference to the actual house at Coole Park

108   7   *friend* : the poem is written to Lady Gregory, to reassure her of the value of her work and the intrinsic greatness she has created.

108   AT GALWAY RACES

This poem was written at Coole in the summer of 1908 according to Hone (*WBY* 225) ; on 21 October 1908 according to Ellmann (*IY* 288). It first appeared in *ER* (Feb. 1909) entitled 'Galway Races'.

5   *We, too* : the poets. An entry of Yeats's Diary of this period compared poets to the aristocracy of birth, and horsemen (cf. line 7), as opposed to merchants and clerks (cf. line 8), are the descendants of the class that honoured bards.

7   *horsemen* : used as symbols of simple, violent and passionate men in 'The Gyres' (*CP* 337)

10–16 *at some new moon . . . sleeping is not death . . . horses* : these lines reflect some of *AV*'s thought and resemble 'The Gyres' (*CP* 337):

> What matter ? Those that Rocky Face holds dear,
> Lovers of horses and of women, shall . . . [disinter]
> . . . The workman, noble and saint, and all things run
> On that unfashionable gyre again.

15–16 *hearteners among men | That ride upon horses* : Maud Gonne (MacBride) noticed the change in his acquaintances :

He found himself among the comfortable and well-fed, who style themselves the 'upper classes', but whom Willie shuddering at the words and discriminating even among them, called 'Distinguished Persons' ; and some undoubtedly deserved the title. (*Scattering Branches. Tributes to the Memory of W. B. Yeats*, ed. Stephen Gwynn (1940) 28)

A FRIEND'S ILLNESS   **109**

This poem was written out three times in Yeats's Diary, in section 52 in [February] 1909. It first appeared in *GH*.

1 *sickness* : the Diary entry for 4 February 1909 reads :

This morning I got a letter telling me of Lady Gregory's illness. I did not recognise her son's writing at first and my mind wandered, I suppose because I am not well. I thought my mother was ill and that my sister was asking me to come at once : then I remembered my mother died years ago and that more than kin was at stake. She had been to me mother, friend, sister and brother. I cannot realise the world without her — she brought to my wavering thoughts steadfast nobility. All the day the thought of losing her is like a conflagration in the rafters. Friendship is all the house I have.

On 6 February [1909] the Diary continues :

Lady Gregory better but writes in pencil that 'she very nearly slipped away'.

Section 50 of the Diary praised Lady Gregory's work (it is printed in *Estrangement*) and section 51 contained one sentence: 'Of Lady

Gregory one can say what Shakespeare or another said, "She died every day she lived".' Section 52 contained the three versions of the poem, and section 53 continued :

> All Wednesday I heard Castiglione's phrase ringing in my memory, 'Never be it spoken without tears, the Duchess is dead,' that slight phrase coming where it did among the numbering of his dead has often moved me till my eyes dimmed ; and I feel his sorrow as though one saw the worth of life fade for ever.

ALL THINGS CAN TEMPT ME

109 This poem was written at Coole Park in the summer of 1908, according to Hone (*WBY* 226). It first appeared in *ER* (Feb. 1909), entitled 'Distraction', the present title being used in *GH*.

1 *tempt me* : Yeats wrote little verse while he was Manager of the Abbey Theatre (1904–10).

2 *woman's face* : Maud Gonne

BROWN PENNY

109 This poem first appeared in *GH* entitled 'The Young Man's Song'.

Responsibilities

SOME of the poems in this volume appeared in *The Green Helmet and Other Poems* (1912), others in periodicals, while public life stirred Yeats into the passionate speech of the poems written about the Lane Gallery which were published as *PWD* in 1913. These particular poems reflect his delight in the patronage given by the rulers of Italian Renaissance Courts, with which he compared the attitude of Ireland's new rich. He weighed the new politicians against the old heroes and found them sadly lacking ; in 'The Fisherman' he contrasted his hopes for Ireland with the reality. His experience of secret societies, committees, public meetings emerged in bitter political rhetoric : there was a bitterly disillusioned note in the love poetry too ; the Celtic trappings were finally, decisively, renounced in 'A Coat' and his own ancestors were given mythological significance, while he continued to write love poems, still deeply moved by the beauty of Maud Gonne and, while angered by the way in which the Irish crowd had behaved to him and to her ('The People'), yet ready to accept her continuing regard for the people as selfless and impressive. These love poems have some gentleness and excitement ; they are also compassionate in their evocation of old memories. There are also poems recording intense personal experiences, such as that superb and timeless poem 'The Cold Heaven'.

[PARDON, OLD FATHERS] [INTRODUCTORY RHYMES] 113

This poem is dated 1912–14 in *Responsibilities and Other Poems* (1916). Ellmann (*IY* 288) dates it December 1913. It first appeared in *RPP*.

1 *old fathers* : the poem was provoked by George Moore's attacks on Lady Gregory and Yeats in portions of *Vale* printed in

ER in January and February 1914 :

As soon as the applause died away, Yeats who had lately returned to us from the States with a paunch, a huge stride, and an immense fur overcoat, rose to speak. We were surprised at the change in his appearance, and could hardly believe our ears when, instead of talking to us as he used to do about the old stories come down from generation to generation he began to thunder like Ben Tillett against the middle classes, stamping his feet, working himself into a great temper, and all because the middle classes did not dip their hands into their pockets and give Lane the money he wanted for his exhibition. When he spoke the words, the middle classes, one would have thought that he was speaking against a personal foe, and we looked round asking each other with our eyes where on earth our Willie Yeats had picked up the strange belief that none but titled and carriage-folk could appreciate pictures. And we asked ourselves why our Willie Yeats should feel himself called upon to denounce his own class ; millers and shipowners on one side, and on the other a portrait-painter of distinction ; and we laughed, remembering A E's story, that one day whilst Yeats was crooning over his fire Yeats had said that if he had his rights he would be Duke of Ormonde. A E's answer was : I am afraid, Willie, you are overlooking your father — a detestable remark to make to a poet in search of an ancestry ; and the addition : We both belong to the lower-middle classes, was in equally bad taste. A E knew that there were spoons in the Yeats family bearing the Butler crest, just as there are portraits in my family of Sir Thomas More, and he should have remembered that certain passages in *The Countess Cathleen* are clearly derivative from the spoons. He should have remembered that all the romantic poets have sought illustrious ancestry, and rightly, since romantic poetry is concerned only with nobles and castles, gonfalons and oriflammes. Villiers de l'Isle Adam believed firmly in his descent, and appeared on all public occasions with the Order of Malta pinned upon his coat ; and Victor Hugo, too, had inquired out his ancestry in all the archives of Spain and France before sitting down to write *Hernani* . . . and with good reason, for with the disappearance of gonfalons and donjons it may be doubted if—— My meditation was interrupted by Yeats's voice.

We have sacrificed our lives for Art ; but you, what have you done ? What sacrifices have you made ? he asked, and everybody began to search his memory for the sacrifices that Yeats had made, asking himself in what prison Yeats had languished, what rags he had worn, what broken victuals he had eaten. As far as anybody could remember, he had always lived very comfortably, sitting down invariably to regular meals, and the old green cloak that was in keeping with his profession of romantic poet he had exchanged for the magnificent fur coat which distracted our attention from what he was saying, so opulently did it cover the back of the chair out of which he had risen. But, quite forgetful of the coat behind him, he continued to denounce the middle classes, throwing his arms into the air, shouting at us, and we thinking not at all of what he was saying, but of a story that had been floating about Dublin for some time. (*Vale* (1947 ed.) 113–15)

The passage continues with a malicious discussion of Dublin criticism of Yeats ('a literary movement consists of five or six people who live in the same town and hate each other cordially'), the allegation that his work was finished, and a view that Yeats's love of Maud Gonne was 'the common mistake of a boy'. The rewritten passages which deal with Lady Gregory and her writing can be read in *Vale* (1947) 122–31, 145–7, Moore altered his suggestion in the *English Review* that she had gone amongst the cottages as a Bible reader when a young woman, with skill, and tongue in cheek :

In her own words, 'early association had so much to do with that religion which is the secret of the heart with God'. In saying as much she wins our hearts, but our intelligence warns us against seduction, and we remember that we may not acquiesce in what we believe to be error.

Cf. notes (p. 140) on 'The Witch' (*CP* 135) and on [Final Rhymes] (*CP* 143). Yeats regarded *Reveries* (part of *A*) which he finished on Christmas Day 1914, as 'some sort of apologia for the Yeats family' (Letter to Lily Yeats, 29 Dec. 1914), and had written earlier in his 1909 Diary that :

Duncan has been looking up my coat of arms for a book plate. I gave him the crest . . . a goat's head on a coronet. He found that a Mary Yeats of Lifford who died in 1673 had the following [coat of arms]. Being a woman there was no crest but the English 'Yates' had the goat's head . . . Can my sister get back to 'Mary Yeates'? Mary is an old family name and we had relations not very far from Lifford in North Sligo.

The Prologue was also intended as a challenge to Moore to speak of his own ancestors. See *Y:M & P* 180, for an extract from Yeats's Diary discussing Moore's family. His revenge came in *DP*.

3 *Old Dublin merchant 'free of the ten and four'*: Jervis Yeats (d. 1712), a Dublin linen merchant supposedly of Yorkshire stock and the first of the Yeats family to live in Ireland. Yeats wrote that the term 'free of the ten and four' applied to merchants who were exempted from certain duties by the Irish Parliament (*RPP*) but a later note, dated 1914, corrected this statement:

'Free of the ten and four' is an error I cannot now correct, without more rewriting than I have a mind for. Some merchant in Villon, I forget the reference, was 'free of the ten and four'. Irish merchants exempted by the Irish Parliament were, unless memory deceives me again — I cannot remember my authority — 'free of the eight and six'.

4 *Galway into Spain*: a good deal of merchandise was carried in sailing vessels between Galway and Spain in the eighteenth and nineteenth centuries.

5 *Old country scholar, Robert Emmet's friend*: Yeats's great-grandfather John Yeats (1774–1846), Rector of Drumcliffe, Sligo, from 1805 till his death. He was a friend of Emmet (1778–1803), the patriot who led a Rebellion in 1803; it failed and Emmet was executed. Yeats's great-grandfather was suspected and imprisoned for a few hours (*A* 21).

6 *to the poor*: he was praised by Rev. T. P. O'Rorke, *History of Sligo : Town and Country*, II 27, for his kindness and charity.

7 *Merchant and scholar*: Jervis Yeats and the Rev. John Yeats

8 *huckster's loin*: merchants had been derided in Yeats's poem 'At Galway Races' (*CP* 108) where they were linked with 'clerks': now they are elevated by being linked with a scholar. A method of

distinguishing between the old and the new middle classes of Ireland was to make a contrast between hucksters and the 'Merchant and scholar'. But line 7 originally read 'Traders or soldiers' and was no doubt emended to sharpen the contrast between his family and the 'hucksters'.

9 *Soldiers*: see line 10. This refers to Yeats's Butler and Armstrong ancestors. Cf. *A* 20, which deals with the military history of the family in vague terms.

10 *a Butler or an Armstrong*: Benjamin Yeats, grandson of Jervis, married Mary Butler, a member of the great Anglo-Irish Ormonde family, and the poet set great store by this connection. The Rev. William Butler Yeats (1806–62), son of the Rev. John Yeats, was the poet's grandfather. He was Rector of Moira, Co. Down, and in 1835 married Jane Grace Corbet, daughter of Grace Armstrong, whose family had strong military traditions. Jane Corbet's brother owned Sandymount Castle, Dublin, where the poet's father, John Butler Yeats, spent much of his time when he was an undergraduate at Trinity College, Dublin. See Jeffares, 'John Butler Yeats' (*IER* 26–8).

11, 12 *Boyne . . . James . . . Dutchman*: the scene of the battle fought on 1 July 1690 in which James II was defeated by William of Orange. Yeats originally thought his ancestors fought on the Jacobite side and lines 9–12 first read as follows :

> Pardon, and you that did not weigh the cost,
> Old Butlers when you took to horse and stood
> Beside the brackish waters of the Boyne,
> Till your bad master blenched and all was lost.

13 *Old merchant skipper*: William Middleton (1770–1832), the poet's maternal great-grandfather, of Sligo. He had a depot in the Channel Islands and brought goods to and from South America. His smuggling developed into a general cargo traffic between Sligo and the Iberian peninsula. He seems to have been a brave man. Cf. T. P. O'Rorke, *History of Sligo : Town and Country*, I, 384.

15 *silent and fierce old man*: Yeats's maternal grandfather, William Pollexfen, a retired sea captain and merchant, a silent and proud

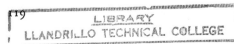

man who had run away to sea as a boy. He was so silent his wife never knew until he was nearly eighty that he had been given the freedom of some Spanish city, a fact he never explained. Yeats was captured by his personality and terrified by it as well : the old man kept a hatchet by his bedside in case of burglars and once the boy saw him hunt men with a horsewhip. Yeats's memories of him were clear : 'Even today when I read *King Lear* his image is always before me, and I often wonder if the delight in passionate men in my plays and in my poetry is more than his memory' (*A* 6 ff.).

18 *wasteful virtues* : probably an implicit comparison with the Middleton relatives in Sligo who were 'liked but had not the pride and reserve, the sense of decorum and order, the instinctive playing before themselves that belongs to those who strike the popular imagination' (*A* 17).

19 *barren passion's sake* : Yeats's unrequited love for Maud Gonne

115 THE GREY ROCK

This poem was written before 1913 but first appeared in *P(Ch)* and *BR* in April 1913.

Title : The Grey Rock is Craig Liath, Carrick-Lee, according to Saul (*PYP* 90), and is Aoife's supposed home near Killaloe.

1–2 *Poets . . . Cheshire Cheese* : poets of the 'nineties, members of the Rhymers' Club which met in an upper room with a sanded floor in the Cheshire Cheese, a Fleet Street chop house. Yeats and Ernest Rhys ((1859–1946), an Anglo-Welsh editor and poet, who became a mining engineer but abandoned this career for writing in 1886 ; he edited the Camelot Series for Walter Scott's publishing house but was best known as the editor of the *Everyman* series) founded the Club (probably in 1891). It had as members Lionel Johnson, Ernest Dowson, Victor Plarr, Ernest Radford, John Davidson, Richard Le Gallienne, T. W. Rolleston, Selwyn Image, Edwin Ellis, and John Todhunter, all of whom 'came constantly for a time'. Arthur Symons and Herbert Horne came 'less constantly, while William Watson joined but never came and

Francis Thompson came once but never joined; and sometimes if
we met in a private house, which we did occasionally, Oscar Wilde
came' (*A* 165). Many of the members were interested in Celtic
literature. Allan Wade adds the names of G. A. Greene and A. C.
Hillier (*L* 181). Elkin Mathews published a *Book of the Rhymers'
Club* in 1892 and Elkin Matthews and John Lane a second volume
in 1894. Ernest Rhys has described the gatherings:

> The first three members were T. W. Rolleston [1857–1920,
> Irish writer, German scholar and editor], W. B. Yeats and
> myself. Each of us asked other Rhymers to come to the club
> suppers, and we soon reached the allotted number of ten.
> Our custom was to sup downstairs in the old coffee-house
> boxes, something like high double-seated pews with a table
> between. After supper, at which we drank old ale and other
> time-honoured liquors, we adjourned to a smoking-room at
> the top of the house, which we came to look upon as our
> sanctum. There long clays or churchwarden pipes were
> smoked, and the Rhymers were expected to bring rhymes in
> their pockets, to be read aloud and left to the tender mercies
> of the club for criticism. (*Everyman Remembers* 105)

10 *Goban*: Goibrui, the ancient Celtic God, whom Yeats mentioned in 'Aristotle of the Books' as 'the legendary mason', and
to whom he attributed legendary wisdom (*M* 66). He was described
as 'bow-legged' in the first published version. He was later known
as an architect and builder.

15 *Slievenamon*: the link between the Gods and the poets of the
Cheshire Cheese is that they each consider man must keep faith
with the eternal powers. Slievenamon is in Tipperary, and was
the site of the god Bodb Derg's palace. Cf. *PYP* 91.

29 *like woman made*: Aoife, a woman of the Sidhe   **116**

32 *for a dead man*: the man who befriended Murrough, the
King of Ireland's son. Cf. lines 71–106.

41 *a woman*: Maud Gonne

47 *lout*: a word Yeats used elsewhere to describe John Mac-
Bride, 'a drunken, vainglorious lout'. Cf. 'Easter 1916' (*CP* 202).

Yeats may be comparing Maud Gonne's briefly successful marriage (1903–5) to Aoife's.

54 *wine or women* : the first may refer to Lionel Johnson, the second to Ernest Dowson. Cf. line 62. Yeats wrote that they were 'dissipated men, the one a drunkard, the other a drunkard and mad about women, and yet they had the gravity of men who had found life out and were awakening from the dream' (*M* 331).

117 62 *Dowson and Johnson* : Ernest Dowson (1867–1900) and Lionel Johnson (1867–1902), both described in Yeats's 'The Tragic Generation'. Johnson drank heavily in his last years, as did Dowson. Johnson lectured Dowson on chastity, 'but the rest of us counted the glasses emptied in their talk'. Dowson 'drunk, desired whatever woman chance brought, clean or dirty' (*A* 308–15). Yeats wrote to his father on 16 February 1910, about these two poets in particular, apropos a lecture he was preparing :

> The doctrine of the group, or rather of the majority of it, was that lyric poetry should be personal. That a man should express his life and do this without shame or fear. Ernest Dowson did this and became a most extraordinary poet, one feels the pressure of his life behind every line as if he were a character in a play of Shakespeare's. Johnson had no theories of any sort but came to do much the same through the example of Dowson and others and because his life grew gradually so tragic that it filled his thoughts. (*L* 548)

Yeats's 'Modern Poetry : a broadcast' also described 'the lucklessness' of the Rhymers' Club, and, in particular, Johnson and Dowson, and estimated their effect on Yeats himself. Cf. *E & I* 491–5.

65–68 *The Danish troop ... King of Ireland's dead* : the Scandinavians began to invade the British Isles from about 800 onwards. They virtually controlled Ireland about 977. Their rule was broken by Malachy, king of Meath, who freed Meath in 980, and Brian Boru, king of Munster, who became High King of Ireland, restored many of the ruined churches and replaced the lost books, and finally defeated the Norsemen at the Battle of Clontarf in 1014. He and his son Murchad fell in the battle.

88 *Aoife*: Cuchulain conquered this Scottish warrior queen, **118**
forcing her to grant him three wishes. She was to become the vassal
of Scatach (a warrior woman of Skye who taught Cuchulain the
art of war), to sleep with him one night, and bear him a son.

125 *rock-born, rock-wandering foot* : there is an implicit comparison **119**
of Maud Gonne (the 'rock-wandering' perhaps a reference to her
love of wandering on Howth's rock paths) and Aoife.

128 *loud host before the sea* : this may refer to Yeats being unpopular
with the I.R.B. and the nationalists. He had accepted a British
Civil List pension in 1910, and was sneered at as 'pensioner Yeats'
by the nationalist press, but these papers had earlier attacked him
over the 'Playboy' controversy of 1907, and his poems dealing
with the Lane controversy had not made him popular. See 'September 1913' (*CP* 120).

TO A WEALTHY MAN WHO PROMISED A SECOND **119**
SUBSCRIPTION TO THE DUBLIN MUNICIPAL GALLERY IF IT
WERE PROVED THE PEOPLE WANTED PICTURES

This poem was dated 8 January 1913 by Yeats, but Ellmann (*IY*
288) dates it 24 December 1912. It first appeared in the *Irish
Times* (11 Jan. 1913) entitled 'The Gift / To a friend who promises
a bigger subscription than his first to the Dublin Municipal Gallery
if the amount collected proves that there is a considerable "popular
demand" for the pictures.' The poem was included in *PWD*
where the 'friend' of the title was altered to 'Man'. Sir Hugh
Lane (1874–1915), Lady Gregory's nephew, offered to give his
collection of French paintings to Dublin if they were properly
housed. He favoured a bridge gallery over the river Liffey,
designed by Sir Edward Lutyens. In disgust at Dublin Corporation's reaction to his proposed gift he placed these pictures in the
National Gallery, London and left them in his will to London, but
before leaving for America on the *Lusitania*, with which he went
down when it was torpedoed by a German submarine, he added
a pencilled codicil to his will leaving the pictures to Dublin. This
was not properly witnessed and the pictures were retained in the
Tate Gallery in London until 1959 when a compromise agreement
was reached by the British and Irish governments by which the
pictures are shared between London and Dublin.

This was the third public controversy which stirred Yeats's imagination, the first being that over Parnell, the second the dispute over Synge's *The Playboy of the Western World.*

In the thirty years or so during which I have been reading Irish newspapers, three public controversies have stirred my imagination. The first was the Parnell controversy. There were reasons to justify a man's joining either party, but there were not to justify, on one side or on the other, lying accusations forgetful of past service, a frenzy of detraction. And another was the dispute over *The Playboy.* There may have been reasons for opposing as for supporting that violent, laughing thing, though I can see the one side only, but there cannot have been any for the lies, for the unscrupulous rhetoric spread against it in Ireland, and from Ireland to America. The third prepared for the Corporation's refusal of a building for Sir Hugh Lane's famous collection of pictures.

One could respect the argument that Dublin, with much poverty and many slums, could not afford the £22,000 the building was to cost the city, but not the minds that used it. One frenzied man compared the pictures to Troy horse which 'destroyed a city,' and innumerable correspondents described Sir Hugh Lane and those who had subscribed many thousands to give Dublin paintings by Corot, Manet, Monet, Degas, and Renoir, as 'self-seekers,' 'self-advertisers,' 'picture-dealers,' 'log-rolling cranks and faddists,' and one clerical paper told 'picture-dealer Lane' to take himself and his pictures out of that. A member of the Corporation said there were Irish artists who could paint as good if they had a mind to, and another described a half-hour in the temporary gallery in Harcourt Street as the most dismal of his life. Someone else asked instead of these eccentric pictures to be given pictures 'like those beautiful productions displayed in the windows of our city picture shops.' Another thought that we would all be more patriotic if we devoted our energy to fighting the insurance act. Another would not hang them in his kitchen while yet another described the vogue of French impressionist painting as having gone to such a length among 'log-rolling enthusiasts' that they even admired 'works that were rejected from the Salon forty years ago by the finest critics in the world.'

The first serious opposition began in the *Irish Catholic*, the chief Dublin clerical paper, and Mr William Murphy the organiser of the recent lock-out and Mr Healy's financial supporter in his attack upon Parnell, a man of great influence, brought to its support a few days later his newspapers *The Evening Herald* and *The Irish Independent*, the most popular of Irish daily papers. He replied to my poem 'To a Wealthy Man' (I was thinking of a very different wealthy man) from what he described as 'Paudeen's point of view,' and 'Paudeen's point of view' it was. The enthusiasm for 'Sir Hugh Lane's Corots' — one paper spelled the name repeatedly 'Crot' — being but 'an exotic fashion,' waited 'some satirist like Gilbert' who 'killed the aesthetic craze,' and as for the rest 'there were no greater humbugs in the world than art critics and so-called experts'. As the first avowed reason for opposition, the necessities of the poor got but a few lines, not so many certainly as the objection of various persons to supply Sir Hugh Lane with 'a monument at the city's expense,' and as the gallery was supported by Mr James Larkin, the chief labour leader, and important slum workers, I assume that the purpose of the opposition was not exclusively charitable.

These controversies, political, literary, and artistic, have showed that neither religion nor politics can of itself create minds with enough receptivity to become wise, or just and generous enough to make a nation. Other cities have been as stupid — Samuel Butler laughs at shocked Montreal for hiding the Discobolus in a lumber-room — but Dublin is the capital of a nation, and an ancient race has nowhere else to look for an education. Goethe in *Wilhelm Meister* describes a saintly and naturally gracious woman, who, getting into a quarrel over some trumpery detail of religious observance, grows — she and all her little religious community — angry and vindictive. In Ireland I am constantly reminded of that fable of the futility of all discipline that is not of the whole being. Religious Ireland — and the pious Protestants of my childhood were signal examples — thinks of divine things as a round of duties separated from life and not as an element that may be discovered in all circumstance and emotion, while political Ireland sees the good citizen but as a man who holds to certain opinions and not as a man of good will. Against all this we have but a few educated men and the remnants of an old traditional culture among the poor. Both were stronger forty years ago, before the rise of our new middle class which made its first public display during the nine years of the Parnellite split, showing how base at moments of excitement are minds without culture. (*RPP*)

(*Note.*—I leave out two long paragraphs ['One could respect . . . not exclusively charitable' *VE* 819–20] which have been published in earlier editions of these poems. There is no need now to defend Sir Hugh Lane's pictures against Dublin newspapers. The trustees of the London National Gallery, through his leaving a codicil to his will unwitnessed, have claimed the pictures for London, and propose to build a wing to the Tate Gallery to contain them. Some that were hostile are now contrite, and doing what they can, or letting others do unhindered what they can, to persuade Parliament to such action as may restore the collection to Ireland.—Jan. 1917) (*Responsibilities and Other Poems*)

1 *You*: the 'wealthy man' is probably Lord Ardilaun, though William Martin Murphy has been suggested by Saul (*PYP* 91). Yeats mentioned Lord Ardilaun in a letter written to Lane on 1 January 1913 : 'I have tried to meet the argument in Lady Ardilaun's letter to somebody, her objection to giving because of Home Rule and Lloyd George, and still more to meet the general argument of people like Ardilaun that they should not give unless there is a public demand' (*L* 573). Yeats also commented in his Notes, apropos William Martin Murphy's reply to 'To a Wealthy Man', 'I was thinking of a very different wealthy man'.

2, 3 *Paudeen's* . . . *Biddy's* : the crowd, the people ; sometimes used contemptuously as of beggars

7 *the blind and ignorant town* : Yeats particularly resented the attacks made on Lane in the *Irish Independent*, William Martin Murphy's paper. Cf. Conor Cruise O'Brien, 'Passion and Cunning : An Essay on the Politics of W. B. Yeats' (*IER* 232 ff.).

9 *Duke Ercole* : Duke Ercole de l'Este (1431–1505), son of Duke Niccolo III and Rizzarda di Saluzzo, was bred at the Neapolitan Court and became Duke of Ferrara. Though his reign was not peaceful his court was renowned for luxury and the brilliancy of its art and letters which the Duke supported generously and with discrimination. Yeats had first read Castiglione's *The Book of the Courtier* in Hoby's translation in 1903 or 1904 (there are many references to it in his 1909–10 Diary). This described the Duke's

court in Ferrara, and Yeats visited Ferrara and Urbino when he went to Italy for the first time with Lady Gregory and her son in 1907.

12   *his Plautus* : the Duke's patronage of the theatre is described by Castiglione and Opdycke's translation of *The Courtier* (1902) mentions this : 'no less than five plays of Plautus being performed during the wedding of his son Alphonso in 1502'. Though Yeats owned a copy of Hoby's translation he seems to have used Opdycke's also, from the notes of which he probably gathered the information about these plays of Plautus.

14   *Guidobaldo* : Guidobaldo di Montefeltro, Duke of Urbino   **120**
(1472–1508), son of Duke Federico de Montefeltro and Battista Sforza, an accomplished niece of the first Sforza Duke of Milan.

15   *That grammar school* : he was highly praised in *The Courtier*. Talents, learning, grave deportment and fluency of speech were required of his courtiers, and the culture and refined manners of his court were renowned. Yeats sees it as a place where youth 'for certain brief years imposed upon drowsy learning the discipline of its joy' (*A* 545).

17   *Urbino's windy hill* : Urbino is superbly situated on the slopes of the Apennines. Castiglione described the palace as

> regarded by many as the most beautiful to be found in all Italy ; and he so well furnished it with everything suitable that it seemed not a palace but a city in the form of a palace ; and not merely with what is ordinarily used, — such as silver vases, hangings of richest cloth-of-gold and silk, and other similar things, — but for ornament he added countless antique statues in marble and bronze, pictures most choice, and musical instruments of every sort, nor would he admit anything there that was not very rare and excellent. Then at very great cost he collected a goodly number of most excellent and rare books in Greek, Latin and Hebrew, all of which he adorned with gold and silver, esteeming this to be the chiefest excellence of his great palace. (Castiglione, *The Courtier*, trans. L. E. Opdycke (1903))

Yeats walked to Urbino from San Sepolcro and described its situation vividly in 'A Tower on the Apennines' (*E & I* 290).

19 *the shepherds' will*: in *BS* Yeats remembered a friend (Lady Gregory) reading out Castiglione's commendations of Urbino and remembered 'a cry of Bembo's made years after, "Would that I were a shepherd that I might look down daily upon Urbino"' (*A* 545). The quotation is also made in *AV*, where men of Phase Three are described as images seen by lyric poets (particularly those of the seventeenth phase, to which Yeats belonged). See *AV* (B) 108–9.

20 *Cosimo*: Cosimo de Medici, exiled in 1433 to Venice

23 *Michelozzo*: an architect and pupil of Brunelleschi. He accompanied Cosimo to Venice and designed many public and private buildings there, returning in triumph with Cosimo in 1434. Yeats probably acquired knowledge of him and his work when in Venice in 1907. He designed, at Cosimo's order and expense, the Library of the Monastery of S. Giorgio Maggiore and the Library of St Mark's, Florence. Lines 21–4 originally ran:

> Unknowing their predestined man,
> So much more time and thought had he
> For Michelozzo's latest plan
> Of the San Marco library.

T. R. Henn, 'The Green Helmet' and 'Responsibilities', (*HG* 41), remarks Cosimo de Medici is Hugh Lane, Michelozzo is Lutyens, the San Marco Library is the projected gallery over the Liffey.

28 *dugs*: the word is a mark of Yeats's new style, and received a veiled reproof in a letter from 'Val d'Arno':

> Mr Yeats draws all his mental nourishment from the dry breasts of Greece, whose views of men and things please him for the simple reason that they equate with the prejudices of the class to which Mr Yeats presumably belongs. (*Irish Times*, 13 Jan. 1913)

32 *the sun's eye*: a reference to the eagle being able to stare unblinkingly at the sun. Cf. line 36 'eagle's nest', and note (pp. 109–110) on 'Upon a House shaken by the Land Agitation' (*CP* 106). The eagle symbolises nobility, activity, greatness, objectivity.

SEPTEMBER 1913   **120**

This poem was dated 7 September 1913 when it first appeared in the *Irish Times* (8 Sept. 1913) entitled 'Romance in Ireland / (On reading much of the correspondence against the Art Gallery)'. In *Nine Poems* (1914) it was entitled 'Romantic Ireland (September 1913)' and the present title was adopted in *RPP*.

1 *you*: the people of Ireland, but particularly the new Catholic middle class which Yeats disliked

2 *greasy till*: the image came from a speech Yeats made in July 1913. He wrote to Lady Gregory that he had spoken with Lane as well as possible subscribers [to the Gallery] in his mind: 'I described Ireland, if the present intellectual movement failed, as a little greasy huxtering nation groping for halfpence in a greasy till but did not add except in thought, "by the light of a holy candle"' (Lady Gregory, *Hugh Lane*, 137).

8 *O'Leary*: John O'Leary (1830–1907) when a medical student   **121** in Trinity College, Dublin, was influenced by the Young Ireland Movement, and became one of the Triumvirate in the Fenian movement which succeeded it. He was arrested in 1865, condemned to twenty years' penal servitude, but set free after serving five years of his sentence, on condition that he did not return to Ireland for fifteen years. He spent his exile in Paris, had a large collection of Irish books and greatly influenced Yeats. (He was also friendly with Yeats's father, John Butler Yeats.) It was through O'Leary's influence that Yeats moved from his father's Home Rule views to a more strongly nationalist point of view. O'Leary, 'the handsomest old man' Yeats had ever seen, was a romantic figure:

> Sometimes he would say things that would have sounded well in some heroic Elizabethan play. It became my delight to rouse him to these outbursts, for I was the poet in the presence of his theme. Once when I was defending an Irish politician who had made a great outcry because he was treated as a common felon, by showing that he did it for the cause's sake, he said, 'There are things that a man must not do to save

a nation.' He would speak a sentence like that in ignorance of its passionate value, and would forget it the moment after. (*A* 95–6)

He despised inferior writing and told Yeats, 'Neither Ireland nor England knows the good from the bad in any art, but Ireland unlike England does not hate the good when it is pointed out to her' (*A* 101). From debates in a Young Ireland Society, from O'Leary's conversation and the Irish books he lent Yeats came all I have set my hand to since' (*A* 101). O'Leary belonged to Yeats's romantic conception of Irish nationality : he — like his disciple the barrister J. F. Taylor — seemed to Yeats to be the last 'to speak an understanding of life and Nationality, built up by the generation of Grattan, which read Homer and Virgil, and by the generation of Davis, which had been pierced through by the idealism of Mazzini, and of the European revolutionists of the mid-century' (*E & I* 246).

16 *in the grave* : Yeats could not bring himself to go to O'Leary's funeral, for he shrank from seeing about his grave 'so many whose Nationalism was different from anything he had taught or that I could share' (*E & I* 246).

17 *the wild geese* : Irishmen who served abroad in the armies of France, Spain, and Austria, largely as a result of the Penal Laws passed after 1691. Sarsfield and 11,000 men left for the French service, out of loyalty to James II, after the Treaty of Limerick was signed in 1691 ; the Irish Brigade fought with the French until the Revolution. In all, it is said that 120,000 'Wild Geese' left Ireland between 1690 and 1730. Cf. Curtis (*HI* 292).

20 *Edward Fitzgerald* : Lord Edward Fitzgerald (1763–98), a romantic figure who served in America, became M.P. for Athy and Kildare, and joined the United Irishmen in 1796. He was president of the military committee and died of wounds received while he was being arrested.

21 *Emmet* : Robert Emmet (1778–1803), who was educated at Trinity College Dublin, led an abortive revolt in 1803, was tried for high treason and executed.

Wolfe Tone : Theobald Wolfe Tone (1763–98), educated at Trinity College Dublin, founded the United Irish Club, was appointed chef-de-brigade in France, and led a French force to Ireland. He was captured in Lough Skilly and condemned by court martial. He is said to have committed suicide in prison.

22 *delirium* : this probably derives from Swinburne's contemptuous comment, in his *William Blake* (1906), vi, on Yeats's Introduction to Blake where he had tried to prove Blake a Celt :

> Some Hibernian commentator on Blake, if I rightly remember a fact so insignificant, has somewhere said something to some such effect that I, when writing about some fitfully audacious and fancifully delirious deliverance of the poet he claimed as a countryman, and trying to read into it some coherent and imaginative significance, was innocent of any knowledge of Blake's meaning. It is possible, if the spiritual fact of his Hibernian heredity has been or can be established, that I was : for the excellent reason that, being a Celt, he now and then too probably had none worth the labour of deciphering — or at least worth the serious attention of any student belonging to a race in which reason and imagination are the possible preferable substitutes for fever and fancy.

Yeats's father drew his attention to this passage (*LTHS* 92–3) : 'It is a reference to you of a particularly insolent and contemptuous sort. . . . His criticism that the Celtic movement puts fever and fancy in the place of reason and imagination is I am afraid a true criticism — as true as to my mind it is obvious,' and Yeats probably remembered his own old love for 'fitfully audacious and fancifully delirious heroes' when he wrote in his notes to *Responsibilities* : 'Neither religion nor politics can of itself create minds with enough receptivity to become wise, or just and generous enough to make a nation. Our new middle class . . . showed . how base at moments of excitement are minds without culture.'

He now contrasts the delirium of his heroes with the uncultured excitement of his own times, using Swinburne's word to exalt the old and belittle the new Ireland.

28 *You'd cry* : modern middle-class Ireland could not understand the love these men had for Ireland. Yeats himself is bound to the wild geese and the martyr heroes by his maddened love for

Maud Gonne which was so linked with his love of Ireland.   A passage in *BS* illustrates this :

> During our first long wait all kinds of pictures had passed before me in reverie and now my imagination renews its excitement.   I had thought how we Irish had served famous men and famous families, and had been, so long as our nation had intellect enough to shape anything of itself, good lovers of women, but had never served any abstract cause, except the one, and that we personified by a woman, and I wondered if the service of woman could be so different from that of a Court.   I had thought how, before the emigration of our poor began, our gentlemen had gone all over Europe, offering their swords at every Court, and that many had stood, just as I, but with an anxiety I could but imagine, for their future hung upon a frown or a smile.   I had run through old family fables and histories, to find if any man of my blood had so stood, and had thought that there were men living, meant by nature for that vicissitude, who had served a woman through folly, because they had found no Court to serve.   (*A* 544–5)

122   TO A FRIEND WHOSE WORK HAS COME TO NOTHING

This poem was dated 16 September [1913] in the Maud Gonne MS. book, and first appeared in *PWD*.

2   *Be secret*: Yeats's note, dated 1922 in *Later Poems* (1922), makes it clear that the poem was written to Lady Gregory, though she thought it written to Sir Hugh Lane.

5–6   *one Who* : William Martin Murphy.   The poem probably relates to the final decision of the Dublin Corporation about the Lane pictures.   Yeats wrote to Lady Gregory on the envelope of a letter posted in London on 1 July 1913 : 'Can you send me I T [*Irish Times*] with final decision of Corporation ?   It may move me to another poem.'

122   PAUDEEN

The MS. of this poem, which was written at The Prelude, Coleman's Hatch, is dated 16 September 1913.   I first appeared in *PWD*.

1 *the fumbling wits, the obscure spite* : this may refer to William Martin Murphy's attack on Yeats's first poem of the series on the Lane controversy, 'To a Wealthy Man . . . ' (*CP* 119). Murphy replied to Yeats's reference to 'Paudeen's pence' in that poem :

> I may here remark that, generally speaking, benefactors have to depend upon posterity for the erection of public monuments to their memory . . . . If 'Paudeen's Pennies', so contemptuously poetised a few days ago in the press by Mr W. B. Yeats, are to be abstracted from Paudeen's pockets, at least give him an opportunity of saying whether he approves of the process or not. . . . Speaking for myself I admire good pictures and I think I can appreciate them but as a choice between the two, I would rather see in the city of Dublin one block of sanitary houses at low rents replacing a reeking slum than all the pictures Corot and Degas ever painted. (*Irish Independent*, 17 January 1913)

2 *our old Paudeen* : see Yeats's note, included in headnote to 'To a Wealthy Man . . .' (*CP* 119) where he alludes to Murphy replying to his poem from 'Paudeen's point of view'

6 *God's eye* : a passage in 'The Stirring of the Bones' may expand the thought. Yeats experienced an emotion which seemed to him what the devout Christian must feel when he surrenders his will to God. He woke next day to hear a voice saying, 'The love of God is infinite for every human soul because every human soul is unique ; no other can satisfy the same need in God'. (*A* 378–9)

TO A SHADE   123

The MS. of this poem is dated 29 September [1913]; it was written at Coole and first appeared in *PWD*. The subject is the blind bitterness with which true benefactors of Ireland have been greeted.

1 *thin Shade* : the poem is addressed to Charles Stewart Parnell (1846–91), the Irish Parliamentary leader repudiated by Gladstone, the Irish Hierarchy, and the Irish Party, because of his affair with Mrs O'Shea. Yeats's view of the deposition of Parnell is given in 'Modern Ireland', *Massachusetts Review* (Winter 1964), 257–9.

2 *monument* : the Parnell monument is situated at the northern end of O'Connell Street, Dublin.

7 *gaunt houses* : of Dublin

9 *A man* : Sir Hugh Lane, whose treatment by his fellow countrymen is compared to that of Parnell. See notes on 'To a Wealthy Man . . .' (*CP* 119).

11 *what* : Lane's proffered gift of the French paintings

17 *Your enemy, an old foul mouth* : William Martin Murphy [see notes (pp. 124–6) on 'To a Wealthy Man . . .' (*CP* 119), 'September 1913' (*CP* 120), 'To a Friend whose Work has come to Nothing' and 'Paudeen' (*CP* 122)], proprietor of the *Irish Independent* and the evening paper, the *Evening Herald*. Murphy had opposed the Lane benefaction ; but he had also opposed Parnell, and supported Tim Healy, who had led the attack on Parnell. He had organised the recent lock-out which Yeats regarded as inhumane as well as an unprincipled attempt to stir up religious passion. (See Conor Cruise O'Brien, 'Politics and Cunning : An Essay on the Politics of W. B. Yeats' (*IER* 230), who quotes Yeats's letter published in *Irish Worker* (1 Nov. 1913).) Yeats's note links Murphy and Healy :

> The first serious opposition [to the Lane gallery] began in the *Irish Catholic*, the chief Dublin clerical paper, and Mr William Murphy the organiser of the recent lock-out and Mr Healy's financial supporter in his attack upon Parnell, a man of great influence, brought to its support a few days later his newspapers *The Evening Herald* and *The Irish Independent*, the most popular of Irish daily papers. He replied to my poem 'To a Wealthy Man' (I was thinking of a very different wealthy man) from what he described as 'Paudeen's point of view', and 'Paudeen's point of view' it was. (*RPP*)

18 *The pack* : this refers to the influence Murphy's two newspapers possessed, and was probably inspired by a quotation from Goethe which 'ran through the papers [during the quarrel over Parnell's grave], describing our Irish jealousy : "The Irish seem to me like a pack of hounds, always dragging down some noble

stag".' (Eckermann, *Conversations with Goethe*, 7 April 1829 (quoted by Yeats in *A* 316).) But Corinna Salvadori, *Yeats and Castiglione* 65, suggests that the image may come from Ugolino's dream in Dante, *La Divina Commedia*, Inferno, Canto XXXIII, 28–36.

19 *Glasnevin coverlet*: Parnell was buried in Glasnevin cemetery, situated in north Dublin, on 11 October 1891. Yeats did not attend the funeral but wrote a poem 'Mourn, and then Onward' on the occasion, which was published in *UI* (10 Oct. 1891).

WHEN HELEN LIVED   **124**

This poem was written between 20 and 29 September 1913 and first appeared in *P(Ch)* (May 1914).

8 *Those topless towers*: cf. Marlowe, *Dr Faustus*, v, 1:

> Was this the face that launched a thousand ships,
> And burnt the topless towers of Ilium?

12 *A word and a jest*: in 'The Death of Synge' Yeats recorded that he had dreamed this thought on 6 July 1909: 'Why should we complain if men ill-treat our Muses, when all that they gave to Helen while she still lived was a song and a jest?' (*A* 521). Yeats's poetry and his work for the literary revival were theoretically for Maud Gonne's sake. The Helen – Maud Gonne symbolism is involved in the poem.

ON THOSE THAT HATED 'THE PLAYBOY OF THE WESTERN   **124**
WORLD', 1907

This poem is written in Yeats's Diary with the date 5 April 1909. It was first published in *IR* (Dec. 1911) entitled 'On those who Dislike The Playboy'.

Title '*The Playboy* . . .': Yeats has described the troubles in 'The Controversy over The Playboy of the Western World':

> On the second performance of *The Playboy of the Western World*, about forty men who sat in the middle of the pit succeeded in making the play entirely inaudible. Some of them brought tin trumpets, and the noise began immediately upon

the rise of the curtain. For days articles in the Press called for the withdrawal of the play, but we played for the seven nights we had announced ; and before the week's end opinion had turned in our favour. There were, however, nightly disturbances and a good deal of rioting in the surrounding streets. On the last night of the play there were, I believe, five hundred police keeping order in the theatre and in its neighbourhood. (*E* 226)

2 *Eunuchs* : Yeats wrote to Lady Gregory on 8 March 1909 telling her he had written a number of notes, in one of which he had compared Griffith and his like to the Eunuchs in Charles Ricketts's picture watching Don Juan riding through Hell. This note was shortly made into the poem. Arthur Griffith (1872–1922) founded the *United Irishman* after returning to Ireland from Africa in 1899 ; he edited this paper and its successor (in 1906) *Sinn Fein.* He was arrested in 1916, released in 1917, was Vice-President of Dail Eireann in 1918, and negotiated the treaty of 1921. He became President of the Dail in 1922 and died that year.

Griffith had attacked Synge's plays. He held that literature should be subordinate to politics (see *L* 422) but Yeats regarded the journalists and political leaders as suffering from a cultivation of hatred which made them regard creative power with the jealousy of the Eunuch (cf. *A* 486). The attack on Synge seemed to him an attack on genius. In his Diary he wrote of the warping of repressed desire, he regarded the sterility of Irish writing and thought as due to sexual abstinence. An entry for 18 May 1910 reads :

> When any part of human life has been left unexperienced there is a hunger for the experience in large numbers of men and if the expression is prevented artificially the hunger becomes morbid and [then] if the educated do not beware is born the ignorant will.

See also the essay ' J. M. Synge and the Ireland of his Time' (*E & I*, 311), where Yeats thought that the young men who had wished 'to silence what they considered a slander upon Ireland's womanhood' had been slowly prepared to adopt this attitude by patriotic but ignoble journalism ever since Synge's *The Shadow of the Glen* had been performed. In a letter to Lady Gregory of 8 March 1908 he recorded writing 'culture is the sanctity of the intellect' and went on to explain that he was 'thinking of men like Griffith and how they can renounce external things without it but not envy, revenge, jealousy and so on' (*L* 525).

Charles Ricketts (1866–1931), whose painting was in Yeats's mind as he wrote the poem, was a close friend, and was also a stage and book designer, a sculptor and critic. He was co-editor of *The Dial* (1889–97). See Yeats's comment on his work in *A* 550. He met Ricketts and Charles Shannon (see *A* 169) frequently. See also *L* for several comments on both artists.

THE THREE BEGGARS   **124**

This poem first appeared in *Harper's Weekly* (15 Nov. 1913).

5   *lebeen-lone* : according to Henn (*LT* 92) probably *libin leamhan*,   **125**
a small fish or minnow

6   *crane* : heron. The symbolic significance of the bird is discussed by Henn (HG 45).

Gort : village in Galway near Coole

8   *King Guaire* : originally Guari, a legendary king of Gort, Co. Galway

THE THREE HERMITS   **127**

This poem was written at Stone Cottage, Sussex, on 5 March 1913 and first appeared in *The Smart Set* (Sept. 1913). Its tone may have resulted from Ezra Pound's influence. He was acting as secretary to Yeats at the time and was urging him to stiffen his style and become harsher in expression. F. F. Farag (*YCE* 43) points out that the poet is presenting different points of view on the question of rebirth. The theory that man cannot reincarnate as animal after reaching the human stage was, he points out, hotly debated in the Theosophical Society. He cites H. P. Blavatsky, *Isis Unveiled*, I 179 and A. P. Sinnett, *Esoteric Buddhism*, 205–6. See lines 22–8 of the poem.

128   BEGGAR TO BEGGAR CRIED

The MS. of this poem is dated 5 March 1913, and it first appeared in *P(Cb)* (May 1914). Hone (*WBY* 301) has suggested its tone was probably caused by the breaking off of a love affair which began in 1910. A telegram was sent to Yeats when he was at Coole by the lady announcing she was pregnant. Yeats thought wrongly that an attempt was being made 'by an unmarried woman past her first youth' to force him into marriage, but this idea like the news in the telegram was wrong. There was a somewhat sardonic reaction on Yeats's part to Lady Gregory's treatment of the situation; she thought Yeats should marry lest some similar upset should disturb his peace in the future. See notes (pp. 149 and 188) on 'The Dolls' (*CP* 149) and 'Presences' (*CP* 174).

4   *make my soul*: a common Irish expression meaning to prepare for death. Yeats used the phrase in 'The Tower', line 181 (*CP* 218) 'Now shall I make my soul.'

129   RUNNING TO PARADISE

This poem was written at Coole on 20 September 1913 and first appeared in *P(Cb)* (May 1914).

9   *skelping*: beating

19   *a bare heel*: as a young man in London, Yeats inked his heels so the holes in his socks would not be noticeable.

20   *old sock full*: of money

130   THE HOUR BEFORE DAWN

The MS. of this poem is dated 19 October 1913. It was written at Coole, and first appeared in *RPP*. T. R. Henn (*HG* 47), thinks the poem may have arisen out of a Jack Yeats illustration of a Cuala Press Broadside, 2 July 1913, entitled 'Two Tinkers'. He also suggests two poems by Yen Hui (in the British Museum).

4   *Cruachan*: Yeats commented that this is pronounced as if spelt 'Crockan' in modern Gaelic. It was Maeve's capital.

8 *Maeve . . . Maines* : Queen of Connaught. The nine Maines were her sons by Ailill. See line 36.

25 *Hell Mouth* : the Cave of Cruachan, known as the Hell gate of Ireland. Cf. *PYP* 97. Line 120 read in the first version 'From the Hell Mouth at Cruachan'.

50 *Goban's mountain-top* : see note on 'The Grey Rock' (*CP* 115). **131** In one version line 54 read, '"That sacred Goban brewed", he cried'.

82–93 Louis MacNeice, *The Poetry of W. B. Yeats*, 113, thought **132** these lines echoed Synge's tramp in *The Shadow of the Glen* :

We'll be going now, I'm telling you, and the time you'll be feeling the cold, and the frost, and the great rain and the sun again, and the south wind blowing in the glens, you'll not be sitting up in a wet ditch, the way you're after sitting in this place making yourself old with looking on each day, and it passing you by. You'll be saying one time, 'It's a good evening, by the grace of God,' and another time 'It's a wild night, God help us ; but it'll pass surely.'

100 *Michael's trumpet* : on the day of Judgement. Cf. line 41, **133** 'The Happy Townland' (*CP* 9).

A SONG FROM 'THE PLAYER QUEEN' **134**

Yeats spent many years working on this play. This song first appeared in *P* (Ch) (May 1914). *The Player Queen* first appeared in 1922. In the play Decima introduces the song, which her husband Septimus has made, as follows :

It is the song of the mad singing daughter of a harlot. The only song she had. Her father was a drunken sailor waiting for the full tide, and yet she thought her mother had foretold that she would marry a prince and become a great queen.

8 *gold and silver* : see note (p. 39) on 'The Man who dreamed of Faeryland' (*CP* 49)

135 THE REALISTS

This poem first appeared in *P* (Ch.) (Dec. 1912).

3   The MS. had a half-scratched-out sentence which ran 'A poet known in France used to sing to women to wive . . .' which suggests a possible French source. Dragons may be derived from memories of paintings of the Perseus–Andromeda or St George legends ; but a possible source may be the legend connected with Innisfree. Russell K. Alspach quotes William Gregory Wood-Martin, *History of Sligo* (1882) for the account (which Yeats knew) of the dragon which guarded the fruit of a tree on the island. The daughter of the chief of the island asked her lover, named 'Free', to get her some. He defeated the dragon, ate the fruit and died of its virtue. She ate it and died across his body. See also *A* 71–2, quoted in notes (p. 34) on 'The Lake Isle of Innisfree' (*CP* 44), and Alspach, *Yeats and Innisfree* (1965), 71.

135 THE WITCH

The first version of this poem is dated 24 May 1912 in Yeats's Diary. The poem first appeared in *P* (Ch.), (May 1914).

1   *rich* : Yeats's financial position had begun to improve after 1910 because of his pension (see note (p. 123) on line 128 'The Grey Rock' (*CP* 115)) and funds from his American lecturing tours. George Moore gave a malicious account of the apparent signs of this in *Vale* :

> We have sacrificed our lives for Art ; but you, what have you done ? What sacrifices have you made ? he asked, and everybody began to search his memory for the sacrifices that Yeats had made, asking himself in what prison Yeats had languished, what rags he had worn, what broken victuals he had eaten. As far as anybody could remember, he had always lived very comfortably, sitting down invariably to regular meals, and the old green cloak that was in keeping with his profession of romantic poet he had exchanged for the magnificent fur coat which distracted our attention from what he was saying, so opulently did it cover the back of the chair out of which he had risen. . . . The poet advanced a step or two nearer to the edge of the platform, and stamping his foot he asked again

what the middle classes had done for Art, and in a towering rage (the phrase is no mere figure of speech for he raised himself up to tremendous height) he called upon the ladies and gentlemen that had come to hear my lecture to put their hands in their pockets and give sovereigns to the stewards who were waiting at the doors to receive them, or, better still, to write large cheques. We were led to understand that by virtue of our subscriptions we should cease to belong to the middle classes, and having held out this hope to us he retired to his chair and fell back overcome into the middle of the great fur coat, and remained silent until the end of the debate. (George Moore, *Hail & Farewell, Vale* 162–3. Text from 1914 ed.)

3 *witch* : originally read 'bitch' in MS.

7 *one long sought* : possibly a reference to Maud Gonne. (Yeats's early courtship was inhibited by his lack of money : 'What sort of wife would she make, I thought, for a poor student.' He did not propose to her for some years after they first met in 1889.) But the poem is a general comment of disillusionment with success.

THE PEACOCK   **135**

This poem first appeared in *P* (Ch) (May 1914).

1 *riches* : cf. the scorn of wealth in 'The Grey Rock' (*CP* 115) '. . . never made a song / That you might have a heavier purse.'

5 *Three Rock* : probably the Three Rock Mountain which overlooks Dublin

THE MOUNTAIN TOMB   **136**

This poem was written at Maud Gonne's house, Les Mouettes, Colville, Calvados in August 1912. It first appeared in *P* (Ch) (Dec. 1912). Yeats's essay 'The Body of the Father Christian Rosencrux' provides an explanation (he was a member of a Rosicrucian order, and had written two pamphlets dealing with its future in 1901) :

The followers of the Father Christian Rosencrux [who reputedly founded in 1484 the Rosicrucian order, which is first mentioned in 1614], says the old tradition, wrapped his imperishable body in noble raiment and laid it under the house of their Order, in a tomb containing the symbols of all things in heaven and earth, and in the waters under the earth, and set about him inextinguishable magical lamps, which burnt on generation after generation, until other students of the Order came upon the tomb by chance. . . .

Yeats used the symbolism of the tomb to describe his own times ; the following passage may shed light on the sense of the poem's 'in vain, in vain . . .', for it shows the futility of housing a body which does not reveal wisdom :

It seems to me that the imagination has had no very different history during the last two hundred years, but has been laid in a great tomb of criticism, and had set over it inextinguishable magical lamps of wisdom and romance, and has been altogether so nobly housed and apparelled that we have forgotten that its wizard lips are closed, or but opened for the complaining of some melancholy and ghostly voice. . . . (*E & I* 196 ff.)

See also Karl Kisewetter, 'The Rosicrucians', *Theosophical Siftings*, III.

136   TO A CHILD DANCING IN THE WIND

This poem was written at Les Mouettes, Colville, Calvados, in December 1912. It first appeared in *P* (Ch) (Dec. 1912).

2   *you*: Iseult Gonne, Maud Gonne MacBride's daughter, who later married the novelist Francis Stuart. For a description of her (probably in 1916 or 1917, when Yeats and she were reading the French religious poets together, see *L* 628–9) in Normandy, see *AV* :

I remember a beautiful young girl singing at the edge of the sea in Normandy words and music of her own composition. She thought herself alone, stood barefooted between sea and sand ; sang with lifted head of the civilisations that there had come and gone, ending every verse with the cry : 'O Lord, let something remain.' (*AV* (B) 220)

137   7   *The fool's triumph* : perhaps William Martin Murphy's campaign against Lane's pictures

8 *Love lost as soon as won* : perhaps a reference to Maud Gonne's marriage which only lasted from 1903 to 1905

9 *the best labourer* : J. Unterecker (*RG* 126) suggests this may refer to Synge's death in 1909.

TWO YEARS LATER   137

This poem was written on 3 December 1912 or 1913 and first appeared in *P* (Ch), (May 1914).

3 *you* : Iseult Gonne

9 *your mother* : Maud Gonne

A MEMORY OF YOUTH   137

The MS. is undated but this poem was probably written on 13 August 1912 and first appeared in *P* (Ch) (Dec. 1912).

5 *her praise* : the poem is written about Maud Gonne.   138

15 *silent as a stone* : the stone image which was associated with Maud Gonne occurs in 'Easter 1916' : 'Too long a sacrifice / Can make a stone of the heart' (*CP* 203). It symbolises love ending in coldness or else a quality of coldness incapable of comprehending the love Yeats professed. It also conveyed a sense of political ruthlessness :

> Hearts with one purpose alone
> Through summer and winter seem
> Enchanted to a stone.   (*CP* 203).
>> Cf. also *E & I* 312–14.

FALLEN MAJESTY   138

This poem was written at Maud Gonne's house, Les Mouettes, Colville, Calvados ; the MS. is dated 1912 and the poem first appeared in *P* (Ch) (Dec. 1912).

1 *crowds gathered* : Yeats's comments on Maud Gonne as a speaker are contained in 'The Trembling of the Veil' :

Her power over crowds was at its height, and some portion of the power came because she could still, even where pushing an abstract principle to what seemed to me an absurdity, keep her own mind free, and so when men and women did her bidding they did it not only because she was beautiful, but because that beauty suggested joy and freedom. (*A* 364)

2 *even old men's eyes* : the line echoes the admiration the elders of Troy felt for Helen, cf. 'When Helen lived' (*CP* 124). But the 'even' has its particular point here. Maud Gonne's attitude in the 'nineties was that of the more violent Fenian movement from which she later retired, and as an incipient stirrer-up of violence she had the disapproval of the older nationalists who deplored the use of force in any attempt to seek independence for Ireland.

5 *lineaments* : a word Yeats found in Blake and found poetically effective

6 *what's gone* : Maud Gonne virtually retired from public life after her marriage in 1903, which lasted until 1905. The crowds are probably those Yeats remembered from his experience while President of the '98 Commemoration Association when he went 'hither and thither speaking at meetings in England and Scotland and occasionally at tumultuous Dublin conventions, and endured some of the worst months of my life' (*A* 355) ; he travelled by rail with Maud Gonne on many occasions and they had stirring conversations about the possibility of uniting the various Irish organisations (*A* 362).

The poem is concerned with how the memory of great beauty lingers on. There may be a hint in line 2 of the Homeric Helen, who lived on through Homer's praise. There is another parallel in the case of Mary Hynes, the peasant girl admired by crowds in much the same way :

. . . I can see at no great distance a green field where stood once the thatched cottage of a famous country beauty, the mistress of a small local landed proprietor. I have spoken to old men and women who remembered her, though all are dead now, and they spoke of her as the old men upon the wall of Troy spoke of Helen, nor did man and woman differ in their praise.
   . . . And there were men that told of the crowds that gathered to look at her upon a fair day, and of a man 'who

got his death swimming a river', that he might look at her. It was a song written by the Gaelic poet Raftery that brought her such great fame, and the cottagers still sing it, though there are not so many to sing it as when I was young. (*A* 561)

The comparisons are clear. Mary, Helen, and Maud moved crowds by their beauty ; they were admired by older people ; and their beauty lives on — Helen had Homer, Mary Raftery and Maud Yeats, through whose words this came about.

FRIENDS

The MS. date of this poem is January 1911 ; it first appeared in *The Green Helmet and Other Poems* (1912)

4   *One* : Mrs Olivia Shakespear (a cousin of Lionel Johnson) whom Yeats first met in London in 1894. They corresponded until her death in 1938 when he wrote 'For more than forty years she has been the centre of my life in London, and during all that time we have never had a quarrel, sadness sometimes, but never a difference.' In 1895 Yeats and she exchanged many letters when he was in Sligo and she sent him the manuscript of her work *Beauty's Hour* while he wrote to her on his ideas of the coincidence of opposites. See note (p. 63) on 'The Lover mourns for the Loss of Love' (*CP* 68).

10   *And one* : Lady Gregory, whom Yeats first met in 1896 and whose house Coole Park he visited during succeeding summers. She got him to help her in collecting folklore and became his ally in the movement to create an Irish theatre. She also helped him to put his 'house in order' and created conditions in which he could work regularly :

> She asked me to return there the next year, and for years to come I was to spend my summers at her house. When I was in good health again, I found myself indolent, partly perhaps because I was affrighted by that impossible novel, and asked her to send me to my work every day at eleven, and at some other hour to my letters, rating me with idleness if need be, and I doubt if I should have done much with my life but for her firmness and her care. (*A* 377)

See also 'Coole Park, 1929' (*CP* 273) and 'Coole Park and Ballylee, 1931' (*CP* 275).

16   *labouring in ecstasy* : Maud Gonne thought that this line referred to the Italian tour which Yeats made in 1907 with Lady Gregory and her son Robert.   The summer gatherings at Coole Park afforded an Irish parallel to Urbino's court.

17   *her that took* : Maud Gonne, whom Yeats first met in 1889 when he was twenty-three.   She married in 1903.

25   *eagle look* : the detachment and objectivity Yeats associated with active rather than contemplative persons.   Yeats was always struck by Maud Gonne's refusal to discuss herself : 'You know I hate talking of myself ; I am not going to let you make me' (*SQ* 330).

140   THE COLD HEAVEN

This poem first appeared in *The Green Helmet and Other Poems* (1912). Maud Gonne asked Yeats its meaning and was told that it was an attempt to describe the feelings aroused in him by the cold detached sky in winter.   He felt he was alone, responsible in his loneliness for all the past mistakes that were torturing his peace of mind. This was a momentary intensity of perception, made more poignant for him by the memory of his lost love.   It has the air of a dream clinging to it and Yeats wrote in 'The Trembling of the Veil' of his belief that after death men live their lives backwards (*A* 378). Henn (*LT* 93) sees in this poem the effect of Yeats's reading of Grierson's edition of Donne.

6   *love crossed long ago* : his love for Maud Gonne

7   *out of all sense and reason* : Henn (*LT* 94) comments that 'out of all sense' is an Irish (and ambiguous) expression meaning both 'to an extent far beyond what common-sense could justify' and 'beyond the reach of sensation'.

10–12   *Confusion of the death-bed over* : it has been suggested by Henn that these ideas are derived from Berkeley, but it is likely Yeats had not read him at this period.

THAT THE NIGHT COME   140

This poem first appeared in *The Green Helmet and Other Poems* (1912).

1   *She* : this poem is written about Maud Gonne.

AN APPOINTMENT   141

This poem was written at Coole Park in 1907 or 1908 : it first appeared in ER (Feb. 1909) entitled 'On a Recent Government Appointment in Ireland'.

1   *government* : Yeats was enraged with Lord Aberdeen and Mr Birrell because they had not given Sir Hugh Lane the position of Curator of the National Museum in Dublin, but had appointed Count Plunkett.

3   *the proud, wayward squirrel* : a squirrel was described more conventionally in *The Island of Statues*, I, iii.

8   *the tame will . . . timid brain* : Lady Gregory described the way Yeats received the news of the appointment :

> It was, in his mind, one of the worst of crimes, that neglect to use the best man, the man of genius, in place of the timid obedient official.   That use of the best had been practised in the great days of the Renaissance.   He had grown calmer before my arrival, [she had telegraphed the news] because when walking in the woods, the sight of a squirrel had given him a thought for some verses, the first he had ever written on any public event : [Lady Gregory had probably not read 'Mourn – and then Onward' which had appeared in the *United Irishman* in 1891, but not been reprinted]. . . . Hugh, having a certain reverence for writers, was pleased, though a little puzzled, by the lines, which do but put in form of fantasy what another poet has called 'the difference between men of office and men of genius, between computed and uncomputed rank.' (*Hugh Lane* 85)

She goes on to describe how Yeats wrote out the poem on a blank leaf of one of his books and wrote above it, 'On the Appointment of Count Plunkett to the Curatorship of the Dublin Museum, by

Mr T. W. Russell and Mr Birrell, Hugh Lane being a candidate'. Yeats wrote a poem on Birrell in his Diary for 16 September 1909 calling it an attempt to put in rhyme a joke Robert Gregory had made at dinner — 'it is too savage to be much good — I had described my old conversation with Birrell.' The title originally read 'On a certain middle-aged office holder' which became 'On a prosperous mimic of others' thought' and the poem ran

> He thinks to set his world aright
> As his [he's ?] no longer parasite
> Now that he's master of the trick
> That turns a flea into a tick.

Yeats decided it was 'not worth giving by itself, would seem mere party politics, but might come in part of old note of conversation at Baily — names left out.' . . . 'Cabinet Minister who had been a lively chatterbox in his youth' would, he thought, be enough of a description.

141   THE MAGI

This poem was written on 20 September 1913 and first appeared in *P* (Ch), (May 1914). The poem is complementary to 'The Dolls' (*CP* 141). After he had made the latter Yeats

> looked up one day into the blue of the sky, and suddenly imagined, as if lost in the blue of the sky, stiff figures in procession. I remembered that they were the habitual image suggested by blue sky, and looking for a second fable called them 'The Magi', complementary forms of those enraged dolls. (*RPP*)

2   *unsatisfied*: the Magi are unsatisfied by the birth of Christ because they represent Yeats's belief that the Christian revelation was not final, that history occurs in alternate movements, or gyres (cf. 'The Gyres' (*CP* 337)). Christ is uncontrollable because he is not final, he has ushered another cycle which will be succeeded by another. Cf. 'Two Songs from a Play' (*CP* 239) and this is probably one of the first poems to be linked with the ideas later expressed in *AV* (A) and *AV* (B), in which Christ is a being of Phase one :

> When the old *primary* becomes the new *antithetical*, the old realisation of an objective moral law is changed into a sub-

conscious turbulent instinct. The world of rigid custom and law is broken up by 'the uncontrollable mystery upon the bestial floor'. (*AV* (B) 105)

Cf. line 8 of 'The Magi', and 'The Second Coming' (*CP* 210), which used the symbol of the rough beast, the antithesis of Christ, bringing in a new era.

7 *Calvary's turbulence* : Yeats wrote that at or near the central point of a lunar month of classical civilisation — the first degree of Aries in the Great Wheel — comes the Christian *primary* dispensation, the child born in the Cavern. 'At or near the central point of our civilisation must come *antithetical* revelation, the turbulent child of the Altar' (*AV* (B) 204). Here Yeats was thinking of symbols discovered by Frobenius in Africa, the cavern being a symbol of nations moving westwards, the Altar (at the centre of radiating roads) being a symbol of nations moving eastwards. For Yeats's use of Christianity see his play *Calvary* (*Four Plays for Dancers* (1921)) and the 'Galilean turbulence' of 'Two Songs from a Play' (*CP* 239).

THE DOLLS   141

This poem was written on 20 September 1913, and first appeared in *RPP*. It is related to 'Beggar to Beggar Cried' (*CP* 128) and 'Presences' (*CP* 174). See pp. 138 and 188.

3 *That* : the baby the woman has brought into the house. There   142
is a parallel passage in Synge, where a woman is blamed for bringing a doll into the house :

> Today a grotesque twopenny doll was lying on the floor near the old woman. He picked it up and examined it as if comparing it with her. Then he held it up : 'Is it you is after bringing that thing into the world,' he said, 'woman of the house ?' (J. M. Synge, *The Aran Islands*, 37)

A COAT   142

This poem was written in 1912 and first appeared in *P* (Ch), (May 1914). It marks Yeats's renunciation of his earlier style.

1 *my song a coat* : two extra lines in a MS. revision of the poem—

> And gave it to my song
> And my song wore it—

make clearer the ambiguity of the first line, which means 'I made a coat for my song'.

3   *old mythologies* : the Gaelic legends Yeats had read in O'Grady's translations, and those of O'Donovan, O'Currie, O'Looney, Mangan, etc. The MS. version of the poem had for this line 'Dragons and Gods and moons'.

5   *the fools* : probably a reference to some of A E's protégés, among them 'Seumas O'Sullivan'. Cf. 'To a poet who would have me Praise certain Bad Poets, Imitators of His and Mine' (*CP* 105).

143   CLOSING RHYME [WHILE I, FROM THAT REED-THROATED WHISPER] or [EPILOGUE]

This poem was written in 1914 and was entitled 'Notoriety (suggested by a recent magazine article)' when it first appeared in The *New Statesman* (7 Feb. 1914).

Title   magazine article : the poem was provoked by an article by George Moore in *ER*. Yeats told Lady Gregory in a letter of 1 February 1914, written on board a Cunard liner (probably the *Lusitania*, though he refers to the *Mauretania* in *L* 586) that he had sent

> that second Moore poem to *The New Statesman* because they happened to ask for something, and asked Ezra [Pound] to see to the proofs. Sturge Moore wanted me to send it to *The English Review* itself but that would have been to condone Harrison's share in the thing. People have constantly spoken to me of the article with indignation.

5–6   *the dull ass's hoof . . . Jonson's phrase* : the phrase is used in 'An Ode to Himself' and in the Epilogue to *The Poetaster* :

> Leave me. There's something come into my thought,
> That must and shall be sung high and aloof,
> Safe from the wolf's black jaw, and the dull ass's hoof.

7   *Kyle-na-no* : one of the seven woods at Coole

8   *that ancient roof* : Coole Park

14   *a post* : in his 1930 Diary Yeats wrote, 'I shall publish when ready — to adapt a metaphor from Erasmus — to make myself a post for dogs and journalists to defile.'

The Wild Swans at Coole

Most of the poems in this volume were written between 1915 and 1918. During this period Yeats emerged from the slough of *Responsibilities*, yet was unhappy — until, after his marriage in 1917, he became preoccupied with writing *AV*. The poems in this volume reflect Yeats's development when placed in chronological order, but he deliberately arranged them differently (seven of the poems written to Maud Gonne, for instance, were written in 1915, but are placed at *CP* 168–174), not wanting people, as he told his wife, to know too much about his personal concerns. The main intellectual interest of the volume lies in the poetry it contains, which deals tentatively with the system of *AV*. In part, Yeats regained his poetic energy (whose loss he had lamented in *The Green Helmet*) by using poetry as a vehicle for his strange thoughts and for his own personal life. After the 1916 Rising he proposed to Maud Gonne (her husband having been shot as one of the leaders), then to her daughter Iseult. He married Georgie Hyde-Lees, whom he had known for some years, in October 1917. He was deeply disturbed after his marriage through a feeling of responsibility for Iseult (the hidden meaning of 'Two Songs of a Fool' (*CP* 190), though some of these turbulent moods were not disclosed until later ; 'Owen Aherne and his Dancers' (*CP* 247) was not published until 1928.) The automatic writing of Mrs Yeats and the creation of *AV* banished his emotional disturbance. There was also the excitement of making Thoor Ballylee habitable. Yeats had been impressed by this tower earlier ; it became increasingly important in his poetry after he bought it in 1917 and began to live in it. The difference is shown in 'Ego Dominus Tuus' (*CP* 180), written in 1915, and 'In Memory of Major Robert Gregory' (*CP* 148) written in 1918.

'Ego Dominus Tuus' is an important poem because it deals with the material of *AV*. Into his poetry came a new kind of strength based upon 'getting it all in order'. The system of *AV* lurks behind many of the later poems even when these are not acting as direct mouthpieces for his thought. The results of his early reading of Theosophy, magic, occultism, Kabbalism, astrology, Blake, Swedenborg, and Boehme all combined steadily with his increasing knowledge of history and philosophy. 'The Double Vision of Michael Robartes' (*CP* 192), for instance, can be clarified by reference to *AV*: it foreshadows the poems to follow such as 'The Second Coming' (*CP* 210) or 'Sailing to Byzantium' (*CP* 217) and 'Byzantium' (*CP* 280), which through their cryptic yet concise confidence convey the excitement of, and impart authority to, Yeats's views.

Besides the innovations in subject matter, the poems in *WSC* reveal Yeats developing his use of ancestors and friends as subjects for poetry: he is now more prepared to delineate details of personality just as he is to use personal names. His regret that his own youth, even if it has been replaced by wisdom, is vanishing is the substance of his personal cry — 'O Heart we are old'. This awareness of approaching age, sharpened by contemplation of Iseult's beauty, echoes through the poems even if momentarily lulled by the symbolism of the Solomon and Sheba poems recording the early years of his marriage. These seemed to combine age and wisdom for a time until, indeed, the old complaint broke out once more in *The Tower* about

> Decrepit age that has been tied to me
> As to a dog's tail.

THE WILD SWANS AT COOLE   **147**

This poem was written in 1916 and first appeared in the *Little Review* (June 1917) where it is dated October 1916. In the first printed version lines 25–30 were placed between lines 12 and 13. Yeats was fifty-one when he wrote the poem, and realised how he had changed since he first visited Coole Park at the age of thirty-two. When he first stayed at Coole he was grieving over Maud Gonne's refusal to return his love: as he recorded in *DP*:

I must have spent the summer of 1897 at Coole. I was involved in a miserable love affair, that had but for one brief interruption absorbed my thoughts for years past, and would for some years yet. My devotion might as well have been offered to an image in a milliner's window, or to a statue in a museum, but romantic doctrine had reached its extreme development. Dowson was in love with a girl in an Italian restaurant, courted her for two years; at first she was too young, then he too disreputable; she married the waiter and Dowson's life went to wreck. . . . My health was giving way, my nerves had been wrecked. Finding that I could not work, and thinking the open air salutary, Lady Gregory brought me from cottage to cottage collecting folk-lore. Every night she wrote out what we had heard in the dialect of the cottages. (*A* 399 ff.)

In 1916 he was still grieving, but a new element had entered into his grief. Now he was troubled by his own lack of concern that Maud, after her husband John MacBride had been shot for his part in the 1916 Rebellion, had refused once more to marry him. Madame MacBride told the present editor in 1944 that she thought Yeats was relieved by this refusal, which was accompanied by her old comment of the 'nineties that neither she nor Yeats was the marrying kind. Romantic love could not be rekindled. Lady Gregory and Mrs Shakespear had each been urging him to marry, to have descendants, to be comfortable. Marriage with Maud, he now realised, could never have been comfortable.

1-4 *trees . . . paths . . . the water*: descriptions of the lake at Coole Park. Cf. Lady Gregory's description:

Our own river that we catch a glimpse of now and again through hazel and ash, or outshining the silver beech stems of Kyle Dortha, has ever been an idler. Its transit is as has been said of human life 'from a mystery through a mystery to a mystery'; suddenly appearing, as a French writer has put down in his book 'dans le beau parc privé de Coole, derrière le village de Kiltartan.' And dipping presently under great limestone flags that form a natural bridge 'la dernière réapparition se fait voir a 350 mètres de là toujours dans le parc de Coole.' Then, flowing free, it helps to form a lake, whose fulness, finding no channel above ground, is forced 'de chercher sa route par les passages souterains de lac vers la mer'; into which it flows under the very shadow of the Dun of the ancient legendary King of Guaire [or Gort]. (*Coole* 27–8)

Cf. 'Coole and Ballylee, 1931' (*CP* 139).

6 *nine-and-fifty swans* : they were there, as Yeats told the late Professor H. O. White (describing the poem as written in a mood of intense depression). Lady Gregory quotes George Moore's description of them :

It was then I forgot Yeats and Edward [Martyn] and everything else in the delight caused by a great clamour of wings, and the snowy plumage of thirty-six great birds rushing down the lake, striving to rise from its surface. At last their wings caught the air, and after floating about the lake they settled in a distant corner where they thought they could rest undisturbed. Thirty-six swans rising out of a lake and floating round it, and settling down in it, is an unusual sight ; it conveys a suggestion of fairyland, perhaps because thirty-six wild swans are so different from the silly China swan which sometimes floats and hisses in melancholy whiteness up and down a stone basin. That is all we know of swans — all I knew until the thirty-six rose out of the hushed lake at our feet, and prompted me to turn to Yeats, saying, You're writing your poem in its natural atmosphere. (*Ave* (1947 ed), 190.)

Lady Gregory adds the following sentence in her quotation from Moore in *Coole* 35 : And Yeats himself in the volume to which he has given their name tells of an October evening when he made the count of a yet greater number. . . .

7, 16 *nineteenth autumn . . . first time* : Yeats's first brief visit to Coole took place in 1896 (he subsequently spent that summer in Paris in a very unhappy state, cf. *A* 343) but these lines refer to 1897, the year he regarded, in *DP*, as altering his life.

19 *lover by lover* : there may be a link between this poem and Shelley's *Alastor* (lines 277 ff.), where in each case the unhappiness of the *persona* is accentuated by the thought of mated swans :

A swan was there,
Beside a sluggish stream among the reeds,
It rose as he approached, and with strong wings
Scaling the upward sky, bent its bright course
High over the immeasurable main.
His eyes pursued its flight :—'Thou hast a home,
Beautiful bird ! thou voyagest to thine home,
Where thy sweet mate will twine her downy neck
With thine, and welcome thy return with eyes
Bright in the lustre of their own fond joy.

And what am I that I should linger here,
With voice far sweeter than thy dying notes,
Spirit more vast than thine, frame more attuned
To beauty, wasting these surpassing powers
In the deaf air, to the blind earth, and heaven
That echoes not my thoughts ?'   A gloomy smile
Of desperate hope wrinkled his quivering lips.
For Sleep, he knew, kept most relentlessly
Its precious charge ; and silent Death exposed,
Faithless perhaps as Sleep, a shadowy lure,
With doubtful smile mocking its own strange charms.

Cf. also Shelley's preface to *Alastor*, describing the poet imagining the Being whom he loves, attaching all of the wonderful, wise or beautiful which could be envisaged by poet, philosopher or lover, to a single image, and then searching in vain for a prototype of his conception.

22   *Their hearts . . . old* : the other love poems in *WSC* written to Maud Gonne ('His Phoenix', 'Broken Dreams', 'A Deep-Sworn Vow', 'Presences', etc.) were composed *before* 1916. But Yeats may have been troubled both by the death of his love for Maud Gonne and by the realisation that Iseult Gonne, to whom he proposed marriage in 1916 and 1917, would think of him as an old man. Cf. 'The Living Beauty', (*CP* 156) and 'A Song' (*CP* 156) or 'Men improve with the Years' (*CP* 152). Throughout the poems of *WSC* runs this grief over the age of the heart. Cf. 'A Song' (*CP* 156), '*O who could have foretold | That the heart grows old?*'

148   28   *By what lake's edge* : Lady Gregory (*Coole* 38) throws light on this query. In August 1928 Yeats saw two swans and three cygnets with them and said, 'I have known your lake for thirty years, and that is the first time a swan has built here. That is a good omen.'

148   IN MEMORY OF MAJOR ROBERT GREGORY

This poem was written by 14 June 1918, and first appeared in *ER* (Aug. 1918). The word 'Major' was not included in the title then, but Yeats's note after the title read : 'Major Robert Gregory, R.F.C., M.C., Legion of Honour, was killed in action on the Italian Front, January 23, 1918'. Yeats wrote four poems in memory of

Robert Gregory; this one, 'Shepherd and Goatherd' (*CP* 159), 'An Irish Airman foresees his Death' (*CP* 152) and 'Reprisals' (unpublished during Yeats's lifetime, see *VE* 791).

1 *our house* : Thoor Ballylee, the Norman tower and cottages Yeats had purchased in 1917, in which he and his family were to spend their summers until 1929. For a detailed description see Mary Hanley, *Thoor Ballylee — Home of William Butler Yeats* (1965). The 'almost settled' describes the period when Yeats and his wife were supervising alterations to the tower to make it habitable and were living in Ballinamantane House which Lady Gregory had lent them.

3 *turf* : peat

3 *tower* : for subsequent treatment of the Tower see *CP* 150, 180, 183, 184, 188, 212, 214, 226, 229, 231, 267, 268, and 269. For other descriptions in which the Tower is not specifically mentioned, see *CP* 221, 227, 229, 232, 265, 268, and 269.

5 *the narrow winding stair* : it gave a name to a subsequent volume of poems, and was associated in Yeats's mind with the spiral movement of the gyres. (For subsequent treatment of the stair see *CP* 221, 227, 229, 232, 265, 268, and 269.)

6 *Discoverers of forgotten truth* : those interested in the occult tradition

8 *All, all* : cf. note on line 21 'Broken Dreams' (*CP* 172)

17–24 *Lionel Johnson* : see note on 'The Grey Rock' (*CP* 115). Yeats met him in 1888 or 1889 and described him in various prose passages. He was a member of the Rhymers' Club (according to Yeats (*E & I* 491) his thought dominated the scene and gave the club its character) and shared a house with Herbert Horne (1864–1916) an architect and writer on art, Selwyn Image (1849–1930) the artist, and others in Charlotte Street, Fitzroy Square, and impressed Yeats with his poise and learning (*A* 168); he had a considerable library, a knowledge of tongues and books which was very great (*A* 306).

157

149 19 *courteous to the worst* : Johnson's courtesy chiefly impressed Yeats, who was conscious of his own provincial clumsiness and lack of self-possession, and envied Johnson his acquaintance with 'everybody of importance'. It was only later he discovered many of Johnson's reported conversations with famous men were imaginary. The worst may refer to Ernest Dowson, Johnson's friend whose life was 'a sordid round of drink and cheap harlots' (*E & I* 492).

19-20 *much falling . . . sanctity* : Yeats described him in 'Ireland after Parnell' :

> He drank a great deal too much, and, though nothing could, it seemed, disturb his calm or unsteady his hand or foot, his doctrine, after a certain number of glasses, would become more ascetic, more contemptuous of all that we call human life. . . . Even without stimulant his theology conceded nothing to human weakness, and I can remember his saying with energy, 'I wish those people who deny the eternity of punishment could realise their unspeakable vulgarity. . . .' He sometimes spoke of drink as something which he could put aside at any moment. . . . (*A* 222)

The 'much falling' may come from his poem 'Mystic and Cavalier' which Yeats quoted in *A* 224. The poem opens :

> Go from me : I am one of those who fall.
> What ! hath no cold wind swept your heart at all,
> In my sad company ? Before the end
> Go from me, dear my friend !

The historical setting of the poem, Yeats thought, was but masquerade, and Johnson rested 'in clouds of doom'. But 'much falling' may also refer to Johnson falling down in a drunken stupor. (See *A* 309.)

22-4 *A long blast . . . consummation* : cf. the last stanza of 'Mystic and Cavalier' :

> O rich and sounding voices of the air !
> Interpreters and prophets of despair :
> Priests of a fearful sacrament ! I come
>   To make with you my home.

25 *John Synge* : Yeats's respect and admiration for John Millington Synge (1871-1909) are well known. He wrote Prefaces to *The*

Well of the Saints (1905) and *Poems and Translations* (1909) and an essay 'J. M. Synge and the Ireland of his Time'. Yeats first met Synge in Paris in 1896 and persuaded him to go to the Aran Islands (see line 30) and find there a life that had never been expressed in literature.

26   *dying*: Yeats's comment upon Synge's poems explains the line:

. . . the greater number were written very recently, and many during his last illness. *An Epitaph* and *On an Anniversary* show how early the expectation of death came to him, for they were made long ago. But the book as a whole is a farewell, written when life began to slip from him. He was a reserved man, and wished no doubt by a vague date to hide, while still living, what he felt and thought, from those about him. I asked one of the nurses in the hospital where he died if he knew he was dying, and she said 'He may have known it for months, but he would not have spoken of it to anyone.' Even the translations of poems that he has made his own by putting them into that melancholy dialect of his, seem to express his emotion at the memory of poverty and the approach of death. . . . (*E & I* 307)

27   *long travelling*: in 'The Tragic Generation' Yeats described Synge in terms of *AV*:

According to my Lunar parable, he was a man of the twenty-third Phase; a man whose subjective lives — for a constant return to our life is a part of my dream — were over; who must not pursue an image, but fly from it, all that subjective dreaming, that had once been power and joy, now corrupting within him. He had to take the first plunge into the world beyond himself, the first plunge away from himself that is always pure technique, the delight in doing, not because one would or should, but merely because one can do. (*A* 344)

30   *a most desolate stony place*: the Aran Islands. Yeats's memories in *BS* illustrate his understanding of what Synge found there:

I had met John Synge in Paris in 1896. Somebody had said, 'There is an Irishman living on the top floor of your hotel; I will introduce you.' I was very poor, but he was much poorer. He belonged to a very old Irish family and, though a simple courteous man, remembered it and was haughty and lonely. With just enough to keep him from starvation and

not always from half-starvation, he had wandered about
Europe, travelling third-class or upon foot, playing his fiddle
to poor men on the road or in their cottages. He was the man
that we needed, because he was the only man I have ever
known incapable of a political thought or of a humanitarian
purpose. He could walk the roadside all day with some poor
man without any desire to do him good or for any reason
except that he liked him. He was to do for Ireland, though
more by his influence on other dramatists than by his direct
influence, what Robert Burns did for Scotland. When Scotland thought herself gloomy and religious, Providence restored
her imaginative spontaneity by raising up Robert Burns to
commend drink and the Devil. I did not, however, see what
was to come when I advised John Synge to go to a wild island
off the Galway coast and study its life because that life 'had
never been expressed in literature'. He had learned Gaelic at
College and I told him that, as I would have told it to any
young man who had learned Gaelic and wanted to write.
When he found that wild island he became happy for the first
time, escaping, as he said, 'from the nullity of the rich and the
squalor of the poor'. He had bad health, he could not stand
the island hardship long, but he would go to and fro between
there and Dublin. (*A* 567–8)

32 *passionate and simple* : Yeats had visited Inishmaan and Inish-
more in 1896, and when he met the oldest man on Inishmaan he
was told by him that 'If any gentleman has done a crime, we'll
hide him. There was a gentleman that killed his father, and I had
him in my own house six months till he got away to America'
(*A* 344). Synge himself was quiet—

timid, too shy for general conversation, an invalid and full of
moral scruple, and he was to create now some ranting bragga-
docio, now some tipsy hag full of poetical speech, and now
some young man or girl full of the most abounding health.
He never spoke an unkind word, had admirable manners, and
yet his art was to fill the streets with rioters, and to bring
upon his dearest friends enemies that may last their lifetime.
(*A* 345)

33 *George Pollexfen* : Yeats's maternal uncle, with whom he spent
holidays as a young man. They experimented with cabbalistic
symbols and studied the visions and thoughts of the Sligo country-

people. See *A* 255–70. George Pollexfen is fully described in *A* 69 as a pessimistic hypochrondiac :

A hypochondriac, he passed from winter to summer through a series of woollens that had always to be weighed ; for in April or May, or whatever the date was, he had to be sure he carried the exact number of ounces he had carried upon that date since boyhood. He lived in despondency, finding in the most cheerful news reasons of discouragement, and sighing every twenty-second of June over the shortening of the days. Once in later years, when I met him in Dublin sweating in a midsummer noon, I brought him into the hall of the Kildare Street Library, a cool and shady place, without lightening his spirits ; for he but said in a melancholy voice, 'How very cold this place must be in winter-time'. Sometimes when I had pitted my cheerfulness against his gloom over the break-fast-table, maintaining that neither his talent nor his memory nor his health were running to the dregs, he would rout me with the sentence, 'How very old I shall be in twenty years'. See also *A* 70–1.

34   *muscular youth* : 'He had once ridden steeple-chases and had been, his horse-trainer said, the best rider in Connacht' (*A* 70).

37   *solid men* : 'He would take to club and dumb-bell if his waist thickened by a hair's breadth, and twenty years after, when a very old man, he had the erect shapely figure of his youth' (*A* 257).

39   *square and trine* : George Pollexfen became interested in astrology and symbolism. He and Yeats used MacGregor Mathers's symbols to induce reveries. At Rosses Point, where George Pollexfen had a small house as a summer residence, Yeats walked by the seashore, his uncle on cliff or sandhill, and Yeats would imagine a symbol and George Pollexfen would notice what passed before his mind's eye, 'and in a short time he would practically never fail of the appropriate vision' (*A* 258 ff.). Yeats thought his uncle's long association with Mary Battle, a second-sighted servant, had led him to believe much in the supernatural world. Cf. 'In Memory of Alfred Pollexfen' (*CP* 175).

46   *dear friend's dear son* : the repetition is reminiscent of line 57   **150** in John of Gaunt's dying speech in *Richard the Second*, II, i, 'This land of such dear souls, this dear dear land.'

47 *Our Sidney*: because Robert Gregory (1881–1918) possessed an Elizabethan versatility of talent, and like Sidney his love of action led him to an untimely death abroad. Gregory was educated at Harrow, New College, and the Slade. He also worked at Jacques Blanche's atelier in Paris; he had an exhibition of paintings in Chelsea in 1914. He was a good shot, a good bowler, a boxer, and a fearless horseman. He joined the 4th Connaught Rangers in 1915, then transferred to the Royal Flying Corps in 1916. He became Chevalier of the Légion d'Honneur in 1917, and was awarded a Military Cross that year also 'for conspicuous gallantry and devotion to duty'. He showed 'the highest courage and skill' as a pilot. He was killed on 23 January 1918 on the north Italian front. Neither Yeats nor his family knew that he had been shot down in error by an Italian pilot.

50 *Were loved by him*: Robert Gregory had encouraged Yeats to buy the tower. He made several drawings of it.

storm-broken trees: the trees are described elsewhere in *CP* 183, 211, 212, 219, 226, and 231.

51–2 *road . . . bridge . . . stream*: are referred to in *CP* 180, 182, 184, 221, 226, 231, and 275.

55 *water-hen*: the water-hens are referred to in *CP* 150, 184, 226, 230, and 275.

57–64 *he would ride*: these lines were added to the poem at the request of Gregory's widow.

65 *a great painter*: Yeats had a painting by Gregory in Riversdale, Rathfarnham, and he recorded his opinion of Gregory's talent elsewhere:

> Robert Gregory painted the Burren Hills and thereby found what promised to grow into a great style, but he had hardly found it before he was killed. His two finished pictures, so full of austerity and sweetness, should find their way into Irish public galleries. (*E & I* 209)

For a discussion of Gregory's work as a painter, see D. J. Gordon and Ian Fletcher, 'Persons and Places' (*IP* 30–4). Three of his paintings are reproduced in that volume on pp. 116, 117, and 118.

83   *dried straw* : Yeats wrote on John Davidson in 'The Tragic   **151**
Generation' in a way which explains something of his attitude to
Gregory's life and work — the image of the 'fire of straw' being
significantly common to the poem and this prose comment on
Davidson :

> I think he might have grown to be a successful man . . .
> violent energy, which is like a fire of straw, consumes in a few
> minutes the nervous vitality, and is useless in the arts.   Our
> fire must burn slowly, and we must constantly turn away to
> think, constantly analyse what we have done, be content even
> to have little life outside our work. . . . A few months after
> our meeting in the Museum, Davidson had spent his inspira-
> tion. 'The fires are out', he said, 'and I must hammer the cold
> iron.' When I heard a few years ago that he had drowned him-
> self, I knew that I had always expected some such end.   With
> enough passion to make a great poet, through meeting no man
> of culture in early life, he lacked intellectual receptivity, and,
> anarchic and indefinite, lacked pose and gesture, and now *no*
> verse of his clings to my memory.   (*A* 318)

There are several passages in Yeats's 1910 Diary which show that
he envied Robert Gregory his lack of introspection.   Gregory
would not 'turn away to think' nor 'constantly analyse' what he
had done nor 'have little life' outside his work.   The stanza emerges
from the thought of stanza VI which showed Yeats could not
become accustomed to the idea of Gregory's death, a thought
which closes the poem in stanza XII.

AN IRISH AIRMAN FORESEES HIS DEATH   **152**

This poem was written in 1918 and first appeared in *WSC*.

1   *I know* : Robert Gregory

3   *Those that I fight* : the Germans

4   *Those that I guard* : the English

5   *Kiltartan Cross* : near Coole.   Lady Gregory's style in her translations is sometimes known as Kiltartan.

152 MEN IMPROVE WITH THE YEARS

This poem was written in 19 July 1916 and first appeared in the *Little Review* (June 1917).

1 *worn out with dreams* : the poem is written about the effect of Iseult Gonne's youth and beauty on Yeats. He endeavours to persuade himself that the wisdom he has won out of the disappointments of life compensates him for the age that prevents him from loving Iseult passionately, 'Delighted to be but wise'. But this theory may be specious. Is it a dream or the truth ? Love crowds in upon his wisdom. The conclusion is very like that of a later poem, 'Politics' (*CP* 392) :

> But O that I were young again
> And held her in my arms !

Cf. also 'The Living Beauty' (*CP* 156) and 'A Song' (*CP* 156) which each record the depressing realisation of age : 'The living beauty is for younger men' and '. . . *who could have foretold | That the heart grows old ?*'

153 THE COLLAR-BONE OF A HARE

This poem was written on 5 July 1916 and first appeared in the *Little Review* (June 1917).

5 . . . *and the dancing* : Cf. a passage in *Visions and Beliefs*, II, 310 : 'always in his [Blake's] boys and girls walking or dancing on smooth grass and in golden light, as on pastoral scenes cut upon wood or copper by his disciples Palmer and Calvert, one notices the peaceful Swedenborgian heaven' (*E* 44). Yeats valued the artists who could delineate a blissful state akin to that of Eden. Cf. lines 64–5 'Under Ben Bulben' (*CP* 397). Cf. also the last stanza of 'John Kinsella's Lament for Mrs Mary Moore' (*CP* 383) for a parallel picture of 'Eden's garden'.

10 *The collar-bone of a hare* : the image probably comes from a peasant story. In 'The Three O'Byrnes and the Evil Faeries'

> a peasant of the neighbourhood once saw the treasure [of the O'Byrnes]. He found the shin-bone of a hare lying on the

grass. He took it up; there was a hole in it; he looked through the hole, and saw the gold heaped up under the ground. He hurried home to bring a spade, but when he got to the path again he could not find the spot where he had seen it. (*M* 87)

13 *where they marry in churches*: the poem expresses a contrast between the ideal world and the real, perhaps sharpened by a situation where Lady Gregory was advising the poet to marry and Mrs Shakespear approved of the idea also. Marriage can seem a very enfettering prospect to a bachelor of fifty-one.

UNDER THE ROUND TOWER   **154**

This poem was written in March 1918 and first appeared in the *Little Review* (Oct. 1918).

4 *Billy Byrne*: there was a Wicklow hero in the 1798 Rebellion who came from Ballymanus and was still a legendary figure in Glendalough legend at the time Yeats stayed there in the Royal Hotel in March 1918.

7–9 *tombstone*: the lines are a description of the Glendalough graveyard, in which the round tower is situated. These slender pencil-shaped stone round towers were built as a defence against the Scandinavian invaders. There are a remarkable number of O'Byrnes and Byrnes buried in the graveyard at Glendalough, Co. Wicklow.

11–13 *sun and moon . . . golden king and silver lady*: cf. 'The Man who dreamed of Faeryland' (*CP* 49). The golden king and silver lady (the sun and moon) symbolise the continual oscillation which is representative of the horizontal movement of the historical cones described in Book V, 'Dove or Swan', cf. *AV* (B).

19 *wild lady*: the moon is 'wild' in 'Solomon and the Witch' (*CP* 199). It becomes 'wilder'. There are sometimes sexual implications in the word in Irish usage.

In Yeats's *Stories of Red Hanrahan* the sun and the moon
are the man and the girl, they are my life and your life, they are travelling and ever travelling through the skies as if under

the one hood. It was God made them for one another. He made your life and my life before the beginning of the world, He made them that they might go through the world, up and down, like the two best dancers that go on with the dance up and down the long floor of the barn, fresh and laughing, when all the rest are tired out and leaning against the wall. (*M* 227–8)

155 SOLOMON TO SHEBA

This poem was written at Glendalough in [March ?] 1918 and first appeared in the *Little Review* (Oct. 1918).

1 *Solomon to Sheba* : Solomon symbolises Yeats, Sheba Mrs Yeats. Cf. 'Solomon and the Witch' (*CP* 199).

7 *theme of love* : in his 1910 Diary Yeats wrote :

It seems to me that true love is a discipline, and it needs so much wisdom that the love of Solomon and Sheba must have lasted, for all the silence of the Scriptures. Each divines the secret self of the other, and refusing to believe in the mere daily self, creates a mirror where the lover or the beloved sees an image to copy in daily life ; for love also creates the Mask. (*A* 464)

156 THE LIVING BEAUTY

The MS. of this poem is dated 1917 and it first appeared in the *Little Review* (Oct. 1918).

Title The Living Beauty : Iseult Gonne (who could not recall when the poem was written). Yeats spent the summer of 1917 at Maud Gonne's house in Colville, Calvados, and renewed his offer of marriage to Iseult, which she finally refused when Maud Gonne and her family arrived in London in September. Yeats had accompanied them ; they were not allowed to proceed to Ireland and Yeats then arranged that Iseult should be given the post of assistant librarian in the School of Oriental Languages. She cried 'because she was so ashamed "at being so selfish" in not wanting me to marry and so break her friendship with me'. See *WBY* 304–6.

1 *the wick and oil are spent* : cf. 'Men improve with the Years' (*CP* 152), 'The Collar-bone of a Hare' (*CP* 153), 'A Song' (*CP* 156) and 'To a Young Beauty' (*CP* 157)

A SONG   **156**

This poem was probably written in 1915 and first appeared in the *Little Review* (Oct. 1918).

3 *dumb-bell and foil* : Yeats did Sandow exercises and Ezra Pound taught him fencing in the winter of 1912–13. Yeats used the image in the essay 'Anima Hominis' :

> I sometimes fence for half an hour at the day's end, and when I close my eyes upon the pillow I see a foil playing before me, the button to my face. We meet always in the deep of the mind, whatever our work, wherever our reverie carries us, that other Will. (*M* 337)

5–6 *the heart grows old* : Saul (*PYP* 104) has compared this refrain with 'Ephemera' (*CP* 16), 'how old my heart' and 'Passion has often worn our wandering hearts'.

TO A YOUNG BEAUTY   **157**

This poem was written in 1918 [probably in the autumn] and first appeared in *Nine Poems* [October] (1918).

1 *Dear fellow-artist* : the poem was written to Iseult Gonne.

3 *every Jack and Jill* : Yeats disapproved of the Bohemian company Iseult Gonne was keeping in Dublin. Maud Gonne had acquired 73 St Stephen's Green, Dublin, which she lent to Yeats and his wife. She had been imprisoned on suspicion in England — having earlier defied the ban on her proceeding to Ireland (imposed in September 1917). Yeats had managed to get her removed to a sanatorium because of her health. By Christmas 1918 Yeats and his wife handed over the house to her

7 *that mirror for a school* : cf lines 14, 15, 50 of 'Michael Robartes and the Dancer' (*CP* 197)

11 *Ezekiel's cherubim* : they are mentioned in Ezekiel ix. 3 ; x. 2, 6, 7, 14, 16, 19 ; xi. 22 ; xxviii. 16 ; xli. 18 ; and are presumably to be taken as more grandiose than the conceptions of Beauvarlet.

12 *Beauvarlet* : Jacques Firmin Beauvarlet (1731–97), a mediocre French painter and engraver. His name appears erroneously as Beaujolet until *Later Poems* (1926).

18 *With Landor and with Donne* : Yeats wrote to Professor Grierson on 14 November 1912 to thank him for his edition of Donne :

> I have been using it constantly and find that at last I can understand Donne. Your notes tell me exactly what I want to know. Poems that I could not understand or could but under- stand are now clear and I notice that the more precise and learned the thought the greater the beauty, the passion ; the intricacy and subtleties of his imagination are the length and depth of the furrow made by his passion. His pedantry and his obscenity — the rock and the loam of his Eden — but make me the more certain that one who is but a man like us all has seen God. (*L* 570)

In a passage in 'The Tragic Generation' Yeats linked capacity for the metaphysical with a vision of evil. Donne could be as physical as he pleased ; because he could say what he pleased : he was not tempted to linger, Yeats thought, between spirit and sense. And Yeats saw in some of his own early work a disagreeable sentimental sensuality. [This might have been in some of the 'nineties poems attacked by Paul Elmer More. Cf. the latter's *Shelburne Essays* (First Series) 181–2.]

> How often had I heard men of my time talk of the meeting of spirit and sense, yet there is no meeting but only change upon the instant, and it is by the perception of a change, like the sudden 'blacking out' of the lights of the stage, that passion creates its most violent sensation. (*A* 326)

It is likely that Yeats read Landor in the winters of 1914, 1915, and 1916. The 'dining' with Landor may be explained by the latter's appearance in *AV* in the same phase, the seventeenth, as Dante and Shelley (and Yeats himself, though this is not explicitly stated). Landor was

> The most violent of men, he uses his intellect to disengage a visionary image of perfect sanity (*Mask* at Phase 3) seen

always in the most serene and classic art imaginable. He had
perhaps as much Unity of Being as his age permitted, and
possessed, though not in any full measure, the Vision of Evil.
(*AV* (B) 144-5)

Cf. the description in 'Anima Hominis' : '. . . Savage Landor
topped us all in calm nobility when the pen was in his hand, as
in the daily violence of his passion when he had laid it down'
(*M* 328)

Landor was also described in 'Anima Hominis' in terms which
gloss Yeats's personal situation — the facing of age — in 1917 :

A poet, when he is growing old, will ask himself if he cannot keep his mask and his vision without new bitterness, new
disappointment. Could he if he would, knowing how frail
his vigour from youth up, copy Landor who lived loving and
hating, ridiculous and unconquered, into extreme old age, all
lost but the favour of his Muses ?

> The Mother of the Muses, we are taught,
> Is Memory ; she has left me ; they remain,
> And shake my shoulder, urging me to sing. (*M* 342)

TO A YOUNG GIRL   **157**

This poem is dated May 1915 in the Maud Gonne Manuscript Book.
Ellmann (*IY* 289) dates it 1913 or 1915. It first appeared in the
Little Review (Oct. 1918).

1 *My dear, my dear* : Iseult Gonne

4 *mother* : Maud Gonne. The 1915 date might suit this poem   **158**
better than the earlier. Yeats did not take seriously the idea that
he had fallen in love with Iseult Gonne until 1916. She proposed
to him in 1915 (but presumably in lighthearted vein) and was
refused because there was too much Mars in her horoscope. Cf.
Y:M & P 190.

THE SCHOLARS   **158**

The manuscript of this poem which I have seen is dated April
1915. Ellmann (*IY* 289) gives 1914 and April 1915. It first
appeared in *Catholic Anthology 1914-1915* (1915).

7 *all cough in ink* : a crossed-out version of this line in the MS. read 'They'll dip in the inkpots to world's end.' The stanza then ran :

> They'd cough in the ink till the world's end
> Wear out the carpet with their shoes
> Earn respect, have no strange friend ;
> If they have sinned nobody knows ;
> Lord what would they say
> Should their Catullus walk that way.

Yeats wrote on the back of this manuscript :

I am doubtful of the last verse. It began with a jerk — what do you think of this ?

> There'll be their life to the world's end
> To wear the carpet with their shoes
> And earn respect ; have no stranger friend ;
> And only sin, when no one knows ;
> Lord what would they say
> Should their Catullus walk that way.

If you choose this end, call it perhaps 'At the British Museum.' I don't like the new fourth line so well I think. Would the old men regret in the new context ?

The softening down took place when Yeats was away from Ezra Pound's influence (information from Mrs W. B. Yeats). See *WBY* 272 for Yeats's friendship with Pound and the winters he spent with him at Stone Cottage, Coleman's Hatch, Sussex.

158 TOM O'ROUGHLEY

This poem was written on 16 February 1918 and first appeared in the *Little Review* (Oct. 1918).

1 *logic-choppers* : Yeats was probably thinking of Newton, Hobbes, and Locke. Cf. a passage in his Introduction to *Fighting the Waves* :

Science has driven out the legends, stories, superstitions that protected the immature and the ignorant with symbol, and now that the flower has crossed our rooms, science must take their place and demonstrate as philosophy has in all ages, that States are justified, not by multiplying or, as it would seem, comforting those that are inherently miserable, but because sustained by those for whom the hour seems 'awful' and by those born out of themselves, the best born of the best.

Since my twentieth year, those thoughts have been in my mind, and now that I am old I sing them to the Garrets and the Cellars :

> Move upon Newton's town,
> The town of Hobbes and Locke,
> Pine, spruce, come down
> Cliff, ravine, rock :
> What can disturb the corn ?
> What makes it shudder and bend ?
> The rose brings her thorn,
> The Absolute walks behind.   (*W & B* 76–7)

4   *An aimless joy is a pure joy* : Yeats wrote in his essay 'Bishop Berkeley' :

In the *Commonplace Book* alone is Berkeley always sincere, and there I find in paragraph 639, 'Complacency seems rather to . . . constitute the essence of volition,' which seems what an Irish poet meant who sang to some girl 'A joy within guides you,' and what I meant when I wrote 'An aimless joy is a pure joy.' Berkeley must have been familiar with Archbishop King's *De Origine Mali* which makes all joy depend 'upon the act of the agent himself, and his election' ; not upon an external object.   The greater the purity the greater the joy.   A Sligo countryman once said to me, 'God smiles even when He condemns the lost.'   (*E & I*, fn. 408).

Cf. also note on line 22 'Demon and Beast' (*CP* 209) :

> For aimless joy had made me stop
> Beside the little lake.

5   *Tom O'Roughley* : he is probably invented as the kind of fool   **159** Yeats had in mind in Phase Twenty-eight of *AV* :

He is but a straw blown by the wind, with no mind but the wind and no act but a nameless drifting and turning, and is sometimes called 'The Child of God'.   At his worst his hands and feet and eyes, his will and his feelings, obey obscure subconscious fantasies, while at his best he would know all wisdom if he could know anything.   The physical world suggests to his mind pictures and events that have no relation to his needs or even to his desires ; his thoughts are an aimless reverie ; his acts are aimless like his thoughts, and it is in this aimlessness that he finds his joy. (*AV* (B) 182)

7–8 '*And wisdom is a butterfly | And not a gloomy bird of prey*': Yeats's note (dated 1928) on 'Meditations in Time of Civil War, VII' read :

> I suppose that I must have put hawks into the fourth stanza because I have a ring with a hawk and a butterfly upon it, to symbolise the straight road of logic, and so of mechanism, and the crooked road of intuition : 'For wisdom is a butterfly and not a gloomy bird of prey.' (*CP*)

159 SHEPHERD AND GOATHERD

This poem was being written on 22 February 1918 and was finished on 19 March 1918 ; it first appeared in *WSC* entitled 'The Sad Shepherd' which was altered in *CP* to the present title.

Title   Shepherd and Goatherd : the poem was written in memory of Robert Gregory. See notes on 'In Memory of Major Robert Gregory' (*CP* 148). Yeats wrote to Lady Gregory on 22 February 1918, 'I am trying a poem in manner like one that Spenser wrote for Sir Philip Sidney', and, on 19 March 1918, 'I have to-day finished my poem about Robert, a pastoral, modelled on what Virgil wrote for some friend of his and on what Spenser wrote of Sidney' (*L* 646 and 647). The poem is nearer to Spenser's *Astrophel* in general spirit, possibly because Yeats knew Spenser better than he knew Virgil (he made a selection for a volume of Spenser's *Poems*, published in 1906), and possibly because the theme of *Astrophel* is nearer to Yeats's subject than is Virgil's Fifth Eclogue (a probable imitation of Theocritus' Elegy on Daphnis, and less personal than Spenser's or Yeats's lament). But the form of the poem is probably derived from Virgil's Eclogue, Virgil using a dialogue between two rustics as a setting for his lament for Daphnis ; Menalcas and Mopsus each sing their own songs as do Yeats's Shepherd and Goatherd (whereas in *Astrophel* the singer repeats a song made by Clorinda, who is not present). There is a further similarity in structure in that the first singer sings of the death, Mopsus of Daphnis, the Shepherd of Gregory, while the second sings of the state after death, Menalcas of the deification of Daphnis, the Goatherd of the Yeatsian reincarnation of Gregory. Yeats brought to the poem his interest in the occult and in mystic thought.

17–20 *He that was best . . . is dead*: Gregory was an excellent **160**
athlete, horseman and shot. Cf. *Astrophel*:

> For both in deeds and words he noutred was.
> Both wise and hardie — too hardie alas !
> In wrestling, nimble ; and in running, swift ;
> In shooting, steddie ; and in swimming, strong ;
> Well made to strive, to throw, to leap, to lift,
> And all the sports that shepheards are among
> In every one, he vanquisht everyone
> He vanquisht all and vanquisht was of none.

21 *he had thrown the crook away*: see notes (pp. 156–63) on 'In
Memory of Major Robert Gregory' (*CP* 148), and cf. *Astrophel*:

> Such skill matcht with such courage as he had,
> Did prick him foorth with proud desire of praise ;
> To seek abroad, of danger nought y'drad
> His mistress' name, and his owne fame to raise.

24 *their loneliness*: Yeats thought that Gregory had captured the
nature of the Galway scene in his paintings and Augustus John
praised his work for conveying its strange quality. See *IP* 31.

25 *his mother*: cf. *Astrophel*:

> For from the time that first the nymph his mother
> Him forth did bring ; and taught her lambs to feed :
> A slender swaine, excelling far each other
> In comely shape, like her that did him breed.

30–2 *when I had neither goat nor grazing*: a reference to Lady
Gregory's friendship with Yeats, her lending him money so that he
could give up journalism (see Hone (*WBY* 195), who writes that it
was not until 1914 that she would accept repayment of a debt
which then amounted to £500) and imposing a routine on him
during his visits to Coole. A letter to Florence Farr indicated
something of his regime there :

After breakfast Chaucer — garden for twenty minutes —
then work from 11 till 2, then lunch, then I fish from 3 till 5,
then I read and work again at lighter tasks till dinner — after
dinner walk. To this I have added Sandow exercises daily.
(*L* 454)

32 *New welcome . . . old wisdom* : refers to his summer visits to Coole Park from 1897 onwards, and 'old wisdom', perhaps, to the folklore she persuaded him to gather with her in the early summers he spent there when he was in ill health and could not work. He wrote elsewhere of their visits to cottages collecting stories :

> As that ancient system of belief unfolded before us, with unforeseen probabilities and plausibilities, it was as though we had begun to live in a dream, and one day Lady Gregory said to me when we had passed an old man in the wood : 'That old man may know the secret of the ages.' (*E* 30)

34 *his children and his wife* : for later mention of Robert Gregory's child Anne see 'For Anne Gregory' (*CP* 277).

161 46 *Old goatherds and old goats* : Wilson (*Y & T* 200) draws attention to 'the Platonic use of sheep and goats as symbols for young and old souls respectively'.

62 *speckled bird* : *The Speckled Bird* was the title of an autobiographical novel Yeats never published.

162 78 *certain lost companions of my own* : possibly those friends lamented in 'In Memory of Major Robert Gregory' (*CP* 148)

80 *the road that the soul treads* : this is autobiographical, and depicts Yeats's interest in the occult.

89 *He grows younger* : this is the main theme of the poem, that Gregory will grow younger and live his life backwards, an idea dealt with in the Introduction to *WWP* in terms of Indian belief, where the unpurified dead

> examine their past if undisturbed by our importunity, tracing events to their source, and as they take the form their thought suggests, seem to live backward through time ; or if incapable of such examination, creatures not of thought but of feeling, renew as shades certain detached events of their past lives, taking the greater excitements first. (*E* 366)

This is a later version of the idea. In an essay on 'Swedenborg, Mediums and Desolate Places' of 1914 Yeats reported country people in the west of Ireland as saying that

> after death every man grows upward or downward to the like-
> ness of thirty years, perhaps because at that age Christ began
> His ministry, and stays always in that likeness; and these
> angels move always towards the 'springtime of their life' and
> grow more and more beautiful, 'the more thousand years they
> live', . . . 'for to grow old in heaven is to grow young.' (*E* 39).

Wilson (*Y & T* 201) traces the idea to Thomas Taylor's *A Dissertation* (1790) quoting a passage dealing with the Orphic theology
which stated that souls under the government of Saturn, who is
pure intellect, instead of progressing from youth to age advance
from age to youth. In the Orphic mysteries the soul in heaven was
represented as a child. Wilson goes on to quote Plato's myth of
two cycles, of Jupiter and Saturn. The latter was the intellectual
world, a prenatal condition from which the soul descended and to
which it returned after death. In the Saturnian kingdom man was
no longer seen advancing to old age but became younger and more
delicate. But in the previous cycle Plato described the world as a
paradise resembling the intellectual condition, and Wilson quotes
this passage from Taylor's *Plato*, IV 123 : 'The white hairs of those
more advanced in years became black, and the cheeks of those that
had beards became smooth, and thus each was restored to the past
flower of his age.' Wilson regards Yeats's commentary on a passage
in Shelley's *Prometheus Unbound* as evidence that Yeats knew the
Platonic myth because, he argues, Shelley drew on this myth of
Plato for Asia's song in *Prometheus Unbound*, and Yeats saw in Asia's
voyage a movement against the current from age to youth, from
youth to infancy, and so to the prenatal condition, 'peopled by
Shapes too bright to see'.

95 *Jaunting, journeying* : jaunting : to take a jaunt for pleasure **163**
(horse-drawn jaunting cars were in common use in Ireland at this
time).

96 *To his own dayspring* : the phrase 'dayspring' is reminiscent of
Yeats's reading in Swedenborg. He quoted the phrase in a letter to
T. Sturge Moore, in a comment on Dowson seeking from religion
'something of that which the angels find who move perpetually,

as Swedenborg has said, "towards the dayspring of their youth"'
(*A* 311), and in *BS* :

> now I am old and rheumatic, and nothing to look at, but my
> Muse is young. I am even persuaded she is like those Angels in
> Swedenborg's vision, and moves perpetually 'towards the day-
> spring of her youth'. (*A* 541)

97   *the loaded pern* : Yeats wrote the following note in 1919 :

> When I was a little child at Sligo I could see above my grand-
> father's trees a little column of smoke from the 'pern mill,'
> and was told that 'pern' was another name for the spool, as I
> was accustomed to call it, on which thread was wound. One
> could not see the chimney for the trees, and the smoke looked
> as if it came from the mountain, and one day a foreign sea-
> captain asked me if that was a burning mountain. (*WSC*)

Cf. line 5 of 'Demon and Beast' (*CP* 209), 'The Fool by the Roadside' (*CP* 247), and 'Hades' bobbin' of 'Byzantium' (*CP* 280).

Cf. Scott's use of the word in *The Antiquary:* ' "I ken naething
about that," said the Gaberlunzie, "but an my auld acquaintance be
hersell, or onything like hersell, she may come to bind us a pirn." '
(Ch. 39).

103   *the close cropped grass* : this may be glossed by Yeats's essay on
Swedenborg, who because he belonged

> to an eighteenth century not yet touched by the romantic
> revival, feels horror amid rocky uninhabited places, and so
> believes that the evil are in such places while the good are amid
> smooth grass and garden walks and the clear sunlight of Claude
> Lorraine. (*E* 37)

Cf. Wilson (*Y & T* 204) who considers that Plato also may have
provided the imagery. He quotes a passage which describes those
distributed about Saturn :

> The inhabitants also are naked and without beds, and for
> the most part are fed dwelling in the open air. The grass like-
> wise springing abundantly from the earth supplies them with
> soft couches. (Taylor, *Plato*, IV 120)

He also draws attention to a passage where Yeats describes how

> always in his [Blake's] boys and girls walking or dancing on
> smooth grass and in golden light, as on pastoral scenes cut upon
> wood or copper by his disciples Palmer and Calvert, one
> notices the peaceful Swedenborgian heaven. (*E* 44)

107 *unwind* : cf. line 97

109–112 these lines are reminiscent of Blake's 'The Mental Traveller'.

115 *new-torn bark* : probably close to Virgil's lines :

> Immo haec in viridi nuper quae cortice fagi
> Carmina descripsi et modulans alterna notavi,
> Experiar.

LINES WRITTEN IN DEJECTION   **163**

This poem was written in 1915 (probably in October) and first appeared in *WSC*.

3 *the moon* : the sun and moon in this poem symbolise objectivity and subjectivity, cf. 'The Man who dreamed of Faeryland' (*CP* 49). At this period of his life Yeats seemed at times to despair of writing poetry ; this poem also carries the dejection of the heart grown old. Cf. 'Men improve with the Years' (*CP* 152), 'The Living Beauty' (*CP* 156) and 'A Song' (*CP* 156).

7 *the holy centaurs* : Yeats wrote elsewhere 'I thought all art should be a Centaur finding in the popular lore its back and its strong legs' (*A* 191).

8 *embittered sun* : it is possible to consider the objective life as destroying the creative element in man. The tasks involved in 'theatre business, management of men' may have seemed objective in comparison to Yeats's earlier life. In *AV* he described a man of the seventeenth phase (to which he belonged) in terms which might suit his own position ('out of phase') at this period of his life :

> If it [the intellect] be out of phase it will avoid the sub-jective conflict, acquiesce, hope that the *Body of Fate* may die away ; and then the *Mask* will cling to it and the *Image* lure it. It will feel itself betrayed, and persecuted till, entangled in *primary* conflict, it rages against all that destroys *Mask* and *Image*. It will be subject to nightmare, for its *Creative Mind* (deflected from the *Image* and *Mask* to the *Body of Fate*) gives an isolated mythological or abstract form to all that excites its hatred. It may even dream of escaping from ill-luck by possessing the impersonal *Body of Fate* of its opposite phase, and of exchanging passion for desk and ledger. Because of the habit of synthesis, and of the growing complexity of the

energy, which gives many interests, and the still faint perception of things in their weight and mass, men of this phase are
almost always partisans, propagandists and gregarious ; yet
because of the *Mask* of simplification, which holds up before
them the solitary life of hunters and of fishers [cf. Yeats's
poem 'The Fisherman' (*CP* 166)] and 'the groves pale passion
loves,' they hate parties, crowds, propaganda. (*AV* (A) 77)

Shelley when 'out of phase' dreamed of converting the world, and
upsetting governments, yet returned 'again and again to these two
images of solitude, a young man whose hair has grown white from
the burden of his thoughts, an old man in some shell-strewn
cave . . .' and the parallel between his life (as seen in these Yeatsian
terms) and Yeats's own can be drawn. In *Estrangement* Yeats
recorded his despair at the apparent dissipation of his poetic skill in
varied work :

> I often wonder if my talent will ever recover from the
> heterogeneous labour of these last few years. The younger
> Hallam says that vice does not destroy genius but that the
> heterogeneous does. I cry out vainly for liberty and have
> ever less and less inner life. Evil comes to us men of imagina-
> tion wearing as its mask all the virtues. (*A* 484)

164 THE DAWN

This poem was written on 20 June 1914 and first appeared in *P* (*Cb*)
(Feb. 1916).

3 *that old queen . . . a town* : the queen was Emain, the town
Emain Macha or Armagh. Emain, daughter of Hugh Roe, claimed
to rule in her father's right after his death, and defeated his brother
Dihorba in battle, married his brother Cimbaeth and captured
Dihorba's five sons by a stratagem. She compelled the five princes
to build her a palace.

4 *With the pin of a brooch* : she marked out the site of the palace
with the bodkin or pin of her cloak — hence the name of her
palace, in latinised form Emania. See Edward Rogers, *Memoir of
Armagh Cathedral* (1882) for further details of the legend.

5–6 *the withered men . . . pedantic Babylon* : a reference to what
Yeats called 'the Babylonian mathematical starlight' in *AV* (B) 268.

11   *the glittering coach* : presumably the chariot of Phoebus, the sun, though the fact that one particular dawn is suggested might imply that that particular dawn had seen Phaëton, the son of Phoebus, on his disastrous attempt to drive the chariot, killed by a thunderbolt hurled by Zeus because Phaëton was likely to set the earth on fire.

ON WOMAN   **164**

This poem was dated 25 May 1914 in the Maud Gonne Manuscript Book ; it first appeared in *P (Ch)* (Feb. 1916). The poem has some of the sardonic realism of 'Beggar to Beggar Cried' (*CP* 128) and 'The Witch' (*CP* 135). It was not written to Mrs Yeats.

11   *Solomon grew wise* : cf. Prov. iv. 5–7   **165**

19   *shuddered in the water* : sexual symbol. Cf. line 23 and 'Leda and the Swan' (*CP* 241)

21   *yawn* : cf. 'Three Things' (*CP* 300), 'And did after stretch and yawn'

30   *the Pestle of the moon* : Yeats's belief in rebirth is qualified — 'if the tale's true'. Cf. Hone (*WBY* 48), who quotes Mohini Chatterjee as saying : 'Everything that has been shall be again.' But the thought here probably relates to Swedenborg. There is an undated entry in the Maud Gonne Manuscript Book which reads :

> . . . O God grant me for my gift not in this life for I begin to grow [old] but somewhere that I shall love some woman, so that every passion, pity, cruel desire, the affection that is full of tears to abasement as before an image . . .

THE FISHERMAN   **166**

This poem was dated 4 June 1914 in the Maud Gonne Manuscript Book, and first appeared in *P (Ch)* (Feb. 1916). The poem has as subject the contrast between an ideal man and the real men of Ireland.

1–8   *him* : the ideal man

4   *grey Connemara clothes* : homespun tweed. See *A* 361 for a comment on this subject.

9–12   *All day . . . and the reality* : the lines refer to the ideal audience, the fisherman — 'What I had hoped 'twoud be / To write for my own race' and to the actual audience, 'the reality', which is so unlike the ideal. The reality is described in lines 13–24.

14   *the dead man* : probably J. M. Synge

167   23–4   *The beating down . . . Art beaten down* : probably a reference to the controversy over the Lane Gallery proposals

25   *a twelvemonth since* : there is an entry in the Maud Gonne Manuscript Book written between 18 and 25 May 1913, a year before 'The Fisherman' was written, which is headed 'Subject for a poem' and runs :

> Who is this by the edge of the stream
> That walks in a good homespun coat
> And carries a fishing [rod] in his hand
> We singers have nothing of our own.
> All our hopes, our loves, our dreams
> Are for the young, for those whom
> We stir into life.   But [there is] one
> That I can see always though he is not yet born
> He walks by the edge of the stream
> In a good homespun coat
> And carries a fishing-rod in his hand.

These lines form the substance of the last sixteen lines of 'The Fisherman' and show that only an imagined person could fulfil the poet's dreams. The germ of the idea can be seen in 'At Galway Races' (*CP* 108), where the horsemen are idealised 'natural' men.

33   *down-turn of his wrist* : Yeats was a good fisherman and this description of skilled casting was praised for its accuracy by Siegfried Sassoon.

167   THE HAWK

This poem first appeared in *P* (*Cb*) (Feb. 1916).

1   *the hawk* : cf. notes on 'Tom O'Roughley' (*CP* 158). In 'Four Years : 1887–1891' Yeats described how he thought that in man

and race there is something called Unity of Being. He thought the enemy of this Unity was abstraction, 'meaning by abstraction not the distinction but the isolation of occupation, or class or faculty'. He then added the first six lines of 'The Hawk'.

15   *Last evening?* : the conversation is not recorded. There is a   **168**
certain amount of self-analysis in Yeats's Diaries where he recorded dissatisfaction with his methods of conversing, particularly in the Arts Club. There is an example of this rethinking of past conversations or debates in *Estrangement*, II. Out of his need to develop a poised personality came the doctrine of the mask: 'Style, personality — deliberately adopted and therefore a mask — is the only escape from the hot-faced bargainers and the money-changers' (*A* 461).

MEMORY   **168**

Ellmann (*IY* 290) dates this poem as 1915–16 ; it first appeared in *P* (*Cb*) (Feb. 1916).

1   *a lovely face* : Mrs Shakespear

5   *form* : the lair in which a hare crouches

6   *the mountain hare* : possibly Iseult Gonne. See notes (pp. 213–14) on 'Two Songs of a Fool' (*CP* 190).

HER PRAISE   **168**

The manuscript of this poem is dated 27 January 1915 ; it first appeared in *P* (*Cb*) (Feb. 1916), entitled 'The Thorn Tree'.

1   *She is foremost* . . . : the poem is about Maud Gonne, who withdrew from public life after her marriage. See *WBY* 210. Yeats sees society as forgetting her but the poor as remembering her. Maud Gonne was well known among the Dublin poor for her charity.

5   *turned the talk* : cf. line 14 'manage the talk'

169 11–18 *I will talk no more . . . But walk* : the original version of these lines ran :

> A man comes hither because of the harsh wind
> I am certain that where he finds the thorn he will stop
> To shelter a while, that puts it into my mind
> To turn the talk until her name has come up.
>
> And being but a ragged man he will know her name
> And be well pleased remembering it, for in old days
> Though she had young men's praise and old men's blame
> Among the poor both old and young gave her praise.

169 THE PEOPLE

The manuscript of this poem is dated 10 January 1915. It first appeared, entitled 'The Phoenix' in *P* (*Ch*) (Feb. 1916).

1 '*What have I earned . . .*' this poem records a conversation with Maud Gonne, who is symbolised by the Phoenix in this poem and 'His Phoenix' (*CP* 170).

2 *all that I have done* : probably a reference not only to Yeats's work for the Abbey Theatre but his earlier work for the literary and political movements.

3 *this unmannerly town* : Dublin, which had failed to appreciate the dramatic work of Synge (and Yeats) and the generosity of Hugh Lane.

4 *most defamed* : perhaps a mixture of dislike of Dublin's malicious gossip, its journalism, and George Moore's writings (see notes) (pp. 115–20 and 150–1) on the 'Introductory Rhymes' and 'Closing Rhymes' of *Responsibilities* (*CP* 113 and 143).

6–9 *I might have lived . . . Ferrara wall* : Wade included a fragment of a letter in his selection, which described a rehearsal at the Gaiety Theatre, Dublin, probably in October 1901, in which Yeats described his longing to get away from his work for an audience which he regarded as unsuitable :

> The kid Benson is to carry in his arms was wandering in and out among the artificial ivy. I was saying to myself 'Here are

we a lot of intelligent people, who might have been doing some
sort of work that leads to some fun. Yet here we are going
through all sorts of trouble and annoyance for a mob that
knows neither literature nor art. I might have been away in
the country, in Italy, perhaps writing poems for my equals
and betters. That kid is the only sensible creature on the stage.
He knows his business and keeps to it.' At that very moment
one of the actors called out 'Look at the goat eating the
property ivy.' (*L* 356)

9 *Ferrara* : Yeats visited the town in 1907. Duke Ercole was an
excellent encourager of the arts. Cf. notes (pp. 123–8) to 'To a
Wealthy Man who promised a second Subscription to the Dublin
Municipal Gallery if it were proved the People wanted Pictures'
(*CP* 119).

11–18 *the unperturbed and courtly images . . . dawn* : the source of
these lines is probably Castiglione's *The Book of the Courtier*. Yeats
possessed Hoby's Elizabethan translation (issued by David Nutt in
1900 with an Introduction by Sir Walter Raleigh), but he seems to
have referred to Opdycke's translation also, published by Duck-
worth in 1902. The following extract is from Opdycke :

. . . the custom of all the gentlemen of the house was to
betake themselves straightway after supper to my lady
Duchess ; where, among the other pleasant pastimes and
music and dancing that continually were practised, sometimes
neat questions were proposed, sometimes ingenious games
were devised at the choice of one or another, in which under
various disguises the company disclosed their thoughts figur-
atively to whom they liked best. Sometimes other discussions
arose about different matters, or biting retorts passed lightly
back and forth. Often devices (*imprese*), as we now call them,
were displayed, in discussing which there was wonderful
diversion, the house being (as I have said) full of very noble
talents. (*The Courtier* (tr. 1902) 12)

The anecdote of the Duchess and her people talking till dawn also
derives from the description of a prolonged evening at Urbino :

My lord Gaspar began making ready to reply, but my lady
Duchess said :
'Of this let messer Pietro Bembo be the judge, and let us
abide by his decision whether or not women are as capable of
divine love as men are. But the controversy between you

might be long, it will be well to postpone it until tomorrow.'

'Nay, until this evening,' said messer Cesare Gonzaga.

'How until this evening?' said my lady Duchess.

Messer Cesare replied:

'Because it is already day'; and he showed her the light that was beginning to come in through the cracks at the windows.

Then everyone rose to his feet in great surprise, for the discussion did not seem to have lasted longer than usual; but by reason of having been begun much later, and by its pleasantness, it had so beguiled the company that they had not perceived the flight of hours; nor was there anyone who felt the heaviness of sleep upon his eyes, which nearly always happens when the accustomed hour of sleep is passed in watching. The windows having then been opened on that side of the palace which looks towards the lofty crest of Mount Catria, they saw that a beautiful dawn of rosy hue was already born in the east, and that all the stars had vanished save Venus, sweet mistress of the sky, who holds the bonds of night and day: from which there seemed to breathe a gentle wind that filled the air with crisp coolness and began to waken sweet choruses of joyous birds in the murmuring forests of the hills hard by.

So, having reverently taken leave of my lady Duchess, they all started towards their chambers without light of torches, that of day being enough for them. . . . (*The Courtier* (tr. 1902) 308)

See also Yeats's comment on Urbino in 'Discoveries' (*ELI* 290 and 293)

170   22   *my phoenix*: Maud Gonne

23   *when my luck changed*: a memory of the unpopularity which greeted Maud Gonne in Dublin. She was seeking a separation from her husband John MacBride in 1905.

27   *after nine years*: this would place the conversation in 1906.

170   HIS PHOENIX

This poem was written in January 1915 and first appeared, entitled 'There is a Queen in China' in *P (Ch)* (Feb. 1916).

1–7   *There is a queen . . . his mind*: the second stanza of the original manuscript version of the poem ran thus:

And every morn and every night some newspaper applauds
The unblemished character, whiteness that has no stain
As though she'd warmed herself in Troy, and there are waggon
   loads
Of Countesses and Duchesses surpassing womankind
Or who have found a painter to make them so for pay
And smooth out stain or blemish with the elegance of his mind.

4 *that sprightly girl*: Leda. Cf. 'Leda and the Swan' (*CP* 241).
Tread (of birds), to copulate.

8 *a phoenix*: Maud Gonne. See the essay on 'Poetry and Tradi- **171**
tion':

> This joy, because it must be always making and mastering,
> remains in the hands and in the tongue of the artist, but with
> his eyes he enters upon a submissive, sorrowful contempla-
> tion of the great irremediable things, and he is known from
> other men by making all he handles like himself, and yet by
> the unlikeness to himself of all that comes before him in a pure
> contemplation. It may have been his enemy or his love or
> his cause that set him dreaming, and certainly the phoenix can
> but open her young wings in a flaming nest; but all hate and
> hope vanishes in the dream, and if his mistress brag of the song
> or his enemy fear it, it is not that either has its praise or blame,
> but that the wings of the holy nest are not easily set afire. The
> verses may make his mistress famous as Helen or give a victory
> to his cause, not because he has been either's servant, but
> because men delight to honour and to remember all that have
> served contemplation. (*E & I* 254–5)

9–11 *their Gaby's laughing eye*: these lines were different in the
original MS. and ran:

> Pavlova is beyond our praise, Gaby's a laughing eye
> Though Ruth St. Denis had no luck she had an Indian charm
> In 1908 or nine Miss Maud Allen had the cry.

9 *Gaby*: Gaby Deslys, a French actress

10 *Ruth St. Denis*: an American dancer

11 *Pavlova*: a famous Russian ballerina (1885–1931)

12 *a player in the States* : Julia Marlowe, whom Yeats saw during his 1903–4 lecture tour in the United States

17 *Margaret . . . Dorothy . . . Mary* : Ellmann (*ED* 73) remarks that this was a list of Ezra Pound's girl friends. In April 1914 Pound married Dorothy Shakespear, daughter of Yeats's friend Mrs Olivia Shakespear. See p. 63 and *PYP* 66–7.

18 *in privacy* : a note in Yeats's handwriting on the final manuscript version of the poem reads : 'When I repeated this to Gogarty [Oliver St. John Gogarty (1878–1957)] he says I spoke of "chastity" not "privacy" and he prefers "chastity".'

172 28 *the simplicity of a child* : cf. 'Against Unworthy Praise' (*CP* 103) where she is described as 'half lion, half child', and 'Long-legged Fly' (*CP* 381) where she is 'part woman, three parts a child'.

29 *that proud look* : cf. 'Upon a House shaken by the Land Agitation' (*CP* 106) with its 'lidless eye that loves the sun'. The eagle is supposed to be able to gaze into the sun unblinkingly.

172 A THOUGHT FROM PROPERTIUS

This poem was probably written before November 1915 and first appeared in *WSC*.

1 *She might* : Maud Gonne

4 *walked to the altar* : the poem probably derives from the second poem in the second book of Propertius. Yeats seems to have selected images from it :

> Why abides such mortal beauty upon earth ? Jupiter, I pardon thy gallantries of olden time. Yellow is her hair, and tapering her hands, tall and full her figure, and stately her walk, worthy the sister of Jove or like to Pallas, when she strides to Dulichian altars, her breast veiled by the Gorgons' snaky locks. Fair is she as Ischomache, heroic child of the Lapithae, the Centaurs' welcome spoil in the revel's midst, or as Brimo when by the sacred waters of Boebeis she laid her virgin body at Mercury's side. Yield now, ye goddesses, whom of old the shepherd saw lay aside your raiment on the heights of Ida ! And oh ! may old age never mar that face, though she reach the years of the Cumaean prophetess. (H. E. Butler's translation)

6   *Pallas Athene* : Yeats described Maud Gonne in terms of Pallas Athene in 'Beautiful Lofty Things' (*CP* 348) : 'Pallas Athene in that straight back and arrogant head.'   When they first met in 1889 she seemed a classical impersonation of the spring, 'the Virgilian commendation "She walks like a goddess" made for her alone.' Cf. *A* 123.

BROKEN DREAMS   **172**

This poem was dated 24 October 1915 in the Maud Gonne Manuscript Book : it first appeared, dated November 1915, in the *Little Review* (June 1917).

1   *your hair* : the poem is written to Maud Gonne.

18   *the poet stubborn with his passion* : Yeats   **173**

19   *chilled his blood* : Yeats was fifty when he wrote the poem

21   *all, all, shall be renewed* : cf. line 8 'In Memory of Major Robert Gregory (*CP* 148) ; line 5 'The Results of Thought' (*CP* 286) ; lines 118–37 'The Shadowy Waters' (*CP* 473) ; line 184 'The Gift of Harun Al-Rashid' (*CP* 511).

28   *your body had a flaw* : in an essay on 'The Tragic Theatre' written five years earlier Yeats praised the attractiveness of the unusual in a beloved, the quality of uniqueness :

> Some little irrelevance of line, some promise of character to come, may indeed put us at our ease, 'give more interest' as the humour of the old man with the basket does to Cleopatra's dying ; but should it come, as we had dreamed in love's frenzy, to our dying for that woman's sake, we would find that the discord had its value from the tune.   (*E & I* 244)

A DEEP-SWORN VOW   **174**

This poem is dated 17 October 1915 in the Maud Gonne Manuscript Book and first appeared in the *Little Review* (June 1917).

1   *you did not keep* : Maud Gonne

2   *That deep-sworn vow* : not to marry

3   *look death in the face* :   the poem may possibly have been inspired by a poem by Arthur Symons because the entry in the Manuscript Book which precedes it reads :

I have just found a scrap of paper in Nan Tobin's writing. It is a poem by Arthur Symons written in his first stages of madness — a state of delirium.   Four lines thus :

> I am undone.   My course shall swiftly run
> Yet lain enrapt in an enchanted swoon
> I die of rapture yet I see that soon
> The fated sisters shall my web have spun.

174   PRESENCES

This poem was dated November 1915 in the Maud Gonne Manu-script Book and first appeared in the *Little Review* (June 1917).

12   *One is a harlot* :   probably the lady referred to by Hone (*WBY* 301).

one a child :   Iseult Gonne

14   *a queen* :   Maud Gonne

175   THE BALLOON OF THE MIND

This poem was written before 1917 and first appeared in the *New Statesman* (29 Sept. 1917).

2   *the balloon of the mind* :   in 'Reveries', written in 1914, Yeats traced a lack of organised thought back to his English schooldays, in the Godolphin School, Hammersmith.   (The similarity of the idea and image in the poem and the prose might argue some closeness in the date of composition) :

I was unfitted for school work, and though I would often work well for weeks together, I had to give the whole evening to one lesson if I was to know it.   My thoughts were a great excite-ment, but when I tried to do anything with them, it was like trying to pack a balloon into a shed in a high wind.   (*A* 41)

He blamed his father for not taking him away from school, this time the High School, Dublin :

He would have taught me nothing but Greek and Latin, and I would now be a properly educated man, and would not have to look in useless longing at books that have been, through the poor mechanism of translation, the builders of my soul, nor face authority with the timidity born of excuse and evasion. Evasion and excuse were in the event as wise as the house-building instinct of the beaver. (*A* 58)

TO A SQUIRREL AT KYLE-NA-NO   **175**

The manuscript of this poem is dated September 1912 and it first appeared in the *New Statesman* (29 Sept. 1917).

Title   Kyle-na-no : one of the seven woods at Coole, spelt 'Kyle-na-gno' in the first printing, later 'Kyle-Na-Gno' until it became Kyle-na-no in *CP*. Cf. 'An Appointment' (*CP* 141).

6   *all I would do* : Yeats's attitude to killing animals emerged early in life :

   I fished for pike at Castle Dargan and shot at birds with a muzzle-loading pistol until somebody shot a rabbit and I heard it squeal. From that on I would kill nothing but the dumb fish. (*A* 55)

ON BEING ASKED FOR A WAR POEM   **175**

This poem was written on 6 February 1915 and first appeared in *The Book of the Homeless* (ed. Edith Wharton, 1916), entitled 'A Reason for Keeping Silent'. The original title was 'To a friend who has asked me to sign his manifesto to the neutral nations.'

1   *I think it better* : Yeats sent the poem to Henry James on 20 August [1915] in a letter from Coole Park and concluded the letter :

   It is the only thing I have written of the war or will write, so I hope it may not seem unfitting. I shall keep the neighbourhood of the seven sleepers of Ephesus, hoping to catch their comfortable snores till bloody frivolity is over. (*L* 600)

IN MEMORY OF ALFRED POLLEXFEN   **175**

This poem was written in August 1916 according to Ellmann (*IY* 290) ; it first appeared in the *Little Review* (June 1917), entitled 'In Memory'.

1 *Five-and-twenty years have gone* : William Pollexfen, Yeats's maternal grandfather, died in 1890. See 'Introductory Rhymes' (*CP* 113) and 'Under Saturn' (*CP* 202).

176 3 *his strong bones* : the use of 'bones' for 'body' in this line may be due to Yeats's memory of his grandfather using the phrase 'I am not going to lie with those old bones' when deciding not to be buried with the Middletons :

> There was a Middleton tomb and a long list of Middletons on the wall, and an almost empty space for Pollexfen names . . . [obviously, as William Pollexfen was the first of the family to settle in Sligo] and already one saw his name in large gilt letters on the stone fence of the new tomb. He ended his walk at Saint John's churchyard [in Sligo] almost daily, for he liked everything neat and compendious as upon shipboard, and if he had not looked after the tomb himself the builder might have added some useless ornament. (*A* 67–8)

4 *his wife Elizabeth* :

> . . . his wife, a Middleton, was gentle and patient and did many charities in the little back parlour among frieze coats and shawled heads, and every night when she saw him asleep [he had a violent temper and kept a hatchet by his bed] went the round of the house alone with a candle to make certain there was no burglar in danger of the hatchet.' (*A* 9)

6 *after twenty years* : George Pollexfen died in September 1910.

9 *And Masons drove* : Yeats described the funeral in a letter of 29 September 1910 to Lady Gregory :

> The funeral was very touching — the church full of the working people, Catholics who had never been in a Protestant church before, and the man next me crying all the time. I thought of Synge's funeral — none at that, after some two or three, but enemies or conventional images of gloom. The Masons (there were 80 of them) had their own service and one by one threw acacia leaves into the grave with the traditional Masonic goodbye, 'Alas my brother so mote it be.' Then there came two who threw each a white rose, and that was because they and he were 'Priori Masons', a high degree of Masonry. (*L* 553)

11 *a melancholy man* : see notes on 'In Memory of Major Robert Gregory' (*CP* 148). George Pollexfen was a hypochondriac, but Yeats wrote, 'it is a curious thing that George who complained so much when well, has always been brave and calm before real calamity' (*L* 551).

13 *Many a son and daughter* : Yeats's 'grandfather's many sons and daughters, came and went' (*A* 10).

15 *The Mall and . . . grammar school* : a street in Sligo and the grammar school which survives today

17 *the sailor John* : John Butler Yeats in a letter written in 1916 to the poet made the point that a sailor's self-control compelled him into personality, alluding to John Pollexfen's stories about his life at sea (*LTHS* 224).

24 *the youngest son* : he 'was stout and humorous and had a tongue of leather over the keyhole of his door to keep the draught out' (*A* 10).

30 *journey home* : Alfred Pollexfen (J. B. Yeats called him 'that mental simpleton Alfred') was married and his wife and children stayed in Sligo while he was away. The lines mean he returned to Sligo at fifty and died ten years later.

37 *A visionary white sea-bird* : Yeats recorded that his sister had **177** (six months before he wrote 'Reveries' in 1914) awoken dreaming that she held a wingless sea-bird in her arms and presently had heard that another uncle had died in his madhouse, 'for a sea-bird is the omen that announces the death or danger of a Pollexfen' (*A* 10). Yeats wrote to Lady Gregory that his sister Lily as well as the nurse heard the Banshee and George Pollexfen died the night after at the same hour the Banshee had cried the night before. He wrote to Lily to say it seemed a fitting thing, as George Pollexfen had an instinctive nature close to the supernatural (*L* 552 and 553).

UPON A DYING LADY **177**

These seven poems were written between January 1912 and July 1914. Section I was written in January 1913, Section II in January

1912, and Section VII probably in July 1914. They first appeared in the *Little Review* (Aug. 1917) under the general title 'Seven Poems', the fourth, fifth and sixth being given numerical subtitles, the other being entitled as in *CP*.

I

Title Her Courtesy : the subject of the poems is the painter Aubrey Beardsley's sister Mabel who had married an actor, George Bealby Wright. She died of cancer in her early forties, and letters Yeats wrote to Lady Gregory on 8 January 1913 and on 11 February 1913 explain the circumstances in which the poems were written :

> My dear Lady Gregory . . . I dined with Lane on Sunday. He is very pleased with the poem which Hone has now. Hone was excited with doing a leader elaborating the thought of the poem. I am not very hopeful. The Corporation has voted about £2000 a year and I told Lane I thought he should consider that as the country's support and not make the action of half a dozen people — who alone have money enough to subscribe £20,000 — the deciding thing. He replied that he hated Dublin. I said so do we. He then said that unless the gallery were built at once it would be a long time before he would have the pleasure of hanging the pictures. I urged him to buy the site himself, if need [be] by selling some of the pictures for the purpose. He said he could buy it without selling any of the pictures but thought it a mistake to do so unless £20,000 was subscribed, so we were back again at the half dozen people. He took all I said in good part and has asked me to invite myself to dinner when I liked. . . .
>
> Strange that just after writing those lines on the Rhymers who 'unrepenting faced their ends' I should be at the bedside of the dying sister of Beardsley, who was practically one of us. She had had a week of great pain but on Sunday was I think free from it. She was propped up on pillows with her cheeks I think a little rouged and looking very beautiful. Beside her a Xmas tree with little toys containing sweets, which she gave us. Mr Davis — Ricketts' patron — had brought it — I daresay it was Ricketts' idea. I will keep the little toy she gave me and I daresay she knew this. On a table near were four dolls dressed like people out of her brother's drawings. Women with loose trousers and boys that looked like women. Ricketts had made them, modelling the faces and sewing the clothes. They must have taken him days. She had all her

great lady airs and asked after my work and my health as if they were the most important things in the world to her. 'A palmist told me,' she said, 'that when I was forty-two my life would take a turn for the better and now I shall spend my forty-second year in heaven' and then emphatically 'O yes I shall go to heaven. Papists do.' When I told her where Mrs Emery was she said 'How fine of her, but a girls' school! why she used to make even me blush!' Then she began telling improper stories and inciting us (there were two men besides myself) to do the like. At moments she shook with laughter. Just before I was going her mother came and saw me to the door. As we were standing at it she said 'I do not think she wishes to live — how could she after such agony? She is all I have left now.' I lay awake most of the night with a poem in my head. I cannot over-state her strange charm — the pathetic gaiety. It was her brother but her brother was not I think loveable, only astounding and intrepid. She has been ill since June last. . . .

My dear Lady Gregory . . . Mabel Beardsley said to me on Sunday 'I wonder who will introduce me in heaven. It should be my brother but then they might not appreciate the introduction. They might not have good taste.' She said of her brother 'He hated the people who denied the existence of evil, and so being young he filled his pictures with evil. He had a passion for reality.' She has the same passion and puts aside any attempts to suggest recovery and yet I have never seen her in low spirits. She talked of a play she wanted to see. 'If I could only send my head and my legs,' she said, 'for they are quite well.' Till one questions her she tries to make one forget that she is ill. I always see her alone now. She keeps Sunday afternoon for me. I will send you the little series of poems when they are finished. One or two are I think very good. (*L* 573-5)

8 *Petronius Arbiter* : a Roman satirist, companion of Nero and author of the Satiricon. He was the director of the pleasures of the Emperor's Court, the *arbiter elegantiae*.

II

2 *doll* : see letters to Lady Gregory quoted above

III

Title *the Dolls'* : made by Ricketts, see letters to Lady Gregory quoted above, and by Edmund Dulac.

178 7   *Longhi* : Pietro Longhi (1702–62), a Venetian genre painter

9   *our Beauty* : see letters to Lady Gregory quoted above

10   *must have like every dog his day* ✦ probably an echo of Paul Fort's phrase, quoted by Yeats in 'Modern Poetry : A Broadcast' :

> And they came back so merrily : all at the dawn of day ;
> A singing all so merrily : '*The dog must have his day !*'

Paul Fort, a French poet, was born in 1872 ; the translation was read by Yeats in one of his brother's *Broadsides* (a mixture of hand-coloured prints and poetry).

V

179 11   *her dead brother's valour* : Aubrey Beardsley (1872–98) was art editor of *The Yellow Book* (1894) and died of consumption at the age of twenty-six.   An unpublished section of the poem ran as follows :

> Although she has turned away
> The pretty waxen faces
> And hid their silk and laces
> For Mass was said to-day
> She has not begun denying
> Now that she is but dying
> The pleasures she loved well
> The strong milk of her mother
> The valour of her brother
> Are in her body still
> She will not die weeping
> May God be with her sleeping.

VI

4–6   *Grania . . . Diarmuid* : see notes (pp. 31–2) on 'A Faery Song' (*CP* 43)

8   *Giorgione* : a famous Venetian painter (*c.* 1478–1510)

9   *Achilles* : Greek hero, son of Peleus and Thetis.   He slew Hector in the siege of Troy (see 'News for the Delphic Oracle' *CP* 376), was wounded in the heel (the rest of his body being invulnerable) by Paris and died.

Timor : Tamburlaine (1336–1405)

Babar : founder of the Moghul Empire in India (1483–1530)

Barhaim : probably Bahram, the great hunter of FitzGerald's *Rubáiyát of Omar Khayyam*

EGO DOMINUS TUUS   **180**

The poem was written by 5 October 1915, though a second manuscript bears the date 5 December 1915. It first appeared in *P* (Ch) (Oct. 1917). In 1925 Yeats wrote : 'I can now, if I have the energy, find the simplicity I have sought in vain. I need no longer write poems like "The Phases of the Moon" [*CP* 183] nor "Ego Dominus Tuus"' (*AV* (A) xii)

Title This comes from Dante. The passage in *PASL* which gives this information indicates the main thought of the poem, that Yeats is open to the power that fills creative men, that the artist has a ,well of strength from which to draw, the source of which he does not know, there being an ununderstood unreality in life :

> How could I have mistaken for myself an heroic condition that from early boyhood has made me superstitious ? That which comes as complete, as minutely organised, as are those elaborate, brightly lighted buildings and sceneries appearing in a moment, as I lie between sleeping and waking must come from above me and beyond me. At times I remember that place in Dante where he sees in his chamber the 'Lord of Terrible Aspect', and how, seeming 'to rejoice inwardly that it was a marvel to see, speaking, he said many things among the which I could understand but few, and of these this : ego dominus tuus' . . . (*M* 325–6)

1 *Hic* : the poem takes the form of a dialogue between *Hic* and *Ille*, the setting the neighbourhood of Thoor Ballylee (which Yeats bought in 1917). Yeats had written to his father that his thought was part of a religion more or less logically worked out :

> A system which will, I hope, interest you as a form of poetry. I find the setting of it all in order has helped my verse, has given me a new framework and new patterns. One goes on year after year getting the disorder of one's own mind in order, and this is the real impulse to create. (Quoted by Hone (*WBY* 305))

He referred to *PASL* (first called 'An Alphabet') in which he developed the theories of the anti-self which are explored in 'Ego Dominus Tuus'. In the poem's dialogue *Hic* defends the objective, *Ille* the subjective. (Contemporary comment in Dublin — Ellmann attributes the quip to Ezra Pound — had it that *Hic* and *Willie* would be more correct nomenclature.) *PASL* affords some explanation of parts of the poem.

2 *wind-beaten tower*: Yeats's Norman tower (Irish, *thoor*) at Ballylee

3 *A lamp*: cf. the symbolism of tower and lamp in 'The Tower' (*CP* 218) and, particularly, notes (p. 268) on the section of 'Meditations in Time of Civil War' (*CP* 225) entitled 'My House' (*CP* 226).

4 *Michael Robartes*: see notes (p. 55) on 'The Lover tells of the Rose in his Heart' (*CP* 62). Michael Robartes appeared in the 'Rose Alchemica' as a mysterious person who persuades the narrator to join a magical society which is attacked in a village riot. Robartes has travelled in the Near East. He and Aherne appear in the Introduction to *AV* where Aherne complains that 'Mr Yeats had given the name of Michael Robartes and that of Owen Aherne to fictitious characters, and made those characters live through events that were a travesty of real events.' In *AV* (A) Robartes is described as finding the *Speculum Anglorum et Hominorum*, written by Giraldus and printed in Cracow in 1594. After this he found an Arab tribe of Judwalis who, though they have lost their sacred book, which was attributed to Kusta ben Luka, a Christian philosopher at the Court of Harun Al-Raschid, remember much of its doctrine, and this doctrine is akin to the material in the book by Giraldus. Yeats agreed to write an exposition of the Giraldus diagrams provided Aherne wrote the Introduction and any notes he pleased. The unreality of this myth-making was acknowledged openly in *A Packet for Ezra Pound* (1929) and in *AV* (B):

> The first version of this book, *A Vision*, except the section on the twenty-eight phases, and that called 'Dove or Swan' which I repeat without change, fills me with shame. I had misinterpreted the geometry, and in my ignorance of philosophy failed to understand distinctions upon which the coherence of the whole depended, and as my wife was unwilling that her share should be known, and I to seem sole author, I

had invented an unnatural story of an Arabian traveller which I must amend and find a place for some day because I was fool enough to write half a dozen poems that are unintelligible without it. (*AV* (B) 19)

The notes (p. 537) on 'The Gift of Harun Al-Rashid' (*CP* 511) should be consulted, and (pp. 204ff.) on 'The Phases of the Moon' (*CP* 183).

5–7 *still trace . . . Magical shapes* : these are the shapes Robartes had previously traced on the Arabian sands :

> many diagrams where gyres and circles grew out of one another like strange vegetables ; and there was a large diagram at the beginning where lunar phases and zodiacal signs were mixed with various unintelligible symbols. (*AV* (A) xviii)

8 *I call to my own opposite* : cf. this passage in Yeats's essay in 'The Death of Synge' :

> I think that all happiness depends on the energy to assume the mask of some other self; that all joyous or creative life is a rebirth as something not oneself, something which has no memory and is created in a moment and perpetually renewed. We put on a grotesque or solemn painted face to hide us from the terrors of judgment, invent an imaginative Saturnalia where one forgets reality, a game like that of a child, where one loses the infinite pain of self-realization. Perhaps all the sins and energies of the world are but its flight from an infinite blinding beam. (*A* 503)

Yeats later referred to this passage ; he had explained that once he had formed the idea of the mask he became over-allegorical and his imagination became sterile, for nearly five years, and he only escaped by mocking his own thought (in *The Player Queen*). He also quoted an earlier comment on the mask :

> If we cannot imagine ourselves as different from what we are, and try to assume that second self, we cannot impose a discipline upon ourselves though we may accept one from others. Active virtue, as distinguished from the passive acceptance of a code, is therefore theatrical, consciously dramatic, the wearing of a mask. . . . (*M* 334)

In the poem we need to read to the end before the full significance of the phrase 'call to my own opposite' can be understood : it is expanded in the final speech of *Ille*: 'I call to the mysterious one . . .'. *Hic*, however, being objective, replies, in effect, 'Why pursue unreality ?'

12 *gentle sensitive mind* : cf. Yeats's comment in 'Anima Hominis' that he began to believe that

> our culture, with its doctrine of sincerity and self-realization, made us gentle and passive, and that the Middle Ages and the Renaissance were right to found theirs upon the imitation of Christ or of some classic hero. Saint Francis and Caesar Borgia made themselves overmastering, creative persons by turning from the mirror to meditation upon a mask. (*M* 333)

This is *Ille's* rejoinder : that there is a lack of inspiration or rapture in contemporary work.

181 19 *Dante . . . found himself* : in a somewhat rhetorical passage in 'Anima Hominis' Yeats wrote of himself when away from others inviting a Marmorean Muse, an art where no thought nor emotion has come to him because another man thought or felt something different :

> . . . for now there must be no reaction, action only, and the world must move my heart but to the heart's discovery of itself, and I begin to dream of eyelids that do not quiver before the bayonet : all my thoughts have ease and joy, I am all virtue and confidence. When I come to put in rhyme what I have found, it will be a hard toil, but for a moment I believe I have found myself and not my anti-self. (*M* 325)

Hic's remarks on Dante finding himself reinforce his earlier comment, but provide an opportunity for *Ille* to develop the idea of the anti-self.

20 *that hollow face* : this line is probably owed to a memory of a sentence by Simeon Solomon (1840–1905), an English painter and draughtsman. Cf. 'Anima Hominis' :

> Some thirty years ago I read a prose allegory by Simeon Solomon, long out of print and unprocurable, and remember or seem to remember a sentence, 'a hollow image of fulfilled desire.' All happy art seems to me that hollow image, but when its lineaments express also the poverty or the exasperation that set its maker to the work, we call it tragic art. Keats

but gave us his dream of luxury; but while reading Dante we never long escape the conflict, partly because the verses are at moments a mirror of his history, and yet more because that history is so clear and simple that it has the quality of art. I am no Dante scholar, and I but read him in Shadwell or in Dante Rossetti, but I am always persuaded that he celebrated the most pure lady poet ever sung and the Divine Justice, not merely because death took that lady and Florence banished her singer, but because he had to struggle in his own heart with his unjust anger and his lust; while, unlike those of the great poets who are at peace with the world and at war with themselves, he fought a double war. 'Always,' says Boccaccio, 'both in youth and maturity he found room among his virtues for lechery'; or as Matthew Arnold preferred to change the phrase, 'his conduct was exceeding irregular.' Guido Cavalcanti, as Rossetti translates him, finds 'too much baseness' in his friend:

> And still thy speech of me, heartfelt and kind,
> Hath made me treasure up thy poetry;
> But now I dare not, for thy abject life,
> Make manifest that I approve thy rhymes.

And when Dante meets Beatrice in Eden, does she not reproach him because, when she had taken her presence away, he followed, in spite of warning dreams, false images, and now, to save him in his own despite, she has 'visited . . . the Portals of the Dead,' and chosen Virgil for his courier? While Gino da Pistoia complains that in his *Commedia* his 'lovely heresies . . . beat the right down and let the wrong go free':

> Therefore his vain decrees, wherein he lied,
> Must be like empty nutshells flung aside;
> Yet through the rash false witness set to grow,
> French and Italian vengeance on such pride
> May fall like Antony on Cicero.

Dante himself sings to Giovanni Guirino 'at the approach of death':

> The King, by whose rich grave his servants be
> With plenty beyond measure set to dwell,
> Ordains that I my bitter wrath dispel,
> And lift mine eyes to the great Consistory. (*M* 329–31)

23 *was the hunger* : in 'Hodos Chameliontos' Yeats wrote of personifying spirits which bring our souls to crisis :

> We have dreamed a foolish dream these many centuries in thinking that they value a life of contemplation, for they scorn that more than any possible life, unless it be but a name for the worst crisis of all. They have but one purpose, to bring their chosen man to the greatest obstacle he may confront without despair. They contrived Dante's banishment, and snatched away his Beatrice, and thrust Villon into the arms of harlots, and sent him to gather cronies at the foot of the gallows, that Dante and Villon might through passion become conjoined to their buried selves, [he wrote earlier that genius is a crisis that joins that buried self (the age-long memorial self that shapes the shell of the mollusc and the child in the womb) for certain moments to our trivial daily mind], turn all to Mask and Image, and so be phantoms in their own eyes . . . but in a few in whom we recognise supreme masters of tragedy, the whole contest is brought into the circle of their beauty. Such masters — Villon and Dante, let us say — would not, when they speak through their art, change their luck ; yet they are mirrored in all the sufferings of desire. The two halves of their nature are so completely joined that they seem to labour for their objects, and yet to desire whatever happens, being at the same instant predestinate and free, creation's very self. We gaze at such men in awe, because we gaze not at a work of art, but at the re-creation of the man through that art, the birth of a new species of man, and it may even seem that the hairs of our heads stand up, because that birth, that re-creation, is from terror. Had not Dante and Villon understood that their fate wrecked what life could not rebuild, had they lacked their Vision of Evil, had they cherished any species of optimism, they could but have found a false beauty, or some momentary instinctive beauty, and suffered no change at all, or but changed as do the wild creatures, or from Devil well to Devil sick, and so round the clock. (*A* 272–3)

26 *Lapo and Guido* : Lapo degli Uberti was said to have been the son of Farinata degli Uberti (the Ghibelline leader of Florence) and father of Fazio degli Uberti, the author of *Dittamondo*, which is thought, according to H. F. Cary, Dante's translator, to approach the *Divina Commedia* in the energy of its style. Guido Cavalcanti (*c.* 1230–1300) was an Italian poet. Yeats may have associated Lapo

and Guido because of a note in Cary's translation of Dante which
he was fond of reading, despite his remark that he was no Dante
scholar and but read him in Shadwell or Dante Rossetti. This note
ran :

> I perceive that some have known the excellence of the ver-
> nacular tongue, namely Guido Lapo. I [Cary] suspect Dante
> here means his two friends Cavalcanti and Uberti ; though this
> has hitherto been taken for the name of one person.

But Lapo Gianni (*c.* 1270–1330) was, like Cavalcanti, also Dante's
friend and contemporary, and he may have been the Lapo intended
by Yeats. See Nicola Zingarelli, 'La Vita, tempe e le opere di
Dante', *Storia Letteraria d'Italia* (Milan 1931) pp. 189, 197, 607 for
discussion of Lapo degli Uberti, and pp. 92, 107, 197, 200, 205, 209,
225, 313, 586, for discussion of Lapo Gianni.

29   *a Bedouin's horse-hair roof* : cf. Shelley's *Queen Mab* :

> Behold yon sterile spot,
> Where now the wandering Arab's tent
> Flaps in the desert blast.

There is a childhood memory which may have recurred to Yeats
which he recounts in 'Reveries over Childhood and Youth' :

> . . . an old white-haired man, who had written volumes of
> easy, too-honeyed verse, and run through his money and gone
> clean out of his mind . . . was known to live in one room
> with a nail in the middle of the ceiling from which innumerable
> cords were stretched to other nails in the walls. In this way
> he kept up the illusion that he was living under canvas in some
> Arabian desert. (*A* 84)

The image of the Arab and his tent recurs in 'Coole Park and
Ballylee, 1931' (*CP* 275).

30   *From doored and windowed cliff* : and the 'stony face' of line 29
may have been suggested by Petra.

33–7   *his lecherous life . . . the most exalted lady* : cf. the passage
quoted above in note on line 20

45   *the fly in marmalade* : a phrase Yeats attributed to Landor, but
in 'The Tragic Generation' he describes Verlaine as using it in a

conversation in Paris in 1895 or 1896 :

> He asked me, speaking in English, if I knew Paris well, and added, pointing to his leg, that it had scorched his leg, for he knew it 'well, too well', and 'lived in it like a fly in a pot of marmalade.' (*A* 341)

182 46 *the rhetorician* : in 'Anima Hominis' Yeats wrote that 'Unlike the rhetoricians, who get a confident voice from remembering the crowd they have won or may win, we [the poets] sing amid our uncertainty'. (*M* 331)

47 *the sentimentalist himself* : in 'Anima Hominis' he also put the view that the sentimentalists are

> practical men who believe in money, in position, in a marriage bell, and whose understanding of happiness is to be so busy whether at work or at play, that all is forgotten but the momentary aim. They find their pleasure in a cup that is filled from Lethe's wharf, and for the awakening, for the vision, for the revelation of reality, tradition offers us a different word — ecstasy. (*M* 331)

48 *a vision of reality* : Yeats wrote that no artist he had read of or known had been a sentimentalist : 'The other self, the anti-self or the antithetical self, as one may choose to name it, comes but to those who are no longer deceived, whose passion is reality.'

51 *dissipation and despair* : Yeats wrote of Johnson and Dowson in 'Anima Hominis' in words which suggest he had them in mind as he wrote these lines :

> Johnson and Dowson, friends of my youth, were dissipated men, the one a drunkard, the other a drunkard and mad about women, and yet they had the gravity of men who had found life out and were awakening from the dream. (*M* 331)

53 *Keats* : *Hic*'s argument is opposed by *Ille*'s interpretation in lines 25–33, of Keats's personality, which can be glossed by Yeats's comment in 'Anima Hominis' :

> I imagine Keats to have been born with that thirst for luxury common to so many at the outsetting of the Romantic Movement, and not able, like wealthy Beckford, to slake it with beautiful and strange objects. It drove him to imaginary

delights ; ignorant, poor, and in poor health, and not perfectly well-bred, he knew himself driven from tangible luxury ;
meeting Shelley he was resentful and suspicious because he,
as Leigh Hunt recalls, 'being a little too sensitive on the score
of his origin, felt inclined to see in every man of birth his
natural enemy.' (*M* 329)

A PRAYER ON GOING INTO MY HOUSE   **183**

This poem was written in 1918, and first appeared in the *Little
Review* (Oct. 1918).

1   *this tower and cottage* : Thoor Ballylee, the Norman tower which
Yeats had bought on or before 17 June 1917 : there were two
cottages adjoining it which were converted. See M. Hanley, *Thoor
Ballylee — Home of William Butler Yeats* (1965) and Sheelah Kirby,
The Yeats Country (1962).

3   *No table or chair or stool* : local craftsmen made heavy beds,
chairs and tables from a local elm tree.

5   *for portions of the year* : refers to the plan Yeats and his wife had
formed of living at Ballylee in the summer months

10–11   *Sinbad the sailor's brought a painted chest,*
       Or image, from beyond the Loadstone Mountain : Henn (*TLT*
263) traces the image to the edition *Sinbad the Sailor and other stories
from the Arabian Nights* which was illustrated by Dulac and quotes a
relevant passage :

'Tell me', I said, 'what is the history of the mountain ?'
'It is black, steep and inaccessible,' he replied. 'On its
summit is a dome of brass, supported by ten pillars of brass ;
and on the dome is a brazen horseman, mounted on a brazen
horse, bearing in his hand a spear of brass, and on his breast
a plate of lead, engraven with mystic signs. Sirs, while that
horseman sits upon his horse, the spell of the loadstone spares
no ship in the surrounding seas, for without iron no ship is
built.'

12   *limb of the Devil* : expression in common use in Ireland

16   *the Red Sea bottom* : cf. the letter to Michael Yeats's school-master, quoted by Hone (*WBY* 420)

183   THE PHASES OF THE MOON

This poem was written in 1918 and first appeared in *WSC*. Yeats's note in *CP*, dated 1922, reads :

> Years ago I wrote three stories in which occur the names of Michael Robartes and Owen Aherne. I now consider that I used the actual names of two friends, and that one of these friends, Michael Robartes, has but lately returned from Meso-potamia, where he has partly found and partly thought out much philosophy. I consider that Aherne and Robartes, men to whose namesakes I had attributed a turbulent life or death, have quarrelled with me. They take their place in a phantas-magoria in which I endeavour to explain my philosophy of life and death. To some extent I wrote these poems as a text for exposition.

This poem deals with one of the central ideas later used in *AV* and in a similar manner to 'Ego Dominus Tuus' (*CP* 180).

2   *He and his friend* : the fanciful introduction to *AV* (A) xx–xxi, supposedly by Aherne, refers to the poem :

> On a walking tour in Connaught we passed Thoor Ballylee where Mr Yeats had settled for the summer, and words were spoken between us slightly resembling those in 'The Phases of the Moon,' and I noticed that as his friendship with me grew closer his animosity against Mr Yeats revived.

184   9   *an otter* : probably based on an early memory of the place, cf. 'an otter hurried away under a gray boulder' (*M* 23)

10   *bridge , . . that shadow is the tower* : a bridge crossed the river which flows past the tower

12   *He* : Yeats

13   *Mere images* : refers to lines 14–18

15   *Milton's Platonist* : an allusion to an illustration by Samuel Palmer (1805–81), water-colour landscape painter and etcher, in

The Shorter Poems of John Milton (1889) entitled 'The Lonely Tower'
which illustrated Milton's *Il Penseroso*, l. 86, 'Some high lonely
tower'. This description accompanied the illustration :

> Here poetic loneliness has been attempted : not the loneliness
> of a desert, but a secluded spot in a genial pastoral country,
> enriched also by antique relics such as the so-called druidic
> stones upon the distant hill. The constellation of the 'Bear'
> may help to explain that the building is the tower of *Il Penseroso*.
> Two shepherds watching their flocks speak together of the
> mysterious light above them.

There is a waning crescent moon in the illustration which connects
with the poem's title — phases of the moon.

16 *Shelley's visionary price* : it is possible Shelley drew upon Milton's
imagery in these lines of *Il Penseroso* :

> Or let my lamp, at midnight hour,
> Be seen in some high lonely tower,
> Where I may oft outwatch the *Bear*,
> With thrice great *Hermes*, or unsphere
> The spirit of *Plato*, to unfold
> What worlds, or what vast regions hold
> The immortal mind that hath forsook
> Her mansion in the fleshly nook ; . . .

Milton's 'lamp at midnight hour' seen 'in some high tower' is
echoed in Shelley's lines in 'Prince Athanase' :

> The Balearic fisher, driven from shore,
> Hanging upon the peaked wave afar,
> Then saw their lamp from Laian's turret gleam,
> Piercing the stormy darkness, like a star, . . .

Milton's reference to the Bear is paralleled by Shelley's 'Bright
Arcturus through your pines is glowing'. Both poets allude to
Plato. Milton seeks to 'unsphere / The spirit of Plato' to discover
what world or regions hold the immortal mind, and Shelley's old
man comforts Prince Athanase with the recollection of 'Plato's
words of light' where Agathon and Diotima seemed 'From death
and dark forgetfulness released'.

Yeats wrote of his mind giving itself

> to gregarious Shelley's dream of a young man, his hair
> blanched with sorrow, studying philosophy in some lonely

tower, or of his old man, master of all human knowledge, hidden from human sight in some shell-strewn cavern on the Mediterranean shore. (*A* 171)

In the copy of Shelley's *Political Works*, which Katharine Tynan gave Yeats in January 1888, p. 510 was turned down opposite the lines which introduce the tower in 'Prince Athanase':

> His soul had wedded wisdom, and her dower
> Is love and justice, clothed in which she sate
> Apart from men, as in a lonely tower,
> Pitying the tumult of their dark estate—

The 'Visionary Prince', like Yeats himself in youth,

> . . . as with toil and travel,
> Had grown quite weak and gray before his time.

In 'Discoveries' Yeats remarked that 'there are many who are not moved as they would be by that solitary light burning in the tower of Prince Athanase, because it has not entered into men's prayers nor lighted any through the sacred dark of religious contemplation' (*E & I* 294).

26–27   . . . *that extravagant style*
         He had learnt from Pater:
a reference to the decorative and involved prose Yeats wrote in the 'nineties, perhaps particularly that of *TSR*.

28   *Said I was dead*: in the story 'Rose Alchemica' (*M* 267 ff.). His end is also alluded to in 'The Tables of the Law' (*M* 293 ff.)

29   *the changes of the moon*: may be traced to Yeats's interest in Chaucer. In 1910 he was 'deep in Chaucer' and extremely interested in 'the eight and twenty mansiouns / That longen to the moon' of *The Frankelyn's Tayle* (lines 1115 ff.)

31   *Twenty-and-eight the phases of the moon*: these are discussed in *AV* (B) 105–84. See also the diagram from *AV* (B) 81, reproduced on p. 540.

32   *The full*: Phase fifteen, complete subjectivity, a phase of complete beauty

the moon's dark : Phase one, a supernatural incarnation, complete objectively, 'Body absorbed in its supernatural environment'. See *AV* (B) 105 and 183–4.

and all the crescents : Phases Two to Eight, Phases Eight to Fourteen, Phases Sixteen to Twenty-two, Twenty-two to Twenty-seven. See the diagram (p. 540).

33 *but six-and-twenty* : see lines 33, 34. Phase one and Phase **185** fifteen are not phases of human life.

36 *the first crescent to the half* : Phases two to eight. See *AV* (B) 105–16. The 'Bodies of Fate' given to these are 'None except monotony', 'Interest', 'Search', 'Natural Law', 'Humanity', 'Adventure that excites the individuality' and 'The Beginning of Strength'.

39 *the moon is rounding* : Phases nine to fourteen. See *AV* (B) 116–37. After Phase eight the 'Bodies of Fate' are 'enforced'.

45 *Athene takes Achilles* : cf. Homer, *Iliad*, XXII, 330 ; or I, 197. Yeats used the image in *The Resurrection* when he wrote 'When the goddess came to Achilles in the battle she did not interfere with his soul, she took him by his yellow hair'. (*C Pl* 587)

46 *Hector is in the dust, Nietzsche is born* : the twelfth phase of *AV* (B) is that of the hero, the man who overcomes himself. 'Solitude has been born at last, though solitude invaded and hard to defend' (*AV* (B) 126–9).

48 *twice born, twice buried* : the full moon is the fifteenth phase : therefore the thirteenth and fourteenth phases must occur first of all, and are subsequently described.

50 *the soul at war* : in *AV* the examples given of the thirteenth phase are Baudelaire, Beardsley and Ernest Dowson. It was the only phase 'where entire sensuality is possible, that is to say, sensuality without the intermixture of any other element' (*AV* (B) 129). The phase is one of emotional morbidity ; there is a

preoccupation with metaphors, symbols and images through which whatever is most morbid or strange is defined.

53 *the frenzy of the fourteenth moon* : the examples of the fourteenth phase given in *AV* are Keats, Giorgione and many beautiful women. In this phase responsibility is dropped. Helen is one of the beautiful women (and perhaps Maud Gonne also) of the phase ; she is imagined as elaborating a delicate personal discipline, and, while seeming an image of softness and quiet she 'draws perpetually upon glass with a diamond' (*AV* (B) 132). Perhaps it is because she desires so little and gives so little that men die and murder in her service. In the poetry of Keats, Yeats wrote, there is, though little sexual passion, an exaggerated sensuousness that compels us to remember the pepper on the tongue as though that were his symbol.

> Thought is disappearing into image ; and in Keats, in some ways a perfect type, intellectual curiosity is at its weakest ; there is scarcely an image, where his poetry is at its best, whose subjectivity has not been heightened by its use in many great poets, painters, sculptors, artificers. (*AV* (B) 134)

58 *becomes an image* : the description of this phase is given in *AV* :

> The being has selected, moulded and remoulded, narrowed its circle of living, been more and more the artist, grown more and more 'distinguished' in all preference. Now contemplation and desire, united into one, inhabit a world where every beloved image has bodily form, and every bodily form is loved. This love knows nothing of desire, for desire implies effort, and though there is still separation from the loved object, love accepts the separation as necessary to its own existence. *Fate* is known for the boundary that gives our *Destiny* its form, and — as we can desire nothing outside that form — as an expression of our freedom. Chance and Choice have become interchangeable without losing their identity. As all effort has ceased, all thought has become image, because no thought could exist if it were not carried towards its own extinction, amid fear or in contemplation ; and every image is separate from every other, for if image were linked to image, the soul would awake from its immovable trance. All that the being has experienced as thought is visible to its eyes as a whole, and in this way it perceives, not as they are to others, but according

to its own perception, all orders of existence. Its own body possesses the greatest possible beauty, being indeed that body which the soul will permanently inhabit, when all its phases have been repeated according to the number allotted : that which we call the clarified or Celestial Body. Where the being has lived out of phase, seeking to live through *antithetical* phases as though they had been *primary*, there is now terror of solitude, its forced, painful and slow acceptance, and a life haunted by terrible dreams. Even for the most perfect, there is a time of pain, a passage through a vision, where evil reveals itself in its final meaning. In this passage Christ, it is said, mourned over the length of time and the unworthiness of man's lot to man, whereas his forerunner mourned and his successor will mourn over the shortness of time and the unworthiness of man to his lot ; but this cannot yet be understood. (*AV* (B) 135–7)

85 *the man within* : Yeats   186

87 *the crumbling of the moon* : the next phase after the fifteenth is one which finds within itself an aimless excitement, and the examples given of it in *AV* are William Blake, Rabelais, Aretino, Paracelsus and some beautiful women. The description in *AV* is lively :

Capable of nothing but an incapable idealism (for it has no thought but in myth, or in defence of myth), it must, because it sees one side as all white, see the other side all black ; what but a dragon could dream of thwarting a St George ? In men of the phase there will commonly be both natures, for to be true to phase is a ceaseless struggle. At one moment they are full of hate — Blake writes of 'Flemish and Venetian demons' and of some picture of his own destroyed 'by some vile spell of Stoddart's' — and their hate is always close to madness ; and at the next they produce the comedy of Aretino and of Rabelais or the mythology of Blake, and discover symbolism to express the overflowing and bursting of the mind. There is always an element of frenzy, and almost always a delight in certain glowing or shining images of concentrated force ; in the smith's forge ; in the heart ; in the human form in its most vigorous development ; in the solar disc ; in some symbolical representation of the sexual organs ; for the being must brag of its triumph over its own incoherence.

Since Phase 8 the man has more and more judged what is

right in relation to time : a right action, or a right motive, has been one that he thought possible or desirable to think or do eternally ; his soul would 'come into possession of itself for ever in one single moment' ; but now he begins once more to judge an action or motive in relation to space. A right action or motive must soon be right for any other man in similar circumstance. Hitherto an action, or motive, has been right precisely because it is exactly right for one person only, though for that person always. After the change, the belief in the soul's immortality declines, though the decline is slow, and it may only be recovered when Phase 1 is passed.

Among those who are of this phase may be great satirists, great caricaturists, but they pity the beautiful, for that is their *Mask*, and hate the ugly, for that is their *Body of Fate*, and so are unlike those of the *primary* phases, Rembrandt for instance, who pity the ugly, and sentimentalise the beautiful, or call it insipid, and turn away or secretly despise and hate it. Here too are beautiful women, whose bodies have taken upon them-selves the image of the True *Mask*, and in these there is a radiant intensity, something of 'The Burning Babe' of the Elizabethan lyric. They walk like queens, and seem to carry upon their backs a quiver of arrows, but they are gentle only to those whom they have chosen or subdued, or to the dogs that follow at their heels. Boundless in generosity, and in illusion, they will give themselves to a beggar because he resembles a re-ligious picture and be faithful all their lives, or if they take another turn and choose a dozen lovers, die convinced that none but the first or last has ever touched their lips, for they are of those whose 'virginity renews itself like the moon.' Out of phase they turn termagant, if their lover take a wrong step in a quadrille where all the figures are of their own composition and changed without notice when the fancy takes them. In-deed, perhaps if the body have great perfection, there is always something imperfect in the mind, some rejection of or inade-quacy of *Mask* : Venus out of phase chose lame Vulcan. Here also are several very ugly persons, their bodies torn and twisted by the violence of the new *primary*, but where the body has this ugliness great beauty of mind is possible. This is indeed the only *antithetical* phase where ugliness is possible, it being complementary to Phase 2, the only *primary* phase where beauty is possible.

From this phase on we meet with those who do violence, instead of those who suffer it ; and prepare for those who love some living person, and not an image of the mind, but as yet this love is hardly more than the 'fixed idea' of faithfulness. As the new love grows the sense of beauty will fade. (*AV* (B) 138–40)

THE CAT AND THE MOON **188**

This poem was written in 1917 when Yeats was staying with the Gonnes in Normandy; it first appeared in *Nine Poems* (1918).

1 *The cat*: Minnaloushe, the Gonnes' black Persian cat. See line 5. Yeats wrote in his Introduction to *The Cat and the Moon*, a play first performed in the Abbey Theatre, Dublin, in 1926, that, as the populace might alter out of recognition or deprive some philosophical thought or verse of its meaning, he had written

a little poem where a cat is disturbed by the moon, and in the changing pupils of its eyes seems to repeat the movement of the moon's changes, and allowed myself as I wrote to think of the cat as the normal man and of the moon as the opposite he seeks perpetually, or as having any meaning I have conferred upon the moon elsewhere. Doubtless, too, when the lame man takes the saint upon his back, the normal man has become one with that opposite, but I had to bear in mind that I was among dreams and proverbs, that though I might discover what had been and might be again an abstract idea, no abstract idea must be present. The spectator should come away thinking the meaning as much his own manufacture as that of the blind man and the lame man [The play deals with an old Irish tradition that a blind man and a lame man dreamed that somewhere in Ireland a well would cure them and set out to find it, the lame man on the blind man's back, the lame man symbolising the body, the blind man the soul. In *DP* Yeats later suggested that the friendship of Edward Martyn and George Moore was symbolised in the play.] had seemed mine. Perhaps some early Christian — Bardaisan had speculations about the sun and moon nobody seems to have investigated — thought as I do, saw in the changes of the moon all the cycles: the soul realising its separate being in the full moon, then, as the moon seems to approach the sun and dwindle away, all but realising its absorption in God, only to whirl away once more: the mind of a man, separating itself from the common matrix, through childish imaginations, through struggle — Vico's heroic age — to roundness, completeness, and then externalising, intellectualising, systematising, until at last it lies dead, a spider smothered in its own web : the choice offered by the sages, either with the soul from the myth to union with the source of all, the breaking of the circle, or from the myth to reflection and the circle renewed for better or worse. For better or worse according to one's life, but never progress as we understand it, never the straight line, always a necessity to break away and destroy, or to sink in and forget. (*E* 402–4)

189 THE SAINT AND THE HUNCHBACK

This poem was written in 1918, and first appeared in *WSC*. The poem epitomises two phases of *AV*, the Hunchback being of Phase twenty-six, the Saint of Phase twenty-seven.

2–5 . . . *great bitterness*
In thinking of his lost renown.
A Roman Caesar is held down
Under this hump : cf. Yeats's prose description in *AV* :

All the old abstraction, whether of morality or of belief, has now been exhausted ; but in the seemingly natural man, in Phase 26 out of phase, there is an attempt to substitute a new abstraction, a simulacrum of self-expression. Desiring emotion the man becomes the most completely solitary of all possible men, for all normal communion with his kind, that of a common study, that of an interest in work done, that of a condition of life, a code, a belief shared, has passed ; and without personality he is forced to create its artificial semblance. It is perhaps a slander of history that makes us see Nero so, for he lacked the physical deformity which is, we are told, first among this phase's inhibitions of personality. The deformity may be of any kind, great or little, for it is but symbolised in the hump that thwarts what seems the ambition of a Caesar or of an Achilles. He commits crimes, not because he wants to, or like Phase 23 out of phase because he can, but because he wants to feel certain that he can ; and he is full of malice because, finding no impulse but in his own ambition, he is made jealous by the impulse of others. He is all emphasis, and the greater that emphasis the more does he show himself incapable of emotion, the more does he display his sterility. If he live amid a theologically minded people, his greatest temptation may be to defy

God, to become a Judas, who betrays, not for thirty pieces of silver, but that he may call himself creator. (*AV* (B) 177–8)

6 *a different plan* : perhaps a reference to the twenty-eight phases of the moon in *AV*. 190

8 *I lay about me with the taws* : taws, a form of birch (cf. the lines in 'Among School Children' :

> Soldier Aristotle played the taws
> Upon the bottom of a king of kings (*CP* 244)

The meaning of the speech of the Saint is clarified in *AV* :

True to phase, he substitutes for emulation an emotion of renunciation, and for the old toil of judgment and discovery of sin, a beating upon his breast and an ecstatical crying out that he must do penance, that he is even the worst of men. He does not, like Phase 26, perceive separated lives and actions more clearly than the total life, for the total life has suddenly displayed its source. If he possess intellect he will use it but to serve perception and renunciation. His joy is to be nothing, to do nothing, to think nothing; but to permit the total life, expressed in its humanity, to flow in upon him and to express itself through his acts and thoughts. He is not identical with it, he is not absorbed in it, for if he were he would not know that he is nothing, that he no longer even possesses his own body, that he must renounce even his desire for his own salvation, and that this total life is in love with his nothingness. (*AV* (B) 180–1)

TWO SONGS OF A FOOL 190

These poems were written between July and September 1918 when Yeats and his wife were living at Ballinamantane House, near Gort, Co. Galway, which Lady Gregory had lent them. They first appeared in *WSC*.

A letter written by Yeats to his father on 17 October 1918 discussed the poem as follows :

Your last letter, however, shows the most curious of all this telepathic exchange. When it came, I said to George [Mrs W. B. Yeats] (without letting her see the date of your letter), 'When did I write my poem of the Hare?' She said 'about September 20th.' Your letter is dated Sept. 22. My memory is that I was full of my subject for some days before Sept. 20th. I send you the two poems. One line, — 'The horn's sweet note and the tooth of the hound,' may have reached you, or the hare's cry — which is to you a symbol of exultation at death. 'The horn's sweet note' might well mean that. Your poem has a fine idea, but I cannot make out whether the symbolising the joy at death by the scream of the hare is, or is not, too strained an idea . . . (*LTHS* 251)

Hone's footnote connecting it with 'The Collar-bone of a Hare' is inaccurate.

I

1 *A speckled cat* : Mrs W. B. Yeats. Cf. a similar joke 'Who can keep company with the goddess Astraea if his eyes are on the brindled cat?' (*Essays 1931–1936*, 3).

a tame hare : Iseult Gonne. The poet's paternal feeling for Iseult appeared in a letter written to Lady Gregory in 1926 :

I believe I was meant to be the father of an unruly family. I did not think that I liked little boys but I liked Shawn [Sean MacBride, Maud Gonne's son]. I am really managing Iseult very well . . . as father, but as father only, I have been a great success. (*WBY* 303)

After his marriage in September 1917 Yeats had a feeling of responsibility for Iseult Gonne. The vague premonition of danger in the first section, more cogent in the second, is like that of 'To a Young Beauty' (*CP* 157).

II

191 2 *slept on my knee* : cf. the lines in 'Solomon to Sheba'
To Solomon sang Sheba,
Planted on his knees. (*CP* 155)

191 ANOTHER SONG OF A FOOL

This poem is not dated ; it first appeared in *WSC*.

1 *butterfly* : cf. 'Tom O'Roughley' (*CP* 158) where the butterfly symbolises the wisdom of wide-ranging thought, and, for butterflies in the tower, cf. also 'Blood and the Moon', III (*CP* 269).

This poem was written in 1919 ; it first appeared in *WSC*.

Title   Michael Robartes : see headnote (p. 55) on 'The Lover tells of the Rose in his Heart' (*CP* 62)

1   *Grey rock of Cashel* : the Rock of Cashel in Co. Tipperary, Ireland, has several ecclesiastical ruins, including the chapel restored by Cormac MacCarthy in the twelfth century. (See the last line of the poem.)

2   *the cold spirits* : these spirits come from the later phases of *AV*.

9   *Constrained* : the third stanza of the poem is quoted to illustrate the adoration of force which comes with the last gyre :

A decadence will descend, by perpetual moral improvement, upon a community which may seem like some woman of New York or Paris who has renounced her rouge pot to lose her figure and grow coarse of skin and dull of brain, feeding her calves and babies somewhere upon the edge of the wilderness. The decadence of the Greco–Roman world with its violent soldiers and its mahogany dark young athletes was as great, but that suggested the bubbles of life turned into marbles, whereas what awaits us, being democratic and *primary*, may suggest bubbles in a frozen pond — mathematical Babylonian starlight.

When the new era comes bringing its stream of irrational force it will, as did Christianity, find its philosophy already impressed upon the minority who have, true to phase, turned away at the last gyre from the *Physical Primary*. And it must awake into life, not Dürer's, nor Blake's nor Milton's human form divine — nor yet Nietzsche's superman, nor Patmore's catholic, boasting 'a tongue that's dead' — the brood of the Sistine Chapel — but organic groups, *covens* of physical or intellectual kin melted out of the frozen mass. I imagine new races, as it were, seeking domination, a world resembling but for its immensity that of the Greek tribes — each with its own Daimon or ancestral hero — the brood of Leda, War and Love; history grown symbolic, the biography changed into a myth. Above all I imagine everywhere the opposites, no mere alternation between nothing and something like the Christian brute and ascetic, but true opposites, each living the other's death, dying the other's life. (*AV* (A) 213–14)

9–16 *Constrained . . . that we obey*: Yeats quoted these eight lines in 'A People's Theatre' to conclude a passage in which he examined the 'two great energies of the world', and distinguished between the arts and 'visible history, the discoveries of science, the discussions of politics'. He saw change as coming from the anti-self of visible history:

> Every new logical development of the objective energy intensifies in an exact correspondence a counter-energy. ... . Are we approaching a supreme moment of self-consciousness, the two halves of the soul separate and face to face? . . . Were it not for that other gyre turning inward in exact measure with the outward whirl of its fellow, we would fall in a generation or so under some tyranny that would cease at last to be a tyranny, so perfect our acquiescence. (*E* 258–9)

18 *A Sphinx*: 'the introspective knowledge of the mind's self-begotten unity.'

193 19 *A Buddha*: 'the outward-looking mind.' Sphinx and Buddha are 'like heraldic supporters guarding the mystery of the 15th phase', and between them the dancer combines intellect and emotion for the moment.

21 *And right between these two a girl at play*: Ellmann (*IY* 255) comments:

> The Sphinx is the intellect, gazing on both known and unknown things ; the Buddha is the heart, gazing on both loved and unloved things ; and the dancing girl, most important of all, is primarily an image of art. She dances between them because art is neither intellectual nor emotional, but a balance of these qualities.

194 56 *Homer's paragon*: Helen of Troy. Cf. 'A woman Homer sung' (*CP* 100), 'No Second Troy' (*CP* 101) and 'When Helen lived' (*CP* 124). The Helen symbol usually suggests Maud Gonne.

Some of the poems in this volume were written in 1916 but not publicly circulated until 1920. His earlier mockery — 'Romantic Ireland's dead and gone' — has vanished, and he records in these poems his clear perception of what was achieved by the Rising, by the leaders who have joined the long procession of Ireland's martyrs. The magnificent poems based on *AV*'s thought blend imaginative experience and explanation in a manner which imparts a sense of revelation. 'A Prayer for my Daughter' (*CP* 211) and 'Demon and Beast' (*CP* 209) while not as completely linked with *AV* as 'The Second Coming' (*CP* 210) are none the less illustrative of how much Yeats's life and thought interacted, how much he resembled at this period the poor man in his poem, who, having roved, loved and thought himself beloved, now 'from a glad kindness cannot take his eyes'.

MICHAEL ROBARTES AND THE DANCER   **197**

This poem was written in 1919 and first appeared in *The Dial* (Nov. 1920).

1   *He* : *He* represents Yeats's views, *She* Iseult Gonne's.

2   *this altar piece* : probably 'Saint George and the Dragon' ascribed to Bordone (*c.* 1500–71) in the National Gallery, Dublin. Henn (*LT* 249) remarks that Cosimo Tura's 'St George and the Dragon', which Yeats saw in Ferrara Cathedral in 1907, may have suggested the idea of the 'altar-piece' which the Bordone is not. Cf. 'Her Triumph' (*CP* 310).

26   *Paul Veronese* : Paolo Veronese, cognomen of Paolo Cagliari   **198** (1525–88), the last great Venetian painter, who settled in Venice in 1555.

29   *lagoon* : at Venice

32   *Michael Angelo's Sistine roof* : Yeats often visited the Sistine Chapel in Rome in 1925, and while there bought reproductions of Michelangelo's 'fabulous' ceiling. See Hone (*WBY* 367–8) and cf. line 45 under 'Ben Bulben' (*CP* 397).

33   *his 'Morning' and his 'Night'* : Yeats saw these paintings in the Medici Chapel, Florence, on his visit there in 1907.

199   SOLOMON AND THE WITCH

This poem was written in 1918, and first appeared in *MRD*.

1   *that Arab lady* : the poem is written about Yeats and Mrs Yeats ; it deals with the possible annihilation of time through a perfect union of lovers. The cockerel thinks that eternity has returned (cf. 'The miracle that gave them such a death' in 'Ribh at the Tomb of Baile and Aillinn' *CP* (327)). It has not, but the lovers try again. The poem is one where meaning is cumulative ; it becomes clearer as the illustrations are developed.

4   *Solomon* : Yeats

6   *Who* : Solomon

9   '*A cockerel . . .*' : Wilson (*YI* 280–1), identifies it as the Hermetic cock.

14   *Chance being at one with Choice* : cf. line 23, and line 58 'All Souls' Night' (*CP* 256). An early use of the two words occurs in *The Island of Statues*, 1, iii, 39 : 'all choice, and give to chance, for guiding chance'. Yeats's note on his play *Calvary* refers to Chance and Choice. He puts the words in the mouth of 'a certain old Arab' :

> I have used my bird-symbolism in these songs to increase the objective loneliness of Christ by contrasting it with a loneliness, opposite in kind, that unlike His can be, whether joyous or sorrowful, sufficient to itself. I have surrounded Him with the images of those He cannot save, not only with the birds, who

have served neither God nor Caesar, and await for none or for a different saviour, but with Lazarus and Judas and the Roman soldiers for whom He has died in vain. 'Christ,' writes Robartes, 'only pitied those whose suffering is rooted in death, in poverty, or in sickness, or in sin, in some shape of the common lot, and he came especially to the poor who are most subject to exterior vicissitude.' I have therefore represented in Lazarus and Judas types of that intellectual despair that lay beyond His sympathy, while in the Roman soldiers I suggest a form of objectivity that lay beyond His help. Robartes said in one of the conversations recorded by Aherne : 'I heard much of *Three Songs of Joy*, written by a certain old Arab, which owing to the circumstances of their origin were considered as proofs of great sanctity. He held the faith of Kusta ben Luki, but did not live with any of the two or three wandering companies of Judwalis. He lived in the town of Hâyel as servant to a rich Arab merchant. He himself had been a rich merchant of Aneyza and had been several times to India. On his return from one of these journeys he had found his house in possession of an enemy and was himself driven from Aneyza by the Wahâbies on some charge, I think of impiety, and it was then he made his first song of joy. A few years later his wife and child were murdered by robbers in the desert, and after certain weeks, during which it was thought that he must die of grief, his face cleared and his step grew firm and he made his second song. He gave away all his goods and became a servant in Hâyel, and a year or two later, believing that his death was near, he made his third song of joy. He lived, however, for several months, and when I met him had the use of all his faculties. I asked him about the 'Three Songs', for I knew that even on his deathbed, as became the votary of a small contentious sect, he would delight in exposition. I said, (though I knew from his songs themselves, that this was not his thought, but I wanted his explanation in his own words) : "You have rejoiced that the Will of God should be done even though you and yours must suffer." He answered with some emotion : "Oh, no, Kusta ben Luki has taught us to divide all things into Chance and Choice ; one can think about the world and about man, or anything else until all has vanished but these two things, for they are indeed the first cause of the animate and inanimate world. They exist in God, for if they did not He would not have freedom, He would be bound by His own Choice. In God alone, indeed, can they be united, yet each be perfect and without limit or hindrance. If I should throw from the dice-box there would be but six possible sides on each of the dice, but when God throws He uses dice that have all numbers and sides. Some worship His Choice ; that is easy ; to know that He has willed for some unknown purpose all that happens is pleasant ; but I have spent my life in worshipping His Chance, and that moment when I understand the immensity of His Chance is the moment when I am nearest Him. Because it is very difficult and because I have put my understanding into three songs I am famous among my people."' (*Four Plays for Dancers*, 1921)

15 *the brigand apple* : that Eve ate, which brought Death into the world and all our woe

17–18 *He that crowed out eternity*
         Thought to have crowed it in : cf. lines 28–9. The world ends or time comes to a stop when a perfect union takes place.

19 *spider's eye* : Henn (*LT* 57) remarks on the complicated nature of the image, alluding to the familiar aspect of the spider, the female destroying the mate after copulation, to Donne's 'spider love that *transubstantiates* all' in 'Twicknam Garden', to the Jacobean use of dried spiders for poison, to the steeping of the spider of jealousy in a man's drink. He adds that Yeats would have known the Arachne in Doré's *Illustrations to Dante* and Blake's 'Black and White Spiders'. He suggests that the image also comes from natural history, the large eye of the spider containing refracting and magnifying lenses which 'gives superbly the capacity of lovers to discover, reflect, enlarge each other's shortcomings'.

200 AN IMAGE FROM A PAST LIFE

This poem was written in September 1919 and first appeared in *N* (6 Nov. 1920). F. F. Farag (*YCE* 43) points out that Tagore's 'In the Dusky Path of a Dream' which Yeats included in the *Oxford Book of Modern Verse 1892–1935*, is a source for the poem's theme. Tagore begins his poem 'In the dusky path of a dream I went to seek the love who was mine in a former life.'

1 *He* : represents Yeats

5 *that scream* : associated with moments of insight or revelation or recollection. Cf. the last line with the scream of Juno's peacock. See note on line 32, 'Meditations in Time of Civil War' III (*CP* 228) and the 'miraculous strange bird' of 'Her Triumph' (*CP* 310).

7 *Image* : see the conclusion to Yeats's note on the poem, quoted below, line 42

8 *She* : represents Mrs Yeats

14 *its lesson* : that happiness is not unalloyed, that other women   **201**
have been loved by the poet

22 *A sweetheart* : this stanza reverts to the romantic languorous language of the early love poetry written to Maud Gonne and 'Diana Vernon', the exception being the adjective arrogant; 'distress', 'loveliness', 'tress', 'starry eddies' and 'paleness' echoing the early poems.

42 *the hovering thing* : the last paragraph of Yeats's note on the poem (here quoted in full) explains this as an 'Over Shadower or Ideal Form' :

Robartes writes to Aherne under the date May 12th, 1917. 'I found among the Judwalis much biographical detail, probably legendary, about Kusta-ben-Luki. He saw occasionally during sleep a woman's face and later on found in a Persian painting a face resembling, though not identical with the dream-face, which was he considered that of a woman loved in another life. Presently he met & loved a beautiful woman whose face also resembled, without being identical, that of his dream. Later on he made a long journey to purchase the painting which was, he said, the better likeness, and found on his return that his mistress had left him in a fit of jealousy.' In a dialogue and in letters, Robartes gives a classification and analysis of dreams which explain the survival of this story among the followers of Kusta-ben-Luki. They distinguished between the memory of concrete images and the abstract memory, and affirm that no concrete dream-image is ever from our memory. This is not only true they say of dreams, but of those visions seen between sleeping and waking. This doctrine at first found me incredulous, for I thought it contradicted by my experience and by all I have read, not however a very great amount, in books of psychology and of psycho-analysis. Did I not frequently dream of some friend, or relation, or that I was at school? I found, however, when I studied my dreams, as I was directed in a dialogue, that the image seen was never really that of a friend, or relation, or my old school, though it might very closely resemble it. A substitution had taken place, often a very strange one, though I forgot this if I did not notice it at once on waking. The name of some friend, or the conceptions 'my father' and 'at school,' are a part of the abstract memory and therefore of the dream life, but the image of my father, or my friend, or my old school, being a part of the personal concrete memory appeared neither in sleep nor in visions between sleep and waking. I found sometimes that my father, or my friend, had been represented in sleep by a stool or a chair, and I concluded that it was the entire absence of my personal concrete memory that enabled me to accept such images without surprise. Was it not perhaps this very absence that constituted sleep? Would I perhaps awake if a single concrete image from my memory came before me? Even these images — stool, chair, etc. were never any particular stool, chair, etc. that I had known. Were these images, however, from the buried memory? had they floated up from the subconscious? had I seen them perhaps a long time ago and forgotten having done so? Even if that were so, the exclusion of the conscious memory was a new, perhaps important truth; but Robartes denied their source even in the subconscious. It seems a corroboration that though I often see between sleep and waking elaborate landscape, I have never seen one that seemed a possible representation of any place I have ever lived near from childhood up. Robartes traces these substitute images to different sources. Those that come in sleep are (1) from the state immediately preceding our birth; (2) from the *Spiritus Mundi* — that is to say, from a general storehouse of images which have ceased to be a property of any personality or spirit. Those that come between sleeping and waking are, he says, re-shaped by what he calls the 'automatic faculty' which can create pattern, balance, etc. from the impressions made upon the senses, not of ourselves, but of others bound to us by certain emotional links though perhaps entire strangers, and preserved in a kind of impersonal mirror, often simply called the 'record,' which takes much the same place in his system [as] the lower strata of the astral light does among the disciples of

Elephas Levi. This does not exhaust the contents of dreams for we have to account also for certain sentences, for certain ideas which are not concrete images and yet do not arise from our personal memory, but at the moment I have merely to account for certain images that affect passion or affection. Robartes writes to Aherne in a letter dated May 15th, 1917 : 'No lover, no husband has ever met in dreams the true image of wife or mistress. She who has perhaps filled his whole life with joy or disquiet cannot enter there. Her image can fill every moment of his waking life but only its counterfeit comes to him in sleep ; and he who classifies these counterfeits will find that just in so far as they become concrete, sensuous, they are distinct individuals ; never types but individuals. They are the forms of those whom he has loved in some past earthly life, chosen from *Spiritus Mundi* by the subconscious will, and through them, for they are not always hollow shades, the dead at whiles outface a living rival.' They are the forms of Over Shadowers as they are called. All violent passion has to be expiated or atoned, by one in life, by one in the state between life and life, because, as the Judwalis believe, there is always deceit or cruelty ; but it is only in sleep that we can see these forms of those who as spirits may influence all our waking thought. Souls that are once linked by emotion never cease till the last drop of that emotion is exhausted — call it desire, hate or what you will — to affect one another, remaining always as it were in contact. Those whose passions are unatoned seldom love living man or woman but only those loved long ago, of whom the living man or woman is but a brief symbol forgotten when some phase of some atonement is finished ; but because in general the form does not pass into the memory, it is the moral being of the dead that is symbolised. Under certain circumstances, which are precisely described, the form indirectly, and not necessarily from dreams, enters the living memory ; the subconscious will, as in Kusta-ben-Luki in the story, selects among pictures, or other ideal representations, some form that resembles what was once the physical body of the Over Shadower, and this ideal form becomes to the living man an obsession, continually perplexing and frustrating natural instinct. It is therefore only after full atonement or expiation, perhaps after many lives, that a natural deep satisfying love becomes possible, and this love, in all subjective natures, must precede the Beatific Vision.

When I wrote An Image from a Past Life, I had merely

begun my study of the various papers upon the subject, but I do not think I misstated Robartes' thought in permitting the woman and not the man to see the Over Shadower or Ideal Form, whichever it was. No mind's contents are necessarily shut off from another, and in moments of excitement images pass from one mind to another with extraordinary ease, perhaps most easily from that portion of the mind which for the time being is outside consciousness. I use the word 'pass' because it is familiar, not because I believe any movement in space to be necessary. The second mind sees what the first has already seen, that is all. (*MRD*)

202 UNDER SATURN

This poem was written in November 1919 and first appeared in *The Dial* (Nov. 1920).

2 *lost love* : for Maud Gonne who consumed his youth

4 *the wisdom that you brought* : perhaps a reference to Mrs Yeats's share in *AV*

5 *the comfort* : in October 1919 Yeats and his wife leased a house in Broad Street, Oxford, and he gave up the rooms in Woburn Buildings which he had rented for twenty years. They did not buy their house in Merrion Square, Dublin, until February 1922.

7 *an old cross Pollexfen* : William Pollexfen, Yeats's maternal grandfather. See note (p. 119) on '*Introductory Rhymes*' (*CP* 113) and 'In Memory of Alfred Pollexfen' (*CP* 175).

8 *a Middleton* : one of Yeats's maternal relatives

9 *a red-haired Yeats* : the Reverend William Butler Yeats, Yeats's grandfather, the 'old country scholar' of 'Introductory Rhymes' (*CP* 113).

202 EASTER 1916

The manuscript of this poem is dated 25 September 1916. Yeats wrote it when he was staying with Maud Gonne MacBride at

Calvados; it first appeared in *Easter, 1916* (1916) an edition of twenty-five copies 'privately printed by Clement Shorter for distribution among his friends' and subsequently in the *New Statesman* (23 Oct. 1920).

This poem, which V. K. Menon, *The Development of William Butler Yeats*, 48, has called a palinode to 'September 1913' (*CP* 120) gives Yeats's reaction to the Easter Rising in Dublin. The Irish Republic was proclaimed on 24 April and the centre of Dublin occupied by the Republicans. They were the Irish Volunteers of the Irish Republican Brotherhood, probably about seven hundred in all. They held out until 29 April. From 3 to 12 May fifteen of the leaders were executed after a series of courts martial. A letter Yeats wrote to Lady Gregory on 11 May shows his sorrow:

My dear Lady Gregory, The Dublin tragedy has been a great sorrow and anxiety. Cosgrave, who I saw a few months ago in connection with the Municipal Gallery project and found our best supporter, has got many years' imprisonment and to-day I see that an old friend Henry Dixon [according to Wade's note, this was Thomas Dickson, the Henry Dixon who took part in the Rising having been released from prison in June 1917, but Edward Malins, *Yeats and the Easter Rising*, 13, has not been able to discover his name among those of the prisoners released at that time] — unless there are two of the name — who began with me the whole work of the literary movement has been shot in a barrack yard without trial of any kind. I have little doubt there have been many miscarriages of justice. The wife of a Belgian Minister of War told me a few days ago that three British officers had told her that the command of the British army in France should be made over to the French generals, and that French generals have told her that they await with great anxiety the result of the coming German attack on the English lines because of the incompetence of the English Higher Command as a whole. Haig however they believed in — he was recommended by the French for the post. I see therefore no reason to believe that the delicate instrument of Justice is being worked with precision in Dublin. I am trying to write a poem on the men executed — 'terrible beauty has been born again.' If the English Conservative party had made a declaration that they did not intend to rescind the Home Rule Bill there would have been no Rebellion. I had no idea that any public event could so deeply move me — and I am very despondent about the future. At the moment I feel that all the work of years has been overturned, all the bringing together of classes, all the freeing of Irish literature and criticism from politics. Maud Gonne reminds me that she saw the ruined houses about O'Connell Street and the wounded and dying lying about the streets, in the first few days of the war. I perfectly remember the vision and my making light of it and saying that if a true vision at all it could only have a symbolised meaning. This is the only letter I have had from her since she knew of the Rebellion. I have sent her the papers every day. I do not yet know what she feels about her husband's death. Her letter was written before she heard of it. Her main thought seems to be 'tragic dignity has returned to Ireland.' She had been told by two members of the Irish Party that 'Home Rule was betrayed.' She thinks now that the sacrifice has made it safe. She is coming to London if she can get a passport, but I doubt her getting one. Indeed I shall be glad if she does not come yet — it is better for her to go on nursing the French wounded till the trials are over. How strange that old Count Plunkett and his wife and his three sons should all be drawn into the net.

I sent on to you yesterday the proof sheets I had finished and fastened up at the start of the Rebellion. I sent a letter with them giving an explanation of what I want you to do. I have been able to do little work lately and that chiefly on *Player Queen* which always needs new touches in its one bad place — first half of second act. Yours W. B. Yeats. (*L* 612–14)

1 *them* : the revolutionaries

4 *eighteenth-century houses* : many Dublin houses were built of granite from the hills, others of limestone from the plains.

203 12 *the club* : probably the Arts Club, of which Yeats was a member. A good description of it (and of Yeats eating two dinners there in one evening) is given in P. L. Dickinson, *The Dublin of Yesterday* (1929), 54.

17 *That woman's days* : Constance Gore-Booth (1868–1927), who married Count Casimir Markievicz. She is described in 'On a Political Prisoner' (*CP* 206) and 'In Memory of Eva Gore-Booth and Con Markiewicz' (*CP* 263). She took part in the Rising ; her

sentence of death was commuted to penal servitude for life and she was later released.

Yeats first met the Gore-Booth sisters in 1894. He stayed at Lissadell, their late-Georgian grey granite house that looks out over Sligo Bay, and, as he wrote to his sister Lily, enjoyed himself greatly :

> They are delightful people. . . . All the while I was at Lissadell I was busy telling stories — old Irish stories — first to one then another and then telling them over again to the sick Miss Gore upstairs. Miss Eva Gore-Booth shows some promise as a writer of verse. Her work is very formless as yet but it is full of very telling little phrases. Lissadell is an exceedingly impressive house inside with a great sitting room as high as a church and all things in good taste. . . . But outside it is grey, square and bare yet set amid delightful grounds. (*L* 239–40)

There is a biography by Sean O'Faolain. See also *IP* 40–3, but the best and fullest accounts of Constance's life are given in Anne Marreco, *The Rebel Countess* (1967) and Jacqueline Van Voris, *Constance de Markievicz in the Cause of Ireland* (1968).

23 *she rode to harriers* : cf. 'On a Political Prisoner' (*CP* 206)

24 *This man* : Patrick Pearse (1879–1916), the founder of St Enda's School for Boys at Rathfarnham, Co. Dublin, was Commandant-General and President of the provisional government in Easter week, and surrendered in the Post Office. He was a member of the Irish Bar, an orator, and had published poetry and prose in Gaelic and English.

26 *This other* : Thomas MacDonagh (1878–1916), a poet, dramatist (his play *When the Dawn is Come* was staged in the Abbey in 1908) and critic whose *Literature in Ireland* was a discerning piece of criticism. He taught English Literature in University College, Dublin. Yeats wrote of him in *Estrangement*:

> Met MacDonagh[1] yesterday — a man with some literary faculty which will probably come to nothing through lack of culture and encouragement. He had just written an article for

[1] Executed in 1916.

the *Leader*, and spoke much as I do myself of the destructive-
ness of journalism here in Ireland, and was apologetic about his
article. He is managing a school on Irish and Gaelic League
principles but says he is losing faith in the League. Its writers
are infecting Irish not only with the English idiom but with the
habits of thought of current Irish journalism, a most un-Celtic
thing. 'The League', he said, 'is killing Celtic civilisation.'
I told him that Synge about ten years ago foretold this in an
article in the *Academy*. He thought the National Movement
practically dead, that the language would be revived but without all that he loved it for. In England this man would have
become remarkable in some way, here he is being crushed by
the mechanical logic and commonplace eloquence which give
power to the most empty mind, because, being 'something
other than human life', they have no use for distinguished
feeling or individual thought. I mean that within his own
mind this mechanical thought is crushing as with an iron roller
all that is organic. (*A* 488)

31   *This other man* : Major John MacBride, Maud Gonne's husband, who had fought against England in the Boer War

33   *most bitter wrong* : probably a reference to the break-up of
MacBride's marriage in 1905

34   *some who are near my heart* : Maud Gonne, and perhaps Iseult
and possibly even Sean MacBride

204   43   *a stone* : hearts enchanted to a stone were Yeats's symbol for
those who had devoted themselves to a cause without thought of
life or love. The stone was a symbol of how politics had affected,
in particular, Maud Gonne. To be choked with hate was the chief
of all evil chances, Yeats wrote in 'A Prayer for my Daughter'
(*CP* 211) with Maud Gonne in mind. Constance Markievicz's mind
had become 'a bitter, an abstract thing' in 'On a Political Prisoner'
(*CP* 206).

58   *a stone of the heart* : the sacrifice referred to is, in particular,
Maud Gonne's long service given to revolutionary ideals. Cf.
E & I 314.

67   *needless death* : the Rising was not generally welcome at first in
Ireland. Edward Malins, *Yeats and the Easter Rising* (1965) 3, has

remarked that there were 100,000 Irishmen serving with the forces of the Crown, and adds, p. 10, that 'within a month the British Government had lit a flame of martyrdom around the leaders, that turned the revolt into a triumphal success, providing an emotional stimulus for the birth of a nation no less than that of Paul Revere and the Minutemen of Lexington'.

68 *may keep faith* : the Bill for Home Rule for Ireland, passed in 1913, had been shelved at the beginning of the 1914–18 war.

76 *Connolly* : James Connolly (1870–1916), a trade union organiser **205** and author of *Labour in Irish History*, founded the *Irish Worker* and Workers' Republic, organised the Citizen Army, and was Commandant in the Post Office during the rising. He was wounded and was brought to his execution in a wheel-chair. He is said to have remarked : 'You can shoot me if you like but I am dying for my country.'

SIXTEEN DEAD MEN   **205**

This poem was written on 17 December 1916 or 1917, and first appeared in *The Dial* (Nov. 1920).

Title Sixteen : Yeats has presumably added Sir Roger Casement (1864–1916) to the fifteen leaders shot in 1916. He was a member of the British Consular Service from 1875 to 1913 ; he joined the Sinn Fein movement in 1914, went to Germany, returned in a submarine to Ireland and was arrested in the south-west. He was tried for high treason in London and hanged. His remains have recently been returned to Ireland.

6 *the boiling pot* : Yeats is emphasising the effect that the executions had had, of making those shot into martyrs.

12 *MacDonagh's* : see note (p. 227) on line 26, 'Easter 1916' (*CP* 202)

16 *Lord Edward and Wolfe Tone* : Lord Edward Fitzgerald and Wolfe Tone, unsuccessful leaders of previous rebellions. See note on 'September 1913' (*CP* 120).

206 THE ROSE TREE

This poem's manuscript is dated 7 April 1917 in the Maud Gonne Manuscript Book. It first appeared in *The Dial* (Nov. 1920).

2 *Pearse to Connolly*: see notes on 'Easter 1916' (*CP* 202)

4 *our Rose Tree*: Ireland, but a different kind of Ireland from the Rose symbolism of the earlier poems. The Rising was a gesture by dedicated men prepared to die for their beliefs, which were based on the idea that the nation needed to be redeemed by blood. Pearse regarded the position of Ireland as one of enslavement, and thought this worse than 'Shedding blood'. See Yeats's 'Modern Ireland' *Massachusetts Review* (winter 1964), 264–5, for a description of Pearse and his belief in 'the blood sacrifice'.

17 *our own red blood*: Pearse wrote that 'Bloodshed is a cleansing and sanctifying thing', *Political Writings*, 99. He thought that it would take 'the blood of the sons of Ireland to redeem Ireland', The theme was an old one. See Georges-Denis Zimmermann, *Irish Political Street Ballads and Rebel Songs* (Geneva, 1966), 71–2. A ballad included in this study, 'Ireland's Liberty Tree', 255 [text in *Harding's Dublin Songster*, new series, 32, 757; sung to tune of 'Norah O'Neal', F. Roche, *Collection of Irish Airs*, 1, 19] seems likely to have influenced Yeats in his composition of 'The Rose Tree':

> A tree has been planted in Ireland,
>   And watered with tears of the brave;
> By our Great-grandsires it was nourished,
>   Who scorned to be held like the slaves.
> The trust they transported to their children,
>   To keep it until they were free,
> And yearly the plant has grown stronger
>   'Tis called 'Ireland's Liberty-Tree!'

> Chorus:
>   Protect then, the tree, sons of Erin,
>   Its branches from traitors keep free,
>   Though Martyrs before ye have perished
>   Neath Ireland's famed Liberty-Tree.

Its roots in the ground firmly woven,
   Unshaken by threat'ning alarm,
Its branches will wave o'er the patriot
   Who dies for his country in arms.
The eyes of the world are upon it,
   And millions beyond the blue sea
Are eagerly waiting to gather
   Beneath Ireland's Liberty-Tree.

Brave Emmet, Fitzgerald and Grattan
   Have died in defence of the tree,
While Shiel and O'Connell predicted
   That the plant would see Ireland free.
Then deem not those patriots dreamers,
   Their prophetic visions could see
That properly nourished, no power
   Could harm Ireland's Liberty-Tree.

Let each son of Erin contribute
   Whate'er in his power doth lie ;
The pure blood of Ireland's Martyrs
   Gave it strength, and it shall never die.
Then gather beneath its broad branches,
   All ye who dare strive to be free,
And Heaven will surely protect those
   Who guard Ireland's Liberty-Tree!

Zimmermann, op. cit., 85, regards Aubrey De Vere's poem 'The Little Black Rose shall be red at last' as the model for 'The Rose Tree' (it is contained in *The Sisters, Inisfail and other poems*, 293). The Liberty-Tree was a patriotic symbol deriving from the 'arbres de la liberté' which appeared in France in 1790, planted to celebrate Revolution and Liberty. They were planted earlier in America, from 1765–75, as symbols of opposition to England. In Ireland the United Irishmen took up the idea in 1792. See Zimmermann, op. cit., 41.

ON A POLITICAL PRISONER 206

This poem was written between 10 and 29 January 1919, and first appeared in *The Dial* (Nov. 1920).

1   *She* : The Countess Markievicz. See note (p. 226) on line 7
'Easter 1916' (*CP* 202). Yeats wrote to Mrs Yeats from Lucan,
Co. Dublin, in 1918 : 'I'm writing one on Con to avoid writing
one on Maud. All of them are in prison. . . .' At this time she
was in Holloway Gaol, having been condemned to life imprisonment for her part in the 1916 Rising. It was at this same time that
relations between Yeats and Maud Gonne were somewhat strained.
In December she had escaped from the nursing home in England
to which she had been transferred from prison on account of her
health. Yeats and his wife had been renting her house, 73 St
Stephen's Green, Dublin, and when she arrived in December Yeats
refused to have her in the house, as his wife was seriously ill with
the devastating influenza then prevalent. Yeats and his wife left
the house shortly afterwards. Another cause of tension between
Yeats and Maud Gonne was the treatment of women prisoners.

207   9   *a bitter, an abstract thing* : cf. 'Easter 1916' (*CP* 202) with its
'stone of the heart' and the dispraise of 'an intellectual hatred' in
'A Prayer for my Daughter' (*CP* 211).

11–12   *Blind and leader of the blind*
Drinking the foul ditch : cf. the blind man and ditch imagery
in 'A Dialogue of Self and Soul', II (*CP* 266).

13   *I saw her ride* : cf. 'Easter 1916' :
. . . young and beautiful
She rode to harriers.

Cf. *Y: M & P* 189 and note on line 16, below. Yeats retailed an
anecdote of a hunt in his broadcast of 10 April 1932 which showed
that he liked the arrogance which accompanied the beauty.

14   *Ben Bulben* : a mountain to the north of Sligo. Cf. 'Under
Ben Bulben' (*CP* 397).

16   *youth's lonely wildness* : D. J. Gordon and Ian Fletcher (*IP* 41)
have written that, for all its gracious leisure, the life of serenity
and opulence at Lissadell could not contain Constance Gore-Booth
and her sister Eva :

The eagerness with which the two girls listened to Yeats in
the bay-windowed room — great windows open to the South

— full of the apparatus of their leisure, must have been an index of their restlessness. Constance, though a famous and reckless horsewoman — Eva too rode fearlessly, but Constance was said to be the finest horsewoman in Ireland — painted, and even those early photographs of her seem to show an element of wilfullness. She always, through gesture or expression, quite deliberately isolates herself from the carefully posed and smiling group.

See also Ian Fletcher, 'Yeats and Lissadell' (*YCE* 62–77).

This poem was written in 1918 and first appeared in *MRD*.

1 *They*: Saul (*PYP* 119), suggests they were the 'crowd' of Dublin Bohemians Constance Markievicz had joined.

6 *The abounding gutter had been Helicon*: perhaps a contrast between the popular press and poetry. Yeats particularly disliked the Sinn Fein press and Arthur Griffith. He wrote, too, of Maud Gonne's activities in 'Poetry and Tradition':

> . . . gradually the political movement she was associated with, finding it hard to build up any fine lasting thing, became content to attack little persons and little things. All movements are held together more by what they hate than by what they love, for love separates and individualises and quiets, but the nobler movements, the only movements on which literature can found itself, hate great and lasting things. (*E & I* 249–50)

Helicon, a mountain in Boeotia, was sacred to the Muses: it had a fountain, Hippocrene, which rose from the ground when struck by the hoof of the horse Pegasus (cf. 'Our colt' in 'The Fascination of What's Difficult', *CP* 104) and this fountain was also sacred to the Muses. The word 'gutter' may well have been used in contrast to Helicon (standing for Hippocrene) to emphasise how far Yeats had moved from his earlier revolutionary belief that 'we must be baptized of the gutter'. But the poem may refer solely to Dublin's would-be writers, artists, etc. See note on line 1.

Truth flourishes where the student's lamp has shone: this is the symbol of 'Ego Dominus Tuus' (*CP* 180) where the lamp 'burns on beside the open book', of 'The Phases of the Moon' (*CP* 183) where 'the light proves that he is reading still'. It is the image of 'mysteriour wisdom won by toil'. See notes (pp. 195–203 and 204–211) on these poems. The 'candle and written page' of 'Meditations in Time of Civil War', II (*CP* 226) are also part of this idea.

208   9   *that have no solitude* : solitude is necessary for the pursuit of wisdom. Cf. the phrase in *AV* (B) 143, which describes Shelley returning 'again and again to these two images of solitude', the young man whose hair has grown white, the old man in the cavern. This occurs when he is 'out of phase' and has been trying to be a man of action, and dreaming of converting the world.

12   *that lamp* : this may link the Miltonic, Shelleyan, Yeatsian image of study with the magical Rosicrucian lamps which also represented a search for hidden truth and were still alight when taken from the tomb of Father Christian Rosencrux. Cf. note (pp. 141–2) on 'The Mountain Tomb' (*CP* 136) and Yeats's essay 'The Body of the Father Christian Rosencrux' (*E & I* 196–7). Yeats asserted that 'wisdom is the property of the dead' in 'Blood and the Moon', IV (*CP* 269).

208   TOWARDS BREAK OF DAY

This poem was probably written in January 1919 and first appeared in *The Dial* (Nov. 1920).

1   *the double of my dream* : the poem is a record of two dreams dreamed by the poet and his wife on the same night when they were staying at the Powerscourt Arms Hotel, Enniskerry, Co. Wicklow, in January 1919. A passage in *AV* (A) describes this kind of experience :

> When two people meditate upon the one theme, who have established a supersensual link, they will invariably in my experience no matter how many miles apart, see pass before the mind's eye complementary images, images that complete one another. One for instance may see a boat upon a still sea full of tumultuous people, and the other a boat full of motionless people upon a tumultuous sea. Even when the link is momentary and superficial this takes place, and sometimes includes within its range a considerable number of people. One, for

instance, will receive from a dream figure a ripe apple, another an unripe ; one a lighted and one an unlighted candle and so on.

On the same night a mother will dream that her child is dead or dying, the child that her mother is dead, while the father will wake in the night with a sudden inexplicable anxiety for some material treasure. I put an experience of the kind into the poem that begins—

Was it the double of my dream, . . .   (*AV* (A) 173)

5   *a waterfall* : possibly the waterfall at Glencar. Wilson (*YI* 259), regards it as an image of the *fons vitae*, the water of life, and argues that the dream indicates that the *summum bonum* of woman's spirituality is outside the scope of sexual possession.

23   *The marvellous stag* : the reference is to the stag in Malory,   **209**
Le Morte d'Arthur, III v, which appeared at the marriage feast of Arthur and Guinevere pursued by a white brachet and thirty couple of running hounds. Unterecker (*RG* 163) draws connections between the dreams : white waterfall, white stag ; water, a female symbol, stag, masculine ; his dream, naturalistic, his wife's, mythological ; his possessive, his wife's detached ; his full of 'over much' love, hers detached ; his water falls, her stag leaps. Wilson (*YI* 258–9) regards the stag image as 'the elusive spiritual beauty which a woman may discern in a man'.

DEMON AND BEAST   **209**

This poem was written on 23 November 1918 and first appeared in *The Dial* (Nov. 1920).

The poem is a description of momentary blessedness. Peter Ure, 'Yeats's "Demon and Beast",' *Irish Writing*, 31 (1955), described the poem as a war between two passions, the demon of hatred and the beast of desire, which he regarded as images of 'a state of intense selfabsorption and subjectivity'.

5   *perned in the gyre* : see note on 'Shepherd and Goatherd' (*CP* 159). To pern is to move with a circular, spinning motion. For gyres see notes on (pp. 215–16) 'The Double Vision of Michael Robartes' (*CP* 192); (pp. 239–44) 'The Second Coming' (*CP* 210); (pp. 284–92) 'Two Songs from a Play' (*CP* 239); and (pp. 435–40) 'The Gyres' (*CP* 337).

10   *Luke Wadding* : a portrait of an Irish Franciscan, born in Waterford 1588, and educated at Lisbon, who became president of the
Irish College at Salamanca. He founded the College of St Isodore
at Rome, where he died in 1657. He presented this College, of
which he was Rector for fourteen years, with 5000 books and 800
manuscripts. The portrait was painted by José Ribera, and is in
the National Gallery, Dublin.

11   *the Ormondes* : portraits of titled members of the Butler family
in the National Gallery, Dublin. Yeats was connected with this
family, see notes (pp. 115–20) on 'Introductory Rhymes' (*CP* 113).
The portraits are part of the Lane Bequest.

13   *Strafford* : Sir Thomas Wentworth, 1st Earl of Strafford (1593–
1641). He was Lord Deputy of Ireland 1632–8, and Charles I's
political adviser. His portrait is in the National Gallery, Dublin,
and is of the school of Van Dyck.

17   *the Gallery* : the National Gallery, Dublin

22   *aimless joy* : cf. note (p. 171) on 'Tom O'Roughley' (*CP* 158).
In *OTB* Yeats wrote :

> The arts are all the bridal chambers of joy. No tragedy is
> legitimate unless it leads some great character to his final joy.
> Polonius may go out wretchedly, but I can hear the dance
> music in 'Absent thee from felicity awhile', or in Hamlet's
> speech over the dead Ophelia, and what of Cleopatra's last
> farewells, Lear's rage under the lightning, Oedipus sinking
> down at the story's end into an earth 'riven' by love ? Some
> Frenchman has said that farce is the struggle against a ridiculous
> object, comedy against a movable object, tragedy against an
> immovable ; and because the will, or energy, is greatest in
> tragedy, tragedy is the more noble ; but I add that 'will or
> energy is eternal delight,' and when its limit is reached it may
> become a pure, aimless joy, though the man, the shade, still
> mourns his lost object. (*E* 448–9)

23   *the little lake* : in St Stephen's Green, Dublin. Yeats and his
wife were living in Maud Gonne MacBride's house, 73 St
Stephen's Green, when he wrote the poem.

27–8   *absurd . . . green-pated bird* : one of the many ducks on the lake

44   *barren Thebaid* : Yeats drew his knowledge of the early Christian monastic movement from two books by the Rev. J. O. Hannay (who wrote his novels under the pseudonym George A. Birmingham), *The Spirit and Origin of Christian Monasticism* (1903) and *The Wisdom of the Desert* (1904).   Hannay's Introduction to the latter, pp. 7–10, stresses the barren nature of the Thebaid.   Cf. Yeats's remark in 'Bishop Berkeley' that he remembered 'that monks in the Thebaid, or was it by the Mareotic Sea, claimed "to keep the ramparts", meaning perhaps that all men whose thoughts skimmed the "unconscious", God-abetting, affected others according to their state, that what some feel others think, what some think others do' (*E & I* 405).

45   *Mareotic Sea* : one of the five regions listed by Hannay where Egyptian monasticism flourished.   Cf. Shelley's *Witch of Atlas*. She glided down the Nile

> By Moeris and the Mareotid lakes
> Strewn with faint blooms like bridal-chamber floors

See note (p. 515) on lines 1–2 of 'Under Ben Bulben' (*CP* 397).

46   *Exultant Anthony* : St Anthony of Coma (240?–345), whose life was described in chapter iv of J. O. Hannay's *The Spirit and Origin of Christian Monasticism*.   Hannay, p. 101, stressed his enthusiasm as an element of his greatness.

47   *twice a thousand more* : a reference to the spread of monasticism. For St Anthony's influence on the Egyptian monastic movement see also A. Cooper Marsdin, *The History of the Island of the Lerins* (1913) and *The School of the Lerins* (1905).

48   *starved* : this was probably suggested by Hannay's chapter on fasting in *The Wisdom of the Desert*, 143–54.

50   *the Caesars* : there is a possible link between St Anthony's connection with the scene of his namesake's disaster.   From Mark Antony to Caesar is an easy transition of thought.   With the idea of the Caesars comes the thought of the effect of Christianity clashing

with the Empire. Christ was seen by Yeats in *PASL* as 'the antithetical self of the classic world' ; he commented that the saint 'whose life is but a round of customary duty, needs nothing the whole world does not need, and day by day he scourges in his body the Roman and Christian conquerors : Alexander and Caesar are famished in his cell' (*M* 337). Cf. notes (pp. 212–13) on 'The Saint and the Hunchback' (*CP* 189) which expresses the same thought and 'Whence had they come?' (*CP* 332) with its 'hand and lash that beat down frigid Rome'.

The Caesars had nothing but their thrones because they did not have the benefit of a check upon their power. The idea is included in 'The Tragic Generation' where 'The typical men of the classical age (I think of Commodus, with his half-animal beauty, his cruelty and his caprice) lived public lives, pursuing curiosities of appetite, and so found in Christianity, with its Thebaid and its Mareotic Sea, the needed curb' (*A* 313). This idea of the curb may have come from a memory of Hannay's assertion in *The Wisdom of the Desert*, 144, that 'the end which the hermits hoped to attain by fasting was the subjugation of the flesh'. The hermit who disdained the exercise of fasting was compared to a horse without a bridle.

The Caesars came between the ideals of Greek religion and Christianity in *AV* :

> God is now conceived of as something outside man and man's handiwork, and it follows that it must be idolatry to worship that which Phidias and Scopas made, and seeing that He is a Father in Heaven that Heaven will be found presently in the Thebaid where the world is changed into featureless clay and can be run through the fingers. (*AV* (A) 185–6)

but their thrones : another passage in *AV* contrasts Christ and Caesar, and deals with the question of Caesar becoming a king. He concludes the section :

> One thinks of Mommsen's conviction that though Caesar chose the lesser of two evils the Roman State was from his day to the end a dead thing, a mere mechanism. (*AV* (B) 244–5)

210 THE SECOND COMING

This poem was written in January 1919 ; it first appeared in *The Dial* (Nov. 1920).

The poem which prophesies the arrival of a new god takes its title from Christian doctrine. (See Kathleen Raine, 'Yeats's Debt to Blake', *Dublin Magazine* (Summer 1966), 40–2, for links between 'The Mental Traveller' and Yeats's system). It blends Christ's prediction of this second coming in Matthew xxiv and St John's description of the beast of the Apocalypse in Revelations. The location of the birthplace in Bethlehem, traditionally associated with the idea of the gentle innocence of infancy and with maternal love, adds horror to the thought of the rough beast. Yeats annotated the poem in terms of the story of the mythical Judwalis and Robartes as follows :

Robartes copied out and gave to Aherne several mathematical diagrams from the *Speculum*, squares and spheres, cones made up of revolving gyres intersecting each other at various angles, figures sometimes of great complexity. His explanation of these, obtained invariably from the followers of Kusta-ben-Luki, is founded upon a single fundamental thought. The mind, whether expressed in history or in the individual life, has a precise movement, which can be quickened or slackened but cannot be fundamentally altered, and this movement can be expressed by a mathematical form. A plant or an animal has an order of development peculiar to it, a bamboo will not develop evenly like a willow, nor a willow from joint to joint, and both have branches, that lessen and grow more light as they rise, and no characteristic of the soil can alter these things. A poor soil may indeed check or stop the movement and a rich prolong and quicken it. Mendel has shown that his sweet-peas bred long and short, white and pink varieties in certain mathematical proportions suggesting a mathematical law governing the transmission of parental characteristics. To the Judwalis, as interpreted by Michael Robartes, all living mind has likewise a fundamental mathematical movement, however adapted in plant, or animal, or man to particular circumstance ; and when you have found this movement and calculated its relations, you can foretell the entire future of that mind. A supreme religious act of their faith is to fix the attention on the mathematical form of this movement until the whole past and future of humanity, or of an individual man, shall be present to the intellect as if it were accomplished in a single moment. The intensity of the Beatific Vision when it comes depends upon the intensity of this realisation. It is possible in this way, seeing that death is itself marked upon the mathematical figure, which passes beyond it, to follow the soul into the highest heaven and the deepest hell. This doctrine is, they contend, not fatalistic because the mathematical figure is an expression of the mind's desire, and the more rapid the development of the figure the greater the freedom of the soul. The figure while the soul is in the body, or suffering from the consequences of that life, is frequently drawn as a double cone, the narrow end of each cone being in the centre of the broad end of the other.

It had its origin from a straight line which represents, now time, now emotion, now subjective life, and a plane at right angles to this line which represents, now space, now intellect, now objective life ; while it is marked out by two gyres which represent the conflict, as it were, of plane and line, by two movements, which circle about a centre because a movement outward on the plane is checked by and in turn checks a movement onward upon the line ; & the circling is always narrowing or spreading, because one movement or other is always the stronger. In other words, the human soul is always moving outward into the objective world or inward into itself ; & this movement is double because the human soul would not be conscious were it not suspended between contraries, the greater the contrast the more intense the consciousness. The man, in whom the movement inward is stronger than the movement outward, the man who sees all reflected within himself, the subjective man, reaches the narrow end of a gyre at death, for death is always, they contend, even when it seems the result of accident, preceded by an intensification of the subjective life ; and has a moment of revelation immediately after death, a revelation which they describe as his being carried into the presence of all his dead kindred, a moment whose objectivity is exactly equal to the subjectivity of death. The objective man on the other hand, whose gyre moves outward, receives at this moment the revelation, not of himself seen from within, for that is impossible to objective man, but of himself as if he were somebody else. This figure is true also of history, for the end of an age, which always receives the revelation of the character of the next age, is represented by the coming of one gyre to its place of greatest expansion and of the other to that of its greatest contraction. At the present moment the life gyre is sweeping outward, unlike that before the birth of Christ which was narrowing, and has almost reached its greatest expansion. The revelation which approaches will however take its character from the contrary movement of the interior gyre. All our scientific, democratic, fact-accumulating, heterogeneous civilisation belongs to the outward gyre and prepares not the continuance of itself but the revelation as in a lightning flash, though in a flash that will not strike only in one place, and will for a time be constantly repeated, of the civilisation that must slowly take its place. This is too simple a statement, for much detail is possible. There are certain points of stress on outer and inner gyre, a division of each, now into ten, now into twenty-eight, stages or phases. However in the exposition of this detail so far as it affects the future, Robartes had little help from the Judwalis either because they cannot grasp events outside their experience, or because certain studies seem to them unlucky. '"For a time the power" they have said to me,' (writes Robartes) '"will be with us, who are as like one another as the grains of sand, but when the revelation comes it will not come to the poor but to the great and learned and establish again for two thousand years prince & vizier. Why should we resist? Have not our wise men marked it upon the sand, and it is because of these marks, made generation after generation by the old for the young, that we are named Judwalis."'

Their name means makers of measures, or as we would say, of diagrams. (*MRD*)

1–2 . . . *widening gyre*

The falcon cannot hear the falconer : originally the falcon was a hawk (see Stallworthy (*BL* 17–18)) but these lines may derive from Dante's description of how he and Virgil reach the eighth circle of Hell seated on Geryon's back. In Cary's translation Geryon moves in wheeling gyres :

> Of ample circuit, easy thy descent . . .
> As falcon that hath long been on the wing

> But lure nor bird hath seen, while in despair
> The falconer cries 'Ah me! thou stoop'st to earth'.

Yeats's falcon also travels in gyres. And the Doré illustration to this part of *The Vision of Hell* shows Geryon emerging from the Abyss with his body shaped like the path of a gyre on a cone. The falcon represents man, present civilisation, becoming out of touch with Christ, whose birth was the revelation which marked the beginning of the two thousand years of Christianity.

211   4   *mere anarchy*: in 'The Trembling of the Veil' Yeats wrote that he had not foreseen (in the 1887–91 period) 'the growing murderousness of the world' (*A* 192) and he went on to quote 'The Second Coming'. He had 'the troubles' in Ireland in mind, no doubt, as well as the Russian Revolution.

A letter was written to George Russell (AE), probably in April 1919, in which Yeats refers to his having sent Russell (who told Iseult Gonne the Russians had only executed 400 people) certain Russian comments on the figure as well as on the figure of 13,000 which was published 'as coming from the Russian government itself'. He continued

> What I want is that Ireland be kept from giving itself (under the influence of its lunatic faculty of going against everything which it believes England to affirm) to Marxian revolution or Marxian definition of value in any form. I consider the Marxian criterion of values as in this age the spear-head of materialism and leading to inevitable murder. From that criterion follows the well-known phrase 'Can the bourgeois be innocent?' (*L* 655–6)

5   *blood-dimmed tide*: cf. 'The Gyres' (*CP* 337) 'Irrational streams of blood are staining earth'

7   *the best*: Henn (*LT* 144) suggests these lines echo Shelley's *Prometheus Unbound*, 625–8.

> The good want power, but to weep barren tears,
> The powerful goodness want : . . .

10   *the Second Coming*:   *AV* contains many passages discussing the succession of civilisations :

> Each age unwinds the threads another age had wound, and it amuses me to remember that before Phidias, and his westward

moving art, Persia fell, and that when full moon came round again, amid eastward moving thought, and brought Byzantine glory, Rome fell ; and that at the outset of our westward moving Renaissance Byzantium fell ; all things dying each other's life, living each other's death. (*AV* (A) 183)

The new era looked likely to be one of irrational force, as another passage pointed out. It is quoted in the note (pp. 215 ff.) on line 9 of 'The Double Vision of Michael Robartes' (*CP* 192) and is particularly germane.

12 *Spiritus Mundi* : 'a general storehouse of images which have ceased to be a property of any personality or spirit'. See the note (pp. 221–4) from *MRD* quoted, line 42 'An Image from a Past Life' (*CP* 200).

14 *A shape with lion body* : lines 13–17 were quoted after the following passage of *AV* :

The approaching *antithetical* influx and that particular *antithetical* dispensation for which the intellectual preparation has begun will reach its complete systematisation at that moment when, as I have already shown, the Great Year comes to its intellectual climax. Something of what I have said it must be, the myth declares, for it must reverse our era and resume past eras in itself ; what else it must be no man can say, for always at the critical moment the *Thirteenth Cone*, the sphere, the unique intervenes. (*AV* (B) 263)

The image, as Peter Ure first pointed out in *TM*, may be related to the Introduction to *The Resurrection* where Yeats wrote : 'I began to imagine, as always at my left side just out of the range of the sight, a brazen winged beast that I associated with laughing, ecstatic destruction' (*E* 393).

Yeats remarked in a footnote that the beast was 'afterwards described in my poem "The Second Coming".' Ure has pointed out (*TM* 46) that this beast probably derived from Yeats's experiences with MacGregor Mathers's symbolism and quotes Yeats's account of how Mathers gave him a cardboard symbol and he closed his eyes :

Sight came slowly, there was not that sudden miracle as if the darkness had been cut with a knife, for that miracle is mostly a woman's privilege, but there rose before me mental images that I could not control : a desert and a black Titan raising himself up by his hands from the middle of a heap of ancient ruins. Mathers explained that I had seen a being of the order of Salamanders because he had shown me their symbol. . . . (*A* 185–6)

17 *desert birds* : these have the ominous aspect of birds of prey : they pick bones bare in *Calvary*.

19 *twenty centuries* : Yeats regarded the Christian era as being of two thousand years, like the era that went before it. Cf. *AV* (B) 267.

21 *rough beast* : Henn (*LT* 145) compares the line 'What from the forest came? What beast has licked its young?' in 'Supernatural Songs' VII (*CP* 331). He comments that the possibilities of the 'rough beast' are endless and suggests that it may be founded on the quotations given above, or on a Blake illustration, or on the man-headed sphinx Sturge Moore drew for a translation of Villiers de L'Isle Adam, or on the brazen winged beasts in Charles Ricketts's illustration for Wilde's *Salome*. Cf. the mystery 'on the bestial floor' of 'The Magi' (*CP* 141). See also S. B. Bushrui, *Yeats's Verse Plays. The Revisions 1900–1910* (1965), 114, who points out that the death speech of the poet in *The King's Threshold* is linked to 'The Second Coming' with its lines :

> He needs no help that joy has lifted up
> Like some miraculous beast out of Ezekiel.

Professor A. M. Gibbs has suggested parallels between the 'rough beast' of this poem and the 'rough beast' in Shakespeare's *Lucrece*. The images of the falcon and the tide of blood were also used by Shakespeare in that poem.

211 A PRAYER FOR MY DAUGHTER

This poem was written between February and June 1919 ; it first appeared in *Poetry* (Nov. 1919).

Title my Daughter : Anne Butler Yeats was born on 26 February 1919. The poem was begun shortly after her birth and finished at Thoor Ballylee, where its scene is set.

4 *Gregory's wood* : Thoor Ballylee was near Lady Gregory's estate, Coole Park.

10   *the tower* : Yeats's tower   **212**

11   *the bridge* : it crossed the stream, which washed one wall of
the tower.

14–16   . . . *future years had come,*
          Dancing to a frenzied drum,
          Out of the murderous innocence
Cf. the foreboding of 'The Second Coming' (*CP* 210) and its
lines :

              The blood-dimmed tide is loosed, and everywhere
              The ceremony of innocence is drowned.

25   *Helen* : the earlier association of Helen and Maud Gonne is a
preparation for lines 57–64.

27   *that great Queen* : Aphrodite, Greek goddess of love, beauty
and fertility.   Hesiod told of her birth from the sea.   Her name
was supposed to be derived from Aphros, meaning foam.   Hence
she was 'fatherless'.

29   *bandy-leggèd smith* : her husband was Hephaestus, the god of fire.

32   *the Horn of Plenty* : Zeus received a cornucopia from Amalthea,
the goat that suckled him : her horns flowed with nectar and
ambrosia.   This is a folk motif, where the possessor can get anything he wants out of the magical object.

33   *In courtesy* : Yeats regarded courtesy and self-possession and
style in the arts as the result of 'a deliberate shaping of all things'.
There is an interesting passage on the role of aristocrats, countrymen and artists in this connection in 'Poetry and Tradition' (*E & I*
251–6), which is echoed in 'The Municipal Gallery Revisited'
(*CP* 368).

37   *for beauty's very self* : probably Maud Gonne is implied.

38   *a poor man* : a reference to Yeats

40   *a glad kindness* : a reference to Yeats's marriage.   Yeats wrote   **213**
to Lady Gregory shortly after his marriage : 'My wife is a perfect

wife, kind, wise and unselfish. I think you were such another young girl once. She has made my life serene and full of order' (*WBY* 307).

51 *prosper but little* : Maud Gonne returned to Ireland in December 1918. Both she and Con Markievicz were in prison afterwards. See note (p. 232) on 'On a Political Prisoner' (*CP* 206).

57 *An intellectual hatred* : Yeats wrote in a Diary in 1910 :

Women because the main event of their lives has been a giving of themselves give themselves to an opinion as if it were a stone doll . . . women should have their play with dolls finished in childhood for, if they play with ideas again it is amid hatred and malice.

In 'The Death of Synge' this appears in a different guise :

F—— is learning Gaelic. I would sooner see her in the Gaelic movement than in any Irish movement I can think of. I fear some new absorption in political opinion. Women, because the main event of their lives has been a giving themselves and giving birth, give all to an opinion as if it were some terrible stone doll . . . to women opinions become as their children or their sweethearts, and the greater their emotional capacity the more do they forget all other things. They grow cruel, as if in defence of lover or child, and all this is done for 'something other than human life'. At last the opinion is so much identified with their nature that it seems a part of their flesh becomes stone and passes out of life. . . . Women should have their play with dolls finished in childish happiness, for if they play with them again it is amid hatred and malice. (*A* 504)

59 *the loveliest woman born* : Maud Gonne, who was hinted at in the Helen symbol in the fourth stanza ; the trouble that Helen had 'from a fool' being paralleled by Aphrodite's choice of Hephaestus and Maud's choice of MacBride as husband.

60 *Plenty's horn* : see note on line 32

66 *radical innocence* : contrasting with the 'murderous innocence' of line 16?

This was written on 9 November 1914 in the Maud Gonne Manuscript Book; it first appeared in *The Dial* (Nov. 1920), with the
title 'A Mediation in Time of War' (probably a misprint), and in
N (13 Nov. 1920).

1   *one throb of the artery*:   William Blake's 'Time' is probably a
source for the poem; it is included in Blake, *Works* (1893) I, 278,
and in Yeats's selection of Blake's *Poems* of 1893:

> Everytime less than a pulsation of the artery
> Is equal in its period and value to six thousand years.
> For in this period the poet's work is done, and all the great
> Events of time start forth and are conceived in such a period,
> Within a moment; a pulsation of the artery.

An essay in *CT*, dated 1902, possibly gives an account of an
experience which has contributed to this poem:

> One day I was walking over a bit of marshy ground close to
> Inchy Wood when I felt, all of a sudden, and only for a second,
> an emotion which I said to myself was the root of Christian
> mysticism. There had swept over me a sense of weakness, of
> dependence on a great personal Being somewhere far off yet
> near at hand. No thought of mine had prepared me for this
> emotion, for I had been preoccupied with Aengus and Edain,
> and with Manannan, Son of the Sea. That night I awoke lying
> upon my back and hearing a voice speaking above me and
> saying, 'No human soul is like any other human soul, and
> therefore the love of God for any human soul is infinite, for no
> other soul can satisfy the same need in God.' A few nights
> after this I awoke to see the loveliest people I have ever seen.
> A young man and a young girl dressed in olive-green raiment,
> cut like old Greek raiment, were standing at my bedside. I
> looked at the girl and noticed that her dress was gathered about
> her neck into a kind of chain, or perhaps into some kind of stiff
> embroidery which represented ivy-leaves. But what filled me
> with wonder was the miraculous mildness of her face. There
> are no such faces now. It was beautiful as few faces are
> beautiful, but it had not, one would think, the light that is in
> desire or in hope or in fear or in speculation. It was peaceful
> like the faces of animals, or like mountain pools at evening, so
> peaceful that it was a little sad. I thought for a moment that
> she might be the beloved of Aengus, but how could that hunted,

alluring, happy, immortal wretch have a face like this? (*M* 68-9)

An essay in *PASL* deals with the same subject:

There are two realities, the terrestrial and the condition of fire.[1] All power is from the terrestrial condition, for there all opposites meet and there only is the extreme of choice possible, full freedom. And there the heterogeneous is, and evil, for evil is the strain one upon another of opposites; but in the condition of fire is all music and all rest. Between is the condition of air where images have but a borrowed life, that of memory or that reflected upon them when they symbolise colours and intensities of fire: the place of shades who are 'in the whirl of those who are fading' and who cry like those amorous shades in the Japanese play:

> That we may acquire power
> Even in our faint substance,
> We will show forth even now,
> And though it be but in a dream,
> Our form of repentance.

After so many rhythmic beats the soul must cease to desire its images, and can, as it were, close its eyes.

When all sequence comes to an end, time comes to an end, and the soul puts on the rhythmic or spiritual body or luminous body and contemplates all the events of its memory and every possible impulse in an eternal possession of itself in one single moment. That condition is alone animate, all the rest is fantasy, and from thence come all the passions and, some have held, the very heat of the body.

> Time drops in decay,
> Like a candle burnt out,
> And the mountains and woods
> Have their day, have their day.
> What one, in the rout
> Of the fire-born moods,
> Has fallen away? ['The Moods' (*CP* 62)] (*M* 356-7)

In the same essay Yeats wrote 'we perceive in a pulsation of the artery, and after slowly decline' (*M* 361). See also his reference to

[1] When writing this essay I did not see how complete must be the antithesis between man and Daimon. The repose of man is the choice of the Daimon, and the repose of the Daimon the choice of man; and what I have called man's terrestrial state the Daimon's condition of fire. I might have seen this, as it all follows from the words written by the beggar in *The Hour Glass* upon the walls of Babylon.

Villiers de l'Isle-Adam quoting Aquinas: 'Eternity is the possession of one's self, as in a single moment' (*E* 37).

TO BE CARVED ON A STONE AT THOOR BALLYLEE   214

This poem was written in 1918, probably between May and July, and first appeared in *MRD*.

2 *old mill boards*: Yeats wrote to John Quinn on 23 July 1918, from Ballylee Castle:

> We are surrounded with plans. This morning designs arrived from the drunken man of genius, Scott, for two beds. The war is improving the work for, being unable to import anything, we have bought the whole contents of an old mill — great beams and three-inch planks, and old paving stones ; and the local carpenter and mason and blacksmith are at work for us. On a great stone beside the front door will be inscribed these lines:
>
> > I, the poet, William Yeats,
> > With common sedge and broken slates,
> > And smithy work from the Gort forge,
> > Restored this tower for my wife George ;
> > And on my heirs I lay a curse
> > If they should alter for the worse,
> > From fashion or an empty mind,
> > What Raftery built and Scott designed.

Raftery is the local builder . . . (*L* 651)

3 *the Gort forge*: the tower was about four miles from the village of Gort.

4 *George*: Mrs Yeats, *née* Bertha Georgina Hyde-Lees. Yeats wrote to his father a week or two after his marriage:

> I am dictating this to my wife. I call her George to avoid Georgie which she has been called hitherto in spite of her protests. I enclose her photograph. She permits me to say that it flatters her good looks at the expense of her character. She is not so black and white, but has red-brown hair and a high colour which she sets off by wearing dark green in her clothes and earrings, etc. (*WBY* 307)

6 *ruin once again*: the tower fell into disrepair after Yeats's death. The last summer the family spent there was in 1929 : its somewhat

isolated situation made it a difficult household to manage, and the damp climate was bad for Yeats's rheumatism. The tower and the cottages have, however, recently been renovated, and the story of this is told in Mary Hanley, *Thoor Ballylee — Home of William Butler Yeats* (1965), which includes photographs of the rooms which now contain replicas of the furniture made for Yeats. See also A. Norman Jeffares, 'Poet's Tower', *Envoy*, v, 20 (July 1951).

Yeats's change of style and his maturity were probably not generally recognised until the publication of *The Tower* in 1928. This volume was a collection of poems which reflect the richness of his life: marriage, a family, senatorship of the Irish Free State, the Nobel Prize for poetry, *AV* published, the discovery of his Anglo-Irish ancestry in politics and literature. There was also the sharpened apprehension, brought by Ireland's civil war, of approaching conflagration in the world and, by approaching age, of ruin and decay. Yeats had become 'a smiling sixty-year-old public man', but with ironic memories of lost youth and love, with the tower to remind him that the glory of a family or a house can vanish, and an idealised Byzantium to set against the realities of living in a country of the young. His verse took on new eloquence, it dealt freely with many of his moods and interests: politics, philosophy, friendship, and love. He wrote of them as they affected his own imaginative life: and his imagination grew stronger as his body decayed: an idea he had seized upon in Blake when he himself was only thirty-four. He looked back on the poetry of *The Tower* in surprise at its bitterness and power, yet it also carried an antithetical view:

> When such as I cast out remorse
> So great a sweetness flows into the breast
> We must laugh and we must sing,
> We are blest by everything,
> Everything we look upon is blest.

SAILING TO BYZANTIUM   217

This poem was written in the autumn of 1926; the two typescripts (there are seventeen other MS. sheets) are dated 26 Sept. 1926. The poem first appeared in *OB*.

Title   Byzantium: Yeats's knowledge of the city was largely derived from reading W. G. Holmes, *The Age of Justinian and Theodora* (1905),

Mrs A. Strong, *Apotheosis and the After Life* (1915), and O. M. Dalton, *Byzantine Art and Archaeology* (1911). He also read Gibbon's *Decline and Fall of the Roman Empire*, *The Cambridge Mediaeval History*, the *Encyclopaedia Britannica* and other general reference works. R. Ellmann has suggested that J. B. Bury the historian, who was Latin master for a time at the High School, Dublin, may first have interested Yeats in Byzantium.

The symbolic meaning of Byzantium can be discovered in Yeats's prose ('Sailing to Byzantium' and 'Byzantium' (*CP* 280) are complementary poems in many respects). In *AV* it was described at about the end of the first Christian millennium. Byzantium is a holy city, as the capital of eastern Christianity, and as the place where God exists because of the life after death Yeats imagines existing there. His description of Byzantium in *AV* shows that he valued the position of the artist in the city :

> I think if I could be given a month of Antiquity and leave to spend it where I chose, I would spend it in Byzantium, a little before Justinian opened St Sophia and closed the Academy of Plato. I think I could find in some little wine-shop some philosophical worker in mosaic who could answer all my questions, the supernatural descending nearer to him than to Plotinus even, for the pride of his delicate skill would make what was an instrument of power to princes and clerics, a murderous madness in the mob, show as a lovely flexible presence like that of a perfect human body.
>
> I think that in early Byzantium, maybe never before or since in recorded history, religious, aesthetic and practical life were one, that architect and artificers — though not, it may be, poets, for language had been the instrument of controversy and must have grown abstract — spoke to the multitude and the few alike. The painter, the mosaic worker, the worker in gold and silver, the illuminator of sacred books, were almost impersonal, almost perhaps without the consciousness of individual design, absorbed in their subject-matter and that the vision of a whole people. They could copy out of old gospel books those pictures that seemed as sacred as the text, and yet weave all into a vast design, the work of many that seemed the work of one, that made building, picture, pattern, metal-work of rail and lamp, seem but a single image ; and this vision, this proclamation of their invisible master, had the Greek nobility, Satan always the still half-divine Serpent, never the horned

scarecrow of the didactic Middle Ages.

The ascetic, called in Alexandria 'God's Athlete', has taken the place of those Greek athletes whose statues have been melted or broken up or stand deserted in the midst of corn-fields, but all about him is an incredible splendour like that which we see pass under our closed eyelids as we lie between sleep and waking, no representation of a living world but the dream of a somnambulist. Even the drilled pupil of the eye, when the drill is in the hand of some Byzantine worker in ivory, undergoes a somnambulistic change, for its deep shadow among the faint lines of the tablet, its mechanical circle, where all else is rhythmical and flowing, give to Saint or Angel a look of some great bird staring at miracle. Could any visionary of those days, passing through the Church named with so un-theological a grace 'The Holy Wisdom', can even a visionary of today wandering among the mosaics at Ravenne or in Sicily, fail to recognise some one image seen under his closed eyelids? To me it seems that He, who among the first Christian communities was little but a ghostly exorcist, had in His assent to a full Divinity made possible this sinking-in upon a supernatural splendour, these walls with their little glimmering cubes of blue and green and gold. (*AV* (B) 279–80) [Ravenne is presumably a misprint for Ravenna.]

In November 1924 Yeats had been ill, out of breath, with high blood pressure, and Mrs Yeats brought him to Sicily where he saw the Byzantine mosaics of Monreale and the Capella Palatina at Palermo. This visit may have revived his memories of the mosaics at Ravenna. He had visited the church of S. Apollinare Nuovo in 1907 and seen its frieze of holy virgins and martyrs. See Gwendolen Murphy, *The Modern Poet*, 153. On 5 September 1926 Yeats wrote to Mrs Shakespear : 'There have been constant interruptions — the last time I wrote a poem about Byzantium to recover my spirits.'

The best comment on the poem, however, is contained in a paragraph Yeats wrote for a broadcast of his poems (B.B.C. Belfast, 8 Sept. 1931) which was not included in the final version of the script :

Now I am trying to write about the state of my soul, for it is right for an old man to make his soul, and some of my thoughts upon that subject I have put into a poem called 'Sailing to Byzantium'. When Irishmen were illuminating the

Book of Kells [in the eighth century] and making the jewelled croziers in the National Museum, Byzantium was the centre of European civilisation and the source of its spiritual philosophy, so I symbolise the search for the spiritual life by a journey to that city.

1 *That country* : Ireland. A version in MS. has 'This is no country for old men'.

old men : Yeats was thinking of the disadvantages of age in relation to love. Early versions of the poem in MSS. show him balancing the young Christ with the ageless pagan gods of Ireland. Then the contrast between the sensual and the soul is developed. There are three discussions of the MSS. versions of the poem : Jeffares, 'The Byzantine Poems of W. B. Yeats', *RES* xxii, 44–52 ; Curtis Bradford, 'Yeats's Byzantine Poems', *PMLA* lxxv, 1, 110–25 and J. Stallworthy, *BL*, 87–136. The last gives the fullest account of the development of the poems.

2 *In one another's arms* : Stallworthy quotes a first and illegible draft in which the poet writes that the time has come to speak of his loves 'in my first youth' and contains these lines 'For many loves have I taken off my clothes' . . . 'but now I will take off my body/That they might be enfolded in that for which they (had longed)'. In 'that', as Stallworthy points out, is probably the poet's soul.

4 *The salmon-falls* : probably a memory of the salmon at Galway (one of the first things Yeats wanted his wife to see when she came to Ireland after their marriage) waiting to leap their way upstream to spawn. George Moore has described Yeats's delight in the Galway salmon weir :

> There were other idlers besides ourselves enjoying the fair weather, and their arms resting on the stone bridge they looked into the brown rippling water, remarking from time to time that the river was very low (no one had ever seen it lower), and that the fish would have to wait a long time before there was sufficient water for them to get up the weir. But my eyes could not distinguish a fish until Yeats told me to look straight down through the brown water, and I saw one, and immediately afterwards a second and a third and a fourth. And then the

great shoal, hundreds, thousands of salmon, each fish keeping its place in the current, a slight movement of the tail being sufficient.

But if they should get tired of waiting and return to the sea?

Yeats is a bit of a naturalist, and in an indolent mood it was pleasant to listen to him telling of the habits of the salmon which only feeds in the sea. If the fishermen were to get a rise it would be because the fish were tired of waiting and snapped at anything to relieve the tedium of existence. . . . (*Salve* 102) 1947 edition

There was also a famous salmon-leap at Leixlip, Co. Dublin, and Cuchulain was famous for his 'salmon-leap', his vigour being compared to that of a bird. In an old Irish song the sensual music of summer is stressed through images of birds and fish :

> The blackbird sings a loud strain
> To him the live world is a heritage
> The sad angry sea is fallen asleep
> The speckled salmon leaps.
>> (*Old Irish Songs of Summer and Winter*, trans. and
>> ed. Kuno Meyer, 1903)

mackerel-crowded seas : probably founded on memories of the mackerel 'coming in' to harbours and shores in the west of Ireland

5 *Fish, flesh, or fowl, commend* : Henn (*LT* 225) compares 'The Dancer at Cruachan and Cro-Patrick' (*CF* 304).

10 *a tattered coat* : cf. 'A Coat' (*CP* 142) and the fourth stanza of 'Among School Children' (*CP* 242) with its 'old scarecrow'

11 *Soul clap its hands and sing* : L. A. G. Strong, *Personal Record*, 32, suggested this image derived from Blake's vision of his brother's soul clapping its hands as it flew up to heaven.

14 *Monuments of its own magnificence* : D. J. Greene suggests that this may derive from Samuel Johnson, *Journey to the Western Islands of Scotland.*

17 *sages standing in God's holy fire* : they are the martyrs in the frieze at S. Apollinare Nuovo at Ravenna. See introductory note to poem

above. In a letter to Mrs Shakespear written on 27 October 1927 Yeats told her that

> When I went to London I had just finished a poem in which I appeal to the saints in 'the holy fire' to send death on their ecstasy. In London I went to a medium called Cooper and on the way called to my people for their especial wisdom. The medium gave me 'a book test' — Third book from R bottom shelf — study — Page 48 or 84. I have only this morning looked it up. The book was the complete Dante designs of Blake. It was not numbered by pages but by plates. Plate 84 is Dante entering the Holy Fire (Purgatorio–Canto 27). Plate 48 is 'The serpent attacking Vanni Fucci.' When I looked this up in Dante I found that at the serpent's sting Vanni Fucci is burnt to ashes and then recreated from the ashes and that this symbolises 'the temporal Fire.' The medium is the most stupid I know and certainly the knowledge was not in my head. After this and all that has gone before I must capitulate if the dark mind lets me. Certainly we suck always at the eternal dugs. How well too it puts my own mood between spiritual excitement, and the sexual torture and the knowledge that they are somehow inseparable! It is the eyes of the Earthly Beatrice — she has not yet put on her divinity — that makes Dante risk the fire 'like a child that is offered an apple.' Immediately after comes the Earthly Paradise and the Heavenly Beatrice. (L 730–1)

19 *perne in a gyre* : see notes (pp. 176 and 235) on 'Shepherd and Goatherd' (*CP* 159) and 'Demon and Beast' (*CP* 209).

218 23–4 *gather me*
        Into the artifice of eternity
Cf. a passage in *The Tables of the Law* where Yeats wrote :

> Just as poets and painters and musicians labour at their works, building them with lawless and lawful things alike, so long as they embody the beauty that is beyond the grave, these children of the Holy Spirit labour at their moments with eyes upon the shining substance on which Time has heaped the refuse of creation ; for the world only exists to be a tale in the ears of coming generations ; and terror and content, birth and death, love and hatred, and the fruit of the Tree, are but instruments for that supreme art which is to win us from life and gather us into eternity like doves into their dove-cots. (M 300–1)

Yeats regarded Justinian's reign in Byzantium as a great age of building in which Byzantine art was perfected. A building like St Sophia preceded the climax of that civilisation. Cf. *AV* (B) 281–2.

27 *such a form as Grecian goldsmiths make* : Yeats's note read : 'I have read somewhere that in the Emperor's palace at Byzantium was a tree made of gold and silver, and artificial birds that sang' (*OB*).

Much speculation has occurred on the subject of the bird's origin. (See Jeffares, 'Yeats's Byzantine Poems and the Critics', *English Studies in Africa*, 1962). T. L. Dume, for instance, in 'Yeats's Golden Tree and Birds in the Byzantine Poems', *Modern Language Notes*, LXVII, 404–7, suggests passages in *The Cambridge Mediaeval History* and Gibbon's *Decline and Fall* as likely sources. Other sources, including the Byzantine, are discussed by Jeffares, 'The Byzantine Poems of W. B. Yeats', *RES*, XXII, 85 (Jan. 1946) 48–9. But the best suggestion put forward is that of E. Schanzer, ' "Sailing to Byzantium", Keats and Anderson', *English Studies*, XLI (Dec. 1960), who thinks Yeats remembered being read, as a child, Hans Andersen's tale 'The Emperor's Nightingale' (probably from the edition which had for cover an illustration of the Emperor and his court listening to the artificial bird). In about 1910 Yeats was told by Eric Maclagan of the well-known passage in Liutprand of Cremona describing the singing bird in the Imperial Palace (referred to in *RES* article cited above).

29–31   . . . *Emperor awake ;*
            Or set upon a golden bough to sing
            To lords and ladies :

see note above.

32 *past, or passing, or to come* : this line echoes the first stanza's 'Whatever is begotten, born, and dies'. Stallworthy (*BL* 99) sees an echo here of Blake's lines:

                Hear the voice of the Bard,
                Who present, past and future, sees ;

The manuscript of the last section is dated 7 Oct. 1925 ; the poem first appeared in *The New Republic* (29 June 1927).

3–6   *Decrepit age . . . imagination . . . the impossible* : Yeats was sixty : he had been ill the previous autumn. The seeming contradiction of having more energy as he grew older is possibly an echo of Blake whom he had quoted in a letter to the *Boston Pilot* in 1889 :

> I have been very near the gates of Death, and have returned very weak, and an old man feeble and tottering, but not in spirits and life, not in the real man, the imagination which liveth for ever. In that I am stronger as this foolish body decays. (*Letters to the New Island*, 42)

8   *rod and fly* : cf. note (pp. 179–80) on 'The Fisherman' (*CP* 166)

9   *Ben Bulben* : mountain to the north of Sligo

11   *bid the Muse go pack* : cf. the final lines of 'Vacillation', VIII (*CP* 285)

12   *Plato and Plotinus* : Yeats wrote in 1928 :

> When I wrote the lines about Plato and Plotinus I forgot that it is something in our own eyes that makes us see them as all transcendence. Has not Plotinus written : 'Let every soul recall, then, at the outset the truth that soul is the author of all living things, that it has breathed the life into them all, whatever is nourished by earth and sea, all the creatures of the air, the divine stars in the sky ; it is the maker of the sun ; itself formed and ordered this vast heaven and conducts all that rhythmic motion — and it is a principle distinct from all these to which it gives law and movement and life, and it must of necessity be more honourable than they, for they gather or dissolve as soul brings them life or abandons them, but soul, since it never can abandon itself, is of eternal being?' (*CP* 533)

Yeats read Plotinus in Stephen MacKenna's translation. A letter from MacKenna to E. R. Debenham, written in October 1926, records MacKenna's pleasure at this :

> Another little encouragement : Yeats, a friend tells me, came to London, glided into a bookshop and dreamily asked for the new Plotinus, began to read there and then, and read on and on till he'd finished (he has really a colossal brain, you know),

and now is preaching Plotinus to all his train of attendant
duchesses : he told my friend he intended to give the winter
in Dublin to Plotinus. (*Journal and Letters of Stephen MacKenna*,
ed. E. R. Dodds, 235)

MacKenna's five-volume translation of Plotinus appeared from
1917 to 1930. Mrs Yeats knew Taylor's translations of *Plotinus*
(*AV* (B) 19). An edition of his *Select Works of Plotinus* was published in 1895 ; his *Five Books of Plotinus* had been published in
1794. Yeats began to read Plato at Lionel Johnson's instigation in
the 'nineties ; he may have used Thomas Taylor's *Plato* (5 vols.,
1804).

17   *the battlements* : on Yeats's tower. He compared winding stairs   **219**
of towers 'to the philosophical gyres' (*CP* 535).

25–9   *Mrs. French* : Yeats wrote that

The persons mentioned are associated by legend, story and
tradition with the neighbourhood of Thoor Ballylee or Ballylee
Castle, where the poem was written. Mrs. French lived at
Peterswell in the eighteenth century and was related to Sir
Jonah Barrington who described the incident of the ears and
the trouble that came of it. The peasant beauty and the blind
poet are Mary Hynes and Raftery, and the incident of the man
drowned in Cloone Bog is recorded in my *Celtic Twilight*.
Hanrahan's pursuit of the phantom hare and hounds is from my
Stories of Red Hanrahan. The ghosts have been seen at their
game of dice in what is now my bedroom, and the old bankrupt man lived about a hundred years ago. According to one
legend he could only leave the Castle upon a Sunday because
of his creditors, and according to another he hid in the secret
passage. (*CP* 532)

Sir Jonah Barrington (whom Mrs Yeats was reading aloud to
her husband at this time) gave a racy description of the incident :

Some relics of feudal arrogance set the neighbours and their
adherents together by the ears. My grandfather (Mr French
of County Galway) had conceived a contempt for, and anti-
pathy to, a sturdy *half* mounted gentleman, one Mr Dennis
Bodkin, who entertained an equal aversion to the arrogance of
my grandfather, and took every possible opportunity of
irritating and opposing him. My grandmother, an O'Brien,
was high and proud, steady and sensible, but disposed to be

rather violent at times, in her contempt and animosities, and entirely agreed with her husband in his detestation of Mr Dennis Bodkin.

On some occasion or other Mr Dennis had chagrined the squire and his lady most outrageously. A large company dined at my grandfather's and my grandmother concluded her abuse of Dennis with an energetic expression that could not have been literally meant, in these words — 'I wish the fellow's ears were cut off! That might quiet him.'

This passed over as usual, the subject was changed, and all went on comfortably till supper ; at which time when everybody was in full glee, the old butler, Ned Regan, who had drunk enough, came in — joy was in his eye — and whispering something to his mistress which she did not comprehend, he put a large snuff box into her hand. Fancying it was some whim of her old domestic, she opened the box and shook out its contents ; when, lo! a considerable portion of a pair of bloody ears dropped on the table! Nothing could surpass the horror and surprise of the company. Old Ned exclaimed, — 'Sure, my lady, you wished that Dennis Bodkin's ears were cut off ; so I told old Gahagan (the gamekeeper) and he took a few boys with him, and brought back Dennis Bodkin's ears — and there they are : and I hope you are plazed, my lady!'

The scene may be imagined ; but its results had like to have been of a more serious nature. The sportsman and the boys were ordered to get off as fast as they could; but my grandfather and grandmother were held to heavy bail, and were tried at the ensuing assizes at Galway. The evidence of the entire company, however, united in proving that my grandmother never had an idea of any such order, and that it was a mistake on the part of the servants. They were, of course, acquitted. The sportsman never reappeared in the county till after the death of Dennis Bodkin, which took place three years subsequently.

The quotation is from Sir Jonah Barrington, *Personal Sketches of his own Time*, 26–7. Torchiana (*Y & GI* 301) points out that Mrs Yeats read to the poet from *Recollections of Jonah Barrington* (Dublin, n.d.). There are slight differences in the text of the latter, pp. 30–1.

33–4 *Some few remembered still when I was young*
     A peasant girl commended by a song : Yeats wrote in the essay 'Dust hath closed Helen's eye' of Mary Hynes and how her memory was 'still a wonder by turf fires'. She died at Ballylee sixty years

before he wrote the essay (in 1900). He heard of her from an old man, an old woman, an old weaver, another old man, two other old women and an old man who lived at Duras.

35   *that rocky place* : the area is one of limestone.

36   *the colour of her face* : Yeats's essay quotes the old man's description 'her skin was like dribbled snow . . . and she had blushes in her cheeks', and the old woman's : 'The sun and the moon never shone on anybody so handsome, and her skin was so white that it looked blue, and she had two little blushes on her cheeks.'

37   *the greater joy* : Yeats commented in his essay :

These poor countrymen and countrywomen in their beliefs, and in their emotions, are many years nearer to that old Greek world, that set beauty beside the fountain of things, than are our men of learning. She 'had seen too much of the world' ; but these old men and women, when they tell of her, blame another and not her, and though they can be hard, they grow gentle as the old men of Troy grew gentle when Helen passed by on the walls. (*M* 28)

39   *Farmers jostled at the fair* : fair in the sense of market. 'And if she went to any kind of meeting, they would all be killing one another for a sight of her, and there was a great many in love with her, but she died young' (*M* 27).

40   *the song* : Raftery's (see note on line 49) capacity for praise and blame was famous.

41–8   *And certain men, being maddened by those rhymes,*   **220**
        Or else by toasting her a score of times,
        Rose from the table and declared it right
        To test their fancy by their sight
        But they mistook the brightness of the moon
        For the prosaic light of day—
        Music had driven their wits astray—
        And one was drowned in the great bog of Cloone

Yeats was told by the old weaver that Mary Hynes was the most beautiful thing ever made:

My mother used to tell me about her, for she'd be at every hurling, and wherever she was she was dressed in white. As many as eleven men asked her in marriage in one day, but she wouldn't have any of them. There was a lot of men up beyond Kilbecanty one night sitting together drinking, and talking of her, and one of them got up and set out to go to Ballylee and see her ; but Cloone Bog was open then, and when he came to it he fell into the water, and they found him dead there in the morning. (*M* 25–6)

49   *the man who made the song* : Anthony Raftery (1784–1834), the blind Gaelic poet.   The Irish poem he wrote on Mary Hynes runs thus :

Going to Mass by the will of God,
The day came wet and the wind rose ;
I met Mary Hynes at the cross of Kiltartan,
And I fell in love with her then and there.

I spoke to her kind and mannerly,
As by report was her own way ;
And she said, 'Raftery, my mind is easy,
You may come to-day to Ballylee.'

When I heard her offer I did not linger,
When her talk went to my heart my heart rose.
We had only to go across the three fields,
We had daylight with us to Ballylee.

The table was laid with glasses and a quart measure,
She had fair hair, and she sitting beside me ;
And she said, 'Drink, Raftery, and a hundred welcomes,
There is a strong cellar in Ballylee.'

O star of light and O sun in harvest,
O amber hair, O my share of the world,
Will you come with me upon Sunday
Till we agree together before all the people ?

I would not grudge you a song every Sunday evening,
Punch on the table, or wine if you would drink it,
But, O King of Glory, dry the roads before me,
Till I find the way to Ballylee.

There is sweet air on the side of the hill
When you are looking down upon Ballylee ;

When you are walking in the valley picking nuts and black-
berries,
There is music of the birds in it and music of the Sidhe.

What is the worth of greatness till you have the light
Of the flower of the branch that is by your side?
There is no god to deny it or to try and hide it,
She is the sun in the heavens who wounded my heart.

There was no part of Ireland I did not travel,
From the rivers to the tops of the mountains,
To the edge of Lough Greine whose mouth is hidden,
And I saw no beauty but was behind hers.

Her hair was shining, and her brows were shining too ;
Her face was like herself, her mouth pleasant and sweet.
She is the pride, and I give her the branch,
She is the shining flower of Ballylee.

It is Mary Hynes, the calm and easy woman,
Has beauty in her mind and in her face,
If a hundred clerks were gathered together,
They could not write down a half of her ways. (*M* 24–5)

52 *Homer* : the connection is a double one. Raftery was blind
and so was Homer. Each sang of a woman who was spoken of in
the same way by the old : Yeats wrote in *BS* of his speaking to old
men and women who remembered Mary Hynes and 'they spoke
of her as the old men upon the wall of Troy spoke of Helen, nor
did man and woman differ in their praise' (*A* 561).

53 *Helen* : Mary Hynes resembled her, see note on line 37. And
Helen is a symbol for Maud Gonne. This leads to the poet himself
in lines 56 ff.

54 *moon and sunlight* : the same imagery is used in 'The Man who
dreamed of Faeryland' (*CP* 49).

57 *Hanrahan* : a character invented by Yeats, who appeared in
Stories of Red Hanrahan (1904) and *TSR* (1907). Lines 57–73 retell
the story entitled 'Red Hanrahan' (*M* 213 ff.) in an abbreviated
form, leaving out mention of the fact that Hanrahan was journeying

to his sweetheart Mary Lavelle when he met the old man in the old bawn. Giles W. L. Telfer, *Yeats's Idea of the Gael* (1965), 92, points out that Hanrahan has a striking resemblance to Eoghan Ruadh O Suileabhan (1748–84).

65   *an old bawn* : this may be a misprint for 'barn' which is used in the prose story 'Red Hanrahan' (*M* 213). Bawn means a fortified enclosure and is used in Spenser's *State of Ireland*, 502b, which Yeats read. It can also mean a cattle ford, a term in use in the south of Ireland. (See *Notes and Queries*, 1, ii, 60.)

69   *a pack of hounds* : a similar trick is described in Lady Gregory, *Gods and Fighting Men*, 109, where several animals and men are created consecutively, who follow each other up into the sky.

221   76   *he was so harried* : this is the old bankrupt man who lived about a hundred years before : see Yeats's note, line 25.

79   *his dog's day* : the phrase may derive from *Hamlet* :

> Let Hercules himself do what he may
> The cat will mew and dog will have his day

or, more likely, from York Powell's translation of Paul Fort :

> And they came back so merrily : all at the dawn of day ;
> A–singing all so merrily : '*The dog must have his day!*'
>
> (*E & I* 498)

85   *whose images* : the ghosts are referred to in Yeats's comments. See note on line 25.

90   *half-mounted man* : the bankrupt owner. The phrase probably derives from Sir Jonah Barrington, op. cit.

91   *rambling celebrant* : Raftery, who was an itinerant poet

92   *the red man* : Red Hanrahan

94   *so fine an ear* : Dennis Bodkin who lost both his ears in Barrington's anecdote

222   105   *Old lecher* : Hanrahan, who turns into Yeats in the next stanza

112 *labyrinth*: cf. 'the labyrinth that he has made/In art and politics' of 'Nineteen Hundred and Nineteen', III (*CP* 235), and the same poem's 'the labyrinth of the wind' (*CP* 237).

114 *woman lost*: Maud Gonne

121 *It is time*: This section of the poem anticipates 'Sailing to Byzantium' (*CP* 217).

123 *that climb the streams*: cf. 'The Fisherman' (*CP* 166).

130-1   . . . *were spat on,*   **223**
     Nor to the tyrants that spat: a private joke referring to friends of Yeats whom he called Spit, Spat and Spat on. Lines 132-3 replaced a line in the MS. 'with nothing on but spats on' referring to a bathing party given by these friends.

132 *The people of Burke and of Grattan*: at this period Yeats was discovering his Anglo-Irish inheritance. In the debate on divorce in the Irish Senate on 11 June 1925, he wound up his speech (the text can be read in *SSY* 90-102) — which argued that to forbid divorce was a measure which the Protestant minority considered grossly oppressive — with a magnificent peroration:

> I am proud to consider myself a typical man of that minority. We against whom you have done this thing are no petty people. We are one of the great stocks of Europe. We are the people of Burke ; we are the people of Grattan ; we are the people of Swift, the people of Emmet, the people of Parnell. We have created the most of the modern literature of this country. We have created the best of its political intelligence.

136 *fabulous horn*: see note (p. 245) on line 32 of 'A Prayer for my Daughter' (*CP* 211)

137 *sudden shower*: this image resembles the first stanza of 'Meditations in Time of Civil War' (*CP* 225).

140 *the swan*: Yeats's note read:

> In the passage about the Swan in Part III I have uncon- sciously echoed one of the loveliest lyrics of our time — Mr

Sturge Moore's 'Dying Swan.' I often recited it during an American lecturing tour, which explains the theft.

THE DYING SWAN

O silver-throated Swan
Struck, struck ! A golden dart
Clean through thy breast has gone
Home to thy heart.
Thrill, thrill, O silver throat !
O silver trumpet, pour
Love for defiance back
On him who smote!
And brim, brim o'er
With love ; and ruby-dye thy track
Down thy last living reach
Of river, sail the golden light —
Enter the sun's heart — even teach,
O wondrous-gifted Pain, teach thou
The god to love, let him learn how.   (*CP* 533)

146–7 *Plotinus' thought*
     And cry in Plato's teeth : cf. note on line 12

158 *learned Italian things* : his visits to Italy, his interest in Dante, in Castiglione, the Italian painters and sculptors

159 *stones of Greece* : he visited the British Museum, and *AV* has several passages on the significance of Greek sculpture. See 'The Statues' (*CP* 375).

224 166 *loophole there* : in the tower

181 *make my soul* : an expression in common use in Ireland, meaning to prepare for death

225 MEDITATIONS IN TIME OF CIVIL WAR

These seven poems were mainly written at Thoor Ballylee during the Irish Civil War of 1922. (The first poem was written in England in 1921). They first appeared in *The Dial* (Jan. 1923).

General Title : Yeats's note reads :

These poems were written at Thoor Ballylee in 1922, during the civil war. Before they were finished the Republicans blew up our 'ancient bridge' one midnight. They forbade us to leave the house, but were otherwise polite, even saying at last 'Good-night, thank you,' as though we had given them the bridge.

The sixth poem is called 'The Stare's Nest by My Window.' In the west of Ireland we call a starling a stare, and during the civil war one built in a hole in the masonry by my bedroom window.

In the second stanza of the seventh poem occur the words 'Vengeance on the murderers of Jacques Molay.' A cry for vengeance because of the murder of the Grand Master of the Templars seems to me fit symbol for those who labour from hatred, and so for sterility in various kinds. It is said to have been incorporated in the ritual of certain Masonic societies of the eighteenth century, and to have fed class-hatred.

I suppose that I must have put hawks into the fourth stanza because I have a ring with a hawk and a butterfly upon it, to symbolise the straight road of logic, and so of mechanism, and the crooked road of intuition : 'For wisdom is a butterfly and not a gloomy bird of prey.' (*CP* 534)

The letters Yeats wrote between April 1921 and November 1922 give some details of his life in the tower during this period. See *L* 680–692.

I

Title Ancestral Houses : the poem perhaps echoes the thought of *AV*, that the new kind of violence which was coming into the world would be unlike the kind of violence which had brought the houses of the rich (in particular the country houses of Ireland) into being. And the present state of the inherited glory of the rich casts doubt upon the value of ancestral houses. Greatness may need violence.

12 *The abounding glittering jet* : Russell K. Alspach, *Yeats and Innis-free* (1965), 78–9, comments on the frequency of the image. He lists the occurrences ; in *The Shadowy Waters* (1906 version), *Poems 1899–1905*, 63 ; the prose essay 'At Stratford-on-Avon', *Ideas of Good and Evil* (1903), 163 ; in this poem ; two occurrences in 'The

Gift of Harun Al-Raschid' (*CP* 511); another in 'The Tower' (*CP* 218) and one in 'Blood and the Moon' (*CP* 267). He regards the fountain and the fountain jet as a symbol for an almost fierce joy in mere living. And Yeats's essay 'The Thinking of the Body' summed up its meaning : 'Art bids us touch and taste and hear and see the world and shrinks from what Blake calls mathematical form, from every abstract thing, from all that is of the brain only, from all that is not a fountain jetting from the entire hopes, memories, and sensations of the body' (*E & I* 292–3).

13 *sea-shell* : the image may derive from Shelley's *The Revolt of Islam* (Canto Fourth, 1):

> Upon whose floor the spangling sands were strown
> And rarest sea-shells, which the eternal flood,
> Slave to the mother of the months, had thrown
> Within the walls of that grey tower.

but see also Canto Seventh, XIII, for the images of shells, a fountain, and 'the state : Of kingless thrones, which Earth did in her heart create.'

Cf. also *The Only Jealousy of Emer* (*C Pl* 281–2).

226 25–9 *gardens where the peacock strays* : these are memories of Lady Ottoline Morrell's house and gardens at Garsington, near Oxford.

II

Title My House : this poem describes Yeats's tower, built by the de Burgo family, mentioned as Islandmore Castle in 1585, and the property of Edward Ulick de Burgo who died in it in 1597. The property is now in trust, and open to the public. See Mary Hanley, *Thoor Ballylee — Home of William Butler Yeats* (1965).

1 *an ancient bridge* : cf. various other references to the bridge in *A Concordance to the Poems of W. B. Yeats* (ed. Parrish and Painter)

4 *the symbolic rose* : see notes (pp. 22 ff.) on 'To the Rose upon the Rood of Time' (*CP* 35). Althea Gyles designed the cover for Yeats's *TSR* and this design has been described well by Joan Coldwell, ' "Images That Yet Fresh Images Beget": A Note on Book-Covers', *The World of W. B. Yeats* (1965), 154:

In the centre of the gold-stamped design is the four-petalled

rose attached to a cross which had been the focal point of the
Poems cover. Now the rose and cross are embedded in the
heart of a serpent-like tree at whose tip appears a trinity of
smaller roses, and beneath these are the kissing faces of a man
and woman.

8   *stilted water-hen* : cf. line 8, 'The Phases of the Moon' (183)

11   *A winding stair* : see notes (p. 319) on *The Winding Stair* (*CP*   **227**
261)

a chamber arched with stone : this was Yeats's bedroom on the first
floor of the tower which he also used as a study. It had an open
fire for turf and an elm-wood bed and wooden ceiling. (See *L* 687.)

14   *Il Penseroso's Platonist* : see note (p. 204) on line 15 'The Phases
of the Moon' (*CP* 183)

18   *Benighted travellers* : cf. Palmer's illustration to Milton's poem,
and the opening lines of 'Ego Dominus Tuus' (*CP* 180) and the
opening and closing lines of 'The Phases of the Moon' (*CP* 183).
Shelley's lines in 'Prince Athanase' may also have been in Yeats's
mind :

> The Balearic fisher, driven from shore,
> Hanging upon the peaked wave afar,
> Then saw their lamp from Laian's turret gleam, . . .

22   *a score of horse* : cf. the 'Rough men-at-arms, cross-gartered to
the knees' of 'The Tower' II (*CP* 221)

28   *My bodily heirs* : Anne Butler Yeats, born 26 February 1919,
and Michael Butler Yeats, born 22 August 1921

III   **227**

2   *Sato's gift* : Yeats wrote a letter to Edmund Dulac on 22 March
1920 which explains how the sword came into his possession :

A rather wonderful thing happened the day before yesterday.
A very distinguished looking Japanese came to see us. He had
read my poetry when in Japan and had now just heard me
lecture. He had something in his hand wrapped up in
embroidered silk. He said it was a present for me. He untied
the silk cord that bound it and brought out a sword which had

been for 500 years in his family. It had been made 550 years
ago and he showed me the maker's name upon the hilt. I was
greatly embarrassed at the thought of such a gift and went to
fetch George, thinking that we might find some way of refusing
it. When she came I said 'But surely this ought always to
remain in your family?' He answered 'My family have many
swords.' But later he brought back my embarrassment by
speaking of having given me 'his sword.' I had to accept it
but I have written him a letter saying that I 'put him under a
vow' to write and tell me when his first child is born — he is
not yet married — that I may leave the sword back to his
family in my will. (*L* 662)

Cf. also the lines describing the sword in 'A Dialogue of Self
and Soul' (*CP* 265) and in 'Symbols' (*CP* 270).

8   *Chaucer had not* : he had, if the sword was made 550 years before
1920 ; but the figure is a round one.

228   9   *Sato's house* : the name of the Japanese who gave the sword to
Yeats was Junzo Sato.

32   *Juno's peacock* : cf. a passage in *AV* :

A civilisation is a struggle to keep self-control, and in this it
is like some great tragic person, some Niobe who must display
an almost superhuman will or the cry will not touch our sympathy. The loss of control over thought comes towards the
end ; first a sinking in upon the moral being, then the last
surrender, the irrational cry, revelation — the scream of Juno's
peacock. (*AV* (B) 268)

IV

2   *my old fathers* : Yeats's father, grandfather and great-grandfather
were educated at Trinity College, Dublin.

3   *a woman and a man* : Anne and Michael Yeats

229   9–12   *And what if my descendants lose the flower*
              Through natural declension of the soul,
              Through too much business with the passing hour,
              Through too much play, or marriage with a fool? : Yeats was
worried about the future of his children, as were many Anglo-

Irish parents at the time of the Treaty and the subsequent civil war. A letter he wrote to Olivia Shakespear on 22 December 1921 put the problem frankly, out of a deep gloom about Ireland and its bitterness :

> In the last week I have been planning to live in Dublin — George very urgent for this — but I feel now that all may be blood and misery. If that comes we may abandon Ballylee to the owls and the rats, and England too (where passions will rise and I shall find myself with no answer), and live in some far land. Should England and Ireland be divided beyond all hope of remedy, what else could one do for the children's sake, or one's own work? I could not bring them to Ireland, where they would inherit bitterness, nor leave them in England where, being Irish by tradition, and by family and fame, they would be in an unnatural condition of mind and grow, as so many Irishmen who live here [he was writing from Oxford] do, sour and argumentative. (*L* 675)

14–18   *Become a roofless ruin that the owl*
        May build in the cracked masonry and cry
        Her desolation to the desolate sky.

        The Primum Mobile that fashioned us
        Has made the very owls in circles move : Yeats may have been remembering Swedenborg's dicta in *Arcana Coelestia*, 5149, that 'gross and dense falsities are signified by owls and ravens ; by owls because they live in the darkness of night, and by ravens because they are black'. The owls 'in circles' almost conform to the cyclic ideas of *AV* and thus prepare us for the 'flourish or decline' of its history.

17   *Primum Mobile* : the Primum Mobile was part of the Ptolemaic system, 'the wheel or rhomb called the Primum Mobile, the motion of which is supposed to cause the revolution of the nine inner spheres round the earth in twenty-four hours'. There is a passage in *Paradise Lost*, VII 449–501, which is explicit :

> Now Heaven in all her glory shone, and rolled
> Her motions, as the great First Mover's hand
> First wheeled their course.

21   *for an old neighbour's friendship* : Lady Gregory's estate, Coole Park, was within walking distance of Ballylee.

22   *a girl's love* : a reference to Mrs Yeats

V

1   *Irregular* : a member of the Irish Republican Army, which opposed the signing of the Anglo-Irish treaty and thus caused the Civil War in 1922.   The Republicans later blew up the bridge beside the tower in the autumn of 1922.   See *L* 692.

6   *A brown Lieutenant and his men* : 'Free Staters' or members of the National Army loyal to the Provisional Government

230   VI

Title   The Stare's Nest : Yeats wrote a long explanation of this poem in *BS* :

> I was in my Galway house during the first months of civil war, the railway bridges blown up and the roads blocked with stones and trees.   For the first week there were no newspapers, no reliable news, we did not know who had won nor who had lost, and even after newspapers came, one never knew what was happening on the other side of the hill or of the line of trees.   Ford cars passed the house from time to time with coffins standing upon end between the seats, and sometimes at night we heard an explosion, and once by day saw the smoke made by the burning of a great neighbouring house.   Men must have lived so through many tumultuous centuries.   One felt an overmastering desire not to grow unhappy or (embittered, not to lose all sense of the beauty of nature.   A stare (our West of Ireland name for a starling) had built in a hole beside my window and I made these verses out of the feeling of the moment :

> > The bees build in the crevices
> > Of loosening masonry, and there
> > The mother birds bring grubs and flies.
> > My wall is loosening ; honey bees,
> > Come build in the empty house of the stare.
> >
> > We are closed in, and the key is turned
> > On our uncertainty ; somewhere
> > A man is killed, or a house is burned,
> > Yet no clear fact to be discerned :
> > Come build in the empty house of the stare.

That is only the beginning but it runs on in the same mood. Presently a strange thing happened. I began to smell honey in places where honey could not be, at the end of a stone passage or at some windy turn of the road, and it came always with certain thoughts. When I got back to Dublin I was with angry people who argued over everything or were eager to know the exact facts : in the midst of the mood that makes realistic drama. (*A* 579–80)

VII

10 *Jacques Molay* : Jacques de Molay was arrested in 1307 and   231
burned in March 1314. See M. Summers, *The Geography of Witch-craft*, 367–76, and Thomas Wright, *Narratives of Sorcery and Magic*. See Yeats's own note quoted in note (p. 267) on general title 'Meditations in Time of Civil War' (*CP* 225).

17–19 *Their legs long, delicate and slender, aquamarine their eyes,*
        Magical unicorns bear ladies on their backs : Henn (*LT* 255) pointed out that these lines describe Gustave Moreau's painting *Ladies and Unicorns* (described in a letter of 8 November 1936, as on a wall of Yeats's house (*DWL* 100)). It is included in the illustrations in Giorgio Melchiori (*WMA* 74–5). These phantoms are 'of the Heart's fullness' in contrast to the brazen hearts which follow, symbols of logic as opposed to intuition.

29 *brazen hawks* : see Yeats's note, quoted in note (p. 267) on gen-   232
eral title 'Meditations in Time of Civil War' (*CP* 225)

32 *clanging wings* : these may be, as Unterecker (*RG* 181) has suggested, a symbol of the emptiness of the coming cycle, which eliminates the subjectivity symbolised by the moon. He draws attention to the last stanza's parody of Wordsworth which, he suggests, Yeats uses 'to celebrate occult investigations of "Demonic images"' . . . and 'to insist that such investigations have brought him intimations of immortality quite as accurate in old age as in youth'.

NINETEEN HUNDRED AND NINETEEN   232

This poem was written in 1919 and first appeared in *The Dial* (Sept. 1921). In *LM* (Nov. 1921) the title was 'Thoughts upon the Present State of the World'.

The poem arose out of 'some horrors at Gort', Co. Galway, see notes on line 25 and lines 26–8.

233 6 *An ancient image* : probably derives from Sophocles, *Oedipus at Colonus*, but the original story is in Herodotus, VIII, 65, where the sacred olive is recounted to have grown a cubit (Pausanias, I, 27, 2, improved on Herodotus' version of the story by making the plant grow a shoot two cubits long on the same day) by the second day after the Persians had sacked and burnt Athens, including the old Erechtheum, which contained the spring of salt water and the sacred olive which were created by Erechtheus and Athene in their rivalry to become deity of the city.   Yeats translated the Sophoclean chorus (*CP* 245) from Paul Masqueray's French translation of *Oedipus at Colonus*.

7 *Phidias* : the famous Athenian sculptor (*c*. B.C. 490–417) ; primarily a bronze-worker, he also acquired his fame from chryselephantine statues, of gold and ivory, of which his Athena Parthenos survives in copies, though his Zeus of Olympia is only a memory. Pericles commissioned him to design the marble sculptures of the Parthenon and he made the models for the sculptors who worked under him.

8 *golden grasshoppers and bees* : from Thucydides I, vi

9–32 *We too had many pretty toys when young:*
A law indifferent to blame or praise,
To bribe or threat; habits that made old wrong
Melt down, as it were wax in the sun's rays;
Public opinion ripening for so long
We thought it would outlive all future days.
O what fine thought we had because we thought
That the worst rogues and rascals had died out.

All teeth were drawn, all ancient tricks unlearned,
And a great army but a showy thing;
What matter that no cannon had been turned
Into a ploughshare?   Parliament and king
Thought that unless a little powder burned
The trumpeters might burst with trumpeting
And yet it lack all glory; and perchance
The guardsmen's drowsy chargers would not prance.

Now days are dragon-ridden, the nightmare
Rides upon sleep: a drunken soldiery
Can leave the mother, murdered at her door,
To crawl in her own blood, and go scot-free;
The night can sweat with terror as before
We pieced our thoughts into philosophy,
And planned to bring the world under a rule,
Who are but weasels fighting in a hole

describe events before 1914 or perhaps before the Boer War.

16   *rogues and rascals had died out*:   Torchiana (*Y & GI* 317) quotes Yeats's speech at the Tailteann Banquet, 2 August 1924, which refers to the 'eighties at this point:

> Everyone, certainly everyone who counted, everyone who influenced events believed that the world was growing better and better, and could not even help doing so owing to physical science and democratic politics, and that dream lasted for many years.

19–20   *no cannon had been turned Into a ploughshare*:   these lines relate to Isaiah ii. 4: 'And they shall beat their swords into plowshares and their spears into pruning hooks: nation shall not lift up sword against nation neither shall they learn war any more.'   Cf. Micah iv. 3 and Joel iii. 10 (where the plowshares are beaten into swords).

21–3   *unless a little powder burned . . . chargers would not prance*:   cf. the speech Yeats made at the Tailteann Banquet, 2 August 1924, quoted in *Y & GI* 317–18:

> A fortnight before the great war a friend of mine was standing beside an English Member of Parliament watching a Review in one of the London Parks.   My friend said as the troops marched past 'It is a fine sight.'   And the Member of Parliament answered 'It is a fine sight, but it is nothing else, there will never be another war.'
>
> 'There will never be another war', that was our opium dream.

25   *Now days are dragon-ridden*:   this stanza refers to atrocities committed by members of the Auxiliaries and the Black and Tans in the pre-Treaty fighting in Ireland.   For details see Brian Graney, 'Days of Terror in South Galway', *Vexilla Regis* (1954–5) 85–98. See note on lines 26–8.

26–8   *a drunken soldiery*
        Can leave the mother, murdered at her door,
            To crawl in her own blood, and go scot-free : these lines also refer
to particularly unpleasant atrocities at Gort. See *WBY* 329 and
Lady Gregory's Journals (ed. Lennox Robinson) 129–46. Mrs Ellen
Quinn was killed by the Black and Tans, and the Loughnane
brothers were murdered and mutilated.

32 *weasels fighting in a hole* : cf. line 92. Yeats had seen weasels
fighting at Coole. Lady Gregory recorded their bad name with
gamekeepers, the need other country people expressed 'to behave
well to them' and the advice of an old acquaintance not to insult
one — 'For they are enchanted and understand all things' (*Coole*
26). Lady Wilde, *Ancient Legends of Ireland*, 179, recorded that they
are 'spiteful and malignant, and old withered witches sometimes
take this form'. Yeats may have been influenced by his reading
of Landor who placed in Sheridan's mouth an argument that there
should be no church establishment for less than one hundred adults :

> But seriously, in turning this acid on such putridity there
> would be a violent fermentation ; there would be animosities
> and conflicts. However, what harm if there should be? Turn
> out the weasel against the rat, and, at least while they are
> fighting, neither of them can corrode the rafters or infect the
> larder. (W. S. Landor, *Collected Works*, 'Conversations with
> Windham and Sheridan', III, 127)

234 43 *That country round* : the burning of the great houses would have
been unthinkable in Ireland before the 'Troubles' and the Civil
War.

49–50 *Loie Fuller's Chinese dancers enwound*
            A shining web, a floating ribbon of cloth : Loie Fuller (b. 1862)
an American dancer who danced 'in a whirl of shining draperies
manipulated on sticks' at the *Folies Bergère* in the 'nineties. Mallarmé wrote about her and Toulouse-Lautrec painted her. Cf.
Kermode, 'Poet and Dancer before Diaghilev', *Partisan Review*
(Jan./Feb. 1961) 48–76 ; *RI* 71 and *IP* 122. She had a troupe of
Japanese dancers.

54 *Platonic Year* : this is derived from Plato. Yeats discussed the
Great Year in *AV* (B) 245–54, basing his ideas on Pierre Duhem,

Le Système du Monde. He also used Cicero's definition :

> But when the whole of the constellations shall return to the positions from which they once set forth, thus after a long interval re-making the first map of the heavens, that may indeed be called the Great Year wherein I scarce dare say how many are the generations of men.

He added his own comment that the Great Year was

> sometimes divided into lesser periods by the return of the sun and moon to some original position, by the return of a planet or of all the planets to some original position, or by their making an astrological aspect with that position ; and sometimes it was dissociated from the actual position of the stars and divided into twelve months, each month a brightening and a darkening fortnight, and at the same time perhaps a year with its four seasons. (*AV* (B) 246)

There are some interesting divergences between the two versions of *AV* in the discussion of Plato's great year. The earlier version speaks of 'the elaborate geometry of *The Timaeus* and certain numerical calculations in *The Republic* of which modern scholars have seventeen incompatible explanations', and continues :

> that no one, not even Plato with all his mathematical calculations, calculated the periods back through the World Year implies an acceptance or half acceptance of that Year, not for its astronomical but for its moral value. Our interest in Plato's comment is precisely that he does use it as we use the lunar phases, as if it were the moving hands upon a vast clock, or a picturesque symbolism that helped him to make more vivid, and perhaps date, developments of the human mind that can be proved dialectically. In the Republic he identifies the passage of his typical community through Timocracy, Oligarchy, Democracy, Tyranny, and so back to Aristocracy again, as a passage through Ages of Gold, Silver, etc., that may have seemed to the eyes of the Sibyl and perhaps to the eyes of Virgil identical with some classification of the Ten Ages : he saw what had seemed *Fate* as *Destiny*. In another passage he makes his typical community bring its different periods to an end by carrying some character to excess, and attributes the changes of the year to a like cause. (*AV* (A) 154–5)

Later he returned to the contrast of the Platonic year :

> The alternation of *antithetical* and *primary* months is certainly Platonic, for his Golden Age men are born old and grow young,

whereas in that which follows they are born young and grow old. He, however, made Gold *antithetical*; upon the other hand the Babylonians had the same alternation but began we are told with Silver and the Moon. (*AV* (A) 157–8)

In *AV* (B) Yeats writes :

Yet Plato's statements are there that scholars may solve the Golden Number, and they have found fourteen different solutions. To Taylor they suggest 36,000 years, 360 incarnations of Plato's Man of Ur. Proclus thought the duration of the world is found 'when we bring into contemplation the numerical unity, the one self-unfolding power, the sole creation that completes its work, that which fills all things with universal life. One must see all things wind up their careers and come round again to the beginning ; one must see everything return to itself and so complete by itself the circle allotted to that number ; or that unity which encloses an infinity of numbers, contains within itself the instability of the Duad and yet determines the whole movement, its end and its beginning, and is for that reason called the Number and the Perfect Number.' It is as though innumerable dials, some that recorded minutes alone, some seconds alone, some hours alone, some months alone, some years alone, were all to complete their circles when Big Ben struck twelve upon the last night of the century. (*AV* (B) 248)

59 *Some moralist or mythological poet* : possibly Shelley in *Prometheus Unbound*, II, v :

> My soul is an enchanted boat,
> Which, like a sleeping swan, doth float
> Upon the silver waves of thy sweet singing ; . . .

235 89 *We, who seven years ago* : these lines measure the decline in British morality since 1914 from the sentiments then expressed and those which later favoured the activities of the Auxiliaries and the Black and Tans.

236 92 *the weasel's twist ; the weasel's tooth* : see note on line 32

93 *mock at the great* : this section of the poem seems to be founded on Yeats's memory of Blake's poem 'Scoffers' with its lines :

> Mock on, mock on, Voltaire, Rousseau,
> Mock on, mock on ; 'tis all in vain ;

> You throw the dust against the wind,
> And the wind blows it back again.

Yeats included this poem in his selection of Blake (Blake, *Poems*
(1893), 108).

97   *the levelling wind* : the wind in this section of the poem and the
next are reminiscent of James Clarence Mangan's 'Gone in the
Wind' with its refrain taken from Rückert :

> Solomon! Where is thy throne? It is gone in the wind.
> Babylon! Where is thy might? It is gone in the wind
> Like the swift shadows of Noon, like the dreams of the Blind,
> Vanish the glories and pomps of the world in the wind.

118   *Herodias' daughters have returned again,*   **237**
      A sudden blast of dusty wind: in a note (pp. 48ff.) quoted in head-
note to 'The Hosting of the Sidhe' (*CP* 61) Yeats wrote that
Sidhe is the Gaelic for wind and that the Sidhe had much to do
with the wind : 'They journey in whirling winds, the winds that
were called the dance of the daughters of Herodias in the Middle
Ages, Herodias doubtless taking the place of some old goddess.'
Yeats may have been thinking of the traditional procession of
witches on St John the Baptist's Eve. See M. Summers, *The
Geography of Witchcraft*, 76, who quotes St Ivo of Chartres on this :

> Certain abandoned women turning aside to follow Satan,
> being seduced by the illusions and phantasms of demons,
> believe and openly profess that in the dead of night they ride
> upon certain beasts with the pagan goddess Diana and a count-
> less horde of women, and that in these silent hours they fly over
> vast tracts of country and obey her as their mistress while on
> other nights they are summoned to pay her homage.

See also M. H. Murray, *The witch cult in Western Europe*, 102. The
legend of the pageant of witches is also to be found in Heine's
Atta Troll, xviii–xx, 67–86. It is possible that Yeats was remembering Arthur Symons's poem 'The Dance of the Daughters of
Herodias' where the daughters dance

> With their eternal, white, unfaltering feet,
> And always, when they dance, for their delight,
> Always a man's head falls because of them.
> Yet they desire not death, they would not slay
> Body or soul, no, not to do them pleasure :

> They desire love, and the desire of men ;
> And they are the eternal enemy.

They are unreal :

> Shapes on a mirror, perishable shapes
> Fleeting, and without substance, or abode,
> In a fixed place.

Symons's lines describe their effect on what men hold dear :

> The wisdom which is wiser than Kings know,
> The beauty which is fairer than things seen,
> Dreams which are nearer to eternity
> Than that most mortal tumult of the blood
> Which wars on itself in loving, droop and die.

128 *That insolent fiend Robert Artisson* : Yeats's note read :

The country people see at times certain apparitions whom they name now 'fallen angels', now 'ancient inhabitants of the country' and describe as riding at whiles 'with flowers upon the heads of the horses'. I have assumed in the sixth poem that these horsemen, now that the times worsen, give way to worse. My last symbol, Robert Artisson, was an evil spirit much run after in Kilkenny at the start of the fourteenth century. Are not those who travel in the whirling dust also in the Platonic Year? — May 1921 (This version follows the text in *The Dial* (Sept. 1921).)

Robert Artisson was the fourteenth-century incubus of Dame Alice Kyteler. Yeats read the MS. accounts in the British Museum of the proceedings against her and her confederates. He also read Dr Carrigan's *History of the Diocese of Ossory* which deals with the events. Thomas Wright edited the MS. for the Camden Society, and his 'Narratives of Witchcraft and Sorcery' in *The Transactions of the Ossory Archaeological Society* (vol. 1), also contain an account of the trial. St John D. Seymour, *Irish Witchcraft and Demonology* (1913) devotes a chapter to Dame Alice Kyteler, whom he describes as the '*facile princeps*' of Irish witches. She was

a member of a good Anglo-Norman family that had been settled in the city of Kilkenny for many years. The coffin-shaped tombstone of one of her ancestors, Jose de Keteller, who died in 128–, is preserved at St Mary's Church ; the inscription is in Norman French and the lettering in Lombardic. The lady in question must have been far removed from the popular concepts of a witch as an old woman of striking ugliness, or else her powers of attraction were very remarkable, for she had succeeded in leading four husbands to the altar. She had been married first, to William Outlawe of Kilkenny, banker; secondly, to Adam le Blund of Callan; thirdly, to Richard de Valle — all of whom she was supposed to have got rid of by poison : and fourthly, to Sir John le Poer, whom it was said she deprived of his sense by philtres and incantations. The Bishop of Ossory at this period was Richard de Ledrede, a Franciscan friar, and an Englishman by birth. He soon learnt that things were not as they should be, for when making a visitation of his diocese early in 1324 he found by an Inquisition, in which were five Knights and numerous nobles, that there was in the city a band of heretical sorcerers, at the head of whom was Dame Alice.

Among the charges laid against this band were two of special significance :

2. They offered in sacrifice to demons living animals, which they dismembered, and then distributed at cross-roads to a certain evil spirit of low rank, named the son of Art.

7. The said dame had a certain demon, an incubus, named Son of Art, or Robin son of Art, who had carnal knowledge of her, and from whom she admitted that she had received her wealth. This incubus made its appearance under various forms, sometimes as a cat, or as a hairy black dog, or in the likeness of a negro (Ethiops), accompanied by two others who were larger and taller than he, and of whom one carried an iron rod.

According to another source the sacrifice to the evil spirit is said to have consisted of nine red cocks, and nine peacocks' eyes.

THE WHEEL   237

This poem was written on 13 September 1921 and first appeared in *SPF*.

Yeats wrote the poem in the Euston Hotel; see Jeffares 'Yeats and his methods of writing verse', *The Permanence of Yeats* (ed. Hall and Steinmann, 1950; 1961). The poem is compared by Saul (*PYP* 127), to a passage in *Mythologies* :

Joachim of Flora acknowledged openly the authority of the Church, and even asked that all his published writings, and those to be published by his desire after his death, should be submitted to the censorship of the Pope. He considered that those whose work was to live and not to reveal were children and that the Pope was their father ; but he taught in secret that certain others, and in always increasing numbers, were elected, not to live, but to reveal that hidden substance of God which is colour and music and softness and a sweet odour ; and that these have no father but the Holy Spirit. Just as poets and painters and musicians labour at their works, building them with lawless and lawful things alike, so long as they embody the beauty that is beyond the grave, these children of the Holy Spirit labour at their moments with eyes upon the shining substance on which Time has heaped the refuse of creation ; for the world only exists to be a tale in the ears of coming generations ; and terror and content, birth and death, love and hatred, and the fruit of the Tree, are but instruments for that supreme art which is to win us from life and gather us into eternity like doves into their dove-cots. (*M* 300–1)

237 YOUTH AND AGE

This poem was written in 1924 and first appeared in *The Cat and the Moon and Certain Poems* (1924).

238 THE NEW FACES

This poem was written in December 1912 and first appeared in *SPF*.

1 *you* : Lady Gregory. Yeats first met her in 1896 when he was thirty-one : she was then 'a plainly dressed woman of forty-five'. See Jeffares, '"The New Faces" a new explanation', *RES*, XXIII, 92 (Oct. 1947).

2 *catalpa tree* : Lady Gregory described it with delight :
We are looking . . . from the bench that is under the shadow of the catalpa tree — 'A weeping ash,' George Moore has called it telling of his quarrels as he sat there with Yeats 'in the warmth and fragrance of the garden,' over that play *Diarmuid and Grania* they were writing, not without differences of opinion. But my own quarrel with him must be for the libel of calling this catalpa by the name of among all trees the one for which I have least affection, even a slight feeling of

dislike. I did not find, or ever plant one here at Coole. . . .

But the catalpa coming as I believe from the gentle Pacific zone has no fault to keep it outside the garden walls. The clean limbs spreading over garden bench and wall give no noxious shade, for the leaves larger than the palm of a man's hand . . . are but few beside those of our native trees. The trusses of white blossom add beauty to their pale green. They cast a pleasant shadow on the long bench and a part of the flower border, yet not such darkness as to check the blossoming of tulip or larkspur, or anemone, or the growth of that delicately leaved laurel painters lay on a poet's brow ; or of rosemary and the sweet tufted herbs. (*Coole* 42–4)

4 *Where we wrought* : Coole Park in general ; but this line may anticipate line 7's 'garden gravel'. This is described by Lady Gregory :

The long grey wall that encloses the garden protects a flower border from the ocean salt, for all the miles between flung in great storms on the very windows of the house, and is itself in part protected by an outer line of great beeches. The seeds of these, flung on to the border, often take root, and appear, two or three inches of forest tree, among the hyacinth and phlox. The ground dips eastward to the orchard, the tennis ground. . . .

Yeats planned many a play or poem pacing up and down this gravelled walk before facing the blank paper on the writing table in his room ; I stealing a pleasant half hour with him between the ordering of the day's meals and the endless answering of letters that falls to a woman's share ; turning just once again towards the great ilex, its silver grey calling to mind that of the olive against the Italian blue. (*Coole* 44–5)

A PRAYER FOR MY SON   238

This poem was written in December 1921 and first appeared in *SPF*.

2 *my Michael* : Michael Butler Yeats was born in August 1921 at Castlebrook House, Thame, Oxfordshire.

10 *Some there are* : Yeats discussed the strange phenomena which accompanied the automatic writing in *AV* :

Sometimes if I had been ill some astringent smell like that of resinous wood filled the room, and sometimes, though rarely, a bad smell. These were often warnings ; a smell of cat's excrement announced some being that had to be expelled, the smell of an extinguished candle that the communicators were 'starved'. A little after my son's birth I came home to confront my wife with the statement 'Michael is ill'. A smell of burnt feathers had announced what she and the doctor had hidden. When regular communication was near its end and my work of study and arrangement begun, I was told that henceforth the Frustrators would attack my health and that of my children, and one afternoon, knowing from the smell of burnt feathers that one of my children would be ill within three hours, I felt before I could recover self-control the mediaeval helpless horror at witchcraft. (*AV* (B) 16)

He continued :

Sometimes my wife saw apparitions : before the birth of our son a great black bird, persons in clothes of the late sixteenth century and of the late seventeenth. There were still stranger phenomena that I prefer to remain silent about for the present because they seemed so incredible that they need a long story and much discussion. (*AV* (B) 17)

239   17   *You* : Christ

26   *Your enemy* : Herod

239   TWO SONGS FROM A PLAY

The poems were written in 1926 with the exception of the latter stanza in II which was probably written in 1930–1. Poem I and the first stanza of II first appeared in *The Adelphi* (June 1927) then in *OB*. The full text first appeared in *Stories of Michael Robartes and His Friends* (1931). There are marked differences between the text of the play in *The Adelphi* and those in other printings, see *VPl.* 900–36.

Yeats's note explained that these two songs are sung by the Chorus of Musicians in *Resurrection*, a play that has for its theme Christ's first appearance to the Apostles after the Crucifixion. The play was meant to be performed in a drawing-room or studio (*OB*) and was first performed in the Abbey Theatre, Dublin, on 20 July 1934. The play deals with Yeats's view expressed in *AV* that

Christianity terminated a 2000-year period of history and ushered in the beginnings of another era with radical violence. His Introduction to the play in *W&B* makes clear his aim :

> This play, or the first sketch of it, more dialogue than play, was intended for my drawing-room, where my *Hawk's Well* had just been played.
>
> For years I have been preoccupied with a certain myth that was itself a reply to a myth. I do not mean a fiction, but one of those statements our nature is compelled to make and employ as a truth though there cannot be sufficient evidence. When I was a boy everybody talked about progress, and rebellion against my elders took the form of aversion to that myth. I took satisfaction in certain public disasters, felt a sort of ecstasy at the contemplation of ruin, and then I came upon the story of Oisin in Tir nà nOg and reshaped it into my *Wanderings of Oisin*. He rides across the sea with a spirit, he passes phantoms, a boy following a girl, a hound chasing a hare, emblematical of eternal pursuit, he comes to an island of choral dancing, leaves that after many years, passes the phantoms once again, comes to an island of endless battle for an object never achieved, leaves that after many years, passes the phantoms once again, comes to an island of sleep, leaves that and comes to Ireland, to Saint Patrick and old age. I did not pick these images because of any theory, but because I found them impressive, yet all the while abstractions haunted me. I remember rejecting, because it spoilt the simplicity, an elaborate metaphor of a breaking wave intended to prove that all life rose and fell as in my poem. How hard it was to refrain from pointing out that Oisin after. old age, its illumination half accepted, half rejected, would pass in death over another sea to another island. Presently Oisin and his islands faded and the sort of images that come into *Rosa Alchemica* and *The Adoration of the Magi* took their place. Our civilisation was about to reverse itself, or some new civilisation about to be born from all that our age had rejected, from all that my stories symbolised as a harlot, and take after its mother ; because we had worshipped a single god it would worship many or receive from Joachim de Flora's Holy Spirit a multitudinous influx. A passage in *La Peau de chagrin* may have started me, but because I knew no ally but Balzac, I kept silent about all I could not get into fantastic romance. So did the abstract ideas persecute me that *On Baile's Strand*, founded upon a dream, was only

finished when, after a struggle of two years, I had made the Fool and Blind Man, Cuchulain and Conchubar whose shadows they are, all image, and now I can no longer remember what they meant except that they meant in some sense those combatants who turn the wheel of life. Had I begun *On Baile's Strand* or not when I began to imagine, as always at my left side just out of the range of the sight, a brazen winged beast [the beast in 'The Second Coming'] that I associated with laughing, ecstatic destruction? Then I wrote, spurred by an external necessity, *Where There is Nothing*, a crude play with some dramatic force, since changed with Lady Gregory's help into *The Unicorn from the Stars*. A neighbourhood inflamed with drink, a country house burnt down, a spiritual anarchy preached! Then, after some years came the thought that a man always tried to become his opposite, to become what he would abhor if he did not desire it, and I wasted some three summers and some part of each winter before I had banished the ghost and turned what I had meant for tragedy into a farce : *The Player Queen*. Then unexpectedly and under circumstances described in *A Packet to Ezra Pound* came a symbolical system displaying the conflict in all its forms :

> Where got I that truth?
> Out of a medium's mouth,
> Out of nothing it came,
> Out of the forest loam,
> Out of dark night where lay
> The crowns of Nineveh.

II

> And then did all the Muses sing
> Of Magnus Annus at the spring.

In 1894 Gorky and Lunacharsky tried to correct the philosophy of Marxian socialism by the best German philosophy of their time, founding schools at Capri and Bologna for the purpose, but Lenin founded a rival school at Paris and brought Marxian socialism back to orthodoxy : 'we remain materialist, anything else would lead to religion.' Four or five years later Pius X saw a Commission of Catholic scholars considering the text of the Bible and its attribution to certain authors and dissolved the Commission : 'Moses and the Four Evangelists wrote the Books that are called by their names ; any other conclusion would lead to scepticism.' In this way did two great men prepare two great movements, purified of modernism, for a crisis when, in the words of Archbishop Downey, they must dispute the mastery of the world.

So far I have the sympathy of the Garrets and Cellars, for they are, I am told, without exception Catholic, Communist, or both! Yet there is a third myth or philosophy that has made an equal stir in the world. Ptolemy thought the precession of the equinoxes moved at the rate of a degree every hundred years, and that somewhere about the time of Christ and Caesar the equinoctial sun had returned to its original place in the constellations, completing and recommencing the thirty-six thousand years, or three hundred and sixty incarnations of a hundred years apiece, of Plato's man of Ur. Hitherto almost every philosopher had some different measure for the Greatest Year, but this Platonic Year, as it was called, soon displaced all others; it was a Christian heresy in the twelfth century, and in the East, multiplied by twelve as if it were but a month of a still greater year, it became the Manvantra of 432,000 years, until animated by the Indian jungle it generated new noughts and multiplied itself into Kalpas.

It was perhaps obvious, when Plotinus substituted the archetypes of individual men in all their possible incarnations for a limited number of Platonic Ideas, that a Greatest Year for whale and gudgeon alike must exhaust the multiplication table. Whatever its length, it divided, and so did every unit whose multiple it was, into waxing and waning, day and night, or summer and winter. There was everywhere a conflict like that of my play between two principles or 'elemental forms of the mind,' each 'living the other's life, dying the other's death.' I have a Chinese painting of three old sages sitting together, one with a deer at his side, one with a scroll open at the symbol of *yen* and *yin*, those two forms that whirl perpetually, creating and re-creating all things. But because of our modern discovery that the equinox shifts its ground more rapidly than Ptolemy believed, one must, somebody says, invent a new symbolic scheme. No, a thousand times no; I insist that the equinox does shift a degree in a hundred years; anything else would lead to confusion.

All ancient nations believed in the re-birth of the soul and had probably empirical evidence like that Lafcadio Hearn found among the Japanese. In our time Schopenhauer believed it, and McTaggart thinks Hegel did, though lack of interest in the individual soul had kept him silent. It is the foundation of

McTaggart's own philosophical system. Cardinal Mercier saw no evidence for it, but did not think it heretical ; and its rejection compelled the sincere and noble Von Hügel to say that children dead too young to have earned Heaven suffered no wrong, never having heard of a better place than Limbo. Even though we think temporal existence illusionary it cannot be capricious ; it is what Plotinus called the characteristic act of the soul and must reflect the soul's coherence. All our thought seems to lead by antithesis to some new affirmation of the supernatural. In a few years, perhaps, we may have much empirical evidence, the only evidence that moves the mass of men to-day, that man has lived many times ; there is some not yet perfectly examined — I think of that Professor's daughter in Palermo. This belief held by Plato and Plotinus, and supported by weighty argument, resembles the mathematical doctrines of Einstein before the experimental proof of the curvature of light.

We may come to think that nothing exists but a stream of souls, that all knowledge is biography, and with Plotinus that every soul is unique ; that these souls, these eternal archetypes, combine into greater units as days and nights into months, months into years, and at last into the final unit that differs in nothing from that which they were at the beginning : everywhere that antinomy of the One and the Many that Plato thought in his *Parmenides* insoluble, though Blake thought it soluble 'at the bottom of the graves.' Such belief may arise from Communism by antithesis, declaring at last even to the common ear that all things have value according to the clarity of their expression of themselves, and not as functions of changing economic conditions or as a preparation for some Utopia. There is perhaps no final happy state except in so far as men may gradually grow better ; escape may be for individuals alone who know how to exhaust their possible lives, to set, as it were, the hands of the clock racing. Perhaps we shall learn to accept even innumerable lives with happy humility ('I have been always an insect in the roots of the grass') and putting aside calculating scruples, be ever ready to wager all upon the dice.

Even our best histories treat men as function. Why must I think the victorious cause the better? Why should Mommsen think the less of Cicero because Caesar beat him? I am satisfied, the Platonic Year in my head, to find but drama. I prefer that the defeated cause should be more vividly described than that which has the advertisement of victory. No battle has been finally won or lost; 'to Garret or Cellar a wheel I send.' (*E* 392–8)

I

1 *a staring virgin*: this stanza draws a parallel between the myth of Dionysus and the death and resurrection of Christ. Ellmann (*IY* 260) draws on Sir James Frazer's *The Golden Bough* (which Yeats read) for this explanation :

Dionysus, child of a mortal Persephone, and an immortal, Zeus, was torn to pieces by the Titans. Athene (the 'staring virgin' of the poems, staring indicating that she acts as if in a trance because the events are pre-ordained) snatched the heart from his body, brought it on her hand to Zeus, who killed the Titans, swallowed the heart, and begat Dionysus again, upon another mortal, Semele. Yeats's introduction (see general note on the poem, above) gives Sir William Crookes, *Studies in Psychical Research* as a source. Sir William Crookes (1832–1919) was an English chemist and physicist.

6–7 *the Muses sing Of Magnus Annus*: they sing of this as a play because they regard the ritual death and rebirth of the god as a recurring event, part of the cycles of history. Ellmann points out that 'both Gods had died and been reborn in March when the sun was between the Ram and the Fish, and when the moon was beside the constellation Virgo, who carries the star Spica in her hand'. In these stanzas Yeats is thinking of Virgil, *Eclogue*, IV, 6, '*Iam redit et Virgo . . .*' where Virgo, daughter of Jupiter and Themis, is the last to leave Earth at the end of the golden age ; but will return, bringing back the golden age. This Virgilian prophesy was later read as a foretelling of the coming of Mary (as Virgo) and Christ, the star of Bethlehem (as Spica) :

'The latest age of Cumean Song is at hand ; the cycles in their vast array begin anew ; Virgin Astrea comes, the reign of Saturn comes, and from the heights of Heaven a new generation of mankind descends. . . . Apollo now is King and in your consulship, in yours, Pollio, the age of glory shall commence and the mighty months begin to run their course.' . . . Three hundred years, two degrees of the Great Year, would but correspond to two days of the Sun's annual journey, and his transition from Pisces to Aries had for generations been associated with the ceremonial death and resurrection of Dionysus. Near that transition the women wailed him, and night showed the full moon separating from the constellation Virgo, with the star in the wheatsheaf, or in the child, for in the old maps she is represented carrying now one now the other. It may be that instead of a vague line, the Sibyl knew some star that fixed the exact moment of transition. I find but four explanations compatible with man's agency, and all four incredible, for Christ being born at or near the moment of transition. (*AV* (A) 152, 156–7)

9–12   *Another Troy . . .*
        Another Argo's painted prow
        Drive to a flashier bauble yet

These lines develop Virgil's *Eclogue*, IV, 31–6:

> Yet shall some few traces of olden sin lurk behind, to call men to essay the sea in ships, to gird towns with walls, and to cleave the earth with furrows. A second Tiphys shall then arise, and a second Argo to carry chosen heroes ; a second warfare, too, shall there be, and again shall a great Achilles be sent to Troy.

Cf. a passage in a rewritten version of 'The Adoration of the Magi' where while one of these old men is reading out 'the Fifth *Eclogue* of Virgil' and falls asleep and 'a strange voice spoke through him, and bid them set out for Paris, where a dying woman would give them secret names and thereby so transform the world that another Leda would open her knees to the swan, another Achilles beleaguer Troy' (*M* 310).

There is another reference to this in *Samhain* (1904): 'for has not Virgil, a knowledgeable man and a wizard, foretold that other Argonauts shall row between cliff and cliff and other fair-haired Achaeans sack another Troy?' (*E* 150).

Yeats is also echoing the imagery of Shelley's *Hellas*, 1060–79, though not its optimistic tone.

240 11   *Another Argo's painted prow* : cf. William Morris, *Life and Death of Jason* Bk. IV, where the prow itself is prophetic :

> For just as a part of the ship Argo, keel or prow, was made of the Dodonaean oak, and Argo's crew heard with astonishment the ship herself prophesy to them on the sea. But Jason

and the builder Argus knew whereby the prow foretold things strange and new.

13   *The Roman Empire stood appalled* : because though there were but six million Christians in the Roman Empire's sixty million, the world was to become Christian, and the Empire to be destroyed by Christianity (a view Yeats shared with Gibbon).

13–16   *The Roman Empire . . .*
       Out of the fabulous darkness called : Ellmann (*IY* 261) remarks that these lines daringly assert a parallelism and even identity between the three pairs, Astraea and Spica, Athene and Dionysus, and Mary and Christ.   Cf. Lady Gregory (*Journal* 263) for an early version reading 'Virgo [the constellation] and the mystic star'.

16   *The fabulous darkness* : from a description of Christianity by Proclus, a fourth-century Neo-platonic philosopher (whom Yeats read in Thomas Taylor's translation of 1816). Cf. Wilson (*Y & T* 59). Cf. *AV* (B) 277 and 278 and *AV* (A) 185 ff.

> . . . the irrational force that would create confusion and uproar as with the cry "The Babe, the Babe, is born" — the women speaking unknown tongues, the barbers and weavers expounding Divine revelation with all the vulgarity of their servitude, the tables that move or resound with raps — but creates a negligible sect.
>
> All about it is an *antithetical* aristocratic civilisation in its completed form, every detail of life hierarchical, every great man's door crowded at dawn by petitioners, great wealth everywhere in few men's hands, all dependent upon a few, up to the Emperor himself who is a God dependent upon a greater God, and everywhere in court, in the family, an inequality made law, and floating over all the Romanised Gods of Greece in their physical superiority . . . the world became Christian and 'that fabulous formless darkness' as it seemed to a philosopher of the fourth century, blotted out 'every beautiful thing', not through the conversion of crowds or general change of opinion or through any pressure from below, for civilisation was *antithetical* still, but by an act of power.

II

3   *Galilean turbulence* : foretold by astronomers in Babylon who reduce man's status by their science ; Man is being taught that he

is nothing in comparison to the universe ; He is becoming feature-less :

> God is now conceived of as something outside man and man's handiwork, and it follows that it must be idolatry to worship that which Phidias and Scopas made, and seeing that He is a Father in Heaven, that Heaven will be found presently in the Thebaid, where the world is changed into a featureless dust and can be run through the fingers ; and these things are testified to from books that are outside human genius, being miraculous, and by a miraculous Church, and this Church, as the gyre sweeps wider, will make man also featureless as clay or dust. Night will fall upon man's wisdom now that man has been taught that he is nothing. . . .
>
> The mind that brought the change, if considered as man only, is a climax of whatever Greek and Roman thought was most a contradiction to its age ; but considered as more than man He controlled what Neo-Pythagorean and Stoic could not — irrational force. He could announce the new age, all that had not been thought of, or touched, or seen, because He could substitute for reason, miracle. (*AV* (B) 273 ff.)

9–16 *Everything that man esteems . . .*
   Man's own resinous heart has fed : these lines praise man who goes on creating heroically despite the fact that all things pass away (cf. *A* 315).

12 *painter's brush* : cf. a passage in 'The Tragic Generation' : 'no school of painting outlasts its founders, every stroke of the brush exhausts the impulse, Pre-Raphaelitism had some twenty years ; Impressionism thirty perhaps' (*A* 315).

240 FRAGMENTS

The date of composition of these poems is probably 1931. The first stanza first appeared in *DM* (Oct.–Dec. 1931) as part of the poet's commentary on *WWP*, the second in *CP*.

1 *Locke* : Yeats hated Locke ; in this he probably followed Blake's example. In his Diary he wrote 'Descartes, Locke and Newton took away the world and gave us its excrement instead' (*E* 325).

2–4 *The Garden died* ;
  God took the spinning-jenny
  Out of his side : the poem is a parody of Eve's coming into
the world in Genesis. In the Introduction to *WWP* Yeats wrote
that he could see

> in a sort of nightmare vision the 'primary qualities' torn
> from the side of Locke, Johnson's ponderous body bent above
> the letter to Lord Chesterfield, some obscure person some-
> where inventing the spinning-jenny, upon his face that look of
> benevolence kept by painters and engravers, from the middle
> of the eighteenth century to the time of the Prince Consort,
> for such as he, or, to simplify the tale—
>   [then follow lines 1–4]   *(E* 358–9)

The spinning-jenny symbolises the Industrial Revolution which
followed on Locke's mechanical philosophy, as Yeats argued in
his essay on Berkeley :

> It is customary to praise English empirical genius, English
> sense of reality, and yet throughout the eighteenth century
> when her Indian Empire was founded England lived for certain
> great constructions that were true only in relation to the will.
> I spoke in the Irish Senate on the Catholic refusal of divorce
> and assumed that all lovers who ignored priest or registrar were
> immoral ; upon education, and assumed that everybody who
> could not read the newspaper was a poor degraded creature ;
> and had I been sent there by some religious organisation must
> have assumed that a child captured by a rival faith lost its soul ;
> and had my country been at war — but who does not serve
> these abstractions? Without them corporate life would be
> impossible. They are as serviceable as those leaf-like shapes
> of tin that mould the ornament for the apple-pie, and we give
> them belief, service, devotion. How can we believe in truth
> that is always moth-like and fluttering and yet can terrify? —
> A friend and myself, both grown men, talked ourselves once
> into a terror of a little white moth in Burnham Beeches. And
> of all these the most comprehensive, the most useful, was
> invented by Locke when he separated the primary and second-
> ary qualities ; and from that day to this the conception of a
> physical world without colour, sound, taste, tangibility, though
> indicted by Berkeley as Burke was to indict Warren Hastings
> fifty years later, and proved mere abstract extension, a mere
> category of the mind, has remained the assumption of science,

the groundwork of every text-book. It worked, and the mechanical inventions of the next age, its symbols that seemed its confirmation, worked even better, and it worked best of all in England where Edmund Spenser's inscription over the gates of his magic city seemed to end 'Do not believe too much': elsewhere it is the grosser half of that dialectical materialism the Socialist Prince Mirsky calls 'the firm foundation-rock of European Socialism,' and works all the mischief Berkeley foretold. (*E & I* 400–1)

241 II

This poem deals with the nature of poetic inspiration and insight. It returns to the belief Yeats held in his youth, that whatever the great poets had affirmed in their finest moments of inspiration was the nearest one could get to an authoritative religion. (Cf. *WBY* 47.) An essay on 'The Symbolism of Poetry' refers to Nineveh :

It is indeed only those things which seem useless or very feeble that have any power, and all those things that seem useful or strong, armies, moving wheels, modes of architecture, modes of government, speculations of the reason, would have been a little different if some mind long ago had not given itself to some emotion, as a woman gives herself to her lover, and shaped sounds or colours or forms, or all of these, into a musical relation, that their emotion might live in other minds. A little lyric evokes an emotion, and this emotion gathers others about it and mëlts into their being in the making of some great epic ; and at last, needing an always less delicate body, or symbol, as it grows more powerful, it flows out, with all it has gathered, among the blind instincts of daily life, where it moves a power within powers, as one sees ring within ring in the stem of an old tree. This is maybe what Arthur O'Shaughnessy meant when he made his poets say they had built Nineveh with their sighing ; and I am certainly never sure, when I hear of some war, or of some religious excitement, or of some new manufacture, or of anything else that fills the ear of the world, that it has not all happened because of something that a boy piped in Thessaly. I remember once telling a seeress to ask one among the gods who, as she believed, were standing about her in their symbolic bodies, what would come of a charming but seeming trivial labour of a friend, and the form answering, 'the devastation of people and the overwhelming of cities.' I doubt indeed if the crude circumstance of the world, which seems to create all our emotions, does more than reflect, as in multiplying mirrors, the emotions that have come to solitary men in moments of poetical contemplation ; or that love itself would be more than an animal hunger but for the poet and his shadow the priest, for unless we believe that outer things are the reality, we must believe that the gross is the shadow of the subtle, that things are wise before they become foolish, and secret before they cry out in the market-place. Solitary men in moments of contemplation receive, as I think, the creative impulse from the lowest of the Nine Hierarchies, and so make and unmake mankind, and even the world itself, for does not 'the eye altering alter all'?

> Our towns are copied fragments from our breast ;
> And all man's Babylons strive but to impart
> The grandeurs of his Babylonian heart.   (*E & I* 157–9)

The only mention of Nineveh made by O'Shaughnessy is his *Ode*, which describes the poets of the ages :

> We, in the ages lying
> In the buried part of the earth
> Built Nineveh with our sighing
> And Babel itself with our mirth ;
> And o'erthrew them with prophesying
> To the old of the new world's worth ;
> For each age is a dream that is dying,
> Or one that is coming to birth.
> (Arthur O'Shaughnessy, *Music and Moonlight*, 2)

The lines on Nineveh and Babel were misquoted in Yeats's *Pages from a Diary Written in Nineteen Hundred and Thirty* (*E* 337).   He wrote another version on this theme in *W & B*:

> Decline of day,
> A leaf drifts down ;
> O dark leaf clay
> On Nineveh's crown!   (*E* 401)

Cf. line 63 'Vacillation' v (*CP* 284).

LEDA AND THE SWAN

This poem was written on 18 September 1923 and first appeared in *The Dial* (June 1924).

Yeats wrote a note to explain that he

wrote Leda and the Swan because the editor [George Russell, A E] of a political review [*The Irishman Statesman*] asked me for a poem. I thought 'After the individualist, demagogic movement, founded by Hobbes and popularised by the Encyclopaedists and the French Revolution, we have a soil so exhausted that it cannot grow that crop again for centuries.' Then I thought 'Nothing is now possible but some movement, or birth from above, preceded by some violent annunciation'. My fancy began to play with Leda and the Swan for metaphor and I began this poem; but as I wrote, bird and lady took such possession of the scene that all politics went out of it, and my friend tells me that 'his conservative readers would misunderstand the poem.'

(The Cat and the Moon and Certain Poems, 1924)

Melchiori (*WMA* 73–114) discusses the genesis and symbolism of the poem very fully. He sees the short poem '.The Mother of God' (*CP* 281) as a Christian counterpart to the Leda annunciation, and he traces the effect of Gogarty's poems on the composition of 'Leda and the Swan' and its imagery, in particular that of 'To the Liffey with the Swans':

> . . . As fair as was that doubled Bird
> By love of Leda so besotten,
> That she was all with wonder stirred :
> And the Twin Sportsmen were begotten.

The poem appears in *AV* (A) heading the section *Dove or Swan* in which Yeats wrote 'I imagine the annunciation that founded Greece as made to Leda, remembering that they showed in a Spartan temple, strung up to the roof as a holy relic, an unhatched egg of hers ; and that from one of her eggs came Love and from the other War'. Cf. also *AV* (B) 268.

Yeats had a coloured photographic copy of Michelangelo's famous picture at Venice, but Charles Madge, the *Times Literary Supplement* (20 July 1962) has argued that an Etruscan bas-relief in the British Museum is closer to the poem's imagery and a more likely source for it than the Michelangelo painting.

7   *that white rush* : Melchiori, *WMA*, draws attention to Spenser, *Prothalamion* 3, 39–45 :

> Two fairer birds I yet did never see :
> The snow which doth the top of *Pindus* strew,
> Did never whiter shew,
> Nor *Jove* himself when he a Swan would be

For love of *Leda*, whiter did appeare :
Yet *Leda* was, they say, as white as he,
Yet not so white as these, nor nothing neare.

10   *The broken wall* : Henn (*LT* 255) quotes Todhunter's *Helena in Troas* which Yeats admired for the link between Leda and Helen of Troy :

O pitiless mischief! Thee no woman bore
Wooed by the billing of the amorous swan.
Yea, Leda bore thee not but Nemesis
To be the doom of Troy and Priam's house.

Henn has also discussed the meaning of the poem :

Two Annunciations form a pattern in history : Leda and the Virgin. The Virgin is linked, mistakenly, to St Anne, *via* Pater's Essay. Both events concern the union of godhead and woman. Both produce momentous births. The eggs of Leda give rise to the fall of Troy ; from them emerge the legend of two destined women Helen and Clytemnestra. Helen has long been a personal symbol for Maud Gonne. The swans are archetypal, everywhere ; in Spenser, emblems, paintings, Celtic myth, and concretely on the Lakes at Coole. The swan stands for power, phallic strength, purity, spirit and spirits (as all white birds), fidelity ; fire and air (as the dove); the ineffable Godhead. In the act of congress the *loosening thighs* and the *white rush* are antithetical aspects. Into the softness and whiteness is concentrated all the sensuality of touch. The outcome of the union is further history or myth, pagan or Christian, Love and War. But what of the woman? Yeats speculates continually on the emotions of woman in such a crisis. Did Leda or Mary by that act become half or wholly divine? Did a god share with beast the lassitude that overcomes all animals, save only the lion and the cock? *Shudder* is of the sexual act, the moment of orgasm, as all husband-men know ; but it is also anticipation in fear. (*LT* 256-7)

ON A PICTURE OF A BLACK CENTAUR BY EDMUND DULAC   **242**

This poem was written in September 1920 and first appeared in *SPF* with the title 'Suggested by a Picture of a Black Centaur'.

Title   Picture of a Black Centaur by Edmund Dulac : The poem, according to Mrs Yeats, was begun in relation to a picture by

Dulac but altered in relation to one by Cecil Salkeld, whose account of the poem's composition appears in *WBY* 326–8 :

Madame Gonne MacBride smiled at me and said : 'Willie is booming and buzzing like a bumble bee . . . that means he is writing something. . . .' To my great surprise, Yeats, who appeared shortly, obviously preoccupied and absent-minded, asked me if I would walk up the glen with him. We walked, treading our way among boulders and small stones along the river bank for nearly half an hour in silence. By that I mean no word was spoken ; but, all the while, Yeats kept up a persistent murmur — under his breath, as it were. Suddenly, he pulled up short at a big stone and said : 'Do you realise that eternity is not a long time but a *short* time . . .?' I just said, I didn't quite understand. 'Eternity,' Yeats said, 'Eternity is in the glitter on the beetle's wing . . . it is something infinitely short . . .' I said that I could well conceive 'Infinity' being excessively small as well as being excessively large. 'Yes,' he said, apparently irrelevantly, 'I was thinking of those Ephesian topers. . . .'

He pulled out of his pocket a very small piece of paper on which he had written 8 lines which had been perhaps ten times corrected. It was almost impossible for me to read a line of it. I only saw one phrase which I knew was obsessing him at that time — for Yeats was at all times a man dominated — sometimes for weeks on end — by a single phrase : this one was 'Mummy wheat' — a phrase destined to appear in a much later poem — a phrase he never forgot.

That night I sat up late, long after the others had gone to bed, and finished a water-colour picture of a weird centaur at the edge of a dark wood : in the foreground, in the shade of the wood, lay the seven Ephesian 'topers' in a drunken stupor, while far behind on a sunny distant desert plain elephants and the glory of a great army passed away into the distance. Next day I showed the picture to Yeats. He looked at it so critically that I suddenly remembered that he had been an Art Student. He peered at me over the top of his glasses. 'Who is your teacher?' he asked. 'Has he told you about values?' 'What are values?' I asked. Yeats laughed his deep ferocious chuckle : 'Do you really tell me you don't know what "values" are?' I said 'No', and waited for instruction. 'Well, I'm certainly not going to tell you ! . . . "Values" were the bane of my youth.' When I walked out with him that day he made no reference to the poem, but talked continuously of the conception of the 'Daimon' which was particularly interesting him at the time : he also told me the history of his play *The Player Queen*, saying (perhaps with a faint reminiscence of Goethe's *Faust* in his head) that he had spent 20 years on the play.

Later that night, W. B. came down to supper with a perfectly clear countenance ; it was plain the poem was finished. He did not speak throughout the meal, yet I felt he would say something before the night was through. When the ladies had withdrawn, he produced a pigskin-covered brandy flask and a small beautifully written manuscript : 'Your picture made the thing clear', he said. 'I am going to dedicate the poem to you. I shall call it The Black Centaur'. . . . It was then for the first time I heard those miraculous lines, one of which is :

Stretch out your limbs and sleep a long Saturnian sleep.

I was impressed and gratified. But when printed in 1928, in *The Tower*, the poem was altered ; it was corrected and it was entitled : 'On a Picture of a Black Centaur by Edmund Dulac'.

7 *mummy wheat* : Yeats implies hidden wisdom which can be ripened centuries after its sowing. When he wrote this poem and 'All Souls' Night' (*CP* 256) where the phrase is used in the second stanza, he was full of the ideas of *AV* and felt that they were revelations of hidden truth which he was bringing into the light out of the darkness where it had been concealed. The image came from his reading of the discoveries in Egyptian tombs (cf. 'The Gyres', *CP* 337).

11 *seven Ephesian topers* : the seven sleepers of Ephesus

AMONG SCHOOL CHILDREN   242

This poem was written on 14 June 1926 and first appeared in *The Dial* (Aug. 1927) and *LM* (Aug. 1927).

A draft in Yeats's white vellum notebook written about 14 March 1926 reads 'Topic for poem — School children and the thought that live [life] will waste them perhaps that no possible life can fulfill our dreams or even their teacher's hope. Bring in the old thought that life prepares for what never happens'. The 'old thought' is probably a memory of ideas written in the Diary begun in 1908. In an unpublished entry, 6 Sept. 1909, Yeats asked himself why life is 'a perpetual preparation for something that never happens'. See also *A* 473 and note on line 39 below.

1 *the long schoolroom* : Yeats visited St Otteran's School, Waterford, in February 1926. This school was run on Montessori principles and Yeats praised its work in the Senate (see *SSY* 111).

2 *a kind old nun* : Rev. Mother Philomena, the Mistress of Schools. See Donald T. Torchiana, '"Among School Children" and the Education of the Irish Spirit', *IER* 123–50.

5–6 *be neat in everything In the best modern way* : the Montessori system emphasised neatness.

243 9–16 *Ledaean body* : Maud Gonne. Leda suggests the story of the eggs and this the Platonic image from the Symposium, 190 ('Plato's parable' of line 15). See note on line 22.

22 *that colour* : Torchiana (*IER* 138–9) makes some interesting remarks on the childlike relationship between Yeats and Maud Gonne. He takes a description of Fionnuala and Aodh from Ella Young's *Celtic Wonder-Tales* (1910) which Maud Gonne illustrated with a recurring motif of a sphere containing two swans intertwined, ultimately blent as one, an obvious symbol of kindred souls (see note on 'Baile and Aillinn' (*CP* 457).

25 *Her present image* : Maud Gonne's appearance at the time he was writing the poem

26 *Quattrocento finger* : this was 'quinto-cento' finger in the early version. It was altered to 'Da Vinci' [Leonardo da Vinci] finger in the version of the poem printed in *LM* (Aug. 1927).

30 *pretty plumage* : Yeats's former raven-coloured hair

32 *scarecrow* : cf. 'Sailing to Byzantium' (*CP* 217)

244 33–40 *What youthful mother, a shape upon her lap*
Honey of generation had betrayed,

And that must sleep, shriek, struggle to escape
As recollection or the drug decide,
Would think her son, did she but see that shape
With sixty or more winters on its head,
A compensation for the pang of his birth,
Or the uncertainty of his setting forth? : Torchiana quotes a
passage from Gentile (*The Reform of Education* 194) which Yeats
read in Dino Bigongiari's translation of 1923 for which Croce wrote
a foreword. (In this book Gentile argues that only our thought
gives unity to material reality, that culture is an activity, a constant
becoming) :

> The mother who tenderly nurses her sick child is indeed
> anxious for the health of the body over which she worries,
> and she would like to see it vigorous and strong. But that
> body is so endeared to her, because by means of it the child is
> enabled to live happily with her ; through it his fond soul can
> requite maternal love by filial devotion ; or in it he may
> develop a powerful and beautiful personality worthy to be
> adored as the ideal creature of maternal affection. If in the
> bloom of physical health he were to reveal himself stupid and
> insensate, endowed with mere instinctive sensuality and bestial
> appetites, this son would cease to be the object of his mother's
> fondness, nay, he would arouse in her a feeling of loathing and
> revulsion. It is this sense of loathing . . . that we . . . feel
> for the human corpse from which life has departed ; for life
> is the basis of every psychological relation, and therefore of
> every possible sympathy. (*IER* 134)

34   *Honey of generation* : this image comes from Porphyry, *On the
Cave of the Nymphs* (1917) 22. Yeats wrote that he found no warrant
in Porphyry for considering it the 'drug' that destroys the 'recollection' of prenatal freedom. He blamed a cup of oblivion given in
the zodiacal sign of Cancer (*CP*). Porphyry's work is a comment,
dedicated to the Nymphs, on the symbolism of Homer's *Odyssey*.
In the cave which Homer described in the thirteenth book of the
Odyssey were bowls and works of divine workmanship in which the
busy bees placed delicious honey. Porphyry gives a long explanation ; he describes the cathartic and preservative functions of
honey and its ebriating effect on Saturn ('the sweetness of honey
signifies, with theologists, the same thing as the pleasure arising
from generation, by which Saturn, being ensnared, was castrated')

and finally links the 'honey of generation' with the aquatic Nymphs. Wilson (*Y & T* 212) explains that in Platonic tradition the soul journeys from the Isles of the Blessed in life ; in death it lives backwards in time and returns to its starting point. The wanderings of Odysseus symbolise life : he returns to Ithaca (which symbolises the Isles of the Blessed) after he has been converted to intellectual life at the Holy City of Phaeacia, but he must return via the cave, where the honey is the pleasure arising from generation and the Nymphs and honey-bees are symbols for two kinds of souls born into the world :

> Since, therefore, honey is assumed in purgations, and as an antidote to putrefaction, and is indicative of the pleasure which draws souls downward to generation ; it is a symbol well adapted to aquatic Nymphs, on account of the unputrescent nature of the waters over which they preside, their putrifying power, and their co-operation with generation. For water co-operates in the work of generation. On this account the bees are said, by the poet, to deposit their honey in bowls and amphorae ; the bowls being a symbol of fountains, and there-fore a bowl is placed near to Mithra, instead of a fountain ; but the amphorae are symbols of the vessels with which we draw water from fountains. And fountains and streams are adapted to aquatic Nymphs, and still more so in the Nymphs that are souls, which the ancients peculiarly called bees, as the efficient causes of sweetness. . . . All souls, however, proceeding into generation, are not simply called bees, but those who will live in it justly and who, after having performed such things as are acceptable to the Gods, will again return (to their kindred stars). . . . We must therefore admit, that honeycombs and bees are appropriate and common symbols of the aquatic nymphs, and of souls that are married (as it were) to (the humid and fluctuating nature of) generation. (Porphyry, *On the Cave of the Nymphs* 23–5)

In his essay on 'The Philosophy of Shelley's poetry' Yeats traced Porphyry's influence on Shelley's cave symbolism, particularly in the Witch of Atlas. Cf. (*E & I* 80–6)

38 *sixty or more winters* : probably derives from John Donne's 'A Song' : 'Till age snow white hairs on thee' according to (*PYP* 131) and possibly to an old beggar telling Lady Gregory she was 'in the winter of her age'.

39   *A compensation* : cf. *At the Hawk's Well* :

> What were his life soon done!
> Would he lose by that or win?
> A mother that saw her son
> Doubled over a speckled shin,
> Cross-grained with ninety years,
> Would cry, 'How little worth
> Were all my hopes and fears
> And the hard pain of his birth.'   (*CPl* 208)

41–8 *Plato thought nature but a spume that plays*
> *Upon a ghostly paradigm of things ;*
> *Solider Aristotle played the taws*
> *Upon the bottom of a king of kings ;*
> *World-famous golden-thighed Pythagoras*
> *Fingered upon a fiddle-stick or strings*
> *What a star sang and careless Muses heard :*
> *Old clothes upon old sticks to scare a bird* : Yeats wrote to Mrs

Shakespear on 24 September 1926 that he was reading Croce, writing verse and hence had nothing to say :

> Here is a fragment of my last curse on old age. It means
> that even the greatest men are owls, scarecrows, by the time their
> fame has come. Aristotle, remember, was Alexander's tutor,
> hence the taws (form of birch)

> > Plato imagined all existence plays
> > Among the ghostly images of things ;
> > Solider Aristotle played the taws
> > Upon the bottom of the King of Kings ;
> > World famous, golden-thighed Pythagoras
> > Fingered upon a fiddle stick, or strings,
> > What the stars sang and careless Muses heard.—
> > Old coats upon old sticks to scare a bird.

Pythagoras made some measurement of the intervals between notes
on a stretched string. (*L* 719)

There is an interesting MS. version of this stanza :

> Caesar Augustus that made all the laws
> And the ordering of everything
> Plato that learned geometry and was
> The foremost man at the soul's meaning
> That golden thighed far famed Pythagoras
> World famous, golden thighed Pythagoras

> Who taught the stars of heaven what to sing
> And the musicians how to measure cords
> Old clothes upon old sticks to scare the birds.

Thomas Parkinson (*YTLP* 101) comments on 'the reasoned rhetorical order' of this draft, from 'the individual soul as seen by Plato to the state as organised by Augustus, to the universe as directed by Pythagoras'. He discusses the unpublished MSS. of the poem in detail, pp. 92–113.

42 *paradigm* : Parkinson (*YTLP* 103) points out that 'paradigm' was Thomas Taylor's favourite term for Archetype or Platonic idea of essence. Yeats used Taylor's translations of Plato and read his other work.

45 *golden-thighed* : the phrase comes from Thomas Taylor's translation of Iamblichus, *Life of Pythagoras*, p. 49 :

> Pythagoras, however, receiving the dart, and neither being astonished at the novelty of the thing, nor asking the reason why it was given to him, but as if he was in reality a god himself, taking Abacis aside, he showed him his golden thigh, as an indication he was not [wholly] deceived [in the opinion he had formed of him].

53 *O Presences* : Parkinson (*YTLP* 105) comments that these can only be taken to mean the statues and children that are knowable by passion, piety, or affection.

245 64 *the dancer from the dance* : Torchiana quotes a passage from Gentile (*The Reform of Education* 228–9), the thought of which he thinks is used by Yeats in the last stanza of the poem :

> The spirit's being is its alteration. The more it *is*, — that is, the more it becomes, the more it lives, — the more difficult it is for it to recognise itself in the object. It might therefore be said that he who increases his knowledge also increases his ignorance, if he is unable to trace this knowledge back to its origin, and if the spirit's rally does not induce him to rediscover himself at the bottom of the object, which has been allowed to alter and alienate itself more and more from the secret source of its own becoming. Thus it happens, as was said of old, that 'He that increaseth knowledge increaseth sorrow.' All

human sorrow proceeds from our incapacity to recognise ourselves in the object, and consequently to feel our own infinite liberty. (*IER* 135)

Parkinson (*YTLP* 108) comments on the final stanza that the problems posed by the poem 'were transported into a world of transcendent possibilities, successes beyond the reach of the divided life embodied in the first four stanzas of the poem and in the aspirations of the great intellects'.

COLONUS' PRAISE   245

This translation of a chorus in Sophocles' *Oedipus at Colonus* was written on (approximately) 24 March 1927, and first appeared in *The Tower* (1928).

Yeats used a French translation by Paul Masqueray as he did not read Greek. (He made a translation of *Oedipus Rex* in 1911–12, but never used it.) His translation of *Oedipus Rex* was first produced at the Abbey Theatre on 6 December 1926. His translation of *Oedipus at Colonus* was produced at the Abbey Theatre on 12 September 1927, and first appeared in *C Pl*.

1   *Colonus* : κολωνὸς ἵππιος, Colonus of the horses, an Attic deme or district, the birthplace of Sophocles (495–406 B.C.), a hill a mile north of Athens

8   *Semele's lad* : Dionysus, son of Zeus and of Semele, a daughter of Cadmus. Hera, who was jealous of her association with Zeus, disguised herself and advised Semele to test the divinity of her lover by asking him to come to her in his true shape. Semele tricked Zeus into granting her whatever she would ask, and she was killed by the fire of his thunderbolts. Zeus put the unborn child in his thigh. He was born at full time, went into Hades and brought Semele up and she became an Olympian goddess.

9   *the gymnasts' garden*: the Lyceum at Athens on the banks of the river Cephisus, a sacred grove

12   *olive-tree* : cf. line 46 'Nineteen Hundred and Nineteen' (*CP* 232).

16 *grey-eyed Athene* : was the patron goddess of Athens ; she produced the olive tree in a struggle with Poseidon for ownership of the land in Attica and won the contest. 'Grey-eyed' was one of the standard descriptions of the goddess.

19 *Great Mother* : Demeter, mourning for Persephone

246 23 *abounding Cephisus* : river in Attica

28 *Poseidon* : Poseidon, god of horses and the sea. See note on line 16.

246 WISDOM

It is not possible to date the composition of this poem accurately ; it probably belongs to the period of 'Two Songs from a Play' (*CP* 239) and first appeared in *OB*.

6–7 *the sawdust from the floor of that working carpenter* : Yeats may have been thinking of pre-Raphaelite paintings, Millais's 'Christ in the house of his parents', for example. The first printed version read for lines 6 and 7

> Dream of shavings on a floor
> And dirty nails of carpenters.

9–13 *In damask clothed and on a seat*
Chryselephantine, cedar-boarded,
His majestic Mother: Henn (*LT* 257) states this is based 'almost beyond doubt' on a poorish seventeenth-century painting by an unknown painter formerly hung in the National Gallery, Dublin, then stored in its cellars and now hung again. It was originally labelled 'The Annunciation' but a more possible title, according to Henn, is 'The Seamless Garment'.

14 *starry towers of Babylon* : Mrs Yeats thinks these came from Yeats's visit to the Ravenna mosaics (1907) cf. 'the Babylonian starlight' of 'Two Songs from a Play' (*CP* 239).

15 *Noah's freshet* : the flood

THE FOOL BY THE ROADSIDE   **247**

This poem's date of composition cannot be determined with accuracy ; it first appeared in *SPF* as 'Cuchulain The Girl and the Fool'. Only lines 18–29 were printed in *CP*. The lines 1–17 appear to deal with an imaginary conversation between Yeats and Iseult Gonne, and are akin to some of the imagery in 'Michael Robartes and the Dancer' (*CP* 197).

5 *upon a spool* : the poem is reminiscent of Plato's spindle in *The Republic* and the pern mill in Sligo (see note (p. 176) on line 97 'Shepherd and Goatherd' (*CP* 159). Cf. notes (pp. 379 ff.) on 'His Bargain' (*CP* 299).

OWEN AHERNE AND HIS DANCERS   **247**

The first part of this poem was written shortly after Yeats's marriage when he and his wife were staying at Ashdown Forest Hotel, Forest Row, on 24 October, and the second on 27 October 1917. It first appeared in *The Dial* (June 1924) with the first section entitled 'The Lover Speaks', the second 'The Heart Replies'.

Title   Owen Aherne : a name for an invented persona : he is described in *The Tables of the Law* (see *M* 293–4). But here he is a disguise for Yeats himself. Henn (*LT* 47) regards the 'Dancers' as 'the delighted senses, the principle of desire'.

1–2   . . . *love had come unsought*
       Upon the Norman upland : a reference to Yeats's love for Iseult Gonne. While the poem describes Yeats's feelings in the summer of 1917 the 'unsought' may refer to Iseult proposing to Yeats in Normandy at the age of fifteen and being rejected 'because there was too much Mars in her horoscope'. Lady Gregory favoured his marrying Iseult.

14   *that young child* : Iseult Gonne. Yeats continually asked her to   **248** marry him in 1917. He delivered an ultimatum to her on the boat when he accompanied Madame MacBride and Iseult to England from France in September 1917. She must make up her mind one

way or the other : he found the situation a great strain and, if she would not marry him, he had a friend who would, a girl strikingly beautiful in a barbaric manner. He must receive her answer within a week. She refused and on 20 October 1917 he married Georgie Hyde-Lees.

19   *the woman at my side* : Mrs Yeats

249   21   *Speak all your mind* : this may refer to the effect of the automatic writing which began *AV* and released much of the poet's tension and unhappiness. Cf. a letter Yeats wrote to Lady Gregory on 29 October 1917 :

> . . . There has been something very like a miraculous intervention. Two days ago I was in great gloom (of which I hope, and believe, George knew nothing). I was saying to myself 'I have betrayed three people' ; then I thought 'I have lived all through this before.' Then George spoke of the sensation of having lived through something before (she knew nothing of my thought). Then she said she felt that something was to be written through her. She got a piece of paper, and talking to me all the while so that her thoughts would not affect what she wrote, wrote these words (which she did not understand) 'with the bird' (Iseult) 'all is well at heart. Your action was right for both but in London you mistook its meaning.' I had begun to believe just before my marriage that I had acted, not as I thought more for Iseult's sake than for my own, but because my mind was unhinged by strain. The strange thing was that within half an hour after writing of this message my rheumatic pains and my neuralgia and my fatigue had gone and I was very happy. From being more miserable than I ever remember being since Maud Gonne's marriage I became extremely happy. That sense of happiness has lasted ever since. The misery produced two poems which I will send you presently to hide away for me — they are among the best I have done.
>
> I enclose a letter of congratulation from Helen Bayly (now Mrs Lawless) you will remember her at Florence. I send it as it shows you how well George is liked — I have had other like testimonies. I think George has your own moral genius. She says by the by that you are the only friend of mine she has never feared. Should have said that after George had written that sentence I asked mentally 'when shall I have peace of

mind' and her hand wrote 'you will neither regret nor repine'
and I think certainly that I never shall again. . . . (*L* 633–4)

A MAN YOUNG AND OLD   **249**

These poems were written in 1926 and 1927 and first appeared in
LM (May 1927) with the title 'Four Essays from the Young
Countryman'. Numbers VI, VII, VIII, and X first appeared under the
title 'More Songs of an Old Countryman' *LM* (April 1926). They
were reprinted under the title 'A Man Young and Old' in *The
Tower* (1928).

I

Title First Love: this poem describes Yeats's youthful love for
Maud Gonne. He wrote a letter to Olivia Shakespear on 7 December 1926 in which he enclosed an early version of the second stanza
of this poem with the comment 'I told you and showed you part
of two series of poems in which a man and a woman in old or
later life remember love. I am writing for each series contrasting
poems of youth' (*L* 720).

8 *heart of stone*: cf. note (p. 228) on line 43 of 'Easter 1916'
(*CP* 202).

II
Human Dignity   **250**

1 *her kindness*: this poem also describes Yeats's love for Maud
Gonne.

3 *no comprehension*: in his Diary for 22 January 1909 Yeats wrote
that Maud Gonne

> never really understands my plans or nature or ideas. Then
> came the thought — what matter? — How much of the best
> I have done and still do is but the attempt to explain myself
> to her? If she understood I should lack a reason for writing,
> and one can never have too many reasons for doing what is so
> laborious. (*WBY* 228)

Cf. the poem 'Words' (*CP* 100).

9 *if I shrieked*: cf. a passage in an unpublished MS. in which
Yeats described his state of mind in 1897: 'I was tortured with

sexual desire and disappointed love. Often as I walked in the woods at Coole it would have been a relief to have screamed aloud.'

III

250 *The Mermaid*

1 *A mermaid* : this refers to Yeats's brief relationship with 'Diana Vernon' in 1896. A literary source may be Lady Gregory, *Visions and Beliefs*, 11 ; 'And there was a boy saw a mermaid down by Spiddal [Galway] not long ago, but he saw her before she saw him, so she did him no harm. But if she'd seen him first, she'd have brought him away and drowned him.'

IV

250 *The Death of the Hare*
This poem was written on 3 January 1926.

2 *The hare* : the hare is Iseult Gonne. Yeats wrote to Maurice Wollman who edited *Modern Poetry 1922–1934* (1935) on 23 September 1935 to say that he didn't want to interpret the poem.

> I can help you to write a note, if that note is to be over your own name, but you must not give me as your authority. If an author interprets a poem of his own he limits its suggestibility. You can say that the poem means that the lover may, while loving, feel sympathy with his beloved's dread of captivity. I don't know how else to put it. (*L* 840–1)

251 12 *the death* : may allude to her marriage to Francis Stuart. See notes (p. 369) on 'Stream and Sun at Glendalough' (*CP* 288) and (pp. 503–4) on 'Why should not Old Men be Mad' (*CP* 388).

V

251 *The Empty Cup*
This poem was probably written in December 1926.

1 *A crazy man* : Yeats

cup : the poem is about Yeats's relationship with 'Diana Vernon' cf. a letter to Olivia Shakespear written on 6 December 1926 :

I came upon two early photographs of you yesterday, while going through my file — one that from *Literary Year Book*. Who ever had a like profile? — a profile from a Sicilian coin. One looks back to one's youth as to [a] cup that a mad man dying of thirst left half tasted. I wonder if you feel like that.

The version of the poem included in the letter ran as follows :

> A madman found a cup of wine
> And half dead of thirst
> Hardly dared to wet his mouth,
> Imagining, moon accurst,
> That another mouthful
> And his beating heart would burst
>
> But my discovery of the change
> For it cannot be denied
> That all is ancient metal now
> The four winds have dried—
> Has kept me waking half the night
> And made me hollow-eyed.   (*L* 721–2)

4 *moon-accursed* : cf. 'First Love' (*CP* 249) and 'Human Dignity' (*CP* 250). The liaison between Yeats and 'Diana Vernon' lasted only a year. Maud Gonne had written to him that she was in London and would come and dine with him, and he had not let her. He was upset by this letter, and when Diana Vernon next came to see him, found he could not answer her and knew there was someone else in his heart. Cf. note (p. 63) on 'The Lover mourns for the Loss of Love' (*CP* 68).

7 *October last* : Yeats had a meeting with 'Diana Vernon' in October 1926.

VI
His Memories   251
It is likely this poem is imaginary or a conflation of various experiences.

VII
The Friends of his Youth   252
This poem was written on 2 July 1926.

VIII
Summer and Spring   253

6–8 . . . *halved a soul*
    And fell the one in t'other's arms
    That we might make it whole : this imagery is related to that of lines 13–17 of 'Among School Children' (*CP* 242), and the imagery of the tree in lines 13–15 is akin to the last stanza of that poem.

IX

253 *The Secrets of the Old*

254 17–18 *bed of straw Or the bed of down* : possibly a cottage or great house antithesis

X

254 *His Wildness*

3–4 *Paris' love That had so straight a back* : a description of Helen or Maud Gonne whose 'straight back' is praised in 'Beautiful Lofty Things' (*CP* 348).

XI

255 *From 'Oedipus at Colonus'*
This poem was written on or before 13 March 1927. See note (p. 305) on 'Colonus' Praise' (*CP* 245).

12 *The second best's a gay goodnight* : Yeats wrote to Olivia Shakespear on 13 March 1927 that the last line was 'very bad Grecian, but very good Elizabethan and so it must stay' (*L* 723).

255 THE THREE MONUMENTS

This poem was written, according to Mrs Yeats, *before* the Irish Senate debate on divorce on 11 June 1925 (not after, as in *WBY* 370 nor, as in *SSY* 98, 'a couple of years later'), and first appeared in *OB*.

2 *Our most renownèd patriots stand* : a reference to the statues of Daniel O'Connell, Charles Stewart Parnell and Lord Nelson in O'Connell Street, Dublin.

4 *stumpier* : Nelson's Pillar (this was recently blown up, and the remains of the elegant column have been removed) which was higher

than the Parnell monument, at the northern end of O'Connell Street (formerly Sackville Street) and the monument to O'Connell at the southern end.

12   *The three old rascals* : Yeats's speech in the Senate was chal-   255
lenging :

> I have said that this is a tolerant country, yet, remembering that we have in our principal streets certain monuments, I feel it necessary to say that it would be wiser if I had said this country is hesitating.
>
> I have no doubt whatever that, when the iceberg melts it will become an exceedingly tolerant country. The monuments are on the whole encouraging. I am thinking of O'Connell, Parnell, and Nelson. We never had any trouble about O'Connell. It was said about O'Connell, in his own day, that you could not throw a stick over a workhouse wall without hitting one of his children, but he believed in the indissolubility of marriage, and when he died his heart was very properly preserved in Rome. I am not quite sure whether it was in a bronze or marble urn, but it is there, and I have no doubt the art of that urn was as bad as the other art of the period. We had a good deal of trouble about Parnell when he married a woman who became thereby Mrs Parnell.
>
> *An Cathaoirleach* : Do you not think we might leave the dead alone?
>
> *Dr Yeats* : I am passing on. I would hate to leave the dead alone. When that happened, I can remember the Irish Catholic Bishops coming out with a declaration that he had thereby doubled his offence. That is, fundamentally, the difference between us. In the opinion of every Irish Protestant gentleman in this country he did what was essential as a man of honour. Now you are going to make that essential act impossible and thereby affront an important minority of your countrymen. I am anxious to draw the attention of the Bishop of Meath to Nelson. There is a proposal to remove Nelson because he interferes with the traffic. Now, I would suggest to the Protestant Bishop of Meath that he should advocate the removal of Nelson on strictly moral grounds. We will then have the whole thing out, and discover whether the English people who teach the history of Nelson to their children, and hold it before the country as a patriotic ideal, or the Bishop of Meath represent, on the whole, public opinion. The Bishop

of Meath would not, like his predecessors in Ireland eighty years ago, have given Nelson a pillar. He would have preferred to give him a gallows, because Nelson should have been either hanged or transported. I think I have not greatly wronged the dead in suggesting that we have in our midst three very salutary objects of meditation which may, perhaps, make us a little more tolerant. (*SSY* 97–8)

256 ALL SOULS' NIGHT
Epilogue to 'A Vision'

This poem was written in November 1920 at Oxford (Yeats wrote 'I have moments of exaltation like that in which I wrote 'All Souls' Night' (*AV* (A) xii)) and it first appeared in *The New Republic* (9 March 1921) and *LM* (March 1921).

1 *Christ Church Bell*: Christ Church, Oxford. Yeats was living there, in Broad Street, when he wrote the poem.

257 21 *Horton's the first*: William Thomas Horton (1864–1919), an Irvingite who produced mystical drawings for *S* in 1896, and for whose *A Book of Images* (1898) Yeats wrote a Preface. Horton also wrote *The Way of the Soul* (1910) with symbolic illustrations; he was influenced by Blake and Beardsley; many of his drawings are preserved in the University of Reading and in Bodley. He is listed among the members of the Order of the Golden Dawn in 1898. See two letters about the Order written to him by Yeats in 1896 (*L* 260–1).

23 *platonic love*: Yeats wrote of him in *AV*:

[He] lived through that strange adventure, perhaps the strangest of all adventures — Platonic love. When he was a child his nurse said to him 'An Angel bent over your bed last night,' and in his seventeenth year he awoke to see the phantom of a beautiful woman at his bedside. Presently he gave himself up to all kinds of amorous adventures, until at last, in I think his fiftieth year but when he had still all his physical vigour, he thought 'I do not need women but God.' Then he and a very good, charming, young fellow-student fell in love with one another, and though he could only keep his passion down with the most bitter struggle, they lived together platonically, and this they did, not from prejudice, for I think they had none, but from a clear sense of something to be attained by what seemed a most needless trampling of the grapes of life. She died and he survived her but a little time during which he saw her in apparition and attained through her certain of the traditional experiences of the saint. (*AV* (A) p. x)

25 *when his lady died*: Audrey Locke died in 1916

35 *a slight companionable ghost*: D. J. Gordon and Ian Fletcher have quoted from a letter that Yeats wrote to Horton after Miss Locke's death: 'She had talent, and great charm and must have been much interwoven in your thought . . . the dead are not far from us . . . they cling in some strange way to what is most deep and still within us.'

They comment that when Horton tried to record this in a self-portrait showing the spiritual presence of the lady, the year after her death, the inadequacy of feeling and will to produce the image is almost desperately apparent (*IP* 103).

40 *a gold-fish swimming in a bowl*: a bowl of goldfish was kept on one of the windows of Yeats's house in Broad Street, Oxford, to amuse Anne Yeats.

41 *Florence Emery*: Florence Farr Emery (d. 1917) first met Yeats in 1890 when she was acting in *A Sicilian Idyll* by John Todhunter (1839–1916); she produced Yeats's *The Land of Heart's Desire* as a curtain raiser at the Avenue Theatre on 29 March 1894, acted the part of Aleel in *The Countess Cathleen* in Dublin 1899, and gave a performance of his *The Shadowy Waters* for a Theosophical Convention at the Court Theatre, London on 8 July 1905. She was a member of the group of students of the occult which centred on MacGregor Mathers, her initials in the Order of the Golden Dawn being S.S.D.D. (Sapientia Sapienti Dona Data). She recited Yeats's poems to the Psaltery and wrote *The Music of Speech* (1909). Ellmann (*Y:M & M* 182) says Yeats had an affair with her after 1903. Shaw described her as

a young independent professional woman, who enjoyed, as such, an exceptional freedom of social intercourse in artistic circles in London. As she was clever, good natured, and very

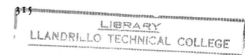

good-looking, all her men friends fell in love with her. This had occurred so often that she had lost all patience with the hesitating preliminaries of her less practised adorers. Accordingly, when they clearly longed to kiss her, and she did not dislike them sufficiently to make their gratification too great a strain on her excessive good nature, she would seize the stammering suitor firmly by the wrists, bring him into her arms by a smart pull and saying 'Let's get it over' allow the startled gentleman to have his kiss, and then proceed to converse with him at her ease on subjects of more general interest. (Hesketh Pearson, *Bernard Shaw: His Life and Personality* (1942) 120–1)

Cf. *Florence Farr, Bernard Shaw and W. B. Yeats*, a volume of letters published by the Cuala Press in 1941.

Yeats described her in 'Four Years : 1887–1891' as possessing

three great gifts, a tranquil beauty like that of Demeter's image near the British Museum Reading-Room door, and an incomparable sense of rhythm and a beautiful voice, the seeming natural expression of the image. . . . Her sitting-room at the Brook Green lodging-house was soon a reflection of her mind, the walls covered with musical instruments, pieces of Oriental drapery, and Egyptian gods and goddesses painted by herself in the British Museum. (*A* 121–3)

46 *teach a school* : Mrs Emery went to teach in a Buddhist Institution, Rasmanathan College, in Ceylon, where she died on 29 April 1917. This was founded by Sri Ponnambalam Ramanathan. For details of her life in Ceylon see Jayanta Padmanabha's articles in the *Ceylon Daily News*, 2 & 3 February 1947 and 29 & 30 April 1947.

49 *foul years* : she was suffering from cancer.

52–3 . . . *discourse in figurative speech*
    By some learned Indian . . . : F. F. Farag (*YCE* 41) suggests that the Indian was Mohini Chatterjee. 'free and yet fast' (line 57) may relate to his view that people do not 'possess even their bodies.'

258 58 *Chance and Choice* : see note (p. 218) on line 14 'Solomon and the Witch' (*CP* 199)

61 *MacGregor* : MacGregor Mathers (1854–1918), originally Samuel Liddle Mathers, studied occultism in London from 1885.

He was appointed Curator of the Horniman Museum at Forest Hill in 1890, lost this post through a quarrel and lived in Paris from (probably) 1894. Interested in Rosicrucianism and Freemasonry, he translated the *Kabalah Denudata*. Yeats wrote of him in 'Four Years : 1887–1891'

At the British Museum Reading-Room I often saw a man of thirty-six, or thirty-seven, in a brown velveteen coat, with a gaunt resolute face, and an athletic body, who seemed, before I heard his name, or knew the nature of his studies, a figure of romance. Presently I was introduced, where or by what man or woman I do not remember. He was called Liddell Mathers, but would soon, under the touch of 'The Celtic Movement', become MacGregor Mathers, and then plain MacGregor. He was the author of *The Kabbala Unveiled*, and his studies were two only — magic and the theory of war, for he believed himself a born commander and all but equal in wisdom and in power to that old Jew. He had copied many manuscripts on magic ceremonial and doctrine in the British Museum, and was to copy many more in Continental libraries, and it was through him mainly that I began certain studies and experiences, that were to convince me that images well up before the mind's eye from a deeper source than conscious or subconscious memory. I believe that his mind in those early days did not belie his face and body — though in later years it became unhinged, as Don Quixote's was unhinged — for he kept a proud head amid great poverty. One that boxed with him nightly has told me that for many weeks he could knock him down, though Mathers was the stronger man, and only knew long after that during those weeks Mathers starved. He had spoken to me, I think at our first introduction, of a society which sometimes called itself — it had a different name among its members — 'The Hermetic Students', and in May or June 1887 I was initiated into that society in a Charlotte Street studio, and being at a most receptive age, shaped and isolated. Mathers was its governing mind, a born teacher and organiser. (*A* 182–3)

61 *from the grave* : he had 'fallen on hard times' and died in 1918.

63 *of late estranged* : Yeats was involved in the split in the Order of the Golden Dawn. Mathers accused Dr Wynn Wescott of forging documents and Yeats was on the committee of the second order (R.R. & A.C.) — The order of Rosae Rubeae and Aureae

Crucis — which investigated this charge. Mathers sent Aleister Crowley to act as his envoy. Mathers and others were suspended from membership of the Second Order by the Committee on 19 April 1900.

He had earlier written several letters to Lady Gregory about the trouble in the Order, about Crowley, 'a person of unspeakable life', and in May 1900 was able to write that

> MacGregor apart from certain definite ill doings and absurdities, on which we had to act, has behaved with dignity and even courtesy. A fine nature gone to wrack. At last we have got a perfectly honest order, with no false mystery and no mystagogues of any kind. Everybody is working, as I have never seen them work, and we have fought out our fight without one discourteous phrase or irrelevant issue. (*L* 344)

Yeat's own view of how the Order of R.R. and A.C. should develop is contained in two pamphlets he wrote, the first, 'Is the order of R.R. and A.C. to remain a magical order?', written in March 1901, and the second, 'A Postscript to Essay called Is the Order of R.R. and A.C. to remain a magical Order?', written on 4 May 1907.

Ellic Howe's book *The Magicians of the Golden Dawn* (1972) lists diary entries of the Second Order which mention Yeats (as DEDI), pp. 290-1. See also George Harper, *Yeats's Golden Dawn* (1974) for a full history of the difficulties within the Order from 1896 onwards.

259 86 *mummy truths* : cf. 'old mummy wheat' in 'On a Picture of a Black Centaur by Edmund Dulac' (*CP* 242)

The Winding Stair, Yeats wrote to Sturge Moore on 26 September 1930 when discussing the design for the cover of the volume, is 'the winding stair of Ballylee enlarged in a symbol but you may not think the stair, even when a mere symbol, pictorial. It might be a mere gyre — Blake's design of Jacob's ladder — with figures, little figures'. Memories became distilled as Yeats grew older, yet the range of his poetry was wide. Longer lyrics and shorter in *The Winding Stair* celebrate his friendships and their results. He remembered the Gore-Booth sisters and weighed up the achievement of Lady Gregory at Coole in noble poems ; and even more condensed personal memories appeared in such poems as 'Quarrel in Old Age' (*CP* 286) ; 'The Results of Thought' (*CP* 286) ; and 'Stream and Sun at Glendalough' (*CP* 288). The dialogue of self and soul developed ; the claims of the supernatural were weighed in 'Byzantium' and 'Vacillation' ; and new characters, Crazy Jane and Old Tom the lunatic, emerged in short poems which dealt with desecration and the lover's night. Deeper reading in philosophy and fresh reading in literature was recorded in such poems as 'The Delphic Oracle upon Plotinus' (*CP* 306) or 'I am of Ireland' (*CP* 303). Indeed Plotinus may have sanctioned the belief that immortality exists, outside the lovers' immediate existence. When Crazy Jane cries to the Bishop

> 'Fair and foul are near of kin
> And fair needs foul'

the poem is based on the thought the lover affirms :

> She would as bravely show
> Did all the fabric fade ;
> No withered crone I saw
> Before the world was made.

263 IN MEMORY OF EVA GORE-BOOTH AND CON MARKIEWICZ

The manuscript of this poem is dated 21 September 1927. The date given in *CP* is October 1927. Mrs Yeats considers that this date was incorrectly supplied; she remembers Yeats working on the poem in November 1927 in Seville. Constance Markievicz died in August 1927, and Eva the year before. It first appeared in *WS*. In a letter of 23 July 1916 Yeats wrote to Eva Gore-Booth 'Your sister & yourself, two beautiful figures among the great trees of Lisadell, are among the dear memories of my youth' (quoted by I. Fletcher (*YCE* 69).

1 *Lissadell*: the Gore-Booth house in Sligo, which Yeats visited in the winter of 1894–5. See notes (p. 227) on line 17 'Easter 1916' (*CP* 202) and (p. 232) 'On a Political Prisoner' (*CP* 206). The house was built in 1832 to the design of Francis Goodwin.

4 *one a gazelle*: Eva, who wrote poetry and later worked for the women's suffrage movement; she read deeply in Indian mysticism and Neoplatonism, and was strongly committed to social work.

7 *The older*: Constance was two years older than her sister. She left Lissadell in 1898 to study painting in Paris. She married Count Casimir Markievicz and they settled in Dublin. See Anne Marreco, *The Rebel Countess* (1967) *passim*.

9 *conspiring*: she gave military training to the Fianna Scouts, worked with Fianna Fail Clubs, and joined the Citizen Army in 1914. She fell deeply under the spell of James Connolly, the Dublin Labour leader. She was deputy leader of the group who held St Stephen's Green in the 1916 Rising. After she was released from prison she busied herself with the affairs of *Cumann na mBan*, was elected an M.P., became the Minister for Labour in *Dail Eireann*, but did not take her seat at Westminster, was gaoled on several occasions. She was reappointed Minister in the second *Dail Eireann* (1921), but supported de Valera and the Republicans at the time of the 1922 Treaty which brought the Irish Free State into being. She fought in the Civil War and won her seat back in 1923. She became ill and died in 1927, her husband and step-son having arrived a few days before from Warsaw.

the ignorant : cf. P. L. Dickinson, *The Dublin of Yesterday*, 92 ff.

27   *till time catch* : cf. 'The Untiring Ones' which has a reference **264**
to God burning up the world with a kiss (*M* 78) ; there is a reference
to God burning Nature with a kiss in the penultimate line of 'The
Man who dreamed of Faeryland' (*CP* 49), and to 'God burning
time' in the penultimate line of 'He tells of the Perfect Beauty'
(*CP* 74). 'The Moods' (*CP* 62) has an image of time dropping in
decay 'Like a candle burnt out' and 'Vacillation' (*CP* 282) has a
brand or flaming breath coming to destroy

> All those antinomies
> Of day and night.

Stanza xi of 'In Memory of Major Robert Gregory' (*CP* 148) has
a similar idea.

30   *the great gazebo* : Ian Fletcher, 'Yeats and Lissadell' (*YCE*
68–9) suggests three meanings for the word : a summer house in
the grounds of Lissadell ; the Anglo-Irish meaning of the word,
e.g. to make a gazebo of yourself or look ridiculous ; and a place
to look from (suggested by Stallworthy (*BL*). The word appeared
first in 1752.

DEATH   **264**

This poem was written on 13 or 17 September 1927 and first
appeared in *WS*.
    This poem was written about the assassination of Kevin
O'Higgins (1892–1927) Vice-President and Minister of Justice in
the Irish Free State, whom Yeats saw as following in the Anglo-
Irish tradition : he added his name to those of Berkeley, Swift,
Burke, Grattan, Parnell, and Augusta Gregory and Synge in a list
which followed a statement in *OTB* that he wrote with two cer-
tainties in mind :

> first that a hundred men, their creative power wrought to the
> highest pitch, their will trained but not broken, can do more
> for the welfare of a people, whether in war or peace, than a
> million of any lesser sort no matter how expensive their educa-
> tion, and that although the Irish masses are vague and excitable

because they have not yet been moulded and cast, we have as good blood as there is in Europe. (*E* 441-2)

O'Higgins was shot on 10 July 1927 at Booterstown, Co. Dublin, on his way to Mass. In the Civil War period the Free State government had executed anyone captured carrying arms and a total of 77 irregulars was executed. O'Higgins had been convinced that this tough policy was correct; and it was thought that he was shot as an act of revenge. Yeats wrote to Olivia Shakespear about the assassination in July or August 1927:

You were right about our peace not lasting. The murder of O'Higgins was no mere public event to us. He was our personal friend, as well as the one strong intellect in Irish public life and then too his pretty young wife was our friend. We got the news just when we reached the Gresham Hotel where we were to dine and we left without dining and walked about the streets till bed-time. The night before George had suddenly called the dog out of the way of what she thought was a motor car — there was no car — and a moment after when inside our own door we both heard two bursts of music, voices singing together. At the funeral at the Mass for the dead I recognised the music as that of the choir which — just before the elevation of the host — sang in just such short burst of song. You will remember the part the motor car had in the murder. Had we seen more he might have been saved, for recent evidence seems to show that those things are fate unless foreseen by clairvoyance and so brought within the range of free-will. A French man of science thinks that we all — including murderers and victims — will and so create the future. I would bring in the dead. Are we, that foreknow, the actual or potential traitors of the race-process? Do we, as it were, forbid the banns when the event is struggling to be born? Is this why — even if what we foresee is not some trivial thing — we foresee too little to understand?

I have finished those love poems — 19 in all — and am now at a new Tower series, partly driven to it by this murder. Next week I must go to Dublin to help vote the more stringent police laws the government think necessary. I hear with anxiety that they will increase the number of crimes punishable by death, and with satisfaction that they will take certain crimes out of the hands of jurors. But I know nothing except what I find in the papers.

I am expecting a visit from my Italian translator — perhaps if we have lived good lives we may be reborn in some peaceful eastern village and have sweethearts with beautiful golden brown skins. (*L* 726–7)

Cf. 'Blood and the Moon' (*CP* 267) which was also written under the stimulus of O'Higgins's assassination.

5–6   *Many times he died*
    Many times rose again: cf. F. F. Farag (*YCE* 41) for the suggestion that this is the same idea of reincarnation expressed in Mohini Chatterjee (*CP* 279), cf. also 'Quarrel in Old Age' (*CP* 286) and 'Under Ben Bulben' (*CP* 397) with its 'two eternities'

11   *He knows death to the bone*: cf. Yeats's letter to Olivia Shakespear written in April 1933:

This country is exciting. I am told that De Valera has said in private that within three years he will be torn in pieces. It reminds me of a saying by O'Higgins to his wife 'Nobody can expect to live who has done what I have.' No sooner does a politician get into power than he begins to seek unpopularity. It is the cult of sacrifice planted in the nation by the executions of 1916. Read O'Flaherty's novel *The Martyr*, a book forbidden by our censor, and very mad in the end, but powerful and curious as an attack upon the cult. I asked a high government officer once if he could describe the head of the I.R.A. He began 'That is so and so who has (the) cult of suffering and is always putting himself in positions where he will be persecuted.' (*L* 809)

A DIALOGUE OF SELF AND SOUL   **265**

This poem was written between July and December 1927, and first appeared in *WS*.

1   *the winding ancient stair*: of Thoor Ballylee

3   *broken, crumbling battlement*: cf. 'I climb to the tower-top and lean upon broken stone', 'Meditations in Time of Civil War', VII (*CP* 231)

9   *The consecrated blade*: see note (p. 269) on 'Meditations in Time of Civil War', III (*CP* 227)

10 *Sato's ancient blade*: Junzo Sato attended a lecture given by Yeats at Portland, Oregon.

13 *That flowering, silken, old embroidery*: Yeats wrote on 2 or 4 October 1927 to Olivia Shakespear to say he had been writing verse: 'a new tower poem "Sword and Tower", which is a choice of rebirth rather than deliverance from birth. I make my Japanese sword and its silk covering my symbol of life' (*L* 729)
The form of the poem may have been suggested by Marvell's 'A Dialogue between the Soul and the Body' (included in Grierson's *Metaphysical Lyrics and Poems* (1921), 163, which Yeats read).

25 *Montashigi*: the maker of the sword, who lived in Osafume

266 32 *the crime*: cf. 'Consolation' (*CP* 310):

> But where the crime's committed
> The crime can be forgot.

33–4 *Such fullness in that quarter overflows*
And falls into the basin of the mind: cf.

> 'Life overflows without ambitious pains;
> And rains down life until the basin spills,'

lines 3–4, 'Meditations in Time of Civil War' (*CP* 225)

267 64 *a proud woman*: Maud Gonne

67–72 *Measure the lot; forgive myself the lot!*
When such as I cast out remorse
So great a sweetness flows into the breast
We must laugh and we must sing,
We are blest by everything,
Everything we look upon is blest: there is a passage in Yeats's essay 'J. M. Synge and the Ireland of his Time' which describes the artist's joy which is of one substance with that of sanctity:

> There is in the creative joy an acceptance of what life brings, because we have understood the beauty of what it brings, or a hatred of death for what it takes away, which arouses within us, through some sympathy perhaps with all other men, an energy so noble, so powerful, that we laugh aloud and mock, in the terror or the sweetness of our exaltation, at death and oblivion. (*E & I* 322)

Cf. 'Vacillation' IV (*CP* 284) for a description of happiness :

> It seemed, so great my happiness,
> That I was blessèd and could bless.

BLOOD AND THE MOON   **267**

This poem was written in August 1927 and first appeared in *The Exile* (Spring 1928).

1   *This place* : Thoor Ballylee

7   *cottages* : the cottages adjoined the tower, and were rethatched by 1919.

12   *Half dead at the top* : the tower was never completely restored ; one room was empty at the top. Concrete was used for the roof rather than an ornate structure designed by Lutyens. Henn (*LT* 13), connects the empty room with the traditional symbol of the Seventh Room in alchemy (referring to *The Chymical Marriage of Christian Rosencrux*) and the ultimate room in St Teresa's *The Interior Castle* (which Yeats had read). He regards the empty room at the top as that in which spiritual revelation is given, and he suggests that 'half dead at the top' refers not to the flat cement roof (as suggested by Hone (*WBY* 331)) but to the impossibility of spiritual enlightenment in this era.

15   *Shelley had his towers* : Yeats wrote an essay on 'The Philosophy   **268** of Shelley's Poetry' in which he discussed this symbol :

> As Shelley sailed along those great rivers and saw or imagined the cave that associated itself with rivers in his mind, he saw half-ruined towers upon the hill-tops, and once at any rate a tower is used to symbolise a meaning that is the contrary to the meaning symbolised by caves. Cythna's lover is brought through the cave where there is a polluted fountain to a high tower, for being man's far-seeing mind, when the world has cast him out he must to the 'towers of thought's crowned powers' ; nor is it possible for Shelley to have forgotten this first imprisonment when he made men imprison Lionel in a tower for a like offence ; and because I know how hard it is to forget a symbolical meaning, once one has found it, I believe

Shelley had more than a romantic scene in his mind when he made Prince Athanase follow his mysterious studies in a lighted tower above the sea, and when he made the old hermit watch over Laon in his sickness in a half-ruined tower, wherein the sea, here doubtless, as to Cythna 'the one mind,' threw 'spangled sands' and 'rarest sea shells.' The tower, important in Maeterlinck, as in Shelley, is, like the sea, and rivers, and caves with fountains, a very ancient symbol, and would perhaps, as years went by, have grown more important in his poetry. (*E &I* 86–7)

Cf. also notes (pp. 199 ff.) on 'Ego Dominus Tuus' (*CP* 180) and (p. 205) on line 16 'The Phases of the Moon' (*CP* 183).

17 *my ancestral stair* : this poem, like 'The Seven Sages' (*CP* 271), expresses Yeats's pride in his intellectual ancestry, the Anglo-Irish Protestant predecessors whom he enumerates in the next line.

He had these men in his mind frequently during his period as a Senator. (In the winter of 1922–3 he met 'the revolutionary soldier' [Capt. D. A. MacManus] who introduced him to Berkeley's works : shortly afterwards Lennox Robinson gave him a two-volume edition of Berkeley.) He regarded them as the founders of Irish thought. In his Introduction to J. M. Hone and M. M. Rossi, *Bishop Berkeley* (1931) he wrote :

> Born in such a community, Berkeley with his belief in perception, that abstract ideas are mere words, Swift with his love of perfect nature, of the Houyhnhnms, his disbelief in Newton's system and every sort of machine, Goldsmith and his delight in the particulars of common life that shocked his contemporaries, Burke with his conviction that all States not grown slowly like forest tree are tyrannies, found in England the opposite that stung their thought into expression and made it lucid. (*E & I* 402)

Yeats had turned from Goldsmith and Burke in his youth because they seemed a part of the English system, while Swift had not been a romantic ; but he changed his attitude to them and wrote in *WB* that now he 'read Swift for months together, Burke and Berkeley less often but always with excitement, and Goldsmith lures and waits' (*E* 344).

He recorded in his 1930 Diary that 'the thought of Swift, enlarged and enriched by Burke, saddled and bitted reality, and that materialism was hamstrung by Berkeley, and ancient wisdom brought back; that modern Europe had known no men more powerful' (*E* 297–8).

18   *the Dean*: Jonathan Swift (1667–1745). Dean of St Patrick's Cathedral, Dublin.

22   *proved the state a tree*: cf. Yeats's comment on 'our tradition' 'that Berkeley was the first to say the world is a vision; Burke was the first to say a nation is a tree. And those two sayings are a foundation of modern thought' (Lady Gregory, *Journals*, 265).
Burke's passage on the oak, *Reflections, Works*, II, 357, inspired several of Yeats's comments on the State: for instance, 'Burke [proved] that the State was a tree, no mechanism to be pulled in pieces and put up again, but an oak tree that had grown through centuries' (*SSY* 172). See also *Pages from a Diary* (*E* 318). Torchiana (*Y & GI* 192–3) has shown that the symbol was used by Yeats in a speech given in 1893, and in another given in 1903–4 (in the latter he said 'A nation is like a great tree . . .'), both before he had read Burke in detail.

25   *God-appointed Berkeley*: Yeats met the true Berkeley, according to Professor A. A. Luce, 'in the pages of the *Commonplace Book* with its snorts of defiance . . . the poet revelled in these note-books, and from them he learned the simple truth which he expressed in the words "Descartes, Locke and Newton took away the world . . . Berkeley restored the world"'. Cf. A. A. Luce, *Berkeley's Immaterialism: a commentary on his Principles of Human Knowledge* (1945).
A speech Yeats delivered on 'The Child and the State' at the Irish Literary Society on 30 November 1925 shows how he thought the main lines of the old Anglo-Irish culture could be extended into the new Catholic nationalist Ireland of his own time:

There are two great classics of the eighteenth century which have deeply influenced modern thought, great Irish classics too difficult to be taught to children of any age, but some day those among us who think that all things should begin with the nation and with the genius of the nation, may press them upon the attention of the State. It is impossible to consider any modern philosophical or political question without being influenced knowingly or unknowingly by movements of thought that originated with Berkeley, who founded the Trinity College Philosophical Society, or with Burke, who founded the Historical. [The College Historical Society, the oldest debating club in the British Isles, which still flourishes in Trinity College, Dublin.] It would be but natural if they and those movements were studied in Irish colleges, perhaps especially in those colleges where our teachers themselves are trained. The Italian Minister of Education has advised his teachers continually to study the great classics, and he adds that those great classics will be as difficult to them as is the lesson to the child, and will therefore help them to understand the mind of a child.

In Gaelic literature we have something that the English-speaking countries have never possessed — a great folk literature. We have in Berkeley and in Burke a philosophy on which it is possible to base the whole life of a nation. That, too, is something which England, great as she is in modern scientific thought and every kind of literature, has not, I think. The modern Irish intellect was born more than two hundred years ago when Berkeley defined in three or four sentences the mechanical philosophy of Newton, Locke and Hobbes, the philosophy of England in his day, and I think of England up to our day, and wrote after each 'We Irish do not hold with this,' or some like sentence.

Feed the immature imagination upon that old folk life, and the mature intellect upon Berkeley and the great modern idealist philosophy created by his influence, upon Burke who restored to political thought its sense of history, and Ireland is reborn, potent, armed and wise. Berkeley proved that the world was a vision, and Burke that the State was a tree, no mechanism to be pulled in pieces and put up again, but an oak tree that had grown through centuries. (*SSY* 171–2)

Swift and Berkeley, 'these two images, standing and sounding together' were combined by Yeats in the Introduction to *Bishop Berkeley* : they concerned all those 'who feel a responsibility for the thought of modern Ireland that can take away their sleep'.

269   28   *Saeva Indignatio* : the phrase is from Swift's epitaph which Yeats translated. See 'Swift's Epitaph' (*CP* 277).

45   *Tortoiseshell butterflies, peacock butterflies* : see Yeats's notes (*CP* 535–6). Butterflies entered the top room of the tower by the loopholes and died against the window panes.

48   *Half dead at the top* : see note on line 12

OIL AND BLOOD   **270**

This poem was probably written in December 1927 and worked over in 1928 and 1929. It first appeared in *WS*.
    Yeats read several books on St Teresa. They were the *Life of St Teresa* (notes by Walter Elliott, 1899) ; *The Book of Foundations* (1913) ; *Life of St Teresa* (1924) ; *The Interior Castle* (1921).

3   *odour of violet* : Lady Lovat writes that
    the wood of the coffin was found to be split and decayed, and the coffin was filled with earth and water but the body of the Saint was intact, her flesh white and soft, as flexible as when she was buried, and still emitted the same delicious and penetrating smell. Moreover the limbs exuded a miraculous oil which bore a similar perfume and embalmed the air and everything with which it came in contact. (Lady Lovat, *The Life of St Teresa*, 606)

Yeats wrote to T. Sturge Moore from Cannes on 2 February 1928 about 'that very British brother of yours' [G. E. Moore, the philosopher] :

    By the bye, please don't quote him again till you have asked him this question : 'How do you account for the fact that when the Tomb of St Teresa was opened her body exuded miraculous oil and smelt of violets?' If he cannot account for such primary facts he knows nothing. (*Y & TSM* 121–2)

5   *the vampires* : Yeats had read Bram Stoker's *Dracula* and Sheridan Le Fanu's vampire story (dramatised by Lord Longford under the title *Carmilla*).

VERONICA'S NAPKIN   **270**

This poem was written at Portofino in 1929 and first appeared in *WMP*.

Title   Veronica's Napkin: Yeats's source for the story of Veronica is not known. The legend is that

> the Holy Face of Veronica is one of the three great, remarkable and very holy relics which the patriarchal Basilica of St Peter of the Vatican preserves with a jealous care, and which have been in every age of the Church, the object of the veneration of the faithful. The Veronica is a veil, or handkerchief, on which is impressed the true likeness of the adorable face of Our Lord and Saviour Jesus Christ, miraculously imprinted, not produced by artificial colours but by the divine power of God the Son made man. . . . From a constant tradition which is founded on the most authentic documents, we are informed that whilst our Saviour was on the way to Calvary loaded with the heavy wood of the cross, the altar on which he was to sacrifice His life for the redemption of mankind, a holy woman, moved by compassion, presented Him a handkerchief, or towel to wipe His face, all covered with sweat, spittle, dust and blood ; and that Jesus, having used it, gave it back to her, having impressed on it His majestic and venerable image, so full of the deep sorrow into which He was plunged by the weight of the sin of the world. (*Veronica or The Holy Face* (translated from the French, 1870), 5)

1   *The Heavenly Circuit* : the title of an essay by Plotinus. Plotinus regarded God as the centre of a perfect circle, and the heavenly bodies rotate about God. The planets are fixed at a particular distance from God. So is the human soul, which circles about him since it cannot coincide with him, though keeps as near to him as it can since he is the being on which all depends. Cf. *Y & T* 207–9.

Berenice's Hair : Yeats used this as a symbol of romantic love in 'Her Dream' (*CP* 299). Berenice II (*c.* 273–221 B.C.) was the daughter of King Magas of Cyrene and Apama the daughter of Antiochus I. Berenice was betrothed to Ptolemy III but when her father died her mother tried to marry her to Demetrius, a Macedonian prince. She led a rebellion against both of them and ordered the death of Demetrius. She married Ptolemy III in 247, and he named a constellation 'Berenice's Curls' after her. Her son Ptolemy IV murdered her after her husband's death. Yeats probably read of her in Catullus LXVI.

2 *Tent-pole of Eden* : possibly the Pole Star

6 *the circuit of a needle's eye* : cf. 'Supernatural Songs' (*CP* 333) with its lines :

> All the stream that's roaring by
> Came out of a needle's eye ;
> Things unborn, things that are gone,
> From needle's eye still goad it on.

7 *a different pole* : the cross

8 *napkin* : the handkerchief Veronica offered to Jesus. Henn (*LT* 260) remarks that there is a picture of the Styrian School in the National Gallery, Dublin, which shows the Apostles setting forth. It bears on the reverse side a large crude painting of St Veronica's napkin.

SYMBOLS   **270**

This poem was written in October 1927 and first appeared in *WMP*.

1–2 *watch-tower*, *A blind hermit* : The source for these lines is probably an experience recorded in 'Discoveries' :

The other day I was walking towards Urbino, where I was to spend the night, having crossed the Apennines from San Sepolcro, and had come to a level place on the mountain-top near the journey's end. My friends were in a carriage some-where behind, on a road which was still ascending in great loops, and I was alone amid a visionary, fantastic, impossible scenery. It was sunset and the stormy clouds hung upon mountain after mountain, and far off on one great summit a cloud darker than the rest glimmered with lightning. Away south upon another mountain a mediaeval tower, with no building near nor any sign of life, rose into the clouds. I saw suddenly in the mind's eye an old man, erect and a little gaunt, standing in the door of the tower, while about him broke a windy light. He was the poet who had at last, because he had done so much for the word's sake, come to share in the dignity of the saint. He had hidden nothing of himself, but he had taken care of 'that dignity . . . the perfection of form . . . this lofty and severe quality . . . this virtue.' And though he had but sought it for the word's sake, or for a woman's praise, it had come at last into his body and his mind. Certainly as he stood there he knew how from behind that laborious mood, that pose, that genius, no flower of himself but all himself, looked out as from behind a mask that other Who alone of all men, the countrypeople say, is not a hair's breadth more nor less than six feet high. He has in his ears well-instructed voices, and seeming-solid sights are before his eyes, and not, as we say of many a one, speaking in metaphor, but as this were Delphi or Eleusis, and the substance and the voice come to him among his memories which are of women's faces ; for was it Columbanus or another that wrote, 'There is one among the birds that is perfect, and one perfect among the fish'? (*E & I* 290–1)

3–5 *All destroying sword-blade still*
     Carried by the wandering fool.

   Gold-sewn silk on the sword-blade : 'probably a thought prompted by Junzo Sato's sword. Cf. 'Meditations in Time of Civil War', III (*CP* 227) and 'A Dialogue of Self and Soul' (*CP* 265).

5 *gold-sewn silk* : the Japanese sword was wrapped in a piece of silk from a Japanese lady's Court dress (*E* 320). Yeats wrote to Olivia Shakespear of the sword and its silk covering being a symbol of life and in a letter to Dorothy Wellesley dated October 1935 commented that the only swashbuckler in his immediate circle

   delighted in those lines about love. He has only two interests, war and women, and that keeps him vital. Do you know my couplet

           The sword, a cross ; thereon He died :
           On breast of Mars the goddess sighed.
                              ['Conjunctions' (*CP* 333)]

That other better couplet

           Gold-sewn silk on the sword-blade
           Beauty and fool together laid.

                                        (*DWL* 33)

It is possible that Yeats was influenced in the cross-sword equation by a passage in G. R. S. Mead, *The Gnostic Crucifixion*, 64 : 'The outer story was centred round a dramatic crisis of death on a stationary cross — a dead symbol and a symbol of death. But the inner rite was one of movement and "dancing", a living symbol and a symbol of life.'

Henn (*LT* 134) regards these couplets as a microcosm of 'A Dialogue of Self and Soul'.

The tower is the emblem of the night of war, of violence, of man's aspirations to philosophy, of the decay of civilisation, of ancient ceremony, disintegrating in the face of the world — 'the broken crumbling battlements'. The tower is night; but its stability is only apparent. Behind it is the cosmic universe, permanent only in 'the star that marks the hidden pole'. The tower becomes astronomical, the departure-point for man's thought facing the universe. Set against it is the objective man, clinging, in old age, to the emblem of love and war, the sword and the embroidery.

SPILT MILK   **271**

This poem was written on 8 November 1930 and first appeared in *WMP*. Yeats wrote to his wife that it was 'the upshot of my talk upon a metaphor of Lady Ottoline's'. Yeats and Walter de la Mare had visited Lady Ottoline Morrell on 7 November 1930.

THE NINETEENTH CENTURY AND AFTER   **271**

This poem was written between January and 2 March 1929 and first appeared in *WMP*.

On 2 March 1929 Yeats wrote to Mrs Shakespear from Rapallo that he had turned from Browning

to Morris and read through his *Defence of Guinevere* and some unfinished prose fragments with great wonder. I have come to fear the world's last great poetical period is over.

> Though the great song return no more
> There's keen delight in what we have—
> A rattle of pebbles on the shore
> Under the receding wave.

The young do not feel like that — George does not, nor Ezra — but men far off feel it — in Japan for instance. (*L* 759)

STATISTICS   **271**

This poem was written in 1931 and first appeared in *WMP*.

271   THREE MOVEMENTS

Yeats wrote a prose version of this poem in his White Manuscript book and dated it 20 January 1932 ; the poem is dated 26 January 1932 by Ellmann (*IY* 267).   It first appeared in *WMP*.

1   *Shakespearean fish*: the prose draft reads: 'Passion in Shakespeare was a great fish in the sea, but from Goethe to the end of the Romantic movement the fish was in the net.   It will soon be dead upon the shore.'   There is a kindred sentiment in the essay on Bishop Berkeley which begins, 'Imagination, whether in literature, painting, or sculpture, sank after the death of Shakespeare' (*E & I* 396).

271   THE SEVEN SAGES

This poem was written on 30 January 1931 and first appeared in *WMP*.

1   *Edmund Burke*: Edmund Burke (1729–97) was educated at Trinity College Dublin, where he founded the College Historical Society, the oldest debating society — it is still flourishing — in the British Isles.   He started the Annual Register, became a powerful and persuasive orator, attacking the Tory government, advocating the cause of the Americans, Catholics and Irish trade.   He impeached Warren Hastings, supported Wilberforce in advocating the abolition of the slave trade, and, disturbed by the excesses of French Revolution, sided with the Tories.   His published works include *A Philosophical Inquiry into the Sublime and the Beautiful* (1796), *Thoughts on the Present Discontents* (1770) and *Reflections on the French Revolution* (1770).

2   *Grattan's house*: Henry Grattan (1746–1820) was educated at Trinity College Dublin.   He carried an address demanding legislative independence for Ireland (1782), and the parliament known as Grattan's Parliament sat during one of Ireland's brief periods of prosperity, but this ended with the passing of the Act of Union in 1800, which Grattan opposed in vain.   He was M.P. for Dublin 1806–20.   Yeats wrote that :

Protestant Ireland should ask permission to bring back the body of Grattan from Westminster Abbey to Saint Patrick's. He was buried in Westminster against the protests of his friends and followers — according to Sir Jonah Barrington, that there might be no place of pilgrimage — abandoned there without bust or monument. I would have him brought back through streets lined with soldiers that we might affirm that Saint Patrick's is more to us than Westminster ; but, though Protestant Ireland should first move in this matter, I would have all descendants of Grattan's party, or of those who voted against the Union, lead the procession. (*E* 296–7)

4   *my great-grandfather's father* : in this poem Yeats is searching for   **272**
his originals :

How much of my reading is to discover the English and Irish originals of my thought, its first language, and, where no such originals exist, its relation to what original did. I seek more than idioms, for thoughts become more vivid when I find they were thought out in historical circumstances which affect those in which I live, or, which is perhaps the same thing, were thought first by men my ancestors may have known. Some of my ancestors may have seen Swift, and probably my Huguenot grandmother who asked burial near Bishop King spoke both to Swift and Berkeley. I have before me an ideal expression in which all that I have, clay and spirit alike, assists ; it is as though I most approximate towards that expression when I carry with me the greatest possible amount of hereditary thought and feeling, even national and family hatred and pride. (*E* 293)

5   *tar-water with the Bishop of Cloyne* : the tar-water in which Bishop Berkeley believed has been described by J. H. Barnard :

His attention was directed to medical matters, and in his attempts to alleviate the sufferings of the sick he discovered, as he thought, a remedy which would cure every ailment under heaven. When among the Indians in America he had heard much of the medicinal properties of tar-water, and trying this, among other drugs, he was led to believe in its efficacy. He was completely led away by this idea, and for years devoted himself to perfecting both the theory and practice of the administration of tar-water. As to theory, he held that tar contained a large amount of the vital element of the universe, and so must be efficacious in prolonging life. In practice he was enthusiastic; he set up a tar-water manufactory in his own house and dosed his friends and neighbours indiscriminately. The virtues of the drug were extolled in his famous work 'Siris; a chain of Philosophical Reflections'; and in this medical tract, where we would least expect it, we have the culmination of his philosophic teaching — It was the most popular of his publications in his own day; but this was as a medical not as a philosophical treatise. Tar-water became a fashionable drug. We read in one of the good Bishop's letters to America: 'My correspondence with patients that drink tar-water obliges me to be less punctual in corresponding with my friends'. Curious stories are told of its efficacy. The famous Irish giant, Magrath, is said to have been brought up in Berkeley's house on tar-water; hence his height 7 feet 10 inches. ('Berkeley', *DUR* March 1885). This article was probably read by Yeats.)

In his essay 'Bishop Berkeley' Yeats asked rhetorically

Did tar-water, a cure-all learnt from American Indians, suggest that though he could not quiet men's minds he might give their bodies quiet, and so bring to life that incredible benign image, the dream of a time that after the anarchy of the religious wars, the spiritual torture of Donne, of El Greco and Spinoza, longed to be protected and flattered? (*E & I* 399. See also *E* 322–4)

6 *Stella*: Swift's name for Esther Johnson whom he first met at Moor Park, Sir William Temple's house. His *Journal to Stella* consists of letters to her and her friend Rebecca Dingley during the period 1710–13. Their friendship lasted throughout Stella's life; their relationship was platonic and has caused much speculation. The best account of Stella is that written by Swift at the time of her death.

8 *Burke was a Whig*: so, initially, was Swift. What Yeats intended is, perhaps, to be discovered in a passage from *OTB*:

A time has come when man must have certainty, and man knows what he has made. Man has made mathematics, but God reality. Instead of hierarchical society, where all men are different, came democracy; instead of a science which had re-discovered *Anima Mundi*, its experiments and observations

confirming the speculations of Henry More, came materialism :
all that Whiggish world Swift stared on till he became a raging
man. The ancient foundations had scarcely dispersed when
Swift's young acquaintance Berkeley destroyed the new for all
that would listen, created modern philosophy and established
for ever the subjectivity of space. No educated man to-day
accepts the objective matter and space of popular science, and
yet deductions made by those who believed in both dominate
the world, make possible the stimulation and condonation of
revolutionary massacre and the multiplication of murderous
weapons by substituting for the old humanity with its unique
irreplaceable individuals something that can be chopped and
measured like a piece of cheese ; compel denial of the immortality of the soul by hiding from the mass of the people
that the grave-diggers have no place to bury us but in the
human mind. (*E* 435–6)

The same basic idea appeared in the Introduction to *WWP*.

'He foresaw the ruin to come, Democracy, Rousseau, the
French Revolution ; that is why he hated the common run
of men—, "I hate lawyers, I hate doctors", he said, "though I
love Dr So-and-so and Judge So-and-so", — that is why he
wrote *Gulliver*, that is why he wore out his brain, that is why
he felt *saeva indignatio*, that is why he sleeps under the greatest
epitaph in history.' The *Discourse of the Contests and Dissensions
between the Nobles and the Commons in Athens and Rome*, published
in 1703 to warn the Tory Opposition of the day against the
impeachment of Ministers, is Swift's one philosophical work.
All States depend for their health upon a right balance between
the One, the Few, and the Many. The One is the executive,
which may in fact be more than one — the Roman republic
had two Consuls — but must for the sake of rapid decision be
as few as possible ; the Few are those who through the possession of hereditary wealth, or great personal gifts, have come
to identify their lives with the life of the State, whereas the lives
and ambitions of the Many are private. The Many do their
day's work well, and so far from copying even the wisest of
their neighbours, affect 'a singularity' in action and in thought;
but set them to the work of the State and every man Jack is
'listed in a party', becomes the fanatical follower of men of
whose characters he knows next to nothing, and from that
day on puts nothing into his mouth that some other man has
not already chewed and digested. And furthermore, from the

moment of enlistment thinks himself above other men and struggles for power until all is in confusion. I divine an Irish hatred of abstraction likewise expressed by that fable of Gulliver among the inventors and men of science, by Berkeley in his *Commonplace Book*, by Goldsmith in the satire of *The Good-Natured Man*, in the picturesque, minute observation of *The Deserted Village*, and by Burke in his attack upon mathematical democracy. Swift enforced his moral by proving that Rome and Greece were destroyed by the war of the Many upon the Few ; in Rome, where the Few had kept their class organisation, it was a war of classes, in Greece, where they had not, war upon character and genius. Miltiades, Aristides, Themistocles, Pericles, Alcibiades, Phocion, 'impeached for high crimes and misdemeanours . . . were honoured and lamented by their country as the preservers of it, and have had the veneration of all ages since paid justly to their memories'. In Rome parties so developed that men born and bred among the Few were compelled to join one party or the other and to flatter and bribe. All civilisations must end in some such way, for the Many obsessed by emotion create a multitude of religious sects but give themselves at last to some one master of bribes and flatteries and sink into the ignoble tranquillity of servitude. He defines a tyranny as the predominance of the One, the Few, or the Many, but thinks that of the Many the immediate threat. All States at their outset possess a ruling power seated in the whole body as that of the soul in the human body, a perfect balance of the three estates, the king some sort of chief magistrate, and then comes 'a tyranny : first either of the Few or the Many ; but at last infallibly of a single person.' He thinks the English balance most perfect in the time of Queen Elizabeth, but that in the next age a tyranny of the Many produced that of Cromwell, and that, though recovery followed, 'all forms of government must be mortal like their authors', and he quotes from Polybius, 'those abuses and corruptions, which in time destroy a government, are sown along with the very seeds of it' and destroy it 'as rust eats away iron, and worms devour wood'. Whether the final tyranny is created by the Many — in his eyes all Caesars were tyrants — or imposed by foreign power, the result is the same. At the fall of liberty came 'a dark insipid period through all Greece' — had he Ireland in his mind also? — and the people became, in the words of Polybius, 'great reverencers of crowned heads'. (*E* 350–3)

16   *Burke's great melody* : Burke devoted his political life to the emancipation of the House of Commons from the control of George III, the emancipation of the American Colonies, the emancipation of Irish trade, parliament and Catholics, the emancipation of India from the rule of the East India Company, and he opposed the Jacobinism of the French Revolution.

18   *Roads full of beggars, cattle in the fields* : Goldsmith depicted rural depopulation in his poem 'The Deserted Village'.

THE CRAZED MOON   **273**

This poem was written in April 1923 and first appeared in *WMP*.

1   *much child-bearing* : Henn (*LT*) has suggested that a passage from Cornelius Agrippa (*Occult Philosophy* II, ch. xxxii), where the moon is described as the life of all the stars, may be the source of this :

> The sun is the lord of all elementary virtues, and the moon by virtue of the sun is the mistress of generation, increase or decrease . . . but the moon, the nighest to the earth, the receptacle of all the heavenly influences, by the sweetness of her course is joined to the sun and the other planets and stars, every month, and being as it were the wife of all the stars and receiving the beams and influences of all the other planets and stars as a conception and imaging them forth to the inferior world as being next to itself, is the parent of all conceptions. (*LT* 174)

Henn also suggests (*LT*, 186) that the moon is womanhood. Mankind seeks for 'the children born of her pain' the events that come from her predestined round. But in the next there is virginal womanhood, and he regards the second stanza as a picture of an earlier richer life and a memory of Constance Gore-Booth, cf. 'On a Political Prisoner' (*CP* 206). And in the third verse woman and circumstance unite.

COOLE PARK, 1929   **273**

This poem was completed at Coole Park on 7 September 1928 and first appeared in Lady Gregory, *Coole* (1931).

A prose draft of the poem reads :

Describe house in first stanza. Here Synge came, Hugh Lane, Shaw Taylor, many names. I too in my timid youth. Coming and going like migratory birds. Then address the swallows fluttering in their dream like circles. Speak of the rarity of the circumstances that bring together such concords of men. Each man more than himself through whom an unknown life speaks. A circle ever returning into itself.

This is discussed by Parkinson (*YTLP* 80–1), who examines the change from the initial idea to final form.

1   *a swallow's flight* : see note on line 17

2   *an aged woman and her house* : Yeats wrote of Lady Isabella Augusta Gregory (1852–1932), translator and dramatist and co-founder of the Abbey Theatre, in *DP*, that when her husband died she had devoted herself to her estate and her son. She was born a Persse, a family that settled in the Irish midlands in the seventeenth century, but had moved to Galway, where Lady Gregory grew up in Roxborough House beside the road from Gort to Loughrea :

The house contained neither pictures nor furniture of historic interest. The Persses had been soldiers, farmers, riders to hounds and, in the time of the Irish Parliament, politicians ; a bridge within the wall commemorated the victory of the Irish Volunteers in 1782, but all had lacked intellectual curiosity until the downfall of their class had all but come. In the latter half of the nineteenth century Lady Gregory was born, an older and a younger sister gave birth to Sir Hugh Lane, and to that John Shawe-Taylor who, by an act of daring I must presently describe, made the settlement of the Land Question possible. (*A* 392–3)

274   9   *Hyde* : Dr Douglas Hyde (1860–1949) Irish poet, translator and scholar, was educated at Trinity College Dublin. He succeeded John O'Leary as President of the Irish National Literary Society. Yeats remarked in *DP* that his presidential lecture on 'The De-Anglicisation of Ireland' led to the foundation in 1893 of the Gaelic League, which was, in Yeats's words, 'for many years to substitute for political argument a Gaelic grammar,

and for political meetings village gatherings, where songs were sung and stories told in the Gaelic language' (*A* 559). Hyde was the first president of Eire (1938–45) and author of *Love Songs of Connaught*. He wrote under the Gaelic name 'An Craoibhin Aoibhin', the pleasant little branch, and lived at French Park, Co. Roscommon. Yeats described him in 1888 as the best of the Irish folklorists : 'His style is perfect — so sincere and simple — so little literary' (*L* 88). His review of Douglas Hyde's *Beside the Fire* was reprinted in the first edition of *CT* under the title 'The Four Winds of Desire'.

10   *That noble blade* : see notes (p. 111) on 'At the Abbey Theatre' (*CP* 107). Yeats described his style in *DP* in connection with a visit Hyde made to Coole Park in 1899 (Lady Gregory had founded a branch of the Gaelic League in her area) :

His ordinary English style is without charm ; he explores facts without explaining them, and in the language of the newspapers — Moore compared one of his speeches to frothing porter. His Gaelic, like the dialect of his *Love Songs of Connacht*, written a couple of years earlier, had charm, seemed all spontaneous, all joyous, every speech born out of itself. Had he shared our modern preoccupation with the mystery of life, learnt our modern construction, he might have grown into another and happier Synge. But emotion and imagery came as they would, not as he would ; somebody else had to put them together. He had the folk mind as no modern man has had it, its qualities and its defects, and for a few days in the year Lady Gregory and I shared his absorption in that mind. When I wrote verse, five or six lines in two or three laborious hours were a day's work, and I longed for somebody to interrupt me ; but he wrote all day, whether in verse or prose, and without apparent effort. Effort was there, but in the unconscious. He had given up verse writing because it affected his lungs or his heart. Lady Gregory kept watch, to draw him from his table after so many hours ; the gamekeeper had the boat and the guns ready ; there were ducks upon the lake. He wrote in joy and at great speed because emotion brought the appropriate word. Nothing in that language of his was abstract, nothing worn-out ; he need not, as must the writer of some language exhausted by modern civilisation, reject word after word, cadence after cadence ; he had escaped our

perpetual, painful, purification. I read him, translated by
Lady Gregory or by himself into that dialect which gets from
Gaelic its syntax and keeps its still partly Tudor vocabulary ;
little was, I think, lost. (*A* 439–40)

11 *There one that ruffled in a manly pose* : Yeats himself. Cf. *A* 457.
The 'pose' included the quality Castiglione described as *sprezzatura*.
Cf. a passage on courtesy in 'The cutting of an Agate' where Yeats
remarked : 'Even knowledge is not enough, for the "recklessness"
Castiglione thought necessary in good manners is necessary in this
likewise, and if a man has it not he will be gloomy and had better
to his marketing again' (*E & I* 256). See Corinna Salvadori, *Yeats
and Castiglione: poet and courtier*, 3 and 12–13.

12 *that slow man* : cf. the extracts from Yeats's 1909 Diary entitled
in published form 'The Death of Synge', and the particular remarks
'For him nothing existed but his thought. . . . He was too confident for self-assertion' (*A* 512)

14 *Impetuous men* : Yeats described John Shawe-Taylor, Lady
Gregory's nephew (1866–1911) in an essay :

> There is a portrait of John Shawe-Taylor by a celebrated painter
> in the Dublin Municipal Gallery, but, painted in the midst of
> a movement of the arts that exalts characteristics above the
> more typical qualities, it does not show us that beautiful and
> gracious nature. There is an exaggeration of the hollows of
> the cheeks and of the form of the bones which empties the
> face of the balance and delicacy of its lines. He was a very
> handsome man, as women who have imagination and tradition
> understand those words, and had he not been so, mind and
> character had been different. There are certain men, certain
> famous commanders of antiquity, for instance, of whose good
> looks the historian always speaks, and whose good looks are
> the image of their faculty ; and these men, copying hawk or
> leopard, have an energy of swift decision, a power of sudden
> action, as if their whole body were their brain.
>   A few years ago he was returning from America, and the
> liner reached Queenstown in a storm so great that the tender
> that came out to it for passengers returned with only one man.
> It was John Shawe-Taylor, who had leaped as it was swept
> away from the ship.

The achievement that has made his name historic and changed the history of Ireland came from the same faculty of calculation and daring, from that instant decision of the hawk, between the movement of whose wings and the perception of whose eye no time passes capable of division. A proposal for a Land Conference had been made, and cleverer men than he were but talking the life out of it. Every argument for and against had been debated over and over, and it was plain that nothing but argument would come of it. One day we found a letter in the daily papers, signed with his name, saying that a conference would be held on a certain date, and that certain leaders of the landlords and of the tenants were invited. He had made his swift calculation, probably he could not have told the reason for it : a decision had arisen out of his instinct. He was then almost an unknown man. Had the letter failed, he would have seemed a crack-brained fool to his life's end ; but the calculation of his genius was justified. He had, as men of his type have often, given an expression to the hidden popular desires ; and the expression of the hidden is the daring of the mind. When he had spoken, so many others spoke that the thing was taken out of the mouths of the leaders ; it was as though some power deeper than our daily thought had spoken, and men recognised that common instinct, that common sense which is genius. Men like him live near this power because of something simple and impersonal within them which is, as I believe, imaged in the fire of their minds, as in the shape of their bodies and their faces.

I do not think I have known another man whose motives were so entirely pure, so entirely unmixed with any personal calculation, whether of ambition, of prudence or of vanity. He caught up into his imagination the public gain as other men their private gain. For much of his life he had seemed, though a good soldier and a good shot, and a good rider to hounds, to care deeply for nothing but religion, and this religion, so curiously lacking in denominational limits, concerned itself alone with the communion of the soul with God. Such men, before some great decision, will sometimes give to the analysis of their own motive the energy that other men give to the examination of the circumstances wherein they act, and it is often those who attain in this way to purity of motive who act most wisely at moments of great crisis. It is as though they sank a well through the soil where our habits have been built, and where our hopes take root or lie uprooted, to the lasting rock and to the living stream. They are those for whom Tennyson claimed the strength of ten, and the common and clever wonder at their simplicity and at a triumph that has always an air of miracle. (*E & I* 343–5)

There is a good brief account of his life in Torchiana (*Y & GI* 44–57).

Sir Hugh Lane (1874–1915), another nephew of Lady Gregory. See notes (pp. 123 ff.) on 'To a Wealthy Man who promised a second Subscription to the Dublin Municipal Gallery if it were proved the People wanted Pictures' (*CP* 119).

17 *like swallows* : this stanza has some points in common with a passage in Pythagoras who wrote :

Receive not a swallow into your house. Explanation — This symbol admonishes as follows : Do not admit to your dogmas a man who is indolent, who does not labour incessantly, and who is not a firm adherent to the Pythagorean sect and endued with intelligence ; for these dogmas require continued and most strenuous attention, and an endurance of labour through the mutation and circumvolition of the various disciplines which they contain. But it uses the swallow as an image of indolence and an interruption of time, because this bird visits us for a certain part of the year, and for a short time, becomes as it were our guest ; but leaves us for the greater part of the year and is not seen by us. (G. R. S. Mead, *The Golden Verses of Pythagoras and Other Pythagorean fragments*, 72)

18 *a woman's powerful character* : Yeats wrote that :

She knew Ireland always in its permanent relationships, associations — violence but a brief interruption —, never lost her sense of feudal responsibility, not of duty as the word is generally understood, but of burdens laid upon her by her station and her character, a choice constantly renewed in solitude. 'She has been', said an old man to me, 'like a serving-maid among us. She is plain and simple, like the Mother of God, and that was the greatest lady that ever lived.' When in later years her literary style became in my ears the best written by woman, she had made the people a part of her soul ; a phrase of Aristotle's had become her motto : 'To think like a wise man, but to express oneself like the common people'. (*A* 395)

26   *those rooms and passages are gone* : the Forestry Department took over the house, garden, fields and woods during Lady Gregory's lifetime : she then rented the house from the Department which sold the house after her death. The purchaser pulled it down.

COOLE PARK AND BALLYLEE, 1931   **275**

This poem was written in February 1931 and first appeared in *WMP*.

1   *my window ledge* : at Thoor Ballylee

4   *'dark' Raftery's 'cellar'* : Raftery, the blind Gaelic poet. See notes (pp. 260–2) on 'The Tower' II (*CP* 219). The limestone is porous and there are several underground rivers in the area. Cf. Lady Gregory's description in *Coole*, quoted in notes (p. 154) on 'The Wild Swans at Coole' (*CP* 147).

8   *the generated soul?* : In 'Earth, Fire and Water' Yeats wrote : 'Did not the wise Porphyry think that all souls come to be born because of water, and that "even the generation of images in the mind is from water"?' (*M* 80). Elsewhere he wrote : 'I think it was Porphyry who wrote that the generation of images in the mind is from water.' The Neoplatonics used water as a symbol of generation, and the passage Yeats had in mind was probably the following :

> For in consequence of containing perpetually-flowing streams of water, it will not be a symbol of an intelligible hypostasis, but of a material essence. On this account also it is sacred to Nymphs, not the mountain *or rural Nymphs*, or others of the like kind, but to the Naiades, who are thus denominated from streams of water. For we peculiarly call the Naiades, and the powers that preside over waters, Nymphs ; and this term also is commonly applied to all souls descending into generation. For the ancients thought that these souls are incumbent on water which is inspired by divinity, as Numenius says, who adds, that on this account, a prophet asserts, that the Spirit of God moved on the waters. The Egyptians likewise, on this account, represent all dæmons and also the sun, and, in short, all the planets . . . not standing on anything solid, but on a

sailing vessel ; for souls descending into generation fly to
moisture. Hence also, Heraclitus says, 'that moisture appears
delightful and not deadly to souls' ; but the lapse into generation is delightful to them. And in another place (speaking of
unembodied souls), he says, 'We live their death, and we die
their life.' Hence the poet calls those that are in generation
humid, because they have souls which are *profoundly* steeped in
moisture. . . . But pure souls are averse from generation ;
so that, as Heraclitus says, '*a dry soul is the wisest.*' Hence, here
also the spirit becomes moist and more aqueous through the
desire of generation, the soul thus attracting a humid vapour
from verging to generation. Souls, therefore, proceeding into
generation are the nymphs called naiades. Hence it is usual
to call those that are married nymphs, as being conjoined to
generation, and to pour water into baths from fountains, or
rivers, or perpetual rills. (Porphyry, *On the Cave of the Nymphs*
15–18)

14 *mounting swan* : in a letter to Mrs Yeats written on 3 February
1932 Yeats told her 'I am turning the introductory verses to Lady
Gregory's 'Coole' (Cuala) into a poem of some length — various
sections with more or less symbolic matter. Yesterday I wrote an
account of the sudden ascent of a swan — a symbol of inspiration
I think' (*WBY* 425).

276 24 *murdered with a spot of ink* : in 'The Irish Dramatic Movement'
Yeats wrote 'Did not M. Tribulat Bonhomet discover that one
spot of ink would kill a swan?' (*E* 90). Henn (*LT* 138) comments
that the allusion must be to Villiers de l'Isle-Adam's satiric novel
M. Triboulat Bonhomet (1887), in which Dr Bonhomet is a hunter of
swans.

26 *somebody that toils from chair to chair* : Lady Gregory

27–28 *Beloved books that famous hands have bound,*
Old marble heads, old pictures everywhere : the house was described by Lady Gregory in *Coole* and Yeats himself described it
in *DP* :

A glimpse of a long vista of trees, over an undergrowth of
clipped laurels, seen for a moment as the outside car approached

her house on my first visit, is a vivid memory. Coole House, though it has lost the great park full of ancient trees, is still set in the midst of a thick wood, which spreads out behind the house in two directions, in one along the edges of a lake which, as there is no escape for its water except a narrow subterranean passage, doubles or trebles its size in winter. In later years I was to know the edges of that lake better than any spot on earth, to know it in all the changes of the seasons, to find there always some new beauty. Wondering at myself, I remember that when I first saw that house I was so full of the mediaevalism of William Morris that I did not like the gold frames, some deep and full of ornament, round the pictures in the drawing-room ; years were to pass before I came to understand the earlier nineteenth and later eighteenth century, and to love that house more than all other houses. Every generation had left its memorial ; every generation had been highly educated ; eldest sons had gone the grand tour, returning with statues or pictures ; Mogul or Persian paintings had been brought from the Far East by a Gregory chairman of the East India Company, great earthenware ewers and basins, great silver bowls, by Lady Gregory's husband, a famous Governor of Ceylon, who had married in old age, and was now some seven years dead ; but of all those Gregorys, the least distinguished, judged by accepted standards, most roused my interest — a Richard who at the close of the eighteenth century was a popular brilliant officer in the Guards. He was accused of pleading ill-health to escape active service, and though exonerated by some official inquiry, resigned his commission, gave up London and his friends. He made the acquaintance of a school-girl, carried her off, put her into a little house in Coole demesne, afterwards the steward's house, where she lived disguised as a boy until his father died. They married, and at the end of last century the people still kept the memory of her kindness and her charity. One of the latest planted of the woods bore her name, and is, I hope, still called, now that the Government Foresters are in possession, 'The Isabella Wood'. While compelled to live in boy's clothes she had called herself 'Jack the Sailor' from a song of Dibdin's. Richard had brought in bullock-carts through Italy the marble copy of the Venus de' Medici in the drawing-room, added to the library the Greek and Roman Classics bound by famous French and English binders, substituted for the old straight avenue two great sweeping avenues each a mile or a little more in length. Was it he or his father who had possessed the Arab horses, painted by Stubbs? It was perhaps Lady Gregory's husband, a Trustee of the English National Gallery, who had bought the greater number of the pictures. Those that I keep most in memory are a Canaletto, a Guardi, a Zurbarán. Two or three that once hung there had, before I saw those great rooms, gone to the National Gallery, and the fine portraits by Augustus John and Charles Shannon were still to come. The mezzotints and engravings of the masters and friends of the old Gregorys that hung round the small downstairs breakfast-room, Pitt, Fox, Lord Wellesley, Palmerston, Gladstone, many that I have forgotten, had increased generation by generation, and amongst them Lady Gregory had hung a letter from Burke to the Gregory that was chairman of the East India Company saying that he committed to his care, now that he himself had grown old, the people of India. In the hall, or at one's right hand as one ascended the stairs, hung Persian helmets, Indian shields, Indian swords in elaborate sheaths, stuffed birds from various parts of the world, shot by whom nobody could remember, portraits of the members of Grillion's Club, illuminated addresses presented in Ceylon or Galway, signed photographs or engravings of Tennyson, Mark Twain, Browning, Thackeray, at a later date paintings of Galway scenery by Sir Richard Burton, bequeathed at his death, and etchings by Augustus John. I can remember somebody saying : 'Balzac would have given twenty pages to the stairs'. The house itself was plain and box-like, except on the side towards the lake, where somebody, probably Richard Gregory, had enlarged the drawing-room and dining-room with great bow windows. Edward Martyn's burnt house had been like it doubtless, for it was into such houses men moved, when it was safe to leave their castles, or the thatched cottages under castle walls ; architecture did not return until the cut stone Georgian houses of a later date. (*A* 388–91)

30 *a last inheritor* : her only child Robert was killed in Italy. See notes (p. 156 on 'In Memory of Major Robert Gregory' *CP* 148). When Lady Gregory sold Coole to the Irish Land Commission and Department of Forestry in 1927 she wrote in her Diary that it

no longer belongs to anyone of our family or name, I am thankful to have been able to keep back a sale for these years past, for giving it into the hands of the Forestry people makes the maintenance of the woods secure and will give employment and be for the good and dignity of the country. As to the house I will stay and keep it as the children's home as long as I keep strength enough and can earn money enough. It had a good name before I came here, its owners were of good, even of high repute ; and that has been continued, has increased, in Robert's time and mine. Perhaps some day one of the children may care enough for it to come back ; they have been happy here. (*Lady Gregory's Journal*, ed. Lennox Robinson, 39)

31 *none has reigned* : cf. Yeats's lines in the play *Purgatory* :

> Great people lived and died in this house ;
> Magistrates, colonels, members of Parliament,
> Captains and Governors, and long ago
> Men that fought at Aughrim and the Boyne. (*C pl* 683)

40 *some poor Arab tribesman* : Yeats had read Doughty's *Arabia Deserta*, but the image may derive from Shelley, cf. note (p. 201) on 'Ego Dominus Tuus' (*CP* 180) and its 'Bedouin's horse-hair roof'.

41 *the last romantics* : cf. stanza VI of 'The Municipal Gallery Revisited' (*CP* 368)

46 *that high horse* : Pegasus. Cf. note (p. 106) on 'The Fascination of What's Difficult' (*CP* 104).

FOR ANNE GREGORY   **277**

This poem was written in September 1930 and first appeared in *WMP*.

Title Anne Gregory : Anne Gregory was Lady Gregory's grandchild.

SWIFT'S EPITAPH   **277**

This poem was first drafted at Coole in 1929 and completed in September 1930. It first appeared in *DM* (Oct.–Dec. 1931).

The Latin epitaph in St Patrick's Cathedral, Dublin, where Swift is buried, reads :

> *Hic* depositum est Corpus
> IONATHAN SWIFT s.t.d.
> Hujus Ecclesiæ Cathedralis
> Decani,
> *Ubi* saeva Indignatio
> Ulterius
> Cor lacerare nequit.
> Abi Viator
> Et imitare, si poteris,
> Strenuum pro virili
> Libertatis Vindicatorem
> Obiit 19° Die Mensis Octobris
> A.D. 1745 Anno Aetatis 78.

See J. V. Luce, 'A note on the composition of Swift's epitaph', *Hermathena*, civ (Spring 1967) 78–81.

Cf. lines 19–20 'Blood and the Moon', ii (*CP* 268).

278 AT ALGECIRAS — A MEDITATION UPON DEATH

This poem was written at Algeciras when Yeats was staying at the Hotel Reina Cristina during November 1928 ; it first appeared in *A Packet for Ezra Pound* (1929) dated 4 February 1929 (Ellmann dated it 23 January 1929 (*IY* 291)) and it is dated November 1928 in *CP*. The title given it in *WMP* was 'A Meditation written during Summers at Algeciras'.

1 *the heron-billed pale cattle-birds* : Yeats watched the birds flying in to roost near the hotel.

11 *Newton's metaphor* : Newton's words were

I do not know how I may appear to the world ; but to myself I seem to have been only like a boy, playing on the seashore, and diverting myself, in now and then finding another pebble or prettier shell than ordinary, while the great ocean of truth lay all undiscovered before me. (David Brewster, *Memories . . . of Sir Isaac Newton* (1855), ii, 407)

12 *Rosses' level shore* : district near Sligo. Cf. lines 14–15 of 'The Stolen Child' (*CP* 20).

16   *Great Questioner* : God. Yeats had been very seriously ill in October 1928. A cold developed into congestion of the lungs and he had been sent to Spain in search of sunshine.

THE CHOICE   **278**

This poem was probably written in February 1931 (it was originally the penultimate stanza of 'Coole Park and Ballylee 1931' (*CP* 275). It first appeared in *WMP*.

MOHINI CHATTERJEE   **279**

This poem is incorrectly dated 1928 in *CP*. Yeats wrote it between 23 January and 9 February 1929, and it first appeared in *A Packet for Ezra Pound* (1929).

Title   Mohini Chatterjee : he was a Bengali Brahmin whom Yeats and his friends in the Hermetic Society invited to come to Dublin ɔ lecture to them in 1885 or 1886 : 'It was my first meeting with philosophy that confirmed my vague speculations and seemed at once logical and boundless' (*A* 91–2). Cf. *CW*, VIII, 279.

1   *if I should pray* : Yeats wrote a note in which he recounted how someone had asked Mohini Chatterjee if we should pray :

but even prayer was too full of hope, of desire, of life, to have any part in that acquiescence that was his beginning of wisdom, and he answered that one should say, before sleeping : 'I have lived many lives, I have been a slave and a prince. Many a beloved has sat upon my knees, and I have sat upon the knees of many a beloved. Everything that has been shall be again.' Beautiful words that I spoilt once by turning them into clumsy verse.

The lines were in 'Kanva on Himself'

> Hast thou not sat of yore upon the knees
> Of myriads of beloveds, and on thine
> Have not a myriad swayed below strange trees
> In other lives? Hast thou not quaffed old wine
> By tables that were fallen into dust
> Ere yonder palm commenced his thousand years.   (*WO*)

Hone commented that the Brahmin had been one of the earliest members of the Theosophical Society in India and taught that everything we perceive exists in the external world; this is a stream which is out of human control, and we are but a mirror, and our deliverance consists in turning the mirror away so that it reflects nothing. He quoted Yeats's lines written out of satisfaction with this philosophy:

> Long thou for nothing, neither sad nor gay.
> Long thou for nothing, neither night nor day,
> Not even, 'I long to see thy longing over,'
> To the ever longing and mournful spirit say.   (*WBY* 48)

17 *Old lovers yet may have*: this is similar to the idea in 'Broken Dreams' (*CP* 172).

> Vague memories, nothing but memories,
> But in the grave all, all, shall be renewed.

280   24 *cannonade*: this echoes the imagery of 'King and no King' (*CP* 102).

280   BYZANTIUM

This poem was written in September 1930 and first appeared in *WMP*.

'Then ill again', Yeats wrote in the Notes to *CP*, 'I warmed myself back into life with "Byzantium" and "Veronica's Napkin", looking for a theme that might befit my years.' He had had Malta fever in the autumn of 1929 at Rapallo.

The prose draft of 'Byzantium' contained in Yeats's 1930 *Diary* ran:

> Subject for a poem.   Death of a friend. . . . Describe Byzantium as it is in the system towards the end of the first Christian millennium.   A walking mummy.   Flames at the street corners where the soul is purified, birds of hammered gold singing in the golden trees, in the harbour [dolphins] offering their backs to the wailing dead that they may carry them to Paradise.
>
> These subjects have been in my head for some time, especially the last.   (*E* 290)

Yeats's view of Byzantium is also given in *AV*:

> I think that if I could be given a month of Antiquity and leave

to spend it where I chose, I would spend it in Byzantium, a little before Justinian opened St Sophia and closed the Academy of Plato. I think I could find in some little wine-shop some philosophical worker in mosaic who could answer all my questions, the supernatural descending nearer to him than to Plotinus even, for the pride of his delicate skill would make what was an instrument of power to princes and clerics, a murderous madness in the mob, show as a lovely flexible presence like that of a perfect human body.

I think that in early Byzantium, and maybe never before or since in recorded history, religious, aesthetic and practical life were one, that architect and artificers — though not, it may be, poets, for language had been the instrument of controversy and must have grown abstract — spoke to the multitude and the few alike. The painter, the mosaic worker, the worker in gold and silver, the illuminator of sacred books, were almost impersonal, almost perhaps without the consciousness of individual design, absorbed in their subject-matter and that the vision of a whole people. They could copy out of old Gospel books those pictures that seemed as sacred as the text, and yet weave all into a vast design, the work of many that seemed the work of one, that made building, picture, pattern, metal-work of rail and lamp, seem but a single image ; and this vision, this proclamation of their invisible master, had the Greek nobility, Satan always the still half-divine Serpent, never the horned scarecrow of the didactic Middle Ages. (*AV* (B) 279)

In 'Modern Ireland' *Massachusetts Review* (Winter 1964), Yeats cancelled this passage, formerly in the MS. :

In my later poems I have called it Byzantium ['it' was 'an example of magnificence : and style, whether in literature or life, comes, I think, from excess, from that something over and above utility, which wrings the heart'], that city where the Saints showed their wasted forms upon a background of gold mosaic, and an artificial bird sang upon a tree of gold in the presence of the Emperor ; and in one poem I have pictured the ghosts swimming, mounted upon dolphins, through the sensual seas, that they may dance upon its pavements.

On 16 April 1930 T. Sturge Moore wrote to Yeats that 'Sailing to Byzantium' had let him down in the fourth stanza 'as such a goldsmith's bird is as much nature as a man's body, especially if it only sings like Homer and Shakespeare of what is past or passing or to come to Lords and Ladies' (*Y & TSM* 162). On 4 October Yeats wrote to Sturge Moore to tell him that 'Byzantium' originated from his criticism of 'Sailing to Byzantium' which had showed Yeats 'that the idea needed exposition'. (*Y & TSM* 164)

1–8　*The unpurged images of day recede;*
　　　The Emperor's drunken soldiery are abed;
　　　Night resonance recedes, night-walkers' song
　　　After great cathedral gong;
　　　A starlit or a moonlit dome disdains
　　　All that man is,
　　　All mere complexities,

　　　The fury and the mire of human veins : the first stanza describes what Stallworthy has called 'the whole, complicated, physical world'; he has suggested that Blake's poem 'London' was in Yeats's mind :

> the hapless soldier's sigh
> Runs in blood down palace walls.

> But most through midnight streets I hear
> How the youthful harlot's curse
> Blasts the new born infant's tear.

Edward Engelberg, *The Vast Design* (1964), 147–8, considers the first two sections of 'Byzantium' echo Dante, *Purgatorio*, VIII 1–12. For other similarities between 'Byzantium' and Dante's *Purgatorio* see F. N. Lees, 'Yeats's "Byzantium", Dante and Shelley', *Notes & Queries* (July 1957), 312–3.

4　*cathedral gong* : Yeats pencilled the word 'gong' in the margin of p. 110 of W. G. Holmes, *The Age of Justinian and Theodora*, opposite this description : 'At the boom of the great *semantron*, a sonorous board suspended in the porch of each church, and beaten with mallets by a deacon.' Wilson regards the gong as being a warning sign, an intimation of the nearness of death (*Y & T* 232–3).

5　*A starlit or a moonlit dome* : the dome of St Sophia

9　*an image, man or shade* : in Yeats's note on his play *The Dreaming of the Bones* he wrote of

the world wide belief that the dead dream back for a certain time, through the more personal thoughts and deeds of life.

The wicked, according to Cornelius Agrippa, dream themselves to be consumed by flames and persecuted by demons. . . . The Shade is said to fade out at last, but the Spiritual Being does not fade, passing on to other states of existence after it has attained a spiritual state, of which the surroundings and aptitudes of early life are a correspondence. (*Four Plays for Dancers* (1931), 77–8)

There is a passage in 'Anima Mundi' which deals with the soul's capacity to mould the body to any shape :

All souls have a vehicle or body, and when one has said that with More and the Platonists one has escaped from the abstract schools who seek always the power of some Church or institution, and found oneself with great poetry, and superstition which is but popular poetry, in a pleasant, dangerous world. Beauty is indeed but bodily life in some ideal condition. The vehicle of the human soul is what used to be called the animal spirits, and Henry More quotes from Hippocrates this sentence : 'The mind of man is . . . not nourished from meats and drinks from the belly, but by a clear luminous substance that redounds by separation from the blood.' These animal spirits fill up all parts of the body and make up the body of air, as certain writers of the seventeenth century have called it. The soul has a plastic power, and can after death, or during life, should the vehicle leave the body for a while, mould it to any shape it will by an act of imagination, though the more unlike to the habitual that shape is, the greater the effort. To living and dead alike, the purity and abundance of the animal spirits are a chief power. The soul can mould from these an apparition clothed as if in life, and make it visible by showing it to our mind's eye, or by building into its substance certain particles drawn from the body of a medium till it is as visible and tangible as any other object. To help that building the ancients offered sheaves of corn, fragrant gum, and the odour of fruit and flowers, and the blood of victims. The half-materialised vehicle slowly exudes from the skin in dull luminous drops or condenses from a luminous cloud, the light fading as weight and density increase. The witch, going beyond the medium, offered to the slowly animating phantom certain drops of her blood. The vehicle once separate from the living man or woman may be moulded by the souls of others as readily as by its own soul, and even, it seems, by the souls of the living. It becomes a part for a while of that stream of images which I have compared to reflections upon water. But how does it follow that souls who never have handled the modelling tool or the brush make perfect images? Those materialisations who imprint their powerful faces upon paraffin wax, leave there sculpture that would have taken a good artist, making and imagining, many hours. How did it follow that an ignorant woman could, as Henry More believed, project her vehicle in so good a likeness of a hare that horse and hound and huntsman followed with the bugle blowing? Is not the problem the same as of those finely articulated scenes and patterns that come out of the dark, seemingly completed in the winking of an eye, as we are lying half asleep, and of all those elaborate images that drift in moments of inspiration or evocation before the mind's eye? Our animal spirits or vehicles are but, as it were, a condensation of the vehicle of *Anima Mundi*, and give substance to its images in the faint materialisation of our common thought, or more grossly when a ghost is our visitor. (*M* 348–50)

11 *Hades' bobbin* : probably taken from Plato's mythology in the myth of Er (see *The Republic* (trans. Davies and Vaughan) § 620). Cf. 'His Bargain' (*CP* 299) where the 'spindle' probably has the same source. G. R. S. Mead compares the soul to a spindle (*Echoes from the Gnosis*, 18). Yeats's draft suggests 'Hades' bobbin' is a spirit :

13 *A mouth that has no moisture and no breath* : cf. Yeats's comment in *WWP*:

The Indian ascetic passing into his death-like trance knows that if his mind is not pure, if there is anything there but the symbol of his God, some passion, ambition, desire, or phantasy will confer upon him its shape or purpose, for he is entering upon a state where thought and existence are the same. One remembers those witches described by Glanvil who course the field in the likeness of hares while their bodies lie at home, and certain mediumistic phenomena. The ascetic would say, did we question him, that the unpurified dead are subject to transformation that would be similar were it not that in their case no physical body remains in cave or bed or chair, all is transformed. They examine their past if undisturbed by our importunity, tracing events to their source, and as they take the form their thought suggests, seem to live backward through time ; or if incapable of such examination, creatures not of thought but of feeling, renew as shades certain detached events of their past lives, taking the greater excitements first. When Achilles came to the edge of the blood-pool (an ancient substitute for the medium) he was such a shade. Tradition affirms that, deprived of the living present by death, they can create nothing, or, in the Indian phrase, can originate no new Karma. Their aim, like that of the ascetic in meditation, is to enter at last into their own archetype, or into all being : into that which is there always. They are not, however, the personalities which haunt the séance-room : these when they speak from, or imply, supernormal knowledge, when they are more than transformations of the medium, are, as it were, new beings begotten by spirit upon medium to live short but veritable lives, whereas the secondary personalities resemble those eggs brought forth without the assistance of the male bird. They, within their narrow limits, create ; they speak truth when they repeat some message suggested by the past lives of the spirit, remembered like some prenatal memory, or when, though such instances must be few, begotten by some spirit obedient to its source, or, as we might say, blessed ; but when they neither repeat such message nor were so begotten they may justify passages in Swedenborg that denounce them as the newspapers denounce cheating mediums, seeing that they find but little check in their fragmentary knowledge or vague conscience.

> Let images of basalt, black, immovable,
> Chiselled in Egypt, or ovoids of bright steel
> Hammered and polished by Brancusi's hand,
> Represent spirits. If spirits seem to stand
> Before the bodily eyes, speak into the bodily ears,
> They are not present but their messengers.
> Of double nature these, one nature is
> Compounded of accidental phantasies.
> We question ; it but answers what we would
> Or as phantasy directs — because they have drunk the blood.
>
> (*E* 366–7)

Wilson (*Y & T* 237) remarks that these lines refer indirectly to Tiresias, Homer's summoner of the shades.

16 *death-in-life* : Stallworthy (*BL* 121) regards this stanza as growing round the nucleus of a Coleridgean image :

> The Nightmare Life-in-Death was she,
> Who thicks man's blood with cold.

And see Denis Donoghue, 'An honoured guest on "The Winding Stair"' (*HG* 116), who quotes the sentence in *The Resurrection* spoken by the Greek student of Heracleitus: 'God and man die each other's life, live each other's death'. He argues that Heracleitus vouched for the superhuman element of the image.

17   *Miracle, bird or golden handiwork*: see notes (p. 257) on lines 27–32 'Sailing to Byzantium' (*CP* 217). The bird may have more symbolical meanings; it might be related to the 'one white fowl wearing a crown' on the highest bough of the Tree of Life which was seen by a young Irishwoman in trance. See 'Magic' (*E & I* 44–5). Kermode distinguishes between the birds in 'Sailing to Byzantium' and that in this poem. (*RI* 87)

281   20   *like the cocks of Hades*: cf. a passage in 'The Adoration of the Magi' where the second of the three old men crowed like a cock and the youngest of them assumed a devil had gone into him. But the voice is that of Hermes, the Shepherd of the Dead (*M* 311–312). Cf. the cockerel in 'Solomon and the Witch' (*CP* 199). Ellmann (*IY* 220) remarks that Yeats is here distinguishing between birds that sing the common strain of the continuing cycle of human lives and those that scorn the cycle and sing only of escape from it.

25   *the Emperor's pavement*: this is probably derived from W. G. Holmes, *The Age of Justinian and Theodora*, 69. Yeats marked this passage in his copy: 'We . . . arrive at the Forum of Constantine, which presents itself as an expansion of the Mese. This open space, the most signal ornament of Constantinople, is called prescriptively the Forum; and sometimes from its finished marble floor "The Pavement".'

25–6   *flit Flames*: cf. 'Anima Mundi' where Yeats describes ghosts held by memories (*M* 354–7) as well as their being refashioned, and the description of the dead 'dreaming back' through their lives in the Notes to *The Dreaming of the Bones* (*Four Plays for Dancers*, 1921).

28   *blood-begotten spirits*: Gwendolen Murphy described them as human ghosts (*The Modern Poet*, 153) and Ellmann (*IY* 221–2) remarked that they have to be immortalised by fire, quoting notes Yeats made for *AV* two years before writing 'Byzantium':

At first we are subject to Destiny . . . but the point in the Zodiac where the whirl becomes a sphere once reached, we may escape from the constraint of our nature and from that of external things, entering upon a state where all fuel has become flame, where there is nothing but the state itself, nothing to constrain it or end it. We attain it always in the creation or enjoyment of a work of art, but that moment though eternal in the Daimon passes from us because it is not an attainment of our whole being . . .

29 *complexities of fury leave* : after purgation. Cf. prose passages referred to in note on lines 25–6.

33 *the dolphin's mire and blood* : cf. Mrs Strong, *Apotheosis and the After Life*, 153, 195, 266. She comments that the dolphin is an 'emblem of the soul or its transit', and states 'The dead man — or his soul — might be conveyed thither by boat, or on the back of a sea monster, a dolphin, sea-horse or triton.' See notes (p. 497) on 'News for the Delphic Oracle' (*CP* 376).

34 *The smithies* : these are derived from W. G. Holmes, *The Age of Justinian and Theodora*, 69.

36 *Marbles of the dancing floor* : see note on line 25

38 *images* : cf. a section of 'Hodos Chameliontos' (*A* 272–4)

THE MOTHER OF GOD   **281**

This poem was written on 3 September 1931 and finally revised on 12 September 1931, and first appeared in *WMP*.

1 *a fallen flare* : Yeats's note reads :

In 'The Mother of God' the words 'A fallen flare through the hollow of an ear' are, I am told, obscure. I had in my memory Byzantine mosaic pictures of the Annunciation, which show a line drawn from a star to the ear of the Virgin. She received the word through the ear, a star fell, and a star was born.

Henn (*LT* 258) suggests as sources Blake's tempera drawing 'Annunciation', in which Gabriel stands with massive eagle wings on the left of the picture, and Charles Ricketts's drawing 'Eros leaving Psyche', in which the departing winged God stands beside the bed and the naked Psyche clutches at his feet.

5 *The Heavens in my womb* : Raymond Lister, 'Beulah to Byzantium . . .' II, *Dolmen Press Yeats Centenary Papers* (1965), suggests that a likely source for this image could have been the Krishna legend that tells of Krishna, when a small boy, eating some dirt and being scolded by his foster mother Yasoda. She ordered him to open his mouth and looked inside to see the whole universe. He refers to W. G. Archer, *The Loves of Krishna* (1957) 32.

282 15 *my hair stand up* : cf. the lines in *The Herne's Egg* :

When beak and claw their work begin
Shall horror stir in the roots of my hair?
Sang the bride of the Herne, and the great Herne's bride   (*C Pl* 664–5)

282 VACILLATION

This poem was written in 1931 and 1932. Section I was written in December 1931. In a letter to Olivia Shakespear of 15 December 1931 Yeats alludes to his having begun 'a longish poem called "Wisdom" in the attempt to shake off "Crazy Jane", and I begin to think I shall take to religion unless you save me from it' (*L* 788). It first appeared in *WMP*. The titles of the sections in the first printing were : I What is Joy ; II The Burning Tree (this included the stanzas numbered II and III in subsequent printings) III (IV subsequently) Happiness ; IV (V subsequently) Conscience ; V (VI subsequently) Conquerors ; VI (VII subsequently) A Dialogue ; VII (VIII subsequently) Von Hügel. The subsequent arrangement first appeared in *WS*. The writing of the poem is discussed by Curtis Bradford (*Yeats at Work*, 128–34) ; Ellmann (*IY* 268–74) ; Jeffares (*Y:M & P* 272–3) ; and Parkinson (*YTLP*, 220–8).

Section IV was written in November 1931 and Section VI between January and March 5 1932, see Ellmann (*IY* 292) ; Section VII was written on 3 and 4 January 1932 and Section VII on 3 January 1932 (*L* 789–90).

282 1 This stanza was enclosed in a letter to Olivia Shakespear written in November 1931 (postmark, 23 November ; letter dated

Last Sunday', but there was another that month) a paragraph of which described the subject of the poem :

> The night before letters came I went for a walk after dark and there among some great trees became absorbed in the most lofty philosophical conception I have found while writing *A Vision*. I suddenly seemed to understand at last and then I smelt roses. I now realised the nature of the timeless spirit. Then I began to walk and with my excitement came — how shall I say ? — that old glow so beautiful with its autumnal tint. The longing to touch it was almost unendurable. The next night I was walking in the same path and now the two excitements came together. The autumnal image, remote, incredibly spiritual, erect, delicate featured, and mixed with it the violent physical image, the black mass of Eden. Yesterday I put my thoughts into a poem which I enclose, but it seems to me a poor shadow of the intensity of the experience. (*L* 785. Wade's footnote is, I think, incorrect)

1 *extremities* : this opening section owes much to Blake's theory of contraries (with which Yeats dealt in the 1893 edition of Blake) and probably to Boehme also. The following passage in Yeats's copy of Denis Saurat, *Blake and Modern Thought* received a pencilled comment :

> Without contraries there is no progression. Attraction and Repulsion, Love and Hate, are necessary to Human existence. From these contraries spring what the religious call Good and Evil. Good is the passive that obeys Reason. Evil is the active springing from Energy. Good is Heaven — Evil is Hell.

Yeats's comment was : 'I think there was no such thought known in England in Blake's day. It is fundamental in Blake.' For the occurrence of the idea in Boehme see H. L. Martensen, *Jacob Boehme : His Life and Teaching*, 77.

II

11 *A tree there is* : this is a tree described in *The Mabinogion*, which Yeats mentioned in an essay 'The Celtic Element in Literature' :

> . . . our 'natural magic' is but the ancient religion of the world, the ancient worship of Nature and that troubled ecstasy before her, that certainty of all beautiful places being haunted, which

it brought into men's minds. The ancient religion is in that passage of the *Mabinogion* about the making of 'Flower Aspect' . . . and one finds it in the not less beautiful passage about the burning tree, that has half its beauty from calling up a fancy of leaves so living and beautiful, they can be of no less living and beautiful a thing than flame : 'They saw a tall tree by the side of the river, one half of which was in flames from the root to the top, and the other half was green and in full leaf'. (*E & I* 176)

(The quotation is from Lady Charlotte Guest, *The Mabinogion, translated from the Red Book of Hergest*, 86)

283   16   *he that Attis' image hangs* : in the procession at the festival of Attis the priest used to hang the god's image on the sacred pine tree.   Ellmann (*IY* 172) suggests that Yeats identifies the poet with the priest, himself castrated like the god (Attis was a vegetation god who castrated himself when Cybele, the earth mother, drove him to frenzy, and his devotees castrated themselves at his March festival) because he conceived of the artist as forced to sacrifice his life for the sake of his art : 'For its sake he becomes one with Attis and in this union, which is also the union of body and soul, he experiences the ecstasy of seeing beyond the cross or gyres into the rose or sphere of things.'   The devotee hanging the image of Attis between the body and soul of the tree rejects normal experiences but knows, according to Ellmann, 'the ecstatic state of non-grief which may be called joy'.   Yeats obtained his main knowledge of the Attis ritual from Sir James Frazer's *Attis, Adonis and Osiris*, 219–49.   Henn (*LT* 259) suggests Julian's 'Hymn to the Mother of God' as a source and Wilson (*YI* 276), mentions Arthur Symons's version of Catullus' 'Attis' (LXVI), and Parkinson (*YTLP* 221) mentions *Hastings' Encyclopaedia of Religion and Ethics* as another source.

17   *That staring fury* : Parkinson (*YTLP* 226) remarks that this is Yeats's way of identifying flame, death and knowledge, each a destructive peril.   'And the blind lush leaf is seen as equally menacing to those who seek revelation beyond grief.'

283   III

This section also answers the query of Section I 'What is joy ?'   It was included with II in the first printed version.

21 *trivial days* : there may be some thought here of the years Yeats spent working for the Abbey Theatre. From 1902 to 1912 he wrote 'little verse and no prose that did not arise out of some need of the Irish players, or from some thought suggested by their work, or in the defence of some friend connected with that work, or with the movement of events that made it possible' (*E & I* 219).

ram them : the image comes from Ben Jonson — Yeats misquoted his *Poetaster* in 'Anima Mundi' : 'Surely of the passionate dead we can but cry in words Ben Jonson meant for none but Shakespeare : "So rammed" are they "with life they can but grow in life with being"' (*M* 360).

27 *Lethean foliage* : Lethe meant oblivion in Greek. In Latin poetry the waters of Lethe, a river in Hades, were drunk by souls about to be reincarnated so they forgot their past lives.

29 *fortieth year* : Yeats had settled on his new bare style by 1905, when he was forty. It is possible that this year, when Maud Gonne and John MacBride separated (but when she, having become a Roman Catholic, would not divorce or be divorced) was indeed a time for testing works of 'intellect or faith'.

IV
35 *fiftieth year* : a passage in 'Anima Mundi' describes this experience :

> At certain moments, always unforeseen, I become happy, most commonly when at hazard I have opened some book of verse. Sometimes it is my own verse when, instead of discovering new technical flaws, I read with all the excitement of the first writing. Perhaps I am sitting in some crowded restaurant, the open book beside me, or closed, my excitement having over-brimmed the page. I look at the strangers near as if I had known them all my life, and it seems strange that I cannot speak to them : everything fills me with affection, I have no longer any fears or any needs ; I do not even remember that this happy mood must come to an end. It seems as if the vehicle had suddenly grown pure and far extended and so

luminous that the images from *Anima Mundi*, embodied there and drunk with that sweetness, would, like a country drunkard who has thrown a wisp into his own thatch, burn up time.

It may be an hour before the mood passes, but latterly I seem to understand that I enter upon it the moment I cease to hate. I think the common condition of our life is hatred — I know that this is so with me — irritation with public or private events or persons. (*M* 364–5)

284 V

50 *Responsibility*: cf. a phrase in the Introduction to Hone and Rossi, *Berkeley* (*E & I* 397) dealing with those who feel a responsibility for the thought of modern Ireland that can 'take away their sleep' and the memory of the '98 riots in *A* 368: 'I count the links in the chain of responsibility, run them across my fingers, and wonder if any link there is from my workshop.'

51 *Things said or done*: cf. 'The Man and the Echo' (*CP* 393)

VI

59 *Chou*: probably, according to Saul (*PYP* 144) Chóu-Kung, a twelfth-century member of the Chou dynasty. Yeats had possibly been reading Richard Wilhelm's translation of *The Secret of the Golden Flower* (*L* 786).

63 *Nineveh*: this probably derives from a memory of Arthur O'Shaughnessy's poem. See note (p. 295) on 'Fragments' (*CP* 240).

285 67 *man's blood-sodden heart*: cf. 'Man's own resinous heart' of 'Two Songs from a Play' (*CP* 239)

VII

72 *The Soul*: Yeats wrote from Coole Park to Mrs Shakespear on 3 January 1932:

I meant to write to you this morning (it is now 3.15) but thought of that sentence of yours [probably she wrote, 'You will be too great a bore if you get religion'] and then wrote a poem, which puts clearly an argument that has gone on in my head for years. When I have finished the poem I began yesterday I will take up the theme in greater fullness. Here is the poem. Heart and Soul are speaking:

Soul. Search out reality, leave things that seem.
Heart. What be a singer born and lack a theme ?
Soul. Ezekiel's coal and speed [speech ?] leaps out anew.
Heart. Can there be living speech in heaven's blue ?
Soul. Knock on that door, salvation waits within.
Heart. And what sang Homer but original sin.

I feel that this is the choice of the saint (St Theresa's ecstasy, Gandhi's smiling face) : comedy ; and the heroic choice ; Tragedy (Dante, Don Quixote). Live Tragically but be not deceived (not the fool's Tragedy). Yet I accept all the miracles. Why should not the old embalmers come back as ghosts and bestow upon the saint all the care once bestowed upon Rameses ? why should I doubt the tale that when St Theresa's tomb was opened in the middle of the nineteenth century the still undecayed body dripped with fragrant oil ? I shall be a sinful man to the end, and think upon my death-bed of all the nights I wasted in my youth. (*L* 789–90)

74 *Isaiah's coal* : cf. Isaiah vi ;

Then flew one of the seraphims unto me, having a live coal in his hand which he had taken with the tongs from off the altar ; and he laid it upon my mouth and said, Lo, this hath touched thy lips, and thine iniquity is taken away and thy sin purged. Also I heard the voice of the Lord saying, 'Whom shall I send, and who will go for us ? Then said I, Here am I ; send me. And he said, Go and tell this people, Hear ye indeed, but understand not ; and see ye indeed, but perceive not.

The change from the Ezekiel of the draft of the poem to Isaiah in the published text may have been because Yeats found von Hügel dealing with Ezekiel in some detail as a representative of the higher elements of religion.

75–6 . . . *Simplicity of fire !* . . . *salvation walks within* : Henn (*LT* 140) cites a passage from *PASL* which is based on Plotinus :

There are two realities, the terrestrial and the condition of fire. All power is from the terrestrial condition, for there all opposites meet and there only is the extreme of choice possible, full freedom. And there the heterogeneous is, and evil, for evil is the strain one upon another of opposites ; but in the condition of fire is all music and all rest. (*M* 356–7)

77 *Homer but original sin ?* : the theme of the poem was epitomised by a remark of Lady Gregory to Yeats a few weeks before she died, that she preferred the poems (in a book Yeats had shown her) which were translated from the Irish, because they came out of original sin. Cf. Frank O'Connor, 'Synge', *The Irish Theatre*, 38.

VIII

The composition of this section is discussed in Bradford, *Yeats at Work* 128–34.

Yeats was reading Baron Friedrich von Hugel's *The Mystical Element of Religion*; this poem's contrast between Homeric and Christian ideas probably came from a passage in von Hugel (186 ff.):

> For the survival after the body's death indubitably attributed to the Psyche in the Homeric poems, is conceived there, throughout, as a miserably shrunken consciousness, and one which is dependent for its continuance upon the good offices bestowed by the survivors upon the corpse and grave. And the translation of the still living Menelaus to Elysium (*Odyssey* IV, 560–8) is probably a later insertion ; it belongs to a small class of exceptional cases ; implies the writer's inability to conceive a heightened consciousness for the soul, after the soul's separation from the body ; and is based not upon any virtue or reward, but upon Menelaus' family-relationship to Zeus. Ganymede gets similarly translated because of his physical beauty. (*Iliad*, XX, 232 ff.)

79 *Accept the miracles*: Yeats wrote in his preface to *The Ten Principal Upanishads* (1937), 10, that '*The Golden Bough* has made Christianity look modern and fragmentary'.

80 *Saint Teresa* : see notes (p. 329) on 'Oil and Blood' (*CP* 270)

82 *self-same hands* : cf. embalmers. Cf. Wilson (*YI* 165), who thinks Yeats 'suggests that the ghosts of ancient Egyptian embalmers may have been sent in the astral body to preserve it' [the body of St Teresa].

286 88 *the lion and the honeycomb* : cf. Judges xiv, 5–18

QUARREL IN OLD AGE

This poem was written in November 1931 and first appeared in
WMP.

1 *her sweetness* : Maud Gonne's. The poem records a quarrel with
her, probably over the treatment of women prisoners on a hunger
strike organised by Mary McSwiney.

3 *blind bitter town* : Dublin. Cf. 'this blind bitter land' of
'Words' (*CP* 100), the 'blind and ignorant town' of 'To a Wealthy
Man who promised a second Subscription to the Dublin Municipal Gallery if it were Proved the People wanted Pictures' (*CP*
119), and 'this unmannerly town' of 'The People' (*CP* 169).

9 *All lives that has lived* : F. F. Farag (*YCE* 41) points out that
the idea of reincarnation gave Yeats hope whenever he felt death
approaching. Cf. 'Mohini Chatterjee' (*CP* 279).

14 *that lonely thing* : cf. 'Broken Dreams' (*CP* 172)

16 *Targeted* : protected as with a round shield or targe. Cf.
Hone (*WBY* 441) who confirms Yeats's approval of the note on
this in *Modern Poetry 1922–1934* (ed. M. Wollman).

like spring : cf. *A* 123, where Yeats described his memory of his
first meeting with Maud Gonne, who seemed 'a classical impersonation of the spring'

THE RESULTS OF THOUGHT   **286**

This poem was written between 18 and 28 August 1931 and first
appeared in *WMP*.

1 *Acquaintance* : not identified

companion : Mrs Shakespear

2 *One dear brilliant woman* : Lady Gregory

287 5 *All, all*: cf. note (p. 187) on line 21. 'Broken Dreams' (*CP* 173)

287 GRATITUDE TO THE UNKNOWN INSTRUCTORS

The date of composition is unknown; the poem first appeared in *WMP*.

1 *they*: those who inspired *AV*. Passages in the Introduction to that work describe how Mrs Yeats surprised the poet on 24 October 1917 by attempting automatic writing:

> What came in disjointed sentences, in almost illegible writing, was so exciting, sometimes so profound, that I persuaded her to give an hour or two day after day to the unknown writer, and after some half-dozen such hours offered to spend what remained of life explaining and piecing together those scattered sentences. 'No' was the answer, 'we have come to give you metaphors for poetry'. (*AV* (B) 8)

> Early in 1919 the communicator of the moment — they were constantly changed — said they would soon change the method from the written to the spoken word as that would fatigue her less, but the change did not come for some months'. (*AV* (B) 9)

> Much that has happened, much that has been said, suggests that the communicators are the personalities of a dream shared by my wife, by myself, occasionally by others. . . . (*AV* (B) 22–3)

287 REMORSE FOR INTEMPERATE SPEECH

This poem was written on 28 August 1931 and first appeared in *WMP*.

1 *the knave and fool*: probably a reference to Yeats's youthful work as a nationalist

288 4 *Fit audience*: probably the friends Yeats made after he was thirty, Lady Gregory in Ireland, and many others in England

8 *hatred*: Yeats wrote on 7 September 1927 to Mrs Shakespear, referring to the 'hatred that is a commonplace here — It lays hold

on our class I think more easily than upon the mass of the people. It finds a more complicated and determined conscience to prey upon.'

10 *fanatic* : Yeats's note reads 'I pronounce "fanatic" in what is, I suppose, the older and more Irish way, so that the last line of each stanza contains but two beats' (*CP* 288)

STREAM AND SUN AT GLENDALOUGH   288

This poem was written on 23 June 1932, and first appeared in *WMP.*

Title Glendalough : in Co. Wicklow. Cf. 'Under the Round Tower' (*CP* 154). Iseult Gonne and her husband Francis Stuart lived at Laragh, a few miles from Glendalough. See notes (p. 310) on 'The Death of the Hare' (*CP* 250) and (pp. 503–4) on 'Why should not Old Men be Mad?' *CP* 388)

Words for Music Perhaps

Yeats wrote in his Introduction to *WS* that in the spring of 1929 :

> life returned to me as an impression of the uncontrollable
> energy and daring of the great creators ; it seemed to me that
> but for journalism and criticism, all that evasion and explana-
> tion, the world would be torn in pieces. I wrote *Mad as the
> Mist and Snow*, a mechanical little song, and after that almost
> all that group of poems, called in memory of those exultant
> weeks *Words for Music Perhaps*.

In a letter of 2 March 1929, Yeats wrote to Mrs Shakespear
from Rapallo that he was 'writing *Twelve poems for music* — have
done three of them (and two other poems) — no [t] so much that
they may be sung as that I may define their kind of emotion to
myself. I want them to be all emotion and all impersonal' (*L* 758).
On 13 September 1929 he wrote to her from Dublin that he would
finish at Rapallo 'the book of thirty poems for music I am more
than half through. "For Music" is only a name, nobody will sing
them' (*L* 769). On 17 August he wrote to her from Riversdale,
Rathfarnham, that the 'Crazy Jane' poems 'and the little group of
love poems that follow are, I think, exciting and strange. Sexual
abstinence fed their fire — I was ill and yet full of desire. They
sometimes came out of the greatest mental excitement I am capable
of' (*L* 814).

These poems were written between 1929 and 1932. See *WBY*
401 for some dates, and ibid., 425, where Yeats's letter (of the
winter of 1931–2) to his wife is quoted : 'I want to exorcise that
slut, Crazy Jane, whose language has become unendurable.' 'Crazy
Jane' was substituted for 'Cracked Mary', the title given in the
first printing.

'Cracked Mary' was an old woman who lived near Lady Gregory
and was 'the local satirist and a really terrible one', as Yeats wrote
in a letter to Mrs Shakespear of November 1931. In this he
described Crazy Jane as more or less founded on this old woman :

who lives in a cottage near Gort. She loves her flower garden — She has just sent Lady Gregory some flowers in spite of the season and [has] an amazing power of audacious speech. One of her great performances is a description of how the meanness of a Gort shopkeeper's wife over the price of a glass of porter made her so despair of the human race that she got drunk. The incidents of the drunkenness are of an epic magnificence.

There is a Jane in 'The Limerick Rake' who may have been a possible source. See Colm O'Loghlain, *Irish Street Ballads*. D. E. S. Maxwell, 'Swift's Dark Grove : Yeats and the Anglo-Irish tradition' (*YCE*, 28–9) suggests the parallels between Yeats's Crazy Jane poems and some of Swift's.

CRAZY JANE AND THE BISHOP   290

This poem was written on 2 March 1929, and first appeared in the *New Republic* (12 Nov. 1930) and *LM* (Nov. 1930). The title was initially 'Cracked Mary and the Bishop'.

1 *the blasted oak* : this was 'the chapel wall' in an early MS. version.

9 *Jack the Journeyman* : Ellmann (*IY* 275), points out that Jack the Journeyman appeared as a character in Yeats's play *The Pot of Broth* (1902), and in a note to that play Yeats remarked that the words and air of the tramp's song in that play, 'There's Broth in the Pot' came from an old woman known as Cracked Mary 'who wanders about the plain of Aidhne, and who sometimes sees unearthly riders on white horses coming through stony fields to her hovel door in the night time.'

CRAZY JANE REPROVED   291

This poem was written on 27 March 1929 and first appeared in the *New Republic* (12 Nov. 1930) and *LM* (Nov. 1930) entitled 'Cracked Mary Reproved'.

2–4 *All those dreadful thunder-stones,*
All that storm that blots the day

Can but show that Heaven yawns : cf. a passage in 'Ireland after Parnell' :

> . . . politics, for a vision-seeking man, can be but half achieve-
> ment, a choice of an almost easy kind of skill instead of that
> kind which is, of all those not impossible, the most difficult.
> Is it not certain that the Creator yawns in earthquake and
> thunder and other popular displays, but toils in rounding the
> delicate spiral of a shell.' (*A* 249)

This suggests that Crazy Jane is being reproved for her choice of lovers.

5 *Europa* : the daughter of Agenor, King of Phoenicia. Zeus fell in love with her, assumed the shape of a bull, and carried her off to Crete : there she became the mother of Minos, Sarpedon, and Rhadamanthus. Zeus' appearance to her as a bull was part of his less serious activity, and ranks, with his production of storms, as inferior to his creation of a shell.

291 CRAZY JANE ON THE DAY OF JUDGMENT

This poem was written in October 1930 and first appeared in *WMP*.

3–4 . . . *the whole/Body and soul* : Saul (*PYP* 147) draws attention to Sir W. Rothenstein, *Since Fifty*, 242, who quoted Yeats's remark that 'the tragedy of sexual intercourse is the perpetual virginity of the souls'.

292 CRAZY JANE AND JACK THE JOURNEYMAN

This poem was written in November 1931 and first appeared in *WMP*.

5 *a skein unwound* : cf. 'His Bargain' (*CP* 299)

293 7 *A lonely ghost* : some of Yeats's ideas about ghosts and their relationships are put in 'Anima Mundi' :

> The dead, as the passionate necessity wears out, come into
> a measure of freedom and may turn the impulse of events,
> started while living, in some new direction, but they cannot
> originate except through the living. Then gradually they

perceive, although they are still but living in their memories, harmonies, symbols, and patterns, as though all were being refashioned by an artist, and they are moved by emotions, sweet for no imagined good but in themselves, like those of children dancing in a ring ; and I do not doubt that they make love in that union which Swedenborg has said is of the whole body and seems from far off an incandescence. Hitherto shade has communicated with shade in moments of common memory that recur like the figures of a dance in terror or in joy, but now they run together like to like, and their covens and fleets have rhythm and pattern. This running together and running of all to a centre, and yet without loss of identity, has been prepared for by their exploration of their moral life, of its beneficiaries and its victims, and even of all its untrodden paths, and all their thoughts have moulded the vehicle and become event and circumstance. (*M* 355–6)

CRAZY JANE ON GOD   **293**

This poem was written on 18 July 1931 and first appeared in *WMP*.

5 *Men come, men go* : the first stanza describes Crazy Jane's realisation that love is transitory, but is yet aware of permanence. Ellmann (*IY* 277) suggests that Yeats originally got the idea from Madame Blavatsky, quoting from Yeats's words in Lady Gregory, *Visions and Beliefs* i, 277 : '. . . she tried to explain predestination, our freedom and God's full knowledge of the use that we should make of it. All things past and to come were present in the mind of God and yet all things were free.'

7 *Banners choke the sky* : a passage in the introduction to *WWP* provides a gloss :

It is fitting that Plotinus should have been the first philosopher to meet his daimon face to face, though the boy attendant out of jealousy or in convulsive terror strangled the doves, for he was the first to establish as sole source the timeless individuality or daimon instead of the Platonic Idea, to prefer Socrates to his thought. This timeless individuality contains archetypes of all possible existences whether of man or brute, and as it traverses its circle of allotted lives, now

one, now another, prevails. We may fail to express an archetype or alter it by reason, but all done from nature is its
unfolding into time. Some other existence may take the
place of Socrates, yet Socrates can never cease to exist. Once
a friend of mine was digging in a long-neglected garden and
suddenly out of the air came a voice thanking her, an old
owner of the garden, she was told later, long since reborn, yet
still in the garden. Plotinus said that we should not 'baulk at
this limitlessness of the intellectual ; it is an infinitude having
nothing to do with number or part' (*Ennead* V. 7. I) ; yet it
seems that it can at will re-enter number and part and thereby
make itself apparent to our minds. If we accept this idea
many strange or beautiful things become credible. The Indian
pilgrim has not deceived us ; he did hear the bed where the
sage of his devotion slept a thousand years ago creak as though
someone turned over in it, and he did see — he himself and
the old shrine-keeper — the blankets all tossed about at dawn
as if someone had just risen ; the Irish countrywoman did see
the ruined castle lit up, the bridge across the river dropping ;
these two Oxford ladies did find themselves in the garden of
the Petit Trianon with Marie Antoinette and her courtiers,
see that garden as those saw it ; the gamekeeper did hear
those footsteps the other night that sounded like the footsteps of a stag where stag has not passed these hundred years.
All about us there seems to start up a precise inexplicable
teeming life, and the earth becomes once more, not in rhetorical
metaphor, but in reality, sacred. (*E* 368–9)

An earlier passage in 'Anima Mundi' dealt with the same idea :

Spiritism, whether of folk-lore or of the séance-room, the
visions of Swedenborg, and the speculation of the Platonists
and Japanese plays, will have it that we may see at certain
roads and in certain houses old murders acted over again, and
in certain fields dead huntsmen riding with horse and hound,
or ancient armies fighting above bones or ashes. We carry
to *Anima Mundi* our memory, and that memory is for a time
our external world ; and all passionate moments recur again
and again, for passion desires its own recurrence more than any
event, and whatever there is of corresponding complacency
or remorse is our beginning of judgement. . . . (*M* 354)

Ellmann (*IY* 277), remarks that the image of the army may derive
from the fact that the original Cracked Mary sometimes saw
'unearthly riders on white horses'.

13–16 *Before their eyes a house*
         That from childhood stood
         Uninhabited, ruinous,

    Suddenly lit up: This is probably the ruined castle referred to in the Introduction to *WWP* quoted above, and it was probably Castle Dargan, near Sligo, also described in Yeats's play *The King of the Great Clock Tower*:

> Castle Dargan's ruin all lit,
> Lovely ladies dancing in it . . .
> . . . Yet all the lovely things that were
> Live, for I saw them dancing there. (*CPl* 640)

This castle is also alluded to, *A* 53. Cf. also *A* 77 and the description of the ruined house 'that was burnt down' in Yeats's play *Purgatory*, a window of which is lit up with a young girl in it (*CPl* 685–7) And cf. the ruined house in 'The Curse of Cromwell' (*CP* 350). There is also a possibility that Yeats had Leap Castle in mind, which 'though burnt down during our Civil War and still a ruin, is haunted by what is called an evil spirit which appears as a sheep with short legs and decaying human head' (*AV* (B) 224). Cf. p. 513.

CRAZY JANE TALKS WITH THE BISHOP

This poem was written in November 1931 and first appeared in *WS*.

3 *Those breasts*: cf. a passage in Synge's translation of Villon's 'An Old Woman's Lamentation':

> 'The man I had a love for — a great rascal would kick me in the gutter — is dead thirty years and over it, and it is I am left behind, grey and aged. When I do be minding the good days I had, minding what I was one time, and that it is I'm come to, and when I do look on my own self, poor and dry, and pinched together, it wouldn't be much would set me raging in the streets.
> Where is the round forehead I had, and the fine hair, and the two eyebrows, and the eyes with a big gay look out of them would bring folly from a great scholar? Where is my straight shapely nose, and two ears, and my chin with a valley in it, and my lips were red and open?
> Where are the pointed shoulders that were on me, and the

long arms and nice hands to them? Where is my bosom was as white as any, or my straight rounded sides?

It's the way I am this day — my forehead is gone into furrows, the hair of my head is grey and whitish, my eyebrows are tumbled from me, and my two eyes have died out within my head — those eyes that would be laughing to the men — my nose has a hook on it, my ears are hanging down and my lips are sharp and skinny.

That's what's left over from the beauty of a right woman — a bag of bones, and legs the like of two shrivelled sausages going beneath it.

It's the like of what we old hags do be thinking, of the good times that are gone away from us, and we crouched on our hunkers by a little fire of twigs, soon kindled and soon spent, we that were the pick of many. (Synge, *Poems and Translations*, 44)

295 16 *The place of excrement* : cf. Blake's line in *Jerusalem* : 'For I will make their places of love and joy excrementitious'

295 CRAZY JANE GROWN OLD LOOKS AT THE DANCERS

This poem was written on 6 March 1929 and first appeared in *The New Republic* (12 Nov. 1930).

1 *that ivory image* : the source of the poem is revealed in a letter Yeats wrote to Mrs Shakespear from Rapallo on 2 March 1929 :

Last night I saw in a dream strange ragged excited people singing in a crowd. The most visible were a man and woman who were I think dancing. The man was swinging around his head a weight at the end of a rope or leather thong and I knew that he did not know whether he would strike her dead or not, and both had their eyes fixed on each other, and both sang their love for one another. I suppose it was Blake's old thought 'sexual love is founded on spiritual hate' — I will probably find I have written it in a poem in a few days — though my remembering my dream may prevent that — by making my criticism work upon it. (At least there is evidence to that effect.) (*L* 758)

The passage on sexual love and spiritual hate in 'Anima Hominis' is concerned with similar matters, where Yeats sees the warfare of man and Daimon as imaged in love. See *M* 336–7.

18 *thraneen* : probably from Synge's *The Playboy of the Western* **296**
World, II, and the phrase means not to care. Thraneen, a small
coin.

GIRL'S SONG **296**

This poem was written on 29 March 1929 and first appeared in the
New Republic (22 Oct. 1930).

11 *an old man young* : this is reminiscent of Blake

YOUNG MAN'S SONG **296**

This poem was written after 29 March 1929, according to Ellmann,
(*IY* 292). It first appeared in the *New Republic* (22 Oct. 1930).

12 *Before the world was made* : cf. 'Before the World was Made' **297**
(*CP* 308)

16 *shall bend the knee* : this phrase frequently occurred in Irish
political oratory in the nineteenth century.

HER ANXIETY **297**

This was written after 17 April 1929, and first appeared in the *New
Republic* (22 Oct. 1930).

HIS CONFIDENCE **298**

This poem was written after 29 March 1929 and first appeared in
the *New Republic* (22 Oct. 1930).

LOVE'S LONELINESS **298**

This poem was written on 17 April 1929 and first appeared in the
New Republic (22 Oct. 1930).

HER DREAM **299**

This poem was written after 29 March 1929 and first appeared in
the *New Republic* (22 Oct. 1930).
  A possible source for the poem is Catullus LXVI.

1-8 *I dreamed as in my bed I lay,*
    All night's fathomless wisdom come,
    That I had shorn my locks away
    And laid them on Love's lettered tomb :
    But something bore them out of sight
    In a great tumult of the air,
    And after nailed upon the night
    Berenice's burning hair : cf. a passage in 'Anima Mundi' :

The soul cannot have much knowledge till it has shaken off the habit of time and of place, but till that hour it must fix its attention upon what is near, thinking of objects one after another as we run the eye or the finger over them. Its intellectual power cannot but increase and alter as its perceptions grow simultaneous. Yet even now we seem at moments to escape from time in what we call prevision, and from place when we see distant things in a dream and in concurrent dreams. A couple of years ago, while in meditation, my head seemed surrounded by a conventional sun's rays, and when I went to bed I had a long dream of a woman with her hair on fire. I awoke and lit a candle, and discovered presently from the odour that in doing so I had set my own hair on fire. I dreamed very lately that I was writing a story, and at the same time I dreamed that I was one of the characters in that story and seeking to touch the heart of some girl in defiance of the author's intention ; and concurrently with all that, I was as another self trying to strike with the button of a foil a great china jar. The obscurity of the 'Prophetic Books' of William Blake, which were composed in a state of vision, comes almost wholly from these concurrent dreams. Everybody has some story or some experience of the sudden knowledge in sleep or waking of some event, a misfortune for the most part, happening to some friend far off. (*M* 358)

8 *Berenice's burning hair* : see note (p. 330) on 'Veronica's Napkin' (*CP* 270)

299 HIS BARGAIN

This poem was written after 29 March 1929 and first appeared in the *New Republic* (22 Oct. 1930). The first version contained six extra lines probably through a printer's error as they are lines 13–18 of 'Young Man's Song' (*CP* 296).

1   *Plato's spindle* : this probably derives from Plato's myth of Er in Book x of *The Republic* (which Yeats's conception of the gyres resembles) :

> For this light binds the sky together, like the hawser that strengthens a trireme, and thus holds together the whole revolving universe. To the extremities is fastened the distaff of Necessity, by means of which all the revolutions of the universe are kept up. The shaft and hook of this distaff are made of steel ; the whorl is a compound of steel and other materials. The nature of the whorl may be thus described. In shape it is like an ordinary whorl ; but from Er's account we must picture it to ourselves under the form of a large hollow whorl, scooped out right through, into which a similar, but smaller whorl is nicely inserted, like those boxes which fit into one another. In the same way a third whorl is inserted within the second, a fourth within the third, and so on to four more. . . . Now the distaff as a whole spins round with uniform velocity ; but while the whole revolves, the seven inner circles travel slowly round in the opposite direction. . . . The distaff spins round upon the knees of Necessity. . . . At equal distances around sit three other personages, each on a throne. These are the daughters of Necessity, the Fates, Lachesis, Clotho, and Atropos . . .
> (*Republic* 616–17, translated by J. L. Davies and D. J. Vaughan).

The lover protests that he has chosen to love only her with whose hair he made the bargain. This choice of faithful love 'before the thread began' may be due to this passage :

> Now the souls, immediately on their arrival, were required to go to Lachesis. An interpreter first of all marshalled them in order, and then having taken from the lap of Lachesis a number of lots and plans of life, mounted a high pulpit and spoke as follows : 'Thus saith the maiden Lachesis, the daughter of Necessity. Ye short-lived souls, a generation of men shall here begin the cycle of its mortal existence. Your destiny shall not be allotted to you, but you shall choose it for yourselves.' (*Republic* 617)

The myth continues to describe the different lives of living things laid before the soul. No settled character of soul was included because the soul inevitably becomes changed with the change of life. The choice 'is apparently the moment when everything is at stake with a man' and

> With iron resolution must he hold fast this opinion when he enters the future world, in order that, there as well as here, he may escape being dazzled by wealth and similar evils ; and may not plunge into usurpations or other corresponding courses of action, to the inevitable detriment of others, and to his own still heavier affliction ; but may know how to select that life which always steers a middle course between such extremes, and to shun excess on either side to the best of his power, not only in this life, but in that which is to come. For, by acting thus, he is sure to become a most happy man.

Yeats did not like the platonic μηδὲν ἄγάν — his lover made his choice 'before the thread began' — but he had made a choice which overrides fate, a choice superior to the common one in which

> Dan and Jerry Lout
> Change their loves about

Plato's story allots the souls a due span of time :

> Now, when all the souls had chosen their lives in the order of the lots, they advanced in their turn to Lachesis, who dispatched with each of them the Destiny he had selected, to guard his life and satisfy his choice. This Destiny first led the soul to Clotho in such a way as to pass beneath her hand and the whirling motion of the distaff, and thus ratified the fate which each had chosen in the order of precedence. After touching her, the same Destiny led the soul next to the spinning of Atropos, and thus rendered the doom of Clotho irreversible. From thence the souls passed straightforward under the throne of Necessity. (*Republic* 620)

This idea was also used in Yeats's play *Diarmuid and Grania* where Diarmuid says to Grania : 'Life of my life, I [k]new you before I was born, I made a bargain with this brown hair before the beginning of time and it shall not be broken through unending time' (*VPl* 1195).

8 *Before the thread began* : Yeats quoted in a letter to Katharine Tynan of June 1891 Mrs Radford's lines :

> The love within my heart for thee
> Before the world was had its birth . . .

And cf. also 'Before the World was Made' (*CP* 308).

11 *A bargain with that hair*: this un-Greek extravagance, typical of the manner in which Yeats could turn from philosophy to love poetry, may be an adaptation of his philosophical sources to another model taken from the love poetry of Hafiz for its image of great and lasting love. (The cynical view of the possibility of this great love is to be found in 'The Fool by the Roadside' (*CP* 247) which uses the same imagery to different ends.) Cf. 'The Tresses of the Hair':

> Hafiz cried to his beloved, 'I made a bargain with that brown hair before the beginning of time, and it shall not be broken through unending time,' and it may be that Mistress Nature knows that we have lived many times, and that whatsoever changes and winds into itself belongs to us. She covers her eyes away from us, but she lets us play with the tresses of her hair. (*E & I* 290)

THREE THINGS   **300**

This poem was written in March 1929 and first appeared in the *New Republic* (2 Oct. 1929).

17 *stretch and yawn*: stretching and yawning are symbols of consummated sex.

LULLABY   **300**

This poem was written on either 20 or 27 March 1929 and first appeared in the *New Keepsake* (London, 1931). Frank O'Connor stated that this poem is based on his translation *Grania* (*Kings, Lords, and Commons*, 49).

Yeats wrote to Olivia Shakespear on 29 March 1929 that this was

> a *Lullaby* that I like. A mother sings to her child [Then followed a version of the poem]. I have done two or three others that seem to me lucky and that does not often happen. Yet I am full of doubt. I am writing more easily than I ever wrote and I am happy, whereas I have always been unhappy when I wrote and worked with great difficulty. I feel like one of those Japanese who in the middle ages retired from the world at 50 or so — not like an Indian of that age to live in jungle but to devote himself 'to art and letters' which was

considered sacred. If this new work do not seem as good as the old to my friends then I can take to some lesser task and live very contentedly. The happiness of finding idleness a duty. No more opinions, no more politics, no more practical tasks. (*L* 760–1)

4 *Paris* : son of Priam, King of Troy, and his wife Hecuba, who was exposed on Mount Ida as it was prophesied he would bring ruin on his country. He was brought up by shepherds, and lived with Oenone, a nymph, until he was appointed to award the prize for beauty to one of the three goddesses, Hera, Athene and Aphrodite. Aphrodite offered him the fairest woman in the world if she gained the prize. Afterwards Paris visited Sparta and persuaded Helen, the wife of King Menelaus, to elope with him. This caused the Greek siege of Troy in which Paris was mortally wounded by an arrow. He was brought to Oenone, but it was too late for her to cure him and in her grief she committed suicide.

301 8 *Tristram* : in Malory's *Morte d'Arthur* Tristram, the son of the King of Lyonesse, is sent to Ireland to be cured of a wound. He falls in love there with La Beale Isoud the King's daughter, but he leaves the court, as he has killed the brother of the Queen of Ireland. He returns to Cornwall and King Mark sends him to Ireland to ask La Beale Isoud to marry King Mark. She marries Mark, but continues relations with Tristram till they are betrayed to Mark. He then leaves Mark's court and falls in love with Isoud la Blanche Mains when fighting for King Howel of Brittany. But he returns to Cornwall, is banished, and is killed by Mark as he sits harping before La Beale Isoud.

Another version of the legend tells how Tristram, wounded by a poisoned arrow in Brittany, sends for La Beale Isoud — she is to come in a ship with a white sail. But when the ship returns Isoud of Brittany tells him the sail is black and he dies. La Beale Isoud discovers his body, lies beside it and dies herself.

9 *potion's work* : see note on line 8

14 *Eurotas* : the main river in Sparta

15   *holy bird* : Zeus who took the shape of a swan. Cf. 'Leda and the Swan' (*CP* 241).

17   *Leda* : Leda, the wife of Tyndareus the King of Sparta, was bathing in the Eurotas when Zeus saw her. She bore Castor and Pollux and Helen to Zeus.

Maud Gonne is described as having a 'Ledaean body' in 'Among School Children' (*CP* 242).

AFTER LONG SILENCE   301

This poem was written in November 1929 and first appeared in *WMP*.

Yeats wrote on 16 December 1929 to Mrs Shakespear from Rapallo to say 'When I first got here I was fairly vigorous though shaky, and wrote this little poem of which I showed you the prose draft' (*L* 772).

The prose draft is quoted by Ellmann (*IY* 280)

> Subject
> Your hair is white
> My hair is white
> Come let us talk of love
> What other theme do we know
> When we were young
> We were in love with one another
> And therefore ignorant

8   *We loved each other* : the poem is written about Yeats and Mrs Shakespear.

MAD AS THE MIST AND SNOW   301

This poem was written on 12 February 1929 and first appeared in *WMP*.

Yeats wrote in *OTB* :

When I began to grow old I could no longer spend all my time amid masterpieces and in trying to make the like. I gave part of every day to mere entertainment, and it seemed when I was ill that great genius was 'mad as the mist and snow'. Already in mid-Renaissance the world was weary of wisdom, science began to appear in the elaborate perspectives of its painters, in their sense of weight and tangibility ; man was looking for some block where he could lay his head. But better than that, with Jacob's dream threatening, get rid of man himself. Civilisation slept in the masses, wisdom in science. Is it criminal to sleep ? I do not know ; I do not say it. (*E* 436)

302 7 *Horace* : Quintus Horatius Flaccus (65–8 B.C.), Roman poet, pardoned after fighting on the losing side at Philippi, and became a friend of Maecenas who gave him a Sabine farm. He wrote satires, odes, epodes, epistles, and the *Ars Poetica*. His lyric poetry had an epicurean bias.

Homer : the Greek epic poet, regarded by the ancients as the author of the *Iliad* and the *Odyssey* (? born between 1050 and 850 B.C.). Seven cities claimed to be his birthplace. Tradition represents him as blind and poor in his old age.

8 *Plato* : the Greek philosopher (427–348 B.C.) was born at Athens or Aegina. He was a pupil and admirer of Socrates and retired to Megara and Sicily after his death, returning to Athens in 386 B.C. to teach in the Academy there. He spent the rest of his life teaching and composing Dialogues in some of which Socrates figures.

9 *Tully's open page* : Marcus Tullius Cicero (106–43 B.C.) became consul in 63 B.C. He was pardoned by Caesar after Pharsalia, having fought on Pompey's side. He attacked Mark Anthony in his Philippic orations, was proscribed by the triumvirate and put to death in 43 B.C. He wrote on rhetoric, political philosophy and moral philosophy. His orations are masterpieces of Latin prose style and his letters give an excellent picture of his life.

302 THOSE DANCING DAYS ARE GONE

This poem was written on 8 March 1929 and first appeared in the *New Republic* (12 Nov. 1930), and *LM* (Nov. 1930).

7–8 *I carry the sun in a golden cup,*
  The moon in a silver bag : cf. 'The Man who dreamed of

Faeryland' (*CP* 49). The first line of the refrain is taken from Ezra Pound's *Cantos* (Notes *CP*).

'I AM OF IRELAND' 303

This poem was written in August 1929 and first appeared in *WMP*. There is a note on the MS. in R. O. Dougan, *W. B. Yeats. Manuscripts and Printed Books exhibited in the Library of Trinity College, Dublin* 1956, 37

1 *I am of Ireland* : Ellmann (*IY* 280) gives an account of Frank O'Connor reading aloud an early fourteenth-century English lyric :

> Icham of Irlande
> Aut of the holy lande of Irlande
> Gode sir pray ich ye
> For of saynte charite
> Come and daunce wyt me,
> in Irlaunde

This version is from J. E. Wells, *Manual of Middle English Writing*, 492. Yeats's note (in *CP*) is that 'the poem is developed from three or four lines of an Irish fourteenth-century dance song somebody repeated to me a few years ago' but the source may be, according to Mrs Yeats, St John D. Seymour's *Anglo-Irish Literature 1200–1582*. In this book there is a passage which may have suggested elements of the poem to Yeats :

> Wells describes a fragment of an English manuscript (1300–1350) containing popular songs, of some of which only a line remains : these, he says, were rude pieces for singing by the roadside or at the ale house as may have been the case with our Kilkenny fragments. One of these is of interest to him, as he considers it to be perhaps the earliest English dance song extant. It is of more interest to us, as it is placed in the mouth of an Irish girl, and so presumably was composed by an Anglo-Irish minstrel.

Here are the elements of the poem : a singing, dancing, Irish girl ; the English crowd by the roadside or in the alehouse ; only one man pays any attention to the girl. Ellmann (*IY* 280–1) comments :

> But only one man listens, and he finds many pretexts for preferring comfortable expedience to the discomforts of idealism. When she repeats her appeal he gives a further reason :

there can be no dancing in a country where all things are awry, and he gives her back her own words by pointing out that there is no time to remedy these things. Yet her cry continues, as if indifferent to his prudential explanations, like the cry of all idealism and heroism.

304 THE DANCER AT CRUACHAN AND CRO-PATRICK

This poem was written in August 1931 and first appeared in *WMP*, with 'Cro-Patrick' spelt as 'Croagh Patrick' in the title. Yeats' note read that 'Cruachan' was pronounced 'Crockhan in modern Gaelic'.

Title Cruachan : see note (p. 138) on 'The Hour before Dawn' (*CP* 130)

Cro-Patrick : a mountain in Connemara. It is near Westport, Co. Mayo, and is a centre for Christian pilgrimage.

1 *I, proclaiming* : St Cellach. Cf. 'An Indian Monk' where Yeats remarks 'Some Irish saint, whose name I have forgotten, sang "There is one among the birds that is so perfect, one among the fish, one perfect among men"' (*E & I* 431).

Another essay in 'Discoveries' puts the question : 'was it Columbanus or another that wrote, "There is one among the birds that is perfect, and one perfect among the fish"?' (*E & I* 291).

There were two Cellachs who should not be confused, one pagan, one Christian. Halt Cellach was the protector of the pagan bards who were overcome by the Christians at the battle of Moyra. Cellach tried to capture Congal, the pagan leader, alive during this battle, but before he could lay hands on him, to quote Sir Samuel Ferguson's *Congal*, p. 132 :

> Sudden and black, the storm came down ; with scourge of hissing hail
> It lashed the blinded, stumbling hosts : a shrill loud whistling wail
> And thundrous clamours filled the sky . . .

305 TOM THE LUNATIC

This poem was written on 27 July 1931 and first appeared in *WMP*.

7 *Huddon and Duddon and Daniel O'Leary*: cf. *AV* (B) 32, where these three characters appear in a poem:

> Huddon, Duddon and Daniel O'Leary
> Delighted me as a child ;
> But where that roaring, ranting crew
> Danced, laughed, loved, fought through
> Their brief lives I never knew.
>
> Huddon, Duddon and Daniel O'Leary
> Delighted me as a child.
> I put three persons in their place
> That despair and keep the pace
> And love wench Wisdom's cruel face.
>
> Huddon, Duddon and Daniel O'Leary
> Delighted me as a child.
> Hard-living men and men of thought
> Burn their bodies up for nought,
> I mock at all so burning out.

Daniel O'Leary (Yeats's footnote to the poem in *AV* reads 'As a child I pronounced the word as though it rhymed to "dairy"') explains himself in the prose of *Stories of Michael Robartes and his friends : an extract from a record made by his pupils* (*AV* (B) 33-55).

The use Yeats made of invented characters may perhaps relate to his experiments in thought transference and interest in complementary dreams. A passage in 'Hodos Chameliontos' shows that his interest in these characters may have come from the experiences of his uncle's second-sighted servant Mary Battle :

> Considering that Mary Battle received our thoughts in sleep, though coarsened or turned to caricature, do not the thoughts of the scholar or the hermit, though they speak no word, or something of their shape and impulse, pass into the general mind ? Does not the emotion of some woman of fashion, caught in the subtle torture of self-analysing passion, pass down, although she speak no word, to Joan with her Pot, Jill with her Pail, and it may be, with one knows not what nightmare melancholy, to Tom the Fool ? (*A* 262)

TOM AT CRUACHAN   306

This poem was written on 29 July 1931 and first appeared in *WMP*.

Title Cruachan: see headnote (p. 386) on 'The Dancer at Cruachan and Cro-Patrick' (*CP* 304).

306 OLD TOM AGAIN

This poem was written in October 1931 and first appeared in *WMP*.

Yeats described the poem in a letter to his wife as 'a reply to the Dancer's Song', probably 'The Dancer at Cruachan and Cro-Patrick' (*CP* 304).

306 THE DELPHIC ORACLE UPON PLOTINUS

This poem was written on 19 August 1931 and first appeared in *WMP*.

This poem is based on the verse oracle, in Porphyry's *Life of Plotinus*, given to Amelius who consulted Delphi to discover where Plotinus' soul had gone after his death. Yeats knew Thomas Taylor's translation of Plotinus and read Dempsey's *The Delphic Oracle* carefully, but the source for this poem, describing the Greek idea of Heaven, is Stephen MacKenna's translation :

> . . . the bonds of human necessity are loosed for you and, strong of heart, you beat your eager way from out the roaring tumult of the fleshly life to the shores of that wave-washed coast free from the thronging of the guilty, thence to take the grateful path of the sinless soul : / where glows the splendour of God, where Right is throned in the stainless place, far from the wrong that mocks at law. / Oft-times as you strove to rise above the bitter waves of this blood-drenched life, above the sickening whirl, toiling in the midmost of the rushing flood and the unimaginable turmoil, oft-times, from the Ever-Blessed, there was shown to you the Term still close at hand : / Oft-times, when your mind thrust out awry and was like to be rapt down unsanctioned paths, the Immortals themselves prevented, guiding you on the straightgoing way to the celestial spheres, pouring down before you a dense shaft of light that your eyes might see from amid the mournful gloom. / Sleep never closed those eyes : high above the heavy murk of the mist you held them ; tossed in the welter, you still had vision ; still you saw sights many and fair not granted to all that labour

in wisdom's quest. / But now that you have cast the screen aside, quitted the tomb that held your lofty soul, you enter at once the heavenly consort : / where fragrant breezes play, where all is unison and winning tenderness and guileless joy and the place is lavish of the nectar streams the unfailing Gods bestow, with the blandishments of the Loves, and delicious airs, and tranquil sky : / where Minos and Rhadamanthus dwell, great brethren of the golden race of mighty Zeus ; where dwells the just Aeacus, and Plato, consecrated power, and stately Pythagoras and all else that form the choir of Immortal Love, there where the heart is ever lifted in joyous festival.

O Blessed One, you have fought your many fights ; now crowned with unfading life, your days are with the Ever-Holy. /

Rejoicing Muses, let us stay our song and the subtle windings of our dance ; thus much I could but tell, to my golden lyre, of Plotinus, the hallowed soul.

Good and kindly, singularly gentle and engaging : thus the oracle presents him, and so in fact we found him. Sleeplessly alert — Apollo tells — pure of soul, ever striving towards the divine which he loved with all his being, he laboured strenuously to free himself and rise above the bitter waves of this blood-drenched life : and this is why to Plotinus — God-like and lifting himself often, by the ways of meditation and by the methods Plato teaches in the Banquet, to the first and all-transcendent God — that God appeared, the God throned above the Intellectual-Principle and all the Intellectual-Sphere. . . .

We are told that often when he was leaving the way, the Gods set him on the true path again, pouring down before him a dense shaft of light ; here we are to understand that in his writing he was overlooked and guided by the divine powers.

'In this sleepless vision within and without,' — the oracle says, 'your eyes have beheld sights many and fair not vouchsafed to all that take the philosophic path' : contemplation in man may sometimes be more than human, but compare it with the True-Knowing of the Gods and, wonderful though it be, it can never plunge into the depths their divine vision fathoms.

Thus far the Oracle recounts what Plotinus accomplished and to what heights he attained while still in the body : emancipated from the body, we are told how he entered the celestial circle where all is friendship, tender delight, happiness and loving union with God, where Minos and Rhadamanthus and Aeacus, the sons of God, are enthroned as judges of souls — not however to hold him to judgment but as welcoming him to their consort to which are bidden spirits pleasing to the Gods — Plato, Pythagoras and all the people of the Choir of Immortal Love, there where the blessed spirits have their birth-home and live in days made happy by the Gods. (S. MacKenna, *Plotinus* 'Porphyry's Life of Plotinus' 22–4; revd. ed. (1946) 16.)

1 *that great Plotinus*: Plotinus (A.D. 205–270) was born in Egypt and studied at Alexandria. He then opened a School at Rome and founded Neoplatonic philosophy; he was a mystic and had knowledge of oriental philosophy.

2 *such seas*: Yeats kept closely to the original, the seas being strengthened by 'buffeted' in the poem. The 'roaring tumult', the 'bitter waves', the 'sickening whirl', the 'rushing flood' and 'unimaginable turmoil' are echoed in this line, for Plotinus was 'tossed in the welter'.

3 *Bland Rhadamanthus*: the adjective may have come from the 'blandishments' of the sentence in MacKenna's translation which precedes the introduction of Rhadamanthus. He, along with Aeacus and Minos, was a judge of souls in the underworld and is bland because he is welcoming Plotinus, not judging him.

4 *the Golden Race*: Porphyry describes Minos, Rhadamanthus and Aeacus, the sons of God, as enthroned as judges of souls: Minos and Rhadamanthus are 'great brethren of the golden race of Zeus'. They looked dim to Plotinus, but they had guided him by pouring down a dense shaft of light that his eyes 'might see from amid the mournful gloom'. While 'tossed in the welter' he still had vision.

5 *Salt blood*: Plotinus was labouring strenuously to free himself and 'rise above the bitter waves of this blood-drenched life'.

307 6–7 *Scattered on the level grass*
   Or winding through the grove: Plotinus having cast the screen aside, enters 'the heavenly consort: where fragrant breezes play'.

8–10   *Plato there and Minos pass,*
         There stately Pythagoras
         And all the choir : cf. MacKenna's translation :

Where Minos and Rhadamanthus dwell, great brethren of the golden race of mighty Zeus ; where dwells the just Aeacus, and Plato, consecrated power, and stately Pythagoras and all else that form the choir of Immortal love, there where the heart is ever lifted in joyous festival.

This is echoed in Yeats's essay 'Bishop Berkeley' as one of his favourite quotations : 'That wave-washed shore . . . the golden race of mighty Zeus . . . the just Aeacus, Plato, stately Pythagoras, and all the choir of immortal love' (*E & I* 409).

A Woman Young and Old

This series of poems was written between 1926 and 1929 ; the 'woman speaks first in youth, then in age' (*WBY* 374). They are, to a certain extent, companion poems to those of *A Man Young and Old*, in *The Tower*, which were written in 1926 or 1927.

308 FATHER AND CHILD

This poem was probably written in 1926 or 1927 ; it first appeared in *WS*.

1 *She hears me* : Anne Butler Yeats, Yeats's daughter

strike the board : an echo of George Herbert's 'The Collar' :
    'I struck the board, and cry'd, No more.'

4 *a man* : the poem records an incident in the Yeats household when Anne, then a child, praised the appearance of a friend, Fergus Fitzgerald.

308 BEFORE THE WORLD WAS MADE

Ellmann (*IY* 292), dates this poem's composition as February 1928. The poem first appeared in *WS*.

7 *I'm looking for the face* : cf. line 12 'Young Man's Song' (*CP* 296) and 'His Bargain' (*CP* 299). Here the woman is searching for her archetypal face. This is parallel to Plato's ideas, though they were abstract. Cf. Grace Jackson, *Mysticism in Yeats and AE in relation to Oriental and American Thought*, 152. There are three possible places in Plato where Yeats might have found a source for his image : *Republic* 597, where Plato applied his theory of ideas to constructing a bed and pointed out that God was the creator of the models of all things ; *Timaeus* 28, where Timaeus

ventures the idea that in making the world God looked to his created pattern ; and *Phaedrus* 250, where Socrates speaks of earthly copies of higher ideas.

A FIRST CONFESSION   309

Ellmann (*IY* 292) gives June 1927 as the date of composition for this poem ; it first appeared in *WS*.

This poem was included in a letter Yeats wrote to Olivia Shakespear from Thoor Ballylee on 23 June 1927 with the introduction 'Here is an innocent little song — one of the first [of] my woman series to balance that of "The Young and Old Countryman"' . . . (*L* 725).

14 *Zodiac* : cf. note (p. 395) on 'Chosen' (*CP* 311)

HER TRIUMPH   310

This poem was written on 29 November 1929 and first appeared in *WS*.

The MS. version of the poem ran as follows :

> I am not evil now ; until you came
> I thought the shamefulest things imaginable
> And they but seemed the sweeter for the shame :
> Thought love the better was it casual :
> I had an opium eating friend, a friend
> Who had drunk to drown a melancholy fit.
> The coils of the dragon had no end
> Its breath had touched me but you mastered it
> And broke the chain and set my ankle free
> Panoplied saint, wing-heeled Persius
> And now we stare at the sea
> And a miraculous strange bird shrieks at us.
>
> I laughed at poet's calls until you came
> And thought a common life more natural
> And Nature but a comedy and a game
> And love the better if but casual.

1   *the dragon's will* : Yeats may have had the picture 'Saint George and the Dragon' (ascribed to Bordone) in mind when he wrote this poem (it is described in 'Michael Robartes and the Dancer' (*CP* 197). It is in the National Gallery, Dublin. Another possible source is Cosimo Tura's 'St George and the Dragon', which Yeats saw in Ferrara Cathedral in 1907. Kathleen Raine, 'Yeats's Debt to Blake' *DM* (Summer 1966) 39, suggests that the dragon reason may be Blake's Urizen.

10   *Saint George or else a pagan Perseus* : see previous note. Yeats had a reproduction (Ed^ne Alinari, p^e 2^a, No. 11884) of Perino del Vaga's *Andromeda and Perseus* from the Papal apartments at Castel S. Angelo, which may have been in his mind when he wrote this poem.

12   *strange bird* : cf. 'Juno's peacock' of 'My Table' (*CP* 227)

310   CONSOLATION

This poem was probably written in June 1927, and it first appeared in *WS*.

    Yeats described the poem as 'one not so innocent' in a letter of 23 June 1927 to Olivia Shakespear (*L* 725).

9   *crime of being born* : cf. 'A Dialogue of Self and Soul' (*CP* 265) with 'the crime of death and birth'

311   CHOSEN

This poem was probably written early in 1926. Yeats wrote to Professor Grierson on 21 February 1926 that he had used the arrangement of the rhymes in Donne's *Nocturnall upon St Lucie's Day* for a poem of his own (*L* 710). 'Chosen' first appeared in *The Winding Stair* (1929) with the title 'The Choice'.

    The writing of the poem is discussed in *BL* 137–63 and Wilson (*Y & T* 205–11) discusses it at length.

1   *chosen* : this may come from Plato's myth of Er, in which the souls of men and women in heaven choose the lots (cf. *LT* 105 and *Y & T* 207) which represent their future destinies.

3   *the whirling Zodiac*: the sun progresses through the whirling zodiac. Yeats's first note on the poem read:

I have symbolised a woman's love as the struggle of the darkness to keep the sun from rising from its earthly bed. In the last stanza of the Choice [the original title of 'Chosen'] I change the symbol to that of the souls of man and woman ascending through the Zodiac. In some Neoplatonist or Hermatist — whose name I forget — the whorl changes into a sphere at one of the points where the Milky Way crosses the Zodiac. (*The Winding Stair* (1929))

The note was expanded in *WS*:

The 'learned astrologer' in *Chosen* was Macrobius, and the particular passage was found for me by Dr. Sturm [Dr F. P. Sturm (d. 1942), a doctor who practised in Lancashire; he published three books of poems and was interested in the occult] that too little known poet and mystic. It is from Macrobius's comment upon 'Scipio's Dream' (Lib. I, Cap. XII, Sec. 5): '. . . when the sun is in Aquarius, we sacrifice to the Shades, for it is in the sign inimical to human life; and from thence, the meeting-place of Zodiac and Milky Way, the descending soul by its defluction is drawn out of the spherical, the sole divine form, into the cone'. Cf. note (p. 358) on line 28, 'Byzantium' (*CP* 280)

16   *both adrift on the miraculous stream*: the Milky Way, a symbol used for the abode of the soul before birth

17   *wrote a learned astrologer*: Wilson (*Y & T* 210) quotes the passage from Macrobius: 'Since those who are about to descend are yet in Cancer, and have not left the Milky Way, they rank in the order of the gods. . . . From the confine, therefore, in which the zodiac and galaxy touch one another, the soul, descending from a round figure which is the only divine form, is produced into a cone' (T. Taylor, *Porphyry*, 187). Wilson points out that Cancer is 'the confine in which the zodiac and galaxy touch one another', where Milky Way and zodiac meet, and Cancer is therefore 'the gate'. The soul passes through it, loses its spherical shape. It descends through the signs; after death it returns through the gate of Capricorn, eventually returning to its source. Wilson remarks (*Y & T* 210), that the harmonious soul is a sphere

and the lovers' souls seem to be united, on their starting point on the Milky Way, 'both adrift' where spiritual and material worlds intersect and the imperfect is turned into the perfect.

18   *The Zodiac is changed into a sphere* : cf. Yeats's explanation of the Thirteenth Cycle or Thirteenth Cone in *AV* :

> It is that cycle which may deliver us from the twelve cycles of time and space.   The cone which intersects ours is a cone in so far as we think of it as the antithesis to our thesis, but if the time has come for our deliverance it is the phaseless sphere, sometimes called the Thirteenth Sphere, for every lesser cycle contains within itself a sphere that is, as it were, the reflection or messenger of the final deliverance.   Within it live all souls that have been set free and every *Daimon* and *Ghostly Self* ; our expanding cone seems to cut through its gyre ; spiritual influx is from its circumference, animate life from its centre. 'Eternity also', says Hermes in the Aeslepius dialogue, 'though motionless itself, appears to be in motion.'   When Shelley's Demogorgon — eternity — comes from the centre of the earth it may so come because Shelley substituted the earth for such a sphere.[1]   (*AV* (B) 210–11).

He also commented on it as follows :

> The *Thirteenth Cone* is a sphere because sufficient to itself ; but as seen by Man it is a cone.   It becomes even conscious of itself as so seen, like some great dancer, the perfect flower of modern culture, dancing some primitive dance and conscious of his or her own life and of the dance.   There is a mediaeval story of a man persecuted by his Guardian Angel because it was jealous of his sweetheart, and such stories seem closer to reality than our abstract theology.   All imaginable relations may arise between a man and his God.   I only speak of the *Thirteenth Cone* as a sphere and yet I might say that the gyre or cone of the *Principles* is in reality a sphere, though to Man, bound to birth and death, it can never seem so, and that it is the antinomies that force us to find it a cone.   Only one symbol exists, though the reflecting mirrors make many appear and all different.   (*AV* (B) 240)

[1] Shelley, who had more philosophy than men thought when I was young, probably knew that Parmenides represented reality as a motionless sphere. Mrs Shelley speaks of the 'mystic meanings' of *Prometheus Unbound* as only intelligible to a 'mind as subtle as his own'.

PARTING   **311**

This poem was written in August 1926 and first appeared in *The Winding Stair* (1929).

The composition of the poem, which is linked with 'A First Confession' (*CP* 309) and 'The Choice' ['Chosen'] (*CP* 311) in Yeats's notes, is discussed in *BL* 138–63.

7   *his loud song* : Hone (*WBY* 433) suggested that there is an echo   **312**
here of *Romeo and Juliet* III, v :

> No, night's bird and love's
> Bids all true lovers rest,
> While his loud song reproves
> The murderous stealth of day.

HER VISION IN THE WOOD   **312**

This poem was written in August 1926, and first appeared in *The Winding Stair* (1929).

14   *a litter with a wounded man* : Ellmann (*IY* 172–3) regards this as a portrayal of the Adonis legend.   Henn (*LT* 260) suggests Adonis, or Diarmuid, who was killed by a boar on a Sligo mountain.   He refers also to the Attis ritual in *The Golden Bough* in section II of 'Vacillation' (*CP* 282).

16   *the beast* : a wild boar killed Adonis, a beautiful youth beloved by Aphrodite.   The flower anemone was said to have sprung from his blood.   He was restored to life by Persephone on condition that he spent six months of the year with her, six with Aphrodite.   (This implied a summer–winter symbol.)   His death and revival were celebrated in various festivals.

20   *Mantegna's thought* : Andrea Mantegna (1431–1506), born near   **313**
Vicenza, left Padua *c.* 1459 where he painted the *Eremitani* frescoes and the *Agony in the Garden*, lived chiefly at Mantua where he painted the *Madonna della Vittoria* and the *Triumph of Caesar*.

25   *all blood and mire* : cf. 'the fury and the mire of human veins' and the dolphin's 'mire and blood' of 'Byzantium' (*CP* 280) and the 'blood and mire' of 'The Gyres' (*CP* 337)

31 *no fabulous symbol* : the body is not that of a god or hero, but of her lover.

313 A LAST CONFESSION

The MSS. dates of this poem are June, July 23 and 24 and August 1926. It first appeared in *The Winding Stair* (1929).

314 12 *Beast gave beast as much* : Henn (*LT* 66) draws attention to Yeats's remark to John Sparrow that the tragedy of sexual intercourse is in the perpetual virginity of the soul, quoted in (*Y:M & P* 267).

23 *bird of day* : cf. the 'most ridiculous little bird' of 'A Memory of Youth' (*CP* 137), the 'miraculous strange bird' of 'Her Triumph' (*CP* 310), and the bird in 'Parting' (*CP* 311). Henn (*LT* 59) remarks that it seems to have among its values a kind of eternalising function : it is not only a link with daytime and the dissipation of the ecstasies of the lovers but it is also

> a half-malicious, half-mystical symbol that suggests a supernatural and eternal commentary on the act. It is 'ridiculous', 'miraculous', 'betraying'. Perhaps it is linked to the golden bird of 'Byzantium' ; something permanent and spiritual, and mocking, beside love's ecstasy.

314 MEETING

The date of composition of this poem is uncertain (probably 1926). It first appeared in *The Winding Stair* (1929).

315 FROM THE 'ANTIGONE'

This translation was made in 1927 or 1928. It first appeared in *The Winding Stair* (1929). Yeats used Paul Masqueray's French translation of the Sophoclean original.

AFTER Yeats had written the last poems of *WS* he thought his inspiration was drying up : for a time he wondered if Lady Gregory's death and the closing of Coole had ended the sub-conscious drama of his imaginative life. Then he returned to verse with 'Parnell's Funeral', in which he 'rhymed passages from a lecture' given in America. In Dublin there followed an intense interlude of politics, and a reawakened interest in *AV* expressed in the *Supernatural Songs* — metaphysical, passionate and a brilliant answer to his earlier worry that perhaps he was too old for poetry.

PARNELL'S FUNERAL   319

This poem was completed in April 1933. Lines 16–23 first appeared, untitled, in *DM* (April–June 1932), as part of the 'Introduction to Fighting the Waves', which was included in *W & B*.

The poem first appeared in entirety in the *Spectator* (19 Oct. 1934) ; and the title given to the first section was 'A Parnellite at Parnell's Funeral'. The second section was entitled 'Forty Years Later'. It also appeared in the *Spectator* (19 Oct. 1934). The second section was untitled in *KGCT*. The first appearance of the whole poem with the present title was in *FMM*. Yeats wrote a commentary on the poem in *KGCT* which reads :

I

When lecturing in America I spoke of Four Bells, four deep tragic notes, equally divided in time, so symbolising the war that ended in the Flight of the Earls ; the Battle of the Boyne ; the coming of French influence among our peasants ; the beginning of our own age ; events that closed the sixteenth, seventeenth, eighteenth and nineteenth centuries. My historical knowledge, such as it is, begins with the Second Bell.

II

When Huguenot artists designed the tapestries for the Irish House of Lords, depicting the Battle of the Boyne and the siege of Derry, they celebrated the defeat of their old enemy Louis XIV, and the establishment of a Protestant Ascendency which was to impose upon Catholic Ireland, an oppression copied in all details from that imposed upon the French Protestants. Did my own great-great-grandmother, the Huguenot Marie Voisin feel a vindictive triumph, or did she remember that her friend Archbishop King had been a loyal servant of James II and had, unless greatly slandered, accepted his present master after much vacillation, and that despite episcopal vehemence, his clergy were suspected of a desire to restore a Catholic family to the English throne. The Irish House of Lords, however, when it ordered the Huguenot tapestries, probably accepted the weavers' argument that the Battle of the Boyne was to Ireland what the defeat of the Armada had been to England. Armed with this new power, they were to modernise the social structure, with great cruelty but effectively, and to establish our political nationality by quarrelling with England over the wool trade, a protestant monoply [monopoly]. At the base of the social structure, but hardly within it, the peasantry dreamed on in their medieval sleep; the Gaelic poets sang of the banished Catholic aristocracy; 'My fathers served their fathers before Christ was crucified' sang one of the most famous. Ireland had found new masters, and was to discover for the first time in its history that it possessed a cold, logical intellect. That intellect announced its independence when Berkeley, then an undergraduate of Trinity College, wrote in his *Commonplace Book*, after a description of the philosophy of Hobbes, Newton and Locke, the fashionable English philosophy of his day, 'We Irish do not think so.' An emotion of pride and confidence at that time ran through what there was of an intellectual minority. The friends who gave Berkeley his first audience, were to found 'The Dublin' now 'The Royal Dublin Society,' perhaps to establish that scientific agriculture described and praised by Arthur Young. The historical dialectic trampled upon their minds in that brutal Ireland, product of two generations of civil war, described by Swift in a well-known sermon; they were the trodden grapes and became wine. When Berkeley landed in America, he found himself in a nation running the same course, though Ireland was too close to England to keep its independence through the Napoleonic Wars. America, however, as his letters show, had neither the wealth nor the education of contemporary Ireland ; no such violence of contraries, as of black upon white, had stung it into life.

III

The influence of the French Revolution woke the peasantry from the medieval sleep, gave them ideas of social justice and equality, but prepared for a century disastrous to the national intellect. Instead of the Protestant Ascendancy with its sense of responsibility, we had the Garrison, a political party of Protestant and Catholic landowners, merchants and officials. They loved the soil of Ireland ; the returned Colonial Governor crossed the Channel to see the May flowers in his park ; the merchant loved with an ardour I have not met elsewhere, some sea-board town where he had made his money, or spent his youth, but they could give to a people they thought unfit for self-government, nothing but a condescending affection. They preferred frieze-coated humanists, dare-devils upon horseback, to ordinary men and women ; created in Ireland and elsewhere an audience that welcomed the vivid imaginations of Lever, Lover, Somerville and Ross. These writers, especially the first have historical importance, so completely have they expressed a social phase. Instead of the old half medieval peasantry came an agrarian political party, that degraded literature with rhetoric and insincerity. Its novels, poems, essays, histories showed Irish virtue struggling against English and landlord crime ; historical characters that we must admire or abhor according to the side they took in politics. Certain songs by Davis, Carleton's *Valentine McClutchy*, Kickham's *Knocknagow*, Mitchel's *History of Ireland*, numberless forgotten books in prose and verse founded or fostered a distortion we have not yet escaped. In the eighties of the last century came a third school : three men too conscious of intellectual power to belong to party, George Bernard Shaw, Oscar Wilde, George Moore, the most complete individualists in the history of literature, abstract, isolated minds, without a memory or a landscape. It is this very isolation, this defect, as it seems to me, which has given Bernard Shaw an equal welcome in all countries, the greatest fame in his own lifetime any writer has known. Without it, his wit would have waited for acceptance upon studious exposition and commendation.

IV

I heard the first note of the Fourth Bell forty years ago on a stormy October morning. I had gone to Kingsto[w]n Pier to meet the Mail Boat that arrived about 6 a.m. I was expecting a friend, but met what I thought much less of at the time, the body of Parnell. I did not go to the funeral, because, being in my sensitive and timid youth, I hated crowds, and what crowds implied, but my friend went. She told me that evening of the star that fell in broad daylight as Parnell's body was lowered into the grave — was it a collective hallucination or an actual event? Years after Standish O'Grady was to write:

'I state a fact — it was witnessed by thousands. While his followers were committing Charles Parnell's remains to the earth, the sky was bright with strange lights and flames. Only a coincidence possibly, and yet persons not superstitious have maintained that there is some mysterious sympathy between the human soul and the elements, and that storm, and other elemental disturbances have too often succeeded or accompanied great battles to be regarded as only fortuitous. . . . Those flames recall to my memory what is told of similar phenomena, said to have been witnessed when tidings of the death of Saint Columba overran the north-west of Europe.'

I think of the symbolism of the star shot with an arrow, described in the appendix to my book *Autobiographies*. I ask if the fall of a star may not upon occasion, symbolise an accepted sacrifice.

Dublin had once been a well-mannered, smooth-spoken city. I knew an old woman who had met Davis constantly and never knew that he was in politics until she read his obituary in the newspaper. Then came agrarian passion; Unionists and Nationalists ceased to meet, but each lived behind his party wall an amiable life. This new dispute broke through all walls; there were old men and women I avoid because they have kept that day's bitter tongue. Upon the other hand, we began to value truth. According to my memory and the memory of others, free discussion appeared among us for the first time, bringing the passion for reality, the satiric genius that informs *Ulysses*, *The Playboy of the Western World*, *The Informer*, *The Puritan* and other books, and plays; the accumulated hatred of years was suddenly transferred from England to Ireland. James Joyce has no doubt described something remembered from his youth in that dinner table scene in *The Portrait of the Artist as a Young Man*, when after a violent quarrel about Parnell and the priests, the host sobs, his head upon the table ; 'My dead King.'

We had passed through an initiation like that of the Tibetan ascetic, who staggers half dead from a trance, where he has seen himself eaten alive and has not yet learned that the eater was himself.

V

As we discussed and argued, the national character changed, O'Connell, the great comedian, left the scene the tragedian Parnell took his place. When we talked of his pride ; of his apparent impassivity when his hands were full of blood because he had torn them with his nails, the proceeding epoch with its democratic bonhomie, seemed to grin through a horse collar. He was the symbol that made apparent, or made possible (are there not historical limbos where nothing is possible ?) that epoch's contrary : contrary, not negation, not refutation ; the spring vegetables may be over, they have not been refuted. I am Blake's disciple, not Hegel's : 'contraries are positive. A negation is not a contrary.' *(KGCT)*

1

1 *the Great Comedian's tomb* : Daniel O'Connell (1775–1847), was educated at St Omer, driven out at the Revolution, read law in London and practised successfully. He killed D'Esterne in a duel, 1815 ; was returned as M.P. for Clare, 1828 ; pushed through Catholic Emancipation, 1829 ; M.P. for Dublin, 1832 ; held balance of power in House of Commons, 1835. He founded the Repeal Association, 1840, and was aided by the *Nation* (founded 1842). He was prosecuted in 1844, his sentence of a year's imprisonment quashed by House of Lords. He quarrelled with the Young Irelanders because of their belief in force. He died on a pilgrimage to Rome, but his body is buried at Glasnevin Cemetery, Co. Dublin. Yeats particularly disliked him, and said of him in a Senate speech :

We never had any trouble about O'Connell. It was said about O'Connell, in his own day, that you could not throw a stick over a workhouse wall without hitting one of his children, but he believed in the dissolubility of marriage, and when he died his heart was very properly preserved in Rome.

I am not quite sure whether it was in a bronze or marble urn, but it is there, and I have no doubt the art of that urn was as bad as the other art of the period. (*SSY* 97–8)

He described him as 'the too compromised and compromising Daniel O'Connell' (*A* 353), and disliked 'the bragging rhetoric and gregarious humour of O'Connell's generation and school' (*A* 195).

4 *a brighter star shoots down* : this is the star, of which Maud Gonne told Yeats, which fell as Parnell's body was lowered into the grave.

7 *the Cretan barb that pierced a star* : this can be explained by a passage in *A* which Yeats annotated very fully. The passage is in 'The Stirring of the Bones' :

As Arthur Symons and I were about to stay with Mr Edward Martyn at Tulira Castle, in Galway, I decided that it was there I must make my invocation of the moon. I made it night after night just before I went to bed, and after many nights — eight or nine perhaps — I saw between sleeping and waking, as in a kinematograph, a galloping centaur, and a moment later a naked woman of incredible beauty, standing upon a pedestal and shooting an arrow at a star. I still remember the tint of that marvellous flesh which makes all human flesh seem unhealthy, and remember that others who have seen such forms have remembered the same characteristic. Next morning before breakfast Arthur Symons took me out on to the lawn to recite a scrap of verse, the only verse he had ever written to a dream. He had dreamt the night before of a woman of great beauty, but she was clothed and had not a bow and arrow. When he got back to London, he found awaiting him a story sent to the *Savoy* by Fiona Macleod and called, I think, *The Archer*. Some one in the story had a vision of a woman shooting an arrow into the sky and later of an arrow shot at a faun that pierced the faun's body and remained, the faun's heart torn out and clinging to it, embedded in a tree. Some weeks later I, too, was in London, and found among Mathers' pupils a woman whose little child — perhaps at the time of my vision, perhaps a little later — had come running in from the garden calling out, 'O, mother, I have seen a woman shooting an arrow into the sky and I am afraid that she has killed God'. I have somewhere among my papers a letter from a very old friend describing how her little cousin — perhaps a few months later — dreamed of a man who shot at a star with a gun and that the star fell down, but, 'I do not think', the child said, 'it minded dying because it was so very old', and how presently the child saw the star lying in a cradle. Had some great event taken place in some world where myth is reality and had we seen some portion of it? One of my fellow-students quoted a Greek saying, 'Myths are the activities of the Daimons', or had we but seen in the memory of the race something believed thousands of years ago, or had somebody — I myself perhaps — but dreamed a fantastic dream which had come to those others by transference of thought? I came to no conclusion, but I was sure there was some symbolic meaning could I but find it. I went to my friend who had spoken to Megarithma, and she went once more into her trance-like meditation and heard but a single unexplained sentence : 'There were three that saw : three will attain a wisdom older than the serpent, but the child will die.' Did this refer to myself, to Arthur Symons, to Fiona Macleod, to the child who feared that the archer had killed God? I thought not, for Symons had no deep interest in the subject, and there was the second child to account for. It was probably some new detail of the myth or an interpretation of its meaning. There was a London coroner in those days, learned in the Cabbala, whom I had once known though we had not met for some years. I called upon him and told all that I have set down here. He opened a drawer and took out of it two water-colour paintings, made by a clumsy painter who had no object but a symbolical record : one was of a centaur, the other of a woman standing upon a stone pedestal and shooting her arrow at what seemed a star. He asked me to look carefully at the star, and I saw that it was a little golden heart. He said : 'You have hit upon things that you can never have read of in any book ; these symbols belong to a part of the Christian Cabbala' — perhaps this was not his exact term — 'that you know nothing of. The centaur is the elemental spirit and the woman the divine spirit of the path Samekh, and the golden heart is the central point upon the cabbalistic Tree of Life and corresponds to the Sephiroth Tiphareth.' I was full of excitement, for now at last I began to understand. The Tree of Life is a geometrical figure made up of ten circles or spheres called Sephiroth joined by straight lines. Once men must have thought of it as like some great tree covered with its fruit and its foliage, but at some period, in the thirteenth century perhaps, touched by the mathematical genius of Arabia in all likelihood, it had lost its natural form. The Sephiroth Tiphareth, attributed to the sun, is joined to the Sephiroth Yesod, attributed to the moon, by a straight line called the path Samekh, and this line is attributed to the constellation Sagittarius. He would not or could not tell me more, but when I repeated what I had heard to one of my fellow-students, a yachtsman and yacht-designer and cabbalist, he said, 'Now you know what was meant by a wisdom older than the serpent'. He reminded me that the cabbalistic tree has a green serpent winding through it which represents the winding path of nature or of instinct, and that the path Samekh is part of the long straight line that goes up through the centre of the tree, and that it was interpreted as the path of 'deliberate effort'. The three who saw must, he said, be those who could attain to wisdom by the study of magic, for that was 'deliberate effort'. I remember that I quoted Balzac's description of the straight line as the line of man, but he could not throw light on the other symbols except that the shot arrow must symbolise effort, nor did I get any further light. (*A* 372–5)

Yeats's notes refer to this vision of an archer :

The description of the vision was not in the first edition of this book, and I add it now on the advice of a man learned in East Mediterranean antiquities, met on a lecturing tour in England, who thought it important, and promised annotation. I would like to give his name, or at any rate to write and ask if I might, but though I have spent several hours in the search I cannot find his letter, nor can I trace him at the house where I thought we met. He was no phantom, though a corre-spondent seems to think so, and I can only offer an apology for my seeming discourtesy. He sent me several pages of notes which I will comment upon and summarise.

(a) *The Child and the Tree*

On a certain night in Devonshire, farmers and farm-labourers and their wives and children perform a ceremony at the finest apple-tree in the orchard. Punch is poured out at the roots and bread put among the branches, and a boy set among the branches 'who is either the tree in boy-form, or the tree in bird-form', and the men fire blank charges at him. All dance round the tree, singing some such rhyme as this :

> 'Here's to thee, good apple-tree,
> To bear and blow apples enow', etc.

(*Transactions of the Devonshire Association*, 1867. Whitcombe, *Bygone Days in Devonshire and Cornwall.*)

'This rhyme calls to mind its ancient prototype, the Hymn of the Kouretes, found at Palaikastro in Crete. The Kouretes "leap" the "full jars and rich fruit crops". Moreover, in a previous stanza is celebrated the baby made immortal for Rhea.'

'This boy finds his analogue in Balder, "who is shot to death that is life by means of a sprig or arrow of mistletoe".'

In my vision, the star is shot by an arrow from a bow, and in one of the children's dreams which I have described, God is shot with an arrow, while in another child's dream, a star is shot with a gun. 'Balder is the tree embodied. His name tells us that. Recent philology has said that the name means, or is related to, apple-tree, Abble, Apfel, etc. But that is not true enough. When the first decipherment of Cretan pictographs is published, it will be seen that his name goes back to the Cretan Apollo who in old Cretan belief was a tree-god.' It is plain too that he is the 'Child hidden in the scented Dikton near Mount Ida' (*Phaen.* 32 ff.) of Aratus' lines, and that part of his significance is solar. 'He was believed to be born and grow up in a year (Aratus ; Callimachus, *Zeus*, 552 ff., etc.) and to die once more. Orpheus made much use of these facts (Lobeck, *Aglaophamus*, i. 552 ff.).'

I had used Hebrew names connected with the symbolic tree, and the star at which the arrow was shot seems to have symbolised Kether, a Sephiroth attributed to the sun, and my invocation had for its object the killing or overcoming in some way of a 'solar influence'.

(b) *The Woman who shot the Arrow*

She was, it seems, the Mother-Goddess, whose representative priestess shot the arrow at the child, whose sacrificial death symbolised the death and resurrection of the Tree-spirit, or Apollo. 'She is pictured upon certain Cretan coins of the fifth century B.C. as a slightly draped, beautiful woman, sitting in the heart of a branching tree. (G. F. Hill, *A Handbook of Greek and Roman Coins*, 163). She goes back to the very earliest form of the religion of Crete, and is, it seems probable, the Tree as Mother, killing the Tree as Son. But she is also Artemis, and there is a beautiful vase at Naples (Reinach, *Répertoire des vases peints grecs*, i. 379. 1) which shows her archaic image upon a tall pillar with a strung bow in her left hand and a *patera* in her right.'

(c) *The Heart torn out*

A Father of the Church, Firmicus Maternus, in his book, *On the Errors of the Profane Religions*, turns the Myth of the Child Slain and Reborn into a story of murder and adultery. The Cretan Jupiter 'made an image of his son in gypsum and placed the boy's heart . . . in that part of the figure where the curve of the chest was to be seen.' It had been kept by his sister, Minerva, and a temple was made to contain the image. There were festivals and noisy processions that followed 'a basket in which the sister had hidden the heart'. 'It may be conjectured, perhaps,' writes my learned man, 'that images were made with a chest cavity to contain the heart of the sacrificed.'

(d) *The Star*

The Star goes right back to the Cretan Mother-Goddess. The later Greek form of it was Asterios or Asterion. The latter, for example, is said to be Jupiter's son by Idaia (Pausanias, ii. 31. 1). 'This Star name did not mean in its primary use any particular star. It appears to have meant the Starry Heavens. . . . Zeus-Asterios is a late Gortynian (Cretan) collocation (Johannes Malala, *Chronicum*, 5). In the earlier thought of Crete, her deified kings bore the same name, Asterion or Asterios (e.g. Bacchylides, frag. 47, and Diodorus, iv. 60).'

(e) *The Centaur*

'There is a fragment of a very early Greek pot showing two roughly drawn centaurs with long thin legs, one of the centaurs touching with his hand a tree which has long leaves and what seems to be a round fruit. Above the centaurs, but apparently separate from the tree, a bird perches on a twig (Salzmann, *Nécropole de Camires*, plate XXXIX).'

(*f*) *Sagitta*

'About the third century B.C. we find Apollo is closely linked with the constellation Sagitta.' I find in a book upon astrology published this year: 'Sagittarius. The symbol is an arrow shot into the unknown. It is a sign of Initiation and Rebirth.' *A Student's Textbook of Astrology*, by Vivian E. Robson, p. 178.

Yeats wrote in August 1896 from Tillyra Castle to William Strang about the beautiful woman. See *L* 266; there is another mention of the woman in 'Anima Hominis':

> Many years ago I saw, between sleeping and waking, a woman of incredible beauty shooting an arrow into the sky, and from the moment when I made my first guess at her meaning I have thought much of the difference between the winding movement of Nature and the straight line, which is called in Balzac's *Séraphita* the 'Mark of Man,' but is better described as the mark of saint or sage. I think that we who are poets and artists, not being permitted to shoot beyond the tangible, must go from desire to weariness and so to desire again, and live but for the moment when vision comes to our weariness like terrible lightning, in the humility of the brutes. I do not doubt those heaving circles, those winding arcs, whether in one man's life or in that of an age, are mathematical, and that some in the world, or beyond the world, have foreknown the event and pricked upon the calendar the life-span of a Christ, a Buddha, a Napoleon : that every movement, in feeling or in thought, prepares in the dark by its own increasing clarity and confidence its own executioner. We seek reality with the slow toil of our weakness and are smitten from the boundless and the unforeseen. Only when we are saint or sage, and renounce experience itself, can we, in imagery of the Christian Cabbala, leave the sudden lightning and the path of the serpent and become the bowman who aims his arrow at the centre of the sun. (*M* 340)

10 *A beautiful seated boy* : cf. Yeats's note, above, on *The Child and the Tree*

13 *the Great Mother* : cf. Yeats's note, above, on *The Woman who shot the Arrow*. A priestess, imaging the Great Mother, shot the arrow.

14 *his heart* : see Yeats's note, above, on *The Heart torn out*

15 *Sicilian coin* : see Yeats's note, above, on *The Woman who shot the Arrow*

17 *strangers* : non-Irish. Emmet and Fitzgerald were killed as rebels ; Tone committed suicide (see notes (pp. 130–1) on 'September 1913' (*CP* 120)) but Parnell was destroyed by the Irish people whose champion he was.

21 *Hysterica passio* : from Lear II, iv, 57. Shakespeare's source was probably Harsnet, *Declaration of Popish Impostures*. Yeats used the phrase in 'Rosa Alchemia' : '. . . I also have felt fixed habits and principles dissolving before a power, which was *hysterica passio* or sheer madness, if you will, but was so powerful in its melancholy exultation that I tremble lest it wake again and drive me from my new-found peace' (*M* 278), and in 'A Bronzed Head' (*CP* 382). The *hysterica passio* of Ireland is alluded to in *Estrangement* (*A* 489) and Yeats used the words in a letter to Dorothy Wellesley :

> I have never 'produced' a play in verse without showing the actors that the passion of the verse comes from the fact that the speakers are holding down violence or madness — 'down Hysterica passio'. All depends on the completeness of the holding down, on the stirring of the beast underneath. (*DWL* 86)

dragged this quarry down : see notes (p. 134) on 'To a Shade' (*CP* 123) which quote Goethe's description of the Irish being like a pack of hounds always 'dragging down some noble stag' (*A* 483)

22 *None shared our guilt* : Yeats wrote to John O'Leary on 22 January 1891 that it would seem plain that a combination of priests with the 'Sullivan gang' [A. M. Sullivan and his brother T. D. Sullivan and their friends and connections by marriage, Tim and Maurice Healey (who were M.P.s) were embittered against Parnell, and A. M. Sullivan controlled the *Nation*, an influential Nationalist weekly paper which voiced their views] is not likely to have on its side in political matters divine justice.' (*L* 163–4)

23 *we devoured his heart* : Parnell is envisaged as being like a god devoured in a ritual. Cf. Yeats's note quoted above on *The Heart torn out*.

320 25 *I thirst for accusation* : Yeats is challenging the Nationalists because they spurned Parnell.

27 *contagion of the throng*: cf. the 'great hatred, little room' of 'Remorse for Intemperate Speech' (*CP* 287)

28 *the rhyme rats hear*: Henn (*LT* 46) suggests as a source for the rats *As You Like It*, III, ii, 170: 'I was never so berhymed since Pythagoras' time that I was an Irish rat, which I can hardly remember', an allusion to the idea of Pythagoras that souls could transmigrate into the bodies of animals. It was popularly believed that Irish witches could use rhymes to kill men and beasts.

II

2 *de Valéra*: Eamonn de Valera (b. 1882), President of Ireland 320 since 1959. He was sentenced to death for his part in the 1916 Rising; this sentence was commuted to life imprisonment, and he was released in 1917. President of Sinn Fein party, 1917–26; President of the Irish Volunteers, 1917–22; imprisoned Lincoln Gaol 1918 and escaped 1919. President of the Fianna Fail party 1926–59. Yeats disliked him for being leader of the anti-treaty party in the Civil War; he thought Olivia Shakespear right (in a letter of February 1933) to compare him to Mussolini or Hitler (*L* 805, but in a letter written in the following month, on 9 March 1933) he told her after an hour's interview with de Valera that he had never met him before and was impressed 'by his simplicity and honesty though we differed throughout. It was a curious experience, each recognised the other's point of view so completely. I had gone there full of suspicion but my suspicion vanished at once' (*L* 806).

Later he wrote to her in April 1933 that:

'This country is exciting. I am told that De Valera has said in private that within three years he will be torn in pieces. . . . No sooner does a politician get into power than he begins to seek unpopularity. It is the cult of sacrifice planted in the nation by the executions of 1916' (*L* 809).

Then on 13 July 1933 he wrote to her again

Politics are growing heroic. De Valera has forced political thought to face the most fundamental issues. A Fascist opposition is forming behind the scenes to be ready should some tragic situation develop. I find myself constantly urging the despotic rule of the educated classes as the only end to our troubles. . . . (*L* 811–12)

Parnell's heart: Charles Stewart Parnell (1846–91), Irish landowner and leader of the Irish Parliamentary Party, who was repudiated by Gladstone, the Irish Hierarchy and the Irish Party when his relationship with Mrs O'Shea became public. See note (p. 133) on 'To a Shade' (*CP* 123), and the poem (written on the day Parnell died) which Yeats published on 10 October 1891 in *UI* but did not reprint. It is included in *VE* 737. See also the later poems on Parnell, 'Come Gather round Me, Parnellites' (*CP* 355) and 'Parnell' (*CP* 359).

5 *Cosgrave*: William T. Cosgrave (1880–1966), who was first, President of Dail Eireann (1922–32) and previously Sinn Fein M.P.: member of Dail Eireann (1922–44).

8 *O'Higgins*: Kevin O'Higgins. See note (p. 321) on 'Death' (*CP* 264).

9 *O'Duffy*: Eoin O'Duffy (1892–1944), member of I.R.A. 1917, head of Irish police in the Irish Free State, Director of the Blue Shirt organisation, later leader of the Opposition United party 1933, and subsequently Brigadier-General in the Spanish Nationalist Army in the Spanish Civil War. A letter Yeats wrote to Olivia Shakespear on 23 July 1933 reveals his attitude to O'Duffy:

> The great secret is out — a convention of blue-shirts — 'National Guards' — have received their new leader with the Fascist salute and the new leader announces reform of Parliament as his business.
> When I wrote to you, the Fascist organiser of the blue shirts had told me that he was about to bring to see me the man he had selected for leader that I might talk my anti-democratic philosophy. I was ready, for I had just re-written for the seventh time the part of *A Vision* that deals with the future. The leader turned out to be Gen[eral] O'Duffy, head of the Irish police for twelve years, and a famous organiser. The man who brought him was one of the two men who came to me when we were threatened with a mutiny in the army. He is an old friend of mine, served in India, is crippled with wounds . . . and therefore dreams an heroic dream. 'We shall be assassinated,' he said, 'but others have been chosen to take our place' — his dream perhaps but possibly not. Italy, Poland, Germany, then perhaps Ireland. Doubtless I shall hate it (though not so much as I hate Irish democracy)

but it is September and we must not behave like the gay young sparks of May or June. Swinburne called September 'the month of the long decline of roses.' The *Observer*, the *Sunday Times*, the only English papers I see, have noticed nothing though Cosgrave's ablest ministers are with O'Duffy. O'Duffy himself is autocratic, directing the movement from above down as if it were an army. I did not think him a great man though a pleasant one, but one never knows, his face and mind may harden or clarify. (*L* 812–13)

Yeats wrote to her about the situation in Ireland on 20 September 1933 ; this letter reveals what Conor Cruise O'Brien ('Passion and Cunning : an Essay on the Politics of Yeats' (*IER* 256)) has called 'the climax' of Yeats's interest in O'Duffy :

I wonder if the English newspapers have given you any idea of our political comedy. Act I. Capt Macmanus, the ex-British officer I spoke of, his head full of vague Facism, got probably from me, decided that Gen[eral] O'Duffy should be made leader of a body of young men formed to keep meetings from being broken up. He put into O'Duffy's head — he describes him as 'a simple peasant' — Fascist ideas and started him off to organise that body of young men. Act II. Some journalist announced that 30,000 of these young men were going to march through Dublin on a certain day (the correct number was 3,000). Government panic. Would not O'Duffy, who had once been head of the army, and more recently head of the police, march on the Government with 30,000, plus army and police ? Result, martial law — in its Irish form — armoured cars in the streets, and new police force drawn from the I.R.A. to guard the government, and O'Duffy's organisation proclaimed. Act III. O'Duffy is made thereby so important that Cosgrave surrenders the leadership of his party to O'Duffy and all the opposition united under him. Two months ago he was unknown, politically . . . (*L* 815). Cf. his letter to Ethel Mannin, 11 Feb. 1937 (*L* 881) for anti-O'Duffy sentiment and horror of modern politics.

12 *bitter wisdom* : Yeats may be referring to Swift's *Discourse of the Contests and Dissensions between the Nobles and the Commons in Athens and Rome*, which was, he wrote in the Introduction to *WMP*, 'published in 1763 to warn the Tory Opposition of the impeachment of Ministers'. He regarded it as Swift's 'one

philosophical work', and sees it as Swift's indictment of the War of the Many against the Few that destroyed Greece and Rome. In Rome there was a class war, in Greece a war upon character and genius. The thoughts he selected from Swift would apply to the situation in Ireland both in Parnell's time and 1933–4; he described Swift's view that the health of all states depends upon a right balance between the One, the Few, and the Many:

> The One is the executive, which may in fact be more than one — the Roman republic had two Consuls — but must for the sake of rapid decision be as few as possible; the Few are those who through the possession of hereditary wealth, or great personal gifts, have come to identify their lives with the life of the State, whereas the lives and ambitions of the Many are private. The Many do their day's work well, and so far from copying even the wisest of their neighbours, affect 'a singularity' in action and in thought; but set them to the work of the State and every man Jack is 'listed in a party', becomes the fanatical follower of men of whose characters he knows next to nothing, and from that day on puts nothing into his mouth that some other man has not already chewed and digested. And furthermore, from the moment of enlistment thinks himself above other men and struggles for power until all is in confusion. (*E* 351)

THREE SONGS TO THE SAME TUNE

These poems were written between 30 November 1933 and February 1934: they first appeared in the *Spectator* (23 Feb. 1934) where Yeats's note after the title read:

> In politics I have but one passion and one thought, rancour against all who, except under the most dire necessity, disturb public order, a conviction that public order cannot long persist without the rule of educated and able men. That order was everywhere their work, is still as much a part of their tradition as the *Iliad* or the Republic of Plato; their rule once gone, it lies an empty shell for the passing fool to kick in pieces. Some months ago that passion laid hold upon me with the violence which unfits the poet for all politics but his own. While the mood lasted, it seemed that our growing disorder, the fanaticism that inflamed it like some old bullet imbedded in the flesh, was about to turn our noble history into an ignoble farce. For the first time in my life I wanted

to write what some crowd in the street might understand and sing; I asked my friends for a tune; they recommended that old march, 'O'Donnell Abu.' I first got my chorus, 'Down the fanatic, down the clown,' then the rest of the first song. But I soon tired of its rhetorical vehemence, thought that others would tire of it unless I found some gay playing upon its theme, some half-serious exaggeration and defence of its rancorous chorus, and therefore I made the second version. Then I put into a simple song a commendation of the rule of the able and educated, man's old delight in submission; I wrote round the line 'The soldier takes pride in saluting his captain,' thinking the while of a Gaelic poet's lament for his lost masters : 'My fathers served their fathers before Christ was crucified.' I read my songs to friends, they talked to others, those others talked, and now companies march to the words 'Blueshirt Abu,' and a song that is all about shamrocks and harps or seems all about them, because its words have the particular variation upon the cadence of 'Yankee Doodle' Young Ireland reserved for that theme. I did not write that song; I could not if I tried. Here are my songs. Anybody may sing them, choosing 'clown' and 'fanatic' for himself, if they are singable — musicians say they are, but may flatter — and worth singing.

The note he appended as 'Commentary on Three Songs' in *P(Cb)* (Dec. 1934) and in *KGCT* read :

For thirty years I have been a director of the Abbey Theatre. It is a famous theatre, known to students of dramatic literature all over the world, but company and building are small, it often turns many away from its cheaper seats. It holds some five hundred persons ; that five hundred, or whatever moiety of it is there on any particular evening, is mainly boys and girls out of the shops and factories. They come again and again to a favourite play, all others are casual or uncertain, except some old adherents who have lasted out the thirty years, and a few students from the National University. If it were in Poland, in Sweden, in some Balkan State, it would have four or five times as many in company, in audience, draw into that audience those that were highly educated or highly placed, have behind it for moments of emergency ample Government support. It would be expected to send its best players now and again to foreign countries that it might raise the prestige of its nation as do the bronze replicas of the

Roman wolf, a master-piece of Etruscan art, the Italian Government has set up in America wherever Italian emigrants are numerous. When I was a foolish lad I hoped for something of the kind. When I founded the Irish Literary Society, the National Literary Society, barred from the Chair politicians and Lord Mayors that literature might live its own sincere life, I hoped for a literature Ireland would honour as Poland honours its literature. Synge, Lady Gregory, A.E. came first; then many novelists and dramatists; Moore and Shaw turned their thoughts to Ireland; nobody could have hoped for so much genius. But most of these writers are better known in other countries, even our novelists who describe in simple vivid speech the circumstance and history of their country, find most of their readers among the Irish in America, and in England; more perhaps among Englishmen and Americans, without Irish blood, than in Ireland. Sometimes I receive a little propagandist paper issued by the Polish Government, written in French, and find there pictures of the noble eighteenth century palace where the Polish Academy of Letters meets. Our not less distingished Academy meets in a room hired for five shillings a night. The explanation is that our upper class cares nothing for Ireland except as a place for sport, that the rest of the population is drowned in religious and political fanaticism. Poland is a Catholic nation and some ten years ago inflicted upon the national enemy an overwhelming, world-famous defeat, but its fanaticism, if it has any, thwarts neither science, nor art, nor letters. Sometimes as the representative of the Abbey Theatre I have called upon some member of Mr Cosgrave's or Mr de Valera's government to explain some fanatical attack — we are a State Theatre though our small subsidy has been lately reduced — once as a member of the Irish Academy to complain of the illegal suppression of a book, and upon each occasion I came away with the conviction that the Minister felt exactly as I felt but was helpless : the mob reigned. If that reign is not broken our public life will move from violence to violence, or from violence to apathy; our [apathy, our (*KGCT*)] Parliament disgrace and debauch those that enter it; our men of letters live like outlaws in their own country. It will be broken when some government seeks unity of culture not less than economic unity, welding to the purpose, museum, school, university, learned institution. A nation should be like an audience in some great theatre — 'In the theatre,'

said Victor Hugo, 'the mob becomes a people' — watching
the sacred drama of its own history ; every spectator finding
self and neighbour there, finding all the world there, as we
find the sun in the bright spot under the burning glass. We
know the world through abstractions, statistics, time tables,
through images that refuse to compose themselves into a
clear design. Such knowledge thins the blood. To know it
in the concrete we must know it near at hand ; religion itself
during our first impressionable years in the dramatis personae
of our own narrow stage ; I think of those centuries before
the great schism had divided the East and West accepted by
Catholic and Protestant alike. Into the drama must enter
all that have lived with precision and energy ; Major Sirr,
picture lover, children lover, hateful oppressor, should he
strike some creative fancy, not less than Emmet and Fitzgerald ; the Ascendency, considering its numbers as fruitful
of will and intellect as any stock on earth, not less than those
Wild Geese, those Catholic gentlemen who, in the words of
Swift, carried into foreign service 'a valour' above 'that of
all nations.'

If any Government or party undertake this work it will
need force, marching men (the logic of fanaticism, whether in
a woman or a mob is drawn from a premise protected by
ignorance and therefore irrefutable) ; it will promise not this
or that measure but a discipline, a way of life ; that sacred
drama must to all native eyes and ears become the greatest of
the parables. There is no such government or party today ;
should either appear I offer it these trivial songs and what
remains to me of life.

April, 1934
P.S. Because a friend belonging to a political party where-
with I had once some loose associations, told me that it had, or
was about to have, or might be persuaded to have, some such
aim as mine, I wrote these songs. Finding that it neither
would nor could, I increased their fantasy, their extravagance,
their obscurity, that no party might sing them.

August 1934
I   (*VE* 835–8)

10   *the tune of O'Donnell Abu* : Michael Joseph McCann, a Young   **321**
Irelander, wrote 'O Domhnaill Abu'. The song (which later
became 'Parnell Abu') was meant to be sung to the tune 'Roderick
Vick Alpine Dhu', the 'Boat Song' in Sir Walter Scott's *Lady of*

the Lake, but it became famous with another tune composed by Joseph Haliday. This information is from Georges-Denis Zimmermann, *Irish Political Street Ballads and Rebel Songs 1780–1900* (Geneva, 1966), 64, 79, 113, who cites *Irish Book Lover*, XXVI, 85, for some of his material.

25–6 Saul suggests a comparison to 'The Night before Larry was stretched', an eighteenth-century ballad : 'He kicked too — but that was all pride.'

II

322   7 '*Drown all the dogs,*' *said the fierce young woman* : see an anecdote quoted in *Y:M & P* 279 :

> Here is our most recent event. . . . Blueshirts are upholders of law, incarnations of public spirit, rioters in the cause of peace and George hates Blueshirts. She was delighted when she caught their [local Blueshirt family] collie-dog in our hen-house and missed a white hen. I was going into town and she said 'I will write and complain ; if they do nothing I will go to the police'. When I returned in the evening she was plunged in gloom. Her letter sent by the gardener had been replied to at once in these words 'Sorry, have done away with collie-dog' — note the Hitler touch — a little later came the gardener and in his presence . . . [four dogs had been drowned]. . . . A fifth had revived when taken out of the water, and (as it was not their dog) but a stray —— had hunted it down the road with a tin can tied to its tail. There was a sixth dog, —— said, but as it had been with her for some time she would take time to think whether to send it to the dogs' home or drown it. I tried to console George . . . after all she was only responsible for the death of the collie and so on — but there was something wrong and at last it came out. The white hen had returned. Was she to write and say so ? I said 'You feel a multimurderess and if you write —— will too.' 'But she will see the hen.' 'Put it in the pot.' 'But it's my best layer.' However I insisted and the white hen went into the pot.

Frank O'Connor tells the story in a more stylised form :

> . . . as a fascist he was the least fanatical of men. Mrs Yeats was on the opposite side, as I was, and one evening he told me a little moral tale to illustrate the virtues of fascism. 'You see, O'Connor, the people next door are Blueshirts. The

Blueshirts keep a dog. George is a De Valeraite and George keeps hens. The fascist dog worries the democratic hens. Today her favourite hen disappeared, and George said, "It's that damn fascist dog!" so she wrote to the neighbours to complain. But you see, O'Connor, to Blueshirts the idea of order is sacred and back comes a note that reads, "Dear Madam, Dog Destroyed." And now George, who is English and very fond of animals, is filled with remorse.'

The following week when we met he began to chuckle. 'O'Connor, remember the fascist dog? Remember the democratic hen? The democratic hen has come home! Now, George is full of guilt and insists on apologising. I won't hear of it. I say, "George, nothing you can do will bring the fascist dog back to life."'

I enjoyed the story, but once more what interests me is the monologue, that telephone conversation of which one hears only part. Could the fascist dog and the democratic hen be the source of the dog and goose of one of his deplorable fascist marching songs — the dog of law drowned by the fierceness of humanitarian sentiments. (*The Backward Look* 181–2)

23   *mock at* : cf. 'Nineteen Hundred and Nineteen' v (*CP* 236)

O'Donnell : Rory O'Donnell (1575–1608). Younger brother of Hugh O'Donnell, whom he succeeded. He visited James I at Hampton Court and was created an Earl, 1603. He attempted to rouse the Catholic Lords to rebel but on discovery of the plot fled to Rome with the Earl of Tyrone, eldest son of the first Earl of Tyrone.

24   *both O'Neills* : probably Shane O'Neill 'the Proud' (*c.* 1530–1567), who was elected 'the O'Neill' in 1559, made his submission to Elizabeth in London 1562 ; he destroyed Scottish settlements in Antrim, but supported Mary Queen of Scots ; he invaded the Pale and burned Armagh 1566 ; he defeated the MacDonnells at Ballycastle but was killed by them at Cushendun in 1567. And probably Hugh O'Neill, the second Earl of Tyrone (b. *c.* 1540). He succeeded to the title in 1585, married Mabel Bagenal 1591 and when her brother refused to hand over her dowry he captured Blackwater fort and ravaged Cò. Louth. He was proclaimed a traitor and elected the O'Neill in 1591. He beat Bagenal at the

Yellow Ford in 1598. Munster rose and O'Neill marched to receive the Spanish force at Kinsale. But his territory was largely taken by English forces when he returned. He was offered reasonable terms by Elizabeth and submitted. James I received him at Hampton Court. After he returned a law suit was referred to the King, and he was informed that this was a plot to trap him, so he and Hugh Roe O'Donnell left Rathmullen in 1607 and settled in Rome. This was known as the 'Flight of the Earls'. His overtures for a return were repulsed·and he died — of melancholia — in 1616.

25 *Emmet* : see notes (p. 118) on 'Introductory Rhymes' (*CP* 113) and (p. 130) on 'September 1913' (*CP* 120)

Parnell : see notes (pp. 133 ff.) on 'To a Shade' (*CP* 123)

III

323 4 *Troy backed its Helen* : line 4 in the first printed version read :
'What's equality ? — Muck in the yard.'

Cf. for the present version 'When Helen lived' (*CP* 124).

7 The refrain originally ran as in the first of these songs :
'*Those fanatics*' etc.

11 *Empty up there at the top* : cf. 'Blood and the Moon' (*CP* 267) with its 'time half dead at the top' and the query in 'Blood and the Moon' IV (*CP*, 269)

Is every modern nation like the tower,
Half dead at the top ?

The idea of this line and line 12 may derive from Swift. See the Introduction to *WWP* and notes (p. 413) on 'bitter wisdom' line 12 'Parnell's Funeral' II (*CP* 320). See also 'Three Marching Songs' II (*CP* 378) : 'What if there's nothing up there at the top ?'

324 ALTERNATIVE SONG FOR THE SEVERED HEAD IN 'THE KING OF THE GREAT CLOCK TOWER'

This poem was probably written in 1934 ; it first appeared in *Life and Letters* (Nov. 1934).

2 *Ben Bulben and Knocknarea* : mountains overlooking Sligo. Cf. 'Under Ben Bulben' (*CP* 397), 'The Hosting of the Sidhe' (*CP* 67) and 'Red Hanrahan's Song about Ireland' (*CP* 90).

5 *Rosses' crawling tide* : sea coast and village near Sligo. Cf. note (p. 13) on line 15 'The Stolen Child' (*CP* 20).

9 *Cuchulain that fought night long with the foam* : cf. 'Cuchulain's Fight with the Sea' (*CP* 37)

11 *Niamh that rode on it* : cf. 'The Wanderings of Oisin' (*CP* 409) for the

> . . . pearl-pale, high-born lady, who rose
> On a horse with bridle of findrinny ;

and the opening lines of Book III (*CP* 431)

> Fled foam underneath us, and round us, a wandering and
> milky smoke,
> High as the saddle-girth, covering away from our
> glances the tide ;

Cf. notes (p. 51) on Niamh in 'The Hosting of the Sidhe' (*CP* 61) and 'Under the Moon' (*CP* 91).

11 *lad and lass* : Naoise and Deirdre when captured by Conchobar (and kept in a guest house in a wood in Yeats's play). Cf. *Deirdre* 432–56. Naoise's speech sees Deirdre and himself re-enacting the situation of Lugaidh Redstripe (a warrior of the Red Branch cycle of tales). Deirdre was formerly Conchobar's ward whom he kept in the hills in the care of an old nurse Lavarcam, intending to marry her. Naoise, one of his warriors, saw her, fell in love with her and ran away with her to Scotland, accompanied by his brothers, the other sons of Usna. When they return to Ireland, and Fergus, their safe-conduct, has had to leave them Naoise says to Deirdre :

> What do they say ?
> That Lugaidh Redstripe and that wife of his
> Sat at this chess-board, waiting for their end.
> They knew there was nothing that could save them,
> And so played chess as they had any night
> For years, and waited for the stroke of sword.
> I never heard a death so out of reach
> Of common hearts, a high and comely end . . .

15   *Aleel, his Countess*: the poet and the heroine in Yeats's play *The Countess Cathleen* (*CPl*) See note (pp. 37 ff.) on 'The Countess Cathleen in Paradise' (*CP* 48).

Hanrahan: cf. note (p. 259) on 'The Tower' II (*CP* 219)

325   19–20   *The King that could make his people stare,*
               Because he had feathers instead of hair: cf. 'The Wisdom of the King' in *TSR* (*M* 165–70).   The child of the High Queen of Ireland was visited by the crones of the grey hawk (the Sidhe), one of whom let a drop of her blood fall on the infant's lips.   Two years later the King died, and the child grew very wise, but the feathers of the grey hawk grew in his hair.   The child was deceived by the poets and men of law about these feathers: they told him everyone else had had feathers too, and ordered that everyone should wear them, but that anyone who told the child the truth should be put to death.   The reason for this was a law that no one who had a bodily blemish could sit on the throne.   The King eventually discovered the truth, ordered that Eochaid should rule in his stead and vanished.

325   TWO SONGS REWRITTEN FOR THE TUNE'S SAKE

These two songs appeared in *Plays in Prose and Verse* (1922), the first song (i.e. lines 1–4, 7–10, 13–16) in *The Pot of Broth* and the second song (i.e. lines 1 and 6–12) in *The Player Queen*.   The second song first appeared in *The Dial* (Nov. 1922), then in *Plays in Prose and Verse*.   The first song is altered more and the variations are to be found in *VE* 550–1.   The revised versions of the first song appeared in *FMM*.

I

1   *Paistin Finn*: a Munster folk tune, sung to a lively air.   It may be a popularised version of a song from the Ossianic cycle as the title means 'Little child of Fionn'.   Fionn was Oisin's father.   Since the Ossianic cycle was more popular than the Ulster cycle it is not unlikely, Dr Brendan Kennelly suggests, that Paistín Finn, which is purely folk, was originally heroic in the Fenian manner.

II

5 *dreepy* : dreary, doleful. From Scots *dree*, to endure or suffer, an archaic word revived by Sir Walter Scott.

A PRAYER FOR OLD AGE   326

This poem was written in 1934 and first appeared in the *Spectator* (2 Nov. 1934).

This poem was provoked by Ezra Pound's condemnation of *KGCT*, and expressed Yeats's dislike of 'intellectual' poetry. 'We only believe,' he wrote in 'The Cutting of an Agate', 'in those thoughts which have been conceived not in the brain but in the whole body' (*E & I* 235). After Lady Gregory's death Yeats had written no verse for two years :

> . . . I had never been so long barren ; I had nothing in my head, and there used to be more than I could write. Perhaps Coole Park where I had escaped from politics, from all that Dublin talked of, when it was shut, shut me out from my theme ; or did the subconscious drama that was my imaginative life end with its owner ? but it was more likely that I had grown too old for poetry. I decided to force myself to write, then take advice. In 'At Parnell's Funeral' I rhymed passages from a lecture I had given in America ; a poem upon mount Meru came spontaneously, but philosophy is a dangerous theme ; then I was barren again. I wrote the prose dialogue of *The King of the Great Clock Tower* that I might be forced to make lyrics for its imaginary people. When I had written all but the last lyric I went a considerable journey partly to get the advice of a poet not of my school [Ezra Pound] who would, as he did some years ago, say what he thought. I asked him to dine, tried to get his attention. 'I am in my sixty ninth year' I said, 'probably I should stop writing verse, I want your opinion upon some verse I have written lately.' I had hoped he would ask me to read it but he would not speak of art, or of literature, or of anything related to them. I had however been talking to his latest disciple and knew that his opinions had not changed : Phidias had corrupted sculpture, we had nothing of true Greece but certain *Nike* dug up out of the foundations of the Parthenon, and that corruption ran through all our art ; Shakespeare and Dante had corrupted literature, Shakespeare by his too

abounding sentiment, Dante by his compromise with the Church.

He said, apropos of nothing, 'Arthur Balfour was a scoundrel,' and from that on would talk of nothing but politics. All the other modern statesmen were more or less scoundrels except 'Mussolini and that hysterical imitator of his Hitler.' When I objected to his violence he declared that Dante considered all sins intellectual, even sins of the flesh, he himself refused to make the modern distinction between error and sin. He urged me to read the works of Captain Douglas who alone knew what caused our suffering. He took my manuscript and went away denouncing Dublin as 'a reactionary hole' because I had said that I was re-reading Shakespeare, would go on to Chaucer, and found all that I wanted of modern life in 'detection and the wild west.' Next day his judgment came and that in a single word 'Putrid.'

Then I took my verses to a friend of my own school, and this friend said 'go on just like that. Plays like *The Great Clock Tower* always seem unfinished but that is no matter. Begin plays without knowing how to end them for the sake of the lyrics. I once wrote a play and after I had filled it with lyrics abolished the play.' Then I brought my work to two painters and a poet until I was like Panurge consulting oracles as to whether he should get married and rejecting all that did not confirm his own desire. (Preface to *KGCT*)

327 CHURCH AND STATE

This poem was written in August 1934 and first appeared in the *Spectator* (23 Nov. 1934) entitled 'A Vain Hope'.

This poem (untitled) followed Yeats's *Commentary on the Three Songs* in *P(Ch)* (Dec. 1934). See notes (pp. 414 ff.) on *Three Songs to the Same Tune* (*CP* 320).

327 SUPERNATURAL SONGS

Yeats wrote a general comment on these poems which was included in *KGCT*:

An Irish poet during a country walk talked of the Church of Ireland, he had preferences for this or that preacher, Archbishop Gregg had pleased him by accepting certain recent Lambeth decrees; one could be a devout communicant and

accept all the counsels before the Great Schism that separated
Western from Eastern Christianity in the ninth century. In
course of time the Church of Ireland would feel itself more in
sympathy with early Christian Ireland than could a Church
that admitted later developments of doctrine. I said that for
the moment I associated early Christian Ireland with India ;
Shri Purohit Swami, protected during his pilgrimage to a
remote Himalyan shrine by a strange great dog that disappeared when danger was past, might have been that blessed
Cellach who sang upon his deathbed of bird and beast ; Bag-
wan Shri Hamsa's pilgrimage to Mount Kaílás, the legendary
Meru, and to lake Manas Sarowa, suggested pilgrimages to
Croagh Patrick and to Lough Derg. A famous philosopher
believed that every civilisation began, no matter what its
geographical origin, with Asia, certain men of science that all
of us when still in the nursery were, if not African, exceedingly
Asiatic. Saint Patrick must have found in Ireland, for he was
not its first missionary, men whose Christianity had come
from Egypt, and retained characteristics of those older faiths
that have become so important to our invention. Perhaps
some man young enough for so great a task might discover
there men and women he could honour — to adapt the
words of Goethe — by conferring their names upon his own
thoughts ; perhaps I myself had made a beginning.

While this book was passing through the press I wrote the
poems for that old hermit Ribh. I did not explain the poems
in *The King of the Great Clock Tower*, nor will I explain these.
I would consider Ribh, were it not for his ideas about the
Trinity, an orthodox man. (*KGCT*)

In the Preface to *FMM* Yeats remarked 'The hermit Ribh in
"Supernatural Songs" is an imaginary critic of St Patrick. His
Christianity, come perhaps from Egypt like much early Irish
Christianity, echoes pre-Christian thought.'

RIBH AT THE TOMB OF BAILE AND AILLINN   **327**

This poem was written by 24 July 1934 and first appeared in
P(Cb) and *LM* in Dec. 1934.

Yeats wrote to Mrs Shakespear on 24 July 1934 :

I have another poem in my head where a monk reads his
breviary at midnight upon the tomb of long-dead lovers on
the anniversary of their death, for on that night they are

united above the tomb, their embrace being not partial but a conflagration of the entire body and so shedding the light he reads by. (*L* 824)

1 *me*: Ribh, an imaginary character, see Yeats's notes quoted above

6 *Baile and Aillinn*: legendary Irish lovers. See Yeats' 'Baile and Aillinn' (*CP* 457) and notes (p. 91) on 'The Withering of the Boughs' (*CP* 87)

8 *the apple and the yew*: to each of the lovers Aengus, God of Love, gave false news of the other's death; they died of broken hearts, and were changed into swans linked by a golden chain. A yew tree grew where Baile's body lay, a wild apple over Aillinn's; their love stories were written on boards made of yew and apple. There is an interesting discussion of the poem in *LT* 311–17.

328 15 *the intercourse of angels is a light*: it is probable that Yeats got this idea from Swedenborg. In 'Anima Mundi' Yeats wrote of the dead 'I do not doubt that they make love in that union which Swedenborg has said is of the whole body and seems from far off an incandescence.' In a letter of 21 February 1933 he wrote to Mrs Shakespear:

> . . . *Louis Lambert* [by Balzac] might have been [an echo] of that saying of Swedenborg's that the sexual intercourse of the angels is a conflagration of the whole being

and on 9 March:

> Yet why not take Swedenborg literally and think we attain, in a partial contact, what the spirits know throughout their being. He somewhere describes two spirits meeting and as they touch they become a single conflagration. His vision may be true, Newton's cannot be. . . .

26–7 *. . . in a circle on the grass; therein*
I turn the pages of my holy book: the light is circular to indicate the perfect harmony achieved by the lovers. It is possible that the idea of putting priest and lovers into one poem came from

Yeats's reading in Japanese plays. In 'Certain Noble Plays of Japan' he wrote :

> The love-sorrows — the love of father and daughter, of mother and son, of boy and girl — may owe their nobility to a courtly life, but he to whom the adventures happen, a traveller commonly from some distant place, is most often a Buddhist priest; and the occasional intellectual subtlety is perhaps Buddhist. The adventure itself is often the meeting with ghost, god, or goddess at some holy place or much-legended tomb; and god, goddess, or ghost reminds me at times of our own Irish legends and beliefs, which once, if may be, differed little from those of the Shinto worshipper. (*E & I* 232)

The *Nishikigi*, in particular, may have influenced him. The tale of the lovers would lose its pathos 'if we did not see that forgotten tomb' (*E & I* 233), and again this passage suggests that the grass may have been suggested by the *Nishikigi* :

> The lovers, now that in an aëry body they must sorrow for unconsummated love, are 'tangled up as the grass patterns are tangled.' Again they are like an unfinished cloth : 'these bodies, having no weft, even now are not come together; truly a shameful story, a tale to bring shame on the gods.' Before they can bring the priest to the tomb they spend the day 'pushing aside the grass from the overgrown ways in Kefu', and the countryman who directs them is 'cutting grass on the hill'; and when at last the prayer of the priest unites them in marriage the bride says that he has made 'a dream-bridge over wild grass, over the grass I dwell in'; and in the end bride and bridegroom show themselves for a moment 'from under the shadow of the love-grass'. (*E & I* 234)

RIBH DENOUNCES PATRICK 328

This poem was written in late July 1934 and first appeared in *LM* and *P* (Ch) in December 1934.

See Yeats's *Commentary on Supernatural Songs* included above. In a letter of 24 July 1934 to Mrs Shakespear he included the second and third verses with the comment that the point of the poem was that 'we beget and bear because of the incompleteness of our love' (*L* 824).

6   *the Great Smaragdine Tablet* : a medieval Latin work on alchemy published in 1541, attributed to the Egyptian Hermes Trismegistus. Yeats's source was probably G. R. S. Mead's *Thrice Greatest Hermes*, Saul (*PYP* 158) suggests that Madame Blavatsky, *Isis Unveiled*, also makes the point that what is below is like what is above.

9   *in their embraces twined* : cf. a sentence in an essay 'What is Popular Poetry ?' : 'I always knew that the line of Nature is crooked, that, though we dig the canal-beds as straight as we can, the rivers run hither and thither in their wildness' (*E & I* 5).
    A similar image exists in *A* 480.

10   *serpent is multiplicity* : cf. a passage in *Discoveries*, 'On the Serpent's Mouth' :

> If it be true that God is a circle whose centre is everywhere, the saint goes to the centre, the poet and artist to the ring where everything comes round again. The poet must not seek for what is still and fixed, for that has no life for him ; and if he did, his style would become cold and monotonous, and his sense of beauty faint and sickly, as are both style and beauty to my imagination in the prose and poetry of Newman, but be content to find his pleasure in all that is for ever passing away that it may come again, in the beauty of woman, in the fragile flowers of spring, in momentary heroic passion, in whatever is most fleeting, most impassioned, as it were, for its own perfection, most eager to return in its glory. Yet perhaps he must endure the impermanent a little, for these things return, but not wholly, for no two faces are alike, and, it may be, had we more learned eyes, no two flowers. It is that all things are made by the struggle of the individual and the world, of the unchanging and the returning, and that the saint and the poet are over all, and that the poet has made his home in the serpent's mouth ? (*E & I* 287–8)

329   RIBH IN ECSTASY

This poem was probably written in late 1934, and first appeared in *FMM*.

1   *you understood* : possibly Maud Gonne, cf. '*Words*' (CP 100) — or else Frank O'Connor, who, when Yeats read 'Ribh denounces

Patrick' to some friends at his home and asked them if they understood it, replied, 'No, I didn't understand a word of it' (*IY* 282).

7   *Those amorous cries* : the poem describes Yeats's own feeling of
unity or happiness — cf. 'Vacillation' IV (*CP* 283) — when he
had written a philosophical poem (Ellmann suggests the previous
one) which is interrupted again by 'the common round of day'.
      In 1934 Yeats underwent the Steinach operation for rejuvenation.

THERE   **329**

This poem's date is not established but it was probably late in
1934 or early in 1935. It first appeared in *FMM*.

1   *There* : this is perfection, the 'sphere' of *AV*'s thirteenth
cone :

      The *Thirteenth Cone* is a sphere because sufficient to itself;
but as seen by Man it is a cone. It becomes even conscious
of itself, as so seen, like some great dancer, the perfect flower
of modern culture, dancing some primitive dance and conscious of his or her own life and of the dance. There is a
mediaeval story of a man persecuted by his Guardian Angel
because it was jealous of his sweetheart, and such stories seem
closer to reality than our abstract theology. All imaginable
relations may arise between a man and his God. I only speak
of the *Thirteenth Cone* as a sphere and yet I might say that
the gyre or cone of the *Principles* is in reality a sphere, though
to Man, bound to birth and death, it can never seem so, and
that it is the antinomies that force us to find it a cone. Only
one symbol exists, though the reflecting mirrors make many
appear and all different. (*AV* (B) 240).

Thomas R. Whitaker, *Swan and Shadow*, 118, remarks that solar
apocalypse, which Yeats terms the 'Sphere' in *AV*, Ribh calls
'There' — the term by which (in the MacKenna translation)
Plotinus refers to the Divine Sphere : 'the Sun, There, is all the
stars ; and every star, again, is all the stars and sun.' There, as
Boehme said 'life windeth itself *Inwards* to the Sun.'

barrel-hoops : possibly a memory of the drowning of the dogs
caused this imagery and that of 'Meru' (*CP* 333) where civilisation
'is hooped together'.

2   *the serpent-tails* : possibly derived from Theosophical reading. Cf. 'Alchemy', *Theosophical Siftings* II (1889–90).

330   RIBH CONSIDERS CHRISTIAN LOVE INSUFFICIENT

This poem was probably written in 1934 and first appeared in *LM* and *P* (Ch) in December 1934.

3   *I study hatred* : cf. 'Remorse for Intemperate Speech' (*CP* 288). Ellmann (*IY* 283) suggests that the poem developed out of some automatic writing of Mrs Yeats. Yeats wrote in a journal of the ideas of a 'communicator' which she was writing down :

> He insisted on being questioned. I asked about further multiple influx. He said 'hate God,' we must hate all ideas concerning God that we possess, that if we did not absorption in God would be impossible . . . always he repeated 'hatred, hatred' or 'hatred of God' . . . said, 'I think about hatred.' That seems to me the growing hatred among men [which] has long been a problem with me.
>
> The soul has to enter some significant relationship with God even if this be one of hatred.

19   *stroke of midnight* : this phrase was used by Yeats in 'The Four Ages of Man' (*CP* 332) ; it implies the end of life.

331   HE AND SHE

This was written before 25 August 1934, and first appeared in *LM* and *P* (Ch) (Dec. 1934).

Yeats wrote to Mrs Shakespear on 25 August 1934 that this poem was on the soul : 'It is of course, my central myth'. The poem relates to *AV*, 'She' being the soul or humanity, following the notes on phases of the moon. Cf. 'The Phases of the Moon' (*CP* 183) for the relationship between these phases and the soul.

331   WHAT MAGIC DRUM?

This poem was probably written in 1934, and first appeared in *FMM.*

This poem deals with the union of some god or hero with (perhaps) a human mother, as in 'Leda and the Swan' (*CP* 241). The poem is also reminiscent of 'The Second Coming' (*CP* 210), the final emphasis on the 'beast' in each case coming as a jolt of horror to the reader.

4   *magic drum* : cf. the 'frenzied drum' of line 15 of 'A Prayer for my Daughter' (*CP* 211)

WHENCE HAD THEY COME?   332

This poem was probably written in 1934 ; it first appeared in *FMM*.

This poem asks what imponderables lie behind the happenings of personal love or general history, behind the system of *AV*'s interpretation of both.   The lovers are but a symbol of love (cf. 'His Bargain' (*CP* 299)) ;   the thought resembles that of the Platonic Idea, and there are parallels between the sexual symbolism of 'Leda and the Swan' (*CP* 241), this poem and 'What Magic Drum ?' (*CP* 331).

THE FOUR AGES OF MAN   332

This poem was written on 6 August 1934, and first appeared in *LM* and *P*(Ch) (Dec. 1934).

Yeats wrote about the poem to Mrs Shakespear in a letter from Riversdale, Rathfarnham, on 24 July 1934 :

> . . . Yes that book is important.   Notice this symbolism
> Waters under the earth ⎫
>   The Earth   ⎬ The bowels etc.   *Instinct*
>   The Water   = The blood and the sex
>   organ   *Passion*
>   The Air   = The lungs, logical thought *Thought*
>   The Fire   =   *Soul*

They are my four quarters.   The Earth before 8, the waters before 15, the Air before 22, the Fire before 1 (See *AV*, page 86).   Note that on page 85 of *A Vision* [this was a wrong reference, corrected later in a letter of 25 July 1934, to p. 35 of *AV* (A) where 'it is there written that in the last quarter of a civilisation (the quarter we have just entered,) the fight is against body and body should win.   You can define soul as "that which has value in itself" or you can say of it "it [is] that which we only know through analogies".'] the conflict on which we now enter is 'against the Soul' as in the quarter we have just left it was 'against the intellect'. The conflict is to restore the body . . .

Later in this letter Yeats wrote :

The Earth = Every early nature-dominated civilisation
The Water = An armed sexual age, chivalry, Froissart's chronicles
The Air = From the Renaissance to the end of the 19th Century
The Fire = The purging away of our civilisation by our hatred (on these two I have a poem)

(*L* 823–5)

In a later letter of 7 August 1934 to Olivia Shakespear, Yeats remarked that he had put into rhyme what he had written in his last letter, and included the poem (with a variant second line 'Body won and values upright') with the comment

They are the four ages of individual man, but they are also the four ages of civilisation. You will find them in that book you have been reading. First age, *earth*, negative functions. Second age, *water*, blood, sex. Third age, *air*, breath, intellect. Fourth age, *fire*, soul etc. In the first two the moon comes to the full — resurrection of Christ and Dionysus. Man becomes rational, no longer driven from below or above. My two plays, of which I send you the *Sunday Times* notices, both deal with that moment — the slain god, the risen god. (*L* 826)

8 *stroke of midnight* : cf. 'Ribh considers Christian Love insufficient' (*CP* 330)

333 CONJUNCTIONS

This poem was written before 25 August 1934 and first appeared in *LM* and *P*(Ch) (Dec. 1934).

Yeats wrote about the poem in a letter to Mrs Shakespear of 25 August 1934 :

. . . I was told, you may remember, that my two children would be Mars conjunctive Venus, Saturn conjunctive Jupiter respectively ; and so they were — Ann the Mars–Venus personality. Then I was told that they would develop so that I could study in them the alternating dispensations, the Christian or objective, then the Antithetical or subjective. The Christian is the Mars–Venus — it is democratic. The Jupiter–Saturn civilisation is born free among the most cultivated, out of tradition, out of rule.

> Should Jupiter and Saturn meet,
> What a crop of mummy wheat !

> The sword's a cross ; thereon He died :
> On breast of Mars the goddess sighed.

I wrote those lines some days ago. George said it is very strange but whereas Michael is always thinking about life Anne always thinks of death. Then I remembered that the children were the two dispensations. Anne collects skeletons. She buries little birds and beasts and then digs them up when worms and insects have eaten their flesh. She has a shelf of very white little skeletons. She has asked leave to go to the geological museum to draw skeletons. Then she loves tragedies, has read all Shakespeare's, and a couple of weeks ago was searching reference books to learn all about the poison that killed Hamlet's father. When she grows up she will either have some passionate love affair or have some close friend that has — the old association of love and death. (*L* 827–8)

2 *mummy-wheat*: the 'old mummy wheat' of 'On a Picture of a Black Centaur by Edmund Dulac' (*CP* 242)

A NEEDLE'S EYE   333

This poem's date is uncertain ; it first appeared in *LM* and *P*(Ch), (Dec. 1934).

2 *needle's eye*: cf. 'the needle's eye' of 'Veronica's Napkin' (*CP* 270)

MERU   333

This poem was probably written between August 1933 and June 1934 ; it first appeared in *LM* and *P*(Ch) (Dec. 1934).

Yeats had finished his study of various authorities and was about to start his Introduction to Shri Purohit Swami's *The Holy*

Mountain (1934) in August 1933 (*L* 813). He sent back the final proofs, having read it all through in June 1934 and described it in a letter of June to Olivia Shakespear as 'one of those rare books that are fundamental' (*L* 823). There is an account of the Swami's experiences in Yeats's Introduction (*E & I* 448–73). The poem envisages man as a destroyer of what he creates, and the hermits learn this truth, of the succession of civilisations.

334 9 *Mount Meru*: Shri Purohit Swami did not accompany his friend who had been ordered in a meditation known as *Savikalpa-Samadhi* 'to seek *Turiya*, the greater or conscious Samadhi at Mount Kailas, the legendary Meru' as he thought himself unworthy (*E & I* 453).

10 *caverned*: see note (pp. 435 ff.) on 'The Gyres' (*CP* 337). The hermits are a new version of Shelley's Ahasuerus, Indian because of Yeats's intensified interest in Indian mysticism and religious thought at the time of writing the poem.

Last Poems

CURTIS BRADFORD in 'Yeats's *Last Poems* Again', VIII, *Dolmen Press Yeats Centenary Papers* (1965) wrote that those poems in *CP* starting with 'The Gyres' and ending with 'Are You Content?' are Yeats's *New Poems*, as published by the Cuala Press in 1938. He points out that the heading *Last Poems* can be properly applied only to those poems Yeats wrote or finished in the last year of his life. They were published in *Last Poems and Two Plays* in the order he intended by the Cuala Press in 1939. Curtis Bradford reproduces the order of Yeats's manuscript list as follows: 1. 'Under Ben Bulben'; 2. 'Three Songs to One Burden'; 3. 'The Black Tower'; 4. 'Cuchulain Comforted'; 5. 'Three Marching Songs'; 6. 'In Tara's Halls'; 7. 'The Statues'; 8. 'News for the Delphic Oracle'; 9. 'The Long-Legged Fly'; 10. 'A Bronze Head'; 11. 'A Stick of Incense'; 12. 'Hound Voice'; 13. 'John Kinsella's Lament etc'; 14. 'High Talk'; 15. 'The Apparitions'; 16. 'A Nativity'; 17. 'Man and Echo'; 18. 'The Circus Animal's Desertion'; 19. 'Politics'; 20. 'Cuchulain's Death'; 21. 'Purgatory'. The list does not include three poems Yeats included in *OTB*: 'Why should not old Men be Mad?', 'Crazy Jane on the Mountain' and 'The Statesman's Holiday'.

THE GYRES

This poem was probably written between July 1936 and January 1937. It first appeared in *NP*.

1 *The gyres*: see note (p. 235) on the gyres, 'Demon and Beast' (*CP* 209) and cf. line 469, 'The Gift of Harun Al-Rashid' (*CP* 513), Line 1, 'The Second Coming' (*CP* 210), line 19, 'Sailing to Byzantium' (*CP* 217), and line 62, 'Under Ben Bulben' (*CP* 397).

Old Rocky Face: there have been several different identifications of this figure. The MS. versions refer to the 'old cavern man' [and Yeats referred to 'the old ascetic of the cavern' (*E & I* 464)] and this suggests that Yeats was remembering Shelley's Ahasuerus, the cavern-dwelling Jew in Hellas :

> I have described what image — always opposite to the natural self or the natural world — Wilde, Henley, Morris copied or tried to copy, but I have not said if I found an image for myself. I know very little about myself and much less of that anti-self : probably the woman who cooks my dinner or the woman who sweeps out my study knows more than I. It is perhaps because Nature made me a gregarious man, going hither and thither looking for conversation, and ready to deny from fear or favour his dearest conviction, that I love proud and lonely things. When I was a child and went daily to the sexton's daughter for writing lessons, I found one poem in her School Reader that delighted me beyond all others : a fragment of some metrical translation from Aristophanes wherein the birds sing scorn upon mankind. In later years my mind gave itself to gregarious Shelley's dream of a young man, his hair blanched with sorrow, studying philosophy in some lonely tower, or of his old man, master of all human knowledge, hidden from human sight in some shell-strewn cavern on the Mediterranean shore. One passage above all ran perpetually in my ears :

> > Some feign that he is Enoch : others dream
> > He was pre-Adamite, and has survived
> > Cycles of generation and of ruin.
> > The sage, in truth, by dreadful abstinence,
> > And conquering penance of the mutinous flesh,
> > Deep contemplation and unwearied study,
> > In years outstretched beyond the date of man,
> > May have attained to sovereignty and science
> > Over those strong and secret things and thoughts
> > Which others fear and know not.

> > MAHMUD
> >
> > > > I would talk
> > With this old Jew.

> > HASSAN
> >
> > > > Thy will is even now
> > Made known to him where he dwells in a sea-cavern
> > 'Mid the Demonesi, less accessible

Than thou or God ! He who would question him
Must sail alone at sunset, where the stream
Of Ocean sleeps around those foamless isles,
When the young moon is westering as now,
And evening airs wander upon the wave ;
And, when the pines of that bee-pasturing isle,
Green Erebinthus, quench the fiery shadow
Of his gilt prow within the sapphire water,
Then must the lonely helmsman cry aloud
'Ahasuerus !' and the caverns round
Will answer 'Ahasuerus !' If his prayer
Be granted, a faint meteor will arise,
Lighting him over Marmora ; and a wind
Will rush out of the sighing pine-forest,
And with the wind a storm of harmony
Unutterably sweet, and pilot him
Through the soft twilight to the Bosphorus :
Thence, at the hour and place and circumstance
Fit for the matter of their conference,
The Jew appears. Few dare, and few who dare
Win the desired communion. (*A* 171–3)

In *AV*, Phase seventeen contains him : 'This *Mask* may represent intellectual or sexual passion ; seem some Ahasuerus or Athanase' (*AV* (B) 141). This phase contained Dante and Shelley, and it was Yeats's phase also :

Because of the habit of synthesis, and of the growing complexity of the energy, which gives many interests, and the still faint perception of things in their weight and mass, men of this phase are almost always partisans, propagandists and gregarious ; yet because of the *Mask* of simplification, which holds up before them the solitary life of hunters and of fishers and 'the groves pale passion loves', they hate parties, crowds, propaganda. Shelley out of phase writes pamphlets, and dreams of converting the world, [a parallel to Yeats's political activity in the 'nineties] or of turning man of affairs and upsetting governments, and yet returns again and again to these two images of solitude, a young man whose hair has grown white from the burden of his thoughts, an old man in some shell-strewn cave whom it is possible to call, when speaking to the Sultan, 'as inaccessible as God or thou'. (*AV* (B) 143)

Cf. also the passage cited by Henn (*LT* 321) from Yeats's *Letters to A E* :

> Had some young Greek found Shelley's 'Ahasuerus' in that shell-strewn cavern, the sage would not have talked mathematics or even 'those strong and secret thoughts . . . which others fear and know not', but given, I think, very simple advice, not indeed fitted to any momentary crisis but fitted perhaps for the next fifty years. (*DM*, July/Sept. 1939)

Henn also quoted a passage from Spengler which blended the symbolism with world events

> The second wave swelled up steeply in the Apocalyptic Currents after 300. Here it was the Magian waking consciousness that arose and built itself a metaphysic of Last Things, based already 'upon the prime symbol of the coming Culture, the Cavern'. (*Decline of the West*, II 249)

Yeats alluded to the symbol of the cavern in connection with Spengler's speculations in *AV* (B) 258–60 : 'The Cavern is Time . . .'.

It is likely, (see notes (p. 434) on 'Meru' (*CP* 333)), that the idea of the cavern and the wise man came back into Yeats's mind as he read of the Indian sages and their pursuit of detached wisdom. Cf. the 'old ascetic of the cavern' (*E & I* 464).

5 *streams of blood* : cf. 'the blood-dimmed tide' of 'The Second Coming' (*CP* 210), 'all that blood was shed' of 'September 1913' (*CP* 120), the various mentions of blood in 'Blood and the Moon' (*CP* 267), how 'base drove out the better blood' in 'The Statesman's Holiday' (*CP* 389). In 'Two Songs from a Play' (*CP* 239)

> Odour of blood when Christ was slain
> Made all Platonic tolerance vain
> And vain all Doric discipline.

6 *Empedocles* : a Greek philosopher (*c.* 490–430 B.C.) who regarded all things as composed of earth, air, fire, and water, mingled by love or separated by strife. Yeats quoted him in the opening of the section of the *Great Wheel* :

I

> 'When Discord', writes Empedocles, 'has fallen into the lowest depths of the vortex' — the extreme bound, not the

centre, Burnet points out — 'Concord has reached the centre, into it do all things come together so as to be only one, not all at once but gradually from different quarters, and as they come Discord retires to the extreme boundary . . . in proportion as it runs out Concord in a soft immortal boundless stream runs in.' And again : 'Never will boundless time be emptied of that pair ; and they prevail in turn as that circle comes round, and pass away before one another and increase in their appointed turn'. It was this Discord or War that Heraclitus called 'God of all and Father of all, some it has made gods and some men, some bond and some free', and I recall that Love and War came from the eggs of Leda.

II

According to Simplicius, a late commentator upon Aristotle, the Concord of Empedocles fabricates all things into 'an homogeneous sphere', and then Discord separates the elements and so makes the world we inhabit, but even the sphere formed by Concord is not the changeless eternity, for Concord or Love but offers us the image of that which is changeless. (*AV* (B) 67–8)

7 *Hector is dead* : cf. 'The Phases of the Moon' (*CP* 183) :

> Athene takes Achilles by the hair,
> Hector is in the dust, Nietzsche is born,
> Because the hero's crescent is the twelfth.

8 *tragic joy* : this brave opposition to decay and death was part of Yeats's mental make-up. Cf. a passage in 'J. M. Synge and the Ireland of his Time' :

> There is in the creative joy of acceptance of what life brings, because we have understood the beauty of what it brings, or a hatred of death for what it takes away, which arouses within us, through some sympathy perhaps with all other men, an energy so noble, so powerful, that we laugh aloud and mock, in the terror or the sweetness of our exaltation, at death and oblivion. (*E & I* 322)

This idea was repeated in *OTB*, where after a side-swipe at 'the vulgar jocularity of certain ignorant Irish dramatists', no doubt contrasted in his mind with Synge, Yeats remarked 'No tragedy is legitimate unless it leads some great character to his final joy'

(*E* 448). See the passage quoted from this essay in note (p. 236) on line 22 'Demon and Beast' (*CP* 209) and note (p. 170) on 'Tom O'Roughley' (*CP* 158).

And he wrote to Dorothy Wellesley on 26 July 1935 that to him 'the supreme aim is an act of faith and reason to make one rejoice in the midst of tragedy' (*DWL* 12).

9 *numb nightmare* : no doubt these lines owed much to Yeats's knowledge of the troubles and the Irish Civil War. Cf. the 'dragon-ridden' days of 'Nineteen Hundred and Nineteen' (*CP* 232), and 'Meditations in Time of Civil War' (*CP* 225).

10 *blood and mire* : cf. note (p. 397) on line 25 'Her Vision in the Wood' (*CP* 312)

11 *What matter ?* : cf. 'Parnell's Funeral' (*CP* 319)
  'What matter for the scene, the scene once gone.'

338 LAPIS LAZULI

Yeats wrote this poem in July 1936 (finishing it on the 25th) : it first appeared in *LM* (March 1938) and the *New Republic* (13 April 1938). For a discussion of its meaning see *IY* 185–7 and Jeffares, 'Notes on Yeats's "Lapis Lazuli"', *Modern Language Notes* (Nov. 1950) and 'The general and particular meanings of "Lapis Lazuli"' in *Yeats: Last Poems* (ed. J. Stallworthy, 1968), 160 ff. See also Edward Engelberg, *The Vast Design*, 170–5.

3 *poets that are always gay* : in 'Modern Poetry : A Broadcast' Yeats quoted the lines :

> Unto us they belong,
>   Us the bitter and gay,
> Wine and women and song.

He referred to Dowson, and remarked that it had never occurred to him to wonder why the Dowson he knew seemed neither gay nor bitter (*E & I* 492). But here the theme of gaiety is linked to the need to face tragedy heroically. Engelberg (*The Vast Design*, 170) remarks that Arnold's essay 'On the Study of Celtic Literature' (which Yeats read as a young man and commented on in his own essay 'The Celtic Element in Literature of 1897') stresses the Celtic origin of the word 'gay'.

5 *if nothing drastic is done* : the Germans reoccupied the Rhineland in 1936; the Italians were invading Abyssinia in 1935; and the Spanish Civil War was a testing ground for new armaments.

6 *Aeroplane and Zeppelin* : the Zeppelin was anachronistic for bombing purposes in 1936 but Yeats had memories of the Zeppelin bombing raids on London in the 1914–18 war. Frank O'Connor, *The Backward Look* (1967), 174, gives an account of how, at the time Yeats was writing a poem to the donor of the piece of lapis lazuli, Edmund Dulac had written to him to express his terror of what was going to happen if London was bombed from the air.

7 *Pitch like King Billy bomb-balls in* : the 'bomb-balls' probably derive from 'The Battle of the Boyne', a ballad included in *Irish Minstrelsy* (1888), an anthology edited by H. Halliday Sparling whom Yeats probably met at the home of William Morris. The anthology contained a poem by Yeats, and an inscribed copy is in the poet's library. Cf. a passage from Elizabeth Yeats's diary for 1888–9 quoted by Joseph Hone, 'A scattered Fair', *The Wind and the Rain* (Autumn 1946), 113. The ballad lines ran :

> King James has pitched his tent between
> The lines for to retire
> But King William threw his bomb-balls in
> And set them all on fire.

The echo is stronger than the original. Yeats calls King William 'King Billy', a name more likely to rouse memories and political associations in Ireland. He also took over the word 'pitch' and used it for the bomb-balls instead of for the tent. It has the touch of violence he required.

11 *That's Ophelia, that Cordelia* : they are implicitly compared with the 'hysterical women' of 1936.

12–15 *Yet they, should the last scene be there,*
The great stage curtain about to drop,

If worthy their prominent part in the play,

Do not break up their lines to weep : these lines are probably an answer to Frank O'Connor, who told Yeats how troubled he was over an unsatisfactory production of Lady Gregory's *Devorgilla* in which the heroine wept at the curtain. He asked Yeats (who had been talking of the lapis lazuli) 'Is it ever permissible for an actor to sob at the curtain of a play ?' and he replied 'Never !' O'Connor remarked, not quite accurately, that this poem renders the lapis lazuli and the Chinese scenes, the bombardment and his own advice to the players, in strict chronological order as though copied from a diary (*The Backward Look* 174–5).

16   *They know that Hamlet and Lear are gay* : in 'A General Introduction for my Work' Yeats wrote that :

> The heroes of Shakespeare convey to us through their looks, or through the metaphorical patterns of their speech, the sudden enlargement of their vision, their ecstasy at the approach of death : 'She should have died hereafter,' 'Of many thousand kisses, the poor last,' 'Absent thee from felicity awhile.' They have become God or Mother Goddess, the pelican, 'My baby at my breast,' but all must be cold ; no actress has ever sobbed when she played Cleopatra, even the shallow brain of a producer has never thought of such a thing. The supernatural is present, cold winds blow across our hands, upon our faces, the thermometer falls, and because of that cold we are hated by journalists and groundlings. There may be in this or that detail painful tragedy, but in the whole work none. I have heard Lady Gregory say, rejecting some play in the modern manner sent to the Abbey Theatre, 'Tragedy must be a joy to the man who dies.' Nor is it any different with lyrics, songs, narrative poems ; neither scholars nor the populace have sung or read anything generation after generation because of its pain. The maid of honour whose tragedy they sing must be lifted out of history with timeless pattern, she is one of the four Maries, the rhythm is old and familiar, imagination must dance, must be carried beyond feeling into the aboriginal ice. Is ice the correct word ? I once boasted, copying the phrase from a letter of my father's, that I would write a poem 'cold and passionate as the dawn.' (*E & I* 522–3)

Cf. also note (p. 439) on 'tragic joy' line 8 'The Gyres' (*CP* 337).

J. Kleinstück, 'Yeats and Shakespeare' (*YCE* 12–14) discusses this poem at length and suggests the 'tragic joy' was owed, in part, to Nietzsche.

24 *It cannot grow* : Engelberg (*The Vast Design*, 171) remarks that 'It' must clearly refer to the 'tragedy wrought to its utmost'.

29 *No handiwork of Callimachus* : cf. a passage in *AV* describing **339** the period 2000 B.C. to A.D. 1 :

> With Callimachus pure Ionic revives again, as Furtwängler has proved, and upon the only example of his work known to us, a marble chair, a Persian is represented, and may one not discover a Persian symbol in that bronze lamp, shaped like a palm, known to us by a description in Pausanias ? But he was an archaistic workman, and those who set him to work brought back public life to an older form. One may see in masters and man a momentary dip into ebbing Asia. (*AV* (B) 270)

See also 'Certain Noble Plays of Japan' :

> It may be well if we go to school in Asia, for the distance from life in European art has come from little but difficulty with material. In half-Asiatic Greece Callimachus could still return to a stylistic management of the falling folds of display, after the naturalistic drapery of Phidias. . . . (*E & I* 225)

37 *Two Chinamen* : this is a description of the piece of lapis lazuli. Cf. a letter of 6 July 1935 in which Yeats describes it :

> . . . someone [Harry Clifton] has sent me a present of a great piece carved by some Chinese sculptor into the semblance of a mountain with temple, trees, paths and an ascetic and pupil about to climb the mountain. Ascetic, pupil, hard stone, eternal theme of the sensual east. The heroic cry in the midst of despair. But no, I am wrong, the east has its solutions always and therefore knows nothing of tragedy. It is we, not the east, that must raise the heroic cry. (*DWL* 8)

IMITATED FROM THE JAPANESE **340**

This poem was written towards the end of December 1936 (see *DWL*, 116) ; the final version was dated 30 October 1937. It first appeared in *NP*.

A letter Yeats wrote to Dorothy Wellesley in December 1936 records the writing of the poem and includes a version slightly differing from that printed in *New Poems*: 'I have been in bed unable to do anything but sleep, yesterday I got up for the first time. I made this poem out of a prose translation of a Japanese Hokku in praise of Spring' (*DWL* 116).

340 SWEET DANCER

This poem was written in January 1937 and first appeared in *LM* (April 1938).

1 *The girl*: Margot Collis, who wrote under the name Margot Ruddock. Yeats wrote an Introduction to a small volume of her verse, *The Lemon Tree* (1937). She took part in some broadcasts of poetry arranged by Yeats in 1937. She is the subject of 'A Crazed Girl' (*CP* 348). Yeats wrote an account of this happening to Mrs Shakespear in a letter of 22 May 1936:

> The girl who is quite a beautiful person came here seven or eight days ago. She walked in at 6.30, her luggage in her hand and, when she had been given breakfast, said she had come to find out if her verse was any good. I had known her for some years and had told her to stop writing as her technique was getting worse. I was amazed by the tragic magnificence of some fragments and said so. She went out in pouring rain, thought, as she said afterwards, that if she killed herself her verse would live instead of her. Went to the shore to jump in, then thought that she loved life and began to dance. She went to the lodging house where Shri Purohit Swami was, to sleep. She was wet through, so Swami gave her some of his clothes; she had no money, he gave her some. Next day she went to Barcelona and there went mad, climbing out of a window, falling through a baker's roof, breaking a kneecap, hiding in a ship's hold, singing her own poems most of the time. The British consul in Barcelona appealed to me, so George and I went there, found her with recovered sanity sitting up in bed at a clinic writing an account of her madness. It was impossible to get adequate money out of her family, so I accepted financial responsibility and she was despatched to England and now I won't be able to afford new clothes for a year. When her husband wrote it had not been to send

money, but to congratulate her on the magnificent publicity. The paragraph you saw is certainly his work. Will she stay sane? it is impossible to know.

When I am in London I shall probably hide because the husband may send me journalists and because I want to keep at a distance from a tragedy where I can be no further help. (L 856)

THE THREE BUSHES   341

This poem was written in July 1936 and first appeared in *LM* (Jan. 1937). It derived from a ballad of Dorothy Wellesley's which Yeats, in Kathleen Raine's words, 'appropriated, worked upon and published as "The Three Bushes" and its accompanying songs'. The story of the poem's elaboration can be read in the poet's correspondence with Dorothy Wellesley:

Riversdale, July 2nd, 1936

. . . I am longing to read your ballad. I will not send you mine until yours is finished.

Yours with love and affection,

W. B. Yeats.

P.S. Just come.

My dear,

Here you have a masterpiece. (I have just put in the rhymes, made it a ballad.)

I

She sent her maid unto the man
   That would her leman be
'O Psyche mimic me at love
   With him I will not lie
'Tis sweetly done, 'tis easy done
   So child make love for me'.

II

'Why will you never meet the dawn,
   Nor light the torch my child?'
Said lover to the serving maid
   'Lie down, lie down you are wild,
O you are wild for love of me
   And I with love am wild'.

III

The black death came or another death
  And took the lady and lord,
The serving maid, the sewing maid
  Sat down to hem the shroud.
'O all goes well, O all goes well
  And I can sing it aloud'.

IV

She that did what she was bid
  Sang to the feather stitch,
'What of the man and the lady
  No matter which is which,
All goes well with a man in the dark,
  And well with the feather stitch'.

This is far better than my laboured livelier verses. This is
complete, lovely, lucky, born out of itself, or born out of
nothing. My blessing upon you and it.

Riversdale,
[July 10, 1936]
Friday.

My dear Dorothy,
  Here is another version of second & third stanzas. I start
changing things because the rhyme of 'lord' & 'loud' etc. is
not admissible in any prosody, then went on to the rest.
Yrs,
W. B. Yeats.

'I go if that candle is lit'
'Lie down, lie down you are wild'
'O you are wild for love of me
And I with love am wild'
'I came to lie with a man in the dark'
'Lie down again dear child'

or

But the black death took the lady & lord
'I sew but what I am bid
And all goes well O all goes well'
But why does she sing so loud
The serving maid, the sewing maid
She that hems the shroud.

446

Penns in the Rocks,
July 14.

My dear W. B.,

I send the revised version of the Ballad, and except for a minor change here or there I regard it as written. Have added lines to fit an air.

May I have yours now? I long to see it.

Loving

D.

P.S. I like my ballad; anyway for the moment.

Riversdale,
[A] Tuesday [in July, 1936]

I have added 'The Three Bushes', etc.

My dear Dorothy,

I send to you what seems to me a better version of the little poem. There is no reason why you should not write a separate poem on the Rose Bushes or rather put what you have written into ballad rhyme. Forgive me for my work on the present poem. I thought from what you wrote that you meant to leave it un-rhymed & I wanted to prove you wrong. Perhaps it will go well with the 'Street Corner Songs' — it has their mood. I have recovered from the shock of your archaic modernity, which for a moment made me lose faith in myself. I now like my long ballad of the Three Bushes again. I have written two other poems on the same theme. I will send all as soon as I can. I think them among my best things. . . .

Poem by Dorothy Wellesley [the footnote reads 'A second version, by W. B. Y.]

I

She sent her sewing girl to the man
That would her leman be
'O Psyche mimic me at love
With him I will not lie
'Tis sweetly done, 'tis easy done
So child make love for me.'

II

'I go, should you light a candle'
'Lie down, lie down you are wild,

O you are wild for love of me
And I with love am wild'
'I came to lie with a man in the dark'
'Lie down again, dear child.'

III

But the black death took the lord & the lady
'Who is singing so loud'
'A sewing girl, a sewing girl
That sings hemming a shroud
'All goes well, O all goes well
And all that I did she bid.'

IV

High up lady, or sewing girl
What does it matter which !
Has found it sweet to lie in the dark
Nor cared who made the match ;
O all goes well in the dark with a man
And well with the feather stitch !

THE THREE BUSHES
(By W. B. Y.)

I

'Man's love that lacks its proper food
None can rely upon
And could you sing no more of love
Your genius would be gone
And could that happen what were you
But a starving man'
　　O my dear, O my dear.

2

'Light no candles in your room'
That lovely lady said
'When twelve o'clock is sounding
I shall creep into your bed
But if I saw myself creep in
I think I should drop dead'
　　O my dear, O my dear.

3

'I love a man in secret
Dear chambermaid,' said she.
'I know that I must drop down dead
If he stop loving me,
Yet what could I but drop down dead
If I lost my chastity ?'
  O my dear, O my dear.

4

'So you must lie beside him
And let him think me there
Maybe we are all the same
Where no candles are,
Maybe we are all the same
When the body's bare.'
  O my dear, O my dear.

5

'No, not another song' said he
'Because my lady came
'A year ago for the first time
At midnight to my room
And I must lie between the sheets
    the clock[1]
When bells[1] begin to boom'
  O my dear, O my dear.

6

'A laughing, crying, sacred song
A leching song' said they.
Did ever man hear such a song ?
No not before that day.
Did ever man ride such a race ?
Not till he rode away.
  O my dear, O my dear.

7

But when his horse had put its hoof
Into a rabbit hole,
He dropped upon his head and died
His lady that saw it all

[1] These are alternative readings.—D.W.

Dropped and died thereon for she
Loved him with her soul.
  O my dear, O my dear.

8

The chambermaid lived on and took
Their graves into her charge
And there two bushes planted,
That when they had grown large
Seemed sprung from but a single root
So did their roses merge.
  O my dear, O my dear.

9

When she was old and dying
The priest came where she was
She made a full confession
Long looked he in her face,
And O he was a good man
And understood her case.
  O my dear, O my dear.

10

He bade them take and bury her
Beside her lady's man
And set a rose tree on her grave
And now none living can
When they have plucked a rose there
Know where its roots began.
  O my dear, O my dear.

THE LADY TO HER CHAMBERMAID
(By W. B. Y.)

What manner of man is coming
To lie between your feet ?

What matter we are but women ;
Wash, make your body sweet,

I shall find a perfume
To scatter on the sheet.

  The Lord have mercy on us.

He shall love my soul as though
Body were not all

He shall love your body
Untroubled by the soul

Love crams his two divisions
Yet keeps his substance whole

  The Lord have mercy on us.

Soul must learn a love that is
Proper to my breast.

Limbs a love in common
With every noble beast

If soul may look and body touch
Which is the more blest ?

  The Lord have mercy on us.

II

When you and my true lover meet
And he plays tunes between your feet,

If you dare abuse the soul,
Or think the body is the whole

I must, that am his daylight lady,
Outrageously abuse the body ;

Swear that he shall never stray
From either neither night and day,

That I may hear, if we should kiss,
That contrapuntal serpent hiss,

You, should hand explore a thigh,
All the labouring heaven sigh.

                    Riversdale,
                         [postmark
                       July 18, 1936]
                         Thursday.

My dear Dorothy,
    You have got me down to fundamental rock. I cannot
say the good is bad or the bad good, even though the good

is by my bitterest enemy, the bad by my dearest friend. When I got your first sketch I went down stairs humming over the opening stanzas, getting the rhymes regular & said to some-body 'I have something here that will not die'. Yet what you send me is bad. What has the beginning to do with the end ? 'With him I will not lie' can only mean (I thought it a masterly simplification) left unqualified that she is not in love with the man, that she does not want him at all. Why then should she in her talk with the briar lament that he was never hers. Why should this be 'truth after death'. Then why should the fact that she never gave herself cause the squire to lose not the lady but Psyche. Then in the last stanza I do not understand why Psyche has a living heart & why she can rise & deck their graves. Of course you know why, but it is not in the poem.

Then look through any old book of ballads & you will find that they have all perfectly regular rhyme schemes.

'O my dear, O my dear'

W. B. Y.

Perhaps your mind is meditative not narrative. I am putting your little poem with its music in one number with my ballad.

Penns in the Rocks,
July.

My dear W. B.

I have this minute received your letter, slanging my 'ballad'. I take your points as they come.

1. It is not obvious that the lady was a minx, a demi-vierge, an 'allumeuse', leading the young man on, letting him down ? A mental baggage, a jade, hussy, slut, demirep, and so on ?

2. *Argument.* So she left it to her maid, when it came to grips.

3. You say why then when the rose tells her the truth does she mind ? Because she, like all the women described above, regrets what she never knew she wanted.

4. The squire of course minded. He had been cheated. (Psyche is merely a symbol.) And he lamented after death. It disturbed his sleep.

5. Why has Psyche a 'living heart' ? Because she loved the man and got what she wanted, and even the bitter truth after death could not destroy her memories. So she rose to deck all their graves.

6. Now as to technical errors about riming ballads. I hadn't attempted a true ballad. Had tried to graft a modern

form upon the skeleton of the old. That is all. I don't
believe in 'going back' in any sense, but this was an experi-
ment. The modern mind cannot perhaps avoid short cuts,
the assumption being that the reader has jumped to it.

I thought your verses very beautiful. Some I thought as
fine as anything you have done. All yesterday I was in
despair about the Muse.

Will you send back that false ballad? Just stick it into an
envelope. I might rewrite it or not. There is something false
in any case about archaic modernity.

Yrs, with affection,

D.

PS. Have you kept the first version of my 'ballad'? I destroyed mine. You called it a 'masterpiece' in your letter of
that date, a fortnight or so ago. I was certainly astonished
at your praise. Could I have that version back too?

Riversdale,

July 21st, 1936.

Dear Lady Dorothy,

I enclose your first draft, which does not differ much from
the second. When I read it I think I only glanced at the end
about the thorntree. I thought that you had put it in because
it was part of the story, and would as a matter of course leave
it out. The first part surprised me, the new point of view and
the absence of rhyme. Just as I thought you would leave
out the end, so I was certain you either intended or could be
persuaded to add rhyme. I ended the poem at 'Sang sewing
maid to shroud'. In those first four verses I found something that had never been sung. The maid who had seemed
'wild with love' was able to 'sing aloud' as she hemmed the
shroud. 'All goes well, Oh all goes well, No matter who she
be, All in the dark unto a man' (I read this to mean 'in the dark
with a man'). She was gay. She was without grief. ——
said once to George Moore 'I wish I had a slave to do this
for me. I would not have to think of him afterwards.' Your
sewing maid gets the same result by being a slave — she had
not to think of him afterwards. He was merely a man in the
dark. In my excitement I began using my acquired skill to
make your meaning plainer than you had made it. I sent
you a first version with rhymes — I thought you would use
it as a quarry for rhyme. Then against my first intention I
sent you what I thought a finished version.

Regular rhyme is needed in this kind of work. The swing of the sentence makes the reader expect it. 'Said lover to the serving maid', ''Tis sweetly done, 'tis easy done' and so on are ballad cadences, and then the six line stanzas suggest ballad stanzas. There is another reason. In narrative verse we want to concentrate the attention on the fact or the story, not on the form. The form must be present as something we all accept — 'the fundamental sing-song'. I do not know a single example of good narrative where the rhyme scheme is varied . . .

. . . Ah my dear how it added to my excitement when I re-made that poem of yours to know it was your poem. I re-made you and myself into a single being. We triumphed over each other and I thought of *The Turtle and the Phoenix*. (*DWL* 69–82)

7 *O my dear, O my dear* : cf. the refrain 'O my dear, my dear' in an untitled poem (*VE* 778) about which Yeats wrote 'one sometimes has need of more lines of the little song, and I have put into English rhyme three of the many verses of a Gaelic ballad' (*CW* iv)

342 55 *Loved him with her soul* : cf. the lines in 'The Lady's First Song' (*CP* 343)

> What hurts the soul
> My soul adores

343 THE LADY'S FIRST SONG

This was written by 20 November 1936 and first appeared in *NP*.
  Yeats wrote of it as 'not in itself very good but it will heighten the drama' [of 'The Three Bushes'] (*DWL* 105).

344 11 *No better than a beast* : cf. 'A Last Confession' (*CP* 313) :

> And laughed upon his breast to think
> Beast gave beast as much.

344 THE LADY'S SECOND SONG

This poem was written in July 1936 and first appeared in *NP*. This poem is quoted in early form in the letters between Yeats and Dorothy Wellesley.   See notes (pp. 445ff.) on 'The Three Bushes' (*CP* 341).

7   *The Lord have mercy on us* :   Henn (*LT* 332) points out that this liturgical refrain 'not only throws forward to the Chambermaid's final confession to the priest, but is a counterpointed gesture, as by some bystander, on the "heresy" that the Lady propounds'.

THE LADY'S THIRD SONG   **345**

This poem was written in July 1936 and first appeared in *NP*.

10   *A contrapuntal serpent* :   a symbol of the Fall and hence, presumably, sex ; contrapuntal because of the opposition of the soul–body conflict.

THE LOVER'S SONG   **345**

This poem was written on 9 November 1936 and first appeared in *NP*.

Yeats wrote on 9 November 1936 to Dorothy Wellesley

After I had written to you I tried to find better words to explain what I meant by the touch from behind the curtain. This morning, this came. [The poem is then quoted].   It is *Matrix* again but air not earth.   In Fragonard's 'Cup of Life' the young man is not in his first youth, his face is lined with thought & that makes that picture too mysterious — a double thirst.   (*DWL* 102)

He had written to her on 8 November 1936

On the other wall are drawings, paintings or photographs of paintings of friends & relatives, & three reproductions of pictures, Botticelli's 'Spring', Gustave Moreau's 'Women and Unicorns', Fragonard's 'Cup of Life', a beautiful young man and girl running with eager lips towards a cup held towards them by a winged form.   The first & last sense, & the second mystery — the mystery that touches the genitals, a blurred touch through a curtain. . . .   (*DWL* 100)

THE CHAMBERMAID'S FIRST SONG   **345**

This poem was written in November 1936 and first appeared in *NP*.

346 10 *Weak as a worm* : cf. Yeats's letters of 15, 20 and 28 November 1936 to Dorothy Wellesley enclosing this poem and 'The Chambermaid's Second Song' (*CP* 346). In reply to Dorothy Wellesley's letter of 25 November 1936 (cf. *DWL* 103–8) protesting against the worm imagery Yeats changed the adjectives in the poems and wrote :

> The 'worm' is right, its repulsiveness is right — so are the adjectives — 'dull', 'limp', 'thin', 'bare', all suggested by the naked body of the man & taken with the worm by that body abject and helpless. All suggest her detachment, her 'cold breast', her motherlike prayer. (*DWL* 108)

He had used the image earlier in 'The Phases of the Moon' (*CP* 183), 'helpless as a worm'.

346 THE CHAMBERMAID'S SECOND SONG

This poem was written in November 1936 and first appeared in *NP*. See notes (pp. 455–6) on 'The Chambermaid's first Song' (*CP* 345).

346 AN ACRE OF GRASS

This poem was written in November 1936 and first appeared in *Atlantic Monthly* and *LM* (April 1938).

2 *An acre of green grass* : Yeats described his new residence, Riversdale, Rathfarnham, Co. Dublin, in letters to Olivia Shakespear in the summer of 1932 : 'There apple trees, cherry trees, roses, smooth lawns and no long climb upstairs (*L* 798) . . . 'I shall have a big old fruit garden all to myself — the study opens into it and it is shut off from the flower garden and the croquet and tennis lawns and from the bowling-green' (*L* 799).

5 *an old house* : Riversdale, which Yeats described in a letter of 8 July 1932 to Mrs Shakespear as leased 'for but thirteen years but that will see me out of life. . . . At any rate the home will be there while the children are being educated and making friends' (*L* 799)

7 *My temptation is quiet* : cf. a passage in a letter to Mrs Shakespear of 25 July 1932 :

I am writing in my new study — sometimes I go out of the glass-door into the fruit garden to share the gooseberries with the bullfinches. I can hear the workmen putting in the electric bells; through the window to my left I can see pergolas covered with roses. At first I was unhappy, for everything made me remember the great rooms and the great trees of Coole, my home for nearly forty years, but now that the pictures are up I feel more content. This little creeper-covered farm-house might be in a Calvert woodcut, and what could be more suitable for one's last decade? George's fine taste has made the inside almost as beautiful as the garden which has some fame among gardeners. (*L* 799)

8   *at life's end*: Yeats had anticipated this stanza — and this situation — in an essay written in February 1917:

A poet, when he is growing old, will ask himself if he cannot keep his mask and his vision without new bitterness, new disappointment. Could he if he would, knowing how frail his vigour from youth up, copy Landor who lived loving and hating, ridiculous and unconquered, into extreme old age, all lost but the favour of his Muses?

> The Mother of the Muses, we are taught
> Is Memory; she has left me; they remain,
> And shake my shoulder, urging me to sing.

Surely, he may think, now that I have found vision and mask I need not suffer any longer. He will buy perhaps some small old house, where, like Ariosto, he can dig his garden, and think that in the return of birds and leaves, or moon and sun, and in the evening flight of the rooks he may discover rhythm and pattern like those in sleep and so never awake out of vision. Then he will remember Wordsworth withering into eighty years, honoured and empty-witted, and climb to some waste room and find, forgotten there by youth, some bitter crust. (*M* 342)

11   *its rag and bone*: cf. 'The Circus Animals' Desertion' (*CP* 391)

> Old kettles, old bottles, and a broken can,
> Old iron, old bones, old rags, . . .

and

> the foul rag-and-bone shop of the heart.

13   *an old man's frenzy*: this may draw on Nietzsche's quotation,   **347**
The Dawn of Day, 21, of Plato's remark that 'All the greatest

benefits of Greece have sprung from madness'. Yeats was re-reading Nietzsche in 1936–7.

19   *Michael Angelo* :   Michelangelo Buonarroti (1475–1564), Italian sculptor, painter and poet.   His patron was Lorenzo de Medici ; his main works include the statue of David (begun 1501), the ceiling of the Sistine Chapel at Rome (1508–12) and the fresco of the Last Judgement on the east wall of the Sistine Chapel (1535–41). Cf. 'Under Ben Bulben' IV (*CP* 399).

20–2   *. . . pierce the clouds,*
          Or inspired by frenzy
          Shake the dead. . . . :   a contented easy old age would lead to the forgetfulness of later generations.   A passage in Nietzsche (*The Dawn of Day*, 369) casts light on this ambition of Yeats's to avoid easy content :

> At this time, too, as the result of the love which all weary and old people feel for enjoyment, such men as those I am speaking of wish to enjoy the results of their thinking instead of again testing them and scattering the seeds abroad once more.   This leads them to make their thoughts palatable and enjoyable, and to take away dryness, coldness, and want of flavour ; and thus it comes about that the old thinker appar-ently raises himself above his life's work, while in reality he spoils it by infusing into it a certain amount of fantasy, sweetness, flavour, poetic mists, and mystic lights.   This is how Plato ended, as did also that great and honest Frenchman August Comte. . . .

24   *An old man's eagle mind* :   this may owe something to Nietzsche's view of genius, *The Dawn of Day*, 347 :

> We have the best reason for speaking of 'genius' in men — for example, Plato, Spinoza, and Goethe — whose minds appear to be but loosely linked to their character and tem-perament, like winged beings which easily separate them-selves from them, and then rise far above them.

347   WHAT THEN ?

This poem was probably written in 1936 ; it first appeared in *The Erasmian* (April 1937).

Yeats described the poem in a letter to Edith Shackleton Heald as 'a melancholy biographical poem' (*L* 895). This poem, like 'An Acre of Grass' (*CP* 346) was inspired by Yeats's re-reading of Nietzsche, the refrain of 'What then?' is similar to Nietzsche's conclusion of *The Dawn of Day*, which is headed 'We Aeronauts of the Intellect':

> All those daring birds that soar far and ever farther into space, will somewhere or other be certain to find themselves unable to continue their flight and they will perch on a mast or some narrow ledge — and they will be grateful even for this miserable accommodation! But who could conclude from this that there was not an endless free space stretching far in front of them, and that they had flown as far as they possibly could? In the end, however, all our great teachers and predecessors have come to a standstill, and it is by no means in the noblest or most graceful attitude that their weariness has brought them to a pause: the same thing will happen to you and me! but what does this matter to either of us? *Other birds will fly farther!* Our minds and hopes vie with them far out and on high; they rise far above our heads and our failures, and from this height they look far into the distant horizon and see hundreds of birds much more powerful than we are, striving whither we ourselves have also striven, and where all is sea, sea, and nothing but sea!
>
> And where then are we aiming at? Do we wish to cross the sea? whither does this overpowering passion urge us, this passion which we value more highly than any other delight? Why do we fly precisely in this direction, where all the suns of humanity have hitherto set? Is it possible that people may one day say of us that we also steered westward, hoping to reach India — but that it was our fate to be wrecked on the infinite? Or, my brethren? or — ?

1 *chosen comrades thought at school*: Yeats went to a dame school in Sligo, next to the Godolphin School, Hammersmith, and then to the High School, Dublin, an Erasmus Smith foundation. *The Erasmian*, in which this poem first appeared, is its school magazine. An article in it by 'John Eglinton' [W. K. Magee], who was there with Yeats, describes the nature of the school in the eighteen-seventies and eighties. See 'Yeats at the High School', *Erasmian*, xxx (June 1939). Charles Johnston would have been one of his closest friends. See notes (pp. 7–8) on 'The Indian upon God' (*CP* 14).

5 *Plato's ghost* : Plato may have been suggested by the passage in Nietzsche quoted in note (p. 458) on line 24, 'An Acre of Grass' (*CP* 346).

12 *A small old house* : Riversdale, Rathfarnham, Co. Dublin. See notes (pp. 456–7) on 'An Acre of Grass' (*CP* 346).

348 BEAUTIFUL LOFTY THINGS

This poem's date of composition is not known, though it was probably written in 1937 (in 'A General Introduction for my Work', written in 1937, Yeats mentions O'Leary, O'Grady, and Lady Gregory in 'II Subject Matter' in ways which are complementary to the poem. See *E & I* 510–16.) It first appeared in *NP*.

1 *O'Leary's noble head* : Yeats called O'Leary 'the handsomest old man' he had ever seen (*A* 94). See notes (p. 129) on 'September 1913' (*CP* 120) for information on O'Leary.

2–4 *My father* : John Butler Yeats (1839–1922). For a brief account of his life see Jeffares, 'John Butler Yeats' (*IER* 24–47). He spoke at the debate in the Abbey Theatre on the issues arising out of the riots about Synge's *The Playboy of the Western World* in 1907: 'No man of all literary Dublin dared show his face but my own father . . .' (*A* 483). The account of the incident given by J. B. Yeats is no less vivid than that given by his son in the poem. He wrote to a friend:

> Of course I did not make a speech in favour of patricide. How could I? Here is what I said. I began with some information about Synge which interested my listeners and then : 'Of course I know Ireland is an island of Saints, but thank God it is also an island of sinners — only unfortunately in this Country people cannot live or die except behind a curtain of deceit.' At this point the chairman and my son both called out, 'Time's up, Time's up.' I saw the lifted sign and like the devil in *Paradise Lost* I fled. The papers next morning said I was howled down. It was worse, I was pulled down. . . . The sentence about the curtain of deceit flashed on my mind at the moment, and was a good sentence, but manifestly a blunder, although I did enjoy it. . . . (*LTHS* 214).

5 *Standish O'Grady* : (1846–1928) an Irish historian and novelist,
author of *The History of Ireland* — *The Heroic Period* (1878), which
had an important influence on the Irish Renaissance. This event
occurred at a dinner given by T. P. Gill, leader writer of the *Daily
Express* in Dublin, in honour of Edward Martyn and Yeats.

The dinner was described by George Moore in *Ave* (1947)
102 ff., and Yeats also dealt with it in *DP* :

> Towards the end of the evening, when everybody was more
> or less drunk, O'Grady spoke. He was very drunk, but
> neither his voice nor his manner showed it. I had never
> heard him speak, and at first he reminded me of Cardinal
> Manning. There was the same simplicity, the same gentle-
> ness. He stood between two tables, touching one or the
> other for support, and said in a low penetrating voice : 'We
> have now a literary movement, it is not very important ; it
> will be followed by a political movement, that will not be
> very important ; then must come a military movement, that
> will be important indeed'. Tyrrell, Professor of Greek in
> Trinity College, known to scholars for his share in the
> Tyrrell–Purser edition of Cicero's Letters, a Unionist, but
> very drunk, led the applause. Then O'Grady described the
> Boy Scout Act, which had just passed, urged the landlords
> of Ireland to avail themselves of that Act and drill the sons
> of their tenants — 'paying but little attention to the age
> limit' — then, pointing to where he supposed England to be,
> they must bid them 'march to the conquest of that decadent
> nation'. I knew what was in his mind. England was deca-
> dent because, democratic and so without fixed principles, it
> had used Irish landlords, his own ancestors or living relatives,
> as its garrison, and later left them deserted among their
> enemies. Tyrrell, understanding nothing but the sweetness
> of that voice, the nobility of that gesture, continued to lead
> the applause. (*A* 423–4)

O'Grady's influence predominated, Yeats recorded, when modern
Irish literature began :

> He could delight us with an extravagance we were too critical
> to share ; a day will come, he said, when Slieve-na-mon will
> be more famous than Olympus ; yet he was no Nationalist
> as we understood the word, but in rebellion, as he was fond
> of explaining, against the House of Commons, not against
> the King. (*E & I* 512).

461

This was an Irish attitude of mind which began with Molyneux's *Case of Ireland Stated* (1691), which argued for the independence of the Irish parliament, and asserted its loyalty to the King, not to the House of Commons in England.

7   *Augusta Gregory* : Lady Gregory told Yeats of this particular threat to her life which occurred in 'the troubles' when she was about seventy. Yeats chose 'eightieth' arbitrarily. She used to sit writing letters before dinner regularly from six to seven every evening when she was at Coole Park. The movement from Standish O'Grady to Lady Gregory is paralleled in 'A General Introduction to my Work' where after describing Standish O'Grady and his cousin as representing the old Irish landowning aristocracy, Yeats went on to describe Lady Gregory as another member of that order, though he distinguished between O'Grady's style, founded on Carlyle, and Lady Gregory's, on the Anglo-Irish dialect of her neighbourhood.

10   *Maud Gonne* : this memory goes back to their walks at Howth (pronounced Hō-th) where Yeats first proposed to her. There are some lyric descriptions of its scenery in *SQ*.

11   *Pallas Athene* : cf. the passage in *A* 123 where 'the Virgilian commendation "She walks like a goddess" [was] made for her alone'. Cf. also 'Her beauty, backed by her great stature . . . her face, like the face of some Greek statue' (*A* 264) and cf. 'The Arrow' (*CP* 85).

348   A CRAZED GIRL

This poem was written at Barcelona in May 1936 and first appeared in *The Lemon Tree* (1937), a book of Margot Ruddock's poems for which Yeats wrote an Introduction. The poem was entitled 'At Barcelona' in that volume.

1   *That crazed girl* : Margot Collis [Ruddock]. See notes (p. 444) on 'Sweet Dancer' (*CP* 340).

349   TO DOROTHY WELLESLEY

This poem was written in August 1936 and first appeared with the title 'To a Friend' in *LM* (March 1938) and *N* (12 March 1938).

7 (*For since the horizon's bought strange dogs are still*): a comma
between 'bought' and 'strange' would clarify the sense. The
original version, included in a letter from Yeats written to Dorothy
Wellesley on 1 August 1936, read 'For since you bought the horizon all is still'. A letter from Dorothy Wellesley dated 4 March
1936 explains the line : 'I have saved by twenty-four hours this
little corner of Sussex from a town of scarlet bungalows. So I
now own the lovely ridge opposite and feel I have done something for "Deserted House"' (*DWL* 53).
In a footnote Dorothy Wellesley remarked : 'I have never understood, however, what he meant by the last half of the line, unless
he had a fantastic idea that after buying the few acres I evicted
the people who lived on it, together with their dogs !' But Yeats
was probably using the present tense as a future. No newcomers'
'strange' dogs would make a noise.

10 *a Great Dane* : Brutus, Dorothy Wellesley's dog, which she
described :

> Brutus himself had a great majesty, both of form and con-
> duct, and Yeats had observed it. When he seemed too tired
> to reach a garden seat, the three of us would walk abreast,
> Yeats's hand and part of his great weight supported on my
> right shoulder, while my left hand and shoulder was supported
> by the great dog. I was always afraid of a landslide, but the
> great hound pacing slowly beside me never let me down.
> The seat was reached, the end achieved, and the tremendous
> Dane would settle down and turn into a piece of black and
> white marble until, our conversation ended, he would help
> us back again to the house. (*DWL* 145–6)

16 *The Proud Furies* : Yeats's letter to Dorothy Wellesley explains **350**
what he meant the poem to achieve :

> We have all something within ourselves to batter down and
> get our power from this fighting. I have never 'produced'
> a play in verse without showing the actors that the passion
> of the verse comes from the fact that the speakers are holding
> down violence or madness — 'down Hysterica passio'. All
> depends on the completeness of the holding down, on the
> stirring of the beast underneath. Even my poem 'To D. W.'
> should give this impression. The moon, the moonless night,

the dark velvet, the sensual silence, the silent room and the violent bright Furies. Without this conflict we have no passion only sentiment and thought. . . .

. . . About the conflict in 'To D. W.', I did not plan it deliberately. That conflict is deep in my subconsciousness, perhaps in everybody's. I dream of clear water, perhaps two or three times (the moon of the poem), then come erotic dreams. Then for weeks perhaps I write poetry with sex for theme. Then comes the reversal — it came when I was young with some dream or some vision between waking and sleep with a flame in it. Then for weeks I get a symbolism like that in my Byzantium poem or in 'To D. W.' with flame for theme. All this may come from the chance that when I was a young man I was accustomed to a Kabalistic ceremony where there were two pillars, one symbolic of water and one of fire. The fire mark is $\triangle$, the water mark is $\triangledown$, these are combined to make Solomon's seal $\Large\hexagon$. The water is sensation, peace, night, silence, indolence ; the fire is passion, tension, day, music, energy. (*DWL* 86–7)

350 THE CURSE OF CROMWELL

This poem was written between November 1936 and 8 January 1937 and first appeared in *A Broadside*, No. 8 (New Series) (Aug. 1937).

Yeats wrote on 8 January 1937 to Dorothy Wellesley 'At this moment I am expressing my rage against the intelligentsia by writing about Oliver Cromwell who was the Lennin of his day — I speak through the mouth of some wandering peasant poet in Ireland' (*DWL* 119).

3 *beaten into the clay* : cf. section v of 'Under Ben Bulben' (*CP* 400) :

> . . . the lords and ladies gay
> That were beaten into the clay

The phrase comes, according to G. B. Saul (*PYP* 176) from Frank O'Connor's translation, *Kilcash* : 'The earls, the lady, the people beaten into the clay.'

11 *He that's mounting up* : cf. 'The Gyres' (*CP* 337). This is a reference to the ebb and flow of civilisations.

18   *the Spartan boy's* : a Spartan boy stole a fox and when appre-
hended let it gnaw him to death under his clothes rather than be
detected in crime.   The story comes from Plutarch, *Lycurgus*.

19   *things both can and cannot be* : this line may derive from Shelley,   351
The Sensitive Plant, 3rd stanza of 'Conclusion' :
>   Where nothing is but all things seem . . .

25   *great house* : cf. Yeats's play *Purgatory*, and notes on 'Crazy
Jane on God' (*CP* 293) with its 'uninhabited, ruinous' house.

32   *What is there left to say* : cf. 'Nineteen Hundred and Nineteen' (*CP* 232), 'What more is there to say ?'

ROGER CASEMENT

This poem was written in November 1936 (the MS. is dated   351
'October/November 1936') and first appeared in the *Irish Press*
(2 Feb. 1937).   A revised version appeared in the *Irish Press* (12
Feb. 1937) ; see notes on line 17.   The ballad was meant to be
sung to the tune of 'The Glen of Aherlow'.

Yeats wrote to Ethel Mannin on 15 November 1936 that he
was in a rage :

> I have just got a book published by the Talbot Press called
> *The Forged Casement Diaries*. It is by a Dr Maloney I knew
> in New York and he has spent years collecting evidence.   He
> has proved that the diaries, supposed to prove Casement 'a
> Degenerate' and successfully used to prevent an agitation for
> his reprieve, were forged.   Casement was not a very able man
> but he was gallant and unselfish, and had surely his right to
> leave what he would have considered an unsullied name.   I
> long to break my rule against politics and call these men
> criminals but I must not.   Perhaps a verse may come to me,
> now or a year hence.   I have lately written a song in defence of
> Parnell (about love and marriage less foul lies were circulated),
> a drinking song to a popular tune and will have it sung from
> the Abbey stage at Xmas.   All my life it has been hard to keep
> from action, as I wrote when a boy, — 'to be not of the
> things I dream.'   (*L* 867–8)

Yeats's letters to Dorothy Wellesley provide a background to this poem and 'The Ghost of Roger Casement' (*CP* 352). He wrote on 28 November 1936

. . . I sent off a ferocious ballad written to a popular tune, to a newspaper. It is on 'The Forged Diaries of Roger Casement' a book published here, & denounces by name —— and —— for their share in abetting the forgeries. I shall not be happy until I hear that it is sung by Irish undergraduates at Oxford. I wrote to the editor saying I had not hitherto sent him a poem because almost [all] my poems were unsuitable because they came out of rage or lust. (*DWL* 107)

The postscript read :

You will not find the four line stanza 'too easy' if you struggle to make your spirit at once natural & imaginative. My 'Casement' is better written than my 'Parnell' because I passed things when I had to find three rhymes & did not pass when I had to find two.

On 4 December he wrote :

I could not stop that ballad if I would, people have copies, & I don't want to. —— belongs to a type of man for whom I have no respect. Such men have no moral sense. They are painted cardboard manipulated by intreaguers. If he had been a man he would before circulating those charges against Casement have asked 'was the evidence shown to Casement ?' & have learned that Casement denied the charges & asked in vain to be shown the evidence. I was present when the Editor of *The Times* spoke of making the same charges in *The Times*. He did not do so, probably because of the infuriated comment of Roger Fry & myself. It was impossible to talk for five minutes to Roger Fry without finding out that he was honest. However I hate 'Leagues of Nations' & Leagues of all kinds & am not likely to be just.

[A discussion of the well-known Casement charge follows.]

But the Casement evidence was not true as we know — it was one of a number of acts of forgery committed at that time. I can only repeat words spoken to me by the old head of the Fenians [John O'Leary], years ago. 'There are things a man must not do even to save a nation.'

By the by my ballad should begin

'I say that Roger Casement
Did what he had to do
But died upon the scaffold,
But that is nothing new.'

I feel that one's verse must be as direct & natural as spoken words. The opening I sent you was not quite natural.

No 1 shall not get the ballad sung in Oxford : that was but a 'passing' thought because I happen to know a certain wild student who would have been made quite happy by the task — the idea amused me.

We will have no great popular literature until we get rid of the moral sycophants. Montaigne says that a prince must sometimes commit a crime to save his people, but if he does so he must mourn all his life. I only hate the men who do not mourn.

Forgive all this my dear, but I have told you that my poetry all comes from rage or lust. (*DWL* 108–9)

On 7 December he wrote

I am upset & full of remorse. You were quite right. I have wronged ——, though not ——. I got in a blind rage & only half read the passage that excited it. . . . All my life I have been subject to these fits of rage though thank God seldom if ever about any matter that effects myself. In this case I lost the book & trusted to memory. I am full of shame. (*DWL* 110)

On 10 December 1936 he wrote :

This post brings me a letter from an Irishwoman in England to whom I had sent the corrected Casement poem, she writes approving of what she supposes to be my hatred of England. It has shocked me for it has made me fear that you think the same. I have written to my correspondent. 'How can I hate England, owing what I do to Shakespeare, Blake & Morris. England is the only country I cannot hate.' She is an extreme revolutionist but writes 'I drank the toast of the king for the first time in my life the other day.' (*DWL* 111)

1 *Roger Casement* : Sir Roger Casement, K.C.M.G. (1864–1916), a British consular official 1895–1913, who joined the Sinn Fein movement in 1914, went to Germany to ask for armed aid, returned in a submarine in 1916 and was arrested in south-west Ireland. He was tried in London on a charge of high treason, found guilty and hanged.

Yeats wrote to Dorothy Wellesley on 8 February 1937

On Feb. 2 my wife went to Dublin shopping & was surprised at the defference everybody showed her in buses & shop.

Then she found what it was — the Casement poem was in the morning paper. Next day I was publicly thanked by the vice-president of the Executive Council, by De Valera's political secretary, by our chief antiquarian & an old revolutionist, Count Plunket, who calls my poem 'a ballad the people much needed'. De Valera's newspaper gave me a long leader saying that for generations to come my poem will pour scorn on the forgers & their backers. The only English comment is in the *Evening Standard* which points out my bad rhymes & says that after so many years it is impossible to discuss the authenticity of the diaries. (The British Government has hidden them for years). (*DWL* 126)

7   *a trick by forgery* : cf. note on line 17. Yeats meant that 'a slander based on forged diaries was spread through the world'.

352   13   *Spring Rice* : Sir Cecil Arthur Spring-Rice (1859–1918), British Ambassador to the U.S. from 1912.

17   *Come Tom and Dick, come all the troop* : in the MS. of the poem an extra stanza was inserted after line 16.

> No, no matter what the names they wear
> A dog must have his day
> And whether a man be rich or poor
> He takes the Devil's pay.

Line 17 originally ran 'Come Alfred Noyes and all the troop' which he altered to 'Come Gilbert Murray, Alfred Noyes'. The first version in the *Irish Press* (2 Feb. 1937) ran 'Come Alfred Noyes and all the troop' but was altered to 'No matter what the names they wear !' in a revised version of the ballad which accompanied Yeats's letter written after Alfred Noyes had written a disclaimer to the *Irish Press*. Yeats's letter was published in the paper on 13 February 1937 :

Dear Sir, I accept Mr Alfred Noyes' explanation and I thank him for his noble letter. I, too, think that the British Government should lay the diaries before some tribunal acceptable to Ireland and to England. He suggests that Dr G. P. Gooch, a great expert in such matters, and I should be 'associated with such an enquiry.' I have neither legal training nor training in the examination of documents, nor have I the trust of the people. But I thank him for his courtesy in suggesting my name.

I add a new version of my song. Mr Noyes' name is left out : but I repeat my accusation that a slander based on forged diaries was spread through the world and that, whatever the compulsion, 'Spring-Rice had to whisper it.' He was an honourable, able man in the ordinary affairs of life ; why then did he not ask whether the evidence had been submitted to the accused ? The British Government would have been compelled to answer.

I was dining with the wife of a Belgian Cabinet Minister after Casement's condemnation, perhaps after his execution, somebody connected with *The Times* was there ; he said they had been asked to draw attention to the diaries. I said it was infamous to blacken Casement's name with evidence that had neither been submitted to him nor examined at his trial. Presently Roger Fry, the famous art critic, came in, and the journalist repeated his statement, and Roger Fry commented with unmeasured fury. I do not remember whether *The Times* spoke of the diaries or not.

Had Spring-Rice been a free man he would have shared my indignation and that of Roger Fry. (*L* 882–3)

24 *That is in quicklime laid* : bodies of those hanged were buried in quicklime within British prisons. Casement's remains were recently returned to Ireland ; he was reburied with military honours in Arbour Hill Barracks, Dublin.

THE GHOST OF ROGER CASEMENT 352

The MS. of this poem is dated October 1936 ; it went through much rewriting and first appeared in *NP*.

This poem is complementary to 'Roger Casement'. It was meant to be sung to the tune of 'The Church's One Foundation'. Yeats wrote to Dorothy Wellesley on 21 December 1936 of the nervous strain caused by writing it (*DWL* 113). He wrote to her on 23 December 1936 :

I will send that ballad but will not be able to do so for a few days. My last typed copies went off to America on Monday & it is always difficult to get a typist who can read my writing or take my dictation. Then you may as well have the two

Casement ballads together, they are meant to support each other. I am fighting in those ballads for what I have been fighting all my life, it is our Irish fight though it has nothing to do with this or that country. Bernard Shaw fights with the same object. When somebody talks of justice, who knows that justice is accompanied by secret forgery, when an archbishop wants a man to go to the communion table, when that man says he is not spiritually fit, when we remember our age old quarrel against gold-brayed and ermine & that our ancestor Swift has gone where 'fierce indignation can lacerate his heart no more', & we go stark, staring mad.

I said when I started my movement in my 25th or 26th year 'I am going to stiffen the back-bone'. Bernard Shaw may have said the same in his youth; it has been stiffened in Ireland with results. I am an old man now & month by month my capacity & energy must slip away, so what is the use of saying that both in England & Ireland I want to stiffen the back bone of the high hearted and high-minded & the sweet hearted & sweet-minded, so that they may no longer shrink & hedge, when they face rag merchants like ——. Indeed before all I want to strengthen myself. It is not our business to reply to this & that, but to set up our love and indignation against their pity & hate — but how I run on — Forgive me. (*DWL* 115)

353 12 *A dog must have his day*: cf. note (p. 194) on line 10, 'Upon a Dying Lady' iii (*CP* 178). This phrase was originally included in the MS. of 'Roger Casement' (*CP* 351). See note (p. 468) on line 17 of that poem.

31 *I poked about a village church*: this stanza echoes Gray's 'Elegy written in a country churchyard.'

> Some village Hampden that with dauntless breast
> The little tyrant of his fields withstood,
> Some mute inglorious Milton, here may rest,
> Some Cromwell guiltless of his country's blood.

See Jeffares, 'Yeats and his methods of writing verse', *The Permanence of Yeats* (ed. Hall and Steinmann, 1950; 1961). Yeats was reading Gray at this period (*OTB* 17).

Yeats's MS. contained the following versions which he eventually discarded.

> For all that Hampden thought
> All that later Milton wrote
>
> It told of all his virtues there
> His words had been his bond
> Of such a man had Milton dreamed
> For such had Hampden planned
>
> For all that Hampden thought
> All that Milton knew
> Had blazed in heart and head
> Although John Hampden's dead.

Another variant of the last stanza described the family tomb :

> It told of all their virtues
> Their glory and estate
> And told it all in Latin
> To give it greater weight.

A contributory source for the introduction of the Casement tomb (apart from the contrast between the quicklime in which Casement was buried and the family tomb in which he might have expected to rest) was probably Thomas Davis's poem on Wolfe Tone, 'Tone's Grave', *National and Other Poems*, 78.

THE O'RAHILLY **354**

This poem was written in January 1937 and first appeared in *NP*. The original refrain was 'Praise the Proud'. The O'Rahilly was killed in the fighting in 1916.

1 *the O'Rahilly* : 'a strikingly handsome young man always dressed in a saffron kilt'. See Arnold Bax, *Farewell my Youth*, 100.

3 *a 'the'* : 'the' is a hereditary title in Ireland.

12 *Pearse and Connolly* : see notes on 'Easter 1916' (*CP* 202)

14 *the Kerry men* : the O'Rahilly was from Kerry and head of his clan.

31 *Henry Street* : a street running at right angles to O'Connell **355** Street, Dublin, beside the G.P.O.

355   COME GATHER ROUND ME, PARNELLITES

This poem was written on 8 September 1936 and first appeared in *A Broadside*, No. 1 (New Series) (Jan. 1937).

1   *Parnellites* :   those who supported Parnell after the O'Shea divorce case and the consequent split in the Irish party.   See *A* 356–7.

11   *fought the might of England* :   Parnell was leader of the Irish parliamentary party, 1880, was imprisoned 1881, threw out the Liberal government, 1885, and supported the Conservatives.   He held the balance of power at Westminster in 1886, and converted Gladstone to Home Rule.

14   *He brought it all to pass* :   Yeats is stressing the strength of Parnell's leadership.

16   *a lass* :   Mrs Kitty O'Shea.   Parnell was co-respondent in the O'Shea divorce case, 1890.   For Yeats's brief account of this see 'Modern Ireland', *Massachusetts Review* (Winter 1964), 257–9.

356   21   *Parnell was a proud man* :   cf. Yeats's account in *AV* of Parnell's passionate pride :

> . . . a follower has recorded that, after a speech that seemed brutal and callous, his hands were full of blood because he had torn them with his nails. . . . Mrs Parnell tells how upon a night of storm on Brighton Pier, and at the height of his power, he held her out over the waters and she lay still, stretched upon his two hands, knowing that if she moved, he would drown himself and her.   (*AV* (B) 124)

25   *The Bishops and the Party* :   Parnell was repudiated by Gladstone and the Irish hierarchy ;   he fought a bitter, but losing fight in 1891.   He died in Brighton in 1891.

27–8   *A husband that had sold his wife*
*   And after that betrayed* :   cf. notes on line 16, and Yeats's letter of 8 September 1936 to Dorothy Wellesley in which he commented on Henry Harrison, *Parnell Vindicated* (1931) and added :

> Mrs O'Shea was a free woman when she met Parnell, O'Shea had been paid to leave her free, and if Parnell had been able to raise £20,000 would have let himself be divorced instead

of Parnell. The Irish Catholic press had ignored his book.
It preferred to think that the Protestant had deceived the
Catholic husband. (*L* 862–3)

Yeats published his own views in 'Parnell' in *Essays 1931 to 1936*
(*E & I* 486–90).

THE WILD OLD WICKED MAN 356

This poem was written when Yeats wanted to go to India with
Lady Elizabeth Pelham. It first appeared in the *Atlantic Monthly*
and *LM* (April 1938). Cf. letters of 21 March, 1 June and 7 July
1937 in Shankar Mokashi-Punekar, *The Later Phase in the Development of W. B. Yeats* (1966), pp. 264–5.

30 *Girls down on the seashore*: this stanza probably is a youthful 357
memory. Cf. this passage in *Reveries*:

> Once when I was sailing with my cousin, the boy who was
> our crew talked of a music-hall at a neighbouring seaport,
> and how the girls there gave themselves to men, and his
> language was as extravagant as though he praised that cour-
> tesan after whom they named a city or the Queen of Sheba
> herself. Another day he wanted my cousin to sail some fifty
> miles along the coast and put in near some cottages where he
> had heard there were girls 'and we could have a great wel-
> come before us'. He pleaded with excitement (I imagine that
> his eyes shone) but hardly hoped to persuade us, and perhaps
> but played with fabulous images of life and of sex. (*A* 75)

43 *all those warty lads*: Yeats wrote on 22 May 1936 to Dorothy 358
Wellesley:

> ... I wrote to-day to Laura Riding, with whom I carry on a
> slight correspondence, that her school was too thoughtful,
> reasonable & truthful, that poets were good liars who never
> forgot that the Muses were women who liked the embrace
> of gay warty lads. I wonder if she knows that warts are
> considered by the Irish peasantry a sign of sexual power?
> Those little poems of yours are nonchalant, & nonchalance
> is declared by Castiglione essential to all true courtiers —
> so it is to warty lads & poets. (*DWL* 63)

THE GREAT DAY 358

This poem was written in January 1937 and first appeared in *LM*
(March 1938), under the title 'Fragments' which included 'Parnell'

(*CP* 359), 'What was Lost' (*CP* 359) and 'The Spur' (*CP* 359). A line which ran 'Many violent leading articles; the cannons shoot' was originally included in the MS.

359 PARNELL

This poem was written in January 1937 and first appeared in *LM* (March 1938). See note (p. 473) on 'The Great Day' (*CP* 358).

359 WHAT WAS LOST

This poem was written in January 1937 and first appeared in *LM* (March 1938). See note (p. 473) on 'The Great Day' (*CP* 358).

The poem relates to the thought of *AV* and, in particular, to a passage in Yeats's Introduction to *The Resurrection*:

> Even our best histories treat men as function. Why must I think the victorious cause the better? Why should Mommsen think the less of Cicero because Caesar beat him? I am satisfied, the Platonic Year in my head, to find but drama. I prefer that the defeated cause should be more vividly described than that which has the advertisement of victory. No battle has been finally won or lost; 'to Garret or Cellar a wheel I send'. (*E* 398)

359 THE SPUR

This poem was written on 7 October 1936, and first appeared in *LM* (March 1938). See note (p. 473) on 'The Great Day' (*CP* 358).

Yeats included this poem in a letter of 9 December 1936 to Dorothy Wellesley, calling it his 'final apology' (*DWL* 110). He had ended a letter of 4 December to her (*DWL* 109) with the remark 'Forgive all this my dear but I have told you that my poetry all comes from rage or lust.' The poem was also included in a letter to Ethel Mannin written on 11 December 1936, prefaced by the sentence 'Certain things drive me mad and I lose control of my tongue' (*L* 872).

359 A DRUNKEN MAN'S PRAISE OF SOBRIETY

The date of composition of this poem is uncertain; it first appeared in *NP*.

10   *dancing like a wave* : cf. 'The Fiddler of Dooney' lines 2 &   **360**
20, 'dance like a wave of the sea' (*CP* 82)

THE PILGRIM   **360**

The date of composition of this poem is uncertain ; it first appeared
in *A Broadside*, No. 10 (N.S.) (Oct. 1937).

6   *Lough Derg* : cf. a passage in *If I were Four-and-Twenty* :

But if I were four-and-twenty, and without rheumatism, I
should not, I think, be content with getting up performances
of French plays and with reading papers. I think I would
go — though certainly I am no Catholic and never shall be
one — upon both of our great pilgrimages, to Croagh Patrick
and to Lough Derg. Our churches have been unroofed or
stripped ; the stained glass of Saint Canice, once famous
throughout Europe, was destroyed three centuries ago, and
Christ Church looks as clean and unhistorical as a Methodist
chapel, its sculptured tombs and tablets broken up or heaped
one on t'other in the crypt ; no congregation has climbed
to the Rock of Cashel since the stout Church of Ireland bishop
took the lead roof from the Gothic church to save his legs :
but Europe has nothing older than our pilgrimages. (*E* 266–7)

7   *the Stations* : the Stations of the cross

16   *A great black ragged bird* : a passage in *If I were Four-and*   **361**
Twenty :

. . . and I would, being but four-and-twenty and a lover of
lost causes, memorialise bishops to open once again that
Lough Derg cave of vision once beset by an evil spirit in the
form of a long-legged bird with no feathers on its wings.
(*E* 267)

COLONEL MARTIN   **361**

This poem was written on 10 August 1937 and first appeared in
A Broadside, No. 12 (N.S.) (Dec. 1937). F. R. Higgins suggested
to Yeats that the refrain should be 'Lullabaloobalo'. A letter
to Edith Shackleton Heald written on 10 August 1937 deals with
the poem :

I have just finished a long ballad — seven eight-line stanzas

— on a Galway story. [There are eight in the printed version.] It has a curious pathos which I cannot define. I have known from the start what I wanted to do, and yet the idea seemed to lie below the threshold of consciousness — and still lies. There is a chorus almost without meaning, followed by concertina and whistle. (*L* 896–7)

and a letter of 13 August 1937 to Dorothy Wellesley described the poem as 'among the best things, almost the strangest thing I have written' (*DWL* 144).

Ellmann provides another version of the story, which Yeats gave in a lecture in 1910 reported by the Dublin *Evening Telegraph*:

Mr Yeats said the thing that was destroying the theatre in Ireland was the substitution of humanitarianism for artistic feeling. The business of art was the exposition of human nature in itself, making us delight in personality, in character, in emotion, in human life, when it is not troubled or persecuted by anything artificial. These things were being crushed away by all kinds of special interests. One man would spend his life in making money; another man would spend his life on a mathematical problem. Human nature should not be merely endured; it should keep its delight, its energy, and its simplicity. He believed that the countryman in Ireland, as the countryman who has kept his simplicity everywhere in the world, had kept his delight in human nature. In proof of this assertion the lecturer related a story which, he said, had been told him by a Galway shepherd, about a certain Colonel Martin, whose wife was unfaithful to him. Colonel Martin discovered his wife in the company of a wealthy neighbour. There were two revolvers on a table, but Colonel Martin did not like to take advantage of an unarmed man. He took other proceedings, and obtained two kegs of gold from the wealthy neighbour. He ordered his man, Tom, to put the kegs on the ass's back, and he went through the streets of Galway distributing the money amongst the poor. The wealthy man had men at every corner ready to attack Colonel Martin, but he could not attack a man who had been so good to the poor. At the end there was no money left, and the man, Tom, said his master would be in want before he died. And he was. That showed how the people delighted in a striking personality. It showed the mysterious love of that mysterious thing, human nature. When they could get free from the daily newspapers, from the rubbish, and get down to this rich soil, there could be a great artistic movement. (*IY* 205–6)

Torchiana (*Y & GI* 335) remarks that the poem is closer to the version in Lady Gregory's *Kiltartan History Book* (1926), and he considers the factual source is contained in the report of a case that came before Lord Kenyon at the Guildhall; this was reported in the *Connaught Telegraph* (22 Dec. 1791) and cited by S. J. Maguire, 'Notes. Martin v. Petrie', *The Galway Reader*, IV (Winter 1954), 122–3. The action was taken by Richard Martin of Dargan against John Petrie of Soho. The jury returned a verdict against Petrie and gave damages of ten thousand pounds. Torchiana mentions two accounts in the possession of the Irish Folklore Commission: James Berry, *Tales of the West. Recollections of Early Boyhood*, 72–4 and 'Tim O'Harte and Colonel Martin' in Sean Mac Giollarnáth, *Annála Beaga o Iorrus Aithneach* (1941), 197–9.

1 *The Colonel*: Richard Martin (1754–1834) was M.P. for Galway, **361** J.P. and High Sheriff of County Galway and Colonel of the Galway Volunteers. He married in 1777 and again in 1796; he was a well-known duellist. See A. E. S. Martin, *Genealogy of the Family of Martin of Ballinahinch Castle* (1890).

71 *from the seaweed*: by gathering it for selling. It is used in **364** the production of edible materials and is still spread on fields in the west of Ireland as a form of manure.

A MODEL FOR THE LAUREATE **364**

This poem was written in late July 1937 and first appeared in *NP*.

Title Laureate: Yeats wrote to Dorothy Wellesley on 26 July 1937: 'Three times I have opened the envelope to add a new version of the enclosed poem. It is the kind of thing I would have written had I been made Laureate, which is perhaps why I was not made Laureate' (*DWL* 141).

The poem was entitled 'A Marriage Ode' in this letter. It was written on King Edward VIII's abdication. Yeats had written earlier, on 21 December 1936, that he thought 'the ex-king's broadcast moving, restrained & dignified & of what I hear the Archbishop's was the reverse' (*DWL* 113). The text of the poem in the letter of 26 July 1937 differs slightly from the unpublished versions.

1 *from China to Peru*: an echo of the opening of Johnson's *The Vanity of Human Wishes*:

> Let observation with extensive view,
> Survey mankind, from China to Peru.

365 THE OLD STONE CROSS

This poem was written between April and June 1937. Yeats began it when staying with Mrs Shakespear at the Chantry House, Steyning, Sussex. It first appeared in *N* (12 March 1938) and *LM* (March 1938).

3 *A journalist makes up his lies*: cf. *OTB*, where Yeats denounced the English mind, which, 'excited by its newspaper proprietors and its schoolmasters, has turned into a bed-hot harlot' (*E* 443).

366 20 *To shuffle, grunt and groan*: Yeats's own method of chanting verse is well known. He was probably influenced by the acting of Heron Allen ('a solicitor, fiddler and popular writer on palmistry') and Florence Farr who both

read poetry for their pleasure. While they were upon the stage [of the Bedford Park Clubhouse] no one else could hold an eye or an ear. Their speech was music, the poetry acquired a nobility, a passionate austerity that made it akin for certain moments to the great poetry of the world. Heron Allen, who had never spoken in public before except to lecture upon the violin, had the wisdom to reduce his acting to a series of poses, to be the stately shepherd with not more gesture than was needed to 'twitch his mantle blue' and to let his grace be foil to Florence Farr's more impassioned delivery. When they closed their mouths, and some other player opened his, breaking up the verse to make it conversational, jerking his body or his arms that he might seem no austere poetical image but very man, I listened in raging hatred. I kept my seat with difficulty, I searched my memory for insulting phrases, I even muttered them to myself that the people about might hear. I had discovered for the first time that in the performance of all drama that depends for its effect upon beauty of language, poetical culture may be more important than professional experience. (*A* 120-1)

In the notes on *KGCT* Yeats wrote that the singer cannot sing poetry and explained how before he 'gave up the fight' he had tried to establish a style of verse speaking with the aid of Florence Farr [see notes (pp. 97-8) on 'The Players ask for a Blessing on the Psalteries and on Themselves' (*CP* 93)]:

I am not musical; I have the poet's exact time sense, only the vaguest sense of pitch; yet I get the greatest pleasure from certain combinations of singing, acting, speaking, drum, gong, flute, string, provided that some or all the words keep their natural passionate rhythm. Thirty years ago I persuaded Florence Farr, beautiful woman, incomparable elocutionist, to rediscover with the help of Arnold Dolmetsch, what seemed the ancient art of singing or speaking poetry to notes: Greek music if Greek music was, as some authorities think, 'regulated declamation.' Many people came to learn but she had only one successful pupil — I think her name was Taylor, I have not heard of her for many years — all others had the sense of pitch without the understanding of words or the understanding of words without the sense of pitch. I gave a number of lectures; Miss Farr spoke or sang to her psaltery passages from Homer, Shelley, Keats or from my own writings. When one spoke to members of the audience they seemed divided like her pupils into musicians who said that she was out of tune and well satisfied readers of poetry. I remember a famous war-correspondent saying, in an aggressive voice as he left the hall 'singing is a decadent art.' It seemed that in the twelfth century everybody had but one set of ears and that it is now possible to have two sets that cannot be pleased at the same time. I was puzzled, sometimes doubtful, but encouraged now and again when some acknowledged authority — I remember a long notice by the musical critic of the *Manchester Guardian* — said that we had discovered a great lost beauty. I, at any rate, keep among my most vivid memories a moment when, during the performance of a Greek play translated by Gilbert Murray, Florence Farr and her one pupil sang or spoke about 'the daughters of the sunset' with alternating voices; so I thought, so I still think, did the ancient world where the poets' 'I sing' seemed but literal truth, hear poetry.

When I had enough knowledge to discover some dramatic form to give her the opportunity she lacked Florence Farr had accepted a post in a Cingalese girls school that she might hide her ageing beauty. (*KGCT*)

In letters to Dorothy Wellesley he returned to his dislike of actors reading poetry :

I have no news except that I went to Richard II last night, as fine a performance [as] possible considering that the rhythm of all the great passages is abolished. The modern actor can speak to another actor, but he is incapable of revery. On the advice of Bloomsbury he has packed his soul in a bag and left it with the bar-attendant. Did Shakespeare in Richard II discover poetic revery ? (*DWL* 145)

366 THE SPIRIT MEDIUM

This poem was written at Penns in the Rocks, Dorothy Wellesley's house in Sussex, and first appeared in *NP*.

4 *Confusion of the bed* : cf. 'The Cold Heaven' (*CP* 140)

6 *Perning* : cf. notes (p. 176) on 'Shepherd and Goatherd' (*CP* 159), (p. 235) 'Demon and Beast' (*CP* 209) and (p. 256) 'Sailing to Byzantium' (*CP* 217).

7 *my body to the spade* : the refrain is a composite picture of Mrs Yeats and Dorothy Wellesley, both gardeners.

11 *Some that being unbegotten* : possibly an echo of Phase one in *AV* :

This is a supernatural incarnation, like Phase 15, because there is complete objectivity, and human life cannot be completely objective. At Phase 15 mind was completely absorbed by being, but now body is completely absorbed in its supernatural environment. The images of mind are no longer irrelevant even, for there is no longer anything to which they can be relevant, and acts can no longer be immoral or stupid, for there is no one there that can be judged. Thought and inclination, fact and object of desire, are indistinguishable (*Mask* is submerged in *Body of Fate*, *Will* in *Creative Mind*), that is to say, there is complete passivity, complete plasticity. Mind has become indifferent to good and evil, to truth and false-hood; body has become undifferentiated, dough-like; the more perfect be the soul, the more indifferent the mind, the more dough-like the body; and mind and body take what-ever shape, accept whatever image is imprinted upon them, transact whatever purpose is imposed upon them, are indeed the instruments of supernatural manifestation, the final link between the living and more powerful beings. There may be great joy; but it is the joy of a conscious plasticity; and it is this plasticity, this liquefaction, or pounding up, whereby all that has been knowledge becomes instinct and faculty. All plasticities do not obey all masters, and when we have con-sidered cycle and horoscope it will be seen how those that are the instruments of subtle supernatural will differ from the instruments of cruder energy; but all, highest and lowest, are alike in being automatic. (*AV* (B) 183–4)

THOSE IMAGES   367

This poem was written on or before 10 August 1937. It first appeared in *LM* (March 1938).

This poem was inspired by a dislike of C. E. M. Joad's talk on politics. Yeats met him during one of his visits to Penns in the Rocks, Sussex, in April 1937. A letter of 13 August 1937 to Dorothy Wellesley indicates the frame of mind behind the poem:

I am well enough to face the public banquet [This was the Banquet of the Irish Academy of Letters held in Dublin on 17 August 1937] and make the necessary senatorial speech. [The speech was included in *A Speech and Two Poems* (1937)]. 'Our movement is essential to the nation — only by songs, plays, stories, can we hold our thirty millions together, [Yeats was thinking of the Irish abroad. See *VE* 839] keep them one people from New Zealand to California. I have always worked with this purpose in my mind.' Yet my dear I am as anarchic as a sparrow. 'For things like these what decent man would keep his lover waiting?' 'Kings and Parliaments,' said Blake, 'seem to me something other than human life,' or as Hugo said, 'they are not worth one blade of grass that God gives for the nest of the linnet.' (*DWL* 142–3)

The poem follows: it 'says what I have just said'.

2   *The cavern of the mind* : a phrase symbolising pure intellect

6   *To Moscow or to Rome* : Mussolini rather than Hitler — after
Abyssinia and the Spanish War — would have seemed the obvious
symbol to use for fascism.

11–12   *The lion and the virgin*
            The harlot and the child

Cf. the final passage of *An Introduction for my Plays*:

> As I altered my syntax I altered my intellect.   Browning
> said that he could not write a successful play because interested
> not in character in action but in action in character.   I had
> begun to get rid of everything that is not, whether in lyric
> or dramatic poetry, in some sense character in action ; a pause
> in the midst of action perhaps, but action always its end and
> theme.   'Write for the ear,' I thought, so that you may be
> instantly understood as when actor or folk singer stands
> before an audience.   I delight in active men, taking the same
> delight in soldier and craftsman ; I would have poetry turn
> its back upon all that modish curiosity, psychology — the
> poetic theme has always been present.   I recall an Indian tale :
> certain men said to the greatest of sages, 'Who are your
> Masters ?'   And he replied, 'The wind and the harlot, the
> virgin and the child, the lion and the eagle.'   (*E & I* 530)

368   THE MUNICIPAL GALLERY REVISITED

This poem was begun in August and completed in early September
1937 ; it first appeared in *A Speech and Two Poems* (1937).

Yeats referred to the poem in his speech at the Banquet of the
Irish Academy of Letters on 17 August 1937 :

> For a long time I had not visited the Municipal Gallery.   I
> went there a week ago and was restored to many friends.   I sat
> down, after a few minutes, overwhelmed with emotion.
> There were pictures painted by men, now dead, who were once
> my intimate friends.   There were the portraits of my fellow-
> workers ; there was that portrait of Lady Gregory, by
> Mancini, which John Synge thought the greatest portrait since
> Rembrandt ; there was John Synge himself ; there, too,
> were portraits of our Statesmen ; the events of the last thirty
> years in fine pictures : a peasant ambush, the trial of Roger

Casement, a pilgrimage to Lough Derg, event after event : Ireland not as she is displayed in guide book or history, but, Ireland seen because of the magnificent vitality of her painters, in the glory of her passions.

For the moment I could think of nothing but that Ireland : that great pictured song. The next time I go, I shall stand once more in veneration before the work of the great Frenchmen. It is said that an Indian ascetic, when he has taken a certain initiation on a mountain in Tibet, is visited by all the Gods. In those rooms of the Municipal Gallery I saw Ireland in spiritual freedom, and the Corots, the Rodins, the Rousseaus were the visiting gods. (*A Speech and Two Poems* (1937))

The best introduction to the poem is Arland Ussher, *Yeats and the Municipal Gallery* (1959). Yeats wrote to Edith Shackleton Heald on 5 September 1937 that he had 'first to make the prose notes and then write the verses at a little over a verse a day' (*L* 898). He described it to her as 'one of his best poems' and in a letter to Dorothy Wellesley on 5 September 1937 called it 'perhaps the best poem I have written for some years, unless the "Curse of Cromwell" is' (*DWL* 144).

2 *An ambush* : possibly Sean Keating's 'The Men of the West'

pilgrims : in 'St Patrick's Purgatory' by Sir John Lavery (1856–1941)

3 *Casement upon trial* : Lavery's 'The Court of Criminal Appeal'. See notes (p. 465) on 'Roger Casement' (*CP* 351) and (p. 469) on 'The Ghost of Roger Casement' (*CP* 352).

4 *Griffith* : see note (p. 136) on line 2, 'On Those that hated "The Playboy of the Western World"' (*CP* 124). The painting referred to is probably the portrait by Lavery but the gallery does include one by Lily Williams.

5 *Kevin O'Higgins* : painted by Lavery. See notes (p. 321) on 'Death' (*CP* 264), and 'Blood and the Moon' (*CP* 267).

8–10 *A revolutionary soldier kneeling to be blessed ;*
An Abbot or Archbishop with an upraised hand
Blessing the Tricolour

This is Lavery's painting, 'Blessing of the Colours', the tricolour being the orange, white and green flag adopted by the Irish Free State after 1922.

12 *terrible and gay* : cf. the 'terrible' beauty of 'Easter 1916' (*CP* 202)

13 *a woman's portrait* : Arland Ussher suggests that this may be a portrait of Lady Beresford by Lavery.

17 *Heart-smitten* : in a letter of 7 September 1937 Yeats wrote to James A. Healey : 'I spoke of my renewed visits to the Municipal Gallery where my friends' portraits were — visits made possible, or at any rate easy, now that I could go by taxi. I spoke of my emotion in the Gallery where Modern Ireland is pictured . . .' (*L* 899).

18 *My heart recovering* : Yeats was suffering from heart trouble at the time of his visit.

21 *Augusta Gregory's son* : Robert Gregory, see notes (p. 156) on 'In Memory of Major Robert Gregory' (*CP* 148). The portrait of Gregory is by Charles Shannon (1863–1937), an English painter and lithographer, a friend of Charles Ricketts and Yeats. Both Shannon and Ricketts (1866–1931), painter, sculptor, art critic, stage designer and co-editor of *The Dial*, were described by Yeats in section XVII of *Four Years* (see *A* 169).

22 *her sister's son, Hugh Lane* : see notes (p. 123) on 'To a Wealthy Man who promised a second Subscription to the Dublin Municipal Gallery, if it were proved the People wanted Pictures' (*CP* 119)

23 *Hazel Lavery living and dying* : she was Sir John Lavery's second wife, born in Chicago, who died in 1935. The 'living' painting is entitled 'Hazel Lavery at her Easel', the dying 'It is finished'.

369 25 *Mancini's portrait* : Antonio Mancini (1852–1930) painted a portrait of Lady Gregory which is hung in the Municipal Gallery.

33 *My medieval knees*: this may refer to Yeats's courtier-like manners. A letter of 25 August 1934 to Mrs Shakespear mentions the Swedish compliment that 'has pleased me better than (any) I have ever had.' A Swede had said to Mrs Yeats : '"Our Royal family liked your husband better than any other Nobel prize winner. They said he has the manners of a Courtier." I would like to think this true but I doubt it — my kind of critical mind creates harshness and roughness' (*L* 827).

34 *that woman, in that household*: Lady Gregory and Coole Park

35 *all lacking found*: this stanza is of 7 lines. In the original version of the poem lines 35–9 had an extra line included and ran differently :

> Honour had lived so long, their health I found.
> Childless, I thought, 'My children may learn here
> What deep roots are,' and never foresaw the end
> Of all that scholarly generations had held dear ;
> But now the end has come I have not wept
> No fox can foul the lair the badger swept :

37 *never foresaw its end*: this stanza is referring to the settled Ireland of Yeats's youth. He was childless when he first visited Coole Park in 1896, and his first child was born in 1919. He did prophesy the end of the house in the last stanza of 'Coole Park, 1929' (*CP* 273).

> When all those rooms and passages are gone,
> When nettles wave upon a shapeless mound
> And saplings root among the broken stone . . .

Lady Gregory was described (because of the death of her only son Robert in Italy in 1917) as 'a last inheritor' in 'Coole Park and Ballylee, 1931' (*CP* 275).

39 *No fox can foul*: an image out of Spenser, referred to in Yeats's essay *Edmund Spenser* (1902), in which he remarks that Spenser's 'The Death of the Earl of Leicester' is 'more than a conventional Ode to a dead patron . . . he laments that unworthy men should be in the dead Earl's place, and compares them to the fox — an unclean feeder — hiding in the lair "the badger swept".' Cf. Unterecker (*RG* 275–6) who comments, 'Echoing

both his own note on Spenser and Spenser himself, Yeats points up the implicit parallel between his own patroness Lady Gregory and Spenser's "great Earl".' The poem in question was included in Yeats's *Poems of Spenser* (1906) 72. See also note on this selection in *B* 233–4.

41 *John Synge, I and Augusta Gregory* : Yeats's view of the people and popular lore is put in *A* 191, and in several essays. See, for instance, 'A People's Theatre' (*E* 244–59) and 'The Galway Plains' in which he wrote of the Galway people as a community 'bound together by imaginative possessions' (*E & I* 213). In *BS* Yeats paid tribute to Lady Gregory and Synge : 'their work and mine has delighted in history and tradition' (*A* 554). Cf. also *A* 395 for her making the people 'a part of her soul'.

44 *Antaeus-like* : Antaeus, son of Poseidon and Earth, when attacked by Hercules drew new strength from his mother whenever he touched the ground.

47 *Dream of the noble and the beggar-man* : in the Introduction to *Fighting the Waves* Yeats mentions Lady Gregory's habit of quoting from Aristotle : 'To think like a wise man, but express oneself like the common people' (*E* 371). He also discussed in this Introduction his own attempt to bring his blank verse as close to common speech as possible (*E* 371).

48 *Synge himself* : cf. line 25 'In Memory of Major Robert Gregory' (*CP* 148). The portrait is by Yeats's father, John Butler Yeats.

that rooted man : Yeats may be referring here to Synge's finding 'his genius and his peace' on Inishmaan and the Blaskets (*E & I* 325).

370 ARE YOU CONTENT ?

This poem's date of composition cannot be determined accurately : it first appeared in *Atlantic Monthly* and *LM* (April 1938).

9–10 *He that in Sligo at Drumcliff*
       Set up the old stone Cross
The Rev. John Yeats (1774–1846), who won the Bishop Berkeley

Medal in Greek while at Trinity College, Dublin, was appointed to the living at Drumcliffe, Co. Sligo, in 1805, and remained as Rector there until his death.

11   *That red-headed rector* : the Rev. John Yeats's son, the Rev. William Butler Yeats (b. 1806), who was a curate in the parish of Moira, Co. Down, before becoming Rector of Tullylish, near Portadown.   In 1835 he married Jane Corbet, whose brother owned Sandymount Castle, Dublin.

13   *Sandymount Corbets* : cf. John Butler Yeats, *Early Memories* (1923), 54–5, where he describes how Robert Corbet (his uncle), once he bought or leased Sandymount Castle, 'began creating all around him beautiful gardens'.
   John Butler Yeats spent most of his time there when he was an undergraduate, and regarded it as his Capua.   When he married he rented 'Georgeville', a house nearby.

14   *Old William Pollexfen* : Yeats's grandfather.   See notes (p. 119) on 'Introductory Rhymes' (*CP* 113).

15   *The smuggler Middleton* : William Middleton (d. 1832), who had a depot in the Channel Islands.   See notes (p. 119) on 'Introductory Rhymes' (*CP* 113).

Butlers far back : see notes (p. 116) on 'Introductory Rhymes' (*CP* 113)

22   *What Robert Browning meant* : the reference is to *Pauline* :   **371**

> . . . an old hunter
> Talking with gods, or a high-crested chief
> Sailing with troops of friends to Tenedos.

It was one of Yeats's favourite quotations (see his *Introduction* to Hone and Rossi, *Berkeley* (1931), (*E & I* 409)).   He also used it in his Introduction to Lady Gregory's *Gods and Fighting Men*, and in *AV*, where the old hunter is seen as an image of peace by men of the opposite phase 'worn out by a wisdom held with labour and uncertainty' (*AV* (B) 110).

371 THREE SONGS TO THE ONE BURDEN

The date of composition is not known; the three songs first appeared in the *Spectator* (26 May 1939).

I

9 *From mountain to mountain ride the fierce horsemen*: possibly a memory of the horsemen described by Mary Battle, the servant of George Pollexfen, Yeats's uncle who lived in Sligo. She described mysterious women as like 'the men one sees riding their horses in twos and threes on the slopes of the mountains with their swords swinging. There is no such race living now, none so finely proportioned' (*A* 266).

Yeats wrote to Ethel Mannin on 11 December 1936:

As a young man I used to repeat to myself Blake's lines

'And he his seventy disciples sent
Against religion and government'

I hate more than you do, for my hatred can have no expression in action. I am a forerunner of that horde that will some day come down the mountains. (*L* 873)

10 *Manannan*: Manannan Mac Lir, the Gaelic god of the sea

19 *Crazy Jane*: an invented character, see notes (p. 370) on *Words for Music Perhaps* (*CP* 290). Cf. also 'Crazy Jane on the Mountain' (*CP* 390).

372 25 *likely couples*: Saul (*PYP* 168) draws attention to the philosophy of the Old Man in *Purgatory*: 'States are justified . . . by . . . the best born of the best' and the quotation from *The Anatomy of Melancholy* in *OTB*: '. . . it were happy for human kind, if only such parents as are sound of body and mind should be suffered to marry' (*E* 418).

II

372 1 *Henry Middleton*: a cousin of the poet, who became a recluse. Hone (*WBY* 21) remarks that he was the original of John Sherman in Yeats's novel *John Sherman*.

3 *A small forgotten house*: 'Elsinore' near Rosses Point, Co. Sligo. It still stands, and is reputed to have been a smuggler's house and haunted.

8 *keys to my old gate*: Hone (*WBY* 22) describes how Yeats and Mrs Yeats visited Henry Middleton in 1919. The gate was locked but Yeats climbed the wall and found his cousin dressed in a white suit in the sitting-room, which was littered with cheap novels and had a butter-churn in the middle of the floor. He said to Yeats, 'You see that I am too busy to see anyone.' In 1930 Michael and Anne Yeats climbed the wall but were turned away by the garden boy when they reached the hall door of the house.

III
2 *Nineteen-Sixteen*: the Easter Rising of 1916; see notes (p. 224) **373** on 'Easter 1916' (*CP* 202). The poem was originally entitled 'An Abbey Player — I meditate upon 1916'. This became 'An Abbey Player and his Song'.

5 *Post Office*: in the centre of Dublin, this building was occupied by the insurgents in 1916.

6 *City Hall*: to the east of the Post Office, where Connolly was in command

11 *Connolly*: James Connolly. See notes on 'Easter 1916' (*CP* 202)

24 *Pearse*: see notes (p. 227) on 'Easter 1916' (*CP* 202). **374**

IN TARA'S HALLS **374**

This poem was written in June 1938 and first appeared in *Last Poems and Two Plays* (1939).

1 *A man*: the MS. version had as first line 'A certain king in the great house at Tara'.

Tara's Halls: Tara, Co. Meath, was once the seat of the High Kings of Ireland. Recent excavations have revealed the site of a palace.

11   *The Sacred House* : the source of the story is uncertain.

375   THE STATUES

This poem was written on 9 April 1938 (but Curtis Bradford suggests April–June 1938), and first appeared in *LM* (March 1939) and *N* (15 April 1939).

The prose draft of the poem reads :

I

They went out in noonday or under the new moon moving with – – – – – [indecipherable] only forms in marble, empty faces, measure Pythagorean perfection only that which is incapable of show is infinite in passion. Only passion sees God. Men were victors at Salamis, and Victory is nothing, now one up, then another, only their cold marble forms could drive back to the vague Asiatic norm. Only they could beat down Nature with their certainty. Weary of victory one went far from all his companions and sat so long in solitude that his body became soft and round, incapable of work or war, because his eyes were empty, more empty than skies at night . . . all men worshipped present deity. Apollo forgot Pythagoras and took the name of Buddha which was victorious Greece in the Asiatic mode. Others stayed away and were made – – – – – [indecipherable] and conquer their sublime emptiness, and in a jungle nigh they saw – – – – – [indecipherable].

II

Where are you now ? It is better that you shed the sunburn and become pale-white ; did you appear in the Post Office in 1916 ? Is it true that Pearse called on you by the name of Cuchulain. Certainly we have need of you. The vague flood is at its. . . . For from all quarters is coming. . . . Come back with your Pythagorean numbers.

A passage in *OTB* gives the poem's meaning :

There are moments when I am certain that art must once again accept those Greek proportions which carry into plastic art the Pythagorean numbers, those faces which are divine because all there is empty and measured. Europe was not born when Greek galleys defeated the Persian hordes at Salamis ; but when the Doric studios sent out those broad-backed marble statues against the multiform, vague, expressive

Asiatic sea, they gave to the sexual instinct of Europe its goal,
its fixed type. (*E* 451)

The poem has been discussed by Hazard Adams, 'Yeatsian art and
Mathematic Form', *Centennial Review* (Winter 1960) 70–88 ; by
Ellmann (*IY* 188–90) ; by V. Koch, *W. B. Yeats, The Tragic Phase*
(1951) 57–75 ; by Unterecker (*RG* 278–81) ; by Peter Ure, '"The
Statues"; a note on the meaning of Yeats's Poem', *RES*, xv
(1949) 254–7 ; by Wilson (*YI* 290–303) ; by E. Engelberg, *The
Vast Design* (1964) 176–210. The last critic offers a view of Yeats's
use of history in this poem and his account on pp. 196–7 and
202–3 is valuable.

1–2   *Pythagoras planned it. Why did the people stare ?*
    His numbers : the Pythagorean doctrine of numbers paved
the way for the art of the Greek sculptors who carved their statues
by exact measurements. Cf. 'Under Ben Bulben' IV (*CP* 399)
lines 42–4.

3   *lacked character* : in *AV* Yeats gave his views of the development of Greek civilisation and pp. 268–72 of the 1937 edition are
a key passage for the understanding of this poem :

> I imagine the annunciation that founded Greece as made to
> Leda, remembering that they showed in a Spartan temple,
> strung up to the roof as a holy relic, an unhatched egg of hers ;
> and that from one of her eggs came Love and from the other
> War. But all things are from antithesis, and when in my
> ignorance I try to imagine what older civilisation that annun-
> ciation rejected I can but see bird and woman blotting out
> some corner of the Babylonian mathematical starlight.
>   Was it because the older civilisation like the Jewish thought
> a long life a proof of Heavenly favour that the Greek races
> thought those whom the Gods love must die young, hurling
> upon some age of crowded comedy their tragic sense ? Cer-
> tainly their tribes, after a first multitudinous revelation —
> dominated each by its *Daimon* and oracle-driven — broke up
> a great Empire and established in its stead an intellectual
> anarchy. At some 1000 years before Christ I imagine their
> religious system complete and they themselves grown bar-
> baric and Asiatic. Then came Homer, civil life, a desire for
> civil order dependent doubtless on some oracle, and then
> (Phase 10 of the new millennium) for independent civil life and

thought. At, let me say, the sixth century B.C. (Phase 12) personality begins, but there is as yet no intellectual solitude. A man may rule his tribe or town but he cannot separate himself from the general mass. With the first discovery of solitude (Phases 13 and 14) comes, as I think, the visible art that interests us most today, for Phidian art, like the art of Raphael, has for the moment exhausted our attention. I recall a Nike at the Ashmolean Museum with a natural unsystematised beauty like that before Raphael, and above all certain pots with strange half-supernatural horses dark on a light ground. Self-realisation attained will bring desire of power — systematisation for its instrument — but as yet clarity, meaning, elegance, all things separated from one another in luminous space, seem to exceed all other virtues. One compares this art with the thought of Greek philosophers before Anaxagoras, where one discovers the same phases, always more concerned with the truth than with its moral or political effects. One longs for the lost dramatists, the plays that were enacted before Aeschylus and Sophocles arose, both Phidian men.

But one must consider not the movement only from the beginning to the end of the ascending cone, but the gyres that touch its sides, the horizontal dance.

> Hands gripped in hands, toes close together,
> Hair spread on the wind they made ;
> That lady and that golden king
> Could like a brace of blackbirds sing.

Side by side with Ionic elegance there come after the Persian wars a Doric vigour, and the light-limbed dandy of the potters, the Parisian-looking young woman of the sculptors, her hair elaborately curled, give place to the athlete. One suspects a deliberate turning away from all that is Eastern, or a moral propaganda like that which turned the poets out of Plato's Republic, and yet it may be that the preparation for the final systematisation had for its apparent cause the destruction, let us say, of Ionic studios by the Persian invaders, and that all came from the resistance of the *Body of Fate* to the growing solitude of the soul. Then in Phidias Ionic and Doric influence unite — one remembers Titian — and all is transformed by the full moon, and all abounds and flows. With Callimachus pure Ionic revives again, as Furtwängler has proved, and upon the only example of his work known to us, a marble chair, a Persian is represented, and may one not discover a Persian symbol in that bronze lamp, shaped like a palm, known to us by a description in Pausanias ? But he was an archaistic workman, and those who set him to work brought back public life to an older form. One may see in masters and man a momentary dip into ebbing Asia.

Each age unwinds the thread another age had wound, and it amuses one to remember that before Phidias, and his westward-moving art, Persia fell, and that when full moon came round again, amid eastward-moving thought, and brought Byzantine glory, Rome fell ; and that at the outset of our westward-moving Renaissance Byzantium fell ; all things dying each other's life, living each other's death.

After Phidias the life of Greece, which being *antithetical* had moved slowly and richly through the *antithetical* phases, comes rapidly to an end. Some Greek or Roman writer whose name I forget will soon speak of the declining comeliness of the people, and in the arts all is systematised more and more, and the antagonist recedes. Aristophanes' passion-clouded eye falls before what one must believe, from Roman stage copies, an idler glance. (Phases 19, 20, 21). Aristotle and Plato end creative system — to die into the truth is still to die — and formula begins. Yet even the truth into which Plato dies is a form of death, for when he separates the Eternal Ideas from Nature and shows them self-sustained he prepares the Christian desert and the Stoic suicide.

I identify the conquest of Alexander and the break-up of his kingdom when Greek civilisation, formalised and codified, loses itself in Asia, with the beginning and end of the 22nd Phase, and his intention recorded by some historian to turn his arms westward shows that he is but a part of the impulse that creates Hellenised Rome and Asia. There are everywhere statues where every muscle has been measured, every position debated, and these statues represent man with nothing more to achieve, physical man finished and complacent, the women slightly tinted, but the men, it may be, who exercise naked in the open air, the colour of mahogany. Every discovery after the epoch of victory and defeat (Phase 22) which substitutes mechanics for power is an elimination of intellect by delight in technical skill (Phase 23), by a sense of the past (Phase 24), by some dominant belief (Phase 25). After Plato and Aristotle, the mind is as exhausted as were the armies of Alexander at his death, but the Stoics can discover morals and turn philosophy into a rule of life.

Among them doubtless — the first beneficiaries of Plato's hatred of imitation — we may discover the first benefactors of our modern individuality, sincerity of the trivial face, the mask torn away. Then, a Greece that Rome has conquered, and a Rome conquered by Greece, must, in the last three phases of the wheel, adore, desire being dead, physical or spiritual force. (*AV* (B) 268–72)

13 *not the banks of oars* : cf. the quotation from *OTB* above. Greek intellect rather than armies conquered the Persians. Salamis, the island which closes the bay of Eleusis on the south, and part of Athens from the time of Solon and Pisistratus, was the site of the battle (Sept., 480 B.C.) in which the Persian fleet was shatteringly defeated by the Athenians.

17 *One image* : Yeats wrote on 28 June 1938 to Edith Shackleton Heald :

'In reading the third stanza remember the influence on modern sculpture and on the great seated Buddha of the sculptors who followed Alexander. Cuchulain is in the last stanza because Pearse and some of his followers had a cult of him. The Government has put a statue of Cuchulain in the rebuilt post office to commemorate this. (*L* 911)

19 *No Hamlet thin from eating flies* : Ellmann (*IY* 189) remarks that Yeats branded Christianity as an Asian importation, the antithesis for Greece and, in the fourth stanza, Ireland : 'For Christianity has no Hamlets, full of their own selves, passionate for knowledge, but only monks with empty eyeballs, contemplating, like the Buddhists, nothingness.' The poem is complementary to a passage in 'Four Years 1887–1891' :

Its [a portrait of William Morris by Watts] grave wide-open eyes, like the eyes of some dreaming beast, remind me of the open eyes of Titian's *Ariosto*, while the broad vigorous body suggests a mind that has no need of the intellect to remain sane, though it give itself to every fantasy : the dreamer of the Middle Ages. It is 'the fool of Faery . . . wide and wild as a hill', the resolute European image that yet half remembers Buddha's motionless meditation, and has no trait in common with the wavering, lean image of hungry speculation, that cannot but because of certain famous Hamlets of our stage fill the mind's eye. Shakespeare himself foreshadowed a symbolic change, that is, a change in the whole temperament of the world, for though he called his Hamlet 'fat' and even 'scant of breath', he thrust between his fingers agile rapier and dagger. (*A* 141–2)

The description of Hamlet thin with eating flies possibly suggested the introduction of Grimalkin (line 24) as it is a common supposition that cats grow thin through eating flies.

20 *Empty eyeballs knew* : cf. a passage in *AV* which culminates in this image :

It is impossible to do more than select an arbitrary general date for the beginning of Roman decay (Phases 2 to 7, A.D. 1 to A.D. 250). Roman sculpture — sculpture made under Roman influence whatever the sculptor's blood — did not, for instance, reach its full vigour, if we consider what it had of Roman as distinct from Greek, until the Christian Era. It even made a discovery which affected all sculpture to come. The Greeks painted the eyes of marble statues and made out of enamel or glass or precious stones those of their bronze statues, but the Roman was the first to drill a round hole to represent the pupil, and because, as I think, of a preoccupation with the glance characteristic of a civilisation in its final phase. The colours must have already faded from the marbles of the great period, and a shadow and a spot of light, especially where there is much sunlight, are more vivid than paint, enamel, coloured glass or precious stone. They could now express in stone a perfect composure. The administrative mind, alert attention had driven out rhythm, exaltation of the body, uncommitted energy. May it not have been precisely a talent for this alert attention that had enabled Rome and not Greece to express those final *primary* phases ? One sees on the pediments troops of marble Senators, officials serene and watchful as befits men who know that all the power of the world moves before their eyes, and needs, that it may not dash itself to pieces, their unhurried, unanxious, never-ceasing care. Those riders upon the Parthenon had all the world's power in their moving bodies, and in a movement that seemed, so were the hearts of man and beast set upon it, that of a dance ; but presently all would change and measurement succeed to pleasure, the dancing-master outlive the dance. What need had those young lads for careful eyes ?

But in Rome of the first and second centuries, where the dancing-master himself has died, the delineation of character as shown in face and head, as with us of recent years, is all in all, and sculptors, seeking the custom of occupied officials, stock in their workshops toga'd marble bodies upon which can be screwed with the least possible delay heads modelled from the sitters with the most scrupulous realism. When I think of Rome I see always these heads with their world-considering eyes, and those bodies as conventional as the metaphors in a leading article, and compare in my imagination vague Grecian eyes gazing at nothing, Byzantine eyes of drilled ivory staring upon a vision, and those eyelids of China and of India, those veiled or half-veiled eyes weary of world and vision alike. (*AV* (B) 275–7)

23 *gong and conch* : cf. the 'great cathedral gong' of 'Byzantium' (*CP* 280)

25–6 *When Pearse summoned Cuchulain to his side,*

What stalked through the Post Office ? : cf. note on line 17 above. Yeats sees Pearse (who was in the General Post Office in the Easter Rising of 1916) as summoning intellectual and aesthetic forces into being, as well as those skills of measuring and numbering, so that the Irish can return to the Pythagorean philosophy, cf. Ure, *RES* (1949) xv, 254–7 and Yeats (*E* 451) 'art must again accept the Greek proportions'.

376 NEWS FOR THE DELPHIC ORACLE

This poem's date of composition is uncertain ; it was probably written during 1938 and first appeared in *LM* (March 1939) and *The New Republic* (22 March 1939).

1 *There all the golden codgers lay* : the 'codgers' are the immortals viewed ironically. The poem is closely related to Porphyry's account of the Delphic oracle on Plotinus. Yeats described MacKenna's translation of it as one of his favourite quotations (*E & I* 409) Cf. notes (p. 388) on 'The Delphic Oracle on Plotinus' (*CP* 306) where the source material is given.

2 *silver dew* : Wilson (*Y & T* 219) thinks this refers to the nectar in the Greek oracle.

5–6 *Man-picker Niamh leant and sighed*
    By Oisin : Yeats introduced figures from Gaelic mythology
into the Greek escatology. See note (p. 51) on Niamh, daughter
of Aengus and Edain, 'The Hosting of the Sidhe' (*CP* 61). Oisin,
the son of Finn, lived with her for three hundred years. Niamh
is described as 'man-picker' because she told Finn

> . . . now I choose . . .
> That I might have your son to kiss.
>
> ('The Wanderings of Oisin' (*CP* 405)).

8–9 *Pythagoras . . . Plotinus* : cf. notes (p. 388) on 'The Delphic
Oracle upon Plotinus' (*CP* 306)

13 *a dolphin's back* : Yeats learned about the dolphins as con-
veyors of the soul after death from Mrs Strong's book *Apotheosis
and the After Life* (cf. notes (p. 359) on 'Byzantium' (*CP* 280)).
In this poem he is also describing some pictures in Rome which
include nymphs, satyrs and dolphins. These are the School of
Raphael from the Papal Apartments at Castel S. Angelo, *Fregio
e ricasco della volta con deita marine e grottesche* (ed. Alinari, 11895,
11896, and 11898).

22 *wades the choir of love* : cf. 'where . . . dwells . . . stately Py-   **377**
thagoras and all else that form the choir of Immortal Love, there
where the heart is ever lifted in joyous festival' (*Plotinus*, tr. Mac-
Kenna, I, 23)

25–6 *Slim adolescence that a nymph has stripped,*
    Peleus on Thetis stares : this relates to Poussin's 'The
Marriage of Peleus and Thetis' which is in the National Gallery
of Ireland. (It is now entitled 'Acis and Galatea'.) The painting
is reproduced in *LT* 233.

31 *Pan's cavern* : Wilson (*Y & T* 222) regards the cavern as
Porphyry's cave on the edge of heaven facing the foam of life,
with one of its mouths in Porphyry facing on the fields of heaven,
and regards Pan as its natural deity because it is a symbol of
generation. He discusses the poem at length, pp. 216–23.

377 THREE MARCHING SONGS

These three poems were written between 3 November 1933 and 27 February 1934, and rewritten in December 1938. They first appeared in *Last Poems and Two Plays* (1939). They are later versions of 'Three Songs to the Same Tune' (*CP* 320).

I

4 *Fled to far countries*: see note (p. 130) on 'Wild Geese' in 'September 1913' (*CP* 120)

378 23–25 . . . *mock at O'Donnell,*
            Mock at the memory of both O'Neills,
            Mock Emmet, mock Parnell: see notes (p. 419) on 'Three Songs to the Same Tune' II (*CP* 322)

II

379 9 *airy spot*: Yeats's note read: '"Airy" may be an old pronounciation of "eerie" often heard in Galway and Sligo.' But it may be an echo of a line in Allingham's 'The Faeries': 'Up the airy mountain'.

21 *nothing up there at the top*: cf. notes (p. 420) on 'Three Songs to the Same Tune' III (*CP* 323)

III

380 23 *the rope gave a jerk there*: cf. note (p. 418) on 'Three Songs to the Same Tune' I (*CP* 323).

381 LONG-LEGGED FLY

This poem was written between November 1937 and April 1938. It was probably completed by 11 April 1938, and first appeared in *LM* (March 1939).

11 *topless towers*: of Troy, Marlowe's phrase in *Dr Faustus*. See note (p. 135) on 'When Helen lived' (*CP* 124).

15 *She thinks*: Maud Gonne. She is similarly described in 'Against Unworthy Praise' (*CP* 104).

23   *the Pope's Chapel*: this stanza describes Michelangelo's paint-   **382**
ings in the Sistine Chapel, Rome.   Cf. 'Under Ben Bulben' IV
(*CP* 399).

A BRONZE HEAD   **382**

The date of composition of this poem is uncertain (probably
1937–8); it first appeared in *LM* (March 1939) and *The New
Republic* (22 March 1937).

1   *right of the entrance*:   of the Municipal Gallery of Modern Art,
Dublin

this bronze head: it is plaster cast painted bronze by Lawrence
Campbell, R.H.A., of Maud Gonne.

7   *Hysterica passio*:   see notes (p. 410) on 'Parnell's Funeral'
(*CP* 319)

8   *No dark tomb-haunter*:   the phrase may derive from Madame
MacBride's habit of wearing black flowing garments and a veil,
as well as of visiting graveyards on political occasions.

13   *Profound McTaggart*:   J. McT. E. McTaggart (1866–1925),
author of *Studies in Hegelian Cosmology* (1901), which Yeats read in
1928.   This poem, however, probably draws on his *Human Immortality and Pre-existence*, 63 :

When science says that a material object — a planet or a
human body — ceases to exist, what does it mean ? It does
not mean that anything is annihilated.   It means that units,
which were combined in a certain way, are now combined
otherwise.   The form has changed.   But everything which
was there before is there now.

Cf. Yeats's remarks in his Introduction to *The Resurrection* :

All ancient nations believed in the re-birth of the soul and
had probably empirical evidence like that Lafcadio Hearn
found among the Japanese.   In our time Schopenhauer
believed it, and McTaggart thinks Hegel did, though lack of
interest in the individual soul had kept him silent.   It is the
foundation of McTaggart's own philosophical system. . . .
All our thought seems to lead by antithesis to some new
affirmation of the supernatural.   (*E* 396–7)

383 A STICK OF INCENSE

The date of this poem's composition cannot be established (probably 1938); it first appeared in *Last Poems and Two Plays* (1939).

2 *empty tomb or Virgin womb*: cf. a similar passage in 'Private Thoughts':

> Among those our civilisation must reject, or leave unrewarded at some level below that co-ordination that modern civilisation finds essential, exist precious faculties. . . . I have noticed that clairvoyance, prevision, and allied gifts, rare among the educated classes, are common among peasants. Among those peasants there is much of Asia, where Hegel has said every civilisation begins. Yet we much hold to what we have that the next civilisation may be born, not from a virgin's womb, not a tomb without a body, not from a void, but of our own rich experience. (*E* 436–7)

383 JOHN KINSELLA'S LAMENT FOR MRS MARY MOORE

This poem was written on 21 or 29 July 1938 and first appeared in *LM* (Dec. 1938). It was originally entitled 'A Strong Farmer's complaint about Death'.

384 11 *What shall I do*: Yeats wrote to Edith Shackleton Heald on 21 July 1938:

> I have just thought of a chorus for a ballad. A strong farmer is mourning over the shortness of life and changing times, and every stanza ends 'What shall I do for pretty girls now my old bawd is dead?' I think it might do for a new *Broadside*. (*L* 912)

385 HOUND VOICE

The date of this poem's composition is uncertain (probably Summer 1938); it first appeared in *LM* (Dec. 1938) and *N* (10 Dec. 1938).

The poem was written in a spirit of mockery.

385 HIGH TALK

This poem was written between 29 July and August 1938 and first appeared in *LM* (Dec. 1938) and *N* (10 Dec. 1938).

1 *high stilts*: Yeats wrote of the 'nineties that (when they were over) 'we all got down off our stilts', and he may here be referring to his own creation of a poetic mythology, cf. line 3, 'no modern stalks upon higher', even though this was less exalted than that of his predecessors. In a letter to Dorothy Wellesley he wrote: 'I have now begun on the stollen [stolen] circus stilts' (*DWL* 182).

5 *piebald ponies*: the poem is reminiscent of some of Jack B.   **386** Yeats's pictures. Cf. 'The Circus Animals' Desertion' (*CP* 391)

9 *Malachi Stilt-Jack*: Malachi was a minor Hebrew prophet. Unterecker (*RG* 286) suggests that he may be 'tied to St Malachy, the twelfth-century saint who assisted Yeats's favourite Irish saint, Cellach'. But the figure is probably an invented one or a memory of some figure in Yeats's youth in Sligo.

THE APPARITIONS   **386**

This poem written in March and April 1938 and first appeared in *LM* (Dec. 1938).

Title The Apparitions: these were a series of death dreams that occurred after Yeats's illness in Majorca in January. Cf. Henn (*LT* 149), who remarks that there were seven apparitions, not fifteen. But see next note.

7 *Fifteen apparitions*: cf. Yeats's letter to Mrs Shakespear of   **387** 11 November 1933:

> Did I tell you that my apparition came a seventh time? As I awoke I saw a child's hand and arm and head — faintly self luminous — holding above — I was lying on my back — a five of diamonds or hearts I was [not] sure which. It was held as if the child was standing at the head of the bed. Is the meaning some fortune teller's meaning attached to the card or does it promise me five months or five years? Five years would be about long enough to finish my autobiography and bring out *A Vision*.

[In fact Yeats lived just a little over five years from November 1933.]

8   *A coat upon a coat-hanger* : Curtis Bradford, 'Yeats's *Last Poems* Again' *Dolmen Press Yeats Centenary Papers* (1965) 274, quotes a sentence from a manuscript book Yeats was using at the time : 'The first apparition was the passage of a coat upon a coathanger slowly across room — it was extraordinarily terrifying.'

21   *increasing Night* : an image for death, cf. 'that great night' line 38, 'The Man and the Echo' (*CP* 393)

387   A NATIVITY

The date of this poem's composition was probably August 1936 ; it first appeared in *LM* (Dec. 1938).

1–2   *What woman hugs her infant there ?*
        Another star . . . : cf. Yeats's notes on *WS* where he commented on 'The Mother of God' (*CP* 281) :

> . . . the words 'a fallen flare through the hollow of an ear' are, I am told, obscure. I had in my memory Byzantine mosaic pictures of the Annunciation, which show a line drawn from a star to the ear of the Virgin. She conceived of the Word, and therefore through the ear a star fell and was born.

3–4   *What made the drapery glisten so ?*
        Not a man but Delacroix : cf. 'Tomorrow's Revolution' (*OTB*)

> We who are opposites of our times should for the most part work at our art and for good manners' sake be silent. What matter if our art or science lack hearty acquiescence, seem narrow and traditional ? Horne built the smallest church in London, went to Italy and became the foremost authority upon Botticelli. Ricketts made pictures that suggest Delacroix by their colour and remind us by their theatrical composition that Talma once invoked the thunderbolt. . . . (*E* 417–18)

Mrs Yeats thinks Yeats included Delacroix for the rotundity of the name. See *LT* 261.

6 *Landor's tarpaulin* : a draft version of the poem contained **388**
these lines :

> What brought that child and woman here ?
> Landor's hammer on the roof
> What can brush the gnats aside ?
> What can keep the rain aloof ?

Yeats told his wife that he took great care to ensure [why ?] that
the insects in this poem were non-stinging.

The Landor image is obscure. Henn (*LT* 261) remarks on the
structure of the poem (the last couplet returns to the Annunciation
of the first) and states that both Landor and Delacroix knew Talma
(line 10). Landor, physically violent, was calm in his writing.
Henn suggests that the tarpaulin on the roof is faintly ridiculous,
'the temporary cover against popular ridicule'.

8 *Irving and his plume of pride* : Sir Henry Irving (1838–1905),
famous actor, *né* Jonathan Henry Brodribb, whom Yeats had
seen acting and had met in his teens with his father. Yeats admired
his 'intellectual pride' (*Plays and Controversies*, 215, and *A* 125).

10 *Talma* : François Joseph Talma (1763–1826), French tragedian. Cf. passage from *OTB* quoted in note on lines 3–4.

11 *the woman* : this reverts to the annunciation of lines 1–2.

WHY SHOULD NOT OLD MEN BE MAD ?   **388**

This poem was written in January 1936, and first appeared in
OTB.

4 *a drunken journalist* : not identified, but R. M. Smylie, editor
of the *Irish Times*, has been suggested.

5 *a girl that knew all Dante once* : Iseult Gonne

6 *a dunce* : Francis Stuart (b. 1902), the novelist and poet, who
married Iseult Gonne in 1920. He is now (1968) married to
Gertrude Meiszner. His autobiography, *Things to live for*, was pub-

lished in 1936. Yeats's views on him changed from time to time. Cf. a letter to Mrs Shakespear of 25 July 1932 :

> Read *The Coloured Dome* by Francis Stuart. It is strange and exciting in theme and perhaps more personally and beautifully written than any book of our generation ; it makes you understand the strange Ireland that is rising up here. What an inexplicable thing sexual selection is. Iseult picked this young man, by what seemed half chance, half a mere desire to escape from an impossible life, and when he seemed almost imbecile to his own relations. Now he is her very self made active and visible, her nobility walking and singing. If luck comes to his aid he will be our great writer. (*L* 799–80)

See also his comment in 'Modern Ireland', *Massachusetts Review* (Winter 1964) 266–7, in which he described him as possessing :

> a style full of intellectual passion and music. . . . He himself is typical of the new Ireland. . . . Shortly after I first met him he spent fifteen months in jail as a political prisoner ; then he was [in] trouble with his Church as one of the editors of a weekly review called in half-a-dozen Catholic papers infamous, immoral, blasphemous. A little later [he] was spending his life under the influence of St John of the Cross in meditation [and] prayer. A little [later] still he owned a racehorse and was betting at the Curragh.

7   *A Helen of social welfare dream* : probably Maud Gonne (though he may have had Constance Markievicz in mind also.) The comma after 'dream' was not in the original MS. Cf. *WBY* 210 for the screaming upon a waggonette, where Hone records how Miss Horniman told Yeats 'the greatest poet is always helpless beside a beautiful woman screaming from a cart'.

389   THE STATESMAN'S HOLIDAY

This poem was completed in April 1938 and first appeared in *OTB*.

A passage in *OTB* explains the mood of the poem (which [untitled] followed this prose passage) :

> In my savage youth I was accustomed to say that no man should be permitted to open his mouth in Parliament until he had sung or written his *Utopia*, for lacking that we could not

know where he was taking us, and I still think that artists of all kinds should once again praise or represent great or happy people. Here in Monte Carlo, where I am writing, somebody talked of a man with a monkey and some kind of stringed instrument, and it has pleased me to imagine him a great politician. I will make him sing to the sort of tune that goes well with my early sentimental poems. (*E* 451–2)

5 *Oscar*: possibly Oscar Wilde, but Saul (*PYP* 173) writes 'presumably Oscar (Tschirky) of the Waldorf (NY)'. But cf. *A* 139 where Yeats remarked '. . . the dinner-table was Wilde's event and made him the greatest talker of his time, and his plays and dialogues have what merit they possess from being now an imitation, now a record, of his talk'.

13 *grass-green Avalon*: the original MS. of the poem contained as refrain 'But a Burne-Jones boat and the grass-green island of Avalon'. Cf. notes (p. 95) on 'Under the Moon' (*CP* 91). Yeats may have had in mind the Burne-Jones designs for Stannon Hall. (These, executed by Morris's company, included the 'Ship of the Knights') or possibly the picture of Arthur in Avalon (1880). Another water-colour was entitled 'The Boat'.

14 *a great Lord Chancellor*: Torchiana (*Y & GI* 356) suggests F. E. Smith, who became Lord Birkenhead. He had been government prosecutor at Casement's trial, had guaranteed the authenticity of Casement's Diaries. Earlier he had worked with Carson to keep Ulster out of any Home Rule settlement. But Torchiana considers that Yeats may have had Lord Glenavy in mind. He points out that Churchill's name appeared in an early MS. of the poem.

15 *the Sack*: a large square bag of wool covered with cloth without back or arms on which the Lord Chancellor sits in the House of Lords

16 *Commanding officer*: Torchiana (*Y & GI* 355) suggests Sir Hubert Gough, loyal to Ulster, who refused to take up defensive positions in Belfast (he commanded the Third Cavalry Brigade

at the Curragh Camp) in March 1914, resigned, was dismissed and reinstated. This Curragh 'mutiny' accelerated the progress of events that led to the 1916 Rising.

18 *de Valéra* : see notes on 'Parnell's Funeral' (*CP* 319)

19 *the King of Greece* : George II, who returned to Greece in 1935 and appointed General Metaxas as head of the government.

20 *the man that made the motors* : probably William Morris, who became Lord Nuffield. Yeats mentions him (*OTB*) as a self-made man whose benefactions would substitute applied science for ancient wisdom in Oxford (*E* 423). Saul (*PYP* 173) suggests Ford as possible.

390 34 *a strutting turkey walk* : possibly a parody of Yeats's own style of walking. Cf. Torchiana, '"Among School Children" and the Education of the Irish Spirit', *IER* 123.

390 CRAZY JANE ON THE MOUNTAIN

This poem was written in July 1938 and first appeared in *OTB*.

1–2 *the Bishop (Said Crazy Jane)* : cf. the earlier poems about Crazy Jane and notes on *Words for Music Perhaps* (*CP* 290). Yeats wrote to Dorothy Wellesley on 13 July 1938 that he was writing a new Crazy Jane poem — 'a wild affair' (*L* 912).

7 *A King had some beautiful cousins* : a reference to the brutal killing of the Tsar and his family, by Commissar Yurovsky and ten Lettish soldiers at Ekaterinburg in July 1918. (See E. M. Almedingen, *The Romanovs* (1966).) Yeats wrote :

I have been told that King George V asked that the Russian royal family should be brought to England. The English Prime Minister refused, fearing the effect upon the English working classes. That story may be no more true than other stories spoken by word of mouth, but it will serve for an example. The average Englishman would think King George's submission, his abandonment of his relations to a fate already foreseen, if proved, a necessary, even a noble sacrifice. It was indeed his submission, his correctness as a

constitutional sovereign that made his popularity so un-
bounded that he became a part of the English educational
system. Some thousands of examinations papers were distributed to schoolchildren in a Northern industrial district
with the question, 'Who was the best man who ever lived?'
The vast majority answered, 'King George the Fifth'. Christ
was runner-up. (E 442–3)

Cf. Dorothy Wellesley's comment on Yeats's visit in July 1938 to
Penns in the Rocks :

. . . he read me a new poem about which he had previously
written, opening thus : 'You won't like this because it
attacks King George V'. 'But I don't care two hoots about
George V,' I replied, angrily realising that this was his first
inevitable attack upon the English, which must continue for
many days. I listened while he read the poem.
   I discovered later that he considers George V should have
abdicated as a protest when his cousin the Czar was dethroned.
'My God!' he said, 'in ancient Ireland such conduct as that
of George V would have been an impossibility,' adding that
'the English should have declared war upon their ally Russia
in 1917'. About all this Yeats was intensely serious. (*DWL*
171)

15   *Great-bladdered Emer* : a footnote in *OTB* reads:

In a fragment from some early version of *The Courting
of Emer*, Emer is chosen for the strength and volume of her
bladder. This strength and volume were certainly considered
signs of vigour. A woman of divine origin was murdered by
jealous rivals because she made the deepest hole in the snow
with her urine. (E 433)

Dorothy Wellesley's comment has a touch of the unintentionally
ludicrous :

When he had read the poem I said, 'What could be better?'
I attempted, however, to point out that 'great-bladdered'
would prove a stumbling-block to any reader not versed in
Irish folklore and suggested 'great bellied' instead, saying
that this would equally well give the same eugenic meaning
without altogether losing the coarseness so necessary to the
poem. 'No, I must have bladder!' he exclaimed. I think
he is right. He went on to tell how in the Irish legend all

other women were jealous of the Queen's power of retention due to the size of her bladder. This was of great importance as seeming a mark of vigour; also how the Queen was able to make a larger hole in the snow than the other women, so that they were jealous, and set upon her and killed her. I suggested he should write a short separate poem on this legend alone, saying that the snow gave the theme its poetry. 'She made a deeper golden hole in the snow' I said. 'Yes', he replied, with intensity. 'Perhaps to-morrow I shall write the poem.' (*DWL* 171–2)

391   17 *Cuchulain*: see note (p. 26) on 'To the Rose upon the Rood of Time' (*CP* 35).

391   THE CIRCUS ANIMALS' DESERTION

The date of this poem's composition is not certain (probably between November 1937 and September 1938. See Curtis Bradford, 'Yeats's *Last Poems* Again', *Dolmen Press Yeats Centenary Papers* (1965) 286): it first appeared in *Atlantic Monthly* and *LM* (Jan. 1939).

5 *Winter and summer*: circuses usually work a half-year season.

6 *My circus animals*: Yeats's early work. The idea of the circus may have come from Yeats's brother's drawings and paintings. Henn (*LT* 271) suggests the illustrations Jack Yeats made for the Cuala Press.

7 *Those stilted boys*: probably the Gaelic figures of Yeats's early poems and plays. Cf. his remark (probably written about the time he composed this poem) that he had given 'certain years to writing plays in Shakespearean blank verse about Irish kings for whom nobody cared a farthing' (*E* 418). Cf. also his remark that at the turn of the century everybody got down off their stilts.

that burnished chariot: probably Cuchulain's

8 *Lion and woman*: this may be a memory of 'Against Unworthy Praise' (*CP* 103), a poem written about Maud Gonne, where she

was described as 'Half lion, half child' and

> Enough if the work has seemed,
> So did she your strength renew,
> A dream that a lion had dreamed
> Till the wilderness cried aloud,
> A secret between you two, . . .

9   *old themes* : the chivalrous love poetry written by Yeats in the 'eighties (in particular, 'The Wanderings of Oisin' (1889)) before he met Maud Gonne in 1889.

10   *that sea-rider Oisin led by the nose* : because he was too chivalrous, and because Niamh fell in love with him and carried him off across the sea to faeryland with her on her horse.   Cf. 'The Wanderings of Oisin' (*CP* 409) and notes (p. 497) on 'News for the Delphic Oracle' (*CP* 376).

11   *three enchanted islands* : Yeats wrote to Katharine Tynan on 6 February 1889, about *The Wanderings of Oisin*, telling her that 'There are three incompatible things which man is always seeking — infinite feeling, infinite battle, infinite repose — hence the three islands' (see Wade, *Letters*, p. 111, and *LKT* 84).

allegorical dreams : Yeats had written to Katharine Tynan in September 1888, that in the second part of 'Oisin' he had

> said several things to which I only have the key.   The romance is for my readers.   They must not even know there is a symbol anywhere.   They will not find out.   If they did, it would spoil the art.   Yet the whole poem is full of symbols — if it be full of aught but clouds.   The early poems I know to be quite coherent, and at no time are there clouds in my details, for I hate the soft modern manner.   (*LKT* 68)

18   *The Countess Cathleen* : Yeats's play which he wrote for Maud Gonne

19–21   *She, pity-crazed, had given her soul away,*   **392**
        But masterful Heaven had intervened to save it.

  I thought my dear must her own soul destroy, : the Countess was like Yeats's early interpretation of Maud Gonne's character. He told her that after they had met in London in 1891 (the year

he first proposed marriage to her) he had come to understand the
tale of a woman selling her soul to buy bread for her starving
people as a symbol of all souls who lose their peace or fineness of
soul or beauty of spirit in political service, but chiefly as a symbol
of her soul that seemed to him incapable of rest. In the play two
agents of the Devil come to Ireland in a time of famine (Maud
Gonne had become ill through overstrain aiding in relief work
among the peasants in Donegal who were threatened with famine)
and take advantage of the starvation of the peasants to offer to
buy their souls for gold. The Countess Cathleen sacrifices her
goods to get money for food for her people. She is about to sell
her soul when the poet Kevin (Aleel) tries to stop her, but in
vain.

21   *my dear* : Maud Gonne

22   *fanaticism and hate* : cf. lines 57–64 'A Prayer for my Daughter'
(*CP* 211) with their terrible indictment of Maud Gonne's political
hatred

25   *the Fool and Blind Man* : characters in Yeats's play *On Baile's
Strand* (1903) where Cuchulain dies fighting the sea.   Birgit
Bjersby (*ICL* 79) remarks that the later Yeats 'admits or rather
wants to tell us that *On Baile's Strand* is a drama in which the
romantic dreams of his youth have found expression and in which
he fights in desperation for his dream world against invading
reality.'   She quotes the conclusion of the 1905 version of the
play (*ICL* 29–30) pointing out the stylistic repetitions in the
closing speeches which culminate in the Blind Man's words :

There will be nobody in the houses. Come this way ; come
quickly ! The ovens will be full. We will put our hands into
the ovens.

27–8   *Heart mysteries there, and yet when all is said*
        It was the dream itself : this may be a reference to Yeats's
personal life after John MacBride married Maud Gonne in 1903.
He took up the management of the Abbey Theatre from 1902 to
1910.

31   *Players and painted stage* : cf. 'The Fascination of What's
Difficult' (*CP* 104) with its 'theatre business, management of

men'; 'At the Abbey Theatre' (*CP* 107); and 'All Things can tempt Me' (*CP* 109) for his views of his work in the Abbey Theatre at the time he was most deeply involved in its work

POLITICS

This poem was written on 23 May 1938 and first appeared in *Atlantic Monthly* and *LM* (Jan. 1939).

A letter to Dorothy Wellesley of 24 May 1938 explains the poem's genesis in terms of Archibald MacLeish's article, 'Public Speech and Private Speech in Poetry', *Yale Review* (Spring 1938):

> There has been an article upon my work in the *Yale Review*, which is the only article on the subject which has not bored me for years. It commends me above other modern poets because my language is 'public'. That word which I had not thought of myself is a word I want. Your language in 'Fire' is public, so is that of every good ballad. (I may send you the article because the criticism is important to us all). It goes on to say that, owing to my age and my relation to Ireland, I was unable to use this 'public' language on what it evidently considered the right public material, politics. The enclosed little poem is my reply. It is not a real incident, but a moment of meditation. . . . P.S. In part my poem is a comment on ——'s panic-stricken conversation.
>
> No artesian well of the intellect can find the poetic theme. (*DWL* 163)

THE MAN AND THE ECHO

This poem was written in July 1938 and revised up to October 1938; it first appeared in *Atlantic Monthly* and *LM* (Jan. 1939).

1 *that's christened Alt*: a rocky fissure on Ben Bulben, perhaps chosen because of its rocky nature, as an Irish equivalent to Delphi. Cf. *Iliad*, IX, 406, where the rocky nature of Delphi is stressed: 'the stone threshold of the archer Phoebus Apollo encompasseth in *rocky* Pytho'.

11 *that play of mine*: *Cathleen ni Houlihan* (1902), which was performed in Dublin in 1902 with Maud Gonne in the title role.

Stephen Gwynn wrote in *Irish Literature and Drama*, 158 :

> The effect of *Cathleen ni Houlihan* on me was that I went home asking myself if such plays should be produced unless one was prepared for people to go out to shoot and be shot. Yeats was not alone responsible ; no doubt but Lady Gregory had helped him to get the peasant speech so perfect ; but above all Miss Gonne's impersonation had stirred the audience as I have never seen another audience stirred.

12 *Certain men the English shot* : probably the leaders of the 1916 Rising, cf. 'Easter 1916' (*CP* 202) (but it could also mean the total effect of the rebellion and 'troubles').

14 *that woman's reeling brain* : Margot (Collis's or) Ruddock's ; see notes (p. 444) on 'Sweet Dancer' (*CP* 340) and (p. 462) on 'A Crazed Girl' (*CP* 348)

16 *a house lay wrecked* : Coole Park. Probably a reflection on the political movements which brought about the end of the 'great houses' in Ireland. The Wyndham Land Purchase Act of 1903 was the turning point in modern Irish history ; through its provisions the large estates were broken up. The Gregory estate was already divided up before English rule in Ireland ended. Cf. notes (p. 109) on 'Upon a House shaken by the Land Agitation' (*CP* 106).

394 22 *bodkin* : symbol of suicide. Cf. *Hamlet*, iii, i : 'When he himself might his quietus make / with a bare bodkin'.

37 *Rocky Voice* : this voice is akin to the figure 'Old Rocky Face' of 'The Gyres' (*CP* 337). See notes (p. 435) on that poem.

38 *great night* : see notes on 'increasing night' line 21, 'The Apparitions' (*CP* 386)

395 CUCHULAIN COMFORTED

This poem is dated 13 January 1939 in *CP* ; it first appeared in *Last Poems and Two Plays* (1939)

The poem is related to Yeats's play *The Death of Cuchulain*. It may be the poem for which Yeats wrote to Edith Shackleton Heald on 1 January 1939 that he was making 'a prose sketch for a poem — a kind of sequel — strange too, something new' (*L* 922). It is possible that it may also be the lyric arising out of the play mentioned in an earlier letter to her of December 1938. The prose draft, according to Mrs Yeats, was dictated on 7 January 1939. See *LT* 338.

Dorothy Wellesley gives an account of the prose version of the poem :

On one of our visits to him at Cap Martin he read the prose theme of a poem he proposed to write in *terza rima* :

A shade recently arrived went through a valley in the Country of the Dead ; he had six mortal wounds, but had been a tall, strong, handsome man. Other shades looked at him from among the trees. Sometimes they went near to him and then went away quickly. At last he sat down, he seemed very tired. Gradually the shades gathered round him, and one of them who seemed to have some authority among the others laid a parcel of linen at his feet. One of the others said : 'I am not so afraid of him now that he is sitting still. It was the way his arms rattled.' Then another shade said : 'You would be much more comfortable if you would make a shroud and wear it instead of the arms. We have brought you some linen. If you make it yourself you will be much happier, but of course we will thread the needles. We do everything together, so everyone of us will thread the needles, so when we have laid them at your feet you will take whichever you like best.' The man with the six wounds saw that nobody had ever threaded needles so swiftly and so smoothly. He took the threaded needles and began to sew, and one of the shades said : 'We will sing to you while you sew ; but you will like to know who we are. We are the people who run away from the battles. Some of us have been put to death as cowards, but others have hidden, and some even died without people knowing they were cowards.' Then they began to sing, and they did not sing like men and women, but like linnets that had been stood on a perch and taught by a good singing master. (*DWL* 193)

20 *our character* : the account of disincarnate state in *AV* (B) **396** 223–5 may be germane to this poem. Yeats is there pondering upon the famous elemental of Leap Castle, and the transformation

of the cowards into birds may echo his suggestions in that portion of *AV* about the spirit's relationship with the Celestial or the Passionate Body.

396 THE BLACK TOWER

This is the last poem Yeats wrote; it is dated 21 January 1939 and first appeared in *Last Poems and Two Plays* (1939)

1 *the old black tower*: this may derive from Browning, though there may also be a hint of Thoor Ballylee.

6 *those banners*: these are the banners of political propaganda.

7 *the dead upright*: Henn (*LT* 251) connects this image with one of Charles Ricketts's illustrations to Oscar Wilde's *Sphinx*, called 'Rose up the Painted Swathéd Dead', though he thinks it may also refer to heroic burial on Knocknarea.

397 24 *the king's great horn*: W. J. Keith, in 'Yeats's Arthurian Black Tower', *Modern Language Notes*, lxxv (Feb. 1960), suggests that this imagery derives from the Arthurian legend that Arthur, Guinevere, all his court and a pack of hounds sleep in a vault beneath the Castle of Sewingshields in Northumberland. The king waits till someone blows the horn which lies on a table and cuts a garter laid beside it with a sword of stone. A farmer found the vault, cut the garter and Arthur woke, only to fall asleep again as the sword was sheathed with these words:

> O woe betide that evil day
> On which the witless night was born
> Who drew the sword — the garter cut
> But never blew the bugle horn.

397 UNDER BEN BULBEN

This poem was completed by 4 September 1938 and first appeared in the *Irish Times*, the *Irish Independent* and the *Irish Press* (3 Feb. 1939).

I

1–2   . . . *what the sages spoke*

Round the Mareotic Lake : see notes (p. 237) on line 44 ff.
'Demon and Beast' (*CP* 209). Yeats wrote of Lionel Johnson
in 'The Tragic Generation' that when he said 'wilderness' he
thought of 'some historical, some bookish desert, the Thebaid,
or the lands about the Mareotic sea' (*A* 307).

3   *the witch of Atlas* : she symbolised the beauty of wisdom in
Shelley's poem of the same name. She was 'a Naiad, and was
born from one of the Atlantides, who lay in a "chamber of grey
rock" until she was changed by the sun's embrace into a cloud'
(*E & I* 84). Yeats wrote of her :

> When the Witch has passed in her boat from the caverned
> river, that is doubtless her own destiny, she passes along the
> Nile 'by Moeris and the Mareotid lakes,' and sees all human
> life shadowed upon its waters in shadows that 'never are
> erased but tremble ever' ; and in 'many a dark and sub-
> terranean street under the Nile' — new caverns — and along
> the bank of the Nile ; and as she bends over the unhappy, she
> compares unhappiness to the strife that 'stirs the liquid sur-
> face of man's life' ; and because she can see the reality of things
> she is described as journeying 'in the calm depths' of 'the
> wide lake' we journey over unpiloted. (*E & I* 85)

5   *those horsemen, by those women* : probably the visionary beings
George Pollexfen's servant Mary Battle described to Yeats :

> 'Some of them have their hair down, but they look quite
> different, more like the sleepy-looking ladies one sees in the
> papers. . . . They are fine and dashing-looking, like the men
> one sees riding their horses in twos and threes on the slopes
> of the mountains with their swords swinging. There is no
> such race living now, none so finely proportioned.' (*A* 266)

11   *Ben Bulben* : this mountain in Sligo was associated with the   **398**
Fianna, the horsemen who served Finn.

II

14–15   *two eternities,*

That of race and that of soul : perhaps this related to Yeats's
idea of the conflict of two states of consciousness, 'beings or

persons which die each others life, live each other's death' (*L* 918). A letter of 22 June 1938 to Dorothy Wellesley puts the same idea : 'This is the proposition on which I write : "There is now over-whelming evidence that man stands between two eternities, that of his family and that of his soul"' (*L* 910).

III

25   *Mitchel* : John Mitchel (1815–1875) replaced Thomas Davis on N, founded the *United Irishman* 1843, was transported, escaped to America, and on his return to Ireland was made an M.P. 'Give us war in our time, O Lord', comes from his famous *Jail Journal*.

30   *his partial mind* : the idea may come from Rilke. Yeats wrote to Ethel Mannin on 9 October 1938 to say he had been rereading an essay on the idea of death in the poetry of Rilke : 'According to Rilke a man's death is born with him and if his life is successful and he escapes mere "mass death" his nature is completed by his final union with it' (*L* 917).

IV

399   41   *fill the cradles* : cf. this imagery in 'The Phases of the Moon' (*CP* 183)

42   *Measurement began our might* : cf. notes on 'The Statues' (*CP* 375)

45   *Michael Angelo* : Yeats kept reproductions of Michelangelo's work in his house and when Shaw's *The Black Girl in Search of God* was banned he brought a reproduction of the Sistine Chapel Adam to the Censorship authorities for purposes of comparison and to show them the error of their ways.

400   62   *Gyres* : see notes (p. 435) on 'The Gyres' (*CP* 337)

64   *Calvert* : Denis Calvert (Calvaert) 1540–1619 was a Flemish painter who founded the School of Bologna and was the master of Guido Reni ; but Yeats is here probably thinking of Edward Calvert (1799–1883) an English visionary artist on whom he once thought of writing a book. Raymond Lister, 'Beulah to Byzan-

tium . . .' *Dolmen Press Yeats Centenary Papers*, II, 36, thinks Yeats read *A Memoir of Edward Calvert by his Third Son* (1893), and points out that Charles Ricketts had an impression of Calvert's line-engraving 'The Bride' and published two of his word-engravings in *The Pageant* in 1897. Calvert and Samuel Palmer were among the group of young men who were disciples of Blake and called themselves 'Ancients'. See a reference to him as a disciple of Blake in *E* 44. Raymond Lister suggests a link between Calvert's 'A Primitive City', Blake's Golgonooza and Yeats's Byzantium. He sees Calvert as looking towards a golden age, like Wilson, Blake, Claude and Palmer. See also Raymond Lister, *Edward Calvert* (1962).

Wilson: probably Richard Wilson (1714–82), British landscape painter. (Yeats refers to George Wilson, a pre-Raphaelite painter, in *A* 156).

Claude: Claude Lorrain (1600–82) landscape artist, master of the picturesque

66 *Palmer's phrase*: cf. Yeats's essay on 'Blake's Illustrations to Dante'. He regarded Palmer as Blake's disciple:

The member of the group [which gathered around Blake in his old age] whom I have already so often quoted has alone praised worthily these illustrations to the first Eclogue [in Thornton's *Virgil*]: 'There is in all such a misty and dreamy glimmer as penetrates and kindles the inmost soul and gives complete and unreserved delight, unlike the gaudy daylight of this world. They are like all this wonderful artist's work, the drawing aside of the fleshly curtain, and the glimpse which all the most holy, studious saints and sages have enjoyed, of the rest which remains to the people of God. (*E & I* 125)

V

78–9 *the lords and ladies gay*
        That were beaten into the clay: Saul (*PYP* 177) has pointed out that the source for these lines is Frank O'Connor's translation *Kilcash*. 'The earls, the lady, the people beaten into the clay.'

VI

84   *Under bare Ben Bulben's head* : in a letter to Ethel Mannin of
22 August 1938 Yeats wrote :

> I am arranging my burial place.   It will be in a little remote
> country churchyard in Sligo where my great grandfather was
> the clergyman a hundred years ago.   Just my name and dates
> and these lines :
>
> > Cast a cold eye
> > On life, on death ;
> > Horsemen pass by.   (*L* 914)

In a letter of 15 August 1938 he had written to Dorothy Wellesley :

> I have found a book of essays about Rilke [R. M. Rilke,
> *Some Aspects and his Mind and Poetry*] waiting me ; one on
> Rilke's ideas about death [by William Rose] annoyed me.
> I wrote on the margin [There follows the epitaph with this line
> prefixed
>
> > 'Draw rein ; draw breath']   (*L* 913)

Hone remarks accurately (*WBY* 473 n) that there is no note on the
margin of Yeats's copy of this book.   Yeats may have derived the
idea of arranging his burial-place from William Pollexfen, his grandfather, who superintended 'the making of his tomb' (*A* 67).

85   *Drumcliff* : a village on the Bundoran Road to the north of
Sligo lying under the slopes of Ben Bulben.   Yeats died at Roquebrune on 28 January 1939.   His body was brought to Ireland in
1948 and re-interred in Drumcliff Churchyard in September 1948.

86   *An ancestor* : the Rev. John Yeats.   See notes (p. 118) to
'Introductory Rhymes' (*CP* 113).

NARRATIVE AND DRAMATIC

The Wanderings of Oisin

This poem was first published in *WO* ; the first version seems to
have been finished in the autumn of 1887 (*LKT* 41). Yeats pre-   **405**
pared it for the printer in the early part of 1888. The poem has
been extensively revised and *VE* 1–63 should be consulted. A
list of variant spellings is given on p. 1. The Gaelic sources are
Oisin i dTir na nOg and *Agallamh na Senorach*. See note on lines
139–45, and Giles W. L. Telfer, *Yeats's Idea of the Gael* (1965).
Yeats departed from the spirit of the Gaelic originals ; he believed
that Irish legends and beliefs resembled those of the east. See
the discussion in *YCE* 45–51, and see also *Y: M&P*, 42–7 and
F. Shaw, 'The Celtic Element in the Poetry of W. B. Yeats', *Studies*
(June 1934).

I

5 *Oisin* : the son of Finn and Saeve (of the Sidhe). His name
means 'the little fawn'. Yeats described him as the poet of the   **409**
Fenian cycle of legend.

13 *Caoilte* : Caoilte Mac Ronain, see notes (p. 78) on 'The Secret
Rose' (*CP* 77). He was Finn's favourite warrior.
Conan : Conan Mail, a braggart Fenian warrior, whom Yeats called
the Thersites of the Fenian cycle

Finn : leader of the Fenians

15 *Bran, Sceolan and Lomair* : Bran and Sceolan were Finn's
cousins, his aunt Uirne having been transformed while pregnant ;
Lomair was one of their three whelps.

16 *Firbolgs* : supposedly prehistoric invaders of Ireland, short and
black-haired. Yeats commented, 'An early race who warred vainly
upon the Fomorians, or Fomoroh, before the coming of the Tuath

de Danaan. Certain Firbolg Kings, killed at Southern Moytura, are supposed to be buried at Ballisodare. It is by their graves that Usheen and his companions rode' (*P* (1895)). He also described them as 'a mythological race'.

17–18 . . . *the cairn-heaped grassy hill*
  Where passionate Maeve is stony-still : Knocknarea, burial place of Maeve. Cf. notes on 'Red Hanrahan's Song about Ireland' (*CP* 90). Yeats commented that 'she is rumoured to be buried under the cairn on Knocknarea. Ferguson speaks of the "shell-heaped cairn of Maeve high up on haunted Knocknarea" but inaccurately for the cairn is of stones' (*P* (1895)). Maeve was 'a famous queen of the Red Branch cycle.'

20 *A pearl-pale high-born lady* : Niamh, daughter of Aengus and Edain ; her name means brightness or beauty. She was described as a child of the Shee (Sidhe) in a line of the version of the poem in *P* (1895).

21 *findrinny* : *findruine*, an alloy. Yeats described it as a kind of red bronze (*P* (1895)) and a kind of white bronze (*P* (1895 ; rev. 1899)). The latter is probably correct.

410 41 *Oscar's pencilled urn* : Oscar was Oisin's son. The lines borrow from Sir Samuel Ferguson's 'Aideen's Grave', the conclusion of which ran :

> A cup of bodkin pencill'd clay
> Holds Oscar ; mighty heart and limb
> One handful now of ashes grey
> And she has died for him.
>
>   (*Lays of the Western Gael*, II, 12–15)

43 *Gabhra* : the Fiana were almost wiped out in a battle here in 284 A.D. The area is near Garristown, in north Co. Dublin. Yeats called it 'the great battle in which the power of the Fenians was broken' (*P* (1895)).

47 *Aengus and Edain* : Aengus was the Celtic god of love and beauty who lived in Tir-nan-Oge, the country of the Young. See notes (p. 96) on 'Under the Moon' (*CP* 91). Edain or Etain was

'a famous legendary queen who went away and lived among the Shee' (*P* (1895)); she 'was lured away by Meder (Midir), King of the Shee' (*P* (1895 ; rev. 1899)). See 'The Two Kings' (*CP* 503–510) which tells of her wooing by Midir through King Eochaid's brother Ardan. The version in 'The Two Kings' departs from the Gaelic original.

53   *the birds of Aengus* : the kisses of Aengus turned into birds and flew around his head. See P. Gurd, *The Early Poetry of William Butler Yeats* (1916), 55 and Yeats's footnote (p. 530) to 'Baile and Aillinn' (*CP* 459).

63   *Danaan* : Tuatha de Danaan, a magical race. See note (p. 36) **411**
on 'The White Birds' (*CP* 46).

71   *brazen bell* : cf. P. Gurd, *The Early Poetry of William Butler Yeats* (1916), 53, who describes as 'oblong and made of iron' the bells introduced into Ireland by St Patrick.

139–145   *. . . now a hornless deer*   **413**
Passed by us, chased by a phantom hound
All pearly white, save one red ear;
And now a lady rode like the wind
With an apple of gold in her tossing hand;
And a beautiful young man followed behind
With quenchless gaze and fluttering hair : this passage owes much to Michael Comyn's 'The Lady of Oisin in the Land of Youth', translated by Brian O'Looney (see *Transactions of the Ossianic Society* IV (1859), 21–5, 117–18, 249, and David Comyn, *Gaelic Union Publications* (1880).

> We saw also, by our sides
> A hornless fawn leaping nimbly
> And a red-eared white dog,
> Urging it boldly in the chase.
> We beheld also, without fiction
> A young maid on a brown steed,
> A golden apple in her right hand,
> And she goes on top of the waves.
> We saw after her,
> A young rider on a white steed.

156   *Almhuin* : Finn's hall, modern Allen   **414**

416 218–20 *Where Aengus dreams . . . world be done*: cf. F. Shaw 'The Celtic Element in the Poetry of W. B. Yeats', *Studies* (June 1934), 272–3, for a discussion of the 'very homely unmysterious Thir na n-Og' described in the original Gaelic poem

239 *this strange human bard*: Oisin's 'stories builded by his words' are earlier described as 'like coloured Asian birds/At evening in their rainless lands' (69–70). Originally, in *WO* (1887) Niamh remarks 'drops of honey are his words.'

421 383 *pale findrinny*: see note on line 21
II

423 The Second Book was thought to derive from the Glaucus episode in *Endymion* by Miss D. M. Hoare, *The Works of Morris and Yeats in Relation to Early Saga Literature* (1937), 114. The hall seemed to Horatio S. Krans, *William Butler Yeats and the Irish Literary Revival* (1904), 69, to come from *Hyperion*. P. Gurd, *The Early Poetry of William Butler Yeats* (1916), 59 suggested that 'the great fortress' was suggested by Shelley's 'Temple of the Spirit' in *The Revolt of Islam*. Saul (*PYP* 180) considers the 'chasm-like portals' called 'the enchanted towers of Carbonek' in Tennyson's 'The Holy Grail' may be echoed here.

I *man of croziers*: St Patrick

425 84 *Seven Hazel Trees*: P. Gurd, *The Early Poetry of William Butler Yeats* (1916), 55, suggests that these are the same as the nine hazel trees of Wisdom of the Tuatha de Danaan. Yeats's note reads:

There was once a well overshadowed by seven sacred hazel trees in the midst of Ireland. A certain lady plucked their fruit, and seven rivers arose out of the land and swept her away. In my poems this is the source of all the waters of this world, which are therefore sevenfold. (*P* (1895))

87 *Aedh*: Irish for Hugh. Aedh is a god of death: 'All who hear his harp playing die. He was one of the two Gods who appeared to Cuhoollin before his death, according to the bardic tale' (*P* (1895)). 'The source is Standish O'Grady, *History of Ireland*' (*P* (1895 ; rev. 1899)).

426 95 *Heber*: Eber, a son of Milesius, who was supposed to rule over southern Ireland after the Milesian invasion. Yeats commented that Heber and Heremon were ancestors of the merely human inhabitants of Ireland (*P* (1895)).

120   *That woman* : the lady of II, line 69. She is 'That maiden'   **427**
in *P* (1895).

128   *Ogham* : an ancient alphabet of twenty characters used in Ireland

Manannan : Manannan Mac Lir, the god of the sea

134   *no milk-pale face* : Christ's

III   **432**

5   *Fenians, and Bran, Sceolan, Lomair* : see note on I, line 15 (p. 521)

49   *sleepers . . . the world began* : early editions read 'sleepers — no,   **435**
neither in house of a cann', cann being explained by Yeats as 'a kind of chieftain'

53   *bell-branch* : 'a legendary branch whose shaking cast all men into a gentle sleep' (*P* (1895))

Sennachies : story-tellers

61   *king*: early editions read 'cann', a chieftain

80   *the name of the demon whose hammer* : Culann, a smith who made   **437**
sword, spear and shield for Conchobar

87   *kings of the Red Branch* : the Ulster cycle of tales

89   *Blanid* : Yeats's note reads 'The Heroine of a beautiful and sad story told by Keating' (*P* (1895)). She was the wife of the King of Munster and was in love with Cuchulain.

Mac Nessa : 'Concobar-Mac-Nessa, Concobar the son of Nessa' (*P* (1895)), King of Ulster

Fergus who feastward : see notes (p. 27) on 'Fergus and the Druid' (*CP* 36). Fergus, Conchobar's stepfather, was under *Geasa* never to refuse an invitation to a feast, and though he was their safe-conduct, he left — though unwillingly — Deirdre and the sons of Usna (who were murdered by Conchobar's men) when Barach invited him (at Conchobar's order) to a feast.

90   *Cook Barach*: see previous note on line 89

438   91   *Dark Balor*: a Formorian King, whom Yeats described as 'The Irish Chimaera, the leader of the hosts of darkness at the great battle of good and evil, life and death, light and darkness, which was fought out on the strands of Moytura, near Sligo' (*P* (1895)).

94   *Grania*:
'A beautiful woman, who fled with Dermot to escape from the love of aged Finn. She fled from place to place over Ireland, but at last Dermot was killed at Sligo upon the seaward point of Benbulben, and Finn won her love and brought her, leaning upon his neck, into the assembly of the Fenians, who burst into inextinguishable laughter.' (*P* (1895))

439   116   *Conan's slanderous tongue*: see note on 1, line 13 (p. 521).

442   152   *keened*: see note (p. 17) on line 22 'The Ballad of Father O'Hart' (*CP* 23)

160   *Rachlin*: Rathlin, island off the coast of Antrim

Bera of ships: Dunboy

443   163   *rath*: an Irish fort

167   *the straw-death*: death in bed

444   179   *Crevroe . . . Knockfefin*: Padraic Colum has informed the editor that Crevroe and Knockfefin are small townlands in Co. Sligo. See note (p. 40) on line 25 'The Man who dreamed of Faeryland' (*CP* 49).

184   *where Maeve lies*: Knocknarea, see note on 1, lines 17–18

445   198   *Hell*: Yeats wrote:
In the older Irish books Hell is always cold, and this is

probably because the Fomoroh, or evil powers, ruled over the
north and the winter.   Christianity adopted as far as possible
the Pagan symbolism in Ireland as elsewhere, and Irish poets,
when they became Christian, did not cease to speak of 'the cold
flagstone of Hell.'   The folk-tales, and Keating in his description of Hell, make use, however, of the ordinary fire symbolism.   (*P* (1895))

446

220   *a hay-cock out on the flood* : perhaps a memory of William Morris,
'The Haystack in the Floods'

The Old Age of Queen Maeve

The poem first appeared in *Fortnightly Review* (April 1903). Lines 1–8 were added in *CP*.

451   11   *Cruachan* : Maeve's palace in Connaught

452   31   *praise another, praising her* : Yeats has been writing about Maud Gonne from 1–10. He addressed her in lines 130–41.

453   58   *White-Horned Bull and the Brown Bull* : the story of the *Táin Bó Cualnge* concerns the cattle raid of Cooley, made by Maeve into Ulster because of a quarrel over these bulls.

   61   *Sidhe* : people of Faery

   69   *Ailell* : Maeve's husband

   71   *Fergus, Nessa's husband* : see notes (p. 27) on 'Fergus and the Druid' (*CP* 36). Conchobar was Ness's son.

   77   *Magh Ai* : Magh aoi, a plain in Co. Roscommon

   78   *of the Great Plain* : the central plain of Ireland

   84   *Aengus* : God of Love

454   92   *the children of the Maines* : Maeve had a son Maine, who was killed by Conchobar. He was married to Ferbe. Saul (*PYP* 96) mentions the tradition of seven Maines, outlawed sons of Maeve and Ailill, who joined in her fight against Ulster and also helped Conaire Mor's foster brothers to raid Erin. There is also traditional authority for eight or nine Maines.

93   *Bual's hill* : Anbual's hill.   He was Etal Anbual, father of Caer.

101   *Aengus of the birds* : see note on line 53 'The Wanderings of Oisin' I (*CP* 409)

130   *Friend* : Maud Gonne   455

141   *that great queen* : Maeve

Baile and Aillinn

Yeats was writing this 'half lyrical half narrative poem' in July 1901 (*L* 353) and it was 'just finished' on 11 August 1901 (*Y & TSM* 2). It first appeared in the *Monthly Review* (July 1902). Yeats wrote a footnote to the poem which ran:

> It is better, I think, to explain at once some of the allusions to mythological people and things, instead of breaking up the reader's attention with a series of foot-notes. What the 'long wars for the White Horn and the Brown Bull' were, and who 'Deirdre the harper's daughter' was, and why Cuchullain was called 'the hound of Ulad,' I shall not explain. The reader will find all that he need know about them, and about the story of Baile and Aillinn itself, in Lady Gregory's 'Cuchullain of Muirthemne', the most important book that has come out of Ireland in my time. 'The Great Plain' is the Land of the Dead and of the Happy; it is called also 'The Land of the Living Heart,' and many beautiful names besides. And Findrias and Falias and Gorias and Murias were the four mysterious cities whence the Tuatha De Danaan, the divine race, came to Ireland, cities of learning out of sight of the world, where they found their four talismans, the spear, the stone, the cauldron, and the sword. The birds that flutter over the head of Aengus are four birds that he made out of his kisses; and when Baile and Aillinn take the shape of swans linked with a golden chain, they take the shape that other enchanted lovers took before them in the old stories. Midhir was a king of the Sidhe, or people of faery, and Etain his wife, when driven away by a jealous woman, took refuge once upon a time with Aengus in a house of glass, and there I have imagined her weaving harp-strings out of Aengus' hair. I have brought the harp-strings into 'The Shadowy Waters,' where I interpret the myth in my own way. (See also *CW* II, which includes *The Legendary and Mythological Foundation of the Plays and Poems*.)

The original story, according to D. M. Hoare, *The Works of Morris and Yeats in Relation to Early Literature*, 116–18, is in *Scél Baili Binn*

Bérlaig, but R. K. Alspach thinks that Yeats's immediate source was
P. Kennedy, *Legendary Fictions of the Irish Celts* (1866).

Title   Baile and Aillinn : Baile was the son of Buan and Aillinn   **459**
the heir of Lugaidh.

4   *Uladh* : Ulster

Buan's son : Buan, an Ulster goddess, the wife of Mesgedra the
king.   Sir Samuel Ferguson, who wrote a poem 'Mesgedra',
described the story : 'In the Conorian cycle, the egg of Leda, so
to speak, is the trophy taken from the dead Mesgedra by Conoll
Cornach under the circumstances which form the subject of this
piece [Mesgedra]' Ferguson, *Poems 1880*, 32.   At Mesgedra's death,
Buan 'lifted up her cry of lamentation and even unto Tara and to
Allen was her cry heard. . . . On the roadside is her grave, even
Coll Buana, "the hazel of Buan" from the hazel that grows through
the grave,' Eleanor Hull, *The Cuchullin Saga in Irish Literature*
(1898), 94.

7   *Aillinn, who was King Lugaidh's heir* : Lugaidh, the son of Curoi
Mac Daire, a Munster king, who went to attack Cuchulain during
the *Táin Bó Cualgne* but, seeing Cuchulain was badly wounded
after his fight with Ferdiad at the Yellow Ford, refrained.   Aillinn
was Lugaidh's daughter

14–15   *the White Horn and the Brown Bull* : see note (p. 528) on line
58 'The Old Age of Queen Maeve' (*CP* 453)

18   *Emain* : Emain Macha, Armagh, the capital of Ulster

21   *Muirthemne* : in Co. Louth.   Cuchulain came from there.

23   *there* : Rosnaree on the River Boyne, where they were to be   **460**
married

25   *there* : Saul (*PYP* 184) glosses as Dundalk

73   *the Hound of Uladh* : Cuchulain, known as the Hound of Culann,   **461**
and as the Hound of Ulster.

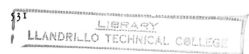

76 *the harper's daughter and her friend* : Deirdre, daughter of Felimid, and Naoise, son of Usna, her lover

79 *betrayed* : see note (p. 525) on Fergus, line 89 'The Wanderings of Oisin' III (*CP* 437).

462 91 *Deirdre and her man* : see note on lines 76

463 117 *Ogham* : see note on line 128 'The Wanderings of Oisin' II (*CP* 423)

123 *the Great Plain* : see Yeats's footnote quoted above

130 *the Hill Seat of Laighen* : ' on the Dublin–Kildare border in the Knockline Mountains

135 *Two swans* : the lovers Baile and Aillinn were changed by Aengus into swans

139 *his changed body* : the old man of lines 25, 47, 100, 113 and 134 reveals himself as Aengus

142 *Edain, Midhir's wife* : see Yeats's footnote quoted above

464 153 *two sweet blossoming apple-boughs* : cf. 'Ribh at the Tomb o Baile and Aillinn' (*CP* 327)

161-3 *Gorias . . . Findrias and Falias . . . And . . . Murias* : see Yeats's footnote quoted above

165 *Cauldron and spear and stone and sword*: Yeats's footnote explains that the Tuatha de Danaan found their talismans in these cities and he gives them as the spear, stone, cauldron and sword. The spear was Lugh's, the stone the *Lia Fail* or Stone of Destiny, brought to Scotland by fifth-century Irish invaders, then brought to England by Edward I and called the Stone of Scone. (It is kept in Westminster Abbey and was removed by Scottish Nationalists in 1950, and spent some time in Scotland before it was brought back to Westminster Abbey by the police.) The cauldron was the Dagda's and the sword Lugh's.

176 *apples of the sun and moon* : cf. notes (pp. 39 ff.) on 'The Man who dreamed of Faeryland' (*CP* 49)

178 *Quiet's wild heart* : quiet is personified also in 'Maid Quiet'   465
(*CP* 78)

180 *glass boat* : see Gurd, *The Early Poetry of William Butler Yeats* (1916), 79 who cites Bonwick, *Irish Druids and Old Irish Religion* (1894), 293

188-93 *a yew tree . . . a wild apple . . . tablets of their board* : cf. notes (p. 426) on 'Ribh at the Tomb of Baile and Aillinn' (*CP* 327)

194 *fighting at the ford* : between Cuchulain and Ferdiad in the *Táin Bó Cualnge*

200 *Beloved* : Maud Gonne

The Shadowy Waters

Yeats probably finished work on *The Shadowy Waters* towards the end of 1899 (*L* 332). Lines 1–44 appeared in *S* (1 Dec. 1900). 'The Harp of Aengus' first appeared in the *North American Review* (May 1900), and the text of the play together with these two poems in *Poems 1899–1905* (1906). The text in *CP* is very different from the original version which is reprinted in *VE* 745 ff. There is a different version in *CPl*, an acting version used at the Abbey Theatre and published by Bullen in 1907.

469 INTRODUCTORY LINES

1 *Coole* : see notes (p. 154) on 'The Wild Swans at Coole' (*CP* 147)

2 *Shan-walla* : old wall

4 *Kyle-dortha* : Kyle, coill, a wood ; dortha, dark

Kyel-na-no : wood of the nuts

7 *Pairc-na-lee* : park or field of the rock

9 *Pairc-na-Carraig* : park or field of the rock

11 *Pairc-na-tarav* : park or field of the bull

13 *Inchy wood* : probably wood of the islands

15 *Biddy Early* : a famous witch in Co. Clare. Cf. *A* 401.

471 THE HARP OF AENGUS

1–2 *Edain came out of Midhir's hill, and lay*
Beside young Aengus in his tower of glass : see Yeats's footnote (p. 530) to 'Baile and Aillinn' (*CP* 459) quoted in notes on that poem.

THE SHADOWY WATERS

A Dramatic Poem

99 *man-headed birds* . . . cf. lines 245–75, 525–31   **477**

118 *All, all*: cf. note on line 137   **478**

137 *all, all*: cf. note (p. 187) on line 21 'Broken Dreams' **479**
(*CP* 172)

169 *hurley*: Irish game (resembling hockey) of some antiquity **480**

386 *a wake*: see note on 'The Ballad of Father O'Hart' (*CP* 23) **490**

389 *the keen*: *caoine*, see notes on 'The Ballad of Father O'Hart'
(*CP* 23)

410 *Iollan*: either Iollan, son of Fergus MacRoy, or Finn's uncle **491**
by marriage, or the Iollann mentioned in the preface to Douglas
Hyde's *Beside the Fire* (1890). There is also an Iolann Iolchrothach,
son of the King of Spain in Irish Folk-Tales collected by Jeremiah **499**
Curlin, edited S. Ó Duilearga.

597 *ancient worm*: probably change and decay. Cf. 'the old worm **499**
of the world' in *The Countess Cathleen*.

The Two Kings

This poem was written in October 1912 and first appeared in *BR* and *P* (*Cb*) (Oct. 1913).

The basic sources are in *The Yellow Book of Lecan* and *The Book of the Dun Cow*. There is a translation in D. M. Hoare, *The Works of Morris and Yeats in Relation to Early Saga Literature*, 124–7 and 151 ff. See also R. I. Best's translation of H. Arbois de Jubainville, *The Irish Mythological Cycle and Celtic Mythology* (1903). Saul (*PYP* 187) cites M. G. MacKimmie *A Study of Yeats's 'The Two Kings'* (1951), an unpublished dissertation in the University of Connecticut.

503 *King Eochaid*: Yeats's footnote reads 'Eochaid is pronounced Yohee'. Eochaid Airem was the High King.

   2 *Tara*: seat of the High King, in Co. Meath

  20 *Mountains of the Moon*: in Ruanda

505 61 *Edain*: Etain, Eochaid's Queen

  79 *Ardan*: Ailill Anguba in the original tale

  83 *Ogham*: see note (p. 525) on line 128 'The Wanderings of Oisin' II (*CP* 427)

506 113 *Loughlan waters*: Norse. 'waters' was originally 'seas'.

507 148–9 *a man . . . unnatural majesty*: Midir, King of the Sidhe

509 202 *Thrust him away*: in the original tale, Edain agrees to return to the land of Faery.

The Gift of Harun Al-Rashid

This poem was written in 1923 and first appeared in *English Life and The Illustrated Review* (Jan. 1924).

Yeats wrote a note which gives a flippant account of his marriage, in *The Cat and the Moon and Certain Poems* (1924) 38 ff. Harun al-Rashid has presented Kusta (who symbolises Yeats) with a new bride:

> According to one tradition of the desert, she had, to the great surprise of her friends, fallen in love with the elderly philosopher, but according to another Harun bought her from a passing merchant. Kusta, a Christian like the Caliph's own physician, had planned, one version of the story says, to end his days in a monastery at Nisibis, while another story has it that he was deep in a violent love affair that he had arranged for himself. The only thing on which there is general agreement is that he was warned by a dream to accept the gift of the Caliph, and that his wife a few days after the marriage began to talk in her sleep, and that she told him all those things which he had searched for vainly all his life in the great library of the Caliph and in the conversation of wise men.

This refers to the automatic writing and the material of *AV*. Cf. *A Packet for Ezra Pound* (*AV* (B) 8–15), particularly the reference to his wife 'in the broken speech of some quite ordinary dream' (22) and the reference to 'an unnatural story of an Arabian traveller which I must amend and find a place for some day because I was fool enough to write half a dozen poems that are unintelligible without it' [*Michael Robartes and his Friends*] (*AV* (B) 19).

6 *banners of the Caliphs hang, night-coloured*: Yeats explained their black colour as mourning for those who had fallen in battle at the establishment of the dynasty. 513

12 *Sappho's song*: Sappho of Lesbos (*fl.* 7th century B.C.), a poetess who used many metres, among them the Sapphic stanza

16   *Treatise of Parmenides* : Parmenides (b. 513 B.C.) founded the Eleatic School of Philosophy (after Elea in Italy) and rejected the theories of Heracleitus.   He regarded the universe as an unchanging continuous indivisible whole.

514   32   *Vizir Jaffer* : perhaps from Jaffier in Otway's *Venice Preserv'd*

517   128   *her sleeping form* . . . : this relates the experiences that went to the making of *AV*. See also notes (p. 220) on 'An Image from a Past Life' (*CP* 200), which include the note Yeats wrote upon it.

519   184   *All, all those gyres and cubes and midnight things*: Yeats's footnote read 'This refers to the geometrical forms which Robartes describes the Judwali Arabs as making upon the sand for the instruction of their young people, and which, according to tradition, were drawn as described in sleep by the wife of Kusta-ben-Luka' (*The Dial* (June 1924)). For *All, all* see note (p. 187) on line 21 'Broken Dreams' (*CP* 173).

Gaelic Names

YEATS commented that when he wrote most of the poems in *P* (1895 ; rev. 1899) he had hardly considered seriously the question of the pronunciation of the Irish words. He had copied at times somebody's perhaps fanciful spelling, and at times the ancient spelling as he found it in some literal translation, pronouncing the words as they were spelt. In 1899 he supposed he would not at any time have defended this system, but he did not then know what system to adopt. He added :

> The modern pronunciation, which is usually followed by those who spell the words phonetically, is certainly unlike the pronunciation of the time when classical Irish literature was written, and, as far as I know, no Irish scholar who writes in English or French has made that minute examination of the way the names come into the rhythms and measures of the old poems which can alone discover the old pronunciation. A French Celtic scholar gave me the pronunciation of a few names, and told me that Mr Whitley Stokes had written something about the subject in German, but I am ignorant of German. If I ever learn the old pronunciation, I will revise all these poems, but at present I can only affirm that I have not treated my Irish names as badly as the mediaeval writers of the stories of King Arthur treated their Welsh names.

In a glossary he gave the old spelling in parentheses wherever he had adopted somebody's phonetic spelling in the poems. Information from this is supplied in this edition. In *CP* he adopted Lady Gregory's spelling of Gaelic names with two exceptions.

> The 'd' of Edain ran too well in my verse for me to adopt her perhaps more correct Etain, and for some reason unknown to me I have always preferred 'Aengus' to her 'Angus'. In her *Gods and Fighting Men* and *Cuchulain of Muirthemne* she went as close to the Gaelic spelling as she could without making the names unpronounceable to the average reader.

APPENDIX II

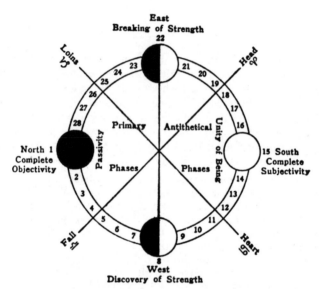

The Great Wheel of the Lunar Phases

Index to Titles

Page numbers in bold are those of the *Collected Poems*; those of the Commentary are in ordinary figures.

Index to Titles

Index to First Lines

Page numbers in bold are those of the *Collected Poems*; those of the Commentary are in ordinary figures.

Index to First Lines

Index to First Lines